HISTORY OF THE
WAR IN SOUTH AFRICA
1899-1902

HISTORY

OF THE

WAR IN SOUTH AFRICA

1899–1902

COMPILED BY DIRECTION OF
HIS MAJESTY'S GOVERNMENT

BY

MAJOR-GENERAL SIR FREDERICK MAURICE, K.C.B.

WITH A STAFF OF OFFICERS

VOLUME III

The Naval & Military Press Ltd

Published by
The Naval & Military Press Ltd
5 Riverside, Brambleside, Bellbrook
Industrial Estate, Uckfield, East Sussex,
TN22 1QQ England
Tel: +44 (0) 1825 749494
Fax: +44 (0) 1825 765701
www.naval-military-press.com

In reprinting in facsimile from the original, any imperfections are inevitably reproduced and the quality may fall short of modern type and cartographic standards.

NOTE.

THE regrettable illness of Major-General Sir Frederick Maurice, K.C.B., which occurred when this Volume was in an early stage of preparation, has unfortunately deprived the Official History of the War in South Africa of his services, and is the cause of the disappearance of his name from the cover and title-page of Volume III.

THE COMPILER.

CONTENTS.

VOLUME III.

CHAP.		PAGE
I.—The Rebellion in the North-West of Cape Colony, October, 1899 to July, 1900	. . . .	1
II.—The Reorganisation at Bloemfontein, March 14th to May 2nd, 1900	. . . . .	27
III.—The Advance from Bloemfontein to Kroonstad	.	40
IV.—The Advance from Kroonstad to Pretoria	. .	65
V.—Operations in the Orange River Colony, May and June, 1900	. . . .	104
VI.—The Defence and Relief of Mafeking	. . .	140
VII.—Colonel Plumer's Operations in Rhodesia	. .	186
VIII.—The Battle of Diamond Hill	. . . .	204
IX.—Operations in the Western Transvaal, June and July, 1900	. . . . . .	226
X.—The Clearing of Northern Natal.	. . .	249
XI.—Operations in the Orange River Colony (*continued*)		286
XII.—Operations in the Eastern Transvaal, June 16th to August 21st, 1900	. . . . .	307
XIII.—Operations in the Orange River Colony. The Pursuit of De Wet and Olivier	. . .	325
XIV.—Operations in the Western Transvaal. The Pursuit and Escape of De Wet	. . . .	335
XV.—Operations in the Western Transvaal, August and September, 1900	. . . . .	357

THE WAR IN SOUTH AFRICA.

CHAP.		PAGE
XVI.—THE ADVANCE TOWARDS KOMATI POORT		380
XVII.—THE ADVANCE TO KOMATI POORT		406
XVIII.—OPERATIONS IN THE EASTERN TRANSVAAL, OCTOBER AND NOVEMBER, 1900		422
XIX.—EVENTS ON JOHANNESBURG—DURBAN LINE, JUNE TO NOVEMBER, 1900		457
XX.—OPERATIONS IN THE ORANGE RIVER COLONY, SEPTEMBER TO DECEMBER, 1900		469
XXI.—OPERATIONS IN THE WESTERN TRANSVAAL, SEPTEMBER TO NOVEMBER, 1900		497

APPENDICES.

NO.		PAGE
1.	LISTS OF STAFFS AND COMPOSITION OF THE FORCES	529
2.	STATES OF STRENGTHS AND CASUALTIES	536
3.	RAILWAY WORK, MAY AND JUNE, 1900	543
4.	THE DEFENCES OF PRETORIA	547
5.	THE DEFENCE AND RELIEF OF MAFEKING. STATES OF STRENGTHS AND CASUALTIES, ETC., ETC.	549
6.	THE CLEARING OF NORTHERN NATAL, CORRESPONDENCE *re* SIR R. BULLER "TO ACT STRICTLY ON THE DEFENSIVE"	552
7.	DISTRIBUTION OF TROOPS ON THE DELAGOA BAY RAILWAY, NOVEMBER 30TH, 1900	553
8.	DISTRIBUTION OF TROOPS ON THE JOHANNESBURG— DURBAN LINE, NOVEMBER, 1900	556
9.	PROCLAMATIONS OF ANNEXATION OF :—	
	(A) ORANGE FREE STATE	559
	(B) SOUTH AFRICAN REPUBLIC	560

LIST OF MAPS AND FREEHAND SKETCHES.
VOL. III.

MAPS.

No. 38.	NORTH OF THE ORANGE FREE STATE AND PART OF THE TRANSVAAL.
No. 39.	THE PASSAGE OF THE ZAND RIVER. *Situation about* 9.45 *a.m.*, May 10th, 1900.
No. 40.	THE PASSAGE OF THE VAAL RIVER. May 24th to 27th, 1900.
No. 41.	THE ACTION AT DOORN KOP. *Situation about* 4 *p.m.*, May 29th, 1900.
No. 42.	THE ACTION AT SIX MILE SPRUIT. *Situation about* 3 *p.m.*, June 4th, 1900.
No. 43.	NORTH-WEST OF CAPE COLONY.
No. 44.	DIAMOND HILL. *Situation about* 3 *p.m.*, June 11th, 1900.
No. 44 (A).	DIAMOND HILL. *Situation on June 12th*, 1900.
No. 45.	NORTHERN NATAL AND PART OF THE TRANSVAAL. *Illustrating Sir R. Buller's advance from Ladysmith into the Transvaal*, May 8th to July 6th, 1900.
No. 46.	LAING'S NEK AND BOTHA'S PASS. June 8th, 1900.
No. 47.	ALLEMAN'S NEK. *Situation about* 3.30 *p.m.*, June 11th, 1900.
No. 48.	EASTERN TRANSVAAL. *Showing the first stage of the combined advance on Komati Poort.* August 6th to 10th, 1900.
No. 49.	BELFAST TO KOMATI POORT. *Showing the second stage of the combined advance on Komati Poort.* September 3rd to 24th, 1900.
No. 50.	THE ATTACK ON BERGENDAL FARM. August 25th, 1900. *Situation prior to the final assault.*
No. 51.	ENVIRONS OF MAFEKING.
No. 52.	DEFENCE OF MAFEKING. *Showing all defence works constructed throughout the siege.* October, 1899, to May, 1900.
No. 53.	BRANDWATER BASIN AND ADJOINING COUNTRY.
No. 54.	NORTH CAPE COLONY AND PART OF THE ORANGE FREE STATE.
No. 55.	INDEX MAP TO VOLUME III.

FREEHAND SKETCHES.

VIEW OF MAFEKING FROM THE SOUTH.
VIEW FROM MAFEKING TO THE SOUTH.
VIEW EAST-SOUTH-EAST FROM LAING'S NEK.
ALLEMAN'S NEK AS SEEN FROM THE SOUTH-WEST.
ZILIKAT'S NEK FROM THE SOUTH.
BRANDWATER BASIN BETWEEN FICKSBURG AND FOURIESBURG.
RETIEF'S NEK.
COUNTRY BETWEEN NAAUWPOORT NEK AND GOLDEN GATE.
VIEW OF THE WITTE BERGEN.
THE BRANDWATER BASIN ABOUT SLAAP KRANZ.
COUNTRY NEAR KOMATI POORT.

MAPS TO VOLUME III.

THE general remarks relative to the mapping of South Africa embodied in the Notes on Maps to Volume I. are applicable also to this Volume.

Map No. 38 was in the first instance prepared from the War Office four-miles-to-one-inch sheets based on the Orange Free State and Transvaal Farm Surveys. It has, however, been checked with the two-miles-to-one-inch Degree sheets which have been published since its original compilation, and all large scale sketches of battle sites, etc., have been incorporated in it. Maps Nos. 39, 40, 41, 42 and 53 have been prepared from the Degree sheets prepared and published since the War; Map No. 43 from the twelve-miles-to-an-inch General Map of Cape Colony prepared in the office of the Surveyor-General of that Colony; Map No. 44 from the Degree sheets and a special sketch of the battle-field made during the War by No. 1 Survey Section Royal Engineers; Map No. 45 from the Cape Colony General Map, on a scale of twelve miles to one inch, and Russell's Official Map of Natal, on a scale of five miles to one inch; Map No. 46 from the Reconnaissance Sketches in North Natal, made in 1896, by Major S. C. N. Grant, R.E.; Map No. 47 from a sketch by Lieut. C. O. Place, D.S.O., R.E.; Map No. 48—the major portion from the four-mile War Office series, but in the North and East from Jeppe's Map of the Transvaal; Map No. 49, also from Jeppe's Map of the Transvaal; Map No. 50 from a sketch made during the War by No. 1 Survey Section Royal Engineers; Map No. 51 from a tracing prepared in the office of the D.A.Q.M.G., Pretoria, from sketches made by Second Lieut. W. H. Tapp, 2nd Dragoon Guards; Map No. 52 from a special survey by Mr. Burnet Adams, A.M.I.C.E.; Map No. 54 is a reprint of No. 35 in Volume II. The eleven panoramic views are from sketches made by the same artist as are those in the two previous Volumes—the late Captain W. C. C. Erskine, Bethune's Mounted Infantry.

THE WAR IN SOUTH AFRICA.

CHAPTER I.

THE REBELLION IN THE NORTH-WEST OF CAPE COLONY.*

OCTOBER, 1899—JULY, 1900.

NOT only ties of blood drew this part of the British South African dominions to the side of the Boer States. Yet these bonds were so strong that both Republican governments, relying upon them as an integral factor of their projected campaign, had many a stand of arms in readiness for distribution amongst the almost exclusively Dutch farmers who peopled this wild and inhospitable district.† But beyond this there had been at work upon the left bank of the Orange influences which would have borne down the scale, even had it wavered. Here, on the fringe of the British administration, its benefits had been less apparent than its restraints; and it is scarcely to be wondered at if many a pure-blooded Boer, passing a narrow, lonely, and almost inaccessible existence, remembered the history of the land rather than its frontiers, and clung to his individuality, which to a Boer was his nationality. To such a man sympathy for grievances, real or imaginary, could be wafted not from the south, but, like the warm wind of South Africa, from the north. Neither grievances nor sympathy were lacking. That the former had nothing to do with any human administration mattered little to sufferers so ignorant and prejudiced, that they were capable of giving credence to the rumour that the Government of Cape Colony was actually paying for the dissemination of disease amongst their

Causes of disaffection.

* See map No. 43.   † See Volume I., page 80.

cattle. Many years of drought, season after season of rinderpest, had embittered those whom these misfortunes had brought almost to the brink of ruin; until, as populations more enlightened have done, they laid the charge to the government within their boundaries, and looked for relief to one without. Nor was the latter backward to sow seed on soil so favourable. Boer agents had long stolen about the districts, planting disaffection where it did not already grow, watering it where it was budding, using it so openly where it grew strongly that, as early as July, 1899, rifles were in the hands of intending rebels; and even, incredible as it may appear, target practice was in full progress on British soil to promote accurate shooting against British soldiers. Such a state of things, much as it may seem to reflect upon the preparedness of the sovereign power, is always to be expected on the borders of great empires, where races mingle, and the shorter arm triumphs temporarily over the longer. At the date mentioned, at any rate, even had there been civil or military machinery to deal with the matter, neither could well have been employed without precipitating the conflict which the British people hoped, and their statesmen were labouring, to avert.

The Boers' first action in the Colony.

Into this fertile field the Boers descended as soon as the declaration of war called them to their harvest. On October 21st General De la Rey entered Vryburg district with some two hundred Transvaalers. He himself moved down to Kimberley almost immediately, but left behind a certain Field Cornet Visser, who speedily enlisted a considerable force of rebels whom he armed from loads of rifles and ammunition sent down from Schweizer Reneke. This force was detailed to take Kuruman; and at the beginning of November Visser moved off, leaving about two hundred men for garrison and patrol duty at Vryburg. The rebels were organised in four commandos, each under an elected field cornet. At the beginning of December Visser's levy amounted to some eight hundred.

In November, the Griqualand West district, also known as the Hay division, was proclaimed Orange Free State territory; and the line of the Orange river was patrolled and watched by Boers despatched from Griquatown. For the moment, however, no large body crossed to the left bank. Yet the British authorities knew well how exposed to invasion were the districts south of the Orange river, and how ripe for rebellion the inhabitants. A small column (about one and three-quarters companies mounted infantry, eighty New South Wales Mounted Rifles, and twenty-five Rimington's Guides), under Lieut.-Colonel E. A. H. Alderson, was therefore sent to Prieska, arriving there and occupying the place on January 3rd, 1900. A few shots were exchanged with Boers, but nothing of importance happened. Alderson and the mounted infantry were withdrawn the same day, but the other troops remained temporarily in garrison. One or two small patrols crossed the river and a few prisoners were taken with some cattle. So weak a garrison, however, ran too great a risk of being cut off, and it was also withdrawn about the 10th. The day after its departure about two hundred Griqualand Boers, under Field Cornet Fouché, crossed the Orange river and entered Prieska, but did nothing beyond destroying telegraphic communication; and after a few days' sojourn in the neighbourhood, they, too, fell back across the river.

The loyalists at Kuruman, against whom Visser was marching, numbered fifty Europeans and thirty coloured men, commanded by Major A. Bates, Cape Police. On November 13th, at 10 a.m., the Boers approached, and fired on the entrenchments until dark. During the night the rebels dug trenches, from which they kept up a heavy fire for the next four days, not venturing to come to close quarters. On November 18th they retired, and were subsequently located by scouts about eighteen miles away. At the end of November they were reinforced by about 130 Griqualand rebels, under Field Cornet Wessels, and again attacked on December 5th. Till December 17th heavy firing was kept up, and four determined assaults were made on the works, all of which were repulsed with loss. The rebels then decided to await the arrival of a gun which had been sent for from Vryburg, and meanwhile continual shooting was carried on by both sides which reduced the ammunition supply of the loyalists to a low ebb. Wessels, owing to supply difficulties, had moved off with the Griqualanders on December 26th towards Dronfield. On the 30th the expected gun arrived, and opening on January 1st, speedily settled the matter. After enduring some eighty rounds, Bates decided to surrender; and the little garrison, with the exception of twelve wounded men, were removed as prisoners of war to Pretoria.

On January 6th the Vryburg rebels left Kuruman and started for Kimberley to join Cronje, taking part in the fighting at Koodoesberg, February 6th—10th. On February 12th they were ordered to Douglas; but the British main advance frightened them back by Barkly West to Fourteen Streams, which was reached February 23rd. They moved to Rooidam early in March, and were joined there by some two hundred more Vryburg rebels, who had previously been doing garrison and patrol duties in their own district. The Vryburgers subsequently took part in the fight at Rooidam on May 5th, and for the remainder of the war formed part of the field army of the Boers. This was the largest of the rebel commandos formed on the western border.

Various levies and their deeds.

Other rebel commandos levied along the western border were as follows:—In the Barkly West district Commandant Van Aswegen raised a commando some three hundred strong in the neighbourhood of Dronfield. These numbers included the force which Field Cornet Wessels had taken to and from Kuruman. In Barkly West also T. De Beer hoisted the Transvaal flag in December, 1899, at Klipdam, near Windsorton, and enlisted a number of local rebels into the Bloemhof and Wolmaranstad commandos. At Olive River, about fifteen miles east-north-east of Douglas, Jan Kolbe, a Free Stater, who, prior to the war, had been a secret agent in the employ of the Republics, was successful in raising a commando over five hundred strong during January, 1900. This commando also joined Cronje and took part in the Koodoesberg fight. After the relief of Kimberley many of them returned to their homes; but some three hundred followed the route taken by Visser's commando, by Barkly West, and reached Fourteen Streams. In November, 1899, Field Cornet Lotter, a blacksmith from

Campbell, formed a laager at Sunnyside, east of Douglas, in the Herbert district, and raised a commando of about two hundred. This party was that eventually surprised and defeated by Colonel Pilcher on January 1st, 1900. (Vol. I., p. 387.) These commandos had all joined the field army of the Republics and had remained north of the Orange river. Soon after the annexation of the districts north of the river, in November, 1899, guards had been posted here and there along the north bank of the Orange at the different ponts and drifts; but with the exception of the brief visit paid by a commando of two hundred Griqualand rebels to Prieska, where they only stayed from January 8th till the 11th, no attempt had been made by the Republics to commandeer in the districts south of the Orange.

To the west of Hopetown the large districts of Prieska and Kenhart, though known to be thoroughly Boer in their sympathies, had been practically left alone by both belligerents. It had been intended to occupy Prieska with a permanent garrison, to deal with any rebel movement in this part of the country, but the necessary troops were never available.

At the beginning of February the British forces, except the containing detachments, were all moving to the front; and the High Commissioner, Sir Alfred Milner, could not conceal his anxiety as to the possible results. On the 4th of February he addressed a memorandum to the Commander-in-Chief, in which he pointed out how great would be the danger of rebellion in the Cape Colony once the British troops should be out of reach, and how that danger would increase with every forward step taken by the army. He suggested that central points should be selected, and entrenched camps formed at each with garrisons of the three arms; and no better plan could have been devised to nip rebellion in the bud before it became formidable. But Lord Roberts, his gaze fixed forward rather than backward, could ill spare the number of troops necessary for such an occupation. The root of the rebellion lay not in Cape Colony, but in Bloemfontein and Pretoria, its branches at Ladysmith and Kimberley; and a blow at these would fell the whole tree. Moreover, Cape

Recommendations by the High Commissioner.

Colony, if at present weakly guarded, would not be so for long. Fifteen batteries of artillery and six battalions of militia were due at Cape Town within a month; these might keep the country quiet until the army in the field could spare time and troops to clear up its rear. Nevertheless, the Commander-in-Chief was by no means blind to the danger to which his lines of communication would be exposed on their passage through regions full of open and secret enemies. But war, especially offensive warfare, is not to be made without great risks; and a plan of campaign based on absolute safety would defeat its own end by becoming interminable.

Encouraged by his success at Magersfontein, Cronje soon sent a commando to strike at the apparently neglected lines of communication in Cape Colony. The detachment consisted of about two hundred Transvaalers, under General Liebenberg, with whom went Commandant Steenkamp, a rebel, who was entrusted with the general direction of operations, and who carried written orders from President Steyn for the annexation of the Colony districts. The plan was to proclaim the northern part of the Colony, to commandeer all available men, and then to act in concert with the commandos east of the railway, under Olivier and Schoeman, their first aim to be at De Aar and other points along the lines of communication. Steenkamp took with him a large supply of ammunition and rifles for the arming of the expected adherents, and made his way through Douglas and Griquatown. Timely information of this movement reached the British Headquarters. To oppose it Colonel E. A. H. Alderson, with six hundred mounted infantry and six guns, was sent, as already related,* to Prieska, which was occupied on January 27th. A position was taken up close to Prieska, with a view to checking a hostile advance from Griqualand West or down the river from the north-east. Three days later, however, this force was recalled to take part in the general advance, and left Prieska for De Aar. An attempt was then made to strike Liebenberg's force in the neighbourhood of Douglas, Brigadier-General R. G. Broadwood, with 1,500 men, moving out to Sunnyside, which he

margin: General Liebenberg's incursion.

* See Volume I., page 439.

reached February 7th; but Liebenberg's force had already gone across the river and Broadwood consequently retired. (Vol. I., p. 442.)

The districts south of the Orange river and west of the railway were now left ungarrisoned, and Liebenberg continued his movement to the south. On February 15th he arrived at Zween Kuil, on the Orange river, about twenty-five miles northeast of Prieska. The following morning, February 16th, Steenkamp, with a posse of Transvaal burghers, rode into Prieska. Proceeding to the public offices, the invader read the annexation proclamation, declaring the Prieska district to be Orange Free State and Transvaal territory, and the flags of the two Republics were hoisted. As in previous cases, according to the terms of the proclamation, anyone unwilling to own allegiance to the Republics was granted eight days in which to cross the border, those who remained being liable to be commandeered. But most of the loyalists had already fled. There were few silent voices in the market square when the Boer national anthem greeted the breaking of the Republican flags. Notices were then despatched in every direction, calling a public meeting to be held at Prieska on February 19th, for the purpose of appointing a military administration. At 3 p.m. on the appointed day the meeting was held. The village was crowded, the inhabitants having come in from all parts of the district. A president was elected, who announced that the object of the meeting was to ascertain public feeling as to going over to the Republics, as to the military law to be applied, and, further, to appoint a military administration. The few loyalists who still remained in the district awaited anxiously the result of this meeting; and for a time those present at the discussion were not without hope, for there were many objections raised. But these arose only from the natural combativeness of Boers in conference. The harvest was ripe. It was known that General Liebenberg, with two hundred Transvaalers and two guns, was on the Orange river, not far away, and that the martial law proclaimed by the Republics would under any circumstances be enforced in the district. To be short, the meeting decided to submit, there being only seventeen dissentient votes. That evening the burghers again met and selected a military committee, who appointed field cornets to call up the burghers in the various divisions of the district; by February 23rd they had succeeded in collecting 150 recruits. These were immediately armed, and started the same evening to join Liebenberg, who was now at Omdraai Vlei. Until the end of the month parties continued to arrive from the outlying districts, and were at once equipped and sent either to join Liebenberg, or to line the borders on either side of Prieska. As for the townsmen, they had been immediately enrolled for the defence of the place, and employed as orderlies and in patrolling.

On February 27th news reached the loyal place of Kenhart that a hostile party from Prieska was advancing on the town. Whereupon a native constable of Kenhart, named McDilling, assembled some twenty-five of the Bastard tribe, who had but four rifles and thirty rounds of ammunition between them, and, acting on his own initiative, lay in wait for the advancing Boers in the sand dunes, a short distance from the town. At about 3 a.m. the Boers advanced, and, being fired on by the Bastards, retired. McDilling, knowing that they would return in strength, then led his little party off; but all were subsequently captured by a strong Boer patrol, which secured also the resident magistrate and the chief constable of the district. Other means of defence Kenhart had none.

The Boers marched in; the annexation proclamation was read; and, as at Prieska, a meeting was called and held on March 2nd, after which commandeering was straightway begun.

On March 8th Steenkamp himself came from Prieska to Kenhart to hasten the commandeering, moving thence to Upington to annex the Gordonia district. While at Kenhart, Steenkamp was visited by a deputation from Calvinia, who begged that their district might not be proclaimed, and urged the rebels to lay down their arms. This deputation remained two days and then returned to Calvinia.

A party of rebels which had already been sent to annex

REBELLION IN NORTH-WEST OF CAPE COLONY. 9

Upington had encamped, on March 3rd, some three miles from the town. Here they were met by the resident magistrate, who vainly endeavoured to persuade them to return to their homes. But Steenkamp and Jooste arrived on the 10th, the proclamation of annexation was read, and the Gordonia district, too, passed to the enemy. The war committee was elected on March 15th and here too fell to commandeering.

In order to assist the British subjects, the German Government in South-West Africa had not only suspended the duty on cattle and sheep, so that those who chose might take refuge in German territory, but had stationed a force of two hundred men near the border, 120 miles north-west of Upington, ready to receive refugees. The English inhabitants all left the district, most of them taking advantage of the asylum offered by their German neighbours. In Gordonia, as in other districts, the Dutch inhabitants were convinced of the ultimate success of the Boers. Many had already voluntarily gone to join the enemy; and at the time of the rebel invasion, the remainder, believing in the reported Boer victories, were in no way unwilling to join the rebels, whose numbers rapidly increased. They were not, however, destined to prove their value in the field. The arrival of Liebenberg and Steenkamp in the Prieska district had been reported to Cape Town; and on February 19th the High Commissioner telegraphed to Lord Roberts, urging that the movement should be promptly checked. *German courtesy to British subjects.*

Lord Roberts was at this time engrossed with the blockade of General Cronje's force in the river bed at Paardeberg. He at once telegraphed orders to Colonel J. Adye, R.A., who was then at Arundel, under Major-General Clements, to proceed to De Aar, and take command of a column for the suppression of the rebel movement. Adye's instructions were to move on Britstown and to prevent disaffection from spreading in the direction of Carnarvon and Victoria West. There was some delay in starting, owing to the fact that the Commander-in-Chief's message to Clements had not been repeated to Brigadier-General H. H. Settle, the general officer commanding at Orange River; but on February 23rd Adye reported that he was ready *The Commander-in-Chief orders the suppression of the rebellion.*

THE WAR IN SOUTH AFRICA.

to start for Britstown. The following day, the Warwickshire mounted infantry company, eighty strong, left De Aar for Britstown, which lay thirty-five miles to the west. A second company was sent on February 25th, but was recalled for service elsewhere on the 26th. On February 27th Lord Kitchener arrived at De Aar, and instructed Adye to proceed with the Field battery then at De Aar to join the mounted infantry company at Britstown, and to drive off any rebels he might find commandeering in that part of the country. The rebel movement was not known to have spread south of Prieska, though at this time Liebenberg was at Omdraai Vlei.

<small>Lord Kitchener arrives at De Aar.</small>

On February 28th, Brigadier-General Settle, upon whom had devolved the pacification of the disaffected region, submitted his plan of action to Lord Kitchener. He proposed first a joint advance by Colonel Sir Charles Parsons from Victoria West to Carnarvon, and by Adye from Britstown, to hold the rebels in check at Houwater. Adye would then advance to Omdraai Vlei, where Settle, moving from Orange River, would meet him and take the two columns on to Prieska. This being approved, Adye left De Aar on February 28th, with the 44th Field battery and two companies of the City Imperial Volunteers, and joined the mounted infantry company at Britstown on March 1st. On the 3rd he received information that the rebels had occupied Houwater, and telegraphed to Settle for reinforcements. In reply, he was informed that a company of South Australian mounted infantry was on the way to join him from Cape Town, but that he was not to wait for them before harassing the enemy. Accordingly, on March 4th, Adye moved from Britstown with the company of Warwickshire mounted infantry and the 44th battery, and, having made a circuit to clear up country in which it was reported that rebels had been looting farms, he encamped at Karee Boosch Poort, a farm about halfway from Britstown to Houwater. The following day he was joined by one of the City Imperial Volunteer companies, which he had called up from Britstown, and spent the day making a personal reconnaissance of the enemy's position. In front of Houwater are a series of defensible ridges, and on the nearest of

<small>Plans for the suppression.</small>

<small>Adye's movements.</small>

REBELLION IN NORTH-WEST OF CAPE COLONY. 11

these a rebel post was observed. Adye then decided to make a reconnaissance in force the following day, with a view to ascertaining the enemy's strength, position and armament. He had no intention of fighting an engagement, having made up his mind, that, unless the enemy had vacated the position, he would retire again to Karee Boosch; and he informed his officers that such were his intentions.

Starting early on March 6th, the force marched without incident until, on arriving within four miles of Houwater, the leading scouts were fired on from the ridge on which the enemy's post had been seen the previous day. Till then the advance had been unobserved, and Adye was now opposite the enemy's left flank. On the guns being brought into action, the enemy's piquets retired, followed by the mounted infantry and City Imperial Volunteers up to the near end of the ridge which they had recently occupied. The enemy then brought up reinforcements and with them a 9-pr. Krupp and a Vickers-Maxim, which engaged the troops in front. At the same time it was reported to Adye that a force of mounted men was working round his left flank, with the evident object of cutting off his line of retreat. Adye then gave the order to retire. Estimating the enemy's strength at three hundred to four hundred men, he considered that with the force at his disposal it would be impossible to push his advance further. Nevertheless, the fire of the enemy's guns was completely kept under by the 44th battery, and there had been no casualties. Once the retirement commenced, the advantages were all on the side of the Boers, who, being mounted, repeatedly got round the flanks of the little detachment, the pace of which was regulated by the tired infantry. The Boers clung to the column to within two miles of the camp at Karee Boosch, when, darkness coming on, they turned back. The casualties during the retirement were three killed, fourteen wounded, and six prisoners. The following day (March 7th), Adye returned with his detachment to Britstown. *His skirmish at Houwater.*

Meanwhile, on March 5th, Settle had also started from Hopetown with a column, consisting of one battery New South Wales artillery, one company Gloucester mounted infantry, Orpen's *Settle's movements.*

Light Horse, and the City Imperial Volunteer cyclists. Karee Kloof or Plaats was reached on March 8th, and a depôt of supplies was formed there. That day information was received that the main body of the rebel force was at Roodepoort, and that detachments, each about three hundred strong, were at Zoutpan and Houwater. The advance was continued, and a small party of rebels was encountered near Schiffer's Pan on March 10th and driven back with loss.

When the news of Adye's affair reached Headquarters, Lord Roberts decided to send his Chief of the Staff, Major-General Lord Kitchener, to superintend the operations west of the railway line, Settle being ordered to suspend all further movements pending his arrival.

Sir C. Parsons' movements.

Sir Charles Parsons, with the southern column, had sent two companies New Zealand Mounted Rifles to Carnarvon, which was occupied on March 8th. The West Australian mounted infantry, which had arrived at Victoria West from Cape Town, left for Vosburg, near Carnarvon, the next day, but were recalled on March 10th, and arrived at Victoria West on March 13th. The force concentrated there on the morning of the 13th consisted of: One company Derby Imperial Yeomanry, two companies Canadian mounted infantry, and two batteries (D. and E.) Royal Canadian artillery. This column marched on the 13th and was followed two days later by the West Australian mounted infantry, who overtook it before reaching Carnarvon, where the force arrived on March 17th.

It was known that the rebels had retired north from Houwater after Adye's skirmish of the 6th. When Lord Kitchener arrived at De Aar on March 10th, he decided to take reinforcements to Britstown, and advance to Houwater, where Sir C. Parsons' column would join him with a view to supporting Settle's advance on Prieska. That day, however, information was received that the rebel commandant at Kenhart was about to descend upon Calvinia. Lord Kitchener, therefore, ordered Sir C. Parsons' column to Van Wyks Vlei, where its presence would check any hostile movement towards Calvinia, trusting to his own strength to support Settle.

REBELLION IN NORTH-WEST OF CAPE COLONY. 13

Immediately on receipt of the news of Adye's encounter, Lieut.-Colonel G. F. C. Mackenzie, with four companies 1st Suffolk regiment, had marched from De Aar to Britstown, which they reached on March 8th. On March 13th Lord Kitchener arrived at Britstown, bringing with him the remainder of the 1st Suffolk regiment, 68th battery Royal Field artillery, Suffolk and Cheshire Imperial Yeomanry, one squadron Nesbitt's Horse, one squadron Kitchener's Horse, and one company South Australian mounted infantry. Already at Britstown were : One company Warwick mounted infantry, 44th battery Royal Field artillery, two companies City Imperial Volunteers, and four companies 1st Suffolk regiment.

<small>Lord Kitchener at Britstown.</small>

Lord Kitchener's instructions to Settle were, to turn the enemy out of Zoutpan, and, moving by Groot Varsh Kuil Drift, to co-operate with his own column in an advance on Prieska. On March 14th Adye was sent on with 550 mounted men to reconnoitre to Houwater, which was occupied by Lord Kitchener the following day. The advance to Prieska *viâ* Roodepoort and Omdraai Vlei was carried out without incident, no enemy being seen. Colonel B. T. Mahon took over command of the advanced cavalry on March 18th, and entered Prieska March 19th. On March 20th Lord Kitchener arrived with one squadron Yeomanry, the 44th battery Royal Field artillery and the 7th Dragoon Guards less one squadron, which, with the 68th battery Royal Field artillery, two companies Suffolk regiment and Yeomanry details, were left at Doornbergfontein. The remainder of the column followed on to Prieska.

<small>At Prieska.</small>

Settle left Karee Kloof, about forty miles south-west of Hopetown, on March 18th, advanced, as instructed, by Zoutpan, and, moving on the right flank and in communication with Lord Kitchener's column, reached Prieska on March 21st. No sign of the enemy had been seen during the advance ; but, as the Commander-in-Chief had foretold, the colony's speediest purge had come not from the south, but the north. After Cronje's capture, repeated orders had been sent from Fourteen Streams to General Liebenberg, telling him to retire immediately, and warning him that he was in imminent danger of being cut off.

<small>The effect of the capture of Cronje.</small>

Liebenberg had consequently fallen back on Prieska, which he reached on March 15th, and that day he heard of the fall of Bloemfontein. He at once sent his wagons, guns and the Transvaal commando across the Orange. The following day he held a council of the rebels whom he had created, and was now about to desert; and, explaining that he was recalled, advised them to await Steenkamp's return. On March 17th he started with his party for Fourteen Streams. The Prieska rebels, seeing their dream vanish with the retiring Transvaalers, at once threw down their arms and dispersed to their farms, to the bewilderment of 150 men of Kenhart, who came to Prieska on March 17th, and seeing the state of affairs, at once returned whence they had come. On March 19th, Jooste at Kenhart wired to Steenkamp at Upington to know what was to be done. The reply pricked yet another hole in the fast subsiding bladder. Jooste was told to destroy all papers, and to instruct every man to look to his own safety. The Kenhart rebels, too, consequently laid down their virgin rifles, and one and all returned to their homes. At Upington Steenkamp had assembled about three hundred men, for the most part unarmed, who were to have been equipped at Prieska. On March 19th he likewise dismissed his flock and fled to Griquatown himself.

While Lord Kitchener and Brigadier-General Settle were advancing on Prieska, Sir C. Parsons' column on the left had reached Van Wyks Vlei after having concentrated at Carnarvon. Owing to difficulties with the water supply, Sir C. Parsons had decided to push forward his column in two divisions. The leading portion, under command of Major M. Cradock, consisted of a company of Canadian and two companies of New Zealand Mounted Rifles, with a section of D. battery Royal Canadian artillery. These left Carnarvon on March 19th, and were followed by the remainder of the column, under Lieut.-Colonel C. W. Drury, on March 21st. On March 22nd Cradock's detachment had reached De Naauwte, and the main body Van Wyks Vlei. Owing to heavy rains the road between Van Wyks Vlei and De Naauwte became impassable for wheeled transport for the next three days. On March 27th the main body advanced as far as Hartebeeste river, which was found to be in flood. Sir C. Parsons then asked for permission to send back Drury's column, and to go on with the remainder from De Naauwte to Kenhart. This proposal having been agreed to, after three days' rest at Hartebeeste river, Drury started with the main body on April 4th, reached Carnarvon on the 7th, and De Aar on April 14th. Cradock's detachment pushed on by forced marches from De Naauwte, and entered Kenhart unopposed on March 31st. There the leaders in the rebel movement were arrested, and some 170 rifles and 20,000 rounds of ammunition were collected from farms in the vicinity. The column remained at Kenhart till April 8th, when, having been relieved, it started for Victoria Road, which was reached on April 17th. The march of Sir C. Parsons' column was made under exceptionally trying conditions. Continuous and heavy rains had rendered the roads most difficult; after leaving De Naauwte the wagons had to be manhandled for some miles through water three feet in depth. Supplies ran short; and from the time of the flooding of the Hartebeeste river, which prevented wagon communication with Van Wyks Vlei, Cradock's force was entirely dependent for forage and rations on such supplies as could be found in the country. There was much sickness among men and horses. In the New Zealand Mounted Rifles alone, as many as seventy out of two hundred men were on the sick list at one time, chiefly suffering from dysentery, and a large percentage of the horses were unfit for work. *Sir C. Parsons at Kenhart.*

To return to Lord Kitchener's column. Finding that the country was clear of any organised rebel bands, Lord Kitchener decided to send Settle with a flying column, one thousand strong, by Upington to co-operate with Sir C. Parsons' column moving on Kenhart; and, leaving Adye with a force of all arms to garrison Prieska, to return himself to De Aar with the remainder of the force. Accordingly on March 22nd Lord Kitchener started back with the 7th Dragoon Guards, and Staffordshire, Hampshire and Suffolk companies of 4th battalion Imperial Yeomanry. Overtaking at Houwater the troops which had been *Lord Kitchener returns to De Aar.*

left at Doornbergfontein, he moved by Britstown, and reached De Aar on March 27th.

Settle's flying column, consisting of one battery New South Wales artillery, one company Gloucestershire mounted infantry, one company Suffolk mounted infantry, 2nd battalion Imperial Yeomanry, Orpen's Light Horse, one squadron Kitchener's Horse, and City Imperial Volunteer cyclists, started on March 22nd with twenty days' supplies, and reached Drachoender on March 25th, progress being much delayed by heavy rains and bad roads. Koegas Pont, fifteen miles from Drachoender, was seized, and orders given for the ponts at Kheis and Groot Drink to be sunk or destroyed. One section of the battery, one and a half squadrons Orpen's Horse, one squadron Imperial Yeomanry, and the Suffolk company mounted infantry, were pushed on *Settle's troops at Upington.* from Drachoender, and entered Upington on March 30th, securing some of the leading rebels and members of the local war committee, who were in the act of leaving the town. The remainder of the column entered Upington on April 2nd. A section of the battery and the Gloucester company mounted infantry were then sent to relieve Sir C. Parsons, and reached Kenhart on April 5th. Sir C. Parsons, as previously related, started three days later with his column for De Aar. To guard against further trouble in these districts, garrisons were now placed at Prieska, Drachoender, Koegas Pont, Upington and Kenhart.

On April 8th, Brigadier-General Settle issued orders and proclamations, dealing with the duties of commandants and the treatment of inhabitants and rebels; these were made known *He is succeeded by Adye.* through the districts. He was shortly afterwards recalled to his duties on the lines of communication, and was succeeded in the command of the north-west districts by Adye. The chief duties of the commandants were connected with the surrendered rebels, who were dealt with according to the evidence against them as to the part they had played. All arms were required to be handed in and all inhabitants to register their names and receive passes.

Although there still remained many disaffected persons, the more determined rebels had all moved north of the Orange.

REBELLION IN NORTH-WEST OF CAPE COLONY. 17

Parties from Griqualand West occasionally appeared on the north bank and exchanged shots with the piquets; and on April 13th a small commando attacked the post at Koegas Pont, which was held by thirty-seven Orpen's Light Horse. The enemy was driven back, Orpen's Horse losing two killed and one wounded. The river at this time of the year was about two hundred yards wide, and could only be crossed at the ponts, of which there were but three between Hopetown and the German frontier, namely, at Prieska, Koegas and Upington. Adye had orders to confine his operations to the south of the river; but when the river had fallen sufficiently to allow of passage by the drifts, he made one or two raids on the right bank, capturing several hundred head of stock and arresting a few farmers who were known to be harbouring rebels. There was no further sign of rebellion south of the Orange. In Griqualand, however, the trouble continued, and in May, Lieut.-General Sir C. Warren was appointed governor of that portion of the Colony, which was well known to him in former campaigns. Early in the month he began the task of suppression; and establishing himself at Belmont on the 6th, he undertook the following scheme of operations:— *Sir C. Warren appointed Governor of Griqualand.*

1. To drive the rebels out of Herbert district as far as the Vaal river and capture Douglas, thus pacifying the whole of the territory east of the Vaal, and securing Hopetown. *His plans.*

2. To attack and drive out the rebels on the Kaap range, and capture Campbell and Griquatown, and liberate all the western portion of Griqualand West.

3. To relieve Kuruman and drive the rebels from Bechuanaland.*

On assuming control he found himself in command of the following troops: One battery Canadian artillery, two companies 8th battalion Imperial Yeomanry, four companies 19th battalion Imperial Yeomanry, eight companies Duke of Edinburgh's

* Sir Charles Warren's report.

Own Volunteer Rifles, one company Warren's Scouts.* To these were subsequently added a detachment of Royal Munster Fusiliers mounted infantry, a section of Cape artillery, and a company of Cape Town Highlanders.

<small>May 15th, 1900. He takes the field.</small>

This force Sir Charles Warren gradually collected at his base at Belmont; and by May 15th he considered that he was strong enough to carry out the first part of his plans. Sending forward half a battalion of the Duke of Edinburgh's Volunteer Rifles to take up a position at Rooipan, he himself followed three days later with one company Imperial Yeomanry, two guns Canadian artillery, thirty police, and the detachment of the Royal Munster Fusiliers mounted infantry. It was reported that Douglas was occupied by about three hundred or four hundred Boers, who could readily be reinforced from Campbell and its vicinity. By a night march made on the 20th, Sir Charles Warren turned the flank of the Boer position on the Kuki Hills, and evaded a concealed entrenchment on the bank of the Vaal which commanded the direct road by which he had been expected to approach. After a few rounds from the artillery, the enemy fled, leaving wagons, Cape carts, personal effects, and ammunition in the laager, besides a considerable number of cattle. Douglas itself was occupied without opposition. In collecting the enemy's cattle a patrol of the Yeomanry had a skirmish the same afternoon on the west of the Vaal, having an officer wounded.

After the capture of Douglas, the country east of the Vaal being now clear of rebels, Sir Charles Warren was able to proceed with the second part of his scheme. The enemy had been reinforced from Griquatown and Campbell, and for a time held a strong position about two and a half miles to the west of Douglas, but evacuated it on the approach of two columns brought against them on the 24th from different directions by Sir C. Warren. Owing to deficiency in transport, it was impossible to make any further advance, and Sir Charles Warren

---

* These scouts, in number about thirty, were chiefly loyal Dutchmen, who, either personally or through their relations, had known Sir Charles Warren during his service in Griqualand some years previously.

remained about five miles west of Douglas. On the 26th, however, he was able to move to a farm called Faber's Put, where there was a good water supply, about twelve miles from Douglas in the direction of Campbell. Here he determined to collect all his forces, with a view to advancing on Campbell by way of Tweefontein. But he was still much hampered by lack of transport; and, indeed, the difficulty of bringing up reserves of food was such that on the 28th there was only one day's supply in hand. On that day a reconnaissance was made for several miles in the direction of Campbell, and some shots were exchanged with the enemy, who everywhere retired. On the 29th a convoy of provisions arrived at Faber's Put, and Sir Charles Warren now prepared to continue his forward movement. In this he was anticipated by the action of the enemy, who took the offensive first.

Surrounded by thick scrub, Sir C. Warren's position at Faber's Put was bounded by low ridges to the north-east and west; and the extent of its front, which faced northwards, was marked by two farmhouses eight hundred yards apart. A shallow valley, trending towards the Vaal river, fell southward from the front between the comparatively high plateaux on the right and left. In this depression lay a garden of fruit trees, and near its northern end was situated the water supply. Most of the infantry were bivouacked near the farmhouse on the right flank, with Sir C. Warren's Headquarters. The men of the Intelligence branch, Warren's Scouts, and the remainder of the infantry were at the north-west farmhouse on the left; the Yeomanry and artillery occupied some kraals in the garden near the water supply, that is, slightly in rear of the rest. The front and flanks were covered by infantry outposts, and the Yeomanry furnished piquets on the high ground to the south-east and south-west. The enemy having concentrated from various quarters to the number of five hundred to six hundred men at Campbell on the night of the 29th of May, their Commandants determined to attack Faber's Put from three sides in the early morning of the 30th. One party, under Forster, composed of men from the northern part of Hay and Barkly West districts, *The Boers decide to attack him.*

was to attack the Headquarters, farmhouse and infantry bivouac. Its first shots were to be the signal to a second party under De Villiers, formed of picked marksmen taken from the country about Campbell and Griquatown, which was then to make its way into the garden from the east, and attack the Yeomanry and artillery. A third division under Venter, composed of men from Postmasburg, was to take possession of the western ridge, and fire into the kraals and artillery bivouac. This programme was begun by a combined movement from the north-east, passing round and to the east of the British position, the two first-named detachments breaking off as they arrived opposite to their points of attack, while the third, by a wide détour to the south, made for the western ridge.

May 30th, 1900. The attack at Faber's Put.

At 5.30 on the morning of the 30th the blow fell. Immediately after reveillé, and before it was yet light, a sudden burst of musketry from the east directed upon the Headquarters and the infantry camp, forced the piquets, which were buried in the thick bush, to fall back. The Volunteers were at once under arms, and two companies with a Maxim gun, under Captain G. Twycross, hurried out in the direction of the firing. One company moved to hold the front and north, the other was kept in reserve. The Boers had made their way through the bush to within 250 yards, and were for pushing on when they were encountered by the two companies of Volunteers, who met them with so much determination that they were speedily driven back to the eastern ridge and over the bushy plain beyond. The shooting at this point, which was very heavy and well directed, ceased about 6 a.m., when Sir C. Warren rode to see that the Yeomanry were on the alert, and the artillery ready for action as soon as there should be sufficient light. On approaching the camp of these units he and his staff were assailed by heavy fire at short range, which wounded both his aides-de-camp, and killed the horse of his chief staff officer. It was clear that the Boers had occupied part of the garden, and Sir C. Warren directed the reserve company of the Volunteers, with all the other infantry at hand, and the Maxim gun, to fire upon the garden and particularly upon its nearer edges. After ten minutes' fusilade he ordered Captain W. V. Simkins with half a company to charge. This party ran upon the garden; but before they could close the enemy fled, followed by the fire of the artillery which came into action beyond the garden. In a few minutes more the whole attack was over.

On the western ridge the chief success of Venter's band was the stampeding of all the horses of the Yeomanry and some of the artillery. Whilst the Boers fired at long range into the camp, some of their more daring men pushed forward and lined a stone-walled cemetery about six hundred yards to the west of the large kraal in which the horses were enclosed. The frightened animals surged up against the wall of the kraal, broke it down and scattered in all directions. It was noticed that few but the English horses belonging to the Yeomanry stampeded; most of the Cape and Hungarian horses did not stray from camp. The Yeomanry then became closely engaged; and eventually, with the assistance of Lieutenant-Colonel S. Hughes and such men as he could collect, drove Venter from the cemetery and his position on the western ridge. In advancing over open ground to the ridge, on which one of their piquets had stubbornly held its own throughout, the Yeomanry suffered many casualties and would have lost even more heavily had not a party under Lieutenant A. W. Huntington covered the flank by firing point blank into the garden. As the attack died away, Sir Charles Warren sent out all the available mounted men, two guns, and two companies of infantry across the veld to the north, in the hope of intercepting the retreating enemy. Unfortunately there were not now available sufficient horses for more than scouting duties, and, though some shells were fired, the pursuit was ineffectual. Every effort was then made to collect the scattered horses, a difficult task, as many had strayed widely, some for over twenty miles. Of the British troops engaged in this brief but spirited affair fifteen were killed and thirty wounded, including Colonel W. A. Spence, Duke of Edinburgh's Own Volunteer Rifles, killed, and four officers wounded. The losses of the Boers were undoubtedly heavy. Thirteen were left dead on the field, and several severely wounded were taken prisoners.

It was subsequently reported that, altogether, at least seventy were killed and wounded.

Its effect on the rebellion. The action at Faber's Put was a fortunate occurrence for Sir Charles Warren; for it solved a problem which was about to present some difficulty. To have himself attacked the Boers in their positions at Campbell and Griquatown would have been a costly manœuvre. That his opponents adopted the unexpected and unusual course of themselves taking the offensive was due to their belief that they only had untried and unsteady troops to deal with. Their mistake, with the serious loss which it involved, had a far-reaching effect, practically deciding the fate of the rebellion, and causing its sudden collapse. On the same day as this action four companies of Paget's Horse arrived at Schmidt Drift, twenty-four miles from Faber's Put. Of these two were brought on to Faber's Put, as was also the garrison that had been left at Douglas. During the next few days Sir C. Warren was fully occupied in accumulating the food and transport necessary to further operations.

Adye in the Prieska district. In connection with Sir Charles Warren's operations north of the Orange river, record must here be made of the action taken by Colonel J. Adye in the Prieska district. By order of the C.S.O., Lines of Communication, on May 19th Adye had consulted with Sir C. Warren how he could most usefully assist that general in his forthcoming operations in Griqualand West. He was informed that this could best be done by clearing the rebels from the country on the north bank of the Orange river for thirty miles north of Prieska, or as far north as Kheis, if sufficient force was available. Adye, having intelligence of the presence of Boer commandos opposite Koegas Pont, and at Groot Drink, decided to move down the river; and, on May 22nd, he marched from Prieska with four guns 44th battery Royal Field artillery, one company Gloucestershire mounted infantry, and a detachment of Nesbitt's Horse. On arrival at Drachoender, he learned that the Boers had moved from Groot Drink to Kheis, had sent patrols across the river, and had done some mischief. He therefore determined to march on Kheis, and drive them from the river at that point. He considered that he would then be

REBELLION IN NORTH-WEST OF CAPE COLONY. 23

at the nearest point on the river to the Kuruman and Langeberg districts, and would be able to threaten the retreat of rebel commandos along the river, either above him or below. He left Drachoender on the 25th, and was followed by the Lancashire Imperial Yeomanry, also by the Warwickshire Imperial Yeomanry, which he had ordered to join him from Kenhart. On the 26th Stof Kraal, a farm on the Orange river, a few miles above Kheis, was reached; and on the 27th Adye was able to reconnoitre the enemy's position, and to form his plan of attack. The rebel laager at Kheis was situated exactly opposite the drift on the north bank of the Orange river, which was here four hundred yards wide. The banks were covered with high trees; in mid-stream lay a large and thickly wooded island, to be crossed in passing from one bank to the other. To have forced this drift in face of an enemy holding the further bank, and perhaps the island, would have been almost impossible for Adye's small force. Fortunately it was ascertained that there was another drift six miles higher up the river at Tesebe, which was not strongly held. Adye, therefore, determined to force a passage at the Tesebe drift with his mounted troops, while his artillery shelled the laager from the opposite bank at Kheis. On the morning of the 28th, he marched from Stof Kraal concealed by the trees that line the river bank. The 44th battery took up a position on the left bank, opposite the rebel laager, escorted by the Warwickshire Yeomanry, who joined the force after a rapid march from Kenhart just as the guns prepared for action. The remainder of the troops were hidden opposite Tesebe Drift.

May 28th, 1900. He crosses the Orange at Tesebe Drift.

As soon as the artillery opened fire musketry was directed upon the enemy's piquet at Tesebe Drift, which, startled by this attack and by the sound of the guns, offered such feeble resistance that Adye was able to cross without any loss. He then moved swiftly down the right bank towards the laager, and found that the shells of the artillery had forced the enemy to evacuate it, and to fall back upon some low, bushy hills to the north. Here the Boers showed every intention of making a stand, and Adye detached the Lancashire Yeomanry, under Captain L. H. Jones, to get round to their left rear, holding back his main attack until this movement was completed. The artillery fire was diverted from the laager to the enemy's new position; and, when Jones closed in and Adye himself advanced, the Boers found themselves enclosed and under long-range artillery fire. Though taken by surprise, they made a determined resistance, under the leadership of a foreigner named Hermann, who was killed. Finally, they broke and fled, abandoning their laager and all that it contained, including one hundred rebel women and children,* a few loyalist prisoners, arms, correspondence, about 30,000 rounds of ammunition, with wagons, carts, baggage and plunder from neighbouring farms. A very large number of cattle and live stock were also taken. The broken nature of the ground and the smallness of his force, prevented Adye from making any effective pursuit.

The affair at Kheis Drift.

Whilst these events were in progress, a misadventure had occurred at Kheis Drift. There the officer in command, seeing that Adye was in full possession of the enemy's laager, and in action beyond it, desired Major J. A. Orr-Ewing, Warwickshire Yeomanry, to ascertain if the drift was practicable, and, if so, to send over and communicate with Adye. In response to a call for volunteers, Lieutenant J. S. Forbes and Corporal A. Baxter attempted to cross to the island in mid-stream. But some of the refugees from the laager were there in hiding, and, at a range of not more than 150 yards, they opened fire upon the daring men, killing their horses. With difficulty the two regained the left bank, where the corporal fell mortally wounded. Orr-Ewing and Private E. P. Ashley, who went to his assistance, were also struck down; and, as they were still being shot at, Civil Surgeon Dun, Lieutenant C. S. Paulet and eight non-commissioned officers and men of the Warwickshire Yeomanry ran forward to help them. They, too, came under a deadly fire, and all, except Lieutenant Paulet and two men, were hit. Major Orr-Ewing, Corporal Baxter and Private W. F. Lane were killed. The rest of the Yeomanry had lined the bank to cover this

* "I was unaware that the laager contained women and children or I should not have shelled it, but fortunately none were hit, having been quickly hidden in a spruit or gully."—Colonel Adye's Report.

attempt, but the enemy were so well concealed that the fire had no effect, nor could the guns be brought to bear on the island. Colonel Adye, fully occupied on the right bank, knew nothing of all this. When he heard of the presence of the enemy on the island, he sent one of his prisoners captured in the laager to try to induce these men to lay down their arms, hoping to avoid loss of life in ejecting them. Six rebels then surrendered, but several others succeeded in escaping.

The total losses to Adye's force in the attack on the laager and at the drift were three officers and five other ranks killed; three officers and fourteen other ranks wounded. The bodies of the Boer leader and some others were found, and several wounded (some mortally) prisoners were taken. The result of this action was that the whole course of the Orange river was, for the time being, free from rebellion. There was no further disturbance till early in 1901, when the thinly inhabited districts again fell into a state of unrest through the action of raiding commandos. *Effect of the action on the rebellion.*

On June 3rd, Sir C. Warren recommenced his forward movement, advancing by Tweefontein and Knoffelfontein to Campbell, which he occupied on the 5th. There were considerable hostile forces in his front; but he was careful to turn all positions that offered opportunity for defence, and the commandos everywhere fell back before him, their rearguard evacuating Campbell only an hour before the British column approached. At Campbell large numbers of the rebels surrendered, giving up arms, horses and equipment. Sir C. Warren was here delayed till the 7th waiting for supplies, but he was able to occupy Griquatown with an advance guard on the 7th, and to go there himself on the 8th. After this date the General was principally engaged in arranging for the effective occupation of the country by establishing garrisons at various points. On June 20th, De Villiers' commando, to the number of two hundred, laid down their arms at Koning; and nothing remained but to bring the country into a settled condition under martial law, before handing it over to Civil Government. On the 24th, Kuruman was occupied, and measures were taken to bring *Sir C. Warren completes his plans* the normal number of police into the district from the lines of communication.

<small>And returns to Cape Town.</small> In July, much of Sir Charles Warren's force was removed for other service, and as his task was successfully completed, and the districts in which he had been employed had passed under the control of the O.C. Lines of Communication, he returned to Cape Town.

CHAPTER II.

THE REORGANISATION AT BLOEMFONTEIN.

MARCH 14TH TO MAY 2ND, 1900.

WHEN Lord Roberts occupied Bloemfontein, on March 13th, 1900, his available strength was 34,000, of which 8,619 men with 7,760 horses belonged to the mounted arms, exclusive of artillery. But neither cavalry nor artillery can be reckoned as fighting units in the field if their horses are unfit for work, and Lord Roberts had now no cavalry, no mounted infantry, and no artillery with horses in effective condition. For the next stage of the campaign—the defeat of the forces which were being gathered for the defence of Johannesburg and Pretoria—Lord Roberts estimated that he would require 50,000 men in all, of whom 15,000 must be properly mounted, exclusive of Imperial Yeomanry, whom he expected to be from 2,000 to 3,000 strong. This was to be the actual striking army; but it was essential also to guard the long and exposed line of communications, and to restore order and establish confidence throughout the broad territory of the Free State. As early as March 24th he announced that he did not expect to be able to move till April 15th; the march did not actually begin till May 3rd. There was more to be done than there is space here to record, though enough will be said, perhaps, to enlighten those who continually wonder at the pauses which occur in the midst of the most successful operations.

The army which marched into Bloemfontein had expended every military requisite except its own spirit and physical fitness. Those remained unimpaired until the arrival at Bloemfontein

The needs of the Army.

relaxed the healthy tension of fighting, and allowed the privations of the past march and the poisonous water of Paardeberg to tell their tale. Then the ranks of the sick were recruited with alarming rapidity, and quite out of proportion to the available means for dealing with so sudden an outbreak, whilst there were many wounded to be nursed. The capture of the convoy at Waterval Drift* had meant the loss of 180,000 rations of bread-stuffs and groceries, 70,200 of preserved meats, 38,792 grain rations and eight wagon loads of medical comforts ; and so rapid had been Lord Roberts' advance, and so difficult the roads behind him, that the Army Service Corps, in spite of extraordinary efforts, had never been able to make good the losses. Fortunately ample supplies were found in Bloemfontein. These were requisitioned on payment, and men and animals at last received full rations. The local manager of the Bank of Africa placed £60,000 in specie at the disposal of Major-General W. F. Kelly, Deputy-Adjutant-General, on his note of hand. The disbursement of this money to the troops on March 26th enabled the men to purchase necessaries to which they had long been strangers. This relief, however, could only be temporary; only a steady flow of stores from the coast would meet the pressing needs. The

The sick and wounded.

ever-increasing number of sick, the difficulty in providing accommodation and care for them, and the deficiency of medical comforts in consequence of the loss of the convoy, rendered urgent the speedy arrival of general hospitals, and with them suitable food. On the first occupation of the town, the only means of providing for the sick and wounded were the Field hospitals, and such buildings in the town as could be equipped. The former had never been intended for the accommodation of patients for more than a few days ; and in them, overcrowded as they were, proper treatment was impossible. More buildings could have been utilised, but neither equipment nor staff was available.† Everything possible was done. All material in the town suitable for the treatment of sick and wounded was bought up, and the Sisters of the Church of England and Roman Catholic convents placed

---

* Volume II., pages 76—8.
† Report of Royal Commission on the care and treatment of the sick and wounded.

THE REORGANISATION AT BLOEMFONTEIN.

their buildings and resources at the disposal of the army authorities. Even more necessary for success in the field was a fresh supply of remounts. The value, and, indeed, the necessity, of mounted troops able to move at full pace had been amply demonstrated by French's successes. But these had been costly in the matter of horseflesh. On February 23rd French had reported "that the cavalry and artillery horses were unequal to a great effort, and that rest and forage were a necessity." Writing to Mr. Rhodes, Lord Roberts said : " Even if I were not detained here by Cronje, I should be unable to move, on account of the crippled state of the horses. For several days they were hard worked, with no grain and very little else to eat. Several of them are too weak for a prolonged effort, and I have sent for all available remounts to get the cavalry division in working order."* Again, Lord Roberts informed Sir Redvers Buller that he would probably be unable to leave Bloemfontein for three weeks or a month, " as I must wait until remounts for the cavalry and artillery arrive."†

Supplies, hospital equipment and necessaries, and remounts were, therefore, the immediate wants ; and, except for what could be obtained by slow moving convoys from the Kimberley line, everything depended on the opening up of the newly-acquired railway. The re-establishment of through railway communication between the Orange Free State and the coast had been always the primary condition of the success of the campaign, and was from the first assumed to be vital to it. On February 20th Lord Roberts informed the Director of Railways of the intended change of the line of communication to the Naauwpoort Junction—Bloemfontein route, adding : " It is of immense importance to the existence of this force that there should be no delay in repairing the railway the moment the enemy is driven north of the river." The advance of Major-General Clements from Arundel and of Sir W. Gatacre through Stormberg on Bethulie‡

Marginal note: Railway communications.

---

* Letter to Mr. Rhodes, February 27th, 1900.

† Telegram from Venter's Vallei, March 12th, 1900.

‡ See Volume II., Chapter XV.

had been pressed mainly for this purpose. As soon as the Boers had been driven back, the Midland Field Railway section made good the railway between Arundel and Norval's Pont, and laid a bridge across the river at this point; the 12th Field company R.E. repaired the line from Stormberg to Bethulie; and the Railway Pioneer regiment, after mending the line between Rosmead and Stormberg, undertook the permanent repairs to the bridges at Norval's Pont and Bethulie. The railway bridges had been badly damaged; and although the line southwards from Bloemfontein was intact, no truck could cross the Orange river until the deviations and makeshift bridges had been finished. Through traffic was opened at Norval's Pont on March 27th, and railway communication was established at Bethulie on the same date, but only by means of shunting trucks by hand across the road bridge.

Change of Base.

On March 18th, Lord Roberts changed his base from Cape Town to Port Elizabeth and East London. This measure much shortened the railway journey, Bloemfontein being by rail 450 and 402 miles from these two ports respectively, as against 750 miles from Cape Town. Moreover, the use of three ports and three lines of railway much relieved the pressure on the western line, which continued to serve that side of the country, and to forward such troops and requisites for Lord Roberts' force as could not be shipped to the new bases without serious delay. There was still great congestion, not only at the ports, into which troops, remounts, and stores of all kinds had been pouring, but at various stations south of the Orange river, where loaded trucks lay in hundreds. There was also a scarcity of engines; there were blocks at the river crossings, and only a single line ran between Springfontein Junction and Bloemfontein; all of which made it at first difficult to do much more than forward enough food for each day. The affairs of Sannah's Post and Reddersburg made it necessary to use the railway for the transport of troops instead of stores, and so hampered the proper working of the line that it was not until April 27th that thirty days' supplies had been collected at Bloemfontein. At the base the officials were puzzled to know in what order and proportion

THE REORGANISATION AT BLOEMFONTEIN. 31

to comply with the multitudinous demands from the front. As the war needs grew more urgent, the sick and wounded in Bloemfontein suffered the more.* Some of the doctors and nurses asked for had been despatched from Cape Town on March 19th and soon afterwards, but in wholly insufficient numbers.

Ammunition was a pressing necessity. As early as February 21st, Lord Roberts had found it necessary to impress on all artillery officers at Paardeberg † the importance of economising ammunition, and the bombardment there had been seriously weakened on that account. Now the cavalry, infantry and artillery all needed replenishment.

The demands for remounts since the later days of February had been incessant. Between March 1st and March 13th, 254 artillery horses, 500 cavalry horses, 728 mounted infantry cobs, 369 Indian ponies, and 572 mules, all to replace casualties, had been issued to Lord Roberts' force. Yet on March 13th there were needed 1,000 cavalry and 500 artillery horses, 1,000 mounted infantry cobs, and 1,000 mules.‡ There was here no miscalculation of supply. The numbers of animals landed in South Africa always exceeded the demand ; but the strain on the railway did not allow the consignments to reach the front as fast as they were called for. Finally, there was a pressing demand for drafts to fill the gaps in the ranks, for reinforcements for the more extensive operations yet to come, and for boots and clothing to enable the army to march. *Remounts.*

Thanks in a great measure to the excellent work done by the railway staffs, both in construction and in the administration of the lines, the supply in all these matters gradually overtook the enormous requisitions ; and Lord Roberts began to build up the reserves which were necessary before he could move forward.

In the meanwhile every effort was being made to re-establish

---

* The condition of the hospitals in Bloemfontein led to the constitution of a Royal Commission in July, 1900, to consider and report upon the care and treatment of the sick and wounded in the campaign then proceeding.

† See Volume II., page 163.

‡ Telegram, March 13th, G.O.C. L. of C., to Secretary of State.

Administration of Bloemfontein.

order in the country, and to restore the ordinary conditions of life in the capital itself. On the entry of the troops into Bloemfontein, Major-General G. Pretyman had been appointed Military Governor; and for dealing with the civil population, Mr. J. A. Collins occupied the post of Landrost. With the assistance of Mr. J. G. Fraser, whose defeat by Mr. Steyn in the last presidential election had thrown the Orange Free State into war, steps were at once taken to open a market for supplies, and to collect the arms of burghers who were induced to surrender by the proclamation of March 15th.* The branch of the National Bank was re-opened for business, and postal service was resumed, the telegraphs being kept still in the hands of the Army. A newspaper† was also started, both as an official organ and in order to publish among the inhabitants true accounts of the situation. Schools were gradually re-opened, and generally a semblance of peace given to the fallen capital. The Cape Police, who had played so prominent a part in the defence of Kimberley, were ordered to return to their regular duties; and a proposal to raise a body of Military Police for service in the Orange Free State was submitted to the High Commissioner.‡ It was decided also that Colonial Volunteer corps should not be employed outside their own colony. In all matters connected with the administration of the conquered territory, Lord Roberts acted in concert with the High Commissioner.

Organisation of mounted troops.

Lord Roberts had further to consider the organisation of his force for the next move, the disposition of troops for the protection of his line of communications, and garrisons for points of importance. Opposition to the advance was expected on the Zand river, where Joubert was reported to have already collected 25,000 men, and to be drawing more commandos to him. The necessity for mobility in flying columns had given little rest to the mounted troops, and still caused loss of horses, which had to be made good. Besides the various drafts the

---

* See Volume II., page 260.

† "The Friend." Produced on March 15th under the joint editorship of Messrs. Rudyard Kipling, Perceval Landon, Julian Ralph, and H. A. Gwynne.

‡ Telegram Lord Roberts to High Commissioner, March 19th.

THE REORGANISATION AT BLOEMFONTEIN.

cavalry received, the 4th brigade, which, in compliance with Lord Roberts' request of January 28th*, had begun to reach the Colony by March 1st; the arrival of small units completed the cavalry division, which by April 14th was organised as follows :—

> 1st brigade (Porter)—6th Dragoon Guards, 2nd Dragoons, 6th Dragoons, New South Wales Lancers, Australian Horse, T. battery R.H.A., D. section Vickers-Maxims.
> 2nd brigade (Broadwood)—Household Cavalry, 10th Hussars, 12th Lancers, Q. battery R.H.A., E. section Vickers-Maxims.
> 3rd brigade (Gordon)—9th, 16th and 17th Lancers, R. battery R.H.A., I. section Vickers-Maxims.
> 4th brigade (Dickson)—7th Dragoon Guards, 8th and 14th Hussars, O. battery R.H.A., J. section Vickers-Maxims.

Such respites as the hard-worked cavalry enjoyed were devoted to re-fitting and re-mounting.

The mounted infantry, in or near Bloemfontein, on March 13th, consisted of Alderson's, Le Gallais', Martyr's and Ridley's commands. Lord Roberts wished to increase their numbers; and as far back as February 24th he had telegraphed from Paardeberg to the G.O.C. at Cape Town to forward without delay all available mounted infantry men who had horses. Telegraphing to Lord Kitchener on February 25th, he alluded to the dwindling numbers, and directed that the Burma mounted infantry, and all companies from the base should be sent on to him. He complained that the mounted troops with him were being wasted for want of proper administration. To check this, various units were amalgamated; and on April 3rd a new organisation, the fourth since the start, was approved for the mounted infantry. It was formed under Major-General I. S. M. Hamilton into a division composed of two brigades, commanded by Major-General E. T. H. Hutton and Colonel C. P. Ridley respectively. Each brigade consisted of four corps, each really

---

* Telegram, January 28th, Lord Roberts to Secretary of State.

a brigade of from three to five regiments. To each brigade was allotted a battery of Royal Horse artillery and two sections Vickers-Maxims.

From February 20th onwards considerable numbers of Imperial Yeomanry arrived in South Africa. Most of them were quite raw, especially in musketry; and all required organising, training, and carefully selected commanders. All this was handed over to Major-General J. P. Brabazon, who sent every unit at once to Maitland camp, near Cape Town, for training before they took their place in the line. By the middle of April about 4,200 Imperial Yeomanry were available; and these, with many still on the sea, were formed into twenty battalions. Six* battalions under Brabazon were ordered to join the main army on April 29th. Exclusive of one thousand Imperial Yeomanry for the Rhodesian Field Force, the total sent out from home was nine thousand. It was at this time that the Secretary of State decided to stop recruiting, his reasons being Lord Roberts' successes, the despatch of the VIIIth division, and the exhaustion of the best material. Lord Roberts agreed that no more Imperial Yeomanry need be sent; for he believed that with the troops then in transit the force in South Africa would be sufficient to finish the war, provided the several corps were fairly maintained by drafts.†

Organisation of the Artillery.
As so many Horse and Field batteries of Royal artillery had been already sent out to South Africa, it was decided,‡ with Lord Roberts' consent, that none should sail with the VIIIth division.§ The loss of the seven R.H.A. guns at Sannah's Post‖

---

* These were the 1st, 4th, 6th, 9th, 11th and 13th battalions. The 7th, 12th, 14th and 19th, under Lord Erroll, were assigned to the Orange Free State; the 3rd, 5th, 10th and 15th, under Lord Chesham, to Kimberley; the 2nd to Sir C. Warren, in Griqualand; the 17th and 18th to Beira; while the 8th, 16th and 20th remained in Cape Colony.

† Telegram, March 18th, 1900, Lord Roberts to Secretary of State.

‡ Telegram, February 26th, 1900, Secretary of State to Lord Roberts. At this date only eighteen Field batteries, of which five were newly raised, were left in Great Britain.

§ Telegram, February 28th, 1900, Lord Roberts to Secretary of State.

‖ See Volume II., Chapter XVII

THE REORGANISATION AT BLOEMFONTEIN. 35

was no impediment. Q. battery was supplied with a 12-pr. gun from Cape Town; to replace the other battery, J. battery, which had previously been armed with 15-pr. guns, received a 12-pr. outfit as soon as it could be sent up from the base. This gave two R.H.A. batteries to each of the four brigades of cavalry. Two Howitzer batteries and a City Imperial Volunteer battery also arrived. On April 14th a corps artillery was formed of J. and M. batteries R.H.A., 43rd, 65th and 87th Howitzer Field batteries, C.I.V. 12½-pr. battery, and the New Zealand Hotchkiss battery.

At the beginning of April, eleven infantry divisions, including the VIIIth (not all landed), were under Lord Roberts' command. Of these, four were in Natal.* Organisation of the Infantry.

De Wet's success in the south-eastern part of the Orange Free State obliged Lord Roberts to call at last for a division from the army of Natal. The recently formed Xth division under Sir A. Hunter was, under orders of April 9th, sent to Cape Colony; with it went the Imperial Light Horse.

At first the units of the VIIIth division (Lieut.-General Sir L. Rundle) disembarked at Cape Town; afterwards the ships, as they arrived, were ordered round to Port Elizabeth and East London. Lord Roberts had originally intended to place this division under Lord Methuen at Kimberley. Finding, however, that his own advance might be delayed by the Boer movements after Sannah's Post, he brought Sir L. Rundle with the fresh division to the Orange Free State. Of the Xth division from Natal, the 6th brigade (Barton) and Headquarters landed at Cape Town, the 5th (Hart) at East London, whence it moved to the relief of Wepener; both ultimately joined at Kimberley.

The addition of these two divisions gave Lord Roberts eight divisions altogether within his immediate sphere of operations. All were brought fairly up to strength by utilising drafts of regulars, some 9,000 of all ranks, twelve battalions of militia numbering about 6,900, and thirty-one companies of volunteers numbering about 3,500.

The ranks of the officers had become seriously depleted, and Officers.

* For composition and commands of Natal Army, see Appendix 1.

Lord Roberts asked for more, especially for mounted infantry. Fifty commissions were placed at the Commander-in-Chief's disposal for appointment amongst all the troops under his command. For mounted infantry, no officers could be sent from home; and it was suggested that, to meet the difficulty, all Imperial officers should be withdrawn from the Colonial forces and revert to regular duties, so as to be available for the purpose. As this could not be carried out, the deficiency of officers continued to be most serious.

The relief of Ladysmith had set free certain officers whom Lord Roberts wished to employ on his staff. During the stay at Bloemfontein the staff was, therefore, remodelled and completed.

On April 18th special orders were issued regulating the railway traffic for conveyance of supplies to Bloemfontein. All trains from Springfontein, with the exception of hospital, mail, and specially authorised trains, were to be exclusively used for the conveyance of supplies. Stores now fast accumulated at Bloemfontein; by May 2nd there was a reserve of forty-five days' food and sufficient equipment to allow the army to advance.

Transport. In order to improve the transport Lord Roberts had at Jacobsdal on February 18th divided the departmental duties, giving Major-General Sir W. Nicholson charge of the transport department, and leaving Colonel W. Richardson to look after the supplies only. On March 23rd Colonel E. W. D. Ward arrived from Ladysmith and took over the duties of Director of Supplies at Headquarters. Colonel Richardson then resumed the post he had previously held of Director of Supplies on the lines of communication and at the base.

When the army arrived at Bloemfontein, certain preparations for the next phase of the campaign were already forward. Whilst the march had been in progress, a reserve of mules, oxen and wagons had been collected. Profiting by experience gained during the march, Lord Roberts utilised the surplus in increasing the transport of the cavalry, the Bearer companies, and the Field hospitals.

THE REORGANISATION AT BLOEMFONTEIN. 37

The mobility of the cavalry had on several occasions been dangerously impaired by lack of forage. It was now enabled to take the field with four, instead of two days' rations and forage, as heretofore.

Owing to the insufficient number of trained Army Service Corps officers, orders were issued on April 17th for the transport with ammunition columns to be taken on charge by the Royal artillery ; and for the Army Service Corps personnel attached to those columns to revert to their Transport companies. Moreover, an order of May 19th sanctioned the re-appointment of regimental officers, to take charge of the transport attached to their units.

The disturbed state of the country made it necessary that the troops to be left behind in the Orange Free State should be fully equipped with transport. This and the provision of transport for the force about to march northwards placed a heavy strain on the department. To quote the Commander-in-Chief's own statement of his difficulties, " To carry the authorised amount of baggage, two days' supplies of food and forage for the infantry and four days' supplies for the mounted corps, as well as to equip the ambulances and the technical vehicles belonging to the Artillery and Engineers, over 22,000 mules, with a corresponding number of wagons, were required. Besides this, 2,500 ox-wagons, with 40,000 oxen, had to be provided for the ammunition and supply columns to carry the reserve ammunition and an average of seven days' reserve supplies."

" During the halt at Bloemfontein, steps had also to be taken to re-mobilise Lord Methuen's division, which had been denuded of most of its mule transport when Lord Roberts moved from the Modder river early in February; to equip with mule and ox transport Sir A. Hunter's division, which had been transferred from Natal to Kimberley ; to provide fifty mule-wagons for the flying column which was being organised for the relief of Mafeking ; and to replace the sixty-seven mule-wagons which were captured by the Boers at Sannah's Post. To satisfy the above demands nearly six thousand mules and four thousand oxen were needed, as well as wagons, harness and establishment."*

Strength of the Army.

By the time that the Commander-in-Chief was prepared to start all this had been collected, except the transport for two days' supplies for the cavalry, which caught up the division at Kroonstad on the way to Pretoria.

The army about to march was composed of three-and-a-half infantry divisions, four cavalry brigades, one division mounted infantry, with forty-two Horse artillery guns, sixty-six Field artillery guns,† ten Naval and siege guns, fourteen Vickers-Maxims, and seventy-three machine guns; with a proportion of Engineer and Medical units, making approximately a total of some 44,000 officers and men and 203 guns.‡

By the 1st May all the important points in the south-eastern districts of the Orange Free State were securely held. The protection arranged for the railway was satisfactory. With a sufficiency of troops equipped and supplied, and his transport practically complete, Lord Roberts felt justified in ordering a forward movement towards Kroonstad.

Preparations completed.

He would have preferred to postpone active operations for a few days longer, in order to perfect his arrangements; but the march from Bloemfontein would have the effect of reducing the opposition to Hunter's advance across the Vaal, and assist Mahon to the relief of Mafeking, about which he was anxious. Orders regulating the general conduct of the movement were issued on April 30th, and the first step forward was made by Ian Hamilton's column moving on Winburg. The Commander-in-Chief with Headquarters left Bloemfontein early on May 3rd. Just before Lord Roberts left Bloemfontein he had verbally told Lieut.-General Kelly-Kenny that his division (the VIth), would for the present remain in the town; but, as the intention

* Lord Roberts' report on Transport to the Royal Commission, dated March 25th 1901.

† Major-General Ian Hamilton in addition borrowed one Field battery from the VIIIth division.

‡ For composition and commands of this, the Natal, and other forces, see Appendix 1.

THE REORGANISATION AT BLOEMFONTEIN.

then was that Sir H. Chermside with the IIIrd division should soon relieve the VIth division, no arrangements were made for Kelly-Kenny to exercise any wider command than that over his own division. As the senior officer on the spot he necessarily assumed general command over all the troops present ; but Major-General Kelly remained to give orders for the line of communications and Kelly-Kenny was left without other special instructions. In order to make intelligible the sequence of events at a later date it is necessary to emphasise this point.

CHAPTER III.

THE ADVANCE FROM BLOEMFONTEIN TO KROONSTAD.*

Lord Roberts leaves Bloemfontein. EARLY on the morning of May 3rd, 1900, the Commander-in-Chief left Bloemfontein, and at Karee Siding placed himself again at the head of the army which he planned to lead to the capital of the Transvaal. Between the two cities lay nearly three hundred miles of rolling country, crossed by many rivers, and by an almost unending series of those low, undefined positions, the attack on which the Boer soldiery knew well how to render slow and costly for their opponents and safe for themselves. At the Zand river, Kroonstad, the Vaal river, Johannesburg and Pretoria itself were stronger lines of resistance, each of which might entail a battle. Behind the Zand the Intelligence Department had information of the presence of 5,000—6,000 Boers with 18 guns, under Commandant-General L. Botha. In the neighbourhood of Kroonstad a similar number of burghers, with eight to ten pieces of artillery, were reported. Smaller detachments, disposed along the railway, linked these bodies together, the nearest being in occupation of Brandfort, five miles north of **The enemy's numbers and positions.** the outposts at Karee Siding. On the right flank of the projected line of advance roamed bodies of varying strength, dangerous more from their mobility, their proximity to the lines of communication, and the quality of their leaders, than their actual numbers, though these were not inconsiderable. Between Thabanchu and Ladybrand hovered Christian De Wet, with a force estimated at between 4,000—6,000 men and eight or ten guns; another commando of one thousand men with two guns

---

* See maps Nos. 38 and 39.

BLOEMFONTEIN TO KROONSTAD. 41

being within reach in the direction of Senekal; and another of about five hundred men with two guns manœuvred between Wepener and Rouxville, in the angle formed by the junction of the Caledon and Orange rivers. The left flank was almost clear; no formed bodies of the enemy existing nearer than Warrenton, where General S. Du Toit, with a reputed four thousand men and nine guns, lay on the Kimberley railway.

Such, generally, was Lord Roberts' first information about the strength and dispositions of an enemy who was, he well knew, neither to be placed nor numbered for more than a few hours at a time, so swift were his movements, so variable his combinations, and so favourable the country to the tactics in which he excelled. How the main Boer forces were manœuvred, often almost bloodlessly, out of one position after another; how the roving bands on the flanks were brushed aside, disregarded in the concentration of purpose which urged forward continually the front of the British army, its flanks often so widely separated across the immense spaces of grass that, had they not been continually controlled by one mind, they would have seemed to be different armies; how this army was kept supplied, despite attacks on the railway, broken bridges and hundreds of shattered culverts, and how finally it marched into Pretoria, destroying for ever the schemes which had summoned it thousands of miles from the mother country, forced to make unwilling war, will now be related.

At Karee Siding the Commander-in-Chief found, on May 3rd, 20,250 officers and men of all arms excepting the cavalry. The latter, handing over Thabanchu to Sir L. Rundle, were only now returning to Bloemfontein to complete their equipment of horses. With the army were 72 Howitzers, Field and Naval guns, 8 Vickers-Maxims, and 49 machine guns.* Lieut.-General Ian S. M. Hamilton, with 14,630 officers and men, 38 guns, 6 Vickers-Maxims, and 20 machine guns† was on the march from Jacobsrust to Isabellafontein, supported by Lieut.-General Sir H. E. Colvile's force of 4,000 officers and men, 14 Field

The British strength.

---

* For full state, see Appendix 2. † For full state, see Appendix 2.

and Naval guns, and 4 machine guns.* Lieut.-General Sir L. Rundle remained at Thabanchu with the VIIIth division and eighteen guns, receiving on May 4th special instructions relative to the guardianship of the lines of communication referred to elsewhere.†

The first step forward, an advance against Brandfort, where lay the southernmost body of the enemy, had already begun when Lord Roberts joined his army at 9.15 on the morning of May 3rd, detailed orders to that effect having been issued by him the previous day. The place was not strongly held. Lulled by the long period of quiet, and unwarned by their Intelligence Department, which here, as elsewhere, though prompt enough to report actual movements of their opponents, remained strangely ignorant of long-continued preparations for movement, the Boers were totally unprepared for a sortie from Bloemfontein, many indeed being absent on furlough. About 450 burghers, composed of the Heidelberg and Blake's Irish commandos (the latter just come from the Biggarsberg), were in the town itself, whilst General De la Rey, with a larger number, occupied a line of rugged kopjes about two miles east of the railway. Three miles to the west and south-west of Brandfort were situated two separated groups of three kopjes each, which stood up boldly from the plain. These were at first unoccupied, but when the British vanguard was descried through the haze, Blake led his Irishmen to the northerly group, and the Heidelbergers, galloping from Brandfort, occupied the southerly, that nearest to the British.

Lord Roberts' army was disposed as follows :—On the west of the line, Major-General E. T. H. Hutton, with the 1st and 3rd corps of mounted infantry and brigade troops, advanced at 5.30 a.m. against the above-described groups of kopjes. Along the line itself, and some distance in rear, the XIth division moved directly upon Brandfort. Eastward of this was Lieut.-General C. Tucker with the 15th brigade and two batteries ; Major-General J. G. Maxwell with the 14th brigade, the

The attack on Brandfort, May 3rd, 1900

---

* For full state, see Appendix 2.   † See pages 105 and 106.

4th and 8th corps mounted infantry (Colonel Henry) and two Vickers-Maxim guns, coming in wide from and slightly to the north-east of Tucker's right flank. The whole movement thus converged upon Brandfort on a wide front. Hutton was first engaged, being opposed with such determination by the enemy on both groups of kopjes opposite to him, that for a time his advance was checked, and he found it necessary to use his G. battery R.H.A. By means of a series of skilful flanking movements, carried out by the 3rd corps mounted infantry on the east, and the 1st corps on the left, the hills were cleared, the New Zealand Mounted Rifles of the first-named corps seizing an opportunity to steal forward along the bush-fringed banks of a spruit which provided a covered way towards Brandfort.

A small body of scouts, under Lieut. C. Ross, a Canadian, trained in seven campaigns with the United States cavalry, had already entered the township about noon; the New Zealanders were soon up, whilst Rimington's Guides, moving between Brandfort and the captured kopjes, won a height commanding the place immediately to the north of it. The enemy then fled, blowing up the bridge, and cutting the telegraph line. So heavy had been the firing on the left, that the 18th brigade of infantry from the XIth division was ordered to support Hutton, who had, however, no need of its services. East of the line De la Rey, employing two guns, opposed the converging advance of the VIIth division by a series of rearguard actions too stubborn to be disposed of summarily. Maxwell, especially, found himself continually checked by the Ermelo men under Grobelaar, and his efforts to close with or outflank the skilful Boer proved unavailing, and were attended by slight losses. Not until sunset was his path clear, the Boers falling back towards Winburg with both their guns, which Maxwell had hoped all day to secure.

Tucker, less stoutly opposed nearer the line by the Wakkerstroom commando, under Greyling, reached his bivouac at Zuurfontein with few casualties, Maxwell halting at Modderfontein, to the north-east. The positions of the rest of the force at nightfall were as follows: The 1st corps mounted infantry, three miles north-west; the 3rd corps mounted infantry, astride the railway two miles north of Brandfort; the XIth division, occupying the town itself.* Ian Hamilton's column, with no more fighting than an affair of cavalry outposts, made Isabellafontein for the night, large bands of the enemy, under Philip Botha, which coalesced at dusk, drifting before him all day. Colvile bivouacked five miles in rear. During the day a railway construction train, following close in rear of the XIth division, repaired the culverts and established railhead at Brandfort whilst the action to secure the place was yet in progress.

Positions, night of May 3rd.

Next day, May 4th, whilst all the troops of the main army stayed in their bivouacs, a reconnaissance of the Vet river was carried out by Hutton's mounted force. A brisk operation, culminating in a spirited charge by the New Zealanders, who secured a ridge above Constantia, pushed the enemy's outlying bodies still further northward, Hutton withdrawing his command to within eight miles of Brandfort for the night. Ian Hamilton's column on the right flank passed a more active day. The enemy, who had been seen to collect on the previous evening, in numbers about 1,500, with three or four guns, were located at daylight upon a big hill, called Bavians Berg, three miles to the north-east, evidently intending to offer battle. Hamilton, though he determined at once to accept the challenge, saw that the position contained peculiar dangers. The hill was too strong for direct attack; to turn it by the east would be to cut himself off from the main army, and expose his communications, whilst the ground to the west formed a trap, in hopes of luring the British into which Botha had doubtless lingered. Here a valley ran northward, narrowing from its mouth, bounded on the east by Bavians Berg, on the west by a long narrow ridge, crenelated by four knolls and their dividing neks; on the north it was closed by a line of kopjes which, connecting the flanking heights, completed a *cul-de-sac*. Nevertheless, though he plainly perceived the dangers, Hamilton decided to adopt this western route, and about 7.30 a.m. ordered the 2nd cavalry brigade under

May 4th, 1900.

Fighting on the right flank; May 4th, 1900.

---

* Casualties, May 3rd—Killed, six men; wounded, one officer and twenty-nine men. The enemy lost less than a dozen men.

BLOEMFONTEIN TO KROONSTAD.

Broadwood and two corps of mounted infantry to the front, the 21st and 19th infantry brigades following in rear. The enemy at once opened with three guns from front and right front; and, as the leading troops penetrated the valley, it was seen that not only was Bavians Berg and its neighbours strongly held, but that numbers of Boers were upon the long ridges on the left, and many more coming up from the direction of Brandfort to reinforce them. Realising that should they succeed in this he would be shut in, Broadwood instantly ordered a squadron of the Royal Horse Guards to charge against the two central knolls of the ridge, of which they were by this time almost abreast. "The Blues," who charged with great dash, were only just in time. As they gained the ridge six hundred Boers were in the act of approaching it from the other side. These, now swerving toward the south, joined their comrades on the lowest point of the ridge, where there was also a gun, and " The Blues " came under a galling fire from right and left. Seeing this, Lieut.-Colonel Lord Airlie, commanding the 12th Lancers, took two squadrons of his regiment and the machine gun to their assistance, coming up on the left. At the same time Lieut.-Colonel N. Legge (6th corps mounted infantry) hurried up the 2nd mounted infantry and Kitchener's Horse to the right of the squadron, anticipating, as " The Blues " had done, by a few moments, a band of Boers who were actually climbing the hill from the west. Thus, though the enemy had gathered in strength on either side of the column, his forces were cut in two, and on one side had no positions. The situation, which a few moments later would have been extremely critical for Hamilton, was in this manner turned to the disadvantage of the enemy, who lost heart and began to waver. Hamilton then sent the infantry to relieve the cavalry on the western ridges, from which the 10th Hussars, assisted by two guns, began to push the Brandfort contingent of Boers back whence they had come ; while Broadwood, riding on to the head of the valley with the rest of his cavalry and two corps of mounted infantry, took up a strong position and opened artillery fire. The Boers now gave back in every direction. At this time MacDonald, coming up on the right rear from Colvile's IXth division, about 2.30 p.m., attacked Bavians Berg, the evacuation of which before a well-delivered onset by the 2nd Black Watch, covered by the two 4.7-in. Naval guns of the division, settled a lively, and at times anxious, engagement in favour of the British column. Arrived at Welkom Drift on the Mangani Spruit, which flowed behind the head of the valley, Hamilton called a halt, the 19th brigade and the mounted troops going into bivouac north of the drift, the 21st brigade on the south.

After dark two small patrols from the 12th Lancers and New South Wales Mounted Rifles sallied out and severed the railway and telegraph in rear of the enemy on the branch line between Winburg and Smaldeel. Early on the morning of May 5th, Lord Roberts wrote to Ian Hamilton, pointing out the necessity for a "supreme effort to run the Boer army down between this and Kroonstad." The enemy's draught and riding animals were reported to be failing, and their guns and wagons would probably fall a prey to hard pressure. Speed, even at the cost of outmarching supplies, was, therefore, essential.* A considerable obstacle confronted the Field-Marshal himself on this morning. This was the Vet river, a stream whose northern banks afforded defences which were not likely to be neglected by an enemy who was obviously bent on fighting delaying actions. The hostile force, of which Hutton had seen something during the reconnaissance of the previous day, numbered about 2,500 men, with eight or ten guns, under De la Rey and Lukas Meyer.† These were actually opposite to Lord Roberts; but Hamilton's success of the day before had thrown back into line with them at least double that number, so that nearly five thousand Boers might have to be reckoned with in a position peculiarly favourable to their tactics. The river ran directly athwart the line of advance. In breadth from thirty to forty yards, it was deeply channelled in the plain, its banks, which were fringed with bush, being in places about twenty feet

---

* No. 017 cipher, May 5th, 1900.

† The presence of Meyer, with 1,000 men and two guns, was not known until next day

deep, and, except at the drifts, almost everywhere sheer. Of the passages, which were few, widely separated, and difficult, only two were then known. Opposite the Boer right, at which flank Lord Roberts decided to strike, Coetzee's Drift lay six miles west of the destroyed railway bridge, Pretorius Drift the same distance downstream (west) of Coetzee's. On the British bank of the river the approaches were perfectly open, except for two small kopjes due south of Coetzee's Drift. On the side of the Boers three considerable hills, two close together to the north-west, and one, the largest, north-east of the drift, commanded the passage; and on them, as well as in the river bed itself, the enemy had gathered in force, having artillery on both groups of kopjes. Coetzee's Drift itself, therefore, was not to be lightly forced, and a turning movement was necessary. Whilst the XIth division, with Maxwell's 14th brigade, preceded by two corps of mounted infantry wide on the right, moved slowly along the eastern side of the railway, Hutton was directed to take his mounted troops north-westerly, to cross the river by whatever drifts he could, and turn the right flank of the enemy on the northern bank. Marching at 7.30 a.m., Hutton quickly covered the fifteen miles to Coetzee's Drift in good time, detaching on his way a troop of the 2nd Canadian Mounted Rifles to seize Pretorius Drift. Soon after noon he was near the river, and a warm fire from the bushy banks and from the kopjes to the north warned him that his passage was to be opposed. *Action on the Vet river; May 5th, 1900.*

Adopting much the same tactics as had proved successful at Brandfort, Hutton now entered upon a succession of bold and rapid manœuvres. Whilst Alderson (1st corps) moved towards the river on the left, that is, between Coetzee's and Pretorius Drifts, Pilcher (3rd corps), advancing on Alderson's right, between him and the railway, about 12.30 p.m., seized, with the Queensland mounted infantry, first the nearer and then the further of the two kopjes on the British side. On the former hill he established a reserve and G. battery R.H.A., which immediately shelled the enemy on the group of hills north-west of the drift. Pilcher then pushed the rest of his men along some dry watercourses down to the river bank, and a brisk exchange of musketry began, which lasted some time, the enemy tenaciously holding the drift. Meanwhile, by a stroke of fortune, Alderson, on the left, who had been advancing with no great prospect of getting in, was told by a Boer prisoner of a little-known drift which lay to his immediate front, that is, about two miles west of Coetzee's Drift, and leading directly outside the enemy's right flank. By this the 1st battalion mounted infantry was directed to cross, covered by the 1st Canadian Mounted Rifles, which advanced to the river side, and even gained a footing on the north bank by the daring action of a party who, led by Lieut. H. L. Borden, swam the stream. As the 1st battalion crossed the drift, a passage only admitting of movement in single file, Hutton, about 3.30 p.m., saw signs of wavering amongst the enemy at Coetzee's Drift. He thereupon ordered his reserve of the New South Wales Mounted Rifles to force the crossing. They delivered their attack with determination, rushing the drift despite heavy fire and lack of cover, much loss being saved by the accurate shooting of two guns of G. battery, and two galloping Maxims, which Pilcher sent forward to the further kopje to cover them at short range. Nor did the New South Wales men stop at the northern bank, but pushed the enemy at the point of the bayonet, not only from the Vet river, but headlong over a spruit which offered a second sunken position to their riflemen. As they did so, the 1st battalion mounted infantry, having made good the passage of the newly-discovered drift, swung in upon the retiring enemy's right, whilst Pilcher's 3rd corps hurried across the river, fell upon his left, and completed his discomfiture. By 4.30 p.m. the neighbourhood of the drift itself was clear. Still the Boers clung to the high hill to the north-east. This, commanding the railway, lay in the way of the main body, and the enemy upon it, about five hundred men with two guns, fired hotly upon the mounted infantry. Just before sundown the 3rd battalion mounted infantry, finely led, dashed around the flank of this height, whilst the New South Wales men, the Queenslanders and New Zealanders attacked it in front.

The Boers, almost surrounded, turned and fled towards

Smaldeel, leaving twenty-six prisoners on the field. Thus a difficult passage was secured by operations the brilliance of which was the more grateful in that it was largely due to the soldiers who of their own free will had come from afar over sea to uphold the Imperial cause. In the evening Lord Roberts, who had missed no detail of the fighting, sent to Hutton hearty congratulations on the " excellent day's work."

With regard to the main body, though the infantry did not come into action, there had seemed every prospect of their having to fight before the passage should be won. Strong bodies of the enemy, upon whom the success of the mounted infantry on the west had little effect, lay along the river east of the railway. With them were four long-range guns, so skilfully concealed and served that their effective practice at seven thousand yards compelled the employment of all the British artillery, heavy and light, before three of them were withdrawn about 4.30 p.m. The fourth continued to fire, until dusk, betraying its flash, disclosed its position, when it was quickly silenced. How expensive an infantry attack on the river might have proved was shown when the lyddite shells, searching the river bed at sunset, drove out some 1,500 Boers who had been in hiding there all day, as Cronje's men had lurked in the low-lying Modder nearly six months earlier. But Lord Roberts had at no time intended to take by assault what he could win by manœuvre. Hutton's operations had practically given him the passage of the Vet; and the XIth division, the Guards' brigade in front, went into bivouac close to the river, having marched some fifteen miles during the day. Two companies of 3rd Grenadier Guards held for the night a kopje on the river which had been captured early in the action by the West Australian mounted infantry. The VIIth division bivouacked at the junction of the Vet river with the Taaibosch Spruit, on the right. At 8 p.m. a patrol made its way around the rear of the enemy, and cut the railway line three miles north of Smaldeel Station. Unfortunately the enterprise was robbed of its reward, the Boers having sent their last train northward earlier in the evening. The patrol rejoined Hutton's force at 9 a.m. the next day. Ten miles eastward Hamilton, gathering the fruits of his success of the previous day, crossed the Vet higher up and entered Winburg unopposed after sixteen miles of marching, his scouts riding into the town at one end as the enemy left it at the other. So close were the adversaries that the bearer of the summons to surrender, and the accompanying trumpeter, were actually caught by Philip Botha, but after some argument released.

<small>May 6th, 1900. The passage of the Vet river.</small>

Next morning, May 6th, Lord Roberts found the Vet river free. Only a few Boers lingered in the bushy country in front of Hutton on the left, and these were easily cleared by his mounted men. The only obstacles were the drifts, which were steep and difficult, and caused much delay, both near the bridge where the XIth division crossed, and four miles up stream where the VIIth division had to make the passage first of the Taaibosch Spruit, and then of the river itself. Smaldeel was reached in the evening, both divisions, with the exception of the 18th brigade of the XIth division, which had been delayed at the Vet, bivouacking about the station. From this place direct telegraphic communication was established with Hamilton at Winburg. That General, who was anxious to reach a drift over the Zand before the enemy should have time to fortify it, marched late on this day with the intention of gaining his point by moonlight. When he had gone nearly eight miles from Winburg, a message reached him from the Commander-in-Chief ordering a halt; and the forces bivouacked at Dankbaarfontein, being replaced at Winburg by Colvile's Highland brigade. Arriving at Winburg, on the 6th, Colvile was informed that his force was to remain as a garrison of that place, collecting supplies and arms from the country round. Here he remained until May 17th.

The Zand river, indeed, seemed likely to prove a barrier requiring careful and combined action. Six thousand men with eighteen guns were reported to be drawn up on its banks, being the joint forces of De la Rey, P. Botha and Grobelaar. On

<small>May 7th, 1900. Reconnaissance of the Zand river.</small>

May 7th, whilst the infantry rested, merely concentrating closer about Smaldeel, Hutton carried out a reconnaissance which confirmed the above estimate. Starting at 6.30 a.m. sixteen miles had been covered with no sign of the enemy, and it was not until

2.30 p.m. that Hutton came in sight of the Boer rearguard and train, which were still upon the south side of the river, upon the north bank of which strong bodies could be seen awaiting them. Hutton promptly tried to cut off the wagons; but his first attempts disclosed the nature of the forces with which he had to deal. Both his flanks were soon threatened by commandos which crossed the river to the assistance of the convoy. These were covered by a steady artillery fire from Field and heavy guns, the latter, which were mounted on railway trucks, completely outranging the Horse artillery battery with the mounted infantry. The enemy, in short, betrayed all his strength in his alarm for his wagons, and Hutton, having gained his object, held his ground until sunset, when he withdrew to Welgelegen Siding and bivouacked.* In his report he estimated the strength of the enemy upon the line of the Zand as six thousand men, with two heavy and eight light pieces of artillery; and the Field-Marshal prepared for a battle. It should be noted that on this day Lieut.-General Sir A. Hunter, on the western line, began his advance on Mafeking from Kimberley and Fourteen Streams.†

On May 8th and 9th French's cavalry division, which, having completed its equipment, had been pressing up by forced marches from Bloemfontein in the wake of the army since the 6th, arrived at the front, in strength some 4,500 sabres,‡ three batteries R.H.A., six Vickers-Maxims, and nine machine guns. Beyond a further reconnaissance by Hutton, who ascertained the arrival on the Zand of considerable Boer reinforcements, coming from the east, the army made no movement on this day; Hamilton also remained quiet at Dankbaarfontein.

May 8th and 9th. Arrival of the cavalry division.

On May 9th Lord Roberts advanced his infantry to within eight miles of the Zand,§ the XIth division, with its Headquarters to Welgelegen Siding, and the VIIth division to Merrie-

---

* Casualties, five men wounded.

† See page 112.

‡ 1st (Porter), 3rd (Gordon) and 4th (Dickson) brigades. For full state, see Appendix 2. Broadwood's 2nd brigade, it must be remembered, had been from the first with Ian Hamilton's column.

§ See map No. 39.

fontein, where it joined hands with Hamilton, who had pushed on in a parallel line to Bloemplaats, less than three miles from the river. Hamilton's march had not been without incident. A Boer force, estimated at from 2,300 to 3,000, which had hung upon his right flank all day, in the afternoon demonstrated against the outposts on that side. Though they were easily repulsed, the presence of so strong a body upon the south bank of the Zand, and outside the extreme right of Lord Roberts' front, seemed to presage difficulty for the morrow's crossing. An important passage, called Junction Drift, lay in front of Hamilton. Anxious to secure it before it became too strong, he sent first the 5th corps mounted infantry and then the 1st Derbyshire regiment to hold it, and by nightfall both banks were in his possession after little opposition. At the same time, Tucker, of the VIIth division, also knowing the value of the drift, and unaware of its seizure by Hamilton, sent the 2nd Cheshire regiment from his 15th brigade to the spot. This battalion found the Derbyshire already in occupation and bivouacked on the southern side. Another drift more to the eastward was also reconnoitred, and the southern bank held by piquets of the mounted infantry. Thus access to the left of the enemy posted along the Zand was assured. On the other flank of the army work equally important was done by the cavalry.

Ian Hamilton reaches the Zand river, May 9th, 1900.

Ten miles west of the railway, a good drift, called Du Preez Laager Drift, crossed the Zand at a point nearly eight miles outside the enemy's right. If it could be seized—Junction Drift being already in British hands—the enemy would be turned by both flanks, and would be forced to leave the line of the Zand. Another drift, close by, called De Klerks Kraal Drift, would also be automatically gained by the capture of Du Preez, thus increasing the power of the force operating on this side to act against the Boer flank. At 5.30 a.m. on the 9th, the 1st cavalry brigade (Porter) left Smaldeel to reconnoitre these drifts. The 4th cavalry brigade (Dickson), which had bivouacked some distance in rear, followed the 1st; the 3rd cavalry brigade (Gordon) being detached altogether from the division for service with the infantry under the immediate orders of the Field-Marshal. At 11 a.m. French, who had followed his advance guard at 7 a.m., was at Kalkoenkrans, five miles south of the river, and half an hour later he received information from the scouts that the Du Preez Laager Drift was unoccupied by the enemy. He immediately ordered a squadron of the Scots Greys to go forward and hold it; and, pushing the rest of the 1st cavalry brigade on after, by 3.30 p.m. was in strong occupation of the drift, keeping the 4th cavalry brigade in support at Kalkoenkrans. De Klerks Kraal Drift was similarly taken into possession. At sunset Hutton's 1st mounted infantry brigade, moving west to Du Preez Laager Drift, was attached to the cavalry, thereafter acting under the orders of French. *Seizure of the Zand drifts, May 9th, 1900.*

These easy seizures of four important avenues of approach threw a new light on the disposition and intentions of the enemy. Only by finding him concentrated could so elusive and mobile an opponent be brought to action and beaten. Lord Roberts began to fear, not that he was to be heavily opposed, but that he would soon hear of the Boers' flight. Information gleaned by French's patrols, the reports of the Intelligence Department, and certain movements of the enemy in front of Hamilton, all seemed now to point to this conclusion, and the Field-Marshal determined to lose no time in closing on the Zand. His plans have been already foreshadowed. They were, briefly, to turn both flanks of the enemy with French's and Hamilton's mounted troops, moving by way of the captured drifts, refusing the centre until the wings should have gained the northern bank on either side. That the passage of the Zand would be effected was almost a certainty, but he hoped to do more. French's orders to the cavalry, issued after an interview with the Chief of the Staff, Major-General Lord Kitchener, on the previous day, foreshadowed operations on the enemy's rear, and the cutting him off from Kroonstad, where another strong defensive position was well known to be. The ground held by the enemy on the north bank was by no means perfect either for defence or for unmolested retirement. The line of the river itself, with its sunken bed and rising background, was strong enough. The

Boer centre, posted opposite the XIth division astride the railway behind Virginia Siding, had little to fear from frontal attack. But on the right, across the Riet Spruit, which bisected the position, a series of isolated kopjes—Dirks Burg Diamond Mine, Vredes Verdrag, Posen Hill, with Kopje Alleen standing isolated four miles to the westward—formed a weakness instead of a security to that flank, for they ran not parallel but at right angles to the Zand, to which they therefore presented but a narrow front. Outside them, two drifts were already in the hands of a large body of British cavalry. The Boer left, stretching across the fronts of Tucker's VIIth division and Hamilton's force at Bloemplaats, was on stronger ground, but was disposed over a distance far too great for its numbers. Here a barrier of kopjes, Doorn Kop—Bosch Kop, lay some three miles north of the river, sending down bluff-ended spurs towards the banks, which were fringed by a broad belt of brushwood. But here, too, the passages were lost to the enemy, and the broken country beyond more suitable to cover attack than defence.

May 10th, 1900.
The action on the Zand river.
At 6 a.m. on May 10th, the whole of Lord Roberts' front moved on the river. On the left French, crossing at Du Preez Laager Drift with the 1st cavalry brigade, followed by Hutton's mounted force and the 4th cavalry brigade, spread northeastward on a wide arc. At 9.45 a.m. the southernmost of the kopjes overlooking the Dirks Burg Diamond Mine on the one side and the Riet Spruit on the other was easily reached. At the left centre the 3rd cavalry brigade and Henry's mounted infantry, preceding the XIth division, moved down the railway towards the drift near the bridge, covered by the artillery fire of the main body. The drift was practically undefended, and the mounted infantry, crossing first, were closely followed by the cavalry, the whole gaining a footing upon the north bank before 8 a.m. The handling of the right centre, the VIIth division, presented more difficulty. No drift lay in front of Tucker, and in order to cross the river he was compelled to diverge northeastward towards Junction Drift—reserved for the passage of the right, under Hamilton. Thither Tucker pushed forward

two batteries to cover the drift, and at 8.30 a.m. sent the 1st East Lancashire regiment and half the 2nd Cheshire regiment across to work on the left flank of Hamilton, some of whose units were already in action on the north bank. Tucker then found another drift, close to Junction Drift, and set the 26th company R.E. to improve both. Hamilton's infantry (21st brigade), arriving at the ford assigned to them, had already passed the river. By 8.30 a.m. the heads of all four divisions of Lord Roberts' wide front were north of the Zand, engaging the enemy with fortunes so various that each must now be separately described.

French, having reached the hills at the junction of the Riet Spruit and the Zand river, sent patrols of the Carabiniers towards Riet Spruit Siding, intending to work round the rear of the enemy. The patrols were met with fire from a force numbering two thousand to three thousand men, who were moving down into the Virginia Siding position, and French, signalling the information to Army Headquarters, made arrangements to cut off their retreat. Leaving the Diamond Mine Hills in charge of the mounted infantry, he moved the 1st cavalry brigade northward, against Vredes Verdrag, on which he ordered an attack by a squadron of the 6th (Inniskilling) Dragoons, one of the Scots Greys, one of Australian Horse, and two troops of the 6th Dragoon Guards (Carabiniers). A desultory fire from two guns posted in front of Kopje Alleen met the brigade as it traversed the open ground, but the Carabiniers, dismounting, gained the southern end of Vredes Verdrag without opposition, and the rest prepared to follow. No sooner were the men on the crest than a body of the enemy, coming forward from the other end of the long feature, attacked them so hotly that, in spite of the covering fire of the Horse artillery, they were forced to fall back on the main body, with all their officers out of action. At the same time, the rest of the brigade, some three-quarters of a mile in rear, were fired upon by a commando which had worked up to their left flank through fields of standing mealies, and Porter had to dismount his command and for a time stand on the defensive around his guns. Dickson soon brought his brigade (4th) up, and was ordered to move wide to the left to envelop the enemy, whilst the 1st corps mounted infantry (Alderson), which arrived with him, was pushed forward in the interval between the cavalry brigades. As Dickson advanced, the Boers, coming out from the crops, fired from the open, and French ordered Dickson to charge. Thereupon the brigade, assuming open order, attempted to ride the enemy down; but the horses were blown with their rapid advance from the river, and the charge, failing to get home, led to the capture of but three prisoners, seven Boers being killed. Whilst the 1st brigade, still under shell fire, then withdrew from its cramped position, the 4th continued the turning movement around Vredes Verdrag, which the enemy abandoned about 2 p.m. French, supported by Hutton on Vredes Verdrag, then pressed on for Posen Hill at the northern end of the ridge, arriving there about 4 p.m. By that time the Boers were in full retreat from their central positions, their rearguard as they passed Vredes Verdrag at 5 p.m. engaging Hutton until nightfall.

Largely owing to these movements, which caused the Boers at Virginia Siding to fear continually for their right flank, the mounted troops in front of the XIth division had a comparatively easy task. After crossing the river, Henry's two corps of mounted infantry moved up the left of the railway, connecting with Hutton, the 3rd cavalry brigade (Gordon) advancing on a parallel line on the right of the railway. R. battery R.H.A. and J., which had been attached this day to the 3rd cavalry brigade, covered the advance of both units. A running fight ensued; but though the enemy, evacuating successive positions, fought only rearguard actions, extreme caution had to be exercised, and four times it was necessary to bring the guns into action to clear the ground. During the advance of the leading cavalry, the 16th Lancers, venturing too far to the north-east, encountered heavy shell and rifle fire, and had to fall back until the batteries and the 9th and 17th Lancers came up in support.

Ian Hamilton, on the right, after he had crossed the river slightly before Tucker and the right centre, had long before daylight sent the remainder of the 21st brigade (Bruce Hamilton) to reinforce the 1st Derbyshire regiment at Junction Drift ; he thus anticipated the enemy, who came down to the deep river bed further eastward, to the number of eight hundred, with the evident intention of flanking the passage. They found the brigade there before them, and, momentarily expecting capture, lay so quiet all day that their presence was actually undiscovered until it was too late to surround them. At dawn the 1st Royal Sussex regiment, issuing from the river under the sharp fire of two guns and two Vickers-Maxims, seized a low ridge on the north bank, about two miles east of the drift and opposite the enemy's right, which, posted on a woody bluff, was nearer to the river than his left. The latter flank, thus obliquely thrown back, seemed to stretch so far eastward that Ian Hamilton, despairing of turning it by a détour, however long, kept his mounted troops in hand on the south bank, with the 19th brigade (Smith-Dorrien), until the infantry attack should have made a breach in the strong position before him. The advance of the 21st brigade from the kopje was made in the following order :— 1st Royal Sussex regiment and 1st Cameron Highlanders in front line, 1st Derbyshire regiment and the City Imperial Volunteers in support. The 1st Gordon Highlanders, from the 19th brigade, were attached to Bruce Hamilton, to assist him by a flank attack ; they extended upon his right. As the infantry advanced, the 76th battery, crossing the stream, came into action upon the ridge on the north bank. At this moment Tucker, coming up to the drift, sent across his 18th battery, escorted by half a battalion Cheshire regiment, to join in the covering fire. As for the rest of Hamilton's artillery, the 74th and 82nd batteries opened from a spur which descended to the south bank on the east of the drift, whilst the two 5-in. guns fired with splendid effect from a site carefully chosen by the General himself higher up the same spur, and four hundred yards in rear. By 9 a.m. a powerful cross-fire was developed. This severely shook the enemy in his positions across the river before the 21st brigade had arrived within striking distance. Then, by a series of brilliant attacks, Bruce Hamilton's battalions began to clear the hills, unchecked by a rolling rifle fire, by that of two guns from the left, or by the rapid shooting of a Vickers-Maxim, which for a time enfiladed the right. The enemy's artillery was soon accounted for. A shell from the 5-in. guns, fired at a range of 7,400 yards, falling sheer into the emplacement of the Vickers-Maxim, killed all the gunners, whom none dared replace. Soon after, the two Boer guns, 6,800 yards westward, fell victims also to the perfect practice of the 4.7-in. and 5-in. guns, a shell from one of which burst between them and silenced both for the rest of the day. Thereafter Bruce Hamilton's infantry carried all before them. At 11 a.m. they were in possession of all the ridges, and the mounted troops, which had begun to cross the drift an hour earlier, took up the pursuit. Meanwhile, about 8.45 a.m., the head of the VIIth division had also crossed the Zand and joined battle on Ian Hamilton's left. After engaging the enemy's guns with the 62nd and 75th batteries (the 18th being already in action) at 9.45 a.m. Tucker sent forward the 15th brigade, supported by the 2nd Hampshire regiment and 1st King's Own Scottish Borderers of the 14th brigade, against Doornkop to his left front, from which were then firing the two pieces soon to be silenced by Ian Hamilton's 5-in. and 4.7-in. guns. The 1st East Lancashire regiment, the first line of the 15th brigade, alone became heavily engaged, and its attack, delivered by three companies in front line, the men extended to ten paces, was rapid and spirited. In spite of a severe fire from a second Vickers-Maxim, concealed on the left, which raked the lines, the battalion drove the enemy from the hill, and captured eleven prisoners. By 11.30 a.m. the front of the VIIth division was clear.

The task of Ian Hamilton on the right proved longer and more difficult. At 11 a.m., whilst his mounted troops were still pressing to the front in pursuit, the same body of the enemy which had annoyed his outer flank during the march of the previous day suddenly fell upon his right rear, which was fortunately guarded by the 10th Hussars and Kitchener's Horse, posted on a kopje about seven miles south-east of Junction Drift. The Boers here brought fresh artillery into action, and the situation seemed at one time to be so threatening that Hamilton despatched two guns to the spot. Though the Boers were eventually driven off, their manœuvre gave them unexpected advantage ; for Broadwood, who was in command of the mounted troops, then engaged in the pursuit, receiving an exaggerated report of this affair, checked his command, in order to be at hand if necessary, and moved somewhat eastward. He thus relaxed his pressure on the retiring enemy, who must otherwise have lost heavily in men, guns and wagons. When undeceived, Broadwood lost no time in pushing again to the front, was in Ventersburg at 2.30 p.m., and, hastening on, regained touch with the Boer rearguard, from which de Lisle's mounted infantry snatched twenty-eight prisoners and five wagons before darkness put an end to the chase. During the day sixty-nine prisoners in all were taken by Hamilton's troops.

Thus the passage of the Zand was won at all points sufficiently early for the infantry to be passed across, and to march eight miles northward before nightfall. The army then bivouacked on a front of over twenty miles, at the following places, from left to right : French (1st and 4th cavalry brigades) and Hutton (1st and 3rd corps mounted infantry) at Zonderhout Farm, ten miles north-west of Ventersburg Road Station, where lay the 3rd cavalry brigade and Henry's 4th and 8th mounted infantry. The latter covered Lord Roberts' Headquarters with the XIth division at Riet Spruit Siding, screening also the VIIth division, which halted on the right about the farm Deelfontein Noord. Hamilton's cavalry occupied Ventersburg and the hills three miles eastward, his 21st brigade reaching Bosch Kop, three miles south-west of the town. The 19th brigade, much delayed at the difficult drift on the Zand, was there overtaken by night, and remained in rear by the river.*

The passage of the Zand river, May 10th, 1900.

The mounted arms were now but one day's march and the infantry two from Kroonstad, the present capital of the Orange Free State, about the defence of which many contradictory

---

* Casualties, May 10th—Killed, one officer, twenty-two other ranks ; died of wounds, one officer, eight other ranks ; wounded, four officers, sixty-six other ranks ; missing, two officers, eleven other ranks ; total, 115.

reports had reached Army Headquarters. A strong position, called the Boschrand, six miles south of the town, lay athwart the approaches to it. This was reported to be entrenched and supplied with artillery. Whatever resistance had been prepared here, Lord Roberts decided to nullify it by a great effort to surround Kroonstad with his cavalry. If this should be successful, and the railway cut north of the town, the flight of the Government officials and the removal of the rolling stock and transport would be prevented; and the more prolonged the opposition on the Boschrand, the more certain would be the fate of those who offered it. At 4.45 on the evening of May 10th, urgent orders were sent to French to get round in rear of Kroonstad and blow up the railway. Though his men and horses were much in need of rest, French, marching at 6.30 a.m., May 11th, without baggage, by 4 p.m. had covered twenty miles, and was in possession of Valsch River Drift, nine miles north-west of Kroonstad, which was thus already partially turned. Soon after he had secured the drift, three thousand Boers with two guns issued from Kroonstad, and made as if to fall upon him, but retired before a display of artillery. Although the cavalry could go no further, the line had still to be destroyed. To effect this French detailed an expedition consisting of fifty picked men from the 1st cavalry brigade and eight mounted Sappers, the whole under command of Major A. G. Hunter-Weston, R.E., accompanied by Mr. F. R. Burnham, a famous scout, trained upon the prairies of America. The enterprise, which was one of exceptional risk, was carried out with great skill, and in all but time, with perfect success. Moving from the drift at 5.30 p.m., and passing through many piquets and scattered knots of Boers, some of whom they captured, and some contrived to avoid, the party reached the railway behind Kroonstad near America Station, only to find the road, which ran parallel to the line, thronged with the retiring enemy. By waiting for intervals in the columns, and taking advantage of the rattling of the ox-wagons and the clamour of the native drivers, two men succeeded in carrying the explosives across the road, laying them on the line, and lighting the fuses, the enemy passing within a

May 11th, 1900.
The cavalry attempt to cut off the enemy.

few yards of them as they worked. Under cover of the confusion caused by the explosions, the party then made off, and after many adventures rejoined French at 2 p.m. on May 12th.

Meanwhile Hutton, supporting French on the west of the line, had followed him as far as Welgelegen, where he bivouacked. The 3rd cavalry brigade, with part of Henry's mounted infantry, moving east of the line, had at the same time preceded the VIIth and XIth divisions, until the Boschrand barred the way. Reconnaissance disclosed upon this position a strong Boer rearguard disposed on both sides of the railway. There ensued a slow artillery duel, which lasted until sunset, when the brigade bivouacked in front of the hills. Of the two infantry divisions in rear, the VIIth halted for the night at Mooiplaats, the XIth with Headquarters near Geneva Siding, both having marched some eighteen miles. On the right Hamilton, still delayed by transport difficulties at the Zand river, did not clear Bosch Kop until 2 p.m. He then covered sixteen miles, half by moonlight, halting at Twistniet at 9 p.m. near to the VIIth division at Mooiplaats.

During the night the enemy evacuated Kroonstad and the Boschrand, Hunter-Weston's party, being unsuspected witnesses of their flight. The burghers, indeed, were in no mood for stubborn resistance. Since their first surprise at Brandfort on May 3rd, the speed and the enveloping nature of Lord Roberts' advance had demoralized them more each day. Whilst the Free Staters now utterly despaired of their country, the men of the Transvaal had no thought but to regain their own territory before a like fate befell it. Not all the exhortations of their most trusted generals, nor even the passionate declamations of President Steyn himself, who had arrived in the town on May 7th, and now hurried to the drifts to stem the flood of retreat, could turn them back to the lines on the Boschrand, where the republican leaders had hoped to give battle. Long before dawn of the 12th, before, unfortunately, the demolition of the line by Hunter-Weston, the last train had steamed northward; then, blowing up the railway bridge, the Boer rearguard cleared Kroonstad, and President Steyn posted for Lindley, proclaiming *The enemy abandons Kroonstad.*

that village his new capital and seat of government. At 6 a.m. on the next day (May 12th) French, reconnoitring on all sides of Kroonstad, found the place abandoned, and went on to Jordaan Siding, five miles northward. On his way thither he was met by the Landrost, who formally surrendered Kroonstad to the forces of Lord Roberts. The 3rd cavalry brigade and Henry's mounted infantry crossed the Boschrand at the same time to one mile south of Kroonstad. Of the infantry, the VIIth division marched sixteen miles to within three miles of the town, bivouacking near Hamilton's column, which came by Trebu and reached Kroonspruit. At 2 p.m. Lord Roberts entered Kroonstad at the head of the XIth division, which, after marching past the Field-Marshal in the Market square, bivouacked north and east of the town.*

<small>May 12th, 1900. Occupation of Kroonstad.</small>

Lord Roberts was now compelled to call a halt. He had far outmarched his rail-head, though the railway repair department, under the directorship of Lieut.-Colonel E. P. Girouard, R.E., following the army, first with a construction train, which was supported by the Railway Pioneer regiment, was putting forth incredible efforts to make good the enormous damage inflicted on the line by the retiring enemy.† Between Bloemfontein and Kroonstad no fewer than twenty-seven spans of four great bridges, some of them seventy feet above the water and totalling 670 feet in width, with twelve piers of massive masonry, lay in ruins in the river beds. Culverts to the number of sixteen had been blown up, most of the water tanks and pumps shattered, rails torn up and twisted, the permanent way and points damaged, signalling instruments broken, in short, all things destroyed with almost as much care and science as had gone to the construction of them. The cavalry division, again, had reached Kroonstad with the loss of nearly half their mobility from wastage in horse-flesh. Of the 5,900 horses which had left Bloemfontein, only 3,470 had survived the march, and nearly 450 of these were reported unfit for further work without a rest. As many as 950

<small>Reasons for a halt there.</small>

---

* For casualties up to the capture of Kroonstad, see Appendix 2.

† For a summary of the work done on the railway during the march see Appendix 3.

BLOEMFONTEIN TO KROONSTAD.   63

had actually died or been destroyed on the way; so heavy is the toll exacted when animals soft from a long sea voyage are forced into long marches and rapid manœuvres, in high altitudes on scant and unaccustomed food, heavily burdened by day and unsheltered by night. For ten days, therefore, whilst these and other deficiencies were made good, the main body remained about Kroonstad, checked more surely by its own needs than if confronted by the strongest hostile fortress.

Although time to get clear and collect himself was thus perforce allowed to the disorganised enemy, Lord Roberts determined at least to give no respite to the fugitive President and State officials of the Orange Free State. On May 14th Lieut.-General Ian Hamilton received orders to push on to Lindley, and thence to Heilbron, to capture whom he might, or at any rate to deny those places to the vagrant coterie who still demanded no more than lodgings in a deserted village street stoutly to proclaim themselves a Government. Hamilton, who was more in want of supplies than any commander, moved six miles on the 15th to Kranzspruit, next day twelve miles to Tweepoort, and on the 17th to Doornkloof, fifteen miles. His cavalry, under Broadwood, operating fourteen miles ahead, entered Lindley on the latter date, after a brush with the enemy outside; and on the 18th the 21st brigade entered the little town, the 19th brigade staying to guard the communications by which a convoy was expected on the Elandspruit, twelve miles westward. Hutton, whose mounted force had suffered much less than the cavalry division from loss of horses, had been sent at his own request, on May 16th, on a wide reconnaissance, which, beginning with a rapid night march, resulted in the capture of several Boer leaders and many prisoners.

May 14th, 1900. Pursuit of the Orange Free State Government.

Remaining at Lindley on the 19th, Hamilton, in pursuance of orders to make next for Heilbron, pushed out northward early on May 20th. A day of brisk, and from the tactical developments of remarkable, fighting followed. The rearguard consisted of the 1st Derbyshire regiment, the 5th mounted infantry, Roberts' Horse, with the 82nd battery R.F.A. No sooner had this force begun to fall back from Lindley, covering

May 19th, 1900. Ian Hamilton at Lindley.

the six miles length of baggage train, than the enemy, under P. De Wet appeared over the ridges southward, and, converging at the gallop, engaged at close quarters the mounted infantry upon the right flank and rear. A long running fight ensued, in which the Boers pressed so hard that they almost over-rode the rearmost mounted infantry, and actually succeeded in getting between the column and the right flank guard, of which they cut off and captured nearly forty men. Nor did they desist until, late in the afternoon, they were rebuffed by the main body and the battery posted on a commanding ridge. Whilst this went on in rear, the van also had become hotly engaged with even larger numbers of the enemy towards the north. As the 10th Hussars, the cavalry screen, approached the Rhenoster river, they came unexpectedly upon about 1,200 Boers with two or three guns, covering the drifts, and suffered severe casualties at the first volley. The enemy then showed a determined and aggressive front, and the column for a time found itself blocked in front and attacked in rear. Just as it seemed as though a set battle would be necessary to get to the Rhenoster, a fortunate coincidence cleared the front as suddenly as it had been obstructed. The 19th brigade, which had remained twelve miles west of Lindley, had marched in the morning to rejoin, not by the road through Lindley, but by a direct route—the third side of a triangle as it were—straight for the point where Hamilton intended to strike the river.

May 20th, 1900. He crosses the Rhenoster. This direction led the brigade precisely against the right flank of the Boers opposing Broadwood. It appeared just as the cavalry were beginning to be pressed. The enemy, completely turned, broke and fled at once, and the column, having by this time also disembarrassed its rear, crossed the Rhenoster, and bivouacked on the northern bank. During the night Hamilton recovered by exchange all his men who had been captured.

CHAPTER IV.

THE ADVANCE FROM KROONSTAD TO PRETORIA.*

LORD ROBERTS was now ready to resume his northward march. Apart from the resting of the soldiers, the arrival of supplies, the reconstruction of the great Valsch bridge, and the approach of the rail-head, the enforced halt had not been unfruitful. Numbers of the enemy had surrendered, and the Field-Marshal had found time to settle many matters of administration both here and in remote quarters of the conquered territory. The army prepared to resume its advance.

In other parts of the theatre of war the situation had everywhere improved. In Natal Sir R. Buller, having swept all before him across the Biggarsberg, had halted in front of Laing's Nek, in order to repair the railway behind, and to clear his right flank of the bands which the speed of his advance had brushed aside. He was in constant communication with Kroonstad; and his army, though fully occupied, and separated from that of Lord Roberts by many leagues and by the Drakensberg, the passes of which were held by the enemy, still formed the true right wing—as the forces of Sir A. Hunter in the Western Transvaal formed the left—of the vast front which the Field-Marshal was impelling northward, a front of nearly 350 miles in extent. Immediate progress by Sir R. Buller was, indeed, uncertain. Laing's Nek was a mighty obstacle, and it grew stronger hourly; yet the Natal army, even if it proved unable to advance on a level with that of Lord Roberts, was strategically most valuable, and there were good hopes for the turning movement which was under discussion by the two Generals.† From the west came at first Situation in other parts of the theatre of war.

---

* See maps Nos. 38, 40, 41 and 42.

† For correspondence between Lord Roberts and Sir R. Buller relative to the latter's plan of campaign in Natal, see Chapter X.

VOL. III. 5

rumours, then confirmation, of the relief of Mafeking.* Further south Sir A. Hunter, having reconstructed the bridge over the Vaal at Fourteen Streams, had pushed back the enemy beyond Christiana, and was marching up the line towards Vryburg; whilst Lord Methuen, similarly freed by the success at Mafeking, moved from Boshof (May 14th) to Hoopstad (May 17th), receiving many surrenders at both places.

<small>Reasons for pressing the advance.</small>

Nevertheless, although the campaign was thus, on the whole, prospering, Lord Roberts was well aware of the dangers of delaying his own advance a day longer than necessary. The recuperative power of the Boers was by no means a determined quantity. If they were blown like clouds before a resolute advance, they gathered as quickly during every lull of the blast; and, still not contemptible in numbers and armament, any strong position might suddenly fortify their uncertain temperament, and induce them to stand to save the capital. That they were then to be respected, and engaged with the greatest caution, many battlefields had proved; now several such positions stood across the road to Pretoria. Already information tended to show that the commandos, eased for a moment of the heavy pressure, were regaining cohesion. Ten to twelve thousand men, with twenty-seven guns, were reported between the Rhenoster and the Vaal; three thousand with ten guns between Klerksdorp and Potchefstroom; and twelve hundred near Heilbron. On May 20th Lord Roberts, who expected to be opposed immediately by seven thousand Boers, with seven guns,† ordered his cavalry to the front. Once more his designs were based on a double turning manœuvre by the cavalry on the west and Hamilton on the east. The mounted troops would have the advantage of gaining touch with Lord Methuen, who had been ordered to march from Hoopstad on Reitzburg, by way of Bothaville. The presence of his column within the zone of operations might prove of infinite value should strong resistance be encountered along the line of the Vaal. It was on this day that Hamilton crossed the Upper Rhenoster, as described at the end of the last chapter.

* See Chapter VI.
† Telegram to Lieut.-General Ian Hamilton, May 19th, 1900.

ADVANCE FROM KROONSTAD TO PRETORIA. 67

He was already well on his way to Heilbron, the turning point of the Boer left flank. French, whose remounts, four hundred in number, only arrived as he was setting out, left Jordaan Siding at 8.30 a.m. with the 1st and 4th cavalry brigades (2,045 officers and men) and Hutton's mounted force (about 2,500 strong); and after an easy march, during which only hostile patrols were met with, reached Kroonbloem north-east of Rhenoster Kop, Hutton halting two miles south of the Kop. Next day, whilst Hamilton—his rearguard still fencing with the enemy—made Witpoort for the night, French moved on, and at noon joined the Carabiniers, who had seized the drift at the junction of the Rhenoster river and Honing Spruit on the previous day. Information which reached him here tended to confirm the estimated strength of the enemy, whose guns were reported to number twenty-six.* May 20th, 1900. The cavalry march.

The 3rd cavalry brigade had also quitted Kroonstad, proceeding to Bosch Kopje, over twenty miles on the Heilbron road, in order to cover the march of a convoy which was about to set out for Hamilton. At the same time the VIIth division closed up to Kroonstad, and Henry's corps of mounted infantry, strengthened by J. battery R.H.A., the 7th Imperial Yeomanry, and other units, moved out to Jordaan Siding, and prepared to screen the progress of the main army. On the 22nd the general advance was resumed. The infantry marched to Honing Spruit and Steenkamp's Pan, with Henry, at Serfontein, five miles in front; the 3rd cavalry brigade covered the right flank at Uitenhage. Hamilton entered Heilbron unopposed, his cavalry pursuing until dark the rearguard of a strong commando with two guns, which fell back northward, abandoning eleven fully-loaded wagons in its retreat. French, crossing the Rhenoster, gained the right flank of the reputed position; but he sighted so few of the enemy, and found so many burghers waiting on their farms to surrender, that, after sifting all information, he reported to Lord Roberts that only a small force remained north of the river.† Lieut. C. Ross, of Hutton's force, scouting boldly May 22nd, 1900. The position on the Rhenoster turned by both flanks.

* Messsage to Chief of Staff, 12 noon, May 21st.
† Telegram to Chief of Staff, 12 noon, May 22nd.

VOL. III.   5*

northward, reported from Reitzburg at 1 p.m. that there were no Boers to be seen south of the Vaal itself. This news, contradicting as it did French's own message of the previous day, and all previously received intelligence, gained little credence at Army Headquarters. It was nevertheless true. Next morning (May 23rd) French, prepared for any eventuality, left his bivouac before daylight. His contact squadrons, ranging far ahead, and preceded by the indefatigable Ross, reached the railway at Leeuw Spruit and Vredefort Road, behind the Rhenoster positions, unopposed, learning that the enemy had passed northward many hours previously. On the previous afternoon Hunter-Weston had sallied out on another expedition to cut the line in rear of the Boers, should they stand on the Rhenoster. At 9 a.m. he returned, reporting that he had located the hostile rearguard at Grootvlei, twenty miles north of the river. The strong line of the Rhenoster, then, had long been abandoned. Whilst French and Hutton halted at Essenbosch, the infantry columns were pushed forward to Roodewal (VIIth division) and Kopjes (XIth division), covered on the right by the 3rd cavalry brigade at Waterval. Hamilton, his rearguard once more engaged as it cleared Heilbron, marched ten miles north-westerly to Driefontein, that is, towards the railway.

May 23rd, 1900. The passage of the Rhenoster.

Lord Roberts' tactics with regard to the Vaal river.

This deflection of Hamilton's line of advance was the first stage of a manœuvre on which the thoughts of the Field-Marshal were now bent. Across his front flowed the Vaal,* a river of the first order, broad and deep, crossed by few and difficult drifts, everywhere defensible, and almost certain to be defended. The Transvaalers, who had so lightly relinquished ridge after ridge, and river-bed after river-bed, any one of which might well have stemmed the fast rising " tide of danger "† which had now almost submerged their comrades of the Free State, had long salved their consciences, and appeased their allies, by promises to stand with resolution behind their

---

* See map No. 40.

† In a telegram to President Kruger, Commandant-General L. Botha had written on April 8th : " . . . I am convinced that the tide of danger lies through the Free State."

ADVANCE FROM KROONSTAD TO PRETORIA.

own strong frontier. The very speed of their retreat from Brandfort, their evident anxiety to preserve commandos and artillery intact, seemed to argue the existence of an ultimate rallying point which could be none other than the Vaal. The reported arrival of two thousand burghers from Natal, the concentration of strong bodies at Vereeniging, Potchefstroom and Klerksdorp, the fortification of the hills between Vereeniging and the Heidelberg railway, all pointed to a determination to keep watch over a wide section of the river. The enemy's main body, a large portion of which had retired from the Rhenoster by train, was posted at Vereeniging, a strong detachment lying at and beyond Englebrecht's Drift, on the eastern side of the railway, in readiness to oppose the passage of Hamilton's force. Immediately on the west of the railway, the Vaal, fringed by intricate country, and crossed by difficult and seldom used drifts, was so lightly guarded, that it was clear that an invasion by this side was not anticipated. On this side, therefore, Lord Roberts decided to strike, and, to effect his purpose, resorted to a device which at once mystified the enemy, and concentrated a force of infantry in the desired direction. On the 24th Ian Hamilton, who had so long formed the extreme right flank, received orders to lead his command diagonally across the front of the army, and advance to the Vaal at Boschbank on May 25th. Crossing there, he would march northward wide around Vereeniging on the 25th, occupy Meyerton on the 27th, and thus, together with the cavalry, who would by that time have come up around his left, stand astride of the line directly behind the main body of the enemy at Vereeniging, which Lord Roberts himself would then attack in front. Before these orders reached Hamilton, French was already across the Vaal.

Leaving Essenbosch at 6 a.m. on the 24th, a march of nearly twenty miles due northward brought him to the banks of the Vaal at Parys, where a good drift was reported to exist. It proved, however, to be difficult and dangerous. Only in single file could the horses be led across the narrow ledge of rough rock, 250 yards long, which zigzagged across the stream. For

May 24th, 1900. The cavalry enter the Transvaal.

wheeled transport, even the lightest, the passage was impossible, and French, anxious to cross before his presence was discovered by the enemy, ordered the 1st cavalry brigade to seek an easier drift up-stream, whilst the 4th brigade wound slowly across at Parys. Not until nearly ten miles of mountainous country had been traversed by the 1st brigade and Hutton's force, was a suitable spot found at Old Viljoen's Drift, five miles south-west of Lindequee. Here, at 4 p.m., the brigade crossed, leaving the baggage in charge of the mounted infantry on the left bank. Meanwhile the 4th brigade, moving up the right bank from Parys, joined the 1st brigade at dusk. A strong position was then taken up covering Old Viljoen's Drift. Thus ended a somewhat anxious day for the cavalry. Only the somnolence of the enemy, who contented himself with guarding Schoeman's Drift, had rendered possible the passage of wide and difficult drifts, and movement through country where a few sharpshooters might have thrown both brigades on the defensive.

Ian Hamilton, continuing his north-westerly movement, halted the 19th brigade at Arcadia, and the 21st brigade four miles north of Vredefort Station, at which place the XIth division and the 3rd cavalry brigade lay that night. The VIIth division bivouacked at Nooitgedacht, slightly to the left rear, and Henry's mounted infantry at Eerstegeluk, in front of the now united forces. During the day Lord Methuen, who had reached Bothaville, had been ordered to desist from his march to the Vaal, and to come in to Kroonstad. Lord Roberts was well aware of the insecurity of his immense and ever-lengthening lines of communication, on either side of which lurked bands of horsemen only awaiting his disappearance north of the Vaal to fall upon the railway. By calling in Lord Methuen to the line these factors of uneasiness would only be diminished, not removed. In any case the Field-Marshal determined not to turn his face from the Transvaal capital, the fall of which would inflict on the enemy a wound deeper than any his own army might receive from behind. On May 25th the main body pushed forward to Grootvlei and Wittepoort, covered by the 3rd cavalry brigade and Henry's mounted infantry at Wolvehoek. Hamilton,

ADVANCE FROM KROONSTAD TO PRETORIA. 71

passing close before the heads of Lord Roberts' columns, crossed the line to Wonderheuvel, sending his mounted troops ahead to Boschbank, where they gained touch with patrols from French's force. The latter moved on Lindequee, the troops advancing along the right bank of the river, their baggage along the left bank, Old Viljoen's Drift having been found too difficult for transport. The Boers from Potchefstroom, awaking to the situation too late, followed in some strength, and Lindequee itself was found weakly held. There was little fighting, and by evening French had his baggage across and was at Zeekoefontein, in a good position to cover Hamilton's passage at Wonderwater Drift. May 25th, 1900. Ian Hamilton transfers his force from right flank to left.

On May 26th French crossed the Rietspruit, pushing back the enemy's scouts and patrols on to Hout Kop, night falling before it could be cleared. A stand by a party of fifty Boers about 4 p.m. was broken up by an onset of five companies of the New Zealand Mounted Rifles, of Hutton's force, the Boer field cornet being wounded and captured, five of his men killed, and three taken prisoners in the affair. French halted at Rietkuil, after learning from his patrols that Vereeniging had been evacuated, and that the enemy, some five thousand in number, were falling back demoralised, on the Kliprivers Berg, a position covering Johannesburg.* Behind French, Hamilton, impeded only by the badness of the drifts and lack of forage, completed his passage of the Vaal at Wonderwater by 7.30 p.m.; whilst the main body, with the Field-Marshal, marched through dusty mealie fields to where the railway crossed the Taaibosch Spruit. May 26th, 1900. Ian Hamilton crosses the Vaal river.

The sudden abandonment of the line of the Vaal, the Rubicon of the Transvaal, was, indeed, significant both to the British and Boer commanders. To Botha it gave warning that even his ceaseless activity, his unsleeping vigilance, his indomitable optimism so long displayed, had been vain to prevent his followers "despairing of the Republic." Now for the first time his telegrams and messages to his subordinates lost, not their authority, for his grip on the helm was firm, nor their clearness The Boers leave the line of the Vaal river.

* Message to Chief of Staff, 8 p.m.

or encouragement, for he kept both his head and his heart, but their patience. There was ample cause. Officers and men alike were failing him. None were to be found where he had ordered them; many were not to be found at all. He had foreseen and provided against the forcing of the drifts about Lindequee; but the commandos at Klerksdorp, Potchefstroom, and on the Gatsrand, had done nothing either to oppose the passage or to harass French when he had crossed. Those around Vereeniging, their fears of being surrounded awakened by the appearance of the 3rd cavalry brigade behind Viljoen's and Englebrecht's Drifts on the east flank, had fallen back before French's scouts had crossed the Rietspruit. The fugitives were already beyond Meyerton when Botha signalled to the heavy artillery at that place to be ready to join him in making a stand.* So many of the burghers had lost their horses that the General now habitually referred to a portion of his forces as "the infantry,"† a term novel, indeed, to an army composed of men who had seldom voluntarily travelled a mile on foot. Already the "last extremity"‡ appeared in sight, and Botha, after telegraphing to the President, advising him to convene an emergency meeting of both Volksraads, followed his demoralised troops northward. In Vereeniging he left Theron and Malan with their corps of scouts, with orders to blow up the railway bridge, and do as much damage as possible before they were forced to depart. He also sent to General De la Rey, at Klerksdorp, entreating him to hasten towards the Gatsrand; and even wired for reinforcements from Natal, where the wavering commandos, still depending on him for orders, and importuning him for assistance, added to his already multitudinous cares.§

Lord Roberts, on the other hand, could now see no obstacle between his troops and Pretoria. An enemy who had run without

* Telegram from Botha to officer in charge of heavy artillery, Meyerton, May 26th.

† Telegrams to State President, May 26th and 27th, and to same and Assistant-General Fourie, May 28th, 1900.

‡ Telegram to State President, May 25th, 1900.

§ Telegram to Assistant-General C. Botha at Laing's Nek, and to Assistant-General Fourie at Charlestown, May 26th, 1900.

ADVANCE FROM KROONSTAD TO PRETORIA. 73

fighting from so strong a defence as the Vaal was not likely to be formidable on the only position now available, the open Rand outside Johannesburg. Pretoria itself, surrounded by heights crowned with modern fortifications, might, indeed, bring him to a pause. The forts erected at such expense were probably armed and manned; four 6-in. guns beside were reported in the neighbourhood of the place, and ten thousand men, with twenty-five guns, were said to be still south of the town. Thus the capital remained an unknown quantity, yet one to be the more easily solved the more speedily it were approached. On May 27th the main body was thrown across the Vaal. The cavalry rode over Hout Kop, which had been evacuated during the night, reconnoitred Meyerton, and then, in accordance with orders received at 10 a.m., pointed due northward for Rietfontein on the Klip river; Hamilton being instructed to follow French by way of Doornkuil. French was opposed throughout his march from Hout Kop. First at Syferfontein, where the road entered a defile, a part of the enemy's rearguard, consisting of about three hundred men with a gun, were dislodged with little difficulty. The Boers then fell back on Vlakfontein, where a second defile carried the track through the eastern arm of the Gatsrand, which, following the bend of the Klip, here curved toward the south, forming a horseshoe of heights. A strong force, the main body of the enemy's rearguard, under Generals Grobelaar, Lemmer and Commandant B. Viljoen, with three guns and two Vickers-Maxims, held the ridges on both sides of the road, and opened a heavy fire. The ground on the right of the road was first cleared by the 1st brigade, not without difficulty, for the Boers were strongly posted. On the heights about Vlakfontein, to the west, the enemy stood stubbornly. A dismounted attack by the Inniskilling Dragoons was driven back; nor could the 4th brigade, which hurried up on the left to reinforce, entirely clear the kopjes, on the northern edges of which the enemy remained until dark with guns and rifles in action. The defile, with its egress towards the Klip, was in French's possession, and his men, who had marched and fought for thirty miles during the day, bivouacked about Vlakfontein. Hutton, with

May 27th, 1900. The British main body crosses the Vaal river.

his mounted troops, after sending forward the 1st battalion M.I. to relieve the cavalry on the positions they had won, halted at Doornkuil for the night. Meanwhile, Hamilton marched uneventfully to Wildebeestfontein; the main body, with the Field-Marshal, crossed the Vaal by drift and pont to Vereeniging, the 3rd cavalry brigade and the 4th and 8th mounted infantry, with J. battery R.H.A., on the right alone meeting with the Heidelbergers, of whom they drove about four hundred pell-mell across Viljoen's and Englebrecht's Drifts to join the northward flight. A false report that the 3rd cavalry brigade had failed to effect a crossing at Englebrecht's Drift had caused the 4th and 8th corps of mounted infantry to be sent post-haste to that drift.

<small>Botha prepares to cover Johannesburg.</small>

On the Boer side Commandant-General Botha, who had been present at the action with his rearguard, seeing that he must lose the Gatsrand, sent urgent messages to De la Rey, who had closed in on Frederikstad, and to Generals Oosthuizen and Du Toit, who had lingered near Potchefstroom, bidding them to make a forced march all night in order to interpose their contingents (the commandos of Krugersdorp, Wolmaranstad, Bloemhof, Rustenburg, Marico, and Potchefstroom) between the British and Johannesburg. He also sent to Johannesburg itself for reinforcements for his crumbling right flank, ordering that all able-bodied men from the mines should be impressed for service. To C. De Wet, who was at Frankfort, he wired that Greylingstad must be cleared of its stores of ammunition, and that an instant plan must be made for attacking the British in rear.* As for the commandos which were streaming past him towards the Rand, he urged them to make one stand for the defence of the city of mines. That entreaties were necessary to induce the keen-witted burghers to draw rein on the Kliprivers Berg was indeed no sign of demoralisation. Truly the ground was favourable to defence, and its configuration perfectly adapted to the protection of Johannesburg. But both flanks of the ridge were exposed, and the line of retreat lay across open country.

Curving from the Vereeniging railway line round the Rand

* Telegrams to Head Commandant C. De Wet, May 26th and 27th.

near Krugersdorp, the Kliprivers Berg,* like a vast "horn- *The Boer position in front of Johannesburg.*
work," covered the approaches to the town from the south and
the south-west; and though of no great height, commanded the
valley of the Klip river, wherein broad and treacherous swamps
obstructed access to the front. On the western flank rose the
hill called Doorn Kop, the scene of a former victory over British
invaders, a victory so recent that its mingled triumph and bitterness might well fire the soul of every burgher who, four years
later, should be called upon to level from its grassy crests the
rifle with which that victory had armed him. On these ridges
some half-dozen commandos were hastily disposed. They were
mostly fresh troops. In spite of the prayers of General Botha,
few of his own burghers turned aside to join the forces of De la
Rey, who had detrained his command at Bank, and of Snyman,
returned inglorious from his failure before Mafeking.† These,
with the Johannesburgers under B. Viljoen, who had only arrived
from Natal the day before to join Grobelaar on the Gatsrand,
and now made ready to give battle for their native town, formed
the main line of defence.

French, who, after the affair in the Gatsrand, had concen- *May 28th, 1900. The cavalry reconnoitre.*
trated at Rietfontein, moved down on the Klip early on the
28th. His approach to the river was unimpeded, for the enemy
had abandoned under cover of darkness the ridges to which
they had clung at nightfall. Yet no sooner were the mounted
brigades across the river than a heavy converging fire from
ten guns on the Kliprivers Berg and supporting heights near
Florida marked the enemy's position and his intention to maintain it. French, determined thoroughly to develop the situation,
reconnoitred with great boldness. Sending the 1st cavalry
brigade and Alderson's corps of M.I., with two Vickers-
Maxims, across at Vanwyksrust, to clear the Boers from the
bushy kopjes which, about Misgund, projected from the Kliprivers Berg and fringed the river, he himself, with the 4th cavalry
brigade and Pilcher's 3rd mounted infantry, moved up-stream
along the northern bank, intending to feel for the enemy's right
flank. Arrived beyond Klipriver's Oog, where the Potchef-

* See map No. 41. † See Chapter VI.

stroom road crossed the stream, he secured a line of kopjes which commanded the drift, facing the heights about Doorn Kop, whence he vigorously shelled the plainly exposed Boer flank. Meanwhile, the 1st cavalry brigade and Alderson's M.I., which were separated from French by the spruit and its marshes, had become so sharply engaged on the right, where they had made good progress up the hill-sides, that the General sent off the 4th cavalry brigade to reinforce, leaving Pilcher to hold the kopjes between the marshes and the Potchefstroom road. A severe shelling, little checked by French's and Hutton's batteries and Vickers-Maxims, pursued the movement of the cavalry across the stream; but the 4th brigade joined the 1st with little loss, and prepared for a further advance.

By this time the enemy's dispositions and intentions were unmistakable, and the mission of the cavalry was accomplished. French, therefore, leaving Hutton with his mounted troops in occupation of the captured kopjes—Pilcher's corps on the kopje south of the Potchefstroom road by Klipriver's Oog, Alderson's at Misgund—withdrew the cavalry across the river to Rietfontein. French received a message from Hamilton, who had come up to Syferfontein, containing orders which had been received from Lord Roberts and his own intentions with respect to them.* Hamilton's movement next day was to be directed on Florida, and this he proposed to effect by a march around the right bank of the Klip, by Doorn Kop, where he would fight if necessary. From the Field-Marshal himself, who had brought the main columns into line with Hamilton at Klip River Station, French had already received general instructions as to his line of advance. Whilst Lord Roberts marched up the line to Elandsfontein and Germiston, thus turning Johannesburg from the east, French, moving round by Florida, whither Hamilton would follow, would make for a point—Driefontein—some ten miles north of the city. The same tactics, in short, as had been successful against so many positions since the army had left Bloemfontein were to be applied to the reduction of Johan-

---

* Message, 9.20 p.m., May 28th, 1900.

nesburg. For their success all depended on the issue of the engagement on the Kliprivers Berg, which seemed imminent.

A night of intense frost followed. At 8 a.m. on May 29th the cavalry, having refilled their wagons with supplies, left Rietfontein, and pushed north-west along the right bank of the Klip towards Doorn Kop and the enemy's right. For some distance this flank march was screened by Hutton's corps holding the kopjes on the left bank. The drift on the Potchefstroom road was gained without fighting, some waterworks at Zuurbekom being seized on the way. Beyond the drift, however, that is, on the kopjes of which the southern prolongation across the Potchefstroom road had been held by Pilcher during the night, the enemy's advanced posts disputed further progress, and a sharp action, carried out with great energy by a dismounted detachment of the 4th brigade, two squadrons 7th Dragoon Guards, and one of the 14th Hussars, was necessary to dislodge them. The Boers were forced back to the Doorn Kop ridges behind, and the 4th brigade, extending to the right, joined hands with Pilcher about 11.30 a.m. thus possessing the whole ridge down to Klipriver's Oog. This ridge lay directly in the face of the main Doorn Kop—Klipspruit—Kliprivers Berg positions, and separated from them by some four thousand yards of open and gently rising ground. The enemy now began a warm converging fire of artillery upon the cavalry. A contact squadron, which endeavoured to feel its way towards Doorn Kop, was furiously shelled; and French, having thus marked the enemy, made good the drift, and secured on the enemy's side of it an excellent base for the operations of the infantry, saw that he could do no more until they arrived. Soon after noon Hamilton rode up in advance of his troops, to confer with the cavalry leader and to view the ground. From the information he had received he had already in great measure grasped the problem before him. Since the chief strength of the Boers lay not on the Kliprivers Berg proper, though that ridge was also strongly occupied, but on the Doorn Kop—Klipspruit kopjes to the west, it was evident that a direct advance by Vanwyksrust and Olifantsvlei would not only involve him in

May 29th, 1900. The battle of Doorn Kop.

ground of extreme intricacy, but would fail to circumvent the enemy who lay between him and Florida, his goal for the day. He had decided, therefore, merely to mask the Boers on the Kliprivers Berg, keeping them from his flank and rear by holding the kopjes on the left bank and all the passages, whilst with the main portion of his force he moved across the easy open ground by Rietfontein and Zuurbekom, endeavouring to work around the Boer right which seemed to be in the air at Doorn Kop. To envelop this flank completely would probably be beyond the reach of the infantry, and would divert them unduly from the line of Florida. This operation French agreed to undertake, Hamilton strengthening him for the purpose with the majority of his own mounted troops, namely, Broadwood's cavalry brigade and de Lisle's mounted infantry.

At 1 p.m. Ian Hamilton's column, which had quitted bivouac at Syferfontein at daylight, reached the river, and, marching upstream along the right bank, relieved the mounted troops on the kopjes on either side of the Potchefstroom road. Thereupon French, assembling his command, re-crossed the Klip and moved towards Zuurbult, sending word to Hutton to withdraw Alderson from the Misgund spur and follow him. Alderson's position, like that of Pilcher on the other side of the marsh, had been of the greatest value, in that it had shielded the flank marches first of the cavalry, and then of Hamilton's column and baggage train. He had been in close touch with the enemy all the morning, and at his first motion of retirement, the Boer firing redoubled upon the 1st battalion M.I. and the 1st and 2nd Canadian Mounted Rifles who composed his corps. Skilfully extricating his men in small parties, Alderson withdrew across the river with trifling loss, and hurried after French.

By the time that the whole of his force had arrived on the kopjes on the left bank of the Klip, Ian Hamilton had decided that, after all, nothing remained to him but a frontal attack on the Doorn Kop—Klipspruit positions. To follow the cavalry in their wide-turning westward movement was now undesirable, or even impossible. The afternoon was wearing on, his men had already been on the march many hours, and the Boer right flank, continually—so French reported—extending westward, would probably in the end still force him to a local frontal attack, however far he might move to outflank it. Moreover, a prolonged movement in that direction would not only isolate him from Lord Roberts and the main body, but would dangerously weaken his hold on the river passages, when the Boers on the main Kliprivers Berg would have easy access to his flank and rear. To attack, then, and at once, was his determination. Nor was there time or scope for subtlety of tactics. Doorn Kop itself, though it was strongly held, and lay on the flank of his projected advance, was too far distant to be struck. He could only trust to French to shake it from the outside, whilst a portion of his own force held it from within. The ridges east of the height he selected as his target. They were sufficiently forbidding in appearance. Rising from the smooth veld some four thousand yards from Hamilton's place of assembly, they curved from Doorn Kop round to the Potchefstroom road, bridging as it were the flats between the bifurcating branches of the Klip river. They were divided, roughly, into two main features; that on the west, an elongated hill broken by several protuberances, being slightly retired from that more to the east, which pointed somewhat forward towards the British position. The crests of both were crowned by long capstones of rock, the eastern hill appearing to be traversed by several such, forming successive defensive walls. In front of both the grass had been burnt, leaving a width of 1,500 yards of ground bare and black. Some 5,000 yards behind the Boer right rose a height called Vogelstruisfontein, from which a heavy gun had fired; behind the left, on a tributary spruit of the Klip, which indented the position, lay Klipspruit Farmhouse. The only circumstance favourable to attack seemed from the British lines to be the existence of dead ground in front of the crests, formed by the rapid fall of the rocks which fringed them. A streamlet, which united with the western arm of the Klip near the drift on the Potchefstroom road, bisected the British position, and formed the dividing line between the brigades. On the west of it was marshalled the 21st brigade (Major-General Bruce Hamilton), consisting of the following battalions :—1st Derbyshire, 1st Royal Sussex, 1st Cameron Highlanders, City Imperial Volunteers (C.I.V.), and the 76th battery R.F.A.; on the east the 19th brigade (Major-General H. L. Smith-Dorrien), consisting of the following battalions :— 2nd Duke of Cornwall's L.I., 1st Gordon Highlanders, Royal Canadians, 2nd King's Shropshire L.I. (the last-named battalion remained on rear and baggage guard during the day; the 81st and 82nd batteries and the 5-in. guns formed the divisional artillery) with the 74th and 81st batteries R.F.A. and the 5-in. guns. Between these wings, by the stream, the Royal Sussex regiment and the 82nd battery R.F.A. were posted to act as column reserve. Whilst Ian Hamilton kept the whole of these troops under his immediate control, the dispositions of the infantry attack were entrusted to Smith-Dorrien, who temporarily handed over his brigade to Lieut.-Colonel J. Spens, of the Shropshire L.I. Orders for battle were quickly issued. Both brigades would advance simultaneously, the 19th brigade against the enemy's left, the 21st brigade against his right centre, refusing Doorn Kop, except in so far as to detach sufficiently to contain it. Bruce Hamilton, indeed, so far from allowing himself to be drawn aside by the commanding hill which overshadowed his left, was instructed to incline rather towards his right, that is, towards the 19th brigade.

At 2 p.m. the word to attack was given. The 21st brigade advanced first, moving northward, parallel to the western arm of the Klip. The City Imperial Volunteers led the way, the Derbyshire being écheloned slightly to their left rear, and the Cameron Highlanders to the right rear. On the other side of the Klip two isolated kopjes rose from the valley which intervened between the flank of the brigade and Doorn Kop. Towards the lower of these, in front of which was situated Doorn Kop Farm, the Derbyshire were almost immediately deflected, and, having secured it and the farm plantations, were disposed to present a front to Doorn Kop. The second kopje, which stood some distance toward the north, was held in strength, the enemy increasing in numbers upon it as the sound of French's guns from far away to the west reached the Boers on the central position, drawing many of them towards Doorn Kop. So warm a fire began to beat upon the flank of the City Imperial Volunteers, who had continued to advance straight forward, that the three leading companies of the battalion, wheeling to the left, were led by Colonel W. H. Mackinnon against the hill, and, after a sharp fight, carried it, some five hundred Boers galloping before them towards Krugersdorp. These operations were effectively covered by four guns of the 76th battery which were pushed forward to the north-western slopes of the kopjes from which the brigade had first emerged. Meanwhile the 19th brigade on the right was plunging deep into action, and Smith-Dorrien, fearing lest the ever-present influence of Doorn Kop might divert—as it had already partially done— the left attack away from the right, thus causing a gap to open between the brigades, after consulting with his Chief, sent word to Bruce Hamilton to stop all further movements towards the west, and to employ his strength in the direction of the right front and the 19th brigade. Under an ever-growing fire of guns and rifles the remaining five companies of the City Imperial Volunteers halted for a time, whilst the Cameron Highlanders came up on the right; and preparations were made for carrying the main ridge, the summit of which was still about a mile distant to the right front. Far to the right, covering the 19th brigade, the 74th and 81st batteries shot rapidly. The 5-in. guns on the right-hand kopje of the British position had already engaged at 8,500 yards the heavy piece on Vogelstruisfontein, silencing it after six rounds, though the smoke from the smouldering grass fires hung like a fog over the battlefield, and rendered sighting most difficult. By 3.30 p.m. although the enemy's artillery was fast dwindling, his musketry was virulent all along the line, and in spite of the shrapnel, swelled rapidly as the brigades closed to the attack. Especially was it severe on the right, opposite the 19th brigade, whose fortunes must now be described.

Shortly after Bruce Hamilton's troops had left cover, Spens

had led his battalions to the front. The Gordon Highlanders and Royal Canadians were in first line, on left and right respectively; the files of their firing lines extended at first to the unusual interval of 30 paces, with 150 paces between lines. The Duke of Cornwall's Light Infantry marched in rear as brigade reserve. The 74th battery, brought forward to the north-east face of the right-hand base kopje, where it was soon after joined by the 81st battery, threw shell over the heads of the infantry at 3,200 yards range. Thus by 2.30 p.m. the whole British line was in motion, and every gun in action. As the van of the 19th brigade drew within 1,800 yards of the position, the peal of the Mausers, which had been sounding loudest from the left, opposite the City Imperial Volunteers, rolled eastward along the ridges until the Boer positions from end to end emitted one steady roar. The valley in front rose in response to a heavy cloud of dust as the multitudinous bullets smote the dry earth, each flinging upward its puff of soil to thicken the yellow mist.

For the men of the 19th brigade there was no cover nor promise of any. The ground was absolutely bare even of ant-hills; the kopje to be stormed, instead of dipping sharply from its crest into dead ground, as had been thought, descended in a gentle, uniform slope from the very summit, along which ran a wall of rocks standing upright on their bases, like the legs of cromlechs, a jagged and formidable parapet. Even before the edge of the burnt, black glacis was reached the losses were numerous, chiefly amongst the Gordon Highlanders, who were full in the face of the storm. The advance of the men of this battalion was deliberate and inflexible. Their pace remained as it had begun, a steady walk; their discipline was so perfect, that an order to change direction, which reached them at the height of the uproar, was obeyed as accurately as though the long unwieldy lines, lashed by bullets, had been the front of a squad upon the drill ground. This occurred about 3 p.m., when Smith-Dorrien, perceiving a divergence between the lines of advance of the two brigades, sent a request to Spens to incline his attack more to the left, as he had already warned Bruce

Hamilton to turn his inward to the right. The message was carried to the front by the brigade-major of the 19th brigade,* who cantered, unhurried and unharmed, along the very front of the firing line, seeking the officer in command. The desired change of direction was promptly effected, and the rear company brought up on the left, to prolong the line towards the 21st brigade. Soon after, the Highlanders and Canadians entered the zone of burnt grass. By this time the intervals had closed considerably, and every burgher sought a target in the light-coloured uniforms, as they stood relieved upon the black background. But the Boers, dismayed by the unwavering nature of the attack, shaken by its very slowness, shot wildly, and though they slew many, stopped but half as many as seemed inevitable, not a tithe enough to keep their stronghold from the grasp of soldiers so resolute. The Canadians, somewhat separated on the right, were better covered by the ground than the Highlanders, and finding temporary shelter in a large stone kraal half way up the face of the hill, suffered far less. More than once they had to look to their outer (right) flank, against which the enemy continually demonstrated from the valley of the eastern arm of the Klip. All attempts on this side they successfully kept at arm's-length by Maxim gun fire. At 3.30 p.m. the Boer artillery was finally silenced. The leading line of the Gordon Highlanders was now within two hundred yards of the crest, under a tempest of fire which had so thinned the front as to render it temporarily unequal to an assault. A brief halt was called, during which the companies in rear hurried up into line. For the first time now reply was made to the hostile musketry, the soldiers sending a blast so fierce and unexpected into the rocks above them that the Boers wavered, many creeping to the rear. Then the battalion, fixing bayonets, charged, and in a moment hurled the enemy back. The Canadians, clambering up on the right, arrived at the top soon after. During the pause which ensued, Spens threw forward the Duke of Cornwall's L.I., who had supported closely, to prolong the line on the left of the Gordon Highlanders. Here they all but joined hands with

* Captain C. P. Higginson, of the King's Shropshire L.I.

two companies of the Royal Sussex regiment from the 21st brigade, who had charged up the left of the hill as the Highlanders had assaulted the centre.

The two brigades of the attack were now, in fact, practically in line over nearly five miles of front. The 21st brigade, with fewer losses, but with scarcely fewer difficulties, had been as successful as the 19th. Inclining slightly to the right, after the deflection of the three companies towards Doorn Kop, the remaining five companies of the City Imperial Volunteers, their right reinforced by the Cameron Highlanders, developed an attack on the westernmost of the two kopjes composing the Boer position. This line was speedily still further prolonged by the well-timed arrival of the Royal Sussex regiment and Marshall's Horse, which Ian Hamilton had kept back under his own hand as a column reserve. These troops, going up on the right of the Cameron Highlanders, so nearly bridged the gap between the brigades, that two companies of the Royal Sussex were diverted to join in the attack on the eastern kopje. To cover the assault, the brigadier then pushed the remaining two guns of the 76th battery (the other four still supporting the Derbyshire on the left rear) to within two thousand yards of the enemy, on whom they opened a telling fire. At the same time the reserve battery (82nd) also moved to the front behind the right of the brigade, and added to the volume of shrapnel searching the crests.

Against much the same opposition as the 19th brigade, Bruce Hamilton's troops won their way forward; using their rifles, however, more freely, and gaining ground by short rushes, instead of the leisurely pace which had marked the advance of the Gordon Highlanders. The two companies of the Royal Sussex, aiding the Highlanders, charged the western face of the eastern kopje under a fire so hot, that the mule, and more than half the crew of the Maxim gun which had accompanied them, were laid low before a round could be discharged. As twilight fell the 21st brigade was upon the ridge. The majority of the enemy, already unsettled by French's outflanking movement, fled; but many only ran back to other lines of rocks in rear, whence they continued to shoot for some time, eventually fading away. The same had occurred in front of the Gordon Highlanders. Here the Boers' second line was dangerously close, and almost as strong as that from which they had been forced. The ridge first captured, indeed, was but a false crest to the hill, the true crest lying some two hundred yards in rear. Behind it the enemy gathered thickly, revealing their numbers by the line of flame from many rifles which illumined the fast-gathering darkness. Soon after 5 p.m. the Highlanders charged once more. A withering volley answered their cheer; but it was the last. The rocks were won in a moment; the Boers, chased by the bayonet, and by magazine fire, rushed down the steep and stony descent which fell behind, and made off across the flat. As they disappeared in the gloom, a body of horsemen appeared galloping across from the left within close range. The cry went up that French's troopers were in pursuit, and the Gordon Highlanders ceased fire. The band, however, were in reality commandos in full flight away from the 21st brigade, and from Doorn Kop, where the cavalry had almost surrounded them. French, with his three brigades of cavalry and two of mounted infantry, had performed an invaluable turning movement with unexpected ease. Circling round Zuurbekom and Zuurbult, where his artillery brushed aside small parties of skirmishers, he swept around Doorn Kop, and by 4 p.m. was well on his way towards Vlakfontein, on the flank of Vogelstruisfontein, where the Boers had placed their reserves and heavy gun. Fearful of being cut off, the commandos on Doorn Kop slipped off eastward, thus easing the pressure on the 21st brigade, and only escaped heavy losses at the hands of the 19th brigade because of the misconception. Those on Vogelstruisfontein fell back northward, French pursuing almost to Roodepoort, whence the practice of two Boer guns showed the presence of a rearguard. With this it was too late to deal. French, having taken prisoner a commandant, an adjutant, and many burghers, then bivouacked on Vlakfontein, Ian Hamilton's victorious brigades finding what shelter they could on the captured positions. During the day their casualties had numbered 141 killed and wounded,* of whom the Gordon Highlanders had lost 98, including ten of their officers.

May 29th, 1900.
Operations of the main body.

On the left, then, Lord Roberts' operations had been crowned with success. Meanwhile those of the main body, carried out almost entirely by the mounted infantry, had been as fruitful and almost bloodless. At 5 a.m. Colonel Henry's brigade of mounted infantry, with J. battery R.H.A., left the bivouac at Klip river, and moved rapidly northward, under orders to try for Elandsfontein, cutting on the way rail and telegraph communication with Natal, Springs and Pretoria. About 7 a.m., as Henry was approaching the Natal Spruit—Heidelberg railway, a train was descried steaming at full speed from the direction of Natal. The 4th and 8th corps of mounted infantry, accompanied by a demolition party of 12th company R.E., galloped their hardest to intercept it, shooting as opportunity offered. Their fire was hotly returned from the windows of the carriages, and after a long chase, which was checked by the intervention of a barbed wire fence, the train escaped, just as the demolition party seemed about to head it off. A force of Heidelbergers under Fourie, posted on some kopjes north of Natal Spruit, and west of the line, then opened upon the pursuers with a long-range Creusot Field gun, a captured British 12-pr., and a Vickers-Maxim. Thereupon Henry occupied high ground between Elsburg and the railway, and sent back for his artillery, which, having been out-distanced, had nearly reached the level crossing at Roodekop Station. The message was expeditiously conveyed by Captain the Duke of Norfolk, who was acting as galloper, and the battery was soon at the front. For a time the enemy's fire was hot, the 12-pr. being especially troublesome, but all three guns were eventually silenced. Meanwhile Henry, taking with him two guns of the battery, pushed on towards Boksburg, which he secured at 1 p.m., a white flag coming out to meet him as he approached. Detailing the 8th mounted infantry to cut the line to Springs, he then turned westward towards Elandsfontein, in front of which he halted on a hill overlooking the

* For full casualty list, see Appendix 2.

ADVANCE FROM KROONSTAD TO PRETORIA. 87

junction, and ordered up the rest of his battery. A 6-in. Creusot gun, mounted on a truck north of Elandsfontein, endeavoured in vain to shell him off. The junction was choked with rolling stock, and Henry, bent on capturing what the army most needed, determined not to relax the pressure. J. battery, coming up, threw shell rapidly by indirect fire on to the line beyond the junction, with the intention of destroying the track. Those in charge of the heavy Boer gun, fearing to be cut off, ceased firing, and steamed northward, just as a party of the 8th mounted infantry dashed in and severed the line. Henry then fell upon Elandsfontein, ousted one band of Boers after another who attempted to stop him from behind the heaps of mine débris which littered the outskirts, and by 3 p.m. was in full possession of this important depôt, securing about one hundred prisoners and the more valuable booty of seven locomotives and a large amount of rolling stock, including six complete trains standing ready for departure. Best of all he had isolated and outflanked Johannesburg itself. In these operations the mounted infantry were supported, though at a considerable distance, by the 3rd cavalry brigade, which had been sent forward from guarding the right flank of the infantry to the sound of the guns about 8.45 a.m. Following much the same line of advance as the mounted infantry, but more toward the east, the cavalry came up with Henry, near Germiston, and bivouacked on the east of the Pretoria line, the mounted infantry halting for the night on the west. As for the infantry divisions, after much delay at the Klip river, caused by a 4.7-in. gun breaking through the frail log bridge, and a brief skirmish in front of Elandsfontein, where thirty-five Boers surrendered to the advance guard, they also moved on to Germiston. There they bivouacked, having out-marched the baggage, which did not arrive that night. Thus ended a successful and eventful day. *May 29th, 1900. Advance to Germiston.*

By this rapid advance against the outskirts of Johannesburg, Lord Roberts had surprised all of his opponents except their General. The stoutly fought battle at Doorn Kop, and French's wide circuit outside it, had drawn all eyes away from the more powerful forces threatening the eastern communications of the city. Ian Hamilton's refusal of the main Kliprivers Berg, increasing the already wide gap between the wings of the invading army, still further drew attention away from the mounted infantry dash on the east of the railway. Botha, nevertheless, had suspected and provided for some such movement. The Heidelbergers had already received orders to entrench strong positions at Natal Spruit—gangs of natives being sent from Elandsfontein to assist—and to patrol with vigilance down the line. The officers on the Kliprivers Berg were warned to keep a vigilant watch toward the east, to guard against being surprised from that side.* On the Zuikerbosch Rand, two field cornetcies were to be posted in observation;† whilst two complete commandos (Bethel and Ermelo) were brought across from the extreme right flank and placed astride of the line north of Elandsfontein.* The withdrawal of these troops from the right was doubtless ordered with more confidence, because the cessation of French's reconnaissance of the 28th had been reported to the Commandant-General as a victory for the Boer arms.‡ Johannesburg, then, seemed well guarded on the east side, or at all events unapproachable without stiff fighting. It was " with sorrow and astonishment "§ that Botha heard of the occupation of Boksburg and Germiston. An eye less quick than his would have perceived that Johannesburg was lost. His fear was not now lest the British should be in Johannesburg but in Pretoria before him;‖ already it was falsely reported to him that strong British columns had passed Elandsfontein and were on the march to the capital.¶ He instantly issued orders for fresh dispositions. At Frederikstad (see map 38) a force of 1,200 men under Du Toit had opportunely arrived from

* Message to Generals De la Rey and Grobelaar, May 28th, 1900.

† Message to General Fourie, commanding the Heidelberg commando, May 28th, 1900.

‡ Telegrams to the State President, May 28th and 29th, 1900.

§ Telegrams to the State President and General De la Rey, May 29th, 1900.

‖ Telegram to General De la Rey, May 29th, 1900.

¶ Message to all officers in the field, May 29th, 1900.

Fourteen Streams.* A detachment had also reported its presence at Klerksdorp. Let these make all haste up to Florida to continue the opposition on the west, whilst the army fell back on Six Mile Spruit. He himself, with a rearguard of five hundred men, would stand across the road to Pretoria. *Botha prepares to cover Pretoria.*

It was characteristic of this type of war that Botha himself spent this night close to Lord Roberts' own Headquarters in the very midst of his enemies. Believing that Smuts was still holding Elandsfontein, he, with his personal staff, galloped straight thither towards dusk, reaching Germiston in the dark. There he found himself surrounded by the British main body. Trusting to darkness he remained still, his party replying to a challenge that they were conductors of the transport of Lumsden's Horse, and had become separated from that corps. Next morning at dawn they rode off towards the dynamite factory, and escaped. *His narrow escape.*

Early on May 30th, Lord Roberts summoned Johannesburg to surrender. There was little hesitation on the part of the town commandant. The city itself was indefensible. The single fort, a far from elaborate structure built around the gaol, had been designed rather to overawe the enemies of the republic within the town than any from without. Its proper armament, four guns and six Maxims, was absent in the field. Moreover, the custody of the gold mines, the assets of seventy-seven companies which were the reputed guardians of twelve hundred and fifty millions of buried wealth, the protection of these stupendous riches from the many proposed and some few actual attempts to destroy them had become almost intolerable, and all but impossible to the Boer authorities, who for the most part sincerely desired to preserve them for the public good. During the morning, Doctor Krause, the commandant, drove out to meet Lord Roberts. After a short interview he agreed to capitulate, stipulating only for one day's grace to enable him to clear the *May 30th, 1900. Fall of Johannesburg.*

* Some of these reinforcements had already come up by train in time only to take part in the flight from Doorn Kop. The use made by General Botha of the Klerksdorp—Johannesburg railway in bringing up first De la Rey's contingent and then that of Du Toit is to be noticed.

town of the bevies of armed men, whom every retiring commando had dropped in the streets and purlieus, many bent on loot, many on the care of their own houses and property, and all very likely, if pressed, to resort to fighting from street to street. For twenty-four hours, therefore, Johannesburg was left in the hands of Krause, who quietly effected an evacuation, to compel which by force of arms would have assuredly entailed considerable losses on the British troops. The army nevertheless did not remain idle throughout the 30th. On the west French's brigades and Hutton's mounted troops, marching early, were in possession of Roodepoort and Florida by 9 a.m., blowing up the line near the former place, thus cutting off seven trains which had remained on the Krugersdorp side, and capturing one in Roodepoort Station itself. Thereafter the cavalry made but slow progress as they penetrated the Witwatersrand by the steep and rocky ground, which was further much intersected by the mine works. The mounted infantry, pushing on more quickly, arrived first on the northern crest of the Witwatersrand, which commanded an extensive view of the northward. Thence Hutton descried a portion of the enemy's rearguard moving away along the Florida—Pretoria road within striking distance. He immediately despatched his command down into the plain in pursuit, sending Alderson to attempt to head the commando, whilst Pilcher followed hard on its track. They came up with the quarry near Klipfontein, and a series of dashing skirmishes ensued, the enemy making desperate efforts to get clear, and developing a hot artillery and Vickers-Maxim fire, which in an hour was quenched by G. and O. batteries R.H.A. Eight ammunition wagons were first captured by the Queenslanders on the left bank of the Little Jokeskei river (see map 38), the 3rd M.I. and a company of New Zealanders seizing some high ground on the right bank. Here they were opposed; but so roughly did they handle the enemy, that he made off, leaving in the hands of Pilcher's men a long-range 75 m/m. gun with its wagon, from which he had been driven by the fire of the batteries. The rest of the M.I., scouring along the road, hustled the Boers as far as the drift over the Jokeskei, where

May 30th, 1900. The mounted infantry pursue.

ADVANCE FROM KROONSTAD TO PRETORIA. 91

they desisted, the enemy presenting on the other side a front too strong to be dealt with by the small numbers available. Hutton then recalled his men, and returned to bivouac near Driefontein with a commandant and forty-five other prisoners, the captured gun, and twelve wagons of stores and ammunition, all obtained at the cost of but one man slightly wounded. French's Headquarters were at Klipfontein for the night.

Some hours before these events, sharp fighting had already been in progress on the opposite flank of the army, nearly fifteen miles away to the east. Here the 3rd cavalry brigade and Henry's M.I. were lying to the north of Elandsfontein, the former on the east of the line, the latter on the west. About 8 a.m. the rearguard collected by Botha, a force of five hundred Boers with three guns and a Vickers-Maxim, attacked the outposts of the cavalry bivouacs, which they pressed hard. To such close quarters did they come in, that R. battery R.H.A. had to shoot from under cover with the shortest fuses, the gun detachments even being withdrawn for a short time, whilst the enemy's automatic gun played accurately on the pieces. The 16th Lancers were hotly engaged, and with loss ; and it was not until the 9th and 17th Lancers came up to reinforce that the enemy were driven off. As they fell back the brigade followed in pursuit, but was soon stopped and ordered to incline toward the west, to gain touch if possible with French. In a short time heliographic communication was established between the cavalry wings, and the brigade, having reached a point south of the dynamite factory, halted for the night.* On the part of the infantry there was little movement during the day. The VIIth division, ordered to support the mounted outposts, proceeded without fighting to a position two miles north-east of Johannesburg. Army Headquarters and the XIth division remained about Germiston. Ian Hamilton, having buried his dead on Doorn Kop, marched up to Florida. *May 30th, 1900. Attack on the cavalry outposts.*

At the stipulated hour on May 31st, Henry's M.I. entered Johannesburg and took over the fort. It contained little but *May 31st, 1900. Occupation of Johannesburg.*

* Casualties 3rd cavalry brigade—Killed, one officer ; wounded, two officers, twenty-four men.

some old guns and rifles and a small store of ammunition. The town was quite orderly, and very little damaged. A proclamation issued by Krause had successfully cleared it of combatants, and the crowds which filled the streets were composed mostly of British loyalists, delighted at the turn of events. At 2 p.m. Lord Roberts led the infantry divisions into the main square. The Republican flag which waved from the Government buildings was hauled down, and replaced by the Union Jack, the troops presenting arms, and bands playing the National Anthem. An outburst of cheering, in which the townspeople joined with the soldiers, greeted the transference to the British Crown of the city, which all knew to be the source and centre of the country's life, the kernel of South Africa, which, like that of many a fair fruit, had not been free from bitterness. The ceremony concluded with a march-past, the divisions defiling before the Field-Marshal. They then proceeded to bivouacs from two to six miles to the north of the town; all but the 15th brigade (Wavell's) of the VIIth division, which remained in garrison.

June 1st and 2nd. Halt at Johannesburg.

Lord Roberts established his Headquarters at Orange Grove.* For the next two days the army made no further advance. The left wing, its mission for the moment accomplished, was drawn in, Ian Hamilton moving to Braamfontein, French and Hutton bivouacking by the side of the 3rd cavalry brigade and Henry's M.I. at Bergvlei, near the dynamite factory. The administration of Johannesburg was actively undertaken, a Military Governor appointed, and Law, Finance, and Police officials selected from the many able men whom the war had scattered over the country. The mines were not neglected. Those which had been kept open by the Republican Government, or by irresponsibles, were closed; on those which had been idle, and had suffered from the irruption of water, pumping operations were ordered to be resumed at once. For the army, supplies were hurried up as rapidly as the enormous damage to the line permitted, and once more the Commander-in-Chief looked towards Pretoria.

Arguments for delaying the advance to Pretoria.

Not in his, but in many minds, grave and not unreasonable doubts had now arisen as to the advisability of pushing on

* See map No. 41.

ADVANCE FROM KROONSTAD TO PRETORIA.

to the capital. Upon the long and solitary line of communication, of which at each remove the army dragged an ever-lengthening chain, his whole force, " living from hand to mouth,"* depended each day for the food of the morrow. And the chain was in daily, nay, hourly, danger of snapping. Guerrilla warfare—the gadfly of regular armies, finding its natural prey in railways, convoys and isolated posts, and born exponents in the horsemen of the Free State—had broken out in the Orange Free State with an activity which was all the more ominous from the presence of the Mina of South Africa, who had already on four occasions disclosed his swift and destructive genius. Christian De Wet, newly invested with the rank of Assistant Commander-in-Chief, lurked to the east of Heilbron. As soon as, pursuant to the instructions received from Botha on May 26th, he had secured the ammunition from Greylingstad, he was ready to carry out the second part of his orders, and initiate a series of raids on the British lines of communication.† His lieutenants were within easy call: Generals P. De Wet, Froneman and P. Botha, near Lindley, J. B. Wessels between that place and Heilbron, P. Roux between Bethlehem and Senekal. They had already taken the offensive. These dispositions were almost accurately reported—in spite of a false despatch coming to hand, detailing a concentration of these Free State leaders between Heidelberg and Standerton—by the Field Intelligence Department in its summary for week ending May 29th. The total number around Heilbron and Lindley were therein estimated at three thousand men, with ten guns. On May 29th a telegram was received at Army Headquarters from Colvile, stating that he was hard pressed by the enemy at Roodepoort, eighteen miles to the south of Heilbron. Next day news that a force of Yeomanry was involved at Lindley, and that Rundle had been checked at Biddulphs Berg, reached the Field-Marshal.‡ There was cause, then, for serious anxiety as to the lines of communication. Neverthe-

* Lord Roberts' despatch, June 1st, 1900.
† See Chapter V.
‡ Telegrams C 1838A and C 1852, May 29th and 30th, to Lord Methuen at Kroonstad. The measures taken are described elsewhere. See Chapter V.

Lord Roberts decides to press on.

less, Lord Roberts, with that disregard of minor troubles when pursuing great ends which had ever distinguished him, determined to fall at once upon the capital. True, the necessity for siege operations before Pretoria would place him in a quandary; but in spite of a host of contradictory reports, his Intelligence Department reported any defence of the forts as exceedingly doubtful.* He knew that the commandos were broken and demoralised; all the rules of war demanded a resumption of the chase. The moral effect of the fall of the capital would be uncertain; but it must certainly be great, if only because the Transvaal Government would be forced to turn vagabond like that of the Orange Free State. Finally, in Pretoria were immured nearly four thousand British prisoners of war, who would be removed out of reach if he delayed, and whose release would not only put an end to much natural triumph on the part of the Boers, but would provide him with a useful reinforcement. On June 2nd two 9.45-in. Howitzers—half of a battery which had been disembarked at Cape Town on May 2nd—as well as four 6-in. Howitzers, arrived at the front. On the same day the army received orders to march.

The Boers in Pretoria.

Meanwhile, in Pretoria itself every man talked loudly of a desperate defence, except the President and the Commandant-General. For what other purpose, demanded the burghers, had the forts been designed, those imposing edifices, which had amazed them by their expense and their seeming strength?† Whilst they thus argued, the two chief officers of the State had already shown the measure of their faith in the costly parapets, President Kruger by vanishing quietly from the town in the evening of May 29th, General Botha by ordering his chief artillery officer to evacuate every magazine, and to despatch the ammunition and all the heavy guns along the eastern line to Middelburg.‡ Kruger was seriously alarmed by a report, in part a true one, that Lord Roberts was about to send a flying column

---

* For a short description of the defences of Pretoria, see Appendix 4.

† Letter from Commandant-General L. Botha to the State President, June 1st, 1900.

‡ Message to Major Wolmarans, State Artillery, June 1st, 1900.

to sever the Delagoa Bay railway, and thus cut off his escape.*
The fact was that at 6 p.m. on June 1st, a party of two hundred
mounted men, under Major Hunter-Weston, R.E., who was
accompanied by Mr. Burnham, the American scout, started
on an expedition to blow up the bridge on the Pretoria—Delagoa
Bay railway at Bronkhorstspruit, about fifty miles distant.
At 9 a.m. on June 2nd the party was discovered and attacked
by greatly superior numbers, being compelled to retire with the
loss of one man killed, four officers (one mortally) and nine men
wounded. The attempt was then abandoned, but it had the
effect of intimidating the President. Another rumour, to the
effect that British troops had landed at Kosi Bay, and were
making for Komati Poort, redoubled his fears. Now, indeed,
for the first time during his long and stormy career the nerve of
the old ruler and warrior seemed on the verge of collapse. Whatever of patriotism and valour had illuminated the Boer arms
—and there had been not a little—nothing had shone more
brightly than the apparent optimism of the President. His
hand, grown too feeble to hold the unerring rifle of former days,
had fought unceasingly for the cause with the pen, pouring out
endless exhortations to keep up the courage of his burghers.
Now, however, unable to endure the knock of war at his very
door, Kruger himself began to talk of surrender, and even wrote
to his brother fugitive, Steyn, that he had convened a council of
war to consider the question of an armistice.† In the meantime, President
leaving his wife in Pretoria, he hurried to Machadodorp. There, Kruger's
his weakness passing away, he established the seat of Govern- flight.
ment; and from his bureau, a saloon carriage which was tele-
graphically connected with the army, endeavoured still to uphold
the rocking edifice of the State, which his ambition had both
built and ruined. General Botha, promising his aged chief to
" remain at his post," turned once more to his almost " unbear-
able task,"‡ and proceeded to the positions at Six Mile Spruit,
the slender but last remaining hope of saving the capital.

* Memoirs of Paul Kruger. Volume II., pages 351 and 352.
† Letter to President Steyn, May 31st, 1900.
‡ Letter to the State President, June 1st, 1900.

June 3rd, 1900.
The army leaves Johannesburg.

On June 3rd Lord Roberts again set his forces in motion. With the same general idea of a westerly turning movement as had been successful at Johannesburg, French and Ian Hamilton were directed to move, first on Rooikrans and Diepsloot respectively, thence on to the Witwaters Berg, at a point near Schurveberg, which would place them well outside Daspoort Fort, the western defence of the capital. French was then to fall upon the line to the north of Pretoria, and sever communication with Pietersburg.* Meanwhile, the main body would follow the Florida—Pretoria road to Leeuwkop and Vlaakplaats,† where the north bank of the Six Mile Spruit would be gained. French crossed the Jokeskei river near Leeuwkop. On arriving at Diepsloot he learned that the only drift on the Crocodile river suitable for the passage of his wagons was at Roodewal, about eight miles due westward. He therefore recrossed the Jokeskei and pushed for the drift, which he reached about noon. Here he received information that the enemy's rearguard, consisting of about 1,500 men, with guns and wagons, was in front of him in the act of falling back through Kalkheuvel to the drift at Welgegund, evidently intending to gain the Witwaters Berg and Pretoria. Towards Kalkheuvel, where the road plunged into a gorge, a moving cloud of dust proclaimed the passage of the convoy, and French despatched the 1st cavalry brigade in pursuit. Two intervening ridges were quickly cleared; and French, hoping to intercept the convoy before it disappeared, called up two hundred of Alderson's corps to the centre, whilst the 1st and 4th cavalry brigades set out to encircle the enemy's right and left flanks respectively. The ground, seamed and broken as it was by spruits, by bushy and bouldered kopjes, prohibited all movements by the cavalry. They were, therefore, recalled to the road along which they continued the chase, the 1st brigade in front, followed by the 4th, Hutton closely supporting. The enemy, consisting of Du Toit's commandos, recently come up from Frederikstad (see page 88), fulfilling admirably their *rôle* of rearguard, stood with seeming

June 3rd, 1900.
The cavalry action in the Kalkheuvel defile.

---

* Orders to Lieut.-Generals Hamilton and French, June 2nd, 1900.
† See maps Nos. 38 and 42.

determination on every favourable feature, and had to be several times dislodged by shell before they yielded the entrance to the gorge, and fell back into its depths. By that time the day was wearing, and French, anxious to make good his point, the outlet and drift at Welgegund, before nightfall, pressed on into the defile. It was deep and narrow, shut in by a double rank of rugged kopjes, such a spot as no burgher of South Africa, any more than the tribesmen of Northern India, could pass by in retreat without setting a trap therein for his pursuers. Thus it happened that, as soon as the advanced patrols reached the centre of the defile, a fierce outburst of guns and small-arms, breaking suddenly from both sides of the road at short range, threw the scouts back on to the head of the column, which seized a rocky rise on the left, where it was soon reinforced by Alderson and artillery. For some time the gorge resounded with a fire-fight of great intensity. During this, Hutton, calling up the New Zealand Mounted Rifles, G. battery R.H.A., and two Vickers-Maxims from his second line, took up a strong supporting position. French then persisted in his determination to win the pass before dark. Two hills, one on either side of the road, commanded the northern outlet. Attacked by the 1st cavalry brigade and Alderson's men, with the 4th cavalry brigade and Hutton's force in support, both heights were occupied with slight loss. The Boers, having extricated their convoy, with the exception of six wagons which they abandoned, drew back clear of the defile at nightfall, keeping an automatic gun in action on the road to the last. The mounted troops then went into bivouac at Kalkheuvel.* During the day French had established heliographic communication with Broadwood, whose brigade was clearing the way for Ian Hamilton. That General, after a fatiguing march, reached Diepsloot according to his orders, whilst Lord Roberts brought the VIIth and XIth divisions to Leeuwkop. On this wing of the army only the 3rd cavalry brigade, on the extreme right, was in action during the day,

---

* Casualties amongst cavalry, June 3rd: Killed, three men; wounded, one officer and five men. Horses, from all causes, forty-eight. Ammunition expended: Shrapnel, 119; Vickers-Maxim, 275; small-arm, 10,141 rounds.

being opposed as it felt its way towards Six Mile Spruit in the late evening.

The Boer position in front of Pretoria.

The dispositions of the enemy as revealed next morning (June 4th) did not foreshadow much opposition.* Two parallel ridges lay to the north of Six Mile Spruit. The southern of these, two miles from the spruit, stretched east to Zwart Kop; the northern and higher ran back without a break to Fort Schanz Kop and Pretoria. The nearer range of the two, from which alone the passage of the spruit could be disputed, was abandoned as soon as J. battery opened. Zwart Kop and the adjacent heights were easily seized about 10.30 a.m. by the mounted infantry in advance of the main body. A hot fire, from about 1,500 yards distance, warned Henry that the enemy were posted on the second ridge. Whereupon, extending his men, the 8th corps to the left, the 4th to the right, he engaged the Boers and awaited the arrival of the VIIth and XIth divisions, J. battery R.H.A. dealing effectually in the meantime with two hostile guns, which opened from 3,700 yards northward. About noon the infantry divisions, which had already marched thirteen miles, reached and crossed Six Mile Spruit almost simultaneously, the XIth division on the right by the bridge on the Germiston road, the VIIth division by the drifts on the tracks from Florida and Johannesburg. No time was lost in pushing to the front. As fast as the infantry relieved his firing line, Henry moved his mounted men and part of J. battery off to the left, with the intention of working around the Boer right, which was on a steep and wooded kopje. The arrival of the heavy artillery, including Captain Bearcroft's, R.N., Naval brigade, with the 18th brigade (Stephenson's) on Zwart Kop, was the signal for a recrudescence of the Boer artillery fire, one of the first shells wounding Commander S. V. Y. de Horsey, R.N., in command of the 4.7-in. Naval guns. The demonstration was speedily quelled by the four guns of J. battery which Henry had left behind. As soon as the 18th brigade was extended along the crest of Zwart Kop —Essex regiment on the left, Welsh on the right—the Guards' brigade moved out to prolong the line of attack eastward, getting

June 4th, 1900. The action on Six Mile Spruit.

* See map No. 42.

astride the Germiston road, and resting their outer flank on a kopje which rose on the right of the road, some six thousand yards from, but out of sight of, Schanz Kop Fort, the southwestern defence of Pretoria. To this kopje went also the Naval 12-prs. and the 83rd and 85th batteries R.F.A. On Zwart Kop itself were posted the 4.7-in. Naval guns, the 5-in. guns of the 36th coy. S.D. R.G.A., and the 84th battery, which from the western slopes fired in a north-westerly direction across the depression, on the other side of which the VIIth division was coming into action. Strong as the right attack was, then, in artillery and position, it was for some time subjected to a ragged fire which, coming as it did chiefly from the left front, was felt most severely by the Essex regiment on that flank, though the batteries were not immune. By a skilful use of indirect fire, the gunners escaped all but trifling losses, whilst the hostile ridges had no respite from their shrapnel. For reasons to be related, the attack here was not pressed home, and the operations were confined to a strong holding action. Schanz Kop Fort, on its towering hill, had been early proved by a few rounds from the 4.7-in. guns at seven thousand yards; its silence removed the last expectation of a formal defence of the capital. Thereafter the heavy guns, throwing shell at nine thousand yards clear over the empty fortress, endeavoured to find the invisible railway station, the destruction of which would put a stop to the process of evacuation which was surely in progress.

Turning now to the VIIth division; the 15th brigade having been left in Johannesburg, there remained of it with Lord Roberts only the 14th brigade (Maxwell's). Its share in the action was little more eventful than that of the XIth division. On crossing Six Mile Spruit Lieut.-General Tucker received a message from the 8th M.I., the left of Henry's force, requesting the assistance of artillery to keep down the severe musketry coming from the wooded kopje held by the Boer right flank. Keeping his infantry under cover, Tucker sent first sections and then the whole of the 75th, 18th and 62nd batteries R.F.A. up to the ridge, disposing them along the summit from left to right in that order. Having beaten down the enemy's fire, Tucker pushed his brigade somewhat more forward, and was about to develop an attack, when an order reached him to delay further operations until the arrival of Hamilton's division in line with his left. For the enemy, either shrinking from the bombardment from Zwart Kop, or hoping to turn the British left by Schurveberg, or perhaps in order to anticipate Henry's own flanking movement in that direction, was by this time drifting westward along the ridges, and bade fair to get outside the 14th brigade. The Field-Marshal, therefore, ordered Tucker to halt, and sent word to Ian Hamilton, who was trending to the left in support of the cavalry, to incline instead to the right, and to come up with all speed to the scene of action. Hamilton had been pursuing a sinuous course. Leaving Diepsloot in the early morning, in accordance with his instructions to follow the wide turning movement of the cavalry, he had already crossed the eastern arm of the Crocodile river, when a message from Headquarters informed him that, as little opposition before Pretoria was expected, he was to retrace his steps, and conform to the march direct on the town. This Hamilton did; and his advance guard reached Mooiplaats Drift just as the fighting across the river began. Having crossed, he ordered his cavalry to bear to the left along the right bank, with the idea of turning by the left the range of hills in front of him. His troops had moved some distance in this direction when, as had occurred to Tucker, a message reached him that Henry's M.I. required support to the eastward. Hamilton's mounted troops, therefore, once more retraced their steps, and climbed the kopjes, to find that Henry, now supported by the VIIth division, was in no danger. Hamilton, wishing to resume his original movement, then drew his horsemen again out to the left, at the same time pushing the 19th brigade forward to a point opposite the enemy's right, leaving the 21st brigade in reserve by the river. Two guns of the 74th battery and a Vickers-Maxim, scaling in a wonderful manner the steep and rocky ridges, went forward with the 19th brigade, and were invaluable in keeping down the Boer fire, which was severe at one thousand yards range. Hamilton, who had early ridden to the front, had at once perceived the weakness of the Boer right, and the possibility of outflanking it. Broadwood, with the cavalry, carrying out the original plan, was by this time circling widely toward the west. But the mounted infantry, under Colonel de Lisle, were at hand, and with them Hamilton decided to effect his purpose. To the left front, a narrow nek, cut like a nick in the ridge, seemed to promise access to the easy ground which bordered on the enemy's position. Towards this de Lisle led his men, about 350 strong. The nek was incredibly steep, especially on the northern side, down which the mounted infantrymen, leading their ponies, scrambled with great difficulty. Once at the bottom and all again in the saddle, de Lisle began to gallop clear round the hostile position, capturing on the way a Maxim gun and two wagon loads of ammunition. The Boers, fearing to be cut off, and already much shaken by the bombardment, fled at full speed, and the 14th and 19th brigades pressed forward at once to occupy the abandoned ground.* Reaching a height overlooking Pretoria, de Lisle, at 4.45 p.m., summoned the city in the name of Lord Roberts to surrender. No answer was returned immediately. About 10 p.m. emissaries from the Transvaal Government came out with proposals for an armistice for the discussion of terms of surrender. The Field-Marshal replied that the capitulation must be unconditional, and that, as his troops had received orders to march at 5 o'clock the next morning, he must receive a reply by that time. At the hour named, the city was formally handed over, and the army advanced on its prize. At 2 p.m. a ceremony similar to that which had been performed at Johannesburg ratified the taking into possession by the British Crown of the Transvaal capital. June 5th, 1900. Fall of Pretoria.

The release of the prisoners, who numbered 3,029 men, proved to be a more dangerous enterprise than the occupation of the city itself. Between nine hundred and one thousand had already been removed out of reach to Nooitgedacht on the Delagoa Bay line. The remainder were interned at Waterval, to the north of Pretoria, and thither—occupying Wonderboom Fort and accepting a hundred surrenders on the way—rode the 1st Release of the British prisoners of war.

* For casualty list, June 4th, see Appendix 2.

cavalry brigade. A train to carry back the captives followed in rear. Directly the men had been freed from their long durance, and were crowding with delight on to the veld, the Boers opened a sudden fire both on them and their liberators from two concealed guns and many rifles. A scene of great confusion followed, and it was with difficulty and some loss that the cavalry withdrew with their convoy of weak and unarmed comrades. The rescue of the officers, 158 in number, was an easier matter. A Boer commando sent to remove them before the fall of the city, had been met with a flat refusal to march on the part of the excited prisoners. Whereupon the burghers, who were on tenterhooks as to their own safety, with singular forbearance departed, leaving the captives to await release.

<small>Considerations on the march from Bloemfontein to Pretoria.</small>

Thus after a march of three hundred miles ended a movement of which neither the magnitude nor the influence on the campaign can be realised at a glance. From its smoothness of execution and its freedom from sanguinary engagements, such an undertaking may appear trifling, just as its effect may seem doubtful from the long continuance of opposition which followed it. That resistance, nevertheless, its source dried up, was to grow weaker daily. In any State, however primitive, the spirit of warfare dwells in the seat of Government, and is in a fair way to be exorcised when that is seized. Though fighting may continue—and it is often more bitter than before—it is like the purposeless struggling of a man who has lost his mind, the proper director of his hands and weapons. Especially was this likely to be the case with the Boers, by nature and training guerrillas, who had throughout assumed but awkwardly the *rôle* of regular troops. Now the opposition of partisans is at all times the least hopeful form of warfare; for guerrilla bands, though they seem to be active and daring, neither can, nor in reality even hope to, accomplish anything vital, and their disjointed efforts become at last a mere nuisance. In aiming at Pretoria, therefore, Lord Roberts, though he left hostile forces in his wake, and secured little more than the city itself, did so with design, for he foresaw that his action would before long bring the pacification of South Africa for the first time within sight.

As for the march itself, the troops only knew its difficulties. Averaging nearly seventeen miles a day, over apparently endless prairies, in blazing sun and bitter cold, swept now by hot and choking dust storms, now by rushes of icy hail, fording rivers and floundering through sand, with scanty food and shelterless bivouacs, their toil had been almost unlightened by anything but hope. Marching, as has been said elsewhere, is the true rigour of campaigning. Of fighting, the welcome relief, Lord Roberts' infantry had too little to lighten the dullness of their task. The country itself but added to the heavy monotony which weighed upon their daily labour. On the vast levels there was nothing to be seen but their own long ranks, no sound to be heard but that of their own footsteps. Silence attended their marches, hunger, fatigue and discomfort their nightly sleeping places. Nevertheless, the fall of the second Boer capital, the mark at which they had aimed so steadfastly, crowned their efforts with honour greater than has been accorded to them, for the blow may truly be said to have reached the heart of the Boer rule in South Africa.

CHAPTER V.

OPERATIONS IN THE ORANGE RIVER COLONY.*

MAY AND JUNE, 1900.

<small>Liability to attack of the lines of communication in the Orange Free State.</small>

NONE knew better than Lord Roberts the dangers to which the disappearance of the army from Bloemfontein would expose his lines of communication. To push the whole of the enemy's strength before him was not to be expected. Forces in retreat before a victorious opponent have a tendency to break up on the flanks and spread outward, even though their centre remain intact; especially was this to be expected with a force so loosely knit as that of the Boers; one, moreover, largely composed of men who would be exceedingly loth to be driven out of their native land. A break back of the Orange Free State commandos, at least, was practically certain. Some, indeed, were already on the British flanks, and out of the zone of the projected drive northward; and there would be more the nearer the invading army approached the Vaal. No line of communication was ever more naked than that on which Lord Roberts depended, and which he was now about to double in length. The railway ran through mid-veld; on the west it was bordered by vast undulating savannahs, sparsely populated, poorly cultivated, and scarcely relieved from solitude by widely separated townships such as Philippolis, Fauresmith, Jacobsdal, Boshof, Hoopstad, Bothaville and Reitzburg. The difficulty of provisioning rendered the railway fairly safe from the descent of large bodies on this side; but a track so long and bare is in jeopardy whilst any hostile band, or even an individual, can

<small>* See map No. 38.</small>

approach it. To the east of the line lay the chief danger. Here stretched both the granary and the manœuvre ground of the Orange Free State, a region dotted with towns and villages wealthy in crops, and abounding in the watercourses, ridges and kopjes on which the Boers had fashioned their favourite tactics. Here men could both hide in safety and subsist in ease ; the harvest of the past year had been too rich for its owners to be willing to desert their stores. The region, in short, formed an irresistible attraction both to farmers and fighting men ; and it flanked the British communications from end to end. How surely Lord Roberts foresaw the probability of trouble is shown by the following extracts from a letter written by him from Brandfort to Lieut.-General Sir L. Rundle at Thabanchu :

"Brandfort, 4th May, 1900.

"It seems clear, from what has happened in the past, that if the enemy get an opportunity, they will again at once invade the south-eastern portion of the Orange Free State. By doing so, they would, strategically speaking, have the best chance of injuring us, and, should they succeed in getting a footing there, our lines of communication would be materially threatened. It would cause great consternation in Cape Colony, and it would be necessary for me to send back troops from the front, which would materially interfere with my plan of campaign. <small>Precautions taken by Lord Roberts</small>

"Under these circumstances, I look to you to take such measures as you may consider necessary to prevent any large body of the enemy being able once more to invest Wepener, or to move towards Smithfield through the Dewetsdorp—Wepener gap.

"As soon as it can be arranged, Chermside with the Headquarters of the IIIrd division will proceed to Bloemfontein, and he will have under his especial charge the line of railway from Bethulie and Norval's Pont up to this point.

"It will be your duty to exercise a vigilant control to

the east of the railway, and prevent the enemy from gaining a footing there.

"My belief is that, as we move north, the Boers will find it necessary to withdraw the whole of their troops now in front of Thabanchu, and also the small bodies now roving about the country south of Dewetsdorp.

"As soon as you are satisfied that they have withdrawn in the manner I anticipate, you should move such a portion of your force as you think necessary to Ladybrand.

"With Thabanchu and Ladybrand occupied in sufficient strength, with Dewetsdorp, Wepener and Smithfield properly garrisoned, with the people disarmed, and their horses taken from them—a measure which is now being thoroughly carried out—the Boers will be quite unable to move down south, and even if they do get there, they will find no armed and mounted burghers to assist them. . . .

"Please keep me fully informed of what goes on. You have a most important task to perform. . . ."

Before quitting Bloemfontein, the Field-Marshal provided for the safety of his communications as far as was possible with the troops at his disposal, leaving Sir L. Rundle with the VIIIth division and Brabant's Colonial division to keep clear the country east of the Waterworks, Kelly-Kenny with the VIth division to watch that between the Waterworks and Bloemfontein, Sir H. Chermside with the IIIrd division to garrison the railway from the capital down to Norval's Pont, and Sir F. Forestier-Walker, with the newly-arrived militia, to hold Cape Colony. Sir H. Colvile, with the Highland brigade of the IXth division, was to follow in support of Ian Hamilton, that is, behind the right flank of the main advance. His movements in the first half of May have been described.

<small>Sir L. Rundle in the south-east.</small> Sir L. Rundle opened the task of isolating the south-east of the Free State by establishing a line from Thabanchu to Ladybrand, which by May 13th he had pushed as far east as Brand's Drift on the Vet river. The enemy had been so threatening on his right flank, that an attempt to double back

OPERATIONS IN THE ORANGE RIVER COLONY. 107

into the Dewetsdorp district had seemed imminent. This activity came to nothing; and on the 13th Sir L. Rundle was able to report a general retirement of the enemy towards Senekal. By May 15th the Colonial division had seized Clocolan, and Sir L. Rundle, to whom in the last few days about 150 burghers had surrendered, joined hands with Sir H. Colvile at Winburg on the 17th. The VIIIth division, now based on Winburg, was extended along a line from Winburg to Clocolan, passing through Brester's Flats and Trommel.

In the meantime Lord Methuen had been assembling his reconstructed division at and near Kimberley. Since the relief of that town, Lord Roberts had kept a strong force in the neighbourhood, partly to isolate a large contingent of the Western Transvaal burghers from the commandos which were gathering along the Pretoria—Bloemfontein railway, partly with a view of succouring Mafeking. As early as March 2nd, the Field-Marshal had requested Lord Methuen to start as soon as possible for Mafeking, *via* Barkly West; but mounted troops were essential for this, and the demand for them in other parts of the theatre of war left none to be supplied. On March 9th Lord Methuen occupied Boshof, and remained in that district collecting supplies, and holding the Boers under Du Toit to their positions about Warrenton.

<small>Lord Methuen in the west.</small>

On April 25th the Commander-in-Chief wrote to Lord Methuen telling him of his intention to relieve Mafeking by means of a flying column, which would be followed along the railway by Sir A. Hunter with the Xth division. Lord Methuen himself was to make all preparations for marching on Hoopstad, as soon as the main advance from Bloemfontein should begin. To this Lord Methuen replied on May 1st that he would require until May 12th to concentrate his division, as some of his troops and ox transport were temporarily attached to Sir A. Hunter. He was able, nevertheless, to demonstrate usefully towards Christiana on May 3rd and 4th, thus assisting both the start of Mahon's column west of the railway, and Sir A. Hunter's passage of the Vaal at Fourteen Streams. Lord Roberts, who was anxious that British troops should appear in as many quarters as possible, then ordered the occupation of Christiana by both Sir A. Hunter and Lord Methuen; but on hearing that this could be done by Sir A. Hunter alone, he directed Lord Methuen to push on at once to Hoopstad. The 1st division marched in two columns; and after covering thirty miles in twenty-three hours over bad ground, arrived at the village at daybreak on May 17th, capturing two commandants and forty burghers. Lord Methuen here received instructions to continue his march on Reitzburg and Parys, by way of Bothaville, which village he occupied on May 24th.

The enemy in the west.

The Boers who had retired before Lord Methuen* and Sir A. Hunter, took up the following positions: General S. P. Du Toit with the Lichtenburg, Wolmaranstad and Bloemhof commandos, reinforced by the Krugersdorpers from Natal—in all some 2,000 men—lay on the north bank of the Vaal at Fourteen Streams. West of Du Toit was Commandant Van Aswegen, with a party of 200 Griqualand West rebels; these were joined on May 4th by a body who had taken up arms under P. J. Liebenberg, when that General invaded the western districts of Cape Colony. General Du Preez, with the Boshof commando—the only Free Staters in the western theatre of war—hovered about Boshof; whilst General A. P. J. Cronje, with the Klerksdorp contingent, 1,200 strong, held Christiana, to keep touch with Du Preez and to reinforce in case of need.

On April 30th the Boer leaders, in consequence of the arrival of the 6th brigade and Headquarters of the Xth division at Dronfield, held a Krijgsraad at Fourteen Streams, to arrange measures to prevent the British from crossing the Vaal. The decision arrived at was that Du Toit was to guard the right; Commandant Oosthuizen, with the Krugersdorp commando, was to hold the positions about Fourteen Streams, supported by A. P. J. Cronje, who would also assist Du Preez in the Boshof district in case of emergency.

Sir A. Hunter's operations in the west.

On May 3rd Lieut.-General Sir A. Hunter left Kimberley for Windsorton Road Station. That point had been already occupied by the 6th brigade (Major-General Barton) and two

* Volume II., pages 332 and 333.

batteries R.F.A. Barton pushed on some seven miles to the drift over the Vaal, leading to Windsorton, and seized it before dark, passing one battalion of infantry over to the right bank. During the afternoon Colonel F. C. Meyrick had arrived, with a squadron 5th regiment of Imperial Yeomanry, who had left Barkly West on May 3rd; he now joined hands with Barton's forces on the right bank of the Vaal. The drift at Windsorton was so bad that the remainder of Barton's troops could not cross, and spent the night on the left bank. On May 4th a second squadron of Yeomanry and two Horse artillery guns joined Meyrick.

As soon as Sir A. Hunter heard that Mahon had a clear start, he decided on a movement up the right bank of the Vaal, from Windsorton to Fourteen Streams, combined with a demonstration at Warrenton, with the object of sweeping the Boers away from Mahon's line of advance. At the same time Lord Methuen arranged to move out of Boshof and threaten the enemy's left flank. At Warrenton was placed the 20th brigade (A. Paget) from Lord Methuen's division, with two batteries of artillery and a 6-in. gun. On May 4th Sir A. Hunter completed the crossing of the Vaal at Windsorton. He then pushed his Yeomanry forward to within two miles of Rooidam, where touch was made with a party of Du Toit's men under Commandant J. Visser. The Boers brought up two guns and opened on the Yeomanry, Visser applying to Du Toit for more men. This was answered by the despatch of Liebenberg and Oosthuizen with about 1,000 men, from the centre to the right. As the object of the Yeomanry was purely reconnaissance, Meyrick withdrew a short distance and bivouacked. The remainder of Sir A. Hunter's troops came up in rear.

At Warrenton, Paget was engaged in shelling the strong position in front of him across the river. Lord Methuen, who had left Boshof, moving in a north-easterly direction, on the 3rd, succeeded completely in his mission of intimidating the Boer left. Such was the effect of his move that Du Preez fell back before him, and by his alarming messages brought out General Cronje from Christiana on the evening of May 4th with 500 men.

Thus by nightfall on the 4th, Sir A. Hunter's plan had succeeded all along the line. He had manœuvred the Boers into scattering their forces; and, better still, he had drawn large bodies of them to the south, thus allowing Mahon to go on his way towards Mafeking in comparative safety.

<small>May 5th, 1900. The action at Rooidam.</small>

At 7.30 a.m. on May 5th, Sir A. Hunter's Yeomanry, with the two guns R.H.A., moved from their bivouac and found the Boers still occupying the ground which they had held the night before. The position at Rooidam consisted of a series of rocky kopjes running from north-west to south-east for a distance of about four miles, the whole of the front being covered with light scrub. The Yeomanry, having re-occupied the forward position in which they had been on the preceding evening, pushed patrols to their front to draw the enemy's fire and halted until the arrival of the infantry. As soon as Sir A. Hunter was informed of the enemy's position, he sent two of his battalions—the 2nd Royal Scots Fusiliers and 2nd Royal Irish Fusiliers—to the east to guard his right and to prevent the Boers coming down on Windsorton. With the 2nd Royal Fusiliers, 1st Royal Welsh Fusiliers, 28th and 78th batteries R.F.A., he pressed on, arriving in front of Rooidam about 11.30 a.m. The primary object of the movement being to clear Mahon's line of advance, Hunter's left was his strategic flank. He at once therefore determined to turn the Boer right, and deployed his troops. On his right, the Royal Irish Fusiliers and the Royal Scots Fusiliers already stood upon the flank of the main artillery position, whence the 28th and 78th batteries R.F.A. now came into action. Their right thus covered, the Royal Welsh Fusiliers formed front to the centre of the enemy's position: upon the left of this battalion the Royal Fusiliers were sent forward in échelon of companies, left refused: Meyrick, with the 5th I.Y., and two guns M. battery R.H.A., was moved from his post of observation across the front to a position upon the outer flank, with orders to develop a turning movement around the Boer right.

When, at 12.30, the whole force advanced, the Yeomanry quickly attained the main tactical point. Galloping towards the flank, the Yorkshire Dragoons, under Major L. E. Starkey,

OPERATIONS IN THE ORANGE RIVER COLONY.

established themselves in a kraal on the enemy's right. A farmhouse some distance on was seen to be the key of this flank, and a dismounted party was sent forward to take it, whilst the Horse artillery guns made a target of the building, from which they drove a small party of Boers. The farm was then occupied, and Meyrick saw at once that it enabled him to look round the enemy's position. Calling up his guns, which commanded the Boer right at effective range, he heavily shelled the slopes.

About noon, Sir A. Hunter ordered the infantry to assault, the Royal Fusiliers and Royal Welsh Fusiliers being detailed by Barton for this purpose. As soon as the advancing lines came within rifle range, the enemy opened a heavy and well-directed fire, which caused several casualties. The ground over which the attacking infantry were passing was devoid of cover; but gradually prolonging their left till their front was an unbroken line, they moved steadily forward against the projecting Boer right. Ordering his battalions to swing up their left, by 2 p.m. Barton had pushed his men within 500 yards of the position. Here he halted whilst his left, seizing rising ground, folded itself further around the flank of the Boers and struck them in rear. The Yeomanry and Horse artillery guns, conforming with the advance, moved rapidly forward upon the outer flank of the infantry, materially supporting the attack by shelling the reverse slopes. At about 3 p.m. the final advance took place. The burghers, alarmed for their line of retreat by the troops on their right, and right rear, and unable to count their opponents' supports in the scattered bush, had already begun to dribble away. A few were caught in the trenches, but by 3 p.m. the commandos had fled, leaving thirteen dead and wounded on the field. The Yeomanry pursued for three miles along the Fourteen Streams road, taking five prisoners and a number of horses, rifles, and a quantity of ammunition. Sir A. Hunter's casualties were one officer and six men killed, three officers and thirty-five men wounded.

Towards the end of April, Major-General Hart's brigade (5th) was still detained in the south of the Orange Free State.* On

Hart joins Sir A. Hunter.

---
* Volume II., page 327.

the 26th the 1st battalion Connaught Rangers and the 2nd battalion Royal Dublin Fusiliers left by train for Kimberley, to join the Xth division, reaching Dronfield the next day. On May 5th, Hart, with the 1st Border regiment, and the brigade supply column, entrained at Bethulie for Warrenton Station, where he arrived on the evening of the 7th, and bivouacked on the south bank of the Vaal. Sir A. Hunter, with the 6th brigade (Barton) and two of Hart's battalions, was encamped on the north side of the river, and was joined by Hart himself on the 8th. The Xth division was now complete, with the exception of the 2nd battalion Somersetshire Light Infantry, left at Smithfield, which rejoined the 5th brigade at Vryburg on May 29th. On May 7th Lord Methuen ordered the 20th brigade (Paget) to concentrate at Windsorton Road, whence it rejoined the Ist division at Boshof.

The railway bridge across the Vaal river at Warrenton was badly broken, and Sir A. Hunter set his men to throwing up defensive works to cover the parties working upon a deviation bridge, and repairing the line, in which tasks the troops also joined, large numbers being daily employed until May 14th, when preparations for the invasion of the Transvaal and the attack on Christiana were completed. On May 15th, leaving the 66th battery R.F.A., one 6-in. gun R.G.A., and the 1st Connaught Rangers to garrison the bridge-head at Fourteen Streams, Sir A. Hunter marched with the Xth division fourteen and a half miles on the road to Christiana. Next day it was discovered that Christiana had been evacuated by the enemy; and the General entered the town, which was surrendered by the Landrost and Public Prosecutor. The Imperial Yeomanry, one Field battery, and the 6th brigade, all under Barton's command, bivouacked near Christiana; whilst Sir A. Hunter, with the remainder of the division, returned to Fourteen Streams, where he arrived at 3 a.m. on the 17th. Barton left Christiana on the same day, and marched across country to the railway at Border and Phokwani Sidings where he arrived two days later.

The pacification of the south-east of the Free State had gone on smoothly. So satisfactory, indeed, appeared the situation, that by May 17th a redistribution of the forces in the Free

OPERATIONS IN THE ORANGE RIVER COLONY.

State was arranged. On that date, Sir H. Colvile, who had remained at Winburg, which was now the chief base of supply for Sir L. Rundle, was ordered to send Major-General MacDonald with two battalions to Ventersburg. Major-General R. A. P. Clements with his brigade (the 12th) was directed to move by train from Bloemfontein to Winburg, whilst Lieut.-General Sir H. C. Chermside with the IIIrd division, who had been operating near Dewetsdorp,* now concentrated at Bloemfontein.

On the 18th MacDonald, with the 2nd Black Watch, 1st Argyll and Sutherland Highlanders, a section of No. 7 company R.E., and twelve men of the Eastern Province Horse, occupied Ventersburg; on the 19th the 2nd Bedfordshire regiment (12th brigade) arrived at Winburg. Sir H. Colvile now received the following instructions from the Chief of the Staff, who was with the main army at Kroonstad :

The Kroonstad area. Sir H. Colvile's orders.

" Now that 12th brigade has commenced to arrive, the remainder of the IXth division will march to Ventersburg, whence your command will move on Lindley under further orders which will be sent you. You should arrange for supplies for this march from Winburg. The 5th battery R.F.A. has been ordered to be railed to Winburg to accompany you, and you should await its arrival before marching. The Field hospital, Highland brigade details and the detachment (62 all ranks) Eastern Province Horse have been ordered to march from here to Ventersburg, starting to-morrow morning; these should arrive 21st at Ventersburg. The 13th battalion of Yeomanry from Bloemfontein has been ordered to join you at Ventersburg, and you will receive further information as to the date of its arrival there."

These orders were supplemented on the 20th by another telegram from the Chief of Staff which ran as follows :

" From Ventersburg the Highland brigade should march to Lindley and thence to Heilbron. Regarding supplies

* For gallantry in these operations Lieut. W. H. S. Nickerson, Royal Army Medical Corps, and Corporal H. Beet, 1st Derbyshire regiment, were awarded the Victoria Cross.

the Director of Supplies will communicate with you on the subject. Take as much as you can from Winburg. Brigade will be concentrated Ventersburg 23rd, reach Lindley 26th and Heilbron 29th."

Sir H. Colvile at once investigated the question of supply, and obtained sufficient for the march to Heilbron. A further telegram informed him that :

" . . . . only two companies of 13th battalion Yeomanry and possibly one mounted company Lovat's Scouts will be able to join you at Ventersburg by 23rd, but the other two companies will follow as soon as possible."

Early on May 21st part of the 5th battery R.F.A. arrived at Winburg ; but as the rest of the battery did not come in until late in the afternoon, Sir H. Colvile decided to defer starting until the next morning.

By the 23rd Sir H. Colvile's force, consisting of 100 Eastern Province Horse, two Naval 4.7-in. guns, 5th battery R.F.A., 7th company R.E., and the Highland brigade, was concentrated at Ventersburg. On the 24th he started for Lindley. It has been seen how that town had been immediately re-entered by the enemy when Ian Hamilton left it. Sir H. Colvile found his entrance resisted, but occupied the place on the 26th. Next morning he resumed his march, bivouacking that night at the Rhenoster river ; and on the 27th continued his advance on Heilbron. Around that place, as at Lindley, the Boers had gathered on Ian Hamilton's withdrawal, and Sir H. Colvile made but little progress on the 28th. The enemy, who was in strength, opposed him stubbornly at Roodepoort, where the losses were two men killed, three officers and thirty men wounded. During the night the Boers retired, leaving Sir H. Colvile to enter Heilbron on the evening of the 29th, thus completing his part of the programme laid down by the Chief of the Staff. It had not been carried out without difficulty. Four well-horsed com-

May 24th, 1900. Sir H. Colvile starts for Lindley and Heilbron.

OPERATIONS IN THE ORANGE RIVER COLONY. 115

mandos—those of Smithfield, Bethlehem, Heilbron and Vrede—had clung throughout to the column, making it feel severely its own weakness in mounted men. Frequently had the infantry to double the toil of long and painful marches by extending for action; and from beginning to end the troops experienced a mortification by no means unknown to their comrades in every part of the theatre of war—that of being helpless, whilst in no real peril, in the presence of the enemy.

During Sir H. Colvile's march the 13th battalion Imperial Yeomanry, which had been allotted to the IXth division, had been making its way up country from Bloemfontein under command of Colonel B. E. Spragge. Owing to delays in supplying the battalion with forage, it was not able to join Sir H. Colvile at Ventersburg on the 23rd, but proceeded, by order of the Chief of Staff, to Kroonstad, where it arrived on May 25th. Instructions were then received "to join General Colvile at Lindley on 26th at latest." This order was unknown to Sir H. Colvile. At Kroonstad, some hours' delay was caused by drawing the two days' forage and rations which Spragge was to carry with him. At about 4 p.m. on May 25th, the battalion, about 500 strong, and composed of the 45th, 46th, 47th and 54th companies, began its forty-seven mile march. After making seven miles it halted for the night. Before daybreak next day the advance was resumed. About mid-day, a small party of Boers drove up to the column in Cape carts, and announced their intention of surrendering. Spragge, having taken their arms, allowed them to go; they returned by a circuitous way to Lindley, whence they had come. The Yeomanry went on and at dark bivouacked eighteen miles west of Lindley.

Spragge's Yeomanry march to catch up Sir H. Colvile.

Sir H. Colvile, moving on the morning of the 27th from the Rhenoster, was in complete ignorance of the fact that Spragge was following him; that officer received in consequence no orders or message from his superior. Early on the 27th, the Yeomanry started again for Lindley. At about 2 p.m., when near the place, Spragge halted his baggage some two miles from the town, whilst he went on with part of his force, sending ahead reconnoitring parties over high ground which lay to the

May 27th, 1900. Spragge finds the Boers in Lindley.

east, and piquets on to the hills above Lindley. Soon after his men entered the town they were fired on from the houses, the reconnoitring party becoming heavily engaged at the same moment. Spragge, realising that a trap awaited him, ordered the troops in the town to withdraw towards the baggage by a drift over the Valsch.

It was now past 5 p.m. The circle of firing which had greeted Spragge's entry into Lindley had plainly declared his situation. With strength only in fact sufficient to protect his own wagons, he was in the presence of superior and equally mobile forces; and the decision to stand on the defensive, which he at once made, was as much from necessity as from choice. In any case he had good reason for deciding to remain where he was. Orders were hourly expected from Sir H. Colvile, who was known to be in the neighbourhood, as also was Sir L. Rundle. His animals, soft from a train journey, had come forty-five miles in forty-eight hours; most of his men had already marched far and fast. He had found a good position for his force, one well provided with water and grazing; and if somewhat too extensive for his numbers, fairly secure unless the Boers should bring artillery against him, an unlikely contingency, in view of Sir H. Colvile's so recent passage through the district. Though he had left Kroonstad with only two days' supplies—expecting to be re-provisioned at Lindley—fears of a shortage of rations had been somewhat allayed by the timely capture of a flock of sheep. Lastly, by resting his men and horses for the night, even if he should have to sacrifice his transport, he had under his hand a body of 500 well-mounted men, on whom he could rely to fight a way back to Kroonstad. He determined, *He decides to stand on the defensive.* then, to stand; and having thrown out piquets on all sides, employed the rest of his command in building sangars from the stones and boulders against a possible attack on the morrow.

The position, which lay between the Kroonstad—Lindley road and the north, or right, bank of the Valsch river, was situated about two miles north-west of Lindley, and consisted of two groups of hills separated by the valley of a streamlet which flowed into the Valsch. On the west bank of this watercourse

OPERATIONS IN THE ORANGE RIVER COLONY.

stood a homestead. The northerly group of hills formed a boulder-strewn plateau which gradually rose to a rocky ridge facing northward. Southward, across the valley, and some half a mile from the plateau, stood the second group of kopjes, which ran north and south, presenting that feature common in South Africa—two conical peaks. These were 200 yards apart, and were the key of the position, although they themselves could be enfiladed from another plateau to the south-west across the Valsch, and from a kopje some 2,000 yards to the north-east.

In the night, during which the Yeomanry were unmolested, Spragge sent a messenger to Sir H. Colvile, and returned to Sir L. Rundle a native whom that General had sent into Lindley to discover if the town was in occupation of the British. His message to Sir H. Colvile ran thus:

> "Found no one in Lindley, but Boers; have 500 men but only one day's food. Have stopped three miles back on Kroonstad road. I want help to get out without great loss.
> "May 27th, 1900."

He informs Sir H. Colvile and Sir L. Rundle.

The native carried the following letter for Sir L. Rundle:

> "Was sent to Lindley with 500 mounted infantry to catch General Colvile. Found him gone and Boers there. Village a nasty place to retire from; have only one day's food and shall find it difficult to get out without help. Am three miles on Kroonstad road.
> "27. 5. '00."

Both these communications were safely delivered, the one to Sir H. Colvile at 7 a.m. on the 28th, the other to Sir L. Rundle at 10 a.m. on the same day.

The presence of the enemy in such strength at Lindley was thus to be accounted for. Lindley, prior to its occupation by Sir H. Colvile, had been for some time the Headquarters of General Marthinus Prinsloo, who exercised general control over the Free Staters in this part of the country, as did C. De Wet

The enemy about Lindley.

in the neighbourhood of Frankfort. On May 26th there were, in or around Lindley, the Smithfield commando under Commandant Potgieter, and a part of the Bethlehem commando under Commandant Michael Prinsloo, in all some 800 men. On Sir H. Colvile's approach Potgieter attempted to check his march without success, his commando dispersing in face of the British advance. The two Prinsloos then left the town, the Commandant joining P. De Wet, who was at that time in laager fifteen miles to the northward, with 1,200 men. Next day P. De Wet sent Commandant Prinsloo with orders to harass Sir H. Colvile's rear, whilst he himself lay in wait to attack his flanks. This Prinsloo it was who, instead of falling on Sir H. Colvile, had encountered the Yeomanry on their entry into Lindley; and his burghers now lay around Spragge.

At daybreak on the 28th firing became general, and was kept up throughout that day and the next, the Boers being reinforced on the 29th by P. De Wet, who left General Prinsloo watching Sir H. Colvile. Little damage was done to the defenders; and Spragge, who had by no means lost confidence in his ability to hold his own, sent the following message on the 30th to Sir L. Rundle, who, however, never received it.

May 29th and 30th, 1900. The enemy reinforced.

" Lindley, 30th May.

" To General Rundle,

" Near Bethlehem.

" I arrived here 27th to join General Colvile. Found no troops, or message, or supplies. Have 500 men and horses, but difficult to get away without losing transport. I have position one and a half miles from town to N.W.; control water and grazing and can take town any day, but it is in a very bad position to hold. I have lots of ammunition, no bread or flour, no corn; can hold on unless they bring guns which they have sent for; tried to get a message to you on 27th, also to General Colvile and Kroonstad; have plenty of fresh meat. I can get out but shall lose in doing so. Heard what we believe to be your force firing near us to S.E. yesterday. If this gets through please assist or tell me which way to operate. The Boers are all round me and have attacked pretty heavily several times. I say nothing about casualties purposely, but am certainly entitled to help. I prefer for obvious reasons not to go into details. Hope you will be able to arrange. Messenger all right.

"B. SPRAGGE, Lt.-Col.

"P.S.—I was sent from Kroonstad with two days' rations, and part of us have marched ninety miles in three days and four nights. Was told should get supplies here. I can attack town any time if I know you are operating the other side. General Prinsloo is in town. Piet De Wet is near here with large commando reported on Heilbron road within few miles."

On May 30th, General Prinsloo arrived with 800 men, three guns, and a Vickers-Maxim. He had left part of his force to hamper Sir H. Colvile at Heilbron, but had been reinforced on his march to Lindley by many farmers who, though they had taken the oath of neutrality, threw to the winds all pledges on the news of a British force in difficulties. Before Prinsloo arrived the Boers had already made demonstrations to the west of the main position, and Spragge ordered Lieut. H. F. Montgomery with sixteen men to seize a kopje held by a small party of the enemy on that side. This was done; but the party was at once exposed to fire from every quarter. They clung on for two hours; but then the Boers, scaling the hill unseen, surrounded the survivors—Montgomery and six men—and took them prisoners. At daybreak on the following day (31st) Captain the Earl of Longford was ordered to recapture the kopje with forty men. The duty was carried out gallantly at the bayonet's point; but Prinsloo had now brought guns into position which suddenly opened from some 3,000 yards to the south-east, and Spragge was compelled to recall Lord Longford's men to aid in the defence of the main entrenchment.

Fighting at Lindley, May 30th, 1900.

Soon afterwards two more guns opened from the north-east at a range of 2,000 yards. These were at once engaged by the two automatic Colt guns accompanying Spragge's party, which forced the Boer pieces to change their position ; but they were soon in action again. The situation was now serious. Exposed to shell fire from two sides, the Yeomanry had no means of reply. The two important kopjes of the group south of the farm, which guarded the water supply and commanded the northerly portion of the defences, were held by one squadron, with two troops of another squadron in reserve. One squadron was divided between the two peaks, an officer being in charge of each kopje, with a connecting post between the two. Below the kopjes were posted the two troops in reserve to this squadron. The Boers, realising the value of these heights, first raked them with artillery, next captured the nearer by a rush. The piquet thereon attempted to fall back on the twin hill, and might have done so had not one of their number, on his own initiative, raised the white flag, and thus forced all to give in. The officer on the other kopje, though now reinforced by the two reserve troops, considered that his own command, too, was in justice included in the surrender, and he laid down his arms, yet another victim to the doubts which modern conditions of battle have introduced into the question of capitulation. The loss of these keys, which were only about a quarter of a mile from the stations of the bulk of the force, made the whole post untenable ; and although fighting was kept up for some time, at about 2 p.m. a general surrender took place, after Spragge had lost seven officers and seventy-three men.

The key of Spragge's position lost. He surrenders.

When Sir H. Colvile received Spragge's message sent on the night of May 27th, he was some eighteen miles from Lindley. The bearers, a corporal and trooper of the 13th battalion Imperial Yeomanry, were closely questioned by himself and his Chief Staff officer, who elicited from the messengers the reassuring statement that there was no firing going on when they had left Lindley, and that, as far as they knew, the road to Kroonstad was open. Sir H. Colvile decided that his proper course was to adhere to his destination, Heilbron, which he was to reach on the 29th. He was still twenty-two miles from that place, and had a numerous enemy to deal with himself, for the Boers had

Sir H. Colvile pursues his march.

strongly attacked his rearguard throughout the preceding day. In his mind was the recollection how the Commander-in-Chief himself had sacrificed factors of value in order not to be distracted from his main object; and he considered that it was now not for him to dislocate possibly higher movements of the game, in which his own division was but a pawn, by turning back to the assistance of a small body of men, whose situation he did not know to be desperate. He proceeded on his way to Heilbron. At the same time he sent the corporal and trooper as well as a native scout to make their way, each by a different route, back to Spragge with the following message:

"Your message received 7 a.m. I am eighteen miles from Lindley and twenty-two from Heilbron, which latter place I hope to reach to-morrow. The enemy are between me and you and I cannot send back supplies. If you cannot join me by road to Heilbron you must retire on Kroonstad, living on country, and if necessary abandon your wagons."

At dusk the messengers returned, having failed to get through to Spragge; and Sir H. Colvile, who by this time had gone a further stage northward, and was now midway between Lindley and Heilbron, marched on, as has been said, into the latter town.

Lieut.-General Sir L. Rundle, who since the 17th had been holding the line Winburg—Trommel—Hammonia, with his own and the Colonial division, had suggested on the 21st to the Chief of the Staff that he should move on Senekal. This proposition was accepted on the 23rd; and two days afterwards the town was occupied, not without loss, as the 34th company Imperial Yeomanry, pressing on into the village in advance of the main body, was surrounded and lost Major H. S. Dalbiac and three men killed, one officer and three men wounded and twelve men taken prisoners. The Colonial division at the same time occupied Ficksburg. Sir L. Rundle remained at Senekal until the 28th, when the native runner whom he had sent to Lindley returned with Spragge's already quoted first message. On receipt of this

Sir L. Rundle's diversion.

Sir L. Rundle decided that, as Spragge had only one day's supply, and Lindley could not be reached in time to help him, the best form of assistance would be to draw off the Boers by demonstrating towards Bethlehem. Leaving Major-General J. E. Boyes in Senekal with one company of Yeomanry, a battery R.F.A. and two battalions, Sir L. Rundle took the Bethlehem road with the following force: 4th battalion and one company 11th battalion Imperial Yeomanry, the 2nd and 79th batteries R.F.A., Driscoll's Scouts, 2nd Grenadier Guards, 2nd Scots Guards, 2nd East Yorkshire regiment, and, to complete the brigade, the 2nd Royal West Kent regiment from Boyes' (17th) brigade. The Yeomanry reconnoitred to the north-west of Biddulphs Berg, and came under rifle and artillery fire. Sir L. Rundle then bivouacked.

May 29th, 1900. The action at Biddulphs Berg.

The Boers on the Biddulphs Berg—Tafel Berg position at this time were some 1,500 strong, commanded by General A. J. de Villiers and Commandant J. Crowther with two guns and a Vickers-Maxim. De Villiers had left his subordinate—Commandant P. H. de Villiers—to watch the movements of General Brabant's Colonial division.

At 6 a.m. on May 29th Sir L. Rundle's troops left bivouac and took up the following positions: One company of Imperial Yeomanry moved towards Tafel Berg; another headed direct for Biddulphs Berg; both units were supported by a detachment of two companies of the 2nd East Yorkshire regiment and two guns which were posted on a hill south-west of Biddulphs Berg. Four companies of the East Yorkshire were placed in charge of the baggage, which was parked about two miles west of Biddulphs Berg. The remaining three companies of Yeomanry were sent to the north-east, to guard the left flank, whilst the rest of the force moved round the northern flank of the Biddulphs Berg preparatory to attacking it from that side. These movements drew fire from two guns, one in a stone kraal near a farm on the north-east of the Biddulphs Berg, the other on a hill somewhat to the east. At 10.30 a.m. the 2nd and 79th Field batteries opened against the farm and the northern face of the Biddulphs Berg. The Boers made no reply and were invisible, though they had been seen moving about in numbers on the mountain shortly before. At 11.30 a.m. the infantry were directed against the farm to clear up the situation. They advanced well extended, the 2nd Grenadier Guards in first line, the 2nd Scots Guards in support, and the 2nd Royal West Kent regiment in reserve. When within some 1,200 yards of the farm the advance was checked by a galling rifle fire, whilst the two Boer guns which had been temporarily silent again came into action, joined by a Vickers-Maxim. Then, as though in league with the adversaries in front, a fierce veld-fire flamed up behind the troops, overtook the fighting line, and not only inflicted severe burns upon many of the soldiers, but destroyed the long grass which formed their only cover.

While the action was in progress, Sir L. Rundle received a telegram from the Chief of Staff, informing him that Clements, and the 12th brigade, was ordered to Senekal, and that the VIIIth division was to move on Ficksburg. This brought to an end Sir L. Rundle's plan of threatening Bethlehem, and at 3.30 p.m. he ordered his troops to withdraw. As the men rose from the ground the Boers redoubled their fire, and the greater number of the casualties occurred at this period. The retirement of the 2nd Grenadier Guards was covered by the other two battalions, and by 6 p.m. the force was back in its camp of the night before. The object of the movement seemed to have been practically attained, for in the afternoon large parties of Boers were seen coming from the direction of Lindley and Bethlehem. The diversion, however, had cost 185 casualties.* The losses of the Boers were slight, but they suffered one important casualty, namely, General de Villiers, who was mortally wounded. There being no doctor with the Boer force, his successor in command arranged with Sir L. Rundle for his removal to Senekal, where he died.

During two or three days before the action at Biddulphs Berg, Brabant, with the Colonial division, had been working to pacify the country between Hammonia and Ficksburg. His patrols were frequently engaged with those of Commandant de Villiers, and in these skirmishes Brabant lost three men killed, six wounded

* See Appendix 2.

and two officers and thirty-eight men captured. His casualties were more than balanced by the surrender of some 170 burghers between May 21st and 31st.

<small>May 28th, 1900.
Lord Methuen called in to Kroonstad.</small>

About this time Lord Methuen, who had reached Bothaville on May 24th, on his way to Reitzburg and Parys, received orders to divert his march on Kroonstad, as there was a rumour that the enemy was gathering for an attack on that important depôt town. Lord Methuen's troops arrived in two columns at Kroonstad on May 28th and 29th, having collected some seventy rifles and destroyed 12,000 rounds of ammunition *en route*. Lord Methuen then received instructions to send Major-General C. W. H. Douglas' brigade with three Yeomanry battalions to Lindley, where, all unknown to Army Headquarters, Spragge was just falling into his predicament. Owing to a scarcity of supplies in Kroonstad, Douglas' brigade was unable to move at once. Late in the evening of the 29th, Sir H. Colvile's message giving his position on the 28th was received. That communication had been intended by the sender only as an explanation to the Chief of the Staff of a possible non-fulfilment of the orders to be at Heilbron by May 29th. It appeared to the Headquarters Staff to be a direct appeal for help, and Lord Methuen was ordered to go with all speed to Sir H. Colvile's assistance, and to take Spragge's Yeomanry with him.

<small>May 30th, 1900.
He starts to extricate Spragge.</small>

Early on the morning of the 30th, Lord Methuen started with the 3rd, 5th, and 10th battalions Imperial Yeomanry, the 4th and 20th batteries R.F.A. and two guns 37th battery, two Vickers-Maxims, and the 9th brigade. Six days' supplies were carried on lightly loaded ox-wagons, which were escorted by a squadron of Yeomanry and an infantry battalion. Ten miles out on the Heilbron road a halt was called, during which Lord Methuen heard of Sir H. Colvile's arrival at Heilbron. At 4 p.m., however, a messenger arrived from Kroonstad with the following telegram from Lord Roberts: " Spragge reported to be in a nasty place . . . . and would find it difficult to get out without help. Methuen should relieve Highland brigade in first instance and then see what can be done for Spragge's Yeomanry." Knowing now that Sir H. Colvile was safe in Heilbron, Lord Methuen

OPERATIONS IN THE ORANGE RIVER COLONY. 125

hurried off at 4.30 p.m. to succour Spragge at Lindley, with the three battalions of Yeomanry, the 4th battery R.F.A., and the two Vickers-Maxims. Douglas followed with the remainder of the force. On the morning of May 31st a message reached Lord Methuen from Spragge saying that he could hold out until June 2nd. Next day, Lord Methuen came in touch with Boers posted in force within eight miles of Lindley. At the same time he learnt that Spragge had surrendered the previous day. Having reconnoitred the hostile position, which was a long low ridge, the nearest of several such ridges covering Lindley from the west, Lord Methuen sent the 5th battalion Imperial Yeomanry, supported by the guns, against the Boers' right and centre, the 10th battalion against their left, whilst the 3rd battalion was ordered to move wide around their right and come in behind them. The ridge was quickly cleared, and occupied by the battery and 3rd and 5th battalions; the 10th battalion guarding the flanks. The 3rd battalion was then pushed forward, and came under artillery and rifle fire. This they silenced, and pressing on, sighted the Boer convoy, which was making off at a great pace. Lieut.-Colonel G. J. Younghusband, in command of the 3rd Imperial Yeomanry, determined to intercept it. Three troops of the Yeomanry managed to scramble down a steep cliff, and galloped into the convoy, cutting off two guns and sixteen wagons only a short distance in rear of the prisoners taken from Spragge. Reinforcements were called for; but the remainder of the troops were fully occupied in clearing the ridges which lay between them and Lindley, and none were sent. Younghusband then took up a position on a knoll, and was soon briskly engaged with the escort to the Boer convoy. At 2 p.m. he was ordered to retire on Lindley, which his small party accomplished with considerable difficulty. His losses during the day were three officers wounded and twenty-three men killed, wounded, or missing. The guns and wagons which he had intercepted escaped out of his hands to the south-east, and eventually joined their convoy. Lord Methuen's horses were now so exhausted that he decided to stop the pursuit at 4 p.m. His troops went into bivouac at Lindley.

June 1st, 1900. Fighting at Lindley.

At this period the principal opponents of the British were A. J. de Villiers, P. De Wet and M. Prinsloo. C. De Wet, with some 800 men, had remained at Frankfort awaiting ammunition which had been promised to him by the Transvaal Government, keeping touch with Pretoria by way of Greylingstad and Heidelberg. It had been agreed, at a meeting held at Vereeniging on May 25th, that on the retirement of the Transvaalers into their own country before Lord Roberts' army, the Free Staters should harry the British communications with Bloemfontein. C. De Wet left Frankfort on May 28th, the day on which his native country was formally proclaimed to be British territory. On the morning of the 30th he reached Lindley. After a consultation with Mr. Steyn, whose camp was about twelve miles north-east of Lindley, De Wet decided to go on and trouble Sir H. Colvile in Heilbron, leaving the greater portion of his men, including some 500 who were without horses, at the President's laager. Striking north-west with the rest of his force—800 in number—De Wet passed the night of June 2nd at Rietfontein, a farm nine miles south of Heilbron. Sir H. Colvile, who had arrived at Heilbron late on the night of May 29th, got into telegraphic communication next day with Kroonstad. His first requirement was a stock of supplies, the town having been cleared by Ian Hamilton and the Boers in turn. He accordingly telegraphed to the Chief of the Staff, asking that a convoy might be sent to him. His telegram concluded with the words: "Yeomanry have not yet joined. Believe they returned to Kroonstad from Lindley." He was answered that the convoy was ready, and that he should make arrangements with railhead for its despatch, adding at the same time, that Lovat's Scouts, some fifty in all, were the only mounted troops available for escort. On receipt of this Sir H. Colvile suggested that the convoy should be escorted by some of Lord Methuen's mounted troops with long-range guns. This telegram was first read by the commandant at railhead, Major R. C. D. Haking, who replied that he only had sixty infantrymen available, but thought that this would be sufficient if Sir H. Colvile would meet the convoy midway between Roodewal and Heilbron. Next day, about 100

OPERATIONS IN THE ORANGE RIVER COLONY. 127

more details having arrived at railhead, Haking decided to despatch the convoy next morning, although no reply had come from Heilbron, owing, as was found later, to the telegraph wire having been cut. On June 2nd the convoy, consisting of sixty wagons, with an escort of 160 men, moved off. Sir H. Colvile had, indeed, sent a telegram to Roodewal ordering the convoy not to start, and that the question of escort should be referred to the Chief of the Staff ; but, owing to the break in the telegraph wire, the message did not reach railhead until June 3rd. In like manner the commandant's announcement of the departure of the convoy was not received by Sir H. Colvile until some days later.

<small>The convoy for Heilbron.</small>

All went well with the convoy until it arrived fourteen miles west of Heilbron on the evening of the 3rd. Then the scouts reported the presence of a strong Boer force three miles ahead. The wagons were immediately laagered, and measures taken for their defence. The escort, without mounted men or artillery, was altogether inadequate for the only defensive position which could be found, but everything possible was done, including attempts to communicate with Heilbron and Vredefort Road. One of the wagon conductors succeeded in reaching the latter place, and reported the situation of the convoy to Major A. E. Haig, who was there in command of some 1,000 details. Haig started off at once with 600 men, at the same time passing on the news to Haking, who had now advanced with railhead to the Kromellenboog Spruit.* On arriving within four miles of the convoy, and hearing no firing, Haig returned to Vredefort Road ; for his men, who were mostly just off ship-board, or fresh from hospital, were out of condition and without rations. On receipt of Haig's message at 7 a.m. on the 4th, Haking sent out 120 mounted infantry, who had just arrived at Kromellenboog Spruit. These failed to join Haig, and did not come across the convoy until too late. At daybreak on the 4th, the conductor who had gone to Haig returned to the convoy with the news that that officer had retired to Vredefort Road. He again went out

---

* This spruit runs into the Vaal just west of Lindequee. It is incorrectly shown as part of the Rhenoster river on map No. 38.

Convoy captured by De Wet.

to seek assistance; but almost immediately a summons arrived from De Wet demanding instant surrender as he had surrounded the convoy with 1,200 men and five guns. No shots were fired and the escort laid down its arms.

Whilst at Rietfontein Farm on June 3rd, De Wet had received from Commandant-General L. Botha an outline of the Transvaal leader's plan of campaign.... "What I desire from your Honour," wrote Botha, "now that the great force of the enemy is here, is to get in behind him and break or interrupt his communications. We have already delayed too long in destroying the railway behind him." Before De Wet could act, his chief scout—a certain G. J. Scheepers—brought in news of the approach of the convoy for Heilbron. Calling up General P. Botha with the mounted men he had left behind in Mr. Steyn's laager, the convoy was quickly in De Wet's hands in the manner described. Having got rid of his prisoners, De Wet was ready to fall upon the railway, in accordance with Botha's suggestion. For this purpose he split his force into three divisions, ordering Commandant Steenkamp with 300 men and a gun to attack Vredefort Road station; General Froneman with 300 men, two guns and a Vickers-Maxim, to seize and destroy the bridge over the Rhenoster river; whilst he himself led about 100 men with one gun against Roodewal station.

Garrisons on the lines of communication.

On May 17th Lord Roberts had made the following arrangements for the safety of the railway. Kroonstad was to be held by the 1st Suffolk regiment and 4th Argyll and Sutherland Highlanders; the reconstructed bridge over the Zand river was watched by the 9th King's Royal Rifles; the 3rd Royal Lancaster regiment was responsible for the safety of the bridge over the Vet river; whilst the railway from Brandfort down to Glen Siding was entrusted to the 3rd East Lancashire regiment. Some changes in these dispositions took place in the next three weeks, the 1st Suffolk regiment leaving for Pretoria, whilst a battalion of militia—the 4th Derbyshire regiment from Bloemfontein—replaced at Zand river the 9th King's Royal Rifles who went on to Taaibosch Spruit. The seizure of the Heilbron convoy on June 4th, and the reported presence of

OPERATIONS IN THE ORANGE RIVER COLONY. 129

such strong hostile bodies in the neighbourhood made the safety of Roodewal station of paramount importance. At that place was collected a large quantity of supplies and ammunition, stored pending the reconstruction of the bridge over the Rhenoster. On June 5th the 4th Derbyshire regiment was moved to Roodewal, the 3rd Royal Lancaster regiment relieving it at Zand River. Vredefort Road station was held by some thirty men, left behind by Major Haig, who had been ordered northward with his 1,000 men, on his return from the attempted rescue of the Heilbron convoy.

The 4th Derbyshire left Zand River by rail on the afternoon of June 5th for Rhenoster River, but was detrained at Roodewal in consequence of a report of an impending attack on that station. During the night the train was stopped by a small party of thirty of the Imperial Yeomanry scouts, under Captain W. Knight (4th Bengal Lancers), who eventually proceeded by road to Roodewal. This place had been hitherto held by two officers and twenty men, details of the Ordnance, Army Service and Post Office Corps, who had improvised rough defences from the heaps of mail bags and bales of clothing which had accumulated. On the arrival of the Derbyshire, two companies were placed on outpost duty, and the rest of the battalion employed in emptying the train, which was then sent back for safety to Kroonstad. The expected attack was not delivered, and the night passed without incident.

Next morning (June 6th) Knight's party passed through Roodewal, and halted at the deviation bridge over the Rhenoster river, four miles to the north, where some kopjes were occupied which commanded the railway about 800 yards north of the stream. All being quiet in the neighbourhood of Roodewal, Major G. E. Wilkinson, the officer in command of the 4th Derbyshire, decided to go on to Rhenoster River, his proper destination. As he had no transport to carry his stores, tents, and other equipment, he telegraphed to Kroonstad for a train. This was sent at once; but owing to long delays at Roodewal, it was not until dusk that the battalion, less one company left to hold Roodewal, arrived at Rhenoster River. In the

June 6th, 1900. The 4th Derbyshire arrive at Rhenoster River.

meantime Knight had thoroughly reconnoitred the ground in the neighbourhood of the bridge, and had discovered small parties of Boers hovering about.

The ground about Rhenoster River bridge was well suited for defence. The kopjes north of the bridge were some two miles long, and so thrown back on either flank that the general outline resembled that of a bridge-head redoubt. The railway ran through a gap in the eastern section of the ridge. Wilkinson, on his arrival, sent one company to piquet the kopjes which had been held by Knight's men, and another to hold the bridge. The remaining five companies were employed unloading the train. During the night desultory shooting was heard; the troops stood to arms; one more company was sent to the bridge, and another to reinforce the piquets on the kopjes. The firing stopped; but at daybreak (June 7th) it was found that the enemy had cut off the piquets on the kopjes, and driven away the two companies holding the bridge. The Boers had, in fact, gained complete command of the camp, and Froneman brought his artillery up and opened fire upon the main body of the battalion. The Derbyshire, raw militia though they were, fought well with their rifles for some hours from the railway embankment; guns they had none, and only the most meagre defences; they fell fast, and at about 10 a.m. were forced to surrender or be totally destroyed. Thus Rhenoster River was accounted for. The shrift of Roodewal was shorter still. The garrison there had been strengthened by a company of the Railway Pioneer regiment, sent up the line on the night of June 5th—6th. At 5.45 a.m. a message was received from C. De Wet demanding the surrender of the post. The summons was refused, and the Boers opened on the defences with a 9-pr. Krupp. This gun was speedily forced out of action, but the surrender at Rhenoster River released three more guns, and their combined fire was too much for the few British rifles. At noon this post also was compelled to capitulate. In much the same manner Commandant Steenkamp overpowered the garrison of Vredefort Road, where thirty men became prisoners.

De Wet's success in this triple raid was none the less brilliant

[Margin note: June 7th, 1900. Rhenoster River, Roodewal and Vredefort Road captured by De Wet.]

OPERATIONS IN THE ORANGE RIVER COLONY.

because of its very facility. He had run little risk at the hands of scattered, inexperienced, and unentrenched troops; and flight could have saved him at any moment from the only real danger, the appearance of a rescuing column from elsewhere. His booty was considerable. He had killed two officers and thirty-six men, wounded five officers and 104 men; into his hands had fallen 486 officers and men. In addition, he had burnt the Rhenoster River bridge, destroyed some ten miles of railway, and, more profitable stroke than all, had captured the supplies and clothing destined for the army in Pretoria.

<small>Losses inflicted by De Wet.</small>

News of these events was quickly in the hands of the Commander-in-Chief. On hearing of the capture of Vredefort Road he ordered the Commandant at Vereeniging to look well to the safety of that place, and with all available troops to hasten southward and restore telegraphic communication with Bloemfontein. He also sent Lord Kitchener with a battery of Field artillery and two battalions of infantry to strengthen the line of communication south of the Vaal. To guard the railway north of that river he stationed Smith-Dorrien's 19th brigade on the line. Lastly, he instructed Lord Methuen, whose column was the nearest mobile force in the Orange Free State, to pursue and take vengeance on De Wet.

Whilst Lord Roberts was thus kept occupied at Pretoria, Kelly-Kenny at Bloemfontein was equally engrossed. On June 6th, hearing that Lord Roberts' communications were in danger, Kelly-Kenny had sent the 2nd East Kent regiment (the Buffs), the 1st Oxfordshire Light Infantry, the 17th battery R.F.A., Prince Alfred's Volunteer Guard M.I., and a company of Imperial Yeomanry to reinforce the 4th Argyll and Sutherland Highlanders holding Kroonstad. Directly Kelly-Kenny heard of the capture of the 4th Derbyshire regiment, he sent Major-General C. E. Knox to take command at Kroonstad, where were stored a vast quantity of supplies, and threw all available troops into Winburg. He also directed Sir L. Rundle to leave his own plans in abeyance in order to cover the eastern approaches to Bloemfontein from Hammonia and Ficksburg, and with the 12th brigade from Senekal. Kelly-Kenny's promptness

<small>Kelly-Kenny strengthens Bloemfontein and Kroonstad.</small>

thus safeguarded Kroonstad at a time when that great depôt was in momentary danger from De Wet, and when its loss would have been a veritable catastrophe.

Bloemfontein was occupied by a strong force of artillery—the City Imperial Volunteer battery, four guns of the 68th battery, two Howitzer batteries, one 6-in. gun and four Vickers-Maxims; but of infantry there was only one battalion—the 2nd Gloucestershire, and of cavalry none at all. This weakness was partially made good by the enrolment of all details and convalescents into a provisional battalion of infantry under Colonel C. J. Long; a cavalry force, similarly improvised, was commanded by Major J. Fowle. Lord Methuen, who had reached Lindley with his Yeomanry on June 1st, was joined there on the 2nd by his 9th brigade (Douglas), and on the 3rd by his 20th brigade (Paget). On June 5th, in consequence of a telegram from Lord Roberts saying that Sir H. Colvile was without supplies at Heilbron, Lord Methuen started thither, taking with him the Yeomanry and 9th brigade, and leaving Paget to garrison Lindley. During the march a number of Boers hung on the column, but there was no serious fighting, and Heilbron was reached on June 7th. On the 9th, C. E. Knox made a reconnaissance from Kroonstad up the railway to America Siding, to find that the enemy had drawn off to the north. That day Lord Methuen left Heilbron with the 9th brigade and Yeomanry. He also took with him from Sir H. Colvile's force fifty of Lovat's Scouts, the 2nd Royal Highlanders (Black Watch), and a section of the 5th battery R.F.A., intending these to escort a convoy back to Heilbron. Lord Methuen had received intelligence from Army Headquarters of the attacks on the railway, together with orders to drive away the marauders. He had got into heliographic communication with Lieut.-Colonel J. Spens, who was in command of the two battalions and the battery which had been brought down the line by Lord Kitchener. On June 10th he reached the railway at Vredefort Road, where he met Lord Kitchener.

June 9th, 1900. Lord Methuen pursues De Wet.

Since his successful foray on the railway De Wet had remained with his prisoners in the neighbourhood of Roodewal, hard by his own farm. On the 9th he had news of Lord Methuen's

OPERATIONS IN THE ORANGE RIVER COLONY. 133

movements; and so exact was his information that he pointed out a safe site for the Imperial Yeomanry hospital during his intended action. This hospital, by good fortune, had appeared in the neighbourhood of Roodewal, and was allowed by the Boer commander to succour the wounded of the 4th Derbyshire. On the morning of June 11th a movement southward from Vredefort Road was begun. Spens, with two battalions, two companies of Yeomanry, and some mounted infantry, marched on the western side of the line; Lord Methuen followed on the eastern. De Wet was found to be holding the kopjes overlooking the Rhenoster river which had been piqueted by the 4th Derbyshire on the night of the 6th. After a pretence at resistance the Boers fell back westwards, their rearguard keeping Spens' mounted men off the British prisoners. Leaving Spens to hold the Rhenoster River bridge, Lord Methuen went on southwards, as he heard that Kroonstad was occupied by the enemy. Next day the report was contradicted, telegraphic communication was established with the town, and Lord Methuen moved south to Honing Spruit. In the meantime De Wet, after being driven from the kopjes of the Rhenoster river, kept to the west of the railway, and, striking to the north-east, decided to profit by his retirement on Frankfort to capture the post at Leeuw Spruit. Here were lying two construction trains full of men and gear employed in the repair of the railway bridge. They were attacked on the night of the 14th; some fifty men and 300 natives of the working parties were taken prisoners; but the rest held out until the arrival of troops from Kopjes station forced the Boers to withdraw.

De Wet declines fighting,

and retires towards Frankfort

Whilst the attention of all in the Orange Free State had been riveted on the doings of De Wet, another Boer raider had appeared upon the scene. When General de Villiers was wounded at Biddulphs Berg the command of the burghers around Senekal fell upon General P. Roux, a "predikant" or minister of that town. Roux selected Virginia (Zand river) Siding for the scene of his operations against the railway. This part of the line was held by four companies of the 3rd Royal Lancaster regiment, twenty mounted infantry of the Royal Irish

covered by another raider.

Rifles, and four companies of the Railway Pioneer regiment, the whole under the command of Lieut.-Colonel J. E. Capper, R.E. News of Roux's approach with 800 men, one gun and two Vickers-Maxims, was received on the night of June 13th, and was at once reported to Kroonstad. At midnight the 1st Oxfordshire Light Infantry was sent by train to Ventersburg Road, and was joined there by the 17th battery R.F.A. and some 200 Imperial Yeomanry. The whole of these troops then proceeded to Riet Spruit. In the meantime, at daybreak on the 14th, Virginia Siding was attacked by Roux. Fighting went on until about noon, when, on the approach of more Yeomanry from the south, the Boers retired, leaving six dead and eleven prisoners on the field. The British losses were two officers and five men killed, one officer and six men wounded.

June, 1900. Distribution of the troops in the Orange River Colony.

After the action of Biddulphs Berg Lieut.-General Sir L. Rundle moved into Senekal, where he was joined by Major-General Clements with the 12th brigade. On May 31st Sir L. Rundle handed over the town to Clements, and, in accordance with orders, took the VIIIth division to Ficksburg. Hammonia was reached on June 2nd without opposition, and the VIIIth division, Colonial division and 12th brigade were employed for the next fortnight in guarding the line Senekal—Ficksburg.

On June 15th the rest of the troops in the Orange River Colony were disposed as follows : Heilbron was occupied by Lieut.-General Sir H. Colvile with the Highland (3rd) brigade ; Lindley by the 20th brigade under Major-General Paget ; Lord Methuen with the 9th brigade was at Kopjes station ; there were small garrisons in Smithfield, Wepener, Dewetsdorp, Winburg and Boshof. Lieut.-General Kelly-Kenny had been placed in command of the lines of communication from Bloemfontein to the Zand river, with Major-General C. E. Knox at Kroonstad, and Major-General R. Allen (22nd brigade) near Winburg ; whilst Lieut.-General Sir H. Chermside superintended the line from the Orange river to Bloemfontein, with Major-General W. G. Knox and the 23rd brigade at Edenburg. Major-General Smith-Dorrien was responsible for the railway north of Kroonstad.

Lord Roberts now planned to bring the Orange River Colony

OPERATIONS IN THE ORANGE RIVER COLONY. 135

into a state of subjection. In a telegram, sent from Pretoria on June 17th to Lord Methuen, Sir L. Rundle, Lord Kitchener, Clements, Sir H. Colvile,* MacDonald, Sir A. Hunter and C. E. Knox, he made known the measures which he now proposed to take " in order to ensure the security of the railway, and to establish order in the north-eastern districts of the Orange River Colony." Lord Roberts' intentions were to provide adequate garrisons for the principal towns and vulnerable points on the railway, and to organise four flying columns to be constantly on the move through the various districts in which the burghers were still in arms. These columns were to be commanded by the following generals: Ian Hamilton, Lord Methuen, Clements and MacDonald, and were to be based on Heidelberg, Rhenoster River, Senekal and Heilbron respectively. All movements were to be completed by June 23rd. The composition of each column and garrison was then given in detail :— {Lord Roberts' plans to subjugate the Orange River Colony.}

Clements' column (Senekal): 700 mounted men from the Colonial division and Imperial Yeomanry, Royal Scots M.I., 8th battery R.F.A., 2nd Bedfordshire, 2nd Worcestershire and 2nd Wiltshire regiments.

Lord Methuen's column (Rhenoster River): Two battalions of Yeomanry, two batteries R.F.A., two Vickers-Maxims, two 5-in. Howitzers, 1st Northumberland Fusiliers, 1st Loyal North Lancashire and 2nd Northamptonshire regiments.

MacDonald's column (Heilbron): Eastern Province Horse and six companies of Yeomanry, one battery R.F.A., and the Highland brigade.

Ian Hamilton's column (Heidelberg): 2nd cavalry brigade, (Broadwood), 3rd cavalry brigade (Gordon), 2nd brigade M.I. (Ridley), three batteries R.F.A., and the 21st brigade (Bruce Hamilton).

Garrison of Lindley: four guns R.F.A., one company of Yeomanry, half battalion of 4th Scottish Rifles and the strongest available battalion of Paget's (20th) brigade.

* Lieut.-General Sir H. Colvile remained at Heilbron until June 27th, when the IXth division having been broken up, he and his staff left for Pretoria. He left Pretoria for England on June 29th.

Garrison of Heidelberg (Transvaal): One company of Yeomanry, two battalions of Major-General Hart's (5th) brigade, one battery R.F.A., all from the Xth division.

Garrison of Frankfort: One company of Yeomanry, the other two battalions of Hart's brigade and one battery R.F.A.

Garrison of Senekal: 700 mounted men and a suitable force to be supplied by Sir L. Rundle.

Garrison of Winburg: To be increased to one battalion by the despatch of half a battalion from Senekal and then to come under Sir L. Rundle's orders.

The telegram ended with instructions as to the movement of the troops to their allotted stations.

On June 20th—21st these instructions were somewhat modified. Paget's brigade was ordered to remain intact at Lindley and act in conjunction with Clements, who was to return to Winburg and clear up the country round that town, and eventually to move on Bethlehem, his place at Senekal being taken by 700 mounted men from Sir L. Rundle's force round Ficksburg. MacDonald, leaving a strong garrison in Heilbron, was directed to join Ian Hamilton moving southwards on Frankfort.

De Wet, after his attack on Leeuw Spruit, had remained in the neighbourhood of his own farm, covering the withdrawal of his prisoners. These he sent back to Reitz, whither the 13th battalion Imperial Yeomanry, captured at Lindley, had also been transferred. The Yeomanry were, however, soon moved on, and were eventually incarcerated at Nooitgedacht in the Transvaal. The occupation of Standerton by General Sir R. Buller, on June 23rd, however, rendered too dangerous the escort of prisoners by this route across the open veld; and the prisoners of the 4th Derbyshire regiment were liberated, after some hard marching, by being put over the Natal frontier on July 8th.

June 19th, 1900. De Wet divides his force.

On June 19th, Methuen, moving towards Heilbron, was apprised of the presence of De Wet on his front. He at once engaged the Boer leader, who, coming between the two fires of Lord Methuen's and Sir H. Colvile's heavy ordnance, had to make off. Dividing his force into two, he himself circled to the

OPERATIONS IN THE ORANGE RIVER COLONY.

north of Heilbron, whilst the other party, under Commandant Nel, struck southward for a short distance.

On June 22nd Nel's commando, some 700 strong with three guns, attacked a post at Katbosch (near Honing Spruit), which was held by two companies of the Shropshire Light Infantry and fifty men of the 2nd battalion Canadian Mounted Rifles. At the same time a train, which was bringing down 400 of the prisoners released from Pretoria, and destined for duty on the lines of communication (commanded by Colonel G. M. Bullock, Devonshire regiment), was attacked in Honing Spruit station itself. A notable engagement ensued. Bullock was a soldier of indomitable spirit, which he had had but one opportunity to display when, at the battle of Colenso, he had been beaten down by a rifle-stock rather than surrender. Once more he found himself in an apparently desperate situation here at Honing Spruit. His troops, men of all corps, hastily armed with different patterns of rifle, were sickly and dispirited from long confinement, and in no condition to meet an enemy elated with recent triumphs, and provided with artillery. Nevertheless, animated by their leader, whose reputation they knew well, they fought stubbornly against the heavy odds, a small party of Canadians especially displaying conspicuous courage. The Boers were held off for hours, and eventually handsomely repulsed, Bullock receiving timely reinforcement from the 14th battalion I.Y. (Colonel A. M. Brookfield) with four guns, in all some 400 mounted men, who had been sent from Kroonstad. *[June 22nd, 1900. One portion attacks Honing Spruit;]*

Major-General Paget, who had remained at Lindley, had been harassed throughout his stay at that village. On June 26th he was attacked by the Boers in force with four guns. His piquets were strongly assailed but kept the enemy out of the town.* Next day the attack was renewed; but Brookfield, arriving for the second time at an opportune moment with 800 mounted men, six guns, and one and a half battalions of infantry, saved the Lindley garrison from a more severe attack threatened by C. De Wet. The garrison's casualties were five men killed, two *[the other threatens Paget at Lindley, June 26th, 1900.]*

---

* For gallantry in this action Private C. Ward, 2nd King's Own Yorkshire Light Infantry, was awarded the Victoria Cross.

officers and thirty-five men wounded. Brookfield's force, which had left Kroonstad on June 25th as escort to a large convoy for Lindley, had been engaged with some 1,500 Boers with two guns throughout its march. His casualties were two men killed, two officers and fourteen men wounded, five missing.

The modifications in the original scheme of distribution which were issued on June 20th and 21st, were designed with a view to driving C. De Wet eastwards towards Bethlehem, and surrounding all the Boer forces in the north-east of the Free State. Briefly the plan was :—Ian Hamilton, with MacDonald's force from Heilbron, was to move south from Heidelberg. The east of the zone of operations was marked by the railway from Durban to Johannesburg, where Sir R. Buller was in occupation of Standerton by June 23rd. To the south was Sir L. Rundle, with his own and the Colonial divisions, to prevent the Boers breaking out in the direction of Thabanchu. North-west of him lay Clements, who had also Paget's brigade ; whilst between Clements and Ian Hamilton, Lord Methuen had to guard against a break back of the enemy westwards, and also to protect the railway from Kroonstad to the Vaal.

Ian Hamilton succeeded by Sir A. Hunter, June 24th, 1900.

On June 23rd Ian Hamilton occupied Heidelberg and chased a Boer force which had been in occupation of it. In this pursuit Hamilton had the misfortune to break his collar-bone by a fall with his horse. Lieut.-General Sir A. Hunter was then placed in command of Hamilton's force, and subsequently took charge of all the troops in the east and north-east of the Orange Free State ; his operations will be described later. Clements, in accordance with the change of plans, had moved from Senekal towards Winburg. On June 24th he arranged to surround a Boer laager at Leliefontein, some fifteen miles north-west of Senekal. For this purpose he called upon Lieut.-Colonel H. M. Grenfell, who had relieved Clements at Senekal, to move with 800 mounted men on June 25th and surprise the laager from the east. The Boers, however, had notice of his coming, and opposed him at dawn, using a gun. They were driven off and pursued to the north and north-east, when Major-General E. Y. Brabant also arrived from Senekal, where he had gone by Sir L. Rundle's order. The

OPERATIONS IN THE ORANGE RIVER COLONY. 139

casualties were two killed, thirteen wounded, twenty missing.* Clements marched back into Senekal on June 27th, and finding Brabant there, made his way northwards towards Lindley next day.

The situation throughout the Orange River Colony† at the beginning of July was shortly as follows: The railway was guarded by detachments of troops, including the British prisoners released at Pretoria, distributed at various posts. On July 6th Lieut.-General Kelly-Kenny was placed in command of the lines of communication from the Orange river to Kroonstad; Lieut.-General Sir H. C. Chermside was given charge of the line from Kroonstad to Pretoria. The VIth division and the IIIrd division had now ceased to exist, even some of the brigades of these divisions being broken up. Of the VIth division the 12th brigade formed part of Clements' column; the 13th brigade, at Kroonstad, had only one of its original battalions at Headquarters, the other three having been transferred to different commands. The 22nd and 23rd brigades were working independently on the line of communication between the Orange river and Kroonstad. In order to assist Lord Methuen in protecting the railway, a force of mounted infantry was organised at Kroonstad and placed under Lieut.-Colonel T. E. Hickman (Worcestershire regiment). It was soon found, however, that the pressure on De Wet was driving him eastward, and Hickman and Lord Methuen were sent to Pretoria and Krugersdorp respectively. As to the districts lying east of the railway, the more important towns between the line and Hunter's columns were occupied by garrisons so as to ensure open communications.

Situation at end of phase.

* The missing men made their way to Ventersburg Road station.

† By proclamation of May 28th, the name of the State was changed to Orange River Colony.

CHAPTER VI.

THE DEFENCE AND RELIEF OF MAFEKING.*

<small>Colonel Baden-Powell's orders.</small>
On July 25th, 1899, Brevet-Colonel R. S. S. Baden-Powell, then in the service of the Colonial Office, landed at Cape Town with instructions :—
(i). To raise two regiments of mounted infantry.
(ii). In the event of war to organise the defence of the Rhodesia and Bechuanaland frontiers.
(iii). As far as possible to keep forces of the enemy occupied in this direction away from their own main forces.

<small>His characteristics.</small>
Such orders, offering unlimited scope for improvisation, were in happy conjunction with the character of the officer called upon to carry them out. The nature of the events which resulted from them render indispensable a brief examination of that officer's personality. Baden-Powell was a soldier of a type which had become uncommon in European service. With him training with and command of regular cavalry, and experience upon the Staff, had been but a foundation, well and truly laid, for those less exact parts of the science of war which had been almost ignored, if not actually disdained, by the military school from which he sprang. That school, with its centuries of honours, he by no means despised; his own regiment, the 5th Dragoon Guards, he had trained in scrupulous accordance with its precepts, and none knew or taught better than he the value of strict regulations. His originality lay in a certain unquenchable and almost exotic attraction towards the unusual in warfare ; in a preference for setting precedents rather than following

---

* See maps Nos. 51 and 52.

THE DEFENCE AND RELIEF OF MAFEKING. 141

them, for making rather than adopting experiments; and he was at once at home with any description of comrades whom the emergency which he courted might produce to meet it. A professional soldier by training, he was a soldier of fortune by predilection; and if, like many such, he was naturally adroit and prompt in minor tactics, his genuine education had endowed him with more soundness of strategy and a stronger grasp of organisation than is usual with leaders of his tendency, whom he excelled much as J. E. B. Stuart (like him an erstwhile officer of Dragoons) excelled the brilliant Turner Ashby of the Confederate forces of 1861. Baden-Powell, whilst strongly resembling Stuart in military qualities, differed in turn from him in that his personal enthusiasm, burning inwards rather than outwards, did not, like Stuart's, immediately set fire to those from whom he had to exact sacrifices; differing, further, from the Virginian because, whilst less exceptionally gifted as a purely cavalry officer, he possessed a more intimate knowledge of the practice of all the arms; so that if he might not, like Stuart, have led a raid around a hostile army, Stuart might not, like him, have organised the defence of an open town.

From the moment of his disembarkation Baden-Powell found full play for his every quality, natural and acquired. For the performance of the first item of his orders, talent untrained would have been sadly at a loss. To raise two serviceable regiments was no easy matter. Certain constitutional difficulties in the way of recruiting in Cape Colony confined him largely to the sparsely inhabited districts on the northern and western borders where, though ne'er-do-wells were to be had in plenty, reliable men were only to be found in regular employment which they were unwilling to throw up for an uncertain prospect of campaigning. Add to the difficulty of recruiting that of obtaining supplies, arms, horses, mules, oxen and money, a task not lightened by the authorities, who wished to avoid expenditure on warlike stores that might never be required; of establishing camping grounds and magazines, of organising cadres which, should they be wanted, would be wanted seriously and at once; of instructing the men in riding, shooting and

His preparations.

manœuvring ; of devising plans whereby a small force could be best adjusted to a vast sphere of operations ; of initiating a system of finance ; and it will be seen that Baden-Powell from the first had scope for the display of one of his peculiar characteristics, that of making bricks without straw against time. The creation of a modern corps demands as much skill, and even more knowledge, than the command of it ; the qualities necessary for both will not often be found in one man. By the end of September Baden-Powell had his two regiments raised, horsed, equipped and trained, their duties assigned, their pay and maintenance provided for, their economy settled and their tactics—much of which were of a peculiar pattern—laid down and fully practised. In completing all this work Baden-Powell had been ably and energetically assisted. His officers were men after his own heart, keen and adventurous, and like himself, animated by that disciplined unrest which not only leads men out of the beaten path, but empowers them to beat out paths of their own. Like himself the majority of his subordinates had old acquaintance with the frontiers along which their work was to lie, knowing both the Boers and the natives of these peculiar districts, where the tides of black and white met but did not mingle in the lonely farms and the unfinished townships ; where the interests of powerful native chiefs, of Boer field cornets, and of British municipalities were in daily contact and not infrequent friction, so that even peace-time was a continual war between tact, suspicion and ignorance. Especially was the native question here paramount ; and in this the interests of the British and Boers at once clashed and were identical. Whilst both desired above all to keep quiescent the warlike tribes, whom the advances of both in past years had thrust mainly out to the westward beyond the railway, and northward across the Limpopo, yet each—foreseeing this to be impossible should conflict arise between themselves—was anxious to impress the tribesmen with his own superiority by initial successes. For this reason, amongst others, Baden-Powell early decided to make Mafeking his own Headquarters. That town was the centre of a district peopled by nearly a quarter of a

Decides to hold Mafeking.

THE DEFENCE AND RELIEF OF MAFEKING. 143

million natives, and itself harboured a black population which outnumbered the white by nearly six to one. Besides this, Mafeking had strategic and other claims to become the pivot of operations. It was the half-way house between Cape Colony and Rhodesia and the outpost for both. It contained large supplies of food, forage and railway material; and though—these things being only of value as means to an end—it is usually a military blunder to allow the guardianship of them to dictate immobility, the loss of them here would have been tantamount to defeat in the eyes of the natives, their transference elsewhere would have taken too long, and their dispersion into weakly guarded posts would have been equivalent to their loss. Finally, and most important, Mafeking was situate on the flank of the Transvaal, impressing Johannesburg and Pretoria along the lines of the Witwatersrand, as Kimberley made its influence felt upon Bloemfontein along the line of the Modder. The enemy, therefore, could not ignore the presence of a British garrison there, and Baden-Powell's object (see No. iii of his orders) was above all to attract attention.

That he might have done so to more advantage by turning the whole of his force into a roving column was a suggestion as alluring as it was impracticable. His information told him that he would be opposed by forces many times greater, better mounted, and more experienced than his own; and these forces were all within a few miles of his lines. He had few spare animals, either draught or riding, no Field artillery and very little transport; his shrift amongst the strong commandos of the western Transvaal would have been short indeed. In any event he would have required a base; and his whole command amounted to little more than the guard of a depôt of moderate size. In order to carry out his orders it was nevertheless necessary to provide a force also for the Rhodesian border. With considerable audacity, considering his remoteness, his own numbers, and those of the enemy, Baden-Powell did not hesitate to divide his small bodies by hundreds of miles. Keeping at Mafeking the newly-raised Protectorate regiment (Lieut.-Colonel C. O. Hore), he ordered the Rhodesia regiment

Sends a force to Rhodesia.

(Lieut.-Colonel H. C. O. Plumer) to Tuli, where it concentrated on October 14th, and thereafter for six months was lost to his sight.*

Mafeking. Baden-Powell had now to call upon all his art for the defence of Mafeking. Without art the place was indefensible, for Nature had done nothing to protect it. Built upon the undulating veld on the right bank of the Molopo river, and on the east of the railway, the town itself presented a square of which each side was about one thousand yards long. Against its southwest angle clustered a large native town or "stadt," inhabited by some six thousand of the Barolong and other tribes, owing allegiance to a headman Wessels. The scattered mass of huts, straggling across the Molopo, had an area many times greater than that of the white town; and, though the natives were loyal and courageous, their presence here was rather a danger than a safeguard to the defence; for their wide-spread village, itself penetrable from the west by way of the steep banks of the Molopo, formed a covered way up to the very boundary of the town itself. Of commanding ground there was little within reach of the place; of defensive works none. What heights existed lay chiefly to the west and south-west of the native village, which they overlooked; whilst two thousand yards to the south-east a small and solitary knoll, called Cannon Kopje, rose from the gently ascending slopes of the veld. On all other sides the environs of Mafeking, from the brickfields to the east round to the Kanya road, and beyond, to the west, were bare; the reservoir, on which the supply of water at first depended, lay out in the open to the north-east, near the racecourse. Thus unprotected against assault, the town, composed of frail mud-bricked tin-roofed houses, was equally at the mercy of artillery fire; and in short seemed to possess no single qualification of a fortress except supply. Of this there was ample stock, partly introduced by Baden-Powell himself, but for the most part in private hands, the stores of Mr. Julius Weil, a notable contractor and merchant of these parts, being particularly well furnished. Space does not

---

* For the operations of Lieut.-Colonel Plumer's force, see Chapter VII.

permit of a specification of all the measures devised by Baden-Powell and his officers for the defence, both during the breathing space before the declaration of war, and subsequently. Let it suffice to say that no less than sixty works (see map No. 52) were erected where none had existed before, all provided with bomb-proofs, the majority connected by telephone and by zig-zags, and hedged in by *abattis* and mines. The water supply, which could not fail to be cut off, was supplanted by the excavation of wells within the perimeter. Across the northern front, the most vulnerable part, an armoured train, improvised on the spot, patrolled along a light railway specially laid down for its use ; whilst inside this the two sides of the town which faced in this direction were fenced in by a zareba of thorn, such as had in the past, and in far regions of the same continent, protected squares of British troops against the rush of Soudanese spearmen.

Altogether the defensive works embraced a perimeter of at first seven, and finally ten miles in extent, an area remarkable indeed in proportion to the numbers available to occupy it.

In all these labours Baden-Powell was keenly seconded by the citizens, and the railway and municipal authorities of Mafeking, who not only freely lent skilled labour, without which much must have been left undone, but of their own volition enrolled over four hundred men, or one-third of the total garrison. Even with their aid the numbers available were only about twelve hundred, composed as follows :—

	Officers.	Men.	
Protectorate Regiment (Lieut.-Colonel Hore)	21	448	Its garrison.
British South Africa Police (Lieut.-Colonel Walford)	10	81	
Cape Police (Inspectors C. S. Marsh and J. W. Browne)	4	99	
Bechuanaland Rifles (Captain B. W. Cowan)	5	77	
The Town Guard	6	296	
Railway and other employés	1	115	
Cape Boy (coloured) contingent	1	67	
Total	48	1,183	

Of these only 576 were equipped with the magazine rifle, the rest carrying the obsolete Martini-Henry single loader. If the rifles were few, of artillery, in the modern sense, there was none. Baden-Powell's repeated requests for proper ordnance had been disregarded, and he had only four 7-pr. guns, one 1-pr. Hotchkiss, and one 2-in. Nordenfeldt, with which to meet the powerful long-ranging weapons known to be with the Boers. Even these feeble and antiquated pieces were scarcely efficient, their carriages being in bad repair, the fittings worn and without duplicates, and the fuses so shrunken with age that they had to be wedged into the shells with paper.

If Britons had long made traditional their readiness to challenge a numerically superior enemy from isolated and ill-equipped outposts, they had seldom done so with more inadequate means than those of Baden-Powell's composite, irregular handful. It will be seen how their historic genius for triumphing in such situations was to be maintained at Mafeking; how, unshackled by the cautious laws of war, they were once more to make good their own peculiar law, that numbers count for little against endurance, or heavy guns against enthusiasm. The British soldier is not versed in the history which his predecessors have made; yet, though Lucknow or Jellalabad are but names to him, he may be trusted to reassert always the spirit of such apparently hopeless defences; and this he did in South Africa at a time when many of his ancestral traits seemed to be obscured in the bewilderment of novel methods of fighting and of an almost unique enemy.

The Boers advance, and surround Mafeking. As war became imminent a cloud of ten thousand Boers, under General Piet Cronje, lowered towards Mafeking and the western border. Cronje, in whom a full share of the stoutness which had delivered his European forefathers from the hand of Spain was leadened with a stupidity which was to drag himself down to ruin, looked upon the open village as a prey to be snapped up in passing. Willing, nevertheless, to acquire an early, if a trifling, plume, he surrounded the town on October 13th, and prepared to enjoy his triumph. With him were the Potchefstroom, Wolmaranstad, Rustenburg, Lichtenburg and Marico commandos, about 6,750 men, with six Krupp and four Vickers-Maxim automatic guns. In co-operation with these the Bloemhof commando, about eight hundred strong, moved upon Vryburg. Early on the morning of this combined advance, the Boers had already won the small success referred to in the account of the defence of Kimberley, when Nesbit was captured with his guns, trucks and detachment near Kraaipan.* For this mischance the troops in Mafeking took revenge next day in the opposite direction. At 5.30 a.m. on the 14th, the patrols reconnoitring toward the north, encountered and drove back a party of Boers who were approaching from the direction of Ramathlabama. The armoured train immediately steamed out in pursuit, carrying fifteen men B.S.A. Police, under Captain A. Williams, a 1-pr. Hotchkiss gun, and a Maxim; and at 6.30 a.m. it became closely engaged with the enemy, who had turned to fight on a good position with about four hundred men, a Krupp gun and a Vickers-Maxim. So heavily sounded the firing in Mafeking that Baden-Powell then despatched "D." squadron, and a troop of "A." squadron of the Protectorate regiment under Captain C. FitzClarence† to support, ordering him to strike hard at the enemy should opportunity offer. On arriving at the scene FitzClarence, dismounting his men on the right of the train, advanced and pressed the Boers persistently until they withdrew their guns, and giving way on his front, drifted out towards his right flank, which they endeavoured to envelop. But FitzClarence, manœuvring brilliantly, and well supported by the armoured train, not only kept the enemy at bay but inflicted far greater losses than he sustained; for the Boers were clumsily handled and fought with little intelligence. Nevertheless, FitzClarence's situation was one of considerable danger; and he would have had difficulty in returning had not Baden-Powell, who was in close touch with the affair by telephone from Mafeking, sent out Lieut.-Colonel Hore with a troop of the Protectorate regiment under Lord C. Bentinck, and

Oct. 14th, 1899. Skirmish to the north.

---

* See Volume II., page 47.

† Captain C. FitzClarence, the Royal Fusiliers (special service), was awarded the Victoria Cross for gallantry on this occasion.

a 7-pr. gun, to cover the retirement. After a hot fight of four hours' duration FitzClarence and the train withdrew, his casualties being two officers wounded, sixteen of other ranks killed and wounded, one missing, and sixteen horses. The enemy lost three times as many in killed alone, including four field cornets; and, staggered by the smartness of the blow, made no attempt to interfere with the retirement. The next day passed quietly, both sides busying themselves in settling into their respective positions. Those of Baden-Powell, too numerous to detail, are seen on the accompanying map (No. 52). Briefly, his works and entrenchments were planned with two objects, an interior line, drawn closely about the town itself, for defence against assault; and an exterior line, widely thrown over all the higher ground on the left bank of the Molopo, embracing the native village and the kopjes commanding it, and circling from west, through north to the east of Mafeking, at an average distance of four thousand yards from the inner defences. This outer line was above all designed for aggression. From the first Baden-Powell, though accepting investment as the best means to his end, placed no faith in a policy of quiescence, determining rather when attack should be threatened to attack first himself, and to meet every new trench of the enemy with a counter-trench, if he could not demolish it before completion. Thus, the dispositions of his numberless small works grew and varied constantly; and if no attempt is therefore made to keep touch with them, it must, nevertheless, be remembered of what importance was the excavation of a few feet of fresh entrenchment or the movement of a squad of men. In a contest of this description a hollow unguarded, a gap unfilled, a fence thrown down, might mean the loss of the place; for the Boers, though they feared to pour over Mafeking in volume, knew well how to trickle through discovered leaks.

Each work, containing fifteen to twenty men, was provided with food and water for two days. Some, and those the most obtrusive, were merely dummy, and their surmounting flag, waving over an empty hole, was to prove the mark of many a Boer shell. Look-out towers, notably one forty feet high on

The defences of Mafeking.

THE DEFENCE AND RELIEF OF MAFEKING.   149

Cannon Kopje, were erected on commanding sites, and these, as well as the majority of the trenches, were connected by telephone with Baden-Powell's Headquarters within the town. Finally shelters had been excavated for the townspeople, and a system of alarm inaugurated whereby in a few moments every soldier was at his post, and every man, woman, and child hidden under shell-proof cover. The duties of Town Commandant were assigned to Lieut.-Colonel C. B. Vyvyan.

On October 16th two Boer guns, opening at 9.20 a.m., threw the first shells into Mafeking from a rise to the north-east. They continued to fire until 2.15 p.m., when a flag of truce from Cronje, who imagined that he saw the town crumbling beneath his ill-aimed projectiles, summoned Baden-Powell to surrender. The Boers utilised the interval of parley, an interval prolonged for transparent attempts at spying on the part of the *parlementaire*, in entrenching closer to the town. By evening they were fairly covered on all sides of it, though even in this, their special faculty, their dispositions seemed marked by a peculiar dullness, and Mafeking was never ringed entirely. On the 17th they seized the waterworks; but the wells in the town and the Molopo, still running full, removed the greatest fear of besieged garrisons. Nor were the occupants of the waterworks allowed to rest within their capture. By day and night patrols of the Cape Police, and the armoured train, which could run to within 2,100 yards, seldom ceased to pester the spot with sudden alarms of rifle and Maxim fire, and the burghers there had little sleep or exercise. On the 20th two thousand men of the strong Potchefstroom commando, with four guns, showed a threatening front from their position on the west. But the prompt manning of every post deterred the enemy, whose withdrawal was further encouraged by the successful practice of a 7-pr. gun and a Maxim. These and many other signs of preparedness began to arouse doubts in Cronje's breast. The dwellers in the open village seemed not only prepared for defence, but disconcertingly eager to attack. Especially was he apprehensive of the mines, which Baden-Powell himself had warned him were sown about the outskirts. For their mysterious power

Oct. 16th, 1899.
The first shell.

an accident had already inspired Cronje with an exaggerated respect. It happened that on the 13th Baden-Powell, wishing to get rid of two trucks of dynamite standing in the siding, had sent them up the line, pushed by an engine which was detached and run backward when the attention of the enemy had been attracted. The Boers immediately attacked the apparently derelict armoured train, and scenting another capture, closed round, shooting rapidly. Soon the trucks blew up with a tremendous explosion, injuring none it is true, but terrifying exceedingly their assailants, whose minds were never thereafter free from the fear of such perilous surprises. Cronje, therefore, decided to keep at arm's length of a garrison which he might have obliterated by numbers alone, and sent to Pretoria for a heavy gun with which to finish the business. On the 23rd the weapon appeared. It was hurriedly emplaced on a height known as Jackal Tree, 3,500 yards south of Mafeking, and at 1.30 p.m. on the 24th threw its first shell into the town, its arrival being heralded on both days by a general bombardment by the various pieces distributed around the arc of investment. These guns, though constantly in movement, were at this time placed approximately as follows :—One on the racecourse, near the reservoir to the north-east of the town ; two on a knoll abreast of Cannon Kopje ; one on either side of the Creusot on the height toward the south ; and three with the Potchefstroom men on the west. Baden-Powell had at this time allocated his 7-prs. as follows :—One on Cannon Kopje, with two Maxims ; one with Major A. J. Godley, Royal Dublin Fusiliers, who commanded the western defences beyond the native village ; one at the brickfields, sweeping the Malmani road ; and one with the reserve in the town. The Maxims, of which he possessed seven, were posted at advantageous spots, such as the angles of the zareba, at the railway bridge, on the Massibi road near the B.S.A. Police Barracks, on the railway beyond the cemetery. He had fully prepared to eke out the scantiness of his armament by its mobility, and at every point of the compass a work was ready for the reception of a gun. Now Cronje, invested by the possession of his cannon with indisputable power

Oct. 23rd, 1899.
A heavy Creusot gun arrives.

THE DEFENCE AND RELIEF OF MAFEKING. 151

over the streets and dwellings of Mafeking, made repeated offers to allow the women and children to depart. The concession was inspired partly by the fact that many of these were of his own race, and partly by his genuine anxiety to avoid waste of life, a humane trait as strongly marked in the otherwise dour general with regard to his enemy as to his own over-shepherded burghers. No leader on the Boer side had a greater unwillingness to cause or suffer losses than he whose fate it was to be to inflict and endure losses as great as any. The non-combatants refused to leave; and Baden-Powell had only to point out their camp, and the position of the Hospital and Convent, each of which was marked by a Geneva flag. The gaol was shown by a yellow flag; and as it was rapidly filling with detected spies, both male and female, avoidance or selection of it as a target was left to the discretion of the Boer artillerists. Spies, indeed, abounded; less of the traitorous sort than of a type inevitable in a frontier town of mixed races, whose citizens were perhaps unaware of their hereditary sympathies until war called upon them to choose definitely which flag they would serve. Some, attempting to serve both, found themselves under the yellow flag of the prison.

On October 25th the enemy made a scrambling demonstration against all sides of the town, feinting with his greatest strength and throwing heaviest shell fire against the native village embracing the south-western angle, whilst he made ready a real attack against the more open western face to the north. But the indignant Barolongs, who had been armed with Snider rifles for their own defence, added their fusilade to that of their white allies; the feinters, handled with unexpected roughness, fell back with loss, and the real attack was abandoned. The various other attacks, awed perhaps by the almost total silence and invisibility of Baden-Powell's men, who lay quiet in their trenches, came to nothing; and but one casualty resulted from the 250 to 300 projectiles which burst amongst the defences. The Boers, on the other hand, lost considerably from timely gusts of Maxim gun fire, which beat upon each skirmishing line as it developed.

A similar display next day (October 26th) was quenched by a heavy downfall of rain. Yet, behind these timorous manœuvrings the enemy was busily stealing ground, especially at the racecourse on the eastern side, across which on the 27th a trench full of marksmen appeared within two thousand yards. Baden-Powell lost no time in dealing a counter-stroke. Detailing three parties, one a squadron of the Protectorate regiment under Captain FitzClarence, another of fifteen men under a sergeant of the Cape Police, and a third of twelve men of the same corps, under Lieutenant Murray, he ordered FitzClarence to attack the trench itself from its southern flank. Beyond this again to the south, and separated from the end of the trench by an interval of open ground, the enemy had a small laager on the verge of the Molopo. This Murray was to distract with rifle fire from the south (left) bank of the Molopo simultaneously with FitzClarence's descent on the trench; whilst the sergeant's posse, moving into the gap between it and the brickfields, was to support both parties. To guide FitzClarence, two lamps, bearing when in line exactly on the flank of the earthwork, were hoisted on the edge of the town, and lighted when the force paraded at 9 p.m. Darkness befriended the dash with which the adventure was carried out. Gaining the flank of the Boer trench undetected, FitzClarence's men were wheeled until they had enveloped the rear of it; then with a shout they fell on with the bayonet. The Boers, who were sleeping under the shelter of sheets of corrugated tin torn from the race stand, had no inkling of their fate until the crash of the soldiers leaping upon their resounding roofs brought them to their feet for an instant before they fell again to the steel. From end to end of the trench the squadron rushed, utterly routing its occupants, of whom few survived. Those in the laager, and in a supporting work in rear, then began a wild fire; but the shooting of Murray's two detachments of Police, coming from different angles, confused still further the half-awakened burghers, who desperately pulled trigger in all directions, believing themselves to be surrounded by a horde of men. Having cleared the trench, FitzClarence blew a whistle, the pre-arranged

Oct. 27th, 1899.
FitzClarence's attack at the Racecourse.

THE DEFENCE AND RELIEF OF MAFEKING. 153

signal for his men to disperse independently back towards the town, whilst the Police continued to pour volleys from the south. Long after all had returned, every Boer position on this side was ablaze with random musketry, which filled the night air with bullets harmless to all but the comrades of those who fired them. Of the sixty burghers reported to have been shot, many must have fallen to the rifles of their own side; for the Protectorate men, though forty Boers succumbed to their bayonets, had not discharged a round. FitzClarence, himself wounded, lost but seventeen of his squadron, six killed, nine wounded, and two missing, losses incurred mostly in the confused *mêlée* which followed his onslaught upon the trench.

This brilliant affair thoroughly, in this quarter at least, shook the enemy, already uneasy from the constant shooting of patrols and the visits of the armoured train. The hoisting on the next night of the same lanterns as had guided FitzClarence, once more drew a prolonged and universal discharge from the trenches; and again on the night of the 30th a false alarm brought thousands of rounds from the same spot. Then the Boers made a determined effort to wipe out the memory of their discomfiture. From the first their estimate of the importance of Cannon Kopje had been plainly shown by the attention it received from the gunners, who expended a vast number of shells upon it, chiefly to the detriment of a sham fort erected outside the real enclosure which crowned the summit. If its value were equally apparent to the defence, less had been done to fortify it than at other parts of the perimeter; and the fort—an open breastwork of stones with a trench in rear, built about an old structure left by Sir C. Warren after a bygone campaign—was neither strong nor skilfully designed. Yet it was the key to Mafeking on this side, commanding the native village, the railway, and main roads to south and east; and, moreover, so looked into the backs of many of the neighbouring defences that its loss would have rendered them untenable. Its garrison consisted of fifty men of the B.S.A. Police under Colonel Walford, with whom also were Captains the Hon. D. Marsham and C. A. K. Pechell. At daylight on October 31st, a cross fire of artillery opened on

Oct. 31st, 1899. Boer attack on Cannon Kopje.

Cannon Kopje, coming from the racecourse, from the direction of Rooigrond, and from the heavy and light pieces in front of Jackal Tree. The aim was accurate, and the fort much knocked about; but the garrison, lying *perdu* in the rearward trench, suffered little. They were, however, unable to reply, and had dismounted their paltry guns for safety. Under cover of the bombardment the enemy gradually developed an attack on both fort and town. Strong bodies went down into the bed of the Molopo to the east and west, ready to rush Mafeking when Cannon Kopje should have fallen. Against the kopje itself three separate parties converged, numbering nearly a thousand men in all, and by 6 a.m. had drawn so near that Walford ordered his men to line the parapet. So doing, they became much exposed, and the shells which fell rapidly into the enclosure began to take effect. In the face of the immense superiority of numbers and armament brought against them their case might well have seemed hopeless. But the Police shot furiously from their splintering pen. The advancing bevies of skirmishers were first brought to a halt, then, aided by a well-served 7-pr. gun which Baden-Powell had sent beyond the southern outskirts, the Police actually drove them back with loss whence they had come. Such a feat was not to be done without cost, and eleven of the small detachment fell, of whom eight were killed. Both the captains perished, but not before their fine example had inspired the rest beyond fear of defeat. Truly did Napoleon rule that in battle a man should never surrender; because he knows not what chance may at the last instant reverse in his favour the most hopeless odds. The achievement of the Police was as notable for its good fortune as its valour; for nothing could have saved them from an enemy but half as resolute as themselves. At 3 p.m. Baden-Powell rode to Cannon Kopje and congratulated the diminished garrison on its service to the town, whose thanks he subsequently voiced in a General Order. Next day a very similar threat was made against the kopje, accompanied as before by a converging fire of all the artillery within range. But the attackers, though they showed in numbers on foot, displayed a not unaccountable disinclination

THE DEFENCE AND RELIEF OF MAFEKING. 155

to close with the silent work; and after hesitating for an hour out of range they finally withdrew, whilst their guns made amends by redoubling the bombardment. Two wagons were then sent up to Cannon Kopje laden with material for improving the defences.

On November 2nd and 3rd Godley's western line of defence was gradually thrown a thousand yards further outward, forestalling the enemy, who had been observed taking up ground for the establishment of a battery, and had even found and disconnected some of the dreaded mines. Godley, pushing forward his men by twos and threes, succeeded in gaining the ridge unobserved, and there excavated a redan for twenty rifles, with breast-high cover backed by a bomb-proof six feet six inches deep, the parapet showing only one foot above the surface.

November, 1899.

On the night of the 4th the enemy, in imitation of their opponents, attempted to run a railway trolley loaded with fused dynamite down the incline into the town. But the trolley, coming soon to a standstill, blew up in the presence of its senders; and sandbags were then placed upon the line to prevent any repetition of the trick. On the 6th the big gun on Jackal Tree was removed and installed in a fresh work three thousand yards east of Cannon Kopje, whence at 3.15 p.m. it resumed the practice which had seldom ceased since the day of its arrival. On the next day Godley, issuing from his lines at 2.30 a.m. with ninety men and three guns, surprised a small laager about three thousand yards in front of his positions on the other side of the Molopo, and scattered it in all directions with rifle and gun fire. As day dawned the enemy quickly gathered to the spot from Cronje's Headquarters, which lay a mile and a half to the south; but Godley drew safely away from before a strong force with the loss of only four men wounded. The Boers sent out three ambulances for their casualties, and vented their annoyance in a hot bombardment of the town which continued with intervals all day.

Some time now elapsed before the belligerents came again to close quarters; and the investment settled down to that period of tense inactivity which to besieged troops has so often seemed more exhausting than shocks and alarms. Long days and nights in all weathers in the trenches, unrewarded by fighting, are the greatest trials of veteran soldiers; to novices, demanding of war but a series of combats and adventures, they are well-nigh insupportable; and on Baden-Powell's troops the duty fell doubly hard by reason of the fewness of their numbers and their inexperience. The enemy, whose constant and apparently aimless movement all around gave hourly but ungratified hopes of encounter, drew closer the line of circumvallation, especially with fresh works at the brickfields, on the railway to the south-west, in front of Godley, and to the north of Mafeking. All of these, as soon as they were discovered, Baden-Powell met with counter-works. Three new redoubts were pushed out into the brickfields, the left of Godley's line was advanced and strengthened, whilst to the north a real redoubt answered, and a dummy work attracted, the fire of the Boers, who had established themselves with two guns in a fort on Game Tree Hill, about two miles north-west of Mafeking. Beyond this there was little to do but to endure the daily and almost incessant bombardment. Shells, of which some hundreds must commonly be launched to kill but one of an army of soldiers in the open field, claim but few victims amongst people so well sheltered as those in the bomb-proofs of Mafeking; but their moral effect, always their chief weapon, might be presumed to be at its greatest when exercised on the unaccustomed nerves of women, children and peaceful civilians, and they condemned to idleness in dark and cheerless refuges. Yet so harmless proved the Boer practice, and so high was the spirit of the non-combatants, that the ringing of the bell which had been adopted as the signal for all to disappear under cover, often, on the contrary, brought everyone out into the open to watch the bursting of the expected projectile, and to gather its fragments. But if the garrison and dwellers in Mafeking found the siege grow tedious, the Boers, confounded that there should be a siege at all, became daily more exasperated. To them the paltry garrison's resistance, even to such futile attempts as they had made to overcome it, seemed incomprehensible, and to their

THE DEFENCE AND RELIEF OF MAFEKING. 157

curiously compounded notions of war, even a little unfair. Letters full of querulous complaints passed frequently from Cronje to Baden-Powell, answered for the most part in a jocular spirit which appeared but another military *inconvenance* to the mirthless Boer. Cronje's reputation was suffering as seriously with his own men as with Baden-Powell's; and he was ready to welcome any excuse for withdrawing from the scene of his failure. Such a pretext was before long afforded by events in the south; and on November 18th Cronje went off with four thousand men and six guns to meet varied fortunes and a dramatic fate elsewhere, leaving General Snyman to carry on the investment of Mafeking. <small>Nov. 18th, 1899. General Cronje departs.</small>

Snyman, possessed of a reputation as great as and even more shadowy than that of his predecessor, had no intention of damaging it by unsuccessful activity. He openly adopted the passive *rôle* of blockader, and from numberless little works and trenches sat down to watch his opponents starve into submission. They for their part languished only from want of excitement; and even their dullness was lightened by a pleasure rare with besieged garrisons—reception of news from outside. For the blockade, the stupidity of its management in no wise removed since Cronje's departure, proved but a slight obstacle to runners and despatch riders, who so often passed in and out from north and south, that Baden-Powell's communication by letter with Plumer, Nicholson, Kimberley, and Cape Town, was scarcely interrupted. For weeks, therefore, there is little to record about the town except that it was still invested, still shelled daily, still unreduced, and every day less likely to be so. By the middle of December the total casualties amongst the white combatants numbered 104, of whom 23 were killed; the black allies had lost 37, whilst 23 non-combatants had been killed and wounded. The food supply remained ample, though in view of the uncertain duration of the siege it was considered wise to assign all foodstuffs to the care of the military authority (Captain C. M. Ryan, A.S.C.), and to place everyone in Mafeking upon a scale of rations. During this period Baden-Powell was so much more aggressive than his opponent, that <small>December, 1899.</small>

it may be almost said that the besiegers themselves were on the defensive. Scarcely a day passed but some new trench or work was driven out to threaten one of the Boers'; marksmen, crawling out to within short range, harried the lines of investment by day and night; and even the gunners of the heavy cannon to the south-east found their operations interrupted by sudden and well-aimed volleys from concealed parties of stalkers. Ammunition for the British 7-prs. had to be carefully husbanded. On December 21st there were but 580 shells (219 common, 295 shrapnel; 66 case) for all four of them. Nevertheless, the little pieces were seldom silent, Major F. W. Panzera, B.S.A. Police, an able officer who commanded all the artillery, contriving to secure results out of all proportion to the calibre of his weapons and the number of rounds expended. What the enemy was unable to do in weeks, Nature on one occasion effected in a few hours, when, on the night of December 5th, a cataract of rain drove the defenders from some of their advanced trenches, many narrowly escaping with their lives from the rush of water. The damage done was great, and took long to repair; but the Boers suffered even more severely, their half-drowned opponents holding them by volleys to their flooded trenches.

Baden-Powell had long heard rumours that disaffection and nervousness were rife amongst the commandos. On December 11th he attempted to increase both by sending forth to the Boer rank-and-file a manifesto in which he pointed out the hopelessness of reducing Mafeking, that thousands of British troops were pouring into the country, and that the burghers would do well to disperse before trouble fell upon them; promising to afford protection in the future to all who acted on his advice. The manifesto was carried out to the laagers by eight mounted orderlies, all of whom returned in safety, good fortune which would scarcely have attended the bearers of such a communication to any enemy but the Boers. On the next day General Snyman and two other commandants replied with not unnatural indignation to what may well have seemed a crowning irregularity on the part of their unconventional adversary. During the following days the interchanges of artillery fire became more frequent.

In these the British 7-prs. were usually the attackers, and met with surprising success, especially at Fort Limestone, in Godley's section, and the brickfields; from before the first of these they forced the Boers to fall back on the 16th, whilst those in front of the brickfields were reduced to silence on both the 16th and 19th, and their works much battered. Such attacks, and there were many more, had invariably the effect of drawing fire from the 94-pr. on the heights to the south-east. But the Boer gunners continued to be hampered by sharpshooters, and by the small pieces on Cannon Kopje, and more than all by a Nordenfeldt which Baden-Powell had posted well forward on the slope near "Boy's H.Q." (see map No. 52), which never ceased to engage its huge opponent in a by no means unequal duel. The shooting from the big gun was further nullified by its very accuracy. Shells from it fell so often upon identically the same spot, notably the north-west corner of the Market Square, that they usually burst innocuously. Once, when the aim was wild, the projectiles, soaring over the brickfields, descended into the Boer commando on the other side, which replied with agitated messages enjoining caution. Thus passed December up to Christmas time. Of Plumer there had been constant news; and when on December 24th Baden-Powell heard that the Boers had fallen back from the Limpopo, he telegraphed his approval of the transference of the Rhodesian force to Palapye. (See page 196.)

Colonel G. L. Holdsworth was at this time already on the western line, engaged in repairing it. In order to draw the enemy away from him, and generally to clear the way for Plumer, Baden-Powell planned a vigorous sally to the north. The main hostile work in this direction was Game Tree Fort, the musketry and light artillery of which had long annoyed the northern defences, and endangered the grazing of cattle. So far as could be seen, the fort appeared to be an open redan of no great strength armed with a small field-piece and a Maxim gun. It lay about three thousand yards from the main line of the northern defences, *i.e.*, Forts Ayr, Millar and Cardigan, and some 850 yards from the nearest point of the railway, which passed to the east of it. On December 25th Baden-Powell issued orders for an attack.

Dec. 26th, 1899. British attack on Game Tree Fort.

The force detailed for the enterprise was 260 men, and was divided into two parts. One, the right wing, consisted of " C." squadron Protectorate regiment (Captain R. J. Vernon, of the King's Royal Rifle Corps), " D." squadron (Captain C. FitzClarence) of the same regiment, the armoured train (Captain A. Williams), manned by twenty men of the B.S.A. Police, and seventy men of the Bechuanaland Rifles (Captain B. W. Cowan), the whole under command of Major Godley. The other body, the left wing, was placed under Lieut.-Colonel Hore, and was composed of three 7-pr. guns, a Maxim, and a troop of the Protectorate regiment as escort, all under Major Panzera, with two troops in reserve. Panzera, leaving one gun in support in Fort Ayr, would push the others as far forward as possible, entrench them under cover of darkness in front of Game Tree, and open fire at dawn. The guns were to be emplaced in échelon, both to minimise the risk from the anticipated attentions of the heavy gun south of Mafeking, and to enable them to swing quickly to the north-west, where a strong Boer laager lay ready either to provide reinforcement, or form an asylum for the occupants of the fort, according as they should stand firm or be ousted. Whilst this was being carried out, the armoured train and the two Protectorate squadrons were to move up the railway, their right protected by a flank guard of the Bechuanaland Rifles, until a point should be reached behind the left of the Boer work. Then, their way having been prepared by Panzera's guns, Vernon and FitzClarence, the latter supporting the former, would lead their men, 120 strong, to the assault, whilst the armoured train lent aid. At 2 a.m. on the morning of December 26th, both wings paraded, Hore at Fort Ayr, and Godley at the Cemetery; Baden-Powell himself repaired to the dummy fort outside the north-west outskirt of Mafeking. Hore's preliminary movements were conducted successfully and without incident; and before daylight Panzera had his guns well covered, the foremost some 1,300 yards from Game Tree. But Godley's party, though likewise undetected in its advance up the railway, found the line freshly destroyed short of the flank of Game Tree, so that the fort could not even be turned, much less taken in reverse, as had been intended. At 4.15 a.m. Hore's artillery began to bombard the work. The slight effect produced by the first shells hinted that Game Tree was enclosed by a parapet of some strength. Panzera was given but little chance of damaging it. It had been arranged that, when the assaulting party was about to close, a whistle from the engine of the armoured train should be the signal for the artillery to cease fire. The guns had been but a short time at work when the whistle was heard, and it was seen that the assault was already in progress. Godley's squadrons, so unfavourably placed by the break in the line, had indeed to attack quickly or not at all. The rear of the fort was now unattainable, and only by speed could they hope to strike even at the flank before reinforcements arrived from the neighbouring laagers. Vernon, therefore, lost no time in leading his men forward by rushes of alternate troops, while FitzClarence's squadron, écheloned slightly to the left rear, covered the advance by volley-firing, pushing on the while in close support of the front lines. From the moment of starting they were heavily fired upon from Game Tree, the musketry swelling at every yard of the advance, until at three hundred yards range it became destructive. The fort was strongly manned; the artillery had first removed all hope of surprise, and then been compelled to cease to play upon the parapet; the Boers, standing to their loopholes, emptied their magazines where they chose, without risk and with a target in every trooper. But Vernon's men, disregarding their losses like veterans, hurled themselves upon the fort, which, had there been a breach, would have been theirs in a few moments. But the work was strong, sunk in the ground, defended by a ditch in front, and in the thick wall above by tiers of loopholes through which protruded the muzzles of many rifles, each discharging bullets at full speed. The three officers, Captain Vernon (already twice wounded), Captain H. C. Sandford and Lieut. H. P. Paton, were first in the ditch; all three fell dead in the act of thrusting their revolvers into the loopholes in endeavours to shoot them clear. The command of the squadron then devolved on a sergeant, Molloy by name, whose leading fell nothing short of the example of his lost officers. Around him the soldiers pressed, some plying their bayonets fruitlessly amongst the Mauser barrels, others endeavouring in vain to force an entrance. But the fort was entirely enclosed; the gorge, which had been open but a few days before, being now as strongly barricaded as the front. One man (Sergeant L. Cooke, Bechuanaland Rifles) actually gained the roof and tried to break it open. But on the heavy superstructure of steel rails, overlaid by sandbags, which had already defied the shells of the artillery, his blows fell powerless. Game Tree, in short, was a heavily armoured blockhouse, and nothing but powerful guns could have brought it down. Meanwhile, FitzClarence's squadron had also rushed in and joined the tumult in the ditch. FitzClarence himself had fallen severely wounded in the open, his place being taken by Lieut. H. Swinburne, who, with Lieut. G. Bridges, finely led the squadron to the assault. But more troops only brought more casualties, and " D." squadron in its turn lost many men as they faced the loopholes, or circled desperately around the fort to find an entry. The attempt had long proved hopeless when the remnants of both units were ordered to draw off. They did so unwillingly, turning constantly to fire as they retreated to over a few hundred yards from the parapet, around which lay nearly fifty of their number;* whilst gallant acts of rescue, too numerous to recount, caused many to linger behind under a very rain of bullets. By this time every Boer laager was in activity, and reinforcements were on the way to the scene from all points of the lines of investment. Baden-Powell sent orders for a general retirement. The 94-pr. cannon on the southeast heights had for some time been playing upon Panzera's guns, and now the heavy shells were turned upon the railway, where the armoured train, carrying back the survivors of Vernon's squadron, was steaming towards the town. From one of these the train narrowly escaped destruction, rapidly as it moved. One body of the enemy approaching from the east was successfully kept off by the Bechuanaland Rifles; another, hovering to the west of Game Tree, hesitated to close; and the

---

* For casualty list, see Appendix 5.

THE DEFENCE AND RELIEF OF MAFEKING.

retreat was safely effected from the very midst of enclosing bands.*

Thus was incurred a reverse with which insufficient reconnaissance, combined with spying from inside the town, had much to do, the behaviour of the assaulting troops nothing. The strengthening of the fort, too elaborate to have been accomplished in haste, bore out the enemy's assertion that he had long expected attack in this quarter; yet means had not been lacking of obtaining more accurate information about a work so small and so close to the lines. That inexperienced soldiers should attack a fortification with such fine resolution was, indeed, the only illumination of a disaster which deprived the garrison of officers and men whose value had been best disclosed by the manner of their death.

December closed darkly; for following the failure at Game Tree, news came to hand of the reverses at Colenso and Stormberg. The only incident of the last days of the year was a determined effort by the Boer 94-pr., a 12-pr. Krupp, and a Vickers-Maxim on the south-east heights, to crush the Nordenfeldt posted outside the southern outskirts; but the trio once more found shot for shot returned by their puny adversary, though the parapet which sheltered the Nordenfeldt was tumbled in upon it by one of the first rounds from the cannon.

Baden-Powell had added to his own armament by the discovery of a smooth-bore barrel of 16-pr. calibre, cast for a ship's broadside nearly a hundred years before. This relic of long-forgotten native wars (it had once belonged to Linchwe's tribe) was rejuvenated by being mounted upon wagon wheels; round shot were made for it, and shells improvised out of the caps of air-condensing cylinders used in the soda-water factory; powder cartridges were sewn by the nuns of the Convent, and finally, after one or two failures, the antique piece, loaded with three pounds of powder, successfully threw a projectile for three thousand yards, and was thereafter enlisted amongst the artillery of the defence, and posted in the bed of the Molopo. Later on,

Artillery make-shifts of the garrison.

---

* Sergeant H. R. Martineau and Trooper H. E. Ramsden, Protectorate regiment, were each awarded the Victoria Cross for gallantry in this action.

the stock of ammunition for the 7-prs., which at the end of December had diminished to some 450 rounds, was also augmented by the resurrection of two hundred shells, which, though they had been buried as useless, were found to give excellent results when altered and fitted with new fuses. A further batch of shells for these weapons was manufactured in Mafeking. Then the supplies of foodstuffs in private hands were found on close investigation to be even fuller than had been reported; so that the New Year found the defence as capable as ever both to strike and to endure.

January, 1900.
The 1st of January, 1900, the eighty-first day of the siege, the enemy celebrated by a combined bombardment with five guns for six hours, the 94-pr. bringing its total expenditure of shell to 635 rounds at the close of the practice. The discovery of a composition of phosphorus in many of the shells disclosed an attempt to fire the town, and Baden-Powell issued instructions to troops and householders to guard against the danger. As a counter-demonstration Baden-Powell, on January 3rd, concentrated four guns, including the old 16-pr., upon the emplacement of the 94-pr. cannon, which was effectually silenced after it had replied with five rounds. About one hundred shells were discharged into the work, and the enemy's gunners were fairly driven from their piece, whilst on the British side only a Nordenfeldt suffered from a shot from a Vickers-Maxim. Again, on the 10th and 13th, the 94-pr. was kept silent, this time by the sharpshooters of the Bechuanaland Rifles, who lay out on the veld all day within medium range of the Boer gunners, whom their accurate marksmanship pinned under cover in a manner very mortifying to the crew of so imposing a weapon. Two days later, finding these continued worries intolerable, the Boers removed altogether the big gun and its attendant Krupp to a position two and a half miles east of Mafeking, having smaller command over the town. When it reopened fire its accuracy

Jan. 20th, 1900. The hundredth day of the siege.
was markedly less than before. January 20th was the one-hundredth day of investment; and Baden-Powell, taking stock of his resources, found that he still had supplies sufficient to last at full rates of issue until March 7th, or at reduced rates up to

THE DEFENCE AND RELIEF OF MAFEKING.

the end of that month. The casualties up to this time had been as follows :—

	Combatants.				Non-combatants.			
	Officers.	Men.	Native Contingent.	Total.	Women and Children.	Natives.	Total.	Total.
Killed	5	49	7	61	4	8	12	73
Wounded	8	82	33	123	2	21	23	146
Missing	1	33	—	34	—	—	—	34
Totals	14	164	40	218	6	29	35	253

On January 24th a message arrived from Lord Roberts, sent through Plumer, who was now at Gaberones. The Field-Marshal congratulated the defenders of Mafeking, and expressed an earnest hope that they would be able to hold out until their relief, which could not be immediate, was effected. At this time the investment was considerably closer than heretofore, and of the runners sent in and out with despatches, many were driven back, and a few taken. The bombardment also increased, falling with special severity upon the hospitals and women's laager, though Baden-Powell had six times already notified Snyman of their position, and protested against his gunners' choice of targets. On January 27th, for one example of many, during nearly an hour every shell burst within a zone fifty yards square inside the women's enclosure. There were many signs that such occurrences, so often repeated, were not altogether the result of chance or carelessness. Many of the inhabitants were in sympathy with the enemy outside, for which it was easy to account, and in communication which it was impossible to sever. More than once the disappearance of the Boer women into bomb-proofs heralded the speedy arrival of shells in their camp; whilst on such mornings male suspects, who were lodged for safety in the gaol by night, were observed not to take advantage of the daily privilege of visiting their families in the women's laager. Finally, when Baden-Powell informed Snyman that he had shut up the suspects in that very laager, shells came no more that way. By night significant lights—what besieged place has been without them?—were seen to flash from upper windows, to be often answered from the Boer lines; whilst mysterious figures, and even a trained messenger dog, were from time to time reported to have vanished past the sentries into the night. In short, there was carried on much secret service, which, though undoubtedly magnified in the minds of the garrison, did indeed tend to hamper the defence and assist the enemy. Such things are the commonplaces of investments; and in a place of such mixed racial sympathies as Mafeking, were to be expected, and rather to be prevented, if possible, than resented. At the end of January Baden-Powell, making a further strict scrutiny of his supplies, discovered that there were still available in the military and Mr. Weil's stores meat for seventy-seven days' and bread for seventy-five days' consumption, besides enough fresh vegetables, groceries, preserved fruits, and even fish, all over and above the stocks in the retail shops of the town. Reduction by starvation, therefore, seemed even more remote than reduction by attack, and almost as remote as relief, of which the events elsewhere in the theatre of war offered little prospect. Indeed, the only shortage in the town had been so far of small change, and this Baden-Powell soon rectified by the issue of bank notes of small face value. Only the natives in the village, deprived of their harvesting and usual work, were in danger of want; but much was done to relieve them by the officer in charge of their affairs. Major H. J. Goold-Adams, the Resident Commissioner of the Protectorate, who organised their rationing, started a system of purchase by tokens, and a soup kitchen for those who were aged or indigent. The settlement, which had given trouble by unruliness during the early days of the siege, had been brought to better order by the deposition of its intemperate and feeble chieftain, a man of stronger character being installed in his place. Thereafter the village, though never an aid to the defence, had ceased to be a danger. It continued to be both an offence and a cause of loss to the Boers. Numbers of their cattle fell into the hands of the expert black raiders, who marauded close to the Boer lines, risking and often losing their lives, but frequently returning the richer by a head or two of Boer stock. The unexpected allegiance of the Barolongs to the British had proved a sore disappointment to the enemy, who on January 30th had the effrontery to send in broad daylight a flag of truce amongst the huts, inviting the headman to bring his people over to the Republican cause. As to the employment of natives in the field, both sides complained bitterly of it, their letters on the subject once actually crossing on the same day. In a matter which both found to be inevitable, neither need be held guilty. Baden-Powell, at any rate, though he had armed and enrolled in five bands nearly five hundred natives, was blameless. If the enemy found it impossible to avoid the neutrals with shot and shell, it was impossible not to allow the sufferers to retaliate ; and though a native armed " for his own defence only " is prone rather to remember the weapon in his hands than the proviso limiting its use, who is to decide which marksman, black or white, fires the first shot of an indiscriminate and well-nigh incessant fusilade ?

Boers attempt to tamper with them.

On January 29th the ancient 16-pr. justified its resuscitation by forcing a laager at the waterworks to pack up and retire out of reach of its bounding shot. The month closed as it had begun, with a bombardment by every Boer gun, now six in number ; each of them during the morning fired a great number of rounds with little damage to the defence. In the evening, when the light was clear for aiming, Baden-Powell made reply with all his artillery, obtaining such good results with his home-made ammunition, that once more the Boers opened with every piece. On this occasion their 14-pr. Krupp, laid by a sure eye from the heights across the Molopo, placed shells through the very loopholes of the work which covered the Nordenfeldt, which was slightly damaged. Matters were soon equalised by the silencing of a hostile Maxim by the 7-pr. in Fort Ayr. Not until long after dark did the artillery duel cease, one of the last shells from the 94-pr., which burst in the town, killing a civilian in the Market Square. The bombardment was resumed on February 1st, when a shell from the Boer cannon, which fired its nine-hundredth round during the day, penetrated a splinter-proof on Cannon Kopje, killing one and wounding two of the garrison.

February, 1900.

Throughout the month of February there was little to record. Daily and often nightly shelling, sleepless vigilance, and the constant round of duty in the trenches formed the life of the garrison, to whom the siege dragged on only less wearily than to the non-combatants condemned at once to inactivity, discomfort, and danger. The enemy's guns, seldom silent, were often moved. On the 14th the 94-pr. appeared on a fresh position four thousand yards due west, opposite Fort Ayr, a range too great for the old 16-pr., which attempted to engage it. The cannon, however, made such poor practice from its new site that, on the 22nd, it was again dragged to the east of the town, to a work half a mile behind its former emplacement in this quarter. The gun, which was evidently deteriorating, shot with less accuracy and less frequently than formerly; though the women's laager continued to be so much its favourite target that the Boer women themselves indited a joint letter to Snyman, entreating him to spare their place of retreat. On several days the great gun was altogether silent. At one time, towards the end of the month, the battery at Jackal Tree also refrained from firing for nearly a week, and it was thought that the guns had been withdrawn. But a dummy truck, armed with a stove pipe to simulate a gun barrel, which Baden-Powell rolled along the line out of the southern outskirts, soon reawakened the Boer pieces. Joined by the 94-pr. they fired heavily for an hour upon the bait. The garrison had now to husband carefully the artillery ammunition, which was being expended so much faster than it could be replaced, that on February 11th but fifty rounds per gun remained in store. Panzera then applied himself to the manufacture of gunpowder, and was soon successful in producing a quality which gave good results with the 7-prs.

Further artillery make-shifts

THE DEFENCE AND RELIEF OF MAFEKING. 169

Next, in conjunction with Mr. Conolly, of the railway workshops, who was serving as a private in the Bechuanaland Rifles, and Mr. Coughlan of the same department, the resourceful Panzera began the construction of a 5-in. Howitzer, of which the barrel was made of a steel tube strengthened by iron rings shrunken on, the breech-block, trunnions and rings of bronze castings. The weapon, begun in the middle of the month, was ready for trial at the end; and, after one preliminary failure, successfully threw an eighteen-pound spherical shell a distance of four thousand yards. Early in February, Mafeking had received some hint of the probable duration of its time of trial by a message from Cape Town, requesting Baden-Powell to make his food last until the end of May. The inhabitants, therefore, resigned themselves to four more months of incarceration, whilst Baden-Powell became anxious as to the supply. Especially was a shortage to be feared in the foodstuffs for the refugee and non-combatant natives, of whom there were very many. For these there were in hand supplies sufficient to last only to the middle of March, and Baden-Powell determined to make every effort to rid himself of as many mouths as possible. At Kanya, Plumer had already laid down stores sufficient to maintain a large number. (See Chapter VII.) With varying success parties of these natives, rationed for the journey and guarded by armed men through the hostile outposts, were sent out of Mafeking on dark nights. Few got through, less because the enemy discovered them than because of their own fears. Not until much later were any considerable bodies induced to depart for good; and, meanwhile, the support of these outcasts was a heavy drain on the resources of the commissariat.

For some time the chief military interest of the siege had been centred on the brickfields on the east side of the town. There the enemy had drawn closer to the defence than at any other point of the perimeter, and had built a strong fort, armed with a 5-pr. gun. His sharpshooters, riflemen of unerring skill, lay out in front amongst the kilns, and from secure shelter annoyed the town with their marksmanship, and gave no rest to the men who held the British defences facing them. Nor, in

Fighting at the Brick-fields.

truth, did the latter allow any. The Cape Police, under Inspector Marsh, sending bullet for bullet, accounted daily for some of their tormentors. With the Police was a contingent of Cape Boys, under Sergeant Currie, a staunch and aggressive band, endowed with particular hatred of the Boers, and adept in this peculiar fighting, with its interminable watching and waiting, the hasty shot and the no less hasty concealment, which constitutes the normal warfare in trenches in close proximity to a vigilant enemy. In the brickfields especially, was the attack upon the defensive. From the night of FitzClarence's onslaught the uneasiness of the Boers' tenure had been shown by the constant false alarms which at the slightest stir in the British lines, at an unusual light, or for no reason whatever, drew from them thousands of rounds wasted in targetless fusilades. Nevertheless, their presence so close to the town was a real danger, and plans were made to turn them out. On the night of February 1st, Panzera and two others sallied, and blew up with dynamite one of the nearest of the kilns in which marksmen had sheltered. Five days later Sergt.-Major Taylor, a practised scout, headed a small party and blew up another kiln, whilst his men by rapid shooting drove the enemy from a covering trench into one more distant, drawing in reply a tremendous but harmless discharge. The kiln, which was only two hundred yards from the enemy's main trench, was then held and arranged for defence; nor could the practice of three guns, including a 12-pr. Krupp which the Boers brought into use on the 11th and following days, shake the troops from their hold on it.

<small>Feb. 23rd, 1900. Sapping begun there.</small>
On February 23rd Baden-Powell, who had personally reconnoitred the narrow space between the belligerents, ordered sapping operations to be begun towards the fort. The work was placed in charge of Lieut. J. A. P. Feltham, of the Protectorate regiment, and proceeded surely, the diggers trenching from behind the shelter of a steel shield. On the night of February 27th Sergt.-Major Taylor and Private Oliphant made their way from the sap into the enemy's lines, crawled from end to end of a communicating trench, and examined the fort, which they found to be open in rear, but protected in front by a high breast-work, and strongly roofed in

overhead. On the night of March 1st the Boers, who had detected the approach to their redoubt, began to drive a sap southward from it towards the river, and across the front of Taylor's Post (see map No. 52). Baden-Powell immediately ordered a cross sap to be run out from the post, so as to intercept that of the Boers, should it be prolonged. On March 3rd the enemy's trench had come so near that the men therein endeavoured to throw hand grenades towards the Taylor's Post sap. Then, working on under cover of fire from the 94-pr., which kept the troops of the defence to their shelters, they in their turn dug across the British sap, and rendered it untenable for a time by building a loopholed work which raked it from end to end. But the sap itself was then blocked midway by a loopholed wall, behind which a few men maintained themselves only one hundred yards from the enemy. During the firing which accompanied these operations, four of the garrison were wounded, one, the bold Sergt.-Major Taylor, mortally. All night, amidst bursts of firing, the dangerous duel of spades went on. On the morning of March 5th, a slip on the part of the defence all but lost them their advantage. The Cape Boys, who were holding the loopholed wall of the sap, retired from it through misapprehension of an order. In a moment the watchful Boers were at their side of the wall, and, supported by heavy shooting from their works in rear, threw dynamite bombs over the barrier, and plied their rifles through the loopholes. News of this misadventure was quickly in Baden-Powell's hands by means of the telephone which had been established at Currie's Post; and he at once sent reinforcements. Then Feltham, throwing dynamite grenades as he ran, headed some of the Bechuanaland Rifles and Cape Boy corps in a rush against the wall, which was regained after it had been for some hours in the enemy's possession. After this the defence of the brickfields was reorganised into three lines, the whole under FitzClarence; the advanced posts, which were only seventy yards from the enemy, being assigned to Feltham, the second line of separate works to Williams of the B.S.A. Police, and the main trench behind all to Inspector Browne, Cape Police. Only one hundred men could be allotted to this

March, 1900.

March 3rd. Close quarters in the Brickfields.

important quarter, viz.: Twelve Bechuanaland Rifles, thirty-eight Cape Police and fifty Cape Boy corps. The defences were much improved, a loophole made of steel plates, with an aperture of only three inches, contributing greatly to the safety of the sharpshooters. In daylight and darkness the shooting across the brickfields went on, the Boers getting so much the worst of the exchanges that, on March 23rd, they altogether abandoned not only their saps and advanced works, but also the redoubt which had been the base of all their operations in this quarter. It was immediately occupied by the British, who found it to consist of a long and deep trench, completely closed in by a parapet and gorge of earth and sandbags, whilst walls of the same materials divided it laterally into about a dozen bomb-proof chambers, the whole being heavily roofed in by sleepers and rails. In one corner a mine of 250 lbs. of nitro-glycerine was discovered lying in wait for the intruders, the wire of which was safely severed. Baden-Powell ordered that most of the work should be demolished, only one angle being retained as a defensible post for a party of his own men: the post was named Fort Browne. In it two emplacements were then built for the reception of a 7-pr. and Panzera's Howitzer, which were mounted therein on the night of March 25th, to be reinforced on the 27th by the old 16-pr. Their combined fire seriously discomposed the main Boer laager, some four thousand yards to the eastward; and the Boers, who replied with every gun, demonstrated strongly on every side of the town with lines of skirmishers. Simultaneously with their abandonment of Fort Browne, the Boers had evacuated the trench near the Malmani road which had been rushed by Fitz-Clarence on the night of October 27th. Since that event the work had been strengthened on the same plan as Fort Browne; and it was now similarly taken over by the Bechuanaland Rifles, and named after the officer whose onslaught upon it had impressed the enemy more than any incident of the siege. From these evacuations, and other signs, it was plain that the numbers of the investing force had decreased. Nevertheless, Baden-Powell still deprecated any attempt by Plumer to relieve him. He was soon justified by the heavy resistance encountered by

March 23rd, 1900. The Boers abandon the Brickfields.

THE DEFENCE AND RELIEF OF MAFEKING. 173

Plumer, when on March 31st he attempted the reconnaissance from Ramathlabama to be described in Chapter VII. The sharpness of that affair, little lessened by a showy demonstration toward the north made by Baden-Powell himself, proved clearly that to attempt to succour Mafeking with a few hundred men was still impracticable. Up to the end of March the losses in the town by rifle and shell fire numbered 389.*

On April 4th, Lieut. F. Smitheman, an officer from the northern force, made his way into Mafeking, and his report of the numbers and armament of Plumer's contingent confirmed the wisdom of keeping it outside. Smitheman, as described elsewhere, usefully employed his influence with the Mafeking natives by inducing many of them to quit the town, thereby much relieving the commissariat. He returned the way he had come on the night of April 7th. Again the besieged settled down to cope with the monotonous difficulties of their situation. As an instance of these may be noted the explosion, by lightning, of nearly the whole of the carefully laid north-east minefield during a storm at night. The occasional flooding out of trenches and shelters by torrential rains was rendered more serious than an annoyance by the consequent destruction of the rapidly diminishing ammunition.

On April 11th the bombardment, which had been too regular to be described daily, was heavier than at any previous period, eight guns and two Maxims joining in belabouring the town for four hours. Thirty of the 350 shells fired fell into the women's laager. A skirmishing advance of the enemy up the Vryburg road was repulsed with loss by a ruse on the part of the occupants of Fort Abrams, who lured the Boers to close range by feigning to have evacuated their post. On the same night the 94-pr., which had thrown nearly 1,500 shells into Mafeking, disappeared for good from the scene of its failure, and was transported to Pretoria. Further cheer was given to the garrison by a graciously appreciative message from Her Majesty Queen Victoria. Beyond this there was little to lighten the prospect for the besieged. Indeed, relief seemed to be yet further off when

April, 1900.

* For details, see Appendix 5.

on April 20th a telegram was received from Lord Roberts, dated the 9th, warning Baden-Powell that if he had not yet joined hands with Plumer, he must be prepared to make his supplies last even longer than the date previously notified, *i.e.*, May 18th. Again, therefore, Baden-Powell examined his resources. So well had Mafeking been stocked before the investment that the quantity of foodstuffs remaining was still sufficient to banish all fear of starvation. On April 23rd, when a board of officers took stock, there were still in hand breadstuffs (oats and meal) sufficient for fifty-two days, and meat for ninety days; horses, donkeys and mules being counted as available for the latter, in addition to cattle, calves and sheep. These supplies were both augmented and varied by devices of the commander, to whom no detail seemed too trifling or too technical for the application to it of his own never-failing resource. Space fails to tell of his numberless experiments, many of them his own, many incited by the contagion of his inventive genius. The discovery by a Cape boy that brawn was to be made from ox-hides, was promptly applied by Baden-Powell to horse-hide with such success that the new ration was more eagerly sought for than any on the list. Twenty-five pounds of brawn were derivable from two hides. A sausage factory was also instituted, the horses again supplying the material, and the product, one thousand pounds per diem, proved as excellent as the brawn. The horses, which were failing too quickly from lack of proper fodder to be of service in the field, were thus able still to sustain their former riders. A new form of biscuit, a new form of bread, both nutritious though economically manufactured from the inferior materials available, were other inventions; whilst "sowen," a porridge made from damaged oats and spent oat-bran, proved a valuable commodity, especially for native consumption. The troops, indeed, thus assiduously cared for, received rations such as have been rarely enjoyed by men so long besieged. The following was the daily issue per head :—

April 23rd, 1900. Supplies in hand. How augmented.

Meat, 1 lb.
Breadstuffs, 6 oz.
Coffee, 2 oz.

Sugar, 1 oz.
"Sowen," 1 quart.
Vegetables, 2 oz.

THE DEFENCE AND RELIEF OF MAFEKING. 175

Yet with all this, the unceasing round of duty, the constant exposure to weather and danger, and the monotony of their incarceration were beginning to tell their tale upon the garrison. Of actual sickness there was not much;* but there was visible in the ranks that inevitable lassitude of men long confined on low diet, which is dreaded by every commander of a beleaguered place as weakening his power both to parry and to thrust. To troops thus situated alacrity is as necessary as courage; should the first become enervated, a place may be lost even if the latter remain. In this matter, too, Baden-Powell had left nothing undone to keep up the spirits of his men and the townspeople. Exhibitions, competitions of all sorts, sports, races, cricket matches, and even balls, had been held from time to time. These entertainments usually took place on a Sunday; for Sundays were observed as a day of rest by both belligerents, by an informal convention only once broken throughout the siege. This concession, though very generally made by the enemy over all the theatre of war, is one very little to be expected from adversaries less strict in religious observances. It was greatly in favour of the defence, for the army which besieges a town, wars as much against the spirits as the bodies of the troops of the garrison, and by conceding anything which may relieve their mental strain gives away much of the advantage of its situation. Unrelenting pressure may quickly become unendurable; that which is periodically relieved may be borne for ever; and it is not too much to say of Mafeking, as of Ladysmith, that the weekly respite of the defenders went far to build up their resistance of the succeeding six days.

<small>Condition of the garrison.</small>

On April 24th, a young Field Cornet, Eloff by name, joined the Boers around Mafeking with a small force. An impatient and somewhat turbulent officer, and possessed of influence in that he was a grandson of President Kruger, he had long burned to win his spurs; and there seemed no better chance than by rousing the drowsy operations against Mafeking which had become the scorn of the rest of the Boer army. Eloff's advent was marked on the 25th by a combined bombardment,

<small>April 24th, 1900. Field Cornet Eloff joins the investing force.</small>

* For sick returns up to end of April, see Appendix 5.

accompanied by a demonstration which was chilled ere half begun, as others had been, by the silence of the works against which it was directed. Thereafter, though there was daily shelling, and fresh influence was discernible by the violation of the Sabbath truce for the first time on May 6th, the Boers remained in their lines for eighteen days. Then Eloff struck his first and last blow at Mafeking.

May, 1900.

May 12th, 1900. Eloff's attack. Before dawn of day on May 12th, a heavy fire breaking out against the eastern defences caused all the troops to stand to arms. For more than an hour the fusilade continued; but no enemy was visible, there were no indications of an attack, and when it finally died away it seemed as though the display was either the usual abortive demonstration, or a feint to distract attention from some other quarter. Baden-Powell took it to be the latter and from his post at Headquarters had sounded the alarm at the first outbreak, and telephoned to the garrisons of the south-western works to be alert. Scarcely had he done so, when Hore, who was with a small detachment in the fortified barracks of the B.S.A. Police, heard a wild shout at the western end of the native village, and looking out, saw flames leap into the air from the same quarter. Close on this came a message from Godley, who commanded the western defences, calling for the reserve squadron to be sent forward with all speed to Hidden Hollow. Next a crowd of men on foot came running out of the village towards the barracks. In the dim light Hore and his companions mistook them at first for Godley's outposts retiring; not until the hurrying figures were within three hundred yards of the post, and had all but surrounded it, were they seen to be those of Boers; whereupon Hore's party, which consisted of two officers and only fifteen men, poured a rapid fire from the loopholes. Behind the foremost Boers, other bands were visible amongst the huts, very many of which were now in a blaze. The whole village was in the hands of the enemy, and Eloff was at the head of the attack.

His plan of attack. That young officer's long examination of the environs of Mafeking had shown him how best to circumvent the ring of small but apparently formidable works which encircled the place, namely,

THE DEFENCE AND RELIEF OF MAFEKING. 177

by way of the deep-cut bed of the Molopo, which threaded its way through the south-western outposts into the encumbering stadt behind. Could he but scatter a force through the mass of huts, a way would be open for reinforcements, the whole line of British outworks would be turned, and he feared little from the inner line, to which, moreover, the buildings and broken ground afforded a well-covered approach. At moonrise, on the night of May 11th, Eloff had led three hundred burghers of the Marico and Rustenburg commandos, with a few French and German volunteers, down to the Molopo, about a mile beyond the outermost British piquets. Before leaving, he had arranged with Snyman that a feint should be made against the opposite side of Mafeking, extracting from that General, whom he held both in contempt and suspicion, a written promise to reinforce him should he succeed in breaking in, an event of which the flames of the burning native village were to be the signal. Arrived at the river, the Boer leader sent all the horses back to the laager, and then with his band crawled cautiously along the river bed until, without being detected, all were through the outposts and in the village. Eloff himself fired the first hut; others were quickly in a blaze; behind the curtain of smoke and flame which the wind blew before them the burghers filtered through the alleys in three separate parties, the natives scattering in terror before them, until soon after dawn they appeared in front of the barracks of the B.S.A. Police, their presence being at the same time discovered by Godley. The fate of Hore and his posse was quickly decided. Surrounded at point-blank range, and driven from the fort itself into the mess-house at the eastern end, they had nothing to do but surrender or be demolished by a single volley. Eloff then filled the out-buildings with his men, and turned to face the town which " having exasperated and detained the Boer generals for seven months was now about to fall."* He only awaited the promised reinforcements to make a final rush. Meanwhile in the doomed place all was activity. Instantly taking in the situation Baden-Powell issued orders rapidly in all directions. Now appeared

He seizes and sets fire to the Native Village.

Baden-Powell's dispositions.

* Boer account.

the extreme value of the system of telephones which he had so carefully installed. Curiously enough the first message which crossed the lines came from a Boer, who from the captured B.S.A. Police barracks himself informed Headquarters that the building had fallen. The line was then disconnected here and switched on to Godley, who was ordered to close up his outposts so as to shut in the bands occupying the native village, and to prevent them being reinforced from outside. Towards Godley then hastened the reserve squadron of the Protectorate regiment, that of the Bechuanaland Rifles, together with the armed Railway division, and the garrison of the hospital redan. Two of Panzera's guns were moved to the western face of the town; the Town Guard was pushed into the Pound at the south-western angle, whilst from the brickfields and Cannon Kopje the Cape Police and the B.S.A. Police were called into Mafeking to act as reserve. With incredible speed these movements were completed. The soldiers of the garrison, overjoyed to be roused from their enforced lethargy, hastened with more than willingness to the threatened quarter. Their enthusiasm communicated itself to the civilians of the town; men of every grade sprang to arms; many who were unpossessed of weapons found rifle and ammunition thrown into their eager and not unpractised hands, and all hurried after the troops to the defences. Even the military prisoners in the gaol, released and armed for the emergency, stood on guard around their place of penance, and rejoiced that its situation close to the threatened boundary of the town allowed them once more to level their rifles against the enemy. Soon so deadly a musketry issued from the western face of Mafeking into the native village, that the Boers therein found themselves imprisoned in the shelters they had won, and began to look anxiously for the promised support. But they looked in vain. Commandos had indeed followed Eloff, but at a distance; and Godley's prompt consolidation of his outposts had completely cut off the reinforcements from their comrades within. Nor did the former make any strenuous effort to break through the barrier, contenting themselves with sparring so timidly with the uninviting line of works, that FitzClarence,

Enthusiasm of the garrison and townspeople.

THE DEFENCE AND RELIEF OF MAFEKING.

who had led the reserve Protectorate squadron to stiffen Godley's front, found that he was not required, and moved back towards Mafeking for fresh orders, driving some more Boers into the barracks on the way. Now, too, Baden-Powell, informed by telephone of the exact situation in the stadt, and how the Boers, though victorious at the barracks, were separated into different bands, pushed forward his Cape Police and Lieut. Feltham's squadron (" C.") Protectorate regiment past the barracks to the north-eastern edge of the village, thus not only threatening Hore's captors, but keeping back their friends behind. Thus about 8.30 a.m. the attack reached high-water mark. The town and every work about it were fully manned, and secure against storming, though assailed by heavy rifle fire and by that of the enemy's guns which from time to time sent a shower of shells over the defences. The Boers in the stadt could now neither advance nor retire; all their detachments had lost touch, whilst between them and their supports intervened the en- *Eloff's men* trenched array of Godley's outposts. Eloff began to be conscious *isolated.* that he had been betrayed; and his situation was unenviable. Of the force he had led into the village two-thirds were beyond his ken; his own party was still scattered about the precincts of the barracks. Fierce shooting beat upon them from the edge of the town, where the troops and citizens, in high spirits and strengthened by breakfast which Baden-Powell had contrived to distribute, fired with deadly aim at every sign of movement. Worse than this was the absence of water for Eloff's men; the water tanks having been perforated by bullets early in the day. There were many wounded, who would have been altogether neglected had not three of the prisoners themselves, viz.:— Veterinary-Lieutenant Dunlop-Smith, Farrier-Corporal Nichols and Mr. Forbes (Canteen keeper), in response to an appeal by Eloff, devoted themselves not only to attending but even to rescuing men who lay wounded in the open. Still more had both burghers and prisoners of war to thank two ladies, Miss Craufurd and Mrs. Buchan, who were in charge of the neighbouring children's hospital, where they received and cared for many wounded Boers, braved the bullets in search of others, and even carried tea across the dangerous level between the two buildings. In spite of their growing danger the burghers fought on well, the majority, indeed, knowing little of the anxieties which had begun to beset their young leader. Meanwhile, Baden-Powell was devising measures to seal their fate and that of every Boer in the stadt. Telephoning to Godley he ordered him to take command of all the troops then in and about the stadt, that is " A." and " B." squadrons Protectorate regiment, to which Baden-Powell added " D." squadron and a 7-pr. gun which he sent from nearer the town. Godley's first care was reconnaissance. So scattered was the enemy, and so encumbered the ground, that it was difficult to mark definitely any hostile body except that in the Police Barracks. Vigorous scouting, however, which was much assisted by the Barolongs, soon cleared up the situation; and it was found that of the three parties which Eloff had led into the village one had ensconced itself in a stone kraal some 600 yards south-west of the barracks, the second upon a bouldered kopje south of the women's laager at Rowland's house, the third being that which was in the barracks, where Hore and his companions were incarcerated. Godley first undertook the kraal, skilfully manœuvring " B." and " D." squadrons until they had surrounded it, whilst a portion of " A." squadron, under Captain Lord Charles Bentinck (9th Lancers), concealed itself near the river to the west of, that is, behind, the threatened spot. The Boers were then summoned to surrender. They refused, and a brief but intense interchange of musketry followed. The Protectorate men, drawing closer, poured in irresistible volleys, and when, after a few moments, they ran upon the kraal, a white flag went up from the interior. Twenty-seven men gave up their arms; and only the personal intervention of Captain F. C. Marsh, the commander of " B." squadron, was able to save their lives from the enraged Barolongs who had accompanied the attack. The Boers on the kopje, refusing likewise to surrender, declined at the same time to be caught like their comrades. Six rounds of shrapnel from the 7-pr. and a rush by the Protectorate squadrons cleared the knoll before the men could come to close quarters, and the burghers scattered westward towards the outlet by which they had come in. But Bentinck, who had lain *perdu* awaiting this, barred the way, and the trapped fugitives turned upon him with desperate shooting. Bentinck, who had but one weak troop with him, was like to have been roughly handled, when through the telephone he received an order from Baden-Powell himself to draw aside and let the enemy through, whilst Godley by the same means was told to press him hard towards the outlet. Thus Baden-Powell, from his post in the town, was able to issue by the telephonic wire tactical orders direct to two separated officers at the very height of a *mêlée* more easily than those officers could repeat them to their own men in the uproar. The Boers then fled away from one party and past the other, suffering severely as they did so. Meanwhile the situation of those at the barracks had been momentarily growing worse. Many of their number, unable to endure longer hunger and thirst and the searching fire, had vanished to the rear, and by dusk, of the 243 burghers whom Eloff had led into the fort, less than 70 exhausted men remained. Until dark these clung to their post. Finally, about 6 p.m., Hore received the surrender of the Field Cornet whose prisoner he had been for more than twelve hours. Five officers and 68 men gave up their arms; and if their defeat was embittered by the knowledge that they had been abandoned by their general, it was enlightened by the admiration of their captors for the gallant part they had played. In all the Boers lost this day some 60 killed and wounded and 108 prisoners, at a cost to the defence of but 4 killed and 10 wounded of white troops, and 8 killed and 10 wounded amongst the natives. *Eloff surrenders.*

Eloff's throw for Mafeking, had it succeeded, had but been made just in time. On May 15th Baden-Powell heard that a column was marching to his relief from the south and was already past Vryburg. As ready as ever to strike, he at once ordered a mobile force of 220 men and two guns to prepare to sally out to co-operate. The relief column in question consisted of 1,100 men and four guns* under Colonel B. Mahon, *May 15th, 1900. News of a relief column.*

* For state, see Appendix 5.

and its origin, and adventures on the march to Mafeking, must be briefly mentioned. Starting from Barkly West* on May 4th, Mahon's column, an offshoot from the force of Sir A. Hunter, followed the line of the Harts river, the enemy, many of whom were near at hand at first, being kept from interfering by Sir A. Hunter's brilliant engagement at Rooidam on the 5th.† The Boers followed Mahon nevertheless, only to find themselves for once quite outmarched, and their several attempts to intercept him many hours too late. On the 7th Mahon was near Taungs, eighty-four miles from his starting-point, on the 9th at Vryburg, and on the 12th about six miles to the west of Motsitlani. Ascertaining here that a strong hostile body, come down from Mafeking, was lying in wait for him across the direct road to Sanie and Mafeking, Mahon on the 13th began a *détour* towards the west which he hoped would carry him past the enemy and bring him abreast of Mafeking at Massibi. The Boers, discovering his change of direction, attacked him sharply at 4 p.m., in bush so thick that his advance guard ran right into the enemy, and for a moment was thrown back. Rallying speedily, the Imperial Light Horse, fresh from the hard-fought fields of Natal, advanced on foot, and after a spirited skirmish cleared the enemy from the road with the loss of thirty-one killed and wounded, in a little more than an hour's close fighting. The Boers lost about the same numbers and drew off altogether. At 5.30 a.m. on May 15th Mahon gained his point at Massibi, having covered more than 230 miles in twelve days with a large convoy through a country so inhospitable that the Boers were to be counted as enemies less formidable than the drought and dust which dogged each day's march. At Massibi junction with Plumer was effected (see Chapter VII); and next day joint operations were undertaken for the immediate relief of the invested town. Mahon, who was in command, formed the combined forces into two brigades, placing his own troops under Lieut.-Colonel A. H. M. Edwards, of the Imperial Light Horse, whilst Plumer remained at the head of the corps which he had led from the banks of the Limpopo down to Ramathlabama. Thus organised, the column advanced

* See map No. 43.   † See page 110.

THE DEFENCE AND RELIEF OF MAFEKING. 183

towards Mafeking along the north (right) bank of the Molopo; Plumer, who sent two squadrons of the B.S.A. Police as right flank-guard across the river, moving on the right of Edwards; the convoy following in rear midway between both. The Boers were now thoroughly aroused, and much mystified by the union of these two bodies from opposite directions. Nevertheless they were still in high hopes, for "the hero,"* General De la Rey, had arrived on the field, and his orders were in cheering distinction from those of the vacillating and incapable Snyman. *General De la Rey arrives before Mafeking.*

De la Rey, assuring his burghers that "all would go well," arranged an enveloping attack, and with more than two thousand men and seven guns at his disposal, drew a formidable semicircle between Mahon and Mafeking. Soon after noon, when the advancing columns were abreast of Sanie, the action began, the outer wings of both brigadiers coming under fire simultaneously. But Mahon, though he could only make way slowly, was never checked. First Edwards, seeing on the left high ground which he thought to be outside the enemy, galloped for it with three squadrons, and gained the top just as the Boers, who had also raced for the point of vantage, reached the foot of the slopes on the other side, where they were immediately met at medium range and driven back. Edwards then sent for the guns of the Royal Horse artillery, and until their arrival was smartly shelled by a 12-pr. Krupp and a Vickers-Maxim. About 2.30 p.m. a strong commando moved to encircle him on the left, a misapprehension of the flank-guard on that side, who mistook the body of horsemen for Plumer's squadrons, allowing the enemy to make some progress around the flank. The despatch of supports soon checked the Boers, who were far from venturesome; and on the arrival of the artillery Edwards ordered a general advance, which forced them back all along his front. Edwards then took up the chase, broke up all opposition, and before 6 p.m. a patrol of the Imperial Light Horse under Major Karri Davis rode into Mafeking, just as a few weeks earlier they had been first to enter Ladysmith. Meanwhile Plumer on the right had had to fight for every yard of the way towards the town, the *Operations outside Mafeking.*

* Boer account.

enemy in front of him taking up position after position, trying every wile to entrap his foremost line. In this at times they almost succeeded. Plumer's casualties were numerous, amongst them falling Major W. D. Bird, who was wounded in seven places. At Israels Farm Plumer was stoutly opposed, a gun and a Vickers-Maxim checking his advance. Mahon sent thither the Royal Horse artillery, who quickly silenced the gun; but the Maxim was inextinguishable, and Mahon ordered forward his infantry detachment under Captain C. C. Carr (Royal Fusiliers) to attack the farm. This was done with great success; the wagon of the Maxim and all its ammunition were captured, and the gun itself was only missed owing to the gathering darkness covering its flight. When all opposition ceased Mahon collected his forces, and rested them prior to advancing finally on Mafeking, which was now seven miles distant. At 12.30 a.m., after carefully reconnoitring the road, he resumed his march, and at 3.30 a.m. on May 17th the column, much exhausted, entered Mafeking.

May 17th, 1900. Relief of Mafeking.

Thus was succoured a place, which originally unfortified, open and unfavourably situated, had withstood with small losses* for 217 days an unremitting investment and a bombardment during which more than twenty thousand projectiles had fallen amongst the defenders. So remarkable an achievement may well produce effects far greater than the actual military gain resulting from it. The latter, indeed, was not momentous; nor could it be. The general who accepts investment, even on so great a scale as Masséna at Genoa, or Bazaine in Metz, inevitably assumes a *rôle* secondary to one who preserves his freedom. If the siege of Mafeking had not been able to absorb sufficient numbers of the enemy to retard seriously the course of the main Federal campaign—as Ladysmith had gone further to do in Natal—it had yet detained many, and had in short justified every reason which had induced Baden-Powell originally to resign himself to it. But more than this; the long struggle to hold and reduce the town had been a combat of sentiment which had little relation to the value of the prize itself. The issue was a triumph and defeat for a greater thing than arms.

Considerations on the siege.

* For total casualties during siege, see Appendix 5.

THE DEFENCE AND RELIEF OF MAFEKING.

Nothing in war is more impressive than a prolonged siege, whether the respective armies be actually engaged in it or only distant spectators. More than a heroic charge, or a pitched battle, does the long-drawn catalogue of the defence's perpetual resistance, disregarded danger and hardship, unquenchable resource and cunning, strike the imagination, until their mere continuance becomes a victory to the side of the defence and a festering sore in that of the attack. The leader who draws up his troops before a place of arms, tacitly promises them its capture; and failure entails a dangerous loss of confidence not only in their own power but in his. Thus so low fell the *moral* of some of Snyman's best commandos after Mafeking was relieved, that they openly mutinied, refusing longer to serve under a leader who had played them false. Finally, the retention of the town, together with the success at Kimberley, had a peculiar significance; for Cronje's commandos had the mortification of witnessing the two chief places of the district which their leader had by proclamation "annexed," maintaining their integrity though superior numbers, armament, positions and mobility did their worst against them.

CHAPTER VII.

COLONEL PLUMER'S OPERATIONS IN RHODESIA.*

For reasons previously given (Volume I., page 36) the British Government had from the first recognised the impossibility of setting apart a large force for a serious defence of Rhodesia. Only Colonel Baden-Powell's levies could be spared in this direction, a force so weak, so hastily enrolled, trained, and equipped, and so certain to be isolated, that it seemed as though nothing but exceptional resource on the part of its leaders could allow it to be of any service, or even save it from destruction. Of such resource the disposition of the handful at the outbreak of war gave early evidence. At Mafeking Baden-Powell had placed himself, courting investment even more deliberately than Sir G. White in Ladysmith, as being the only method of detaining a large number of the enemy from raiding down the open roads into the Colony.

At that time Lieut.-Colonel H. C. O. Plumer, with the Rhodesia regiment, was on the march from Buluwayo to Tuli, prepared for the threefold task of watching the border, co-operating with Baden-Powell, and playing on the nerves of the Transvaal by incursions across her northern frontier.

For a full exposition of Baden-Powell's plan of campaign the reader is referred to Chapter VI. It need only be pointed out again how daring was his very presence so far north of the Orange river; how effectually at Mafeking he threatened the heart of the northern Republic at the moment when it

---

* See General Map of South Africa in Volume I. map-case. Any names not shown thereon are described relative to places which are marked upon the map.

beat most confidently; and, finally, how the manipulation of Plumer's contingent made that hostile State raise a guard also towards its unprotected head.

At a period when the art of war seemed to have not yet re-awakened in the British councils, such adroit tactics, waiting on strategy so bold, were as remarkable, despite the smallness of the scale and scope of each, as they will be seen to have been successful. Plumer's orders, received from Baden-Powell, were as follows:— Colonel Plumer's orders.

"The duty of the force under your command is:—

"1. To defend the border as far as it can be carried out from the neighbourhood of Tuli as a centre.

"2. By display of strength to induce the Boers to detail a strong force to protect their northern district.

"3. To create diversions in the north of the Transvaal, co-operating with the invasion of the south by our main force, if necessary advancing into the Transvaal for the purpose. No portion of your force is to cross the frontier till you receive orders. Instructions will be sent to you as to the date for co-operation with the other column."

Plumer's command consisted at first of five squadrons of the Rhodesia regiment, and about one hundred men of the British South Africa Police, with the following semi-obsolete artillery: One $12\frac{1}{2}$-pr. Maxim Nordenfeldt, two $2\frac{1}{2}$-in. muzzle-loading screw guns, and two .45 Martini-Henry Maxim guns on Naval carriages. Later on, as will be seen, this force received additional strength; but during October, when the initiative lay with the enemy, when all seemed uncertain except the perilous predicament of British rule in South Africa, the discrepancy between Plumer's force and the task which it was enjoined to perform was striking enough. To "defend a border" as long as the railway from London to Aberdeen, to "display strength," and to "create diversions," with one weak regiment composed of novices, these were orders which nothing but success could justify. What force the enemy would detach against Plumer could not be guessed. It was characteristic of the boldness of the scheme that the larger the numbers he could draw upon his little band, the better would he effect his purpose.

<small>Oct. 14th, 1899. Plumer at Tuli.</small>

On October 14th Mafeking was shut up; and Plumer, who concentrated at Tuli on the same day, found himself with only five hundred men on a frontier as many miles in length. Across his front, flowing down the second great fissure of the upper tableland, stretched the river Limpopo, separating Rhodesia from the Transvaal. Around its vast arc, from Mafeking to the Portuguese border, watch was to be kept under conditions which might well have seemed impossible. The stream, as variable as any of the mercurial waterways of South Africa, though never dry, was passable at almost any point except during the brief seasons of flood. The woods and thickets of

<small>Difficulties of country</small>

thorn which fringed its banks made reconnaissance difficult and surprise easy. Dense bush, interspersed with craggy kopjes, hampered movement north of the river, which here and there spread into swamps, as fruitful in sickness to Europeans as in mealies to the natives who cultivated their margins.

On their side of the Limpopo the Boers had even greater difficulties to contend with than their opponents. Between the south bank of the river and the Blaauwberg and Zoutpansberg mountains lay that strange region of salt "pans," and of gigantic trees (baobab) bearing fruit as acrid as the waters which nourished them. This belt of country was in reality as effective a protection to Rhodesia as the Karroos to Cape Colony. Almost waterless in winter, and in the summer permeated by the noxious exhalations from the saline ponds, important military operations were well-nigh impossible, and, as will be seen, even on a small scale, proved too much for both belligerents.

In the matter of munitions, Plumer had at first the advantage of his opponents, inasmuch as six weeks' supplies had been collected at Tuli before his arrival. When, however, the western line ceased to be available, an arrangement of extra-

<small>and of supply.</small>

ordinary difficulty had to be adopted. Supplies had then to be sent by sea from Durban to Beira, conveyed thence by rails of different gauges to Marandellas, on the Sabi River railway;

thence to Buluwayo by wagon, and again by the same slow process on to Tuli and the front, a distance of 450 miles over tracks of the roughest description. The difficulties attending this transport, surely almost unique in its complexity, were ably overcome by Colonel J. S. Nicholson, Commandant-General of the British South Africa Police, who acted as base commandant at Buluwayo. The Boers, on the other hand, who drew upon Pietersburg for sustenance, though they bewailed the "fearful length"* of their communications, had to traverse less than 150 miles from base to front; yet, in truth, the tract to be covered offered almost every obstacle to transport by draught. From the outset, too, they were prejudiced by the incompetence of their leaders; and, in their inhospitable terrain, were haunted by fears alike of fever, of drought, and of an onslaught by the natives of Bechuanaland. Thus both sides, though neither was fully aware of the other's difficulties, laboured under disabilities which deprived them of the power to venture far afield into hostile territory.

Plumer's first care was for the drifts covering Tuli. Six vulnerable points existed, viz. (from east to west):—(a) Baine's Drift, to the west of the Maklutsi river; (b) the junction of the Maklutsi and Limpopo; (c) the Pont by which the road from Baine's Drift along the south bank was carried across the river; (d) Rhodes Drift, twenty miles due south of Tuli; (e) the junction of the Shashi and the Limpopo; (f) Masibi Drift, twenty-five miles east of Rhodes Drift, and (g) Middle Drift, fifteen miles east of Masibi. Though the enemy had reached the line of the river on October 16th—his vedettes at the Pont even shouting across in the night their intention to come over next day—Plumer's force was too weak to enable him to hold all these passages. Leaving a squadron of the Rhodesia regiment with the British South Africa Police in Tuli, he at first posted one squadron at the Shashi junction, keeping three others together on some kopjes a mile north of Rhodes Drift,

Plumer's dispositions.

---

* Letter from Assistant-General Grobelaar to the Government, Pretoria, November 11th, 1899.

the river bank itself there and at the Pont being indefensible. A squadron which had started for the Maklutsi junction was recalled on the Boers showing, in number about five hundred, opposite the Pont. They, too, had established themselves a mile from the bank, their position being ascertained by a patrol on the 18th. Another reconnaissance by a small party on October 22nd was roughly handled, being hustled back to the river with the loss of an officer (Captain L. D. Blackburn, Scottish Rifles), several men, and horses. Meanwhile reports had come in of the approach of the enemy in strength on both sides; on the west by way of Selika towards Palapye, and from Brack River to Masibi Drift on the east. The former place was out of reach; and though a reconnaissance of Masibi on the 19th discovered no Boers to be yet in that direction, all information pointed to an augmentation of the enemy to about 1,700 men along the frontier. The manœuvring was thus bearing good fruit; but in country so blind as the Limpopo valley they who play the part of lure run the greater risks the more successful their deception; and on October 22nd, Plumer, fearing lest his squadrons at Rhodes Drift should be cut off from their base, ordered them to fall back on Tuli. This was done during the night.

On the 24th Plumer, receiving reiterated warnings of a threat to Palapye, despatched a squadron (Captain K. MacLaren) to Maklutsi village, to remain in observation of the western section of the native border. Simultaneously, however, it was reported that the Boers in front of him, so far from advancing, had withdrawn the bulk of their forces towards Pietersburg. Thereupon, on October 27th, a squadron (Lieut.-Colonel J. A. Spreckley) was sent to reoccupy the drifthead at Rhodes Drift; another squadron (Major W. D. Bird) proceeding to the Maklutsi confluence, where a post was established under the imposing wall of rock which here overhangs the river bed. A reconnaissance across the river at the Pont disclosed the enemy still in occupation of their kopjes, though apparently in diminished numbers, the patrol losing four men as it returned. Both the Shashi and Maklutsi posts meanwhile remained clear, so far as could be ascertained by the little scouting possible.

However, the crisis of the situation, such as it was, was only now about to develop. Plumer, in his *rôle* of borderer, was meeting with more success than he imagined. From the outset the Boers had been actuated by a very real fear of invasion from the north, a fear increased by Plumer's skilful disguise of his weakness, and the topographical difficulties of reconnoitring him. The dread, too, of an incursion by the regiments of the native Chieftains, Khama and Linchwe, whose hostility to the Republics was notorious, was ever present with the northern commandos. To meet both dangers, the entire Zoutpansberg commando, 1,300 men, with three guns, under Van Rensburg, had proceeded early in October to the Brack river, thirty miles south of Rhodes Drift, where was established the advanced post whose skirmishes with Plumer's patrols have been related. At the same time, Assistant-General Grobelaar, the commander of the whole military district, had himself taken nearly six hundred men, with two guns, to the confluence of the Palala river and the Limpopo, that is, opposite Selika, with the double object of watching the natives and maintaining touch with a Boer post which was in occupation of Sekwani, some 140 miles to the south, on the Marico river, abreast of Gaberones. He was thus exactly midway between Sekwani and Rhodes Drift, and could reinforce either. Hearing of the retirement of Plumer's squadrons from Rhodes Drift—the natives meanwhile appearing inert—Grobelaar, with an eye to taking the offensive, despatched 160 picked men with one gun to join the Zoutpansbergers, remaining himself at Selika.

His success in impressing the enemy.

On November 2nd the commando, about four hundred men, with two guns, suddenly crossed the river at Rhodes Drift. Circling round Spreckley's squadron, which was stationed a mile north of the drift, the Boers then bore down on Tuli. Between that place and the river, and four miles north of the latter, stood a building called Bryce's Store, where a convoy of eight wagons for Spreckley, escorted by twenty-six men, had just arrived. It was immediately attacked by overwhelming numbers, and

Nov. 2nd, 1899. The Boers cross the Limpopo.

captured after a gallant resistance, the escort losing their officer, a chaplain* and six men prisoners. The remainder, of whom four were wounded, scattered and made their escape to Tuli. The Boers then turned on Spreckley. His position was critical in the extreme. His line of retreat was cut off, his defences exposed in rear, and though cover was found for the men, nearly all his animals were soon killed by shell fire, and escape seemed impossible. The Boers, however, considering the squadron as now practically taken, contented themselves with shooting, and made no attempt to close. Until nightfall Spreckley's men lay motionless. Then, stealing through the bush, they made down-stream for Masibi Drift, struck northward there, passed clear around the Boers in the dark, and on the morning of November 3rd arrived safely at Tuli, bereft of everything but their rifles. In this affair the Boers, who had lost three men, took nine wagons, seventy horses, and one hundred mules, the additional wagon being that of Major Bird's detachment at the Maklutsi confluence, which had been sent in to refill.

Escape of the British outpost.

Next morning the Boers shelled Spreckley's evacuated position until noon, when, discovering the bird had flown, they desisted, and set about entrenching themselves at Bryce's Store. Tuli seemed now to be in considerable danger; and Plumer, recalling Bird, concentrated in daily expectation of attack. Its delay was more unaccountable to the British than to their opponents. Mismanagement, timidity, and divided counsels reigned supreme in the Zoutpansberg laager. The Boer leaders, having allowed what was already in their grasp to escape, were little fitted to lay hands on prizes farther away. Failing totally, indeed, to grasp the true object of their presence on the northern frontier, they knew not whether to advance or retire; their troubles being intensified by the difficulties of the region in which they found themselves. It was not until Grobelaar himself, wearying of inaction at Selika, came up along the river with nearly four hundred men, that spirit was infused into the operations. Thoroughly comprehending his mission, he came with a vigorous conception. This was nothing less than

Plumer concentrates at Tuli.

---

* The chaplain, the Rev. J. W. Leary, was released on arrival at Pretoria.

the capture of the forces at Tuli, followed by the destruction of the western railway line,* measures which, if successful, would assuredly have laid at his mercy the British frontier, and safeguarded his own. The plan, however, was promptly vetoed by his Government. The danger to the Republics, wrote the State Secretary,† lay clearly not in the north, but in Natal and Cape Colony where the British armies were mustering. Grobelaar must let Tuli go, and content himself with observing the line of the river with three detachments of four hundred men apiece, each with a gun, to be placed :—(a) near the Saltpan below the Zoutpansberg; (b) on the Palala river, opposite Selika; (c) on the Matlabas river (a branch stream opposite Palla), thus connecting by a chain of patrols the post at Sekwani with that at Rhodes Drift, nearly three hundred miles distant. Grobelaar was even deprived of the five hundred men remaining over after this arrangement, they being ordered to ride at once for Pretoria. Thus it was that the expected blow did not fall upon Tuli. Subsequently the Boer detachments were still further reduced; and by November 27th it seemed to Plumer as though the main body had fallen back altogether. Bryce's Store, Rhodes Drift and the Pont were alike evacuated; there were no Boers reported at Middle Drift, Masibi Drift, Baine's Drift or the Shashi and Maklutsi confluences. Opposite Selika only was there any strength, and a remnant of the retiring force was said to have lingered on the Brack river.

<small>Grobelaar's aggressive plans.</small>

<small>He is forbidden to carry them out.</small>

In order to clear up the situation, on December 1st Plumer led a reconnaissance across the river towards Pietersburg. He found the country clear down to the Brack river, and a sufficient reason—if none other had existed—for the departure of the enemy, in the total absence of water, which compelled him to return after an exhausting march. He had now to reconsider his position. The Boers had gone, and with them his occupation. Three courses were open to him; one to follow

<small>Dec. 1st, 1899. Plumer discovers the Boer retreat.</small>

* Letter from Assistant-General Grobelaar to Government, Pretoria, November 13th, 1899.

† Letter from State Secretary, Pretoria, to Assistant-General Grobelaar, November 13th, 1899.

them to Pietersburg ; another to repair to the western line and endeavour to open communication with, if not relieve, Mafeking. The third alternative, that of abiding blindly by his original instructions, and remaining where he was, was at once dismissed. Whilst he considered, the Limpopo itself practically decided his action by coming down in flood (December 6th), threatening to cover the drifts with many feet of roaring water. Next, the Pont, under the circumstances the only available means of transit, was found to be rotten and unserviceable ; and to repair it, or construct rafts, would take a fortnight. Pietersburg, then, was out of the question. Even supposing the river could be crossed, there would lie between him and Pietersburg 135 miles of tracks deep either in sand or mud, according to the weather ; and it would take another nine days to reach the town. Finally, Pietersburg did not seem to offer any telling objective ; and it was certain that his force could not stay there for want of supplies. In all these circumstances Plumer decided to transfer his force from Tuli to the western line, *viâ* Palapye to Mochudi. There were, indeed, other reasons for such a movement, besides the above and the desire to assist Mafeking. For their inception it is necessary to revert to an earlier period.

He decides to leave the line of the Limpopo.

Ever since the beginning of the war, Colonel Nicholson had maintained troops on the western line, which, by means of armoured trains, patrolled and repaired the line from Magalipsi (opposite Selika) southward, and endeavoured as far as possible to preserve the integrity of the native boundaries. In this they were not, as, indeed, they could not be, entirely successful. The Boers, who lived in daily fear of a native rising, went far to foment what their leaders sincerely desired to avert by repeated acts of aggression, firing on parties of native labourers, looting kraals, and even on one occasion shelling a kopje well within the confines of the neutral territory (November 7th). The native chiefs' conviction that they were to be invaded was thus strengthened ; and, pinning their allegiance to the British, they responded by massing their fighting men opposite the Boer detachments, and preparing to defend their frontiers. Further quarrels then arose about the use of water supply, about natives

The Native question in the west.

who had been taken prisoners, about the robbery of horses, and other matters.

So high rose the mutual exasperation that on November 10th, Segali, the brother of Linchwe, requested permission to fall upon the Boer laager at Sekwani. This was refused by the Administrator. On the 22nd, Colonel G. L. Holdsworth, who had arrived to take command at Magalipsi on the 4th, having obtained information about the laager in question, in his turn asked leave to attack it, which was granted. To assist him, he was further authorised to make use of Linchwe's men, their co-operation being intended to be confined to services as guides and transport assistants. Although this limitation was not made clear in the telegraphic instructions sent to Holdsworth, that officer, during an interview with the natives prior to the affair, impressed on them the necessity of their remaining on their own side of the border, and that they were not to fire unless ordered. Early on the morning of November 25th, Holdsworth, who had been much misled as to the strength and position of the Boer laager, delivered his attack. At the first shots Linchwe's men got out of hand, crossed the Marico, and firing wildly in all directions, got in front of Holdsworth and ruined his plans. They then attacked the laager, killing some of the enemy, and finally looted the few houses which were scattered along the valley. Holdsworth, therefore, relinquished his attempt, and returned to Mochudi, where the armoured train awaited him.*

Nov. 25th, 1899.
The affair at Sekwani.

After this unfortunate occurrence, the friction between Boers and natives naturally increased. On November 30th the Boers shelled the native village of Sekwani, which lay on the left bank of the Marico. Then, in the first week of December, when tidings of the affair of the 25th had reached Nylstroom, the whole of the Waterberg commando, six hundred in number, under Commandant Lombard, were despatched from that place on a punitive expedition.

* For full accounts of this incident, and the correspondence prior and subsequent to it, see Volume of South African Telegrams—No. 634, Colonial Office, September, 1901, pp. 81, 235, *et seq.*

On December 18th they attacked and burned the native village, losing eight men, and slaying many of the blacks in a fierce fight around the drift. They then threatened Mochudi, Linchwe's capital, where Holdsworth still was with two hundred of the Southern Rhodesia Volunteers. In the face of the Boer success at Sekwani, Holdsworth, if unsupported, would be compelled to fall back 120 miles to Magalipsi, that being the nearest watering place; the territories of Linchwe and Khama would be open to the Boers; the line would be destroyed, and the difficulty of opening communication with Mafeking doubled.

<small>Dec. 18th, 1899. The Boers retaliate.</small>

Immediately on receipt of this news, Plumer—who had meanwhile again reconnoitred the Pietersburg road, finding no enemy within thirty-five miles of the river—ordered eighty-five men of MacLaren's squadron at Maklutsi village to march at once for Palapye, whence they would proceed by train to Mochudi. He himself prepared to follow with the remainder of his force, which at this time numbered in all 480 men with 400 horses. As Tuli and Rhodes Drift could not be left unguarded, he decided to leave at the former place 120 men with a 12½-pr. Field gun and a Maxim; at Maklutsi twenty men would remain from the departing squadron. On December 27th and the four following days the force set out in small detachments on a march of 175 miles to Palapye. The operation, which in inexperienced hands might have resulted in confusion, was smoothly carried out. Owing to the fatal effects of the sun on draught oxen in this region, the parties marched only in the cool of the early morning and late evening. As they drew westward the country became easier, the dense bush giving place to more open country about Maklutsi, whence, on approaching Khama's country, it expanded again into broad and breezy uplands which were welcome indeed to men who had been stifling in the bush of the Limpopo. At Palapye the entraining operations, admirably organised, caused no delay; and by January 10th, 1900, the whole force had reached a point 22 miles north of Mochudi, that is, some 160 miles from Mafeking.

<small>Dec. 27th, 1899. Plumer marches for the west.</small>

On his arrival Plumer found the situation as follows:—At

PLUMER'S OPERATIONS IN RHODESIA. 197

Sekwani, forty miles to the east, some two hundred Boers with two small guns were occupying fortified ridges on either bank of the Marico river. These were of the original post at that place, the Waterbergers having been summoned southward after their act of vengeance. Another party of two hundred to three hundred men of the Rustenburg commando, with one 75 m/m. ($12\frac{1}{2}$-pr.) Vickers-Maxim, a Vickers-Maxim automatic, and a machine gun, were covering the railway station and water supply at Crocodile Pools, nine miles south of Gaberones. These were an advanced party of the main Rustenburg laager, which, lying three miles to the south, towards Ramutsa, relied for support on the commandos investing Mafeking, seventy-eight miles distant. Plumer had now, after his junction with Nicholson's detachment, about one thousand men under his command (of whom about 750 were available for operations), with one 2.5-in. gun, one 7-pr. (black powder) and two Maxims; he had also two fighting trains, one armoured, the other partially so. On January 13th—15th he pushed his force forward to Gaberones, occupied the fort and station, and on the 17th established an advanced post of 240 men of the Rhodesia regiment, under Major Bird, on a line of kopjes about six miles south of Gaberones, covering a demolished iron railway bridge upon which repairs were commenced soon after. Here Bird was in touch with the foremost Rustenburgers, who for the next few days shelled his sangars steadily but harmlessly with their Field guns. Beyond this nothing occurred until January 23rd, when Bird, reinforced by one hundred men, issued from his lines at 3 a.m., drove in the enemy's outposts, and endeavoured to look into his works. Heavy rain, however, frustrated his purpose; and Bird returned without loss, though shells fell amongst his men. Next day a $12\frac{1}{2}$-pr. gun, similar to that used by the enemy, arrived from Tuli, another 2.5-in. gun coming to hand on the 28th. Bomb-proofs having been constructed, on the 31st a duel ensued with the Boer pieces which, though the fort which contained them was slightly damaged, had the better of things from the superiority of their ammunition, Plumer's proving defective.

On February 4th the largest Boer gun was struck by a

The situation in the west.

Jan. 13th, 1900. Plumer at Gaberones.

shell which silenced it for six days. On the 5th Plumer, who was in frequent communication with Baden-Powell, received information that bodies of the enemy were leaving Mafeking to reinforce those at Crocodile Pools. He, therefore, made arrangements to attack the latter before they could be strengthened. But two attempts to sally from his lines were prevented by torrential rains; and on the 7th the Boer reinforcements arrived, in number two hundred to three hundred men. Nevertheless, Plumer, preferring to make rather than await attack, persisted in his plan; and on the night of the 11th despatched two hundred men (140 Rhodesia regiment, 30 of the Southern Rhodesia Volunteers, 30 British South Africa Police), under Bird, to attack the fort. Bird, who had closely reconnoitred the approaches, set out at 11 p.m.; and at 3.45 a.m. on the 12th deployed his party at the foot of the kopje undetected. The dense bush and enormous boulders which covered the knoll broke up his formation from the outset; during the climb the men lost touch with their officers and each other, and only about fifty arrived with Bird near the top, where the glacis had been cleared. Meanwhile the Boers had awakened, and fired furiously. Their volleys tore through the thickets of undergrowth, the dark recesses of which flashed with innumerable sparks as the bullets smote the concealed rocks. A mine, too, laid some distance down the hillside, exploded with a vivid flame and loud report, fortunately after all had passed it by; and thereafter the Boers depressed the muzzle of their Field piece, and hurled down shell into the peopled bush almost at their feet. But Bird, undaunted, attempted still to rush the fort, followed by the few who had succeeded in forcing their way upward. Ten yards from the work a barbed wire had been stretched. Here, of the four officers who accompanied him, one (Captain S. G. French, Royal Irish regiment) was killed and two others wounded; and Bird, seeing that but some half-dozen soldiers were now with him, realised that his enterprise had failed, and ordered all to the foot of the hill. Under the gusts of firing which swept through the bush, he rallied his bewildered men, and led them from the place, regaining his lines at 6 a.m.

Feb. 11th, 1900. Attack on a Boer fort.

PLUMER'S OPERATIONS IN RHODESIA. 199

with the loss of an officer and four men killed, two officers and sixteen men wounded, and five missing. Of the latter three were wounded, and after being handed over by the enemy, subsequently died.

Four days later the Boers in their turn took the offensive, shelling the British trenches so rapidly that an attack seemed imminent. The expectation was strengthened by the discovery of a strong band concealed behind a kopje well in advance of their own lines on Plumer's right flank. The demonstration came to nothing, however, and the enemy fell back. Plumer had now begun to fear that the forces opposed to him were strong enough to bar the direct road to Mafeking. He had early foreseen the possibility of such a contingency, and to meet it had arranged with a local chief, Bathoen by name, to facilitate the concentration of supplies at his capital, Kanya, a considerable settlement of the Bangwaketse tribe, lying some seventy-five miles north-west of Mafeking. By adopting this village as a base, it might be possible to turn the Boers at Ramutsa, and assist Mafeking in spite of them. Thither on February 12th proceeded a convoy of ten wagons, followed by eleven more on the 17th, and by a further sixteen on the 20th. By that time the enemy had got an inkling of the project, and despatched a force ten miles westward to intercept any further convoys. Kanya was now, however, almost sufficiently supplied; and on February 25th the Boers, realising that they had been outwitted, abandoned all their positions north of Ramutsa, and retired to Lobatsi, thirty miles south of that place. Plumer, first forwarding one more convoy to Kanya, immediately followed up the enemy; and on March 6th was at Lobatsi, which was evacuated before his arrival. Here he learned that, except for a party of two hundred to three hundred, laagered about twenty miles north-east, under Schwartz, all the commandos had retired on Mafeking. He then felt his way still further southward; and on March 13th his advance guard, under Lieut.-Colonel W. Bodle, came once more in touch with the enemy at Pitsani Bakluku (Pothlugo).

Plumer establishes an auxiliary base.

March 6th, 1900. Plumer at Lobatsi.

His movements were now causing serious alarm to the Boer

forces which were engaged in investing Mafeking; and Snyman, ordering Schwartz to co-operate, sent a strong detachment northward. On March 15th Bodle's advance guard was sharply attacked and retired to Lobatsi with seven casualties. The Boers pushing on, then shelled Lobatsi,* which they endeavoured to surround. Next day, Schwartz moved in with his band towards the line, and made as if to get between Lobatsi and Ramutsa. Now Lobatsi, lying in a hollow encircled by hills, was unfavourable for defence; or if defended, would so lock up the whole available force as to render all further advance impossible. Plumer, therefore, desiring above all things to preserve his freedom, decided to get clear whilst he could. At this juncture the value of the auxiliary base at Kanya became apparent. Sending Holdsworth up the line, with 350 men, a $12\frac{1}{2}$-pr. and a 7-pr. gun to block the railway at Crocodile Pools, Plumer himself with 560 men, two 2.5-in. guns and a Maxim, drew aside to Kanya, intending thence to descend again upon Mafeking by Moshwane and the Molopo river. The manœuvre was safely effected by both detachments during the night of March 16th, the Boers knowing so little of it that they bombarded the empty position at Lobatsi all the next morning. On ascertaining the facts, they returned to Mafeking. On the evening of March 19th Plumer set out again for Mafeking. On the 21st he reached a point (Sefetili) five miles south of Moshwane, and thirty miles north-west of Mafeking. Here he entrenched his force, and threw out patrols to Ramathlabama, Pitsani and Jan Massibi's, finding no enemy at any of these places. He was still in constant communication with Baden-Powell,† to whom, on the 23rd, he sent a message offering, if need be, to advance at once. In his reply, received five days later, Baden-Powell stated that his circumstances were not critical, nor such as to justify an immediate attack by so small a force. Casting about for an objective, Plumer next decided

Marginalia:
- Snyman detaches troops to oppose him.
- March 16th, 1900. Plumer moves to his auxiliary base.
- March 19th, 1900. And sets out by a new route for Mafeking.

---

* Casualties—One officer (Lieut. A. J. Tyler, West Riding regiment) killed.

† Despatches had been received from that officer on the following dates:—January 21st to February 2nd, three messages; February 8th, 15th, 20th, 28th, March 2nd, 9th, 23rd.

to reconnoitre the Marico district, intending if possible to reach Zeerust, where a small Boer force was reported. Starting on the 26th with three hundred men, he marched *via* Korwe. Zeerust, however, was found to be too distant; so, turning northward twelve miles short of it, the force passed through Gopani, and regained Kanya on the 28th. This reconnaissance had the effect of inducing Snyman again to detach from his command in a northerly direction.

March 28th, 1900. Returns to his base.

On arrival in camp Plumer received news from Mafeking that a relief column from Lord Roberts' army had been sighted at Vryburg a week previously. Concluding that the column must now be considerably nearer, Plumer sent out a chosen runner to gain touch with it, and lost no time in taking measures of co-operation. This he proposed to effect by way of Jan Massibi's and the Molopo; but in order to mislead Snyman, he moved first (March 30th) direct on Ramathlabama, and thence next day to within six miles of Mafeking. He arrived in sight of the besieged town at 2.30 p.m. But the enemy, not yet feeling any pressure from the south, poured out in strength against him, bore heavily on his front, turned both his flanks, and pressing hard, fairly chased the force back to Ramathlabama, which was reached about 6 p.m. Nor did the fight end there. So close on his heels was the pursuit, that Plumer, who was himself slightly wounded, ordered a retirement to the base camp at Sefetili. This the main body effected without further adventure. But the Boers and the rearguard entered Ramathlabama at almost the same moment; and Bird, who had throughout the day been conspicuous for his resource, had some difficulty in getting his men away. The force eventually gained its camp having sustained forty-nine casualties,* out of a strength of 350. That it had been extricated without losses still more severe was owing only to the masterly handling of the squadrons in successive rearguard positions. The Boers also suffered severely, and returned to Mafeking, having

March 31st, 1900. Again advances, but is checked at Ramathlabama.

Falls back to Sefetili.

---

* Killed, two officers, six N.C.Os. and men; wounded, three officers, twenty-six N.C.Os. and men; missing, one officer (wounded), eleven N.C.Os. and men (six wounded).

shown one of those flashes of skill and daring which are peculiarly dangerous in an enemy prone to long periods of lethargy and irresolution. They continued to be thoroughly uneasy at the proximity of Plumer's column. On April 2nd Snyman himself again took eight hundred men with three guns on a reconnaissance up to Ramathlabama; and thereafter he established a fresh laager in observation between Mafeking and Sefetili.

From Baden-Powell now came messages deprecating any further attempts at his relief, beyond the passing into Mafeking of supplies if possible.* On April 4th Lieutenant F. Smitheman of the Rhodesia regiment, an officer of considerable influence amongst the natives of the district, made his way into Mafeking, and persuaded the headmen of the Barolong tribe, who inhabited the place, to allow their people to get out and join Plumer. As a result, a steady exodus began, which, very little interrupted by the enemy, by the end of the siege had lightened Baden-Powell's commissariat of 1,200 mouths. Endeavours to drive cattle into the town were less successful, the Boers usually capturing the droves; Baden-Powell, however, was in no urgent need of supplies. Meanwhile the Boers were decreasing daily around Mafeking; by the middle of April they numbered about three thousand. No further tidings had come to hand about the relief column from the south which had been reported at Vryburg on March 29th, until, on April 15th, the runner who had been then sent out by Plumer, returned. His report in great measure accounted for the strength and determination of the enemy in the affair at Ramathlabama on March 31st. On that date the column in question had been still far south of the Vaal, which was not crossed until April 7th. From that point its progress was conjectural, though other runners were sent out in the hopes of opening communication. It was not until May 12th that certain news came to hand in the shape of a telegram received from Lord Roberts, warning Plumer that the column might be expected in the neighbourhood of Mafeking about the 15th. This intimation was followed next day by the arrival of two

May 12th, 1900. Plumer receives certain news of Mahon's relief column.

* For this and other references to Mafeking, see Chapter VI.

messengers from the column itself, and on the 14th by a note from Colonel Mahon, who was in command, containing instructions for a junction on the Molopo river. That evening Plumer sallied out with all his forces. During his six weeks' stay at Sefetili he had received considerable reinforcements, consisting of two hundred men of the British South Africa Police with one 2.5-in. gun, and fifty men of the Mashonaland squadron of the Rhodesia regiment. Finally, on the very day of his departure, he was joined by C. battery Royal Canadian Field artillery (four guns), escorted by one hundred dismounted men of the 3rd Queensland mounted infantry. Sickness, however, had been rife amongst both men and horses of his original force, so that despite the reinforcements, he could muster no more than 800 effective men, of whom only 450 were mounted. With these, and eight guns, he marched all night to Jan Massibi's, twenty-eight miles, where at daylight on the 15th he joined hands with Mahon, and relieved Mafeking in the manner already described. Such a union of small, unsupported forces, which had started from bases more than 650 miles apart, in hostile territory, with a mobile and undefeated enemy in the field, may be illuminative alike of the enterprise of one belligerent and the supineness of the other, of the vastness of the theatre of war, and of the mingled difficulty and immunity which characterised the tactics of this singular campaign.

<small>May 15th, 1900. Plumer joins Mahon in relief of Mafeking.</small>

CHAPTER VIII.

THE BATTLE OF DIAMOND HILL.*

<small>Effect of the fall of Pretoria.</small>

WHILST Lord Roberts paused for a few days to adjust the disordered city of Pretoria, the Boers fell back in dejection toward the east. The loss of the capital, though their leaders made light of it in speech and proclamation, had, indeed, robbed them of more than a seat of Government—of more, even, than a moral rallying point. These deprivations are always rather civil than military, demoralising, perhaps, to a populace, but possibly affecting little an army still in the field with a set task before it. By the fall of Pretoria, however, Botha's commandos lost not only these—for they themselves were the populace—but also their *raison d'être* as military forces, than which no consciousness is more enervating to soldiers. No troops, moreover, could have been quicker than the Boers to grasp this sudden reduction to futility. Their individual intelligence, their skill in warfare which they had exerted to the utmost with no better result than this, their knowledge of the theatre of war, and their rapid information of events all over it, all conspired to reveal to them unmistakably their real situation. They who had stood fruitlessly on guard along strong frontiers, in front of two capitals, and around three besieged towns, could feel as little hope as pride in being called upon now to cover nothing but a fugitive Government installed in a railway carriage. Yet beyond this there seemed nothing left to do. Many, misliking the prospect, made for their homes; many surrendered; the remainder, about seven thousand men with twenty guns, drew

---

* See maps Nos. 44 and 44 (a).

THE BATTLE OF DIAMOND HILL.

rein at the exhortations of their generals, and faced the lost capital on a position fifteen miles eastward.

It was characteristic of the native military acumen of the Boers that at this dark moment all eyes turned for light to the Orange Free State. The British, invulnerable in front, now trailed lines of communication of an immense length. They had marched many hundreds of miles; their supplies, both of food and clothing, their numbers, and health, must be at a low ebb. Best of all, the disconcerting mobility of the cavalry had now, surely, almost disappeared from lack of horse-flesh. " Horses," wrote the President to one of his generals, " are lying dead in one row from Kroonstad. . . . . The troops are even riding mares with foals following." And as for the infantry, they are " weary, done up, and without food . . . can scarcely keep up any longer, and are longing for the war to cease."* Now, therefore, was the time to strike at the rear of this exhausted host, to break the slender tube by which it drew in strength, sustenance and speed, and, if the truth must be spoken, to turn its gaze away from a beaten army which could no longer look it in the face. Such were the hopes and fears which, animating those who stayed by Botha, caused them to call to General C. De Wet in the south for help. Nor did they call in vain. Already, on June 5th, De Wet had followed up his capture of Spragge's Yeomanry by surrounding a convoy of fifty wagons, escorted by two hundred Highlanders, which was on its way to join Colvile at Heilbron. The whole fell into his hands. How, on June 7th and following days, he swooped upon the line at various points, destroying the track and bridges, putting a thousand men *hors de combat*, and burning immense quantities of ammunition, clothing and foodstuffs, is told elsewhere. To compare smaller things with greater, Stonewall Jackson himself had not at Manassas,† thirty-eight years earlier, fuller temporary possession of his enemy's communications than had the Free State leader during the second week of June, 1900.

De Wet's successes.

---

* Letter from President Kruger to General Grobelaar, June 10th, 1900.

† August 27th, 1862.

These feats, though they revived somewhat the failing spirits of Botha's troops, disturbed but little the British Commander-in-Chief. He had fully foreseen them; and despatching southward Lord Kitchener and a column,* under Smith-Dorrien, to re-establish his broken connection, he turned to push Botha further from the city. With this end in view he had disposed his troops from the moment of the capture of Pretoria. Two brigades of cavalry and two of mounted infantry were already at Silverton and Koedoes Poort; Ian Hamilton, intended to act once more upon the flank, had been dropped at Irene. On June 7th, leaving Maxwell with the 14th brigade to garrison Pretoria, Lord Roberts moved out eastward with the XIth division, screening his front from Doorn Poort down to Irene with mounted men. Next day, whilst the XIth division advanced to Silverton, French took the 1st and 4th cavalry brigades and Hutton's force of mounted men northward to Kameel Drift, where fifty Boers came into his bivouac and gave up their arms. Hamilton, from Irene, sent his infantry (21st brigade) and artillery (76th and 82nd R.F.A.) to Garsfontein, and his cavalry (2nd and 3rd cavalry brigades) and mounted infantry to Zwavel Poort, where contact with the hostile outposts was gained. These movements were closely observed by the enemy. At 11 a.m. a 6-in. Creusot gun, mounted on a railway truck, opened fire from Pienaar's Poort on the XIth division at Silverton, a distance of nearly five and a half miles. Pole-Carew replied with two 5-in. guns, one of which, after twelve rounds, burst a shell between the rails thirty yards in front of the muzzle of the cannon at 9,680 yards range, destroying the track, whereupon the Boer gunners withdrew their piece.

Lord Roberts marches eastward.

For the next two days no movements beyond reconnaissance were undertaken, and this for two reasons. In the first place, Lord Roberts, anxious to prevent the degeneration of the campaign into that aimless and bitter guerrilla contest which from

---

* Composition: 19th brigade with the 1st Suffolk regiment; 74th battery R.F.A., four guns 81st battery R.F.A., 8th mounted infantry, mounted infantry of the C.I.V., section 7th company R.E.

THE BATTLE OF DIAMOND HILL. 207

history and the character of his opponents he knew to be imminent, was at this time in negotiation with Botha on the subject of a general capitulation. This, indeed, he might have brought about, seeing that the spirit of the burghers and their leaders had never been more faint, had not the successes of De Wet supervened at this critical moment, interfering even more with the British Commander-in-Chief's negotiations than with his communications. Cheered by tales of captured battalions, of sacked trains, of destroyed railways, Botha turned a deaf ear, and announced his intention of fighting to the last. This being so, extreme caution became necessary. Lord Roberts' field army, depleted by the wastage of his long march, and by garrisons and railway guards dropped on the way, numbered now no more than about sixteen thousand men. The enemy, it is true, possessed but half this number; but he was stretched out on either side of Pienaar's Poort in positions almost unassailable in front, the flanks of which were hard to find.

Botha, in fact, for so many months student perforce of turning movements, had determined on this occasion not to be outflanked at any cost; and he followed every investigation to the north by French's patrols, and to the south by the scouts of Ian Hamilton, by a corresponding drawing out of his wings, until his men were entrenched over twenty-five miles of intricate and mountainous country. His line of defence, which faced nearly due west, was bisected by the Pretoria—Delagoa Bay railway, which, at Pienaar's Poort, penetrated the barrier by a deep ravine. North of the Poort a range of heights ran brokenly up to Krokodil Spruit, lofty everywhere, but especially formidable where, at the uppermost extremity, it was gathered into a triplet of peaks, Louwbaken-Kameelfontein Ridge—Krokodilspruit Hill. Below the western foot of these ran the level and open Kameelfontein Valley, some seven miles long and two to three broad, entrance to which from the British side was by a drift immediately below Louwbaken. Thus ramparted on one margin, the valley was on its opposite edge walled in by the isolated Boekenhoutskloof Ridge, forming a defile as dangerous from its surroundings as it appeared tempting as an avenue

Commandant-General Botha's dispositions.

around the Kameelfontein Ridges. The Boekenhoutskloof Ridge, projecting westward, formed a strong outwork in advance of the flank of the main position, of which it raked the narrow approaches as a caponiere rakes the ditch. Nevertheless, it was not at first held by the enemy, Snyman, who was posted on the extreme right, contenting himself with watching the exit of the valley from the hills above and eastward of Krokodilspruit Drift. There he joined hands with De la Rey, who occupied the Kameelfontein section, their combined forces amounting to some four thousand men with eleven to fifteen guns.

In the Boer centre, guarding either side of Pienaar's Poort, rose two tall and elongated features, the southernmost standing also over the pass of Donker Poort. Southward of this again, ground equally high trended slightly eastward, parallel to the Pienaar's river, by Donkerhoek and Diamond Hill to Mors Kop, throwing bushy spurs of such proportions down to the gorge about Mooiplaats, Kleinfontein and Tweedracht, that it was hard to say which formed the stronger holds, the underfeatures or the main kopjes behind. From Mors Kop the heights held by the enemy then curled south and west by Kameelzyn Kraal, encircling the head streams of the Pienaar's river, and connecting the Diamond Hill range with another running parallel some seven miles to the westward. These westerly heights, which tumbled to the Pienaar as confusedly as their counterparts across the ravine, were cloven at two points, Zwavel Poort and Tyger Poort. Parties of Boers, lying out far in advance of their left flank, held the hills around the source of the Pienaar's river almost up to Tyger Poort.

Lord Roberts' intentions.

To assail decisively this colossal assemblage of natural fortifications was not Lord Roberts' purpose. He knew it to be impossible with the numbers at his disposal, and limited his expectations to manœuvring the enemy further from Pretoria. Foreseeing, too, that he would be able to inflict only slight actual losses, he wished to avoid heavy damage himself. He decided, therefore, to withhold his centre, any attack by which would commit him to a frontal assault on the almost impregnable Pienaar's Poort, and to make play with his wings. How far

THE BATTLE OF DIAMOND HILL. 209

and in what strength the enemy's flanks extended he was uncertain. Of this, as was usually the case with his mobile opponents, an engagement itself could be the only trustworthy reconnaissance.

Before daylight on June 11th Lieut.-Generals French and Ian Hamilton simultaneously broke their bivouacs at Kameel Drift and Garsfontein on either flank, and pushed out, the former north-east towards the Kameelfontein Valley, the latter south-east on Zwavel Poort. French led out the 1st (Porter) and 4th (Dickson) cavalry brigades and Hutton's two mounted corps (Alderson and Pilcher), with fifteen guns, of which three were Vickers-Maxim automatic. But his regiments had been reduced by wastage to little more than the strength of squadrons, and mustered scarcely eight hundred mounted men in all, Hutton's force numbering about 650. French's object was to circle completely round the Boer right—thought to rest about Krokodil Spruit—and once behind it, to drop down the line of the Elands river on to the railway near Elands River station; such tactics, in short, though on a wider scale, as had secured safe passage over so many rivers and had turned so many positions during the preceding weeks. But here, among these rugged uplands, were dangers of a different nature to those encountered on the undulating plateaux which carried the Orange and the Vaal. French was no stranger to such risks; the earliest days of the war had found him campaigning in country almost similar. From the time of Lombard's Kop and Colesberg, he had been acquiring a mastery over the Boer tactics which was now to stand him and his force in good stead. He approached his task with wariness, using special circumspection with regard to the alluring funnel of the Kameelfontein Valley. One hazard was unavoidable, namely, the passage of the drift below Louwbaken by which the valley was to be entered. To make this good was absolutely necessary, and trusting to speed, French pushed rapidly across it—the 7th Dragoon Guards scouting in front—momentarily expecting an attack from Louwbaken. But De la Rey had unaccountably neglected to occupy on that height the point which commanded the drift as the gateway

Events of June 11th; on the left.

tower of a castle commands the drawbridge. In full daylight French got safely across. Even then the enemy gave no sign for some time. It was not until 8 a.m. when the advanced scouts, skirting the spurs, were some way up the valley, that the column was checked by a hot fire from Krokodilspruit Hill, the northernmost of the triple peaks. It was as if De la Rey had purposely left open the mouth of the defile, hoping to entice the cavalry beyond recall into the throat. In spite of French's caution, he might actually have succeeded had his colleague Snyman earlier occupied the Boekenhoutskloof Ridge on the other side of the valley. Only now did that uniformly unfortunate tactician bethink himself of such a manœuvre, and his commando, cantering in a body westward across the head of the valley, passed in full view of French, who instantly appreciated the net thus spread in his sight. Calling up O. battery R.H.A. (Major Sir John H. Jervis-White-Jervis) and two Vickers-Maxim guns, whose shells first checked and then deflected northward the knots of horsemen, he detached the 1st cavalry brigade westwards towards a line of kopjes above Roodeplaats, with orders to seize the Boekenhoutskloof Ridge and forestall Snyman. As Porter left to carry this out, the enemy made strenuous efforts to be first on the ground, shelling Porter's brigade from Krokodilspruit Hill, and pushing skirmishers forward from the northern end of Boekenhoutskloof. But Jervis' rapid and accurate practice continually sent them to cover, and Porter was able to gain ground. Meanwhile the 4th cavalry brigade, remaining on the right, was getting from moment to moment deeper into action. The Boer riflemen, shooting as before chiefly from the north of the Kameelfontein Ridge, crept near through the scrub, and aided by guns of all calibres on the height above, threw on the defensive the outnumbered cavalry, who had scarcely a hundred men in the firing line. Now, too, a heavy cannon, concealed in the kopjes above Edendale, six miles to the southeast, began to drop shell clear over Louwbaken on to the spurs along which the dismounted troops were skirmishing, so that they were under fire from both flanks.

Dickson, deploying the whole of his attenuated brigade, then occupied the slopes and summit of Louwbaken; shortly afterwards two companies of Alderson's corps climbed to the top in support of the cavalry. A little later, about 10 a.m., Alderson sent two more companies on to Louwbaken, Pilcher's 3rd corps being held in reserve at the foot; and the right flank at least seemed fairly secure. Thereupon the Boers, still bombarding furiously from Krokodilspruit Hill, detached parties circuitously round by the east, and attempted to envelop Louwbaken. This French and Hutton countered promptly from opposite directions, the former despatching G. battery R.H.A. out to the left, in order to discover a spot whence Krokodilspruit Hill could be shelled; Hutton at the same time throwing the 1st mounted infantry battalion against the sharpshooters to the east, who were soon brought to a halt, the situation here being further secured by the arrival of the 2nd Canadian Mounted Rifles by the side of the troops already on Louwbaken. By this time G. battery, which had started first, had so smothered Krokodilspruit Hill with shrapnel sent from Boekenhoutskloof that the Boer fire therefrom had slackened considerably. Nevertheless, it was still hot over all this part of the field, and the success of Porter's enterprise to the westward was anxiously awaited. Smartly shelled as it crossed the valley, the 1st cavalry brigade gained the west slopes of Boekenhoutskloof, and for two hours was engaged in a running fight over the ridge. Every knob and depression upon it was held by the enemy and had to be made good, and, though the brigade attacked with vigour, and G. and O. batteries assisted with a searching fire, it was 1 p.m. before Porter, having cleared the ridge up to Doornfontein, was himself firmly enough on it to be able to protect the other brigade from being outflanked. Beyond this nothing more could be done, and even so much success was surprising. The situation of the cavalry was not enviable. Had it not been for the fine tenacity of the 4th brigade in refusing to be shot off from Louwbaken, it might well have been almost desperate. The artillery ammunition was well-nigh exhausted. The Boers, greatly outnumbering their opponents, clung fast, and were not only not to be driven further, but themselves attempted many counter-attacks, which more than once placed the British force in jeopardy. Moving their mounted men and numerous guns rapidly about the field—the gunners of the distant piece near Edendale still co-operating with wonderful intelligence—they left no means untried to shake the cavalry from their hold. Especially fierce was an attack by three guns upon O. battery R.H.A. about 2.30 p.m., which, though speedily quelled, cost the battery, whose fighting had been the admiration of all, still further casualties. Thus, with incessant firing, with alarms from all sides, with constant changes of target, and, for the British, without one moment's respite for food or rest, passed the rest of the day, the last shot sounding only at fall of night. The men then bivouacked where they lay, so closely locked with the enemy that during the night the Boer sentries shouted jests across the narrow space which divided the lines. So much for the fortunes of the British left attack on June 11th. It had plainly reached the limits of its strength, and French, reporting to the Commander-in-Chief, gave no hopes of being able to do more than hold his own.

Events of June 11th; on the right. Throughout this long-drawn combat, Ian Hamilton had been fighting on the opposite flank, more than twenty miles to the southward. His troops consisted of the 2nd cavalry brigade (Broadwood), 3rd cavalry brigade (Gordon), 2nd mounted infantry brigade (Ridley), R. and Q. batteries R.H.A., 76th and 82nd batteries R.F.A., K. section Vickers-Maxim automatic guns, two 5-in. guns, and the 21st infantry brigade (Bruce Hamilton). Like French, Hamilton aimed at the Boer flank, but was equally uncertain where it rested, or whether, indeed, there would prove to be any definite flank at all. In the billowing country before him, sinking first to the Pienaar's River gorge, thence rolling upward to the cliff-like Diamond Hill ridges behind, broken everywhere by under-features, trenched with watercourses, and thicketed with scrub, in such a maze who could say where bands of well-mounted scouts would be found, or if found, how long they would remain? Hamilton's first point was to gain an inlet into this confused stronghold, and of the two at his disposal—Zwavel Poort and Tyger Poort—he selected the

THE BATTLE OF DIAMOND HILL. 213

former and nearer, Tyger Poort being probably in the hands of the enemy. At daybreak the 2nd cavalry brigade, followed by the 3rd cavalry brigade, the mounted infantry and the 21st infantry brigade, passed through the defile, and, turning south-eastward at its exit, struck for the enemy's side of Tyger Poort. The Derbyshire regiment, with two guns of the 76th R.F.A., detached at Zwavel Poort, under Colonel G. G. Cunningham, moved parallel to the rest, but on the western side of the long ridge which connected the two Poorts, the hope being to catch the occupants of Tyger Poort between the two converging forces. The 2nd cavalry brigade was first at the Poort about 7 a.m., its scouts being immediately engaged. The Boers here, who were merely a screen, were easily dispersed by shell-fire, and scattered southward. Broadwood then halted to wait for Gordon's 3rd cavalry brigade, which was intended to hold the ground on the right flank of the advance. On its arrival he pushed on eastward towards Tweedracht, leaving Gordon, in his turn, to await relief by Cunningham's approaching detachment. During the time which necessarily elapsed before this could be effected, Broadwood, advancing alone, found himself beset on every side. Even before he crossed the Pienaar's river the enemy's gunners, sighting his movement from the Diamond Hill ridges, burst shell so rapidly over his squadrons that Broadwood, expecting to be attacked from the main position, detached Ridley's mounted infantry to watch his left. He was immediately set upon from precisely the opposite direction, that is, from his right rear, where bodies of the enemy, drifting away from the still stationary brigade of Gordon, had gathered in the increasing interval between the two brigades. The 10th Hussars were thereupon directed to take ground to the right to hold them in check, whilst the remainder went on under a steady bombardment. Soon after crossing the river, Broadwood became aware that, as he had anticipated, strong bodies of the enemy were hurrying down from Diamond Hill to dispute his advance. They were soon directly athwart his path. He therefore halted and ordered a section of Q. battery R.H.A. to go forward and brush them away. The guns advanced, escorted by but a few cavalry.

Then the Boers, in minor tactics quick as ever to espy an opening, rushed in to short range, began a withering fire, and, in conjunction with another strong body which at this moment attacked Broadwood's right flank, bade fair to sweep the gunners and their escort from the field. The loss of an instant would have lost the guns, and Broadwood sent word by a galloper to the 12th Lancers to charge the Boers in front, and ordered the Household Cavalry to fall on those shooting from the right. Lieut.-Colonel the Earl of Airlie, commanding the 12th Lancers, was in the act of forming the troopers nearest to him into line for a charge when Broadwood's messenger reached him. So scattered were the weak squadrons that it was impossible to muster instantaneously any considerable body. Lord Airlie could display but sixty men or so, of whom ten were of the 10th Hussars. At the head of these he rode for the enemy, his men cheering as they urged their enfeebled Argentine horses to a gallop. The Boers, having emptied their magazines, melted away, taking refuge on a knoll behind; only a few fell to lance or sabre, but the guns were saved. Then Lord Airlie, coolly watching on all sides even whilst he galloped, descried another hostile body hastening up against his handful from the left flank. To be caught by them would mean destruction, and, his task being accomplished, he ordered "files about." As the troopers wheeled, the enemy, now reinforced on the knoll, reopened a ravaging fire. The soldiers, trained to be as slow in retreat as swift in advance, started back at the regulation trot, and reiterated orders were needed to induce them to break into a gallop. Men and officers were struck down, amongst the latter, shot through the heart, their commander himself, a cavalry leader of fine attainments, and much beloved. Two horses had already fallen under him this day. In all, amongst the sixty officers and men who took part in this adventure, there were sixteen casualties and many more in horses.

As for the Boers on the right, they dispersed in all directions before the onset of the Household Cavalry, who were disappointed in their attempt to close. Thereafter in this part of the field supervened a condition of stalemate; neither

THE BATTLE OF DIAMOND HILL.

belligerent gained or yielded any further ground throughout the day, both meanwhile maintaining a hot and unceasing fire. Gordon, after handing over Tyger Poort to Cunningham, did, indeed, make some little way. He was engaged continuously and with loss until he regained touch with Broadwood in the afternoon. He was then posted so as to fend the enemy off the right flank, and keep the infantry attack from being molested. Thus, on both widely-separated wings, Lord Roberts' cavalry, rather outflanked than outflanking, was blocked; and, should he decide to persist, his tactics would have to be transformed from a manœuvre of envelopment by the mounted troops to one of penetration by the infantry.

Inside the guard formed by the cavalry brigades, Ian Hamilton in due time developed his attack. The 21st brigade was reduced in strength already by the absence of the Derbyshire regiment, and Bruce Hamilton had further to leave the Cameron Highlanders on rearguard in front of Zwavel Poort. In pursuance of orders from Ian Hamilton, he advanced first towards Boschkop with the City Imperial Volunteers, the Royal Sussex regiment, and the 76th and 82nd batteries Royal Field Artillery, the same troops which had gone into action under his command on the left at Doorn Kop in the previous month. Their task here seemed far more formidable than in that brilliant affair. Forced now by the successful tactics of the Boer flankers to advance against instead of around the main position, the whole strength of that range of precipices stood arrayed against them. North of Donker Poort, the end of the long kopje, plunging to the gorge, presented a perpendicular face of rock, crowned by a mass of boulders. To the south of this, and nearer, towered the Donkerhoek—Diamond Hill ridges, separated by a narrow valley from the confused terrain which concealed the Boer *tirailleurs* lurking east of the Pienaar's river. There were thus, so to speak, three ascending decks of defence, increasing in weight of metal as they mounted. Gaining Boschkop and the right bank of the Pienaar's without opposition—for here the hostile skirmishers, overlapped by the cavalry, had fallen back—Bruce Hamilton turned on Kleinfontein, where the enemy had disposed his first line along a low ridge covered with boulders and brushwood. It was admirably adapted for their purpose. A narrow valley, the bed of a tributary watercourse, bounded its southern foot, and would have to be crossed by the attack; another, running up to Donkerhoek behind, provided a well-covered way of retreat, whilst the very lowness of the kopjes allowed the guns of the lofty main position, about a mile in rear, to shoot over them and play upon the ground in front. Thus, for a delaying action the ridge was perfect, and the five or six hundred Boers upon it intended no more. Their tenure was, indeed, brief enough. Deploying his troops—Royal Sussex regiment on the left, City Imperial Volunteers on the right, with the 76th and 82nd batteries between, and Legge's mounted infantry on the right flank of all—Bruce Hamilton pushed them gradually but uninterruptedly towards the kopjes, covered by the 5-in. guns, which, from the ridge overlooking Boschkop three miles east of Zwavel Poort, bombarded the crest of the main ridges at ten thousand yards. A universal fire of guns and small arms from every part of the Boer positions within sight and range contested his advance; the Field artillery, which took post on the high right bank of the Pienaar's, being especially belaboured by the hostile gunners. The batteries were so well hidden, however, that they suffered little loss, and so well served that the defenders of Kleinfontein wavered from the first. About 2.30 p.m. the Royal Sussex, pressing back the Boer right, had won the western end of the ridge; the City Imperial Volunteers, whose object—the enemy's left—lay more distant, being still too far back for close battle. The Royal Sussex, therefore, were ordered to wheel to their right and sweep the ridge from west to east. Whilst they did this, under heavy fire, the City Imperial Volunteers drew nearer, the Field batteries redoubled their practice, whilst the 5-in. gunners, shortening their fuses to four thousand yards, scoured the reverse of the kopjes. At 4 p.m. the Boers, loosing their hold, galloped to the rear. The Kleinfontein Ridge was then occupied from end to end, and Ian Hamilton immediately turned to examine the heights of Diamond Hill.

THE BATTLE OF DIAMOND HILL. 217

Their menacing faces were still a mile distant. Legge, ordered to lead his mounted infantry forward to test their strength, was stopped after a very short advance by a prohibitive fire. Only two battalions, both fatigued, were available for attack; and dusk was coming on. The General, therefore, had to be content with what he had won, and leaving outposts on the captured ridges, ordered his men into bivouac at Boschkop, where the Derbyshire regiment rejoined Bruce Hamilton's brigade from Tyger Poort. More, in fact, had already been accomplished than had been expected. Lord Roberts, finding his blows countered on both flanks, had no intention of incurring the heavy losses inevitable to frontal attack, and had sent instructions to Ian Hamilton not to press home. By the time the order reached that General the Kleinfontein Ridges had been seized, and the attack was too deeply and too successfully committed to be withdrawn. Bruce Hamilton's brigade was, nevertheless, obviously too weak to push on unaided, and it was decided that at least two battalions of the Guards from the XIth division should reinforce him for next day's operations.

Whilst matters had thus fared on either wing, the fighting in the centre had been confined to long-range artillery fire. There the XIth division, under Pole-Carew, had all day been held in leash pending the development of the flanking movements. Posting Captain Bearcroft's two 4.7-in. Naval guns, escorted by half the 1st Yorkshire regiment, near the Zwartkoppies before daybreak, Pole-Carew disposed his brigades from Marks' Farm down to Mooiplaats—the 18th brigade on the left, the Guards' brigade on the right. South of Mooiplaats the West Australian mounted infantry and North Devon Imperial Yeomanry linked the Guards with Ian Hamilton's troops of the right attack; whilst north of Marks' Farm Colonel Henry, with J. battery R.H.A., two Colt guns and about seven hundred men of the 4th mounted infantry, 7th Imperial Yeomanry, Tasmanian mounted infantry and Victorian Mounted Rifles, bridged the gap between the XIth division and the left attack of French. All day the bluejackets of the 4.7-in. guns lay in wait for the enemy's 6-in. piece, every attempt of which to come into action from the

Events on June 11th; in the centre.

recesses of Pienaar's Poort they foiled with well-placed lyddite. From under a kopje some three thousand yards south-east of them the 5-in. guns bombarded the ridges between the two Poorts. But no forward movement was undertaken. Henry, attempting to penetrate northward, was checked, as Legge more to the south had been, by greatly superior forces posted with artillery about Frans Poort; and though from dawn to dark Pole-Carew kept his men in readiness for an instant advance, he had to go into bivouac without fighting.

The results of the fighting on June 11th. The results of the day were thus disappointing. The vastness of the enemy's extension had upset all calculations. The British line of battle now stretched twenty-five miles from flank to flank; yet at both extremities it was overlapped, and not weakly opposed in the centre. Night fell, therefore, on a somewhat dubious situation. Only on the left, it is true, was any part of the enormous front in actual risk during the hours of darkness. There, where the soldiers of French and De la Rey lay within point-blank range, a counter-attack was possible at any moment, and both combatants passed an uneasy night. The rest of the force, secure enough in its bivouacs, was concerned chiefly with the fortunes of the morrow, when the frowning heights, of which a foothill alone had required a whole day to capture, must either be forced or declined.

June 12th, 1900. Events on the right. At 6 a.m. on June 12th, Bruce Hamilton reoccupied his outpost line along the kopjes in front of Kleinfontein. He had already received orders from Ian Hamilton to press the attack against Diamond Hill—which had been marked as the key to the Boer left defence—and to endeavour to strike at the railway behind it. The hill was plainly held in strength, and Bruce Hamilton was instructed to defer his stroke until the arrival of the battalions of Guards, the promised reinforcements from the centre. Whilst waiting for them Ian Hamilton called the 5-in. guns from the west of Boschkop, and posted them on the plateau close behind the infantry, who were deployed as follows along the Kleinfontein Ridges:—Royal Sussex regiment on the left, City Imperial Volunteers in the centre, half battalion Derbyshire regiment slightly apart on the right, the other half of this corps

THE BATTLE OF DIAMOND HILL.

being placed behind the centre in reserve. The 76th and 82nd batteries were posted in front of the 5-in. guns at the head of a small valley enclosing a tributary of the Pienaar's river; de Lisle's mounted infantry, which was not part of the 21st brigade, on the extreme right faced the heights about Rhenosterfontein, and the Cameron Highlanders remained guarding the communications near Zwavel Poort. Whilst the 21st brigade took up these positions, under a slow long-range musketry and shell fire from the enemy, Pole-Carew at Marks' Farm was making arrangements to assist the coming attack. Extending the 18th brigade as before, he despatched southward the Guards' brigade under Major-General Inigo Jones, with orders to cross the river at Mooiplaats and place his brigade at the service of Ian Hamilton. In addition to his four battalions, Inigo Iones took with him the 83rd battery R.F.A., two Naval 12-pr. guns and the two 5-in. guns, the place of the latter below Zwartkoppies being taken by the two 4.7-in. guns, which were drawn southward for the purpose. At 10.15 a.m. Jones crossed the Pienaar's, leaving the 5-in. guns on the left bank, whence at 6,500 yards they began to throw shell into the ravine of Donker Poort. He dropped here also the Scots Guards, as a link between his own force and the Divisional Headquarters, and with the rest of his brigade pushed on south-eastward in the following battle order:—First and second lines, the 1st and 2nd Coldstream Guards; the 3rd Grenadier Guards being écheloned as third line on his left rear. At 12.45 p.m. the Guards came into touch with the 21st brigade. Bruce Hamilton immediately ordered the attack on Diamond Hill, the 2nd Coldstream coming up on the left rear of the Royal Sussex to support his fighting line. The 1st Coldstream, continuing on their south-easterly route, passed Bruce Hamilton's reserve, and moved forward to the ground quitted by the City Imperial Volunteers as that battalion advanced with its brigade.

Diamond Hill proved a surprisingly easy capture. The enemy upon it, shaken beyond endurance by the incessant downpour of shrapnel, fell away on either side before the 21st brigade had come within close range, some making for the

Capture of Diamond Hill.

fortified wall of Donker Poort, others eastward, across the front of the Derbyshire, towards the heights around the head of the Honde river, whence two guns and a Vickers-Maxim played in enfilade on Bruce Hamilton's advancing lines. The real combat began when, about 1.30 p.m., the crest of Diamond Hill had been won. The summit and the long plateau of Donkerhoek running from it were alike almost clear of the enemy. But the afore-mentioned hills to the east now swarmed with sharpshooters; the lofty ramparts of the Poort itself, which overlooked the whole of the plateau, were thickly manned and backed by a numerous artillery. A serious fire beat crosswise upon the plateau, and Bruce Hamilton saw that further progress would be costly. There was, however, no time for delay. Unless the plateau could be secured at once, it might easily be lost, or, at any rate, denied to him by fire alone. The artillery had now moved forward. Sending word to the nearest battery to come up to the summit at once, Bruce Hamilton, about 3.15 p.m., pushed his battalions across Donkerhoek to its northern edge, where there was good cover; the 2nd Coldstream Guards opportunely supported the Royal Sussex on the left, and the 1st Coldstream closed the gap between the City Imperial Volunteers and the Derbyshire on the right. Soon, in response to the call, the 82nd battery (Major W. H. Connolly), having climbed the steep side of Donkerhoek, was upon the plateau eight hundred yards behind the firing line along the crest. The battery was wholly exposed. The Boers, both riflemen and gunners, shot fast from their tower-like stronghold down upon the guns drawn up across the bare ground, a target plainer by far than the recumbent and nearly invisible infantry. But the 82nd replied rapidly at 1,850 yards range, and the roll of the Mausers, though it never ceased, thinned perceptibly in volume. The battery here lost an officer killed, six men wounded and eight horses. Shortly afterwards additional artillery help was at hand at even closer range on the left. So early as 2 p.m. Inigo Jones, having summoned half the Scots Guards from Mooiplaats, had advanced in closer support to the Kleinfontein Ridges, sending on ahead the 83rd battery and the Naval 12-prs.,

THE BATTLE OF DIAMOND HILL. 221

whose practice did much to tame the shooting both from Donker Poort and the eastern hills.

When the 2nd Coldstream had come at close quarters with the enemy on the northern edge of Donkerhoek by the side of Bruce Hamilton's men, Jones, about 4.30 p.m., sent the 83rd battery (Major H. Guthrie-Smith) forward, two guns going almost into the firing line, between the Coldstream and the Royal Sussex. To climb thither alone was a feat. To serve the pieces there with effect, to challenge and master the rifle within medium rifle-range was a daring exploit. At no more than nine hundred yards range the gunners of the 83rd battery dealt shrapnel all over the hostile trenches, and, together with their comrades of the 82nd battery on the right rear, kept silent half the Mausers on the brow of Donker Poort. A little before this de Lisle, on the right flank, noticing the evil effect of the cross fire from the eastern kopjes above Rhenosterfontein, decided to attempt to extinguish it by a dash with his mounted infantry. Clearing a path with a stream of shells from two Vickers-Maxim automatic guns, he galloped straight at the ridges, and rushed the crest with little loss. A galling fire met him there, and he was unable to push further. He had, however, done his work; the Boers fell back and pestered no more the flank of the infantry. Bruce Hamilton, thus relieved, still hoped to win his mark before dark. To assail the Poort by shock tactics was out of the question. The deep gorge yawning between his front line and the embattled commandos of itself reduced such a plan to a counsel of desperation. Half the amount of resistance he was now encountering would fill the ravine with dead, and there would be no extricating an attack once launched. He, therefore, sought for an opening towards the north-east—that is, around the Boer left—where the ground, subsiding gently towards the railway, seemed to offer facilities for a rapid forward swing of his right. But here, too, he found himself forestalled. The enemy, as usual even more watchful of low ground than of high, had driven across the flats trenches to which there was no approach without hard and protracted fighting. For that neither time nor light remained; and once more night fell, with much accomplished, but much more, apparently, remaining to be undertaken before victory should be won.

June 12th, 1900. Events on the left. In other parts of the field this day the operations had remained at a standstill, awaiting the issue of the infantry attack. On neither flank, indeed, was there much scope for activity. French, faced by even greater numbers and two more guns than on the previous day, was more concerned with holding his own than with aggression. His artillery was almost silent from lack of shell. His troops were everywhere reduced to the defensive tactics of infantry, and only their stubborn endurance in this partly unaccustomed capacity kept them from being overpowered by the superior forces which manœuvred around them. A long day's continuous bombardment and musketry left them, not, it is true, in possession of new ground, but still clinging firmly to the old, in itself an achievement as valuable as it was meritorious; for disaster on the left flank would have imperilled the weakened centre and laid open the road to Pretoria. So precarious seemed the situation here that, at 5 p.m., the Commander-in-Chief informed French that he intended to send a battalion of infantry to Derde Poort, to be used by him either as a support in case of advance or as a rallying-point should the cavalry have to fall back. So, too, with the mounted troops on the right. Suffering less from fire than French's men, though they were never free from it, Broadwood's regiments were equally unable to make progress, de Lisle's mounted infantry alone from this force taking its important part in the action.

June 12th, 1900. The centre. In the centre Pole-Carew had never ceased to bombard with the 4.7-in. guns Pienaar's Poort and the ridge between it and Donkerhoek, and, though not permitted to advance, had contrived to clear away with his mounted infantry the skirmishers who fringed the low ground at the base of the Boer position.

During the night of the 12th Generals Pole-Carew and Ian Hamilton concerted measures for clinching the matter definitely on the morrow. De Lisle's capture of the kopje to the east had provided a valuable *point d'appui*. This it was proposed to utilise for a stroke not at the impregnable Donker Poort, but directly at

THE BATTLE OF DIAMOND HILL. 223

the railway behind it, the nearest part of which was under four
miles distant. To cover this movement, and to establish Plans for
superiority of fire from the south, the 5-in. guns were sent June 13th.
across the river from Mooiplaats to join Inigo Jones at Donkerhoek. The Guards' brigade was ordered to take over Donkerhoek
from the 21st brigade, which, thus relieved, would concentrate
above Rhenosterfontein preparatory to an advance northward.
Pole-Carew himself intended to lead forward in the centre the
18th brigade, covered by the 4.7-in. Naval guns; and it was
hoped that the enemy, engaged in front, held in flank, and
menaced in rear, would give way.

No sooner had these arrangements been carried out than The Boers
they were rendered unnecessary. At dawn on June 13th the disappear.
piquets all along the British front reported that the Boers had
vanished; the growing light revealed every road leading eastward to be filled with their retreating transport. The long campaign, then, if, as the Boers boasted, it had not vanquished their
arms, had begun to wear down their endurance. Men who had
once fought without pause for weeks against far greater odds in
battalions and guns, now, after the strain of but two days, broke
from positions as strong as any in South Africa—this, too, when
in parts of the field they were still successful. Such troops were,
indeed, ripe for the hopeless resort to guerrilla warfare.

Ian Hamilton went immediately in chase. Preceded by
de Lisle's mounted infantry, he marched through the abandoned trenches as far as Elands River station, where he halted
for the night. The mounted infantry pressed on under inter- The pursuit.
mittent fire from the 6-in. Creusot gun, which was receding
eastward from Pienaar's Poort in a railway truck. Near
Bronkhorstspruit the 6th mounted infantry and the West Australian mounted infantry ran down the Boer rearguard of three
hundred men, which was laagered in apparent unconsciousness
of such close pursuit. In a few moments twenty thousand
rounds of ammunition, discharged at utmost speed at a medium
range, broke up the mass of men and animals, the survivors
flying in all directions. Further to the right Broadwood's
cavalry drove stragglers before them across the Honde river up

to the railway below Witfontein, being then recalled to bivouac at Elands River. In the centre the 18th brigade and Henry's mounted infantry remained on the ground of the previous day. On the left, French, now supported at Derde Poort by the Lincolnshire regiment, the 75th battery and De Montmorency's Scouts, all come out from Pretoria, during the day worked his way around the heights which had seemed likely to block him for ever. The country in rear proved too difficult for speed; the enemy had a long start, and at nightfall French desisted from pursuit along the line of Elands River, his own Headquarters being at Tweefontein.

Thus a few hours had completely transformed the situation. The great barrier was now behind instead of before the British army; the enemy, in full flight eastward, lightened at every mile the anxiety which, whilst he was near, had weighed upon the capital. The Commander-in-Chief's purpose was accomplished even more thoroughly than he had expected, and he ordered his forces back to Pretoria for their much-needed rest and refitting. On June 14th French's brigades returned to Kameel Drift and those of Hutton to Derde Poort. The withdrawal of Ian Hamilton's troops was less easy; for ten miles in front of him Broadwood and de Lisle were still hanging on to the Boer rearguard, and could not be left unsupported. On the morning of June 15th the enemy had drawn off too far to be harassed longer with safety, the mounted troops returned, and Ian Hamilton marched back along the Pretoria road to Marks' Farm. On the next day all were back in Pretoria, Henry alone being left with five hundred mounted infantry and J. battery R.H.A. on the Pienaar's Poort ridges, as a look-out toward the east.

Recall of the forces.

The casualties in the British force during these operations— about one hundred and eighty all ranks*—were little indication of the closeness and continuity of the fighting. The very magnificence of the country about Diamond Hill was a safeguard from heavy losses. It is not rough boulders and precipitous hills which, if properly undertaken, are most costly to capture. The amount

---

* See Appendix 2.

of cover against firearms which these afford is of as much advantage to patient and skilfully-led assailants as to the defenders. Far more deadly ground to approach under modern conditions is that which presents no features, and, therefore, gives neither a target for the attacker's guns and rifles, nor protection from the undiscoverable weapons of the defence. Thus there had been many more dangerous actions than this of Diamond Hill, though few more hardly fought, and more nearly lost.

CHAPTER IX.*

OPERATIONS IN THE WESTERN TRANSVAAL.

JUNE AND JULY, 1900.

Separation of the Boer forces.

On the day the main British army crossed the Vaal, the military combination of the Boer Republics practically came to an end. The Free Staters remained south of the river, which severed alike their forces and interests from those of the Transvaalers, who prepared to defend only their own endangered territory.

This separation arose less from the military organisation than the social conditions of the Republics. To serve on commando out of his own district had never been a congenial duty to a burgher; to leave his own State altogether to fight in defence of another had never even crossed his mind. The resulting schism had been clearly foreseen, and its moral effects carefully discounted by the Boer leaders. The two Governments—they had announced—agreed that, when the invaders entered the Transvaal, the Free State commandos should not follow them; not because of any difference with their brethren of the Transvaal, but purely on strategical grounds. The British were to have an enemy behind them as well as in front. Such a plan, new in the campaign, but ancient in history, was indeed no unskilful conversion of necessity to virtue; and to it were to be owed some of the most troublesome episodes of the war.

After the surrender of Johannesburg and the entry of the British Commander-in-Chief into Pretoria on June 5th, 1900, the process of disintegration continued. Defeat scattered the Transvaal forces far and wide; and the organised resistance of the separate commandos was weakened by the growing lack of

* See map No. 38.

control. A large number of the men still under arms fled eastwards to form the last prop of President Kruger's tottering and fugitive Government. Others went to the west; very many returned to their homes. As in the Orange Free State after the fall of Bloemfontein, the Transvaal burghers began to desert their commandos and take refuge on their farms. The numbers in the field were greatly reduced. Many surrendered and took the oath of neutrality. Pretoria, in spite of its impressive fortifications, had fallen, almost without a shot; and the news of its easy occupation staggered both Republics, astounding, as is commonly the case, distant spectators even more than the men who had witnessed the catastrophe. In the Orange Free State, all the influence of the leading men was required to induce the burghers to continue the war in the face of such a disaster.

Terms of peace were being everywhere eagerly discussed. The *Peace mooted.* first sign of this mood had appeared at an interview between Sir R. Buller and Assistant-Commandant-General C. Botha, near Laing's Nek, when a three days' armistice was agreed upon to allow of discussion amongst the commandos, and to give them time to communicate with the Government.* Three days later General P. De Wet, brother of the Free State generalissimo, had gone to Lindley to confer with Lord Methuen as to terms of surrender, obtaining a six days' cessation of hostilities to enable him to consult with Mr. Steyn. On June 8th Lord Roberts himself ordered that no avoidable hostilities were to be undertaken in the neighbourhood of Pretoria, as negotiations with President Kruger were taking place. Nothing, indeed, came of these parleyings; and if they showed that the idea of submission was current amongst the separate parts of the Boer body politic, the depression of the fighting men was too transitory to survive negotiations of any duration. Nor was the pledge of one man binding on another. In the loosely organised forces it was open to any leader in difficulties to make the best terms he could for his own particular body of men, with no reference or prejudice to other commandos outside the danger zone. Lord Roberts

* See Chapter X.

was well aware of this; and he carefully limited the cessation of active operations to the immediate neighbourhood of Pretoria.

Notwithstanding the breakdown of negotiations, a speedy end of the war was something more than a mirage. Sir Redvers Buller's entry into the South-eastern Transvaal on June 11th,* and the advance of Lord Roberts along the Delagoa railway would certainly place Botha's forces between two fires, and might compel surrender. Everywhere patrols heard from farmers how they were weary of the war, and wanted nothing but to settle down quietly in their homes. Favourable reports from the Western Transvaal at this period confirmed the impression that no operations of any magnitude would be necessary in that area, thus leaving Lord Roberts free to deal with the remnants of the Boer forces to the east of Pretoria. Telegraphing to Sir R. Buller on June 20th the Commander-in-Chief said: " The outlying districts will settle down soon enough when we have beaten the enemy now in the field; the Free Staters are now the only ones giving much trouble, but until they have been brought to terms there is little chance of the Transvaalers giving in." In short, all the omens encouraged the Commander-in-Chief to think that his task was near its end, and the Home Government shared that view. All that now seemed needed was the same systematic patrolling of the unsettled districts of the Transvaal as had once more been begun in the Orange Free State. On June 5th, the western area was divided into military districts, in order to carry out the pacification. The Marico district, including the towns of Mafeking, Zeerust, Lichtenburg, and later Rustenburg, was assigned to Major-General R. S. S. Baden-Powell, with a force consisting of 1,100 Rhodesian Volunteers and Police, a battery of Canadian artillery and three other guns. Lieut.-General Sir A. Hunter, with the Xth division, was to command the area Ventersdorp — Potchefstroom — Klerksdorp; Major-General H. H. Settle, with Headquarters at Vryburg, was to be responsible for the south-west.

* See Chapter X.

OPERATIONS IN THE WESTERN TRANSVAAL. 229

The distribution of the British forces in other parts of the theatre of war at this time was as follows: Lord Roberts' main army, consisting of four brigades of cavalry, four companies of Imperial Yeomanry, a mounted infantry division made up of eight corps, two infantry divisions, and two unattached infantry brigades, was around Pretoria. Sir R. Buller was at Ingogo. Sir F. Carrington's force was partly disembarking at Beira, partly écheloned along the line Umtali—Buluwayo. Lord Methuen was escorting supplies to Heilbron, which Sir H. Colvile much needed. Sir C. Warren was at Campbell, in Griqualand, in general command of the region south of the Orange river. Sir L. Rundle and Major-General E. Y. Brabant were about Hammonia. Distribution of the British forces early in June, 1900.

The general situation resembled that which had followed the capture of Bloemfontein. Now, as then, the problem was the more complicated because the desire for peace on the part of the Boer farmers was perfectly genuine; and once more the distribution of the British army was devised more to take advantage of its opponents' inclination to peace than to the best military advantage. Once more, therefore, opportunities were given of which a few irreconcilable patriots made use; and, as before, their partial success at once revived the spirit of their weaker brethren. The resulting captures by surprise of weak posts and parties would have been of little importance had they not refilled and inspired the wasted ranks of resistance, and pulled down the white flag from many a Boer farm. Steyn and De Wet in the Orange Free State, Botha and De la Rey in the Transvaal, were striving hard to keep alive the drooping spirits of their compatriots; but not until the vulnerable points of the British line of communications had been successfully attacked did their exhortations fall on willing ears. The means for a renewal of the conflict were always at hand. The fact that a burgher had surrendered his arms was no proof that he had given up *all* his arms. There were few who had not two or three rifles more; and the oath of allegiance counted for nothing against an appeal to the sacred duty of patriotism. These sudden changes from farmer to soldier added enormously to the Taken advantage of by the enemy.

difficulties of the campaign. Dispersed British detachments, engaged in peaceful relations with the inhabitants, were always liable to sudden surprises by overwhelming numbers springing in a night from a friendly countryside. This was no miracle, but merely the working of the territorial machinery of the Boer organisation. Every farmer belonged to a commando; and when the corps from which he had deserted approached his unprotected dwelling, very little persuasion or force was needed to induce him to resume his place in it. When Pretoria fell there were few more than 1,200 Boers present with commandos in the whole country between Mafeking and the capital. When Mafeking had been relieved, General Snyman's disappointed and semi-mutinous force had trekked eastwards, breaking up into its component commands. The strongest was one of 300 men, under Commandant Piet Kruger at the Magato Nek in the Magaliesberg, with an advanced post at Elands River, on the Zeerust—Rustenburg road. It was reported that even General De la Rey's men from Lichtenburg were at that time willing to lay down their arms. The Marico commando was at Bethanie; and Commandant T. De Beer was north of Pretoria with 200 men. To deal with such parties as these was not likely to present difficulty; and it was anticipated that the west would soon be at peace. The south-west was reported entirely clear of the enemy, except at Klerksdorp and Buffelsdoorn, where the local commandos were surrendering by order of Commandant Andries Cronje. To prepare for extended patrolling, Baden-Powell had divided his command into two parts—one for the field, the other to garrison posts. The former was made up of two mobile columns, one under Colonel H. C. O. Plumer, consisting of 500 mounted men of the Rhodesia regiment, with four guns of the Royal Canadian artillery, and two mountain guns; the other under Lieut.-Colonel A. H. M. Edwards, who had with him 360 men of the Imperial Light Horse and two 1-pr. Vickers-Maxims. For these columns there was a small reserve of 100 mounted men of the British South Africa Police, and the remaining two guns of the Canadian battery. Mafeking and Zeerust were each held

OPERATIONS IN THE WESTERN TRANSVAAL. 231

by 200 dismounted men of the Protectorate and Rhodesia regiments respectively, and two 7-pr. guns; while detachments of 100 men and one gun were at Otto's Hoop and Lobatsi. These detachments were required to check raiding by natives—mostly Barolongs from Mafeking—and to collect horses, transport and supplies.

The Xth division, under Lieut.-General Sir A. Hunter, consisted of Brigadier-General B. T. Mahon's cavalry, the 28th, 66th and 78th batteries Royal Field artillery, and the 5th and 6th infantry brigades, under Major-Generals A. F. Hart and G. Barton respectively. Marching from various points of assembly between Warrenton and Vryburg, the division concentrated at Lichtenburg without opposition on June 7th. Du Toit's commando retired before it and joined T. De Beer's men north of the Magaliesberg, near Pretoria. The railways east and west of this part of the theatre of war were in full working order. Communication was re-opened between Kimberley and Buluwayo on June 6th. Major-General Smith-Dorrien, with the 19th brigade, was in charge of the line from Vereeniging to Pretoria, with detachments at the important points. The VIIth division under Lieut.-General C. Tucker, garrisoned Johannesburg and Pretoria, each with a brigade. An advance eastwards by Baden-Powell's force and the Xth division, marching parallel, promised to clear the Western Transvaal and drive wandering bands to the railway, where they could be stopped and disarmed.

June 7th, 1900. Occupation of Lichtenburg.

In the north-west of the Republic there were no British troops. Such of Sir F. Carrington's mounted force as had landed at Beira, and concentrated at Buluwayo, did no more than watch the drifts over the Limpopo river, the frontier of the Transvaal. Sir F. Carrington's force numbered some 4,000 men, and was made up of the 17th and 18th battalions I.Y., 2,100 Bushmen from the Australian colonies, Tasmania and New Zealand, and a specially enlisted corps of Imperial Bushmen about 1,900 strong. With the force were ten 15-pr. Q.F. guns and eight Vickers-Maxims; but there were only fifty trained artillerymen to work them. Volunteers from the New Zealand Bushmen were afterwards drilled as gunners, and became efficient. The 1st brigade of Bushmen, 1,200 strong, was under the command of Colonel G. A. L. Carew; the 2nd brigade, mainly Imperial Bushmen, was commanded by Colonel Raleigh Grey. The duty assigned to Sir F. Carrington was that of threatening the enemy from the north, preventing them retreating in that direction, and safeguarding Rhodesia from native risings. When the Limpopo is in flood, Rhodes Drift and Baine's Drift are for 200 miles the only passable outlets from the Transvaal. Five hundred men at each of these fords would therefore effectually close Rhodesia.

Sir F. Carrington's real difficulties lay in the nature of the country, which has been fully described in the narrative of Plumer's operations in the same district.*

Occupation of Potchefstroom, June 11th, 1900.

From Lichtenburg, the Xth division marched to Ventersdorp; and Mahon's advanced troops, reinforced by the Imperial Light Horse in place of the Kimberley Mounted Corps left behind, occupied Potchefstroom on June 11th. They were followed next day by the 6th (Barton) brigade. On entering the town, the former capital of the Transvaal, the 2nd battalion Royal Scots Fusiliers hoisted the very Union Jack which had waved over Pretoria during the siege of 1881; a relic preserved by the regiment, which had formed part of the old garrison. Two battalions, one battery and one squadron were left to hold the town. The other two battalions were sent to Frederikstad and Klerksdorp.

With the 5th brigade and the cavalry, Sir A. Hunter marched northwards on June 16th. The railway was not available, as the bridge at Bank Station had been blown up on June 14th.

Surrender of Krugersdorp, June 18th.

Krugersdorp surrendered on June 18th, and the troops entered the town next morning. There Hunter received orders to move to Springs and Heidelberg, leaving troops to hold Krugersdorp. These were furnished by Barton, who detailed as garrison the 1st Royal Welsh Fusiliers and half a battalion Royal Scots Fusiliers. The movement of Sir A. Hunter's division made it necessary to withdraw all but a fragment of the Klerksdorp garrison; and, later, to move the whole of the 6th brigade from

* See Chapter VII.

OPERATIONS IN THE WESTERN TRANSVAAL.

the Potchefstroom district, leaving only seventy men in the town itself. At Germiston, on the way to Heidelberg, Mahon's cavalry, with the 1st Border regiment and 1st Connaught Rangers, were withdrawn from the division and called in to Pretoria. During the march, Sir A. Hunter was ordered to take over command of Lieut.-General Sir Ian Hamilton's force, in consequence of the riding accident which had recently incapacitated Hamilton. The Xth division was now astride the central railway, Barton's brigade (the 6th), with the 78th Field battery and a company of Yeomanry, remaining as garrison at Krugersdorp.

Meanwhile Baden-Powell, moving on Sir A. Hunter's left, sent his column along the two roads which converge on Rustenburg, the most important town in the Western Transvaal. This place had a sentimental value in the eyes of the "Dopper" Boers, for it had been the country home of President Kruger, and the interests of the district were closely bound up with those of the dominant clique. Distant about sixty miles by road from Pretoria, and fifty from the nearest railway station at Krugersdorp, Rustenburg was an isolated spot. The district lying shut in behind the mountain barrier of the Magaliesberg, was thus cut off from every influence which had tended to dispose the burghers of many less secluded districts to more friendly relations with their conquerors. The southern arm of the range runs westward from Pretoria for twenty miles to Haartebeestpoort, where the Crocodile river makes its way through a narrow cañon. Beyond this gorge the range bends south-west for thirty-five miles, and then turns sharply to the north-west. The southern slopes are for the most part steep; west of the Crocodile river they become rugged, broken and precipitous. The range is impassable for troops everywhere except at certain defiles, the possession of which, by one belligerent or the other, dictated the tactics of the campaign which now followed. Close to Pretoria are Horne's Nek and Wonderboom Poort. Both of these were part of the local defences of the capital. Westwards from Pretoria the first pass is Zilikat's (Mosilikatze's) Nek. Seven miles further on, and three beyond the river, is

Commando Nek, where the main road from Pretoria to Rustenburg crosses the mountains. Thence to the end of the range there are only two passes available for troops and wheel traffic, viz.: Olifants Nek, in the angle of the sharp turn to the north-west, and Magato Nek, in the north-western arm itself, eight miles north-west of Rustenburg. Thus, in the ninety miles of the western arm of the range there are but four passes practicable for wheels; and only five cattle-paths between Commando and Olifants Neks.

<small>Occupation of Rustenburg, June 14th, 1900.</small> Marching from Zeerust, Baden-Powell's northern column (Plumer) crossed the Magaliesberg at Magato Nek, and occupied Rustenburg without opposition on June 14th, a garrison of 100 men of the Southern Rhodesian Volunteers, under Lieut.-Colonel G. L. Holdsworth, having been left at the drift over the Elands river. The other column kept to the south of the Magaliesberg to keep touch with Hunter. It rejoined Baden-Powell and the rest of the force at Rustenburg on the 21st, going by Olifants Nek.

From Rustenburg, Baden-Powell, who had brought thither 600 mounted troops on June 17th, rode in with a small escort to see the Commander-in-Chief. At Bokfontein he met a force under Major-General E. T. H. Hutton, which had come from Pretoria to join him. It consisted of the 1st battalion mounted infantry, the Canadian Mounted Rifles, the New Zealand Mounted Rifles, 2nd Lincoln regiment, 18th battery R.F.A., in all 1,062 men, with six guns and two machine guns. Finding Commando and Zilikat's Neks unoccupied, and seeing no sign of the enemy in the mountains, Hutton marched northwards on June 18th, as far as Zoutpans Drift, where Lieut. F. V. Young, of the Manitoba Dragoons, guided by Sergeant Vaughan, with two of Hutton's Scouts, and a small detachment of the 1st Canadian Mounted Rifles, captured without loss two Field guns, one of which was said to have been taken from the Jameson raiders of 1896. Amongst the dozen men in the successful party were found representatives of no less than ten different regiments of Canadian militia. Hutton's column then returned to Pretoria.

At this period, provisions for the Rustenburg troops were drawn from Mafeking and Zeerust, and the necessary escorts for the convoys used up a large part of the small garrison. Early in July, Lord Roberts desired that a move should be made from Rustenburg to Warmbad, in conjunction with a brigade from Pretoria, so as to clear that section of the country. For this purpose 2,000 mounted men of the Imperial Bushmen Corps and two Maxims were ordered to be detached from Sir F. Carrington's command at Buluwayo, and to join Baden-Powell's force. Patrolling and raiding widely in every direction, the latter force awaited its reinforcements at Rustenburg for a fortnight, receiving surrenders and collecting arms. All was quiet up to the end of June, and a deceptive calm fell upon the districts west of the central railway. Krugersdorp alone, on account of the sullen demeanour of its inhabitants, seemed to require watching, and it was judged inexpedient to withdraw the garrison. Towards the beginning of July, parties of armed Boers began to collect at various places in the west, and there were signs of some considerable movement of the enemy north of Pretoria. The Scots Greys were accordingly sent to Waterval, and the 14th Hussars to Derde Poort. Boers in large parties were moving beyond Lord Roberts' northern flank, and it became clear that Botha, having failed to breast the British advance, hoped to relieve the pressure by rousing the farmers in the north and west. General De la Rey, with 2,000 men and five guns, was sent to the neighbourhood of Rustenburg, and Commandant Grobelaar, with 500 men and two guns, to threaten Pretoria from the north. Simultaneously, General Lemmer appeared south of Olifants Nek, and the Hekpoort men, south-west of Commando Nek, formed themselves into a force under the local Field Cornet, Sarel Oosthuizen. Another commando was known to have crossed the Vaal river at Venterskroon, south-east of Potchefstroom. Three hundred men of the Royal Scots and Royal Welsh Fusiliers, with sixty Imperial Yeomanry and two guns were, therefore, sent from Krugersdorp, under the command of Captain A. P. G. Gough, to reinforce the seventy men at Potchefstroom. To meet the new developments further south, Sir F. Carrington, with all the troops he could collect, was ordered to Mafeking to strengthen the line between that town and Rustenburg. Four companies of Yeomanry from Sir C. Warren's force, near Kuruman, were directed to concentrate at Vryburg, and to march to Klerksdorp under command of the Earl of Erroll; and Major-General Smith-Dorrien, with two battalions of his 19th brigade (2nd Shropshire Light Infantry and 1st Gordon Highlanders) went from Irene to Krugersdorp to operate towards Hekpoort. Meanwhile, on July 2nd, Baden-Powell, who was not yet strong enough to advance on Warmbad, drew nearer to Pretoria as a preliminary measure, and occupied Zilikat's and Commando Neks, each with two squadrons (Rhodesians) and two Royal Canadian guns, keeping the rest of his force midway between the two Neks at Rietfontein.

Occupation of Zilikat's and Commando Neks, July 2nd, 1900.

One of his squadrons had been left behind at Rustenburg, under Lieut.-Colonel C. O. Hore, to await the arrival of the Imperial Bushmen and the supply train from Mafeking. Detailed reports now came in that the town was to be attacked, and Hore's squadron, too weak to hold it, was ordered to fall back along the Zeerust road. The telegraph line was cut behind them, and a strong patrol of 140 men, under Major the Hon. A. H. C. Hanbury-Tracy, Royal Horse Guards, was detached by Baden-Powell to repair it, and to keep open communication with the west. Shortly after this patrol arrived at Rustenburg, a small commando attempted to enter the town from the south-east; but, finding it held by Hanbury-Tracy's detachment, retired to Olifants Nek. Lord Roberts, in consequence of these indications of unrest, had decided that Baden-Powell's force should return to Rustenburg. Meanwhile Hanbury-Tracy was ordered to remain there. At daybreak on July 7th, the threatened attack suddenly developed. Lemmer, having moved up from Olifants Nek, called on Hanbury-Tracy to surrender. His refusal was followed promptly by an assault. Lemmer tried to rush the kopjes to the south-west, and made persistent efforts to pass round to the wooded positions on the north. At the crisis of the fight two squadrons 1st Imperial Bushmen, under Colonel H. P. Airey, after a forced march of forty-eight miles from near

Boers attempt to recapture Rustenburg, July 7th, 1900.

Otto's Hoop, arrived on the field, and threw themselves into the engagement on either flank, when the enemy retired with a loss of five prisoners. Other reinforcements now began to arrive, amongst them Baden-Powell who, relieved at Zilikat's Nek, marched into Rustenburg, where there were now concentrated 1,500 men and fourteen guns. He sent out four squadrons of Bushmen to Magato Nek. Lemmer's commando had fallen back to Olifants Nek and as it was known to now number 700 men, Rustenburg was prepared for defence. Elsewhere there were signs of trouble, and a series of small engagements took place on July 11th.

The 7th Dragoon Guards (350 strong) were sent, on July 7th, with one section of O. battery R.H.A., to take the place, near Waterval, of the Scots Greys, in the outpost line north of Pretoria, held by the cavalry division. Their post was at Onderste Poort, between Waterval and Wonderboom Fort, ten miles from Pretoria, on an isolated range of kopjes parallel to and north of the Magaliesberg. On July 10th it was reported that a party of the enemy was occupying a farm near the eastern end of the kopjes, which Lieut.-Colonel W. H. M. Lowe, who was in command of the regiment, determined to attack the following morning. He obtained the sanction of Major-General J. B. B. Dickson, commanding the 4th cavalry brigade, then at Kameel Drift, and Dickson also undertook to support him. An hour before dawn on July 11th, " C." squadron (Captain J. E. F. Dyer) marched eastwards with three troops along the northern side of the line of kopjes, and one troop (Captain B. E. Church) along the southern side. On arriving near the Nek, Church's troop dismounted and occupied a donga, opening fire at daylight on the enemy in the farm. The Boers, who had been reinforced during the night, replied heavily to the troop from the front and left rear, stampeding the horses.

Affair at Onderste Poort, July 11th, 1900.

The officer who commanded the advance troop on the northern side had been directed to close that end of the Nek. Expecting the co-operation of a squadron of the 14th Hussars from the 4th brigade, and espying some khaki-clad and helmetted figures, he rode up to them, waved his hand to draw their attention, and was immediately severely wounded. The troop was driven back and rejoined Dyer. Meanwhile, a considerable number of the enemy, estimated at 300 men, with two guns, appeared from the north-east, and interposed between the three troops north of the ridge and Church's men.

An officer and two men were slain; another officer was mortally wounded; all the ammunition was expended. The troopers, unable any longer to defend themselves, surrendered, all but a few. The expected help from Kameel Drift had not come, for the squadron of the 14th Hussars, sent by Dickson, was beset in its turn and forced to retire; and Dyer's three troops fell back on the remainder of the regiment, which had moved up in support. At 11 o'clock, as the numbers of the enemy had greatly increased, Lieut.-Colonel Lowe vacated the whole position, removing all the stores and wagons to Derde Poort, nearer Pretoria. Another cavalry regiment, a battery of artillery and two battalions of infantry were sent to strengthen the post. Grobelaar's commando remained in the neighbourhood till July 15th, when Brigadier-General B. T. Mahon's force reached Derde Poort.

The enemy's success at Onderste Poort and the movements of Grobelaar's commando were serious menaces to Pretoria from the north. The new distribution had warded off the danger; but for the time Lord Roberts' scheme for clearing the northern district by the march on Warmbad could not be carried out.

Affair of Zilikat's Nek July 11th, 1900.

West of Pretoria the enemy was yet more successful. The Scots Greys, under Lieut.-Colonel the Hon. W. P. Alexander, when relieved at Waterval by the 7th Dragoon Guards, with two sections of O. battery R.H.A. (Major Sir J. Jervis-White-Jervis), had taken over the western passes vacated by Baden-Powell when he returned to Rustenburg. One squadron and two guns were left at Zilikat's Nek under Major H. J. Scobell; another, with the regimental machine gun, was placed at Commando Nek, and the remainder of the regiment and two guns were posted between the passes on a hill commanding the bridge over the Crocodile river. Persistent rumours of attack were current; and, as the mounted force was required to join a column forming under Smith-Dorrien, five companies of the 2nd battalion Lincolnshire, under Colonel H. R. Roberts, were ordered from Pretoria to relieve the cavalry. These reached Zilikat's Nek during the afternoon of July 10th, and their commanding officer was shown the disposition of the outposts. He decided to keep three companies at Zilikat's Nek, and send the other two to Commando Nek. Owing, however, to the lateness of the hour and the distance already covered by these two companies, they were halted for the night about half a mile in rear of the rest of the battalion. The line of outposts extended some 800 yards to the right of the north entrance of the Nek, and 400 yards to the left. Scobell had constantly employed fifty-five men actually on piquet out of the seventy-five carbines available. The Lincolnshire companies were very weak, and at first only thirty men (one company) were detailed for outpost duty, reinforced later on by fifteen men; another company took up an outpost line to the right rear of the bivouac, owing to a report of an impending attack from that side. As the squadron of the Scots Greys and the two guns had not to join the rest of the mounted force till the following morning, they remained on the Nek for the night in support of the infantry. Sangars, with wire entanglements, had been made for the guns, but the bush in front had not been cleared for a width of more than two hundred yards. Overlooking the piquet line were two high peaks some 400 yards to the right. They commanded the whole position, but were left unoccupied.

At daybreak next morning Mauser fire broke from the peaks, and the outpost commander, Captain L. Edwards (Lincolnshire), was at once reinforced. Shortly after, a Boer force, of about 300 men, bringing a gun and a Vickers-Maxim, made an enveloping attack, despite the fire of the Scots Greys on the right, and of the infantry supports which were pushed forward on the left. The guns in the centre were only able to deliver a few rounds, as the enemy, who was able to approach under cover to within 200 yards, shot so fast that the gunners could not show themselves above the sangars. Having overpowered the piquets on the right, the Boers charged the guns and captured the gun detachments. On the left, the Lincolnshire men, having expended their ammunition, fell back slowly before another strong party, and by 5 p.m. the Nek was lost. Roberts, himself wounded, gave the order to surrender; and the whole squadron of the Scots Greys, with the commanding officer, the adjutant and eighty-four men of the Lincolnshire, were made prisoners.

The other casualties of the battalion were an officer and twenty men killed, three officers and twenty-four men wounded. The squadron of the Scots Greys lost two officers and one man killed, and one officer and sixteen men wounded. Lieut.-Colonel Alexander had been warned to withdraw any small isolated detachments which might be liable to surprise. At 6 a.m. he reported to Pretoria that the Nek was attacked. He remained in his position near the bridge over the Crocodile river with his guns trained on Commando Nek. At 8.45 a.m., in response to a message sent by orderly by Colonel Roberts, the two guns, with a small escort, came into action against the high ground east of Zilikat's Nek. There they remained until 10 a.m. when they were recalled because of the approach of Boers towards them. At 1 p.m. the two companies originally destined for Commando Nek, which had been engaged in firing on the western end of the Nek, fell back on Alexander's party. In the meantime Alexander had sent to the squadron at Commando Nek, ordering it either to retire on him, or make its way back to Pretoria. The latter course was pursued. When the post was beyond rescue, Alexander occupied a watching position south of Zilikat's Nek, and retired towards Pretoria at sundown. He had moved but a few miles, when he met 450 mounted infantry, 500 infantry and four guns, which had left Pretoria at 2 p.m., under command of Colonel J. W. Godfray, King's Own Scottish Borderers. The disaster had thus been due more to lack of co-operation between the detachments than to want of support.

It had been arranged that a column should march from Krugersdorp to co-operate with Baden-Powell's force against Lemmer's commando at Olifants Nek. Accordingly, on July 11th, Major-General Smith-Dorrien, with the 2nd Shropshire

Light Infantry and 1st Gordon Highlanders of the 19th brigade, and the 19th company (Lothian and Berwickshire) Imperial Yeomanry, with a Colt gun and two guns of the 78th battery R.F.A.—1,350 men in all—left for Hekpoort, where they were to be joined by the Scots Greys and two of the Horse artillery guns from Zilikat's Nek. The country immediately north of Krugersdorp is difficult and broken. Beyond, the high and precipitous Witwaters Berg barred the way, trending from near Zeekoehoek for many miles in a south-easterly direction, and rendering it necessary for the heights to be crowned before a direct advance could be made to Hekpoort. Scouting near Onrust, nine miles from Krugersdorp, the Yeomanry were met with heavy fire from hills 2,000 yards from their right flank. Sir J. Miller, commanding the mounted troops, immediately led his Yeomanry towards a high ridge as yet unoccupied, while the Gordon Highlanders and the two guns opened fire on the enemy to the right front. The Boers then galloped across a broad nek to forestall the Yeomanry, and to bring a cross-fire on the guns from both flanks. The section of artillery was too far forward, and before the order to withdraw was received, the enemy had opened fire at a range of 900 yards. Teams and limbers had been placed under cover some 600 yards to the rear. After the guns had been in action for half an hour, only three of the personnel remained unwounded; in trying to remove the guns, both the teams were disabled. Lieut. A. J. Turner, the commander of the section, had been one of the first wounded; notwithstanding a second wound, he continued to work one of his guns himself till the last moment before ceasing fire. When signalling for assistance the officer was struck for the third time; then the non-commissioned officers in charge of each weapon, although themselves wounded, disabled the pieces. The attempt to withdraw them had to be abandoned for the time. Next a small party of the Gordon Highlanders, under the adjutant, Captain W. E. Gordon, with the assistance of the unwounded gunners, made gallant but ineffectual efforts to save the guns, Captain D. R. Younger, Captain P. S. Allan and several men bringing one wagon back. Captain Younger and three men were

<small>Affair at Onrust, July 11th, 1900.</small>

killed.* Lieut.-Colonel J. Spens, Shropshire Light Infantry, was now directed to send two of his companies to a kopje a mile and a half to the right, to outflank the Boers, the rest of his battalion remaining to guard the baggage, which had been parked on the road. At about 12.45 p.m., the enemy, having completely silenced the guns, worked round to the left and opened a long-range fire on the transport. The baggage was moved with difficulty further to the west, under cover of a frontal attack made by the Shropshire upon the ridge. During the afternoon the Boers crept up into a position whence they were able to pour a heavy enfilade fire into the Gordon Highlanders, who had remained covering the guns; but the battalion had erected good sangars, and suffered little loss. As soon as it was dark, the Boers came down the hill to within 300 yards of the Highlanders, and the voices of their leaders, shouting the command "Vorwarts!" were distinctly heard; but the burghers could not be induced to rush the defences, although they fired heavily upon them. An outburst of rapid independent musketry from the Gordon Highlanders threw back the wavering enemy.

During the day, Smith-Dorrien learned what kept the Scots Greys and Horse artillery guns from meeting him at Hekpoort. He therefore decided to retire on Krugersdorp; but as the guns could not be moved till after nightfall, he halted, and asked Major-General Barton to send a force from Krugersdorp to co-operate. By 8 p.m. the guns were withdrawn, and the force reached Krugersdorp at 4 a.m. The casualties, in addition to those already mentioned, were two officers and thirty-five men wounded, of whom seventeen belonged to the Royal artillery.

<small>Effect of above incidents.</small>
The incidents of Onderste Poort, Zilikat's Nek and Onrust, insignificant as they were in themselves, proved that an offensive spirit was by no means dead in the Boer ranks. The mischief of such affairs lay in the exaggerated importance which was attached to them by the farmers, and in the consequent change in their attitude. Encouraged by the success of his enterprise west of Pretoria, Botha proposed to transfer more men to that

* Captain Gordon and Captain Younger (posthumous), were awarded the Victoria Cross.

OPERATIONS IN THE WESTERN TRANSVAAL.

area, in order to save as many as possible from being hemmed in against the Portuguese frontier. In a telegram to Lieut.-General French on the 11th, Lord Roberts wrote: " The enemy are evidently in considerable strength all along our left flank with the intention of working round our left rear. This movement must be checked without delay. . . . Now that the enemy has been driven off by you from our right front . . . order in at once (to Pretoria) the four battalions of infantry and two of the 5-in. guns, and come in yourself to take command of the cavalry on the northern flank."* Lieut.-General Ian Hamilton's column, of which Colonel Hickman's mounted infantry formed part, was also sent north of Pretoria. Still Rustenburg was threatened, and General De la Rey, holding the passes of the Magaliesberg, was free to go as he chose into the Hekpoort district to commandeer the farmers; it was imperative that the force at Krugersdorp should be increased. Lord Roberts proposed, therefore, to bring up Smith-Dorrien's force to Pretoria, sending Hart's stronger brigade from Heidelberg to relieve him. Sir R. Buller, however, found himself unable to replace Hart at Heidelberg, and the transfer of the 5th brigade was cancelled, Smith-Dorrien's battalions remaining for the time at Krugersdorp. Thither, with a force so much reduced as to be a division only in name, Lord Methuen was ordered on July 12th. He marched from Lindley with seven days' supplies for Kroonstad. The Ist division now consisted of 1,200 mounted troops, 2,400 rifles, twelve Field guns, two 5-in. Howitzers, two Vickers-Maxims, and nine machine guns, and was made up of the 5th, 10th and 15th battalions Imperial Yeomanry, a detachment of mounted infantry and Warwick's Scouts, the 4th, 20th and 38th batteries Royal Field artillery, three sections 11th Field company R.E., the 1st battalion Northumberland Fusiliers, the 2nd Northamptonshire, and the 1st battalion Loyal North Lancashire. Owing to lack of rolling stock at Kroonstad, the movement was seriously delayed, the transport having to go by road; and the division as a whole was not at Krugersdorp till a week later. Then it started for Hekpoort together with Smith-Dorrien's

Ist division concentrates at Krugersdorp, July 18th, 1900.

* See page 313.

brigade, while Barton provided a garrison for Krugersdorp. The force marched in two columns; the right consisting of two and a half battalions of infantry, viz.: the 9th brigade, less a half battalion Northumberland Fusiliers with the left column, two guns of the 38th battery R.F.A., one section of Howitzers, one section Field company R.E., and a half squadron Imperial Yeomanry, under Major-General Douglas; the left, under Lord Methuen, was made up of Smith-Dorrien's two battalions, the 4th Field battery, one section of Howitzers, the rest of the R.E., and the remainder of the Yeomanry. A few of the enemy were observed on the scene of the action of July 11th; but they soon left, making but slight resistance at the entrance to Zeekoehoek Pass, and in the kopjes near Wagenpadspruit. Lord Roberts had intended Lord Methuen and Baden-Powell to co-operate against Lemmer's force at Olifants Nek, Baden-Powell blocking the northern, while the marching columns attacked the southern entrance of the pass. Lord Methuen had informed Baden-Powell on the 18th that his columns would attack the Nek from the south-east at daybreak on the 21st. At 8.30 a.m. on that date a telegram was also received at Rustenburg, confirming the instructions for an early attack. Finally, to make sure that there should be no mistake, Lord Roberts himself telegraphed to Baden-Powell the exact date of Lord Methuen's arrival; and when Lord Methuen's columns, leaving Wagenpadspruit at 5 a.m. on July 21st, neared Olifants Nek, they fully anticipated shutting up the Boers in the pass. At 7.30 a.m. the enemy was discovered, barring all the approaches upon a strong position in front of the Nek itself, flanked by high hills with kopjes rising in the midst of the pass.

July 21st, 1900. Attack on Olifants Nek by Lord Methuen.

At eight o'clock they opened fire and brought two Vickers-Maxims into action, which were answered by those with the column, and soon after by the guns. The Northumberland Fusiliers and Northamptonshire regiment of Douglas' (9th) brigade on the left, and the Shropshire Light Infantry of Smith-Dorrien's force on the right, cleared the hills with trifling loss, reaching the summit at 9.30 a.m., and the rest of the column advanced into the pass at eleven o'clock. The Boers were shelled

OPERATIONS IN THE WESTERN TRANSVAAL. 245

as they retired, and one of their gun-carriages was smashed. After a half-hearted resistance the commandos fled, most of them retreating through the Nek and dispersing in the thick bush beyond. The Yeomanry occupied the pass about 12.30 p.m., at which hour Baden-Powell's guns were heard in action from ground some 2,000 yards to the north-east of the pass.

To carry out the idea of co-operation on the pre-arranged date, the commander at Rustenburg had issued orders, in which the duties of the garrison had been stated thus :

1. To hold Rustenburg,
2. To hold Magato Nek in case Lord Methuen failed to get through Olifants Nek, and
3. To help Lord Methuen by making a diversion against Olifants Nek.

For the last and most immediate object, Colonel H. C. O. Plumer was placed in command of three squadrons Rhodesia regiment, three squadrons Protectorate regiment, one squadron Victorian Mounted Rifles, and four guns of the Royal Canadian artillery. A careful look-out was to be kept for any other hostile forces, especially towards the east, where a commando was known to be hovering. The unmolested journey of two cyclists, who had gone round by Elands river and arrived at 8.30, bringing the telegram from Lord Methuen, proved that little need be feared from the westward, and the brigade of Bushmen at Magato Nek could be safely left in their strong entrenchments without anxiety. {Baden-Powell co-operates from Rustenburg.}

The sound of Lord Methuen's guns, which had opened fire about 8.30 a.m., was not heard by the Rustenburg force till 10.30. The Boers had then begun to vacate their position ; when Plumer's force moved towards the Nek, they were in full retreat, and the arrival of the column only hastened their flight. Lord Methuen's losses were two men killed and four wounded. Of the Boers, five dead were found, and four prisoners were taken, a small price for extricating 500 or 600 men from a defile at either end of which stood superior forces. That afternoon at 4.30, as Baden-Powell's force turned back to Rustenburg, a large convoy of the enemy's wagons was reported twelve miles to the south-east, moving eastwards.

A detachment of 300 Imperial Bushmen, under command of Colonel H. P. Airey, left Rustenburg the same evening to clear the Boers off the Zeerust road, and to bring up a large convoy from Elands River. After crossing the Selous river they were fired at. The column bivouacked in a safe spot, and marched next morning towards the Boer laager. The enemy, becoming aware that their camp had been discovered, had inspanned during the night and moved to a fresh site on a kopje 500 yards from the Zeerust road. Airey's force, passing this unsuspected position, was received with heavy fire. The squadrons dismounted and extended for attack, but could neither advance nor retire. Many of their horses were shot, and the remainder stampeded. Reinforcements of 560 men and two guns, made up of two squadrons of Imperial Bushmen, with detachments of the Protectorate and Rhodesia regiments and British South Africa Police, came promptly out from Rustenburg; on their arrival at a ridge overlooking the position, the enemy retired, taking with them 200 of the Bushmen's horses. In this brush one officer and five men were killed, twenty-six men were wounded, nine missing, and an officer afterwards died of his wounds. The convoy could not get through, and remained at Elands River; but, as Baden-Powell had still sixteen days' supplies at Rustenburg after replenishing Lord Methuen's force, no anxiety was felt on that score. After joining hands, it had been arranged that Lord Methuen's and Baden-Powell's combined commands should proceed to Pretoria. Lord Methuen decided to leave a garrison at Olifants Nek. For this duty, the 1st battalion Loyal North Lancashire regiment was detailed from the 9th brigade, with two guns and twenty-five mounted men from Rustenburg, the whole under the command of Colonel R. G. Kekewich, Loyal North Lancashire regiment.

Events further south, however, brought about a change of plan. The day after Lord Methuen left Krugersdorp, the enemy south of the town fired with a Krupp gun upon a hospital train taking convalescents, under the Red Cross flag, from Potchef-

OPERATIONS IN THE WESTERN TRANSVAAL. 247

stroom to Johannesburg. The rails having been torn up near Bank Station, the train ran off the line, and was captured. A commando of 200 men under Commandant Douthwaite was also reported near Potchefstroom, with intent to attack that place as soon as they were joined from the north-east by the Losberg men. In the meantime they destroyed the railway line near Frederikstad, and cut the telegraph wires. The garrison at Potchefstroom, thus isolated, was directed to prepare for attack by entrenching as strongly as possible. Klerksdorp, thirty miles to the southwest, with its small garrison of forty men of the Kimberley Mounted Corps, surrendered on July 24th to a Boer force of 600 men and three guns, under General Liebenberg.

Trouble therefore hung over the Mooi River valley, and energetic measures were taken to meet it. Lord Methuen's force, including Smith-Dorrien's brigade, was recalled from Olifants Nek, and instructed to move at once to Bank Station. Sir F. Carrington was ordered to hasten to Mafeking, so that he might co-operate with Baden-Powell, who was to remain at Rustenburg. Brigadier-General Lord Erroll, who had arrived at Lichtenburg, with two squadrons of Imperial Bushmen, four companies of Paget's Horse, and four Vickers-Maxims, was sent to Otto's Hoop; and the garrison of Heilbron, about 1,000 strong, including the City Imperial Volunteers, and a provisional battalion of two officers and 325 men, was brought by rail to Krugersdorp to strengthen Barton's command.

On July 24th, Baden-Powell reported a concentration of the enemy north-east of Rustenburg, and a movement westward along the north of the Magaliesberg. Six commandos, aggregating between 2,000 and 3,000 men with eight guns, were known to be in the neighbourhood, and a captured Boer artillery officer stated that General De la Rey had 2,000 men and six guns at Wolhuter's Kop, on the Rustenburg—Pretoria road. As it was not clear whether Grobelaar's commando had moved east or west from Waterval, Colonel T. E. Hickman's mounted infantry, temporarily reinforced by the 2nd battalion Duke of Cornwall's Light Infantry and the 18th battery Royal Field artillery, on July 25th was sent from Pretoria towards the junction of the

and in the Rustenburg area.

Six Mile Spruit and the Crocodile river, to reconnoitre Zilikat's and Commando Neks. The Crocodile river was in flood, and the neks could not be properly reconnoitred from the south; the column returned to Pretoria, moving next day along the valley to the north of the Witwaters Berg. From this range a clear view was obtained of the Boer laager, and it was ascertained that the enemy were holding the passes with 2,000 men and seven guns. In short, the situation in the Western Transvaal appeared so disturbed, and the Boers in such strength, that on July 30th the Commander-in-Chief ordered Ian Hamilton's force, now arriving at Pretoria from the Eastern line, to move thence on Commando Nek.

CHAPTER X.

THE CLEARING OF NORTHERN NATAL.*

ON the relief of Ladysmith, the enemy had vanished so completely that the armies of Natal which had for so many months lain within range of his rifles, now failed to catch sight of his rearguard. Although, truly, the defeated Boers found themselves unharried by even the semblance of pursuit, their flight was surprising enough, alike from its celerity and its completeness. The raising of a siege in the face of a victorious field army has been commonly a most expensive operation. Lines of investment long held are in danger of becoming inert. Within them collect inevitably quantities of guns, ammunition, stores and personal belongings; behind them an ever-increasing mass of transport and impedimenta, which require the most assiduous care to maintain them in readiness to move. Yet on March 2nd only a few of the Boers' rearmost wagons, with a paltry escort, were visible at the head of the Van Reenen's Pass,† and but a few tons of stores fell into the hands of the 3rd mounted brigade at Modder Spruit Siding next day. On the 5th, the 14th Hussars patrolled to Elandslaagte without opposition, occupied it, and were joined on the 6th by the entire 1st cavalry brigade, on the 7th by the 4th infantry brigade and the 7th battery R.F.A., on the 8th and following days by four Naval 12-pr. guns, the 2nd infantry brigade and the rest of the IInd division. Of the remainder of the troops, the 7th and 8th brigades, the

The enemy's retreat from Ladysmith.

---

* See maps Nos. 45, 46 and 47.

† Telegram No. 214, Sir R. Buller to Lord Roberts, March 2nd, 1900.

infantry of Ladysmith (now formed into a IVth division under Major-General the Hon. N. G. Lyttelton) and the 5th and 6th brigades (now the Xth division under Major-General Sir A. Hunter) remained in the vicinity of Ladysmith, which they surrounded with posts; whilst on March 6th and 7th the Vth division (Lieut.-General Sir C. Warren) with the 14th Hussars, but without the divisional troops, quitting the Natal forces, moved towards the coast for embarkation to East London, in response to orders by Lord Roberts,* who was anxious to reinforce General Gatacre, on the Stormberg.†

The needs of the Natal Army.

Now ensued a long period of inaction. Though Sir R. Buller himself was anxious to press on immediately, either to Dundee and Newcastle, or through the Drakensberg Passes into the Orange Free State,‡ there were many reasons why such activity at this time was undesirable, or even impossible. Those connected with the situation of the armies under Field-Marshal Lord Roberts will be detailed later. Apart from these, there was much to do before Sir R. Buller's own forces could regain their mobility and efficiency, both considerably impaired by the wear and tear of three months' unrelenting campaigning. The garrison of Ladysmith had emerged from the trenches composed of practically nothing but sick men. On March 2nd the Principal Medical Officer reported that another month must elapse before the soldiers would be fit for service. Only two hundred nearly useless horses remained to the cavalry. The Ladysmith troops had therefore to be scattered into clean and healthy camps to recuperate, the 7th brigade going to Arcadia, the 8th brigade to Colenso, the cavalry dividing to both places to await drafts of fresh horses. The evacuation of the town, and the Intombi Hospital where the sick numbered over two thousand, presented a more difficult problem. The patients were for the most part in a deplorable condition, and it was necessary to remove them at once. But all the railway bridges and culverts were destroyed;

---

* Telegrams No. C. 186, 24/2/00; No. C. 315, 3/3/00 and No. C. 344, 6/3/00.

† The Vth division rejoined the Natal force before the end of March. See page 252.

‡ Telegrams No. 214, 3/3/00 and No. 217, 5/3/00, Sir Redvers Buller to Lord Roberts

and though as early as the 9th a train was run from the left bank of the Tugela to Ladysmith, the northward transit of army stores made heavy demands upon the line. Nevertheless it was contrived to convey the patients southward at the rate of nearly one hundred a day; on March 19th a temporary bridge was open for traffic, by the side of the vast structure lying demolished in the river bed at Colenso. The road bridge, restored to working order on March 2nd, had done much to assist transport by rendering possible a link of wagon traffic between rail-head at Colenso and the resumption of the line on the north bank. By the 27th Intombi was empty, and the sick and wounded were distributed amongst various hospitals in Natal; the convalescent, and those requiring a period of rest, were accommodated in a spacious camp in the magnificent air of Mooi River.

The needs of the relief column, though the sick list was not small, were chiefly in the matter of drafts, horses, clothing and supplies. On the 14th arrived the first of many reinforcements from the home Volunteer Forces, soldiers whose quality was best evinced by the readiness with which they acquired much of the skill and steadiness of the veteran campaigners whom they joined. These, with the drafts from the depôts, it was necessary first to transport to the front, then to train and accustom to the conditions of active service. Both the railway officials, who hurried supplies up unceasingly, and the staffs of all units found the period of delay under the Biggarsberg by no means an interval of idleness; and by the exertions of both, the Natal armies were gradually fully equipped and fitted for further service. General Sir G. White, with Major-General Ian Hamilton, Colonel Sir H. S. Rawlinson and other officers of the Ladysmith Staff, left Natal on March 9th, in accordance with orders from Lord Roberts, and proceeded to Cape Colony. On March 11th the officers and bluejackets of H.M.S. *Terrible* rejoined their ship; all but twenty-five men of the Natal Naval Volunteers also returned from the front, leaving the strength of the Naval brigade at 117 officers and men. The forces of Sir G. White and Sir R. Buller were now welded into a manageable whole by a re-organisation of units,* which was completed on March 27th.

During this period the front of the army covered a somewhat weak line from Tabanyama, Blaauwbank and Smith's Crossing on the left, whence the 3rd mounted brigade watched the Drakensberg Passes, through Intintanyoni and Elandslaagte, where lay the IInd division with two 4.7-in. and four 12-pr. Naval guns, screened by the 1st cavalry brigade, round to Job's Kop on the right, where a force of the Colonial contingent, five squadrons Bethune's M.I., one squadron Umvoti Mounted Rifles, two 12-pr. and two 7-pr. guns, and six companies Imperial Light Infantry under Lieut.-Colonel E. C. Bethune (16th Lancers), had been detached to observe Pomeroy, to cover the right flank, and to check disaffection in the Umvoti district, where the sympathies were largely Boer. This detachment had been out since the first week of February. The Vth division, in accordance with events to be related in their place, returned to Ladysmith from the coast, where it had been in process of embarkation, on the 22nd—24th, and went into camp temporarily near Surprise Hill, being there rejoined by the divisional troops. Of the newly-formed Xth division, the 6th brigade came up to Modder Spruit on March 12th, the 5th brigade joining the IInd division at Elandslaagte on the 24th.

<small>The Boers stand on the Biggarsberg.</small> Before the middle of March the position of the enemy became well defined. Finding himself unpursued, he had retreated no further northward than the Biggarsberg Range† which, situated some miles north of Ladysmith, completely traversed the apex of Natal from the Drakensberg mountains to the Buffalo river. Upon this formidable barrier the Boer army, consisting at this time of about 16,000 men with thirty guns, had now entrenched itself, its right resting upon the Cundycleugh Pass, its left upon the Van Tonder's Pass, Beith, and Helpmakaar; the centre rested between the points where the Newcastle road and

---

* For details, see Appendix 1.

† The decision to stand at the Biggarsberg was made by Commandant-General Joubert at the last council of war presided over by him (he died at Pretoria on March 27th), held at Glencoe on March 10th.

THE CLEARING OF NORTHERN NATAL. 253

the railway pierced the mountains, and was especially strong. In advance of the right wing, patrols and posts held the Drakensberg down to Van Reenen's Pass; whilst strong detachments, entrenched at Pomeroy and Helpmakaar, not only covered the roads approaching the left flank, but in some measure threatened also those leading around the British right in the direction of Weenen and Greytown. The Boer reserves lay at Dundee, where supporting positions had been prepared on Indumeni in front of the town, and Impati behind it. The position, the front of which was largely protected by the Sunday's and Waschbank rivers, was of immense topographical strength, and though of an extent very great for the numbers available, the burghers could rely on their mobility to enable them to man in time any threatened point, since from the commanding crest of the Biggarsberg no movement of their opponents could be concealed from them.

In these situations the opposed armies lay inactive throughout March and the early portion of April, with no more fighting than that provided by affairs of patrols amongst the foothills which fringed the Sunday's river. The delay, however, whilst it strengthened and equipped Sir R. Buller's forces, became every day more to the disadvantage of the enemy. Lord Roberts was marching fast through the Orange Free State; and his progress, as he had foretold, drew large numbers of Boers from Sir R. Buller's front, where they might have been dangerous, to his own, where they only added to the confusion prevailing in the face of his irresistible advance. Approximately half the entire Boer force upon the Biggarsberg had disappeared in this manner by the end of March, when there still remained six thousand to seven thousand men.* In the British lines the chief events of importance were the opening of the Sunday's River bridge for traffic on April 2nd, the arrival of the Vth division at Elandslaagte on April 4th—5th, and the departure of the Xth division for East London *viâ* Durban between April 5th—9th. On the latter date the 1st cavalry brigade (Burn-Murdoch) in front of Elandslaagte exchanged positions with the 3rd mounted

They diminish in numbers.

* Telegram from General Botha, April 8th, 1900.

brigade (Lord Dundonald) from the west of Ladysmith, the 2nd cavalry brigade (Brocklehurst) taking up a line of observation on the east and north-eastern side of Ladysmith at Pound Plateau.

<small>April 10th, 1900. They attack the British camp.</small>

On April the 10th, the enemy, coming down from the highest crest of the Berg, opened fire with three guns at 7.30 a.m. on the camp of the IInd division at Elandslaagte, at a range of about five thousand yards, at the same time engaging with rifle fire the mounted piquets posted along the Sunday's river. The attack, which was directed by General Botha in person, had been carefully prepared, in the full hopes of luring Sir R. Buller into giving battle in the open. A strong force was held in readiness to oppose him, and the commandos in the Drakensberg Passes had been ordered to make a simultaneous demonstration against Ladysmith. Though the effects of the bombardment were insignificant,* it was evident that the camp would be no longer tenable in its exposed situation, and Sir R. Buller, who had arrived at Elandslaagte that morning, decided to withdraw into a better defensive position. Covered by the mounted brigade, and the 2nd brigade, which occupied the kopjes above Sunday's River bridge, becoming slightly engaged with the Boer sharpshooters, and by the 10th brigade on Jonono's Kop, the main body retired in a leisurely manner after dark, and was disposed before dawn upon a strong line based upon the kopjes on which the action of October 21st, 1899, had been fought, these ridges having a greater command facing northward than southward. The enemy made no further demonstrations; and the following days were devoted to the occupation of a more permanent defensive line. By the fresh arrangements, the IInd division was on the 16th withdrawn to Surprise Hill, leaving behind, however, the 2nd Scottish Rifles, and 1st battalion Rifle Brigade to be attached to the Vth division, in completion of the strength of the 10th brigade.

Upon the Vth division then devolved the task of covering the front. On the 20th its commander, Sir C. Warren, left to

---

* Casualties, April 10th—Killed, two men of the Naval brigade; wounded, one officer and eight men.

THE CLEARING OF NORTHERN NATAL.   255

take up an appointment in Cape Colony, and was succeeded by Major-General Hildyard, whose brigade (2nd) passed to Lieut.-Colonel E. O. F. Hamilton, of the 2nd Queen's (R. W. Surrey) regiment. Hildyard now disposed the Vth division along an extremely strong position, which had been chosen before Warren's departure, extending from Jonono's Kop on the left, the lofty summit of which was occupied by units of the 11th brigade, through Woodcote Farm, the Collieries, and Elandslaagte, to the kopjes on which French's battle had been fought six months before, where the 10th brigade lay on the right, the 3rd mounted brigade camping in support on the Modder Spruit. On April 21st, the numbers of the enemy were still further lessened by about three thousand men, who quitted Natal for the Orange Free State. Possibly to cover their departure, the Boer gunners on the Berg opened fire upon the outposts about Elandslaagte Collieries. At the same time strong mounted bodies moved so threateningly towards the British left, that not only was the 3rd mounted brigade sent up to that flank, but the IInd division in Ladysmith was ordered out, and held in readiness to support. The day closed quietly, however, and until the end of the month nothing further occurred in Natal.

Early in May Sir R. Buller began a movement which had far-reaching effects. From the moment of his arrival in Ladysmith he had cast about for fresh employment. The defeated commandos had disappeared; and Sir R. Buller, perhaps conceiving their disorder to be greater than it was, at once matured plans, not only for the clearance of Northern Natal, but for the actual invasion of hostile territory. On March 3rd he telegraphed to Field-Marshal Lord Roberts as follows :* Sir R. Buller's projects after the relief of Ladysmith.

" . . . My own view would be that we should send three brigades to re-occupy Northern Natal, restore order, and repair the railway, and with two divisions attack the three passes, Tintwa, Van Reenen's, and Bezuidenhout, and pass

---

* No. 214, March 3rd, extract. With reference to the following correspondence, it has not been thought necessary to quote *in extenso*, or in some cases to quote at all, the communications, the dates and numbers of which are given in footnotes.

through one of them the division you wish* to your side, or, in the event of your not wanting a division, that the force kept should re-occupy Northern Natal, and the Wakkerstroom-Vryheid district of the Transvaal. . . ."

From this view Lord Roberts, then at Osfontein, dissented, telegraphing on March 3rd :†

" I do not think it would be wise now to embark on extensive operations in Natal, which is evidently extremely suitable for the enemy's tactics and very difficult for our troops. To force the passes of the Drakensberg would undoubtedly be a very hazardous operation, and would probably enable the Boers, with a small force, to hold up a very much larger number of men for some considerable time. The force in Natal three months ago consisted of four divisions of infantry, and two brigades of cavalry. It is probably now not of greater strength than three divisions of infantry, and one brigade of cavalry, besides local mounted troops ; two of these divisions, with the brigade of cavalry, should, I imagine, suffice for the pacification of such portion of Natal as would ensure the safety of the railway toward Van Reenen's Pass, on the understanding that the Natal Field Force is to act strictly on the defensive,‡ until such time as the operations of this column have caused the enemy to withdraw altogether from, or considerably reduce their numbers in, the Drakensberg Passes. The remaining division should be despatched at once to East London. . . ."

On March 5th, Sir R. Buller again telegraphed, submitting further suggestions :§

" . . . The Boers are in full retreat, and it is highly

---

* Lord Roberts (C. 186, of February 24th) had telegraphed as follows :—" As soon as you have relieved Ladysmith, I hope you will be able to send me a division of infantry." The despatch of the Vth division to the coast on March 6th was in accordance with this request. The reasons for its return on the 22nd will appear later.

† No. C. 315, March 3rd.

‡ See Appendix 6.

§ No. 217, March 5th.

THE CLEARING OF NORTHERN NATAL.

desirable to re-occupy Dundee, and if possible Newcastle. . . . I am now through the mountains, and I can get round the Biggarsberg through a fairly open country. . . . I propose to move forward as soon as I have got boots for the men, and to re-occupy Dundee and open the coal mines; this is the best defensive measure I can take."

To this Lord Roberts replied* on the following day, approving the new plan as regards Dundee and Newcastle, but reiterating the undesirability of attempting the passes of the Drakensberg. On March 7th, Sir R. Buller telegraphed† that in his opinion to take the Drakensberg Passes would be an easier task than the Biggarsberg, with the additional advantage that the occupation of Harrismith would materially assist the operations of Lord Roberts himself. The railway line to that town once open, Sir R. Buller estimated, in a later communication, that he might be able to supply Lord Roberts' army at the rate of some four hundred tons per diem.‡ To this Lord Roberts§ agreed, intimating, however, that owing to the probable difficulties of supply, only one division should be employed on the operation.|| This force Sir R. Buller declared¶ to be insufficient for the task, and in a few days reverted to his project of forcing the enemy north of Newcastle before attempting the Drakensberg, which he proposed to do with two divisions.** Lord Roberts at first approved;†† but becoming aware of the increasing strength of the enemy on his own front, in the Ladybrand district, subsequently came to the conclusion that a movement on Harrismith was imperative. He therefore instructed Sir R. Buller to relinquish the Newcastle plan, and to "move with all speed, and as strong as possible, in the direction of Van Reenen's."‡‡ In acknowledging these orders, Sir R. Buller felt it his duty to inform Lord Roberts that his instructions

* No. C. 349, March 6th.
† No. 219, March 7th.
‡ No. 226, March 24th.
§ No. C. 654, March 25th.
|| No. C. 669, March 26th.
¶ No. 230, March 27th.
** No. 234, March 31st.
†† No. C. 789, April 1st.
‡‡ No. C. 798, April 2nd.

involved " some risk to his force, and considerable risk to Natal."*
Two days later, however, Lord Roberts, modifying his plans in
accordance with the development of the tactical situation in
the Orange Free State, abandoned the idea of forcing the passes,
and requested Sir R. Buller to send at once the Xth division and
the Imperial Light Horse to East London.† This division
was embarked on the next day, and Sir R. Buller remained in
his positions.

The time, in fact, had not been ripe for co-operation between
the widely separated armies of Lord Roberts and Sir R. Buller;
and it was not until May that the success of his right wing, and
his preparedness at Bloemfontein, enabled the Commander-in-
Chief to utilise the Natal army as a unit in his general scheme
of advance. The part designed for it to play was of the first
importance; for already the Field-Marshal foresaw that he
would eventually have to depend upon Natal as his base of
supply.‡ On May 2nd, he sent the following communication
to Sir R. Buller :§

" A force, under command of General Ian Hamilton, successfully cleared large numbers of the enemy out of the Hout Nek,
ten miles north of Thabanchu, yesterday. This force will now
advance on Winburg, and another, which I accompany, will
move simultaneously along the line of railway. You should
occupy the enemy's attention on the Biggarsberg, and, as their
numbers decrease, which they assuredly will, move your troops
towards the Transvaal, repairing the railway as you advance.
Please let me know what you hope to do in this respect."

Sir R. Buller, in reply,‖ whilst remarking that for such operations he was short of his proper strength, signified his readiness
to start in four days, and turned immediately to the arrange-

* No. 235, April 2nd.
† No. C. 844, April 4th.
‡ No. 568, Lord Roberts to Secretary of State for War.
§ No. C. 1419, May 2nd.
‖ No. 252, May 3rd.

THE CLEARING OF NORTHERN NATAL. 259

ments for the combined advance of two divisions. Briefly, his design was to turn the left flank of the enemy on the Biggarsberg with the IInd division, moving by Helpmakaar and Beith, the right covered by Bethune's force from the lower Tugela, the left by the Vth division, which marching synchronously, would advance up the railway by Wessels Nek and Waschbank, repairing the line *en route*. The IVth division would remain for the present in reserve in its positions around Ladysmith, where the men were slowly recovering from the exhaustion of the siege.

The IInd division, therefore, its divisional cavalry increased by a squadron 13th Hussars, and one of the 19th Hussars, left its camp about Surprise Hill on May 7th;* was at Modder Spruit on the 8th, at Pieters Farm on the 9th, and at the Sunday's River camp on the 10th. Here the following units were attached to act with the division in the impending operations: The 3rd mounted brigade, the 61st Howitzer battery, two 4.7-in. and four 12-pr. guns, manned by the Royal Garrison artillery,† three Vickers-Maxim (" pom-poms ") and the 4th Mountain battery. This force carried five days' supplies, one day's on the soldier, one in the regimental transport, and three days' in the supply column. On the day previous to this concentration, Major-General H. J. T. Hildyard, in anticipation of the eastern movement of the IInd division, had slightly extended his line in that direction by sending the 2nd Middlesex regiment to a spur, upon which he also arranged gun emplacements, overlooking the valley of the Waschbank.

On the night of the 10th, orders for the march were issued by Sir F. Clery, commanding the IInd division. Sir R. Buller assumed command on the next day, and the columns, screened by Lord Dundonald's 3rd mounted brigade, crossed, and camped on the east bank of the Waschbank river, only a few Boers

May 11th, 1900.
Sir R. Buller marches against the Biggarsberg.

---

* On this night an abortive attack was made on the piquets at the Elandslaagte Collieries by a commando of foreigners.

† After the relief of Ladysmith, the Naval detachments of both H.M.S. *Powerful* and *Terrible* had rejoined their ships, leaving at the front ten officers and fifty men of H.M.S. *Forte*, *Philomel* and *Tartar* under Captain E. P. Jones, R.N. These sufficed to man two 4.7-in. and four 12-pr. guns, the remainder being handed over to three companies Royal Garrison artillery.

encountering the advance guard of Natal Carbineers. Simultaneously with this movement, Hildyard prolonged his line still further by despatching the 2nd Dorset regiment to occupy the summit of Indoda Mountain, which had been temporarily piqueted by Lord Dundonald; and from this lofty hill, which was only to be scaled by a most difficult climb, the Dorset regiment maintained touch with the left of Sir R. Buller's column. On the 12th, the latter, as before watched rather than opposed by small bands of the enemy, reached Vermaaks Kraal, having left behind a small force with two guns at the Waschbank; whilst Bethune, coming up from Tugela Ferry, halted at a point four miles south of Pomeroy, where the enemy unmasked two heavy guns and a Vickers-Maxim.

Sir R. Buller was now confronted by the Berg which, separated from his camp by a deep valley, stood up like a wall athwart his line of advance. At Helpmakaar the main crest-line, the trend of which west of the town had been south-east and north-west, curved sharply southward about seven thousand yards from the camp at Vermaaks Kraal, forming a vast curl or crook which terminated roughly about Pomeroy. Within the concavity thus formed a high, precipitous hill, called Uithoek, connected to the Berg in rear by a col, soared boldly and commanded the whole of the interior of the semi-circle of heights. About three thousand yards to the eastward of this a nek carried the road from Pomeroy up to Helpmakaar; and here, commanded by General Lukas Meyer, was posted the extreme left of the enemy's forces on the Biggarsberg, consisting of the Johannesburgers, under B. Viljoen, and the Swaziland Police, under C. Botha, both with two guns in the Van Tonders Pass; of portions of the Zoutpansberg, Germiston-Boksburg and Lynch's Irish commandos between Beith and Helpmakaar, and at the latter place the Piet Retief commando, with two guns, under Engelbrecht; in all some 1,500 men. With that neglect or unwillingness to occupy detached outworks which had more than once characterised the Boers during the Natal campaign, Uithoek itself was left almost undefended. But though it was supposed to be practically insurmountable from his side, Sir R. Buller, perceiving in it the key

THE CLEARING OF NORTHERN NATAL. 261

to the flank of the Berg, decided to make it his first objective. During the night, which the enemy illumined by setting fire to the grass along the whole crest of the range, two 4.7-in. guns were emplaced on rising ground in front of the camp, and orders were issued for an advance next day. A message to this effect was despatched to Bethune, who was ordered to co-operate, and at once pushed out towards the crest of the Berg. At dawn on the 13th, as the rear of the column was leaving bivouac, the enemy opened with two quick-firers at seven thousand yards' range. The 4.7-in. guns were in the act of limbering up to march, but coming quickly into action, their third round silenced the enemy's pieces. Then, whilst the infantry formed up for attack at Vermaaks Kraal, Lord Dundonald, moving out south-eastward, felt his way cautiously towards Uithoek, Thorneycroft's M.I. scouting in front of the 3rd mounted brigade. During the first portion of this movement little opposition was encountered, and Thorneycroft's adventurous soldiers were soon scaling the precipitous sides of Uithoek. By 9 a.m. a company stood upon the summit. Across on the Berg, two rows of hostile trenches on opposite sides of Helpmakaar Nek, and three long-range guns commanded the causeway formed by the connecting col, and a severe action seemed imminent. At 9 a.m. the infantry were ordered to advance, and by 11.30 a.m. Hamilton's 2nd brigade, headed by the 2nd Queen's regiment, was also on the summit of Uithoek, which was taken over from the mounted infantry. Lord Dundonald, moving his command around the southern slopes of the hill, where he was somewhat covered from the view of the enemy on the Berg, then made for the high ground south of Helpmakaar Nek, swung northward at the foot, and pushed straight for the first row of trenches, which blocked the road. As he turned thus, Bethune's force, pressing along the Pomeroy road, came up into line, joined hands with the 3rd mounted brigade, and the two units dashed in company up the flank of the Biggarsberg at full gallop. This timely co-operation completely surprised the Piet Retief men, who, though reinforced from the centre, after a feeble stand hurriedly abandoned the trenches south of Helpmakaar Nek,

May 13th, 1900. The action at Helpmakaar.

falling back to those to the north. Here for the first time the opposition became too serious to be dealt with solely by the mounted troops. Three guns opened from the position, and a sharp rifle fire proved the enemy to be numerous in the trenches and rocky outcrops, which commanded the road and the col of Uithoek. A. battery R.H.A., which attempted to silence the hostile artillery from a position close in rear of the mounted infantry firing-line, came under so rapid and accurate a bombardment from a Vickers-Maxim and other pieces, that it was ordered to retire, which was only done by man-handling the guns. Not until the 12-prs., served by No. 2 company W.D. R.G.A., came into action at four thousand yards range was the enemy's artillery silenced. Meanwhile the 2nd Queen's regiment, supported at intervals by four companies 2nd Devonshire regiment, had pushed forward to the eastern crest of Uithoek, the summit of which was found to be flat, arriving there about 1.30 p.m. From here their fire commanded not only the col, but the road beyond; and the Boers retiring towards Helpmakaar before the advance of the mounted troops, suffered loss from the fire of their Maxim gun. The remainder of the 2nd brigade, following the route taken earlier by Lord Dundonald below Uithoek, were upon the high ground behind the mounted troops by 3.30 p.m. Half an hour later artillery, including a Vickers-Maxim, now for the first time sounding its strange racket from the British lines in Natal, came up to the same point. A bombardment of the trenches in front of Helpmakaar commenced, and continued until nightfall, when the whole force bivouacked in its positions, the van of the mounted troops in the abandoned trenches, the 2nd brigade partly on the summit of Uithoek and partly on the main ridge, the 4th brigade and the remainder of the mounted troops in the valley below Uithoek.

Chase of the enemy.

During the night the enemy evacuated Helpmakaar and fell back towards Beith. By his bold and rapid manœuvring, therefore, Sir R. Buller had already attained more than half his object; the Biggarsberg was turned, and a northward march would now cut the communications of the Boers who were upon it. Soon after dawn next day (May 14th), Lord Dundonald's scouts were moving on either side of the Beith road, the 2nd brigade, Corps artillery, 4th brigade and the baggage marching along the road in the order named. Through Helpmakaar and beyond there was no sign of the enemy other than the immense grass fires which he had lighted behind him. The whole veld was ablaze, and Lord Dundonald's troopers rode on continually enwrapped by flames and dense smoke. Pushing forward, nevertheless, with extraordinary rapidity, the screen of extended scouts were soon below Spion Kop,* a commanding hill situated on the west of the Dundee road some three miles north of Helpmakaar; but here a sudden outburst of Mausers warned them that a Boer rearguard was in position. Lord Dundonald despatched the South African Light Horse to turn the enemy's right, and Gough's mounted infantry towards the left flank, opening from his own centre heavy fire upon Spion Kop with dismounted riflemen and A. battery R.H.A. The effect was immediate. The Boers, abandoning their strong position, continued their flight northward, and Dundonald pushed on hard after. Two miles farther, in front of Beith, Colonel Lynch (Irish commando), commanding the Boer rearguard, turned and attempted a stand. But Dundonald's cantering troopers were upon him before he had time to steady his command in the position, and the same tactics as had been employed at Spion Kop sent him immediately galloping northward with loss. Viljoen's guns, for the sake of which Lynch had halted, narrowly escaped capture, as Viljoen, who had only just been informed of the flight from Helpmakaar, hurried his force from Van Tonders towards the road, to avoid being caught in flank. Once more Dundonald pressed on in pursuit, now along the same road as that by which Yule had retired southward on October 22nd, 1899. After nine more miles had been covered, the enemy was found to be standing again at Blesboklaagte, whence two guns opened upon Dundonald's van. The position here was immensely strong; night was falling, horses and men were weary after their incessant galloping, the mounted brigade was now

* Not to be confounded with the mountain to the south-west of Ladysmith, the scene of the fighting of January 24th, 1900.

twenty-five miles from its starting point of the morning, and the infantry, halting at Beith, were far behind. Here Dundonald received a message from Sir R. Buller, congratulating him on his success, and ordering a temporary cessation of the pursuit. Recalling a party of Natal Carbineers who had started off to attempt to cut the line north of Glencoe, Dundonald left a strong piquet in observation, and went into bivouac at Myer's Farm. A patrol from the piquet, which stole into Dundee during the night, reported it empty of the enemy, and it was evident that there would be little further opposition.*

The success of the previous day had, in fact, caused a general flight from the Biggarsberg. By the evening of the 14th not a Boer gun remained on the main position, and many of the commandos had already recoiled as far northward as Laing's Nek.

May 15th, 1900. Sir R. Buller enters Dundee.

Dundonald, moving early on the 15th, entered Dundee unopposed at 9 a.m., Sir R. Buller himself an hour later, and by 1 p.m. the head of the infantry column, which had covered sixteen miles since 6 a.m., following Dundonald, marched in by the same road. At Dundee the force remained on the 16th, men and horses obtaining a breathing-space, whilst the supply columns filled up with three days' provisions. On the 17th, a fourteen-mile march brought the main body to Dannhauser, whilst the mounted troops, pushing on, actually had an advanced squadron of Thorneycroft's M.I., accompanied by some of the Head-quarter Intelligence Staff, in Newcastle at 10 p.m. They learned that the enemy had passed through that morning in full retreat for Laing's Nek. Next day the infantry marched twenty-four miles, following Dundonald, who had started at 3 a.m., to Newcastle. Here the 2nd brigade remained on the 19th, the 4th brigade moving on in support of Dundonald, who at 7 a.m. started to reconnoitre the vast position of Laing's Nek, which now loomed close in front. Very brief investigation sufficed to convince Dundonald that the enemy was upon it in force. Large numbers were observed all along the high ground from Majuba to Pougwana mountains; gun emplacements were being openly dug; and when, in accordance with his orders,

* Casualties, May 14th—Seventeen men wounded.

THE CLEARING OF NORTHERN NATAL. 265

Dundonald, after shelling the crest, commenced to withdraw to the Ingogo, strong bodies of Boers emerged from behind the Nek, and threatened both his flanks. Supported by the 4th brigade, the cavalry, maintaining posts at Mount Prospect, then went into bivouac below the Schuins Hoogte ridge, the scene of Sir George Colley's memorable action in 1881. Sir R. Buller, in view of the possibility of prolonged operations before the formidable Nek, decided to halt until he had concentrated his forces, and brought up rail-head closer to the troops. He himself returned to Newcastle, leaving Sir F. Clery in command at the front. May 19th, 1900. And pauses in front of Laing's Nek.

It is necessary now to relate briefly the movements of the Vth division, which at the time when the IInd division crossed the Waschbank on May 11th, had remained with its flanks upon Indoda, and Jonono's Kop.

On May 14th, the 2nd Dorset regiment on Indoda was joined by the 2nd Middlesex regiment, and four Naval 12-pr. guns. On the 15th the 11th brigade occupied the hills west of Wessels Nek, the 10th brigade bivouacking on the heights east of the Nek. The division reached the line Meran—Waschbank without opposition on the 16th; and next day Elandslaagte was finally evacuated by the departure of the supply park northward with six days' supplies, and two 4.7-in. Naval guns. On the 18th the Vth division marched to Hatting Spruit, *viâ* the Glencoe Pass; and here, and at Glencoe, it remained until May 23rd, labouring daily from dawn to dark at completing the repair of the railway, and employing its transport in forwarding supplies to Newcastle. Hildyard's command had thus formed the pivot throughout of Sir R. Buller's flanking march, the two forces traversing the Biggarsberg and arriving in front of Laing's Nek simultaneously by different routes. During the remainder of May there was considerable activity in progress behind the front line on the Ingogo heights. On the 23rd the IVth division and the 1st* and 2nd cavalry brigades, which had remained about Movements of the Vth division on the flank.

---

* Consisting at this moment of the Royal Dragoons only; the 5th Dragoon Guards had already proceeded to Dundee on the 20th, and the 13th Hussars were left at Ladysmith, rejoining the brigade later.

Ladysmith, received orders to move to the front. There were left in charge of Ladysmith the 5th Lancers, 13th Hussars, 1st Gloucester regiment, 1st Royal Inniskilling Fusiliers, 1st Manchester regiment, and 19th and 73rd batteries, all under Colonel C. M. H. Downing, R.A. The infantry of the IVth division were at Ingagane on the 26th, at Newcastle on the 27th; the cavalry (Royal Dragoons) halting at Dannhauser on the 25th, with orders to watch the Buffalo drifts; whilst the 2nd cavalry brigade reached Ingagane on the 27th, the rail-head being completed up to that place on the same day. The Vth division moved forward simultaneously, and on the 27th lay at Newcastle. The army of Natal was thus rapidly concentrating once more in preparation for the extensive operations which seemed likely to ensue.*

May 20th, 1900.
Affair at Vryheid.

Meanwhile an unfortunate incident had occurred wide on the right flank. After its highly successful co-operation with Buller's mounted troops at Helpmakaar, the force under Lieut.-Colonel E. C. Bethune (356 men with two Hotchkiss guns), had left Dundee on the 17th, crossed the Buffalo by Vant's Drift, and, in pursuance of orders to make a reassuring demonstration in Zululand, had proceeded to Nqutu to re-establish the magistracy, receiving there, on May 19th, orders to come in to Newcastle. Bethune marched next day; but on arriving at the Blood river received intelligence that the town of Vryheid, which was said to contain valuable stores, had been abandoned by the enemy, and was at his mercy. He thereupon determined to occupy it. Later, information showed that a Boer commando had laagered six miles to the south of the town; but as they were reported to be only Natal rebels, and without guns, Bethune persevered in his plan, and gained touch with the enemy south of Vryheid. Owing, however, to the lack of caution of his leading squadron, which, galloping through the enemy's screen, found itself ambushed beyond it, Bethune's plan of attack became disarranged at the outset, and he was compelled to employ his whole force to extricate his skirmishers. This was only effected with extreme difficulty, and Bethune had to

* For a Field state of the army at this period, see Appendix 2.

retire to Nqutu, with a loss of three officers and eighteen men killed, two officers and twenty-three men wounded, and eighteen men missing. In consequence of this affair the 5th Dragoon Guards at Dundee were reinforced by the Royal Dragoons. On June 1st both regiments, operating from Dundee and Dannhauser, crossed the drifts of the Buffalo, advanced over the Doorn Berg, and threw squadrons across the Blood river without meeting with serious opposition.

Besides the enemy at Vryheid, there was at this time a force of some 1,500 on Lukas Meyer's old camping-ground of October, 1899, the Doorn Berg, eastward of De Jager's Drift. These demonstrated strongly from time to time against Sir R. Buller's right rear. So unsafe, indeed, appeared this flank, that on May 27th, Sir R. Buller sent two columns across the Buffalo. One, consisting of the 11th (Wynne) brigade, with two 4.7-in. and four 12-pr. Naval guns, and the South African Light Horse, under Hildyard, crossing by Wools Drift, marched on Utrecht on the 29th, and two days later received the surrender of that town. The other column—18th Hussars, two batteries R.F.A., a Howitzer battery, two 12-pr. guns (R.G.A.), one Vickers-Maxim, and the 8th infantry brigade—under Lyttelton, crossed the river by Inchanga Drift, eighteen miles (direct) south-east of Wools Drift, and entering Transvaal soil, supported Hildyard; whilst the 1st cavalry brigade from both banks of the river watched all the drifts to the south. The effect of these diversions was that the enemy, some two thousand in number, under General Grobelaar, of Vryheid, evacuated the Doorn Berg, and retired behind Utrecht, the pressure on the outposts and the danger to the nearly-repaired railway ceasing with their withdrawal. *The right flank cleared.*

Since May 15th Sir R. Buller had been in frequent communication on the subject of his next advance with Lord Roberts, who was then at Kroonstad. The alternatives were obviously threefold: To attack Laing's Nek frontally, to turn it on the left by Botha's, or another of the Drakensberg Passes, or on the right from the direction of Utrecht. The topographical difficulties of the country east of Mount Pougwana, on which was *The problem of Laing's Nek.*

emplaced a 6-in. Creusot gun, and the intervention of the Buffalo river, with its few and uncertain drifts, rendered the last-named the least practicable of these alternatives. Sir R. Buller himself, having good evidence of the demoralisation of the commandos which had run before him from the Biggarsberg, favoured at first a direct attack on the Nek,* even though reconnaissance showed it to be held in strength; but as the delay at Ingogo was prolonged unavoidably by the extensive damage done to the railway, the difficulty of bringing up supplies, and the necessary eastern diversions, the consolidation and increase of the forces upon Laing's Nek became unmistakable; and on May 20th Sir R. Buller reported the position as now "unassailable."† Lord Roberts had intimated from the first‡ the strategical advantage of a western turning movement *viâ* the Drakensberg Passes into the Orange Free State about Vrede. Such an operation, coinciding, as it might, with his own irruption into the Transvaal, could not fail to be of great moral effect, and if turned eventually upon Standerton, would result in addition in isolating any Boer forces remaining upon Laing's Nek, cutting their communicating railway, and imperilling their rolling stock and transport, if not their own safety.

To these views Lord Roberts adhered throughout the correspondence which followed, and Sir R. Buller, though he could not promise synchronous action, decided upon a plan which he had always had in mind.

Sir R. Buller attempts to negotiate. First, however, Sir R. Buller, still hopeful of the enemy's demoralisation, determined to see whether he could not obtain by negotiation what would certainly prove a heavy task for his arms. On May 30th, he despatched a message to Commandant C. Botha, who was now in command of the entire Boer forces on the Nek, informing him of Lord Roberts' passage of the Vaal, and pointing out the inutility of further resistance. In reply, Botha, having communicated with his Government, consented

---

* Telegrams Nos. 255, May 18th; 257, May 22nd.

† Telegram No. 256, May 20th.

‡ No. C. 1615, May 15th.

THE CLEARING OF NORTHERN NATAL. 269

to discuss the matter with Sir Redvers. On June 2nd the Generals met beween the outposts, and Sir R. Buller propounded certain terms of surrender. Botha would promise nothing on his own responsibility, and having obtained a three days' armistice, for further communication with his chiefs, returned to his lines, which hourly increased in strength. He soon received a message from Commandant-General Louis Botha, strongly disapproving of the armistice, which, wrote the Boer leader, could only cover some "deep stratagem" on the part of the British General.* Three days later C. Botha sent his answer— a decided negative—into the British lines; and Sir R. Buller, who had employed the time thus gained in hurrying all his forces and supplies to the front, moved his Headquarters up from Newcastle to Ingogo, and was again prepared for active operations. His plans were already formulated, the ground being well known to him from his experience of former campaigns in this region. Having called in Hildyard's and Lyttelton's detached forces, and concentrated his cavalry, on June 6th he flung the South African Light Horse at Van Wyk's Hill, ousted the Boer piquets which held it, and despatched Major-General Talbot Coke with three battalions† of the 10th brigade and a battery to occupy it under Hildyard's direction, thus possessing himself of the command of the southern side of the mouth of Botha's Pass. Across the road which traversed the defile stood Spitz Kop, a conical hill, behind which, and divided from it by a deep gorge, the main Drakensberg swept northward with many a bold spur and profound re-entrant, but for some distance with only one well-marked peak, that of Inkweloane, which stood nearly ten thousand yards from the southern wall of the Pass. Upon this, upon all the level but indented crest-line south of it, and upon Spitz Kop, ran the Boer trenches; not continuous, but scattered irregularly along the points of command, and too extensive to be more than thinly occupied. There were a few gun-pits, but they held nothing more formidable than Vickers-Maxims; only upon Inkweloane itself were emplaced two long-

June 6th, 1900.
Seizure of Van Wyk's Hill.

* Telegram of June 2nd, 1900.
† 2nd Dorset, 2nd Middlesex, 1st Royal Dublin Fusiliers, 13th battery R.F.A.

range Field guns. The relative positions of the opposing forces on the night of June 6th were somewhat curious. Since the Inkweloane range protruded due southward from Laing's Nek, the Boer right now pointed directly towards the British on Van Wyk, separated from them by the mouth of the Pass. The enemy here and on Laing's Nek thus occupied two sides of a triangle, and within the angle, but secure from either side, a British detachment perched upon the lofty summit of Inkwelo,* from below which four heavy guns replied to the plunging bombardment of a 6-in. Creusot gun upon Pougwana Mountain, over twelve thousand yards to the north-east.

Van Wyk gained, heavy artillery was in the act of moving towards it, when the enemy, coming across from Spitz Kop, made an attempt to re-capture the position under cover of the blazing grass. Talbot Coke, however, who had been left in command of the hill with the battalions of his brigade and the 13th battery R.F.A., easily repulsed the attempt;† and during the night two 4.7-in. and two 12-pr. guns were hauled into position near the summit by the men of the 2nd Royal Lancaster regiment; and two more of the former and four of the latter type of guns were placed on the road below the north-eastern spurs, whence they commanded the whole pass, Spitz Kop, and the opposite crest-line of the Berg. Meanwhile, the enemy, nonplussed by this sudden loss of the key of the entire position, drew back to Spitz Kop as their foremost line, leaving the Pass itself untenanted. On June 7th Hildyard, to whom the conduct of the operations had been delegated, issued orders for a general attack on the Pass, of which the following is a summary. Whilst Talbot Coke maintained his position on Van Wyk, with the 10th brigade, and all the above-mentioned artillery, except the 13th battery, the 11th brigade (Wynne), with the 13th and 69th batteries R.F.A., supported by the 2nd brigade (E. O. F. Hamilton), with the 64th and 7th R.F.A. and 61st Howitzer batteries,

* This mountain had been occupied on May 25th by two companies of the 2nd Rifle Brigade, supported by the remainder of the 4th brigade, with whom, on shelves below the summit, were two 4.7-in., two 12-pr. guns and two 5-in. guns (16th W.D. R.G.A.).

† Casualties—One killed, ten wounded.

THE CLEARING OF NORTHERN NATAL.

would carry out the assault, covered by the fire of all the heavy artillery, whose positions for the sake of clearness may be here more detailed. Two 5-in. guns were on the southernmost spur of Inkwelo and two on the western edge of the Schuins Hoogte ridges; two 4.7-in. (R.G.A.) and four 12-pr. (Naval) on the north-eastern spur of Van Wyk; two 4.7-in. and two 12-pr. (Naval) on the summit, and six heavy pieces (R.G.A.) upon the shelves of Inkwelo. Prior to the infantry movements, the South African Light Horse would advance to test Spitz Kop, whilst the 3rd mounted brigade, with A. battery R.H.A., under Lord Dundonald, based on De Wet's Farm, would operate upon and protect the right of the infantry attack, watch the Hart River valley, towards Quaggas Nek, avoiding close quarters until the situation became assured. The 2nd cavalry brigade would cover the left. On what had been the extreme right, but would become the right rear of the projected attack, Lyttelton would demonstrate on the kopjes east of the Buffalo river with two battalions and two 12-pr. guns (R.G.A.), so as to engage the attention of the enemy upon Laing's Nek.

At 10 a.m. on June 8th, whilst all the artillery opened fire, the South African Light Horse moved from their bivouac at Yellowboom Farm straight upon Spitz Kop, which they occupied without fighting. Thereupon the infantry, marching—the 11th brigade from Yellowboom Farm, the 2nd brigade from Schuins Hoogte—deployed for attack below Van Wyk, and at 10.45 a.m. faced north-west, the 11th brigade on the left of the 2nd brigade, the 13th and 69th batteries coming into action north of the main Botha's Pass road. A very slight shell fire opposed the early stages of the advance, which was carried out in wide extension and deep intervals; and despite the excessive steepness of the mountains at this point, the infantry advance was regular and rapid, the 11th brigade passing by the west of Spitz Kop, on which a Vickers-Maxim gun had been placed, the 2nd brigade by the east. Not until the troops were upon the crest of the Berg (about 2 p.m.) and had already occupied many of the advanced trenches, did the Boers open fire seriously with guns and rifles both from Inkweloane and from the rear of the plateau, and for

June 8th, 1900. Attack and capture of Botha's Pass.

a time a brisk fire-fight ensued. But the enemy was already completely out-manœuvred. The men of the 3rd mounted brigade, climbing with surprising celerity from below Inkweloane, up the precipitous sides of which they actually hauled two guns of the R.H.A. battery, had already enfiladed his left before the infantry made themselves felt; the 11th brigade was in a strong fire position upon his right by 3 p.m.; the 2nd brigade had broken his front, and the practice of the heavy artillery was accurate and incessant. By 4 p.m. all opposition had ceased, and the Boers recoiled, hidden by hundreds of acres of flaming grass, with the smoke of which all the crest of the Berg was obscured. The 2nd cavalry brigade, which had been hampered by bad ground, arriving on the summit in the evening, pushed out some five miles in pursuit, returning eventually to bivouac with the rest of the force. Thus, with little loss,* was effected the capture of Botha's Pass, and the road into the Orange Free State was open.

On June 9th the main body remained in its elevated and bitterly cold bivouac on the summit of the Berg, awaiting the supply column, which struggled with difficulty up the mountainous road. Meanwhile the 11th brigade moved five miles north-westerly, in which direction the defenders of Botha's Pass had fallen back. On the 10th Sir R. Buller resumed the general advance, the South African Light Horse and 10th brigade leading; the objective was a prominent hill situated near the junction of the Klip river and the Gansvlei Spruit. This was found to be occupied by the Boer rearguard, which was speedily driven off by the South African Light Horse and artillery. The former, pushing on into high ground beyond the Spruit, found another detachment of the enemy somewhat strongly posted, and a sharp engagement, in which a squadron of the 18th Hussars lent valuable assistance, was necessary to dislodge him.† Behind this party a body of Boers, estimated at over three thousand horsemen, was seen to halt, and apparently dispose itself in

* Casualties—Killed, two men; wounded, one officer and twelve men.

† Casualties—Six killed, ten wounded. Boer losses—Ten killed; wounded, unknown.

THE CLEARING OF NORTHERN NATAL. 273

the high ground to the northward, about Alleman's Nek. The army bivouacked about the kopje, a severe frost prevailing.

Sir R. Buller was now bent on making Charlestown and Volksrust as quickly as possible, for only thus could be achieved the object of the entire operation, *i.e.*, the turning of the stronghold of Laing's Nek. Speed was essential. He himself was now wide of his line of communications; only a weak detachment remained in front of the strongly-garrisoned Nek; most important of all, delay would soon divulge to the Boer forces entrenched between the Drakensberg and Pougwana the movement which was circumventing them, even if they had not already divined it, in which case the Nek would be evacuated long before he could hope to arrive behind it.

Between Sir R. Buller's army and Volksrust now intervened but one obstacle. But it was no trifling one, and here again delay, as the lessons of the Natal campaign had more than once shown, might render it all but insuperable. Springing from the Drakensberg range at Majuba and Iketeni Mountains, a bold spur ran in a north-westerly direction, bridging, as it were, the wide valley which rolled between the Drakensberg and the subsidiary range of the Verzamel Berg in the Transvaal. This spur, therefore, ran directly athwart the Volksrust road, which at the afore-mentioned Alleman's Nek surmounted it by a deep cleft, flanked by almost precipitous bluffs. Here was then a strong position; and Sir R. Buller's information ran that the enemy was now upon it in sufficient force to form a strong detached right flank-guard to the commandos upon Laing's Nek itself. The occupation of Alleman's Nek could only have been recent; Sir R. Buller determined on attacking before the enemy had time to entrench. At dawn on June 11th his forces set out for the attempt.

Between the bivouac at Gansvlei Spruit and Alleman's Nek lay more than seven miles of country, so undulating that many of the ridges might themselves have constituted positions; and it was necessary to make them all good in succession. The heavy artillery was first disposed upon the high ground north of the bivouac, and thus covered, the 11th brigade moved out at 7 a.m.,

June 11th, 1900.
The action at Alleman's Nek.

entering into the hill and dale bordering the right of the Volksrust road north of the Gansvlei Spruit. Wynne had received orders to halt when he had gained a position enabling the rest of the force to pivot on him, and point on Alleman's Nek. The 2nd cavalry brigade operated simultaneously on the left flank, the 3rd mounted brigade on the right; and to the South African Light Horse was entrusted the guardianship of the rear, by no means the least vulnerable portion of the force at this period. The 11th brigade found the ridges clear, and accordingly halted when some five miles from Alleman's Nek; at 11 a.m. the heavy artillery was ordered forward to a second position, and the 2nd and 10th brigades, marching with it, were about 1 p.m. concentrated under cover of the last roll of the ground which separated them from Alleman's Nek.

At this stage, the cavalry on both flanks ran into the enemy simultaneously, the 3rd mounted brigade on the right becoming actively engaged in the broken ground south-east of Alleman's Nek, whilst on the left Brocklehurst's cavalry brigade commenced desultory skirmishing with scattered bands of Boers who seemed to be riding out from the Orange Free State. At 1.30 p.m. the enemy on the Nek itself gave the first sign of his presence by opening a hot fire with a long-range Field piece and two Vickers-Maxims upon the 3rd mounted brigade and the foremost batteries (A. R.H.A. and 61st Howitzer), which were settling into the second position upon the brow of the rise which covered the two brigades of the attack. A duel then ensued; A. battery R.H.A. shelled the enemy in front of the cavalry on the right, the Howitzers the Nek itself, the Boers returning an accurate and rapid fire. The rest of the heavy guns came up at 2 p.m., and their overwhelming bombardment at 4,000 to 6,000 yards at once caused a slackening of the enemy's practice, which at 2.30 p.m. temporarily ceased.

At that hour the infantry received the order to advance to the attack. Their task seemed no light one. Four thousand yards away across a smooth and open bowl of grass, along the bottom of which wound the dry bed of a spruit, Alleman's Nek rose abruptly in two cliffs or bluffs, between which the

THE CLEARING OF NORTHERN NATAL.   275

road climbed by a glacis totally destitute of cover to the indentation which carried it over the summit. Below the western rampart of the Nek, which stretched without interruption for nine miles westerly, and, therefore, could not be turned, lay two small kopjes, separated from the main feature by a ravine wherein were many riflemen and a gun. The brow of the cliff above them was also lined by marksmen. The eastern side of the Nek rose as an outwork of the Drakensberg, running plateau-wise in to the main range at Iketeni; immediately in front of it stood up like a barbican a tall conical kopje, connected to a similarly shaped peak upon the mass behind by a deeply-bowed saddle. Both kopje and plateau were strongly held, some two thousand Boers in all being upon the position from end to end, composed of the following commandos ; Carolina, Lydenburg, and portions of Johannesburg, Pretoria, Zoutpansberg and Swaziland Police, with four guns. They were for the most part unentrenched, but possessed of so much natural cover and command, that entrenchments could scarcely have added greatly to their power or security. Formidable though the position therefore appeared, it had this unaccustomed advantage to the attackers, that it was well defined. The infantry moved straight upon their allotted points of attack. On the right (south) of the Volksrust road, the 10th brigade was directed upon the conical bastion of the southern side of the Nek, the 2nd Dorset regiment, and 1st Royal Dublin Fusiliers in front line on left and right respectively, the 2nd Middlesex regiment supporting. On the north side of the road, with its right upon it, the 2nd brigade steered upon the bluffs overhanging the western side of Alleman's Nek, disposing in first line the 2nd East Surrey regiment on the right, the 2nd Queen's regiment on the left (each with two companies in front, two in support and five in reserve), and in support on the left rear, the 2nd West Yorkshire regiment. The 2nd Devonshire regiment of this brigade did not accompany the assaulting column, half being detached as escort to the guns, and half with a Vickers-Maxim to form a left flankguard upon a kopje about a mile north-west of the artillery position, in which direction hovered some Boer scouts. The whole attack was again under the direction of Lieut.-General Hildyard. The emergence of the infantry from behind cover on to the slopes leading down to the spruit was plainly discernible by the enemy, who opened a warm fusilade of rifles and automatic guns as soon as the foremost lines came within range. Especially severely fell this at first upon the 2nd brigade, which, moving over open grass-land, received the fire, not only from the Boers to its immediate front, the western heights of the Nek, but also from those upon the eastern walls, upon the conical kopje, its connecting saddle, and upon the cliff behind. At 3.15 p.m. the 2nd brigade was in the dry donga which traversed the hollow; and from here, whilst a Vickers-Maxim opened from an advanced position between the battalion supports, the supports themselves began a rapid covering fire at 1,200 yards, directed chiefly across the Nek on to the conical kopje and its saddle. At the same time almost the whole of the artillery, light and heavy, turned in the same direction, and the enemy's cross-fire upon the 2nd brigade perceptibly diminished, though it was still too powerful for the advance to be at once resumed. The 10th brigade on the other side of the road, though more sheltered at first, soon encountered far graver difficulties. The object of the left battalion, the Dorset, was the conical outwork from which poured a heavy fire, in spite of the tremendous artillery bombardment which was converting it into a smoking pile. The Dorset regiment, followed at three hundred yards distance by the Middlesex, attacked with resolution, and without a check, though the slopes were steep, and a wire fence at the bottom of the valley had been marked as a range by the Boer riflemen and gunners. At 3.30 p.m. the 7th and 64th Field batteries and two 12-pr. guns were moved into a position well forward on the left rear of the 2nd brigade; and their shells, sweeping the Boer left in enfilade, greatly assisted the assault on the detached kopje. At 3.40 p.m. the summit of the cone was rushed, the shells from the heavy guns bursting in the enemy's lines only a few feet in front of the foremost rank of the assault. In front of the Dorset regiment now stretched the concave saddle which connected the hill just won to the second conical eminence

THE CLEARING OF NORTHERN NATAL. 277

projecting from the face of the mountain behind; and so hot a fire poured from both the eminence and mountain that heavy losses seemed about to be the price of further progress. Sending word at 4.15 p.m. to Lieut.-General Hildyard, who promptly ordered the artillery to turn on the new target, Talbot Coke reinforced the Dorset regiment with first the front line, and subsequently with all the second line save two and a half companies of the Middlesex regiment, and immediately pushed on. The assault was brilliantly delivered. Advancing by a succession of short charges, the Dorset regiment, well supported by the Middlesex, swept across the intervening saddle, carried the rear kopje, and clambering up the rugged precipice behind, were upon the main crest-line by 5 p.m., the enemy flying before them. *The assault.*

In this attack, the 1st Royal Dublin Fusiliers, the third battalion of the brigade, had taken no part. Their orders had been to work in line with the right of the Dorset regiment and to threaten the Nek behind the foremost kopje, whilst the Dorsets assaulted it in front. The battalion had not advanced far before it found itself enfiladed from the right by a warm and increasing fire from that portion of the Boer line opposite Dundonald's mounted infantry; and imperceptibly the advance of the Fusiliers deflected eastwards towards a kopje in the valley which faced the enemy's rifles. An interval, therefore, began to open between their left and the right of the Dorset regiment; and so rapidly did this increase, that about 4 p.m., Talbot Coke, having vainly attempted to call up the regiment by flag signal, despatched his brigade-major to bring it back to its proper line of advance. The officer did not come up with the Dublin Fusiliers before they, trending still further to the right,* had become involved in Dundonald's part of the action, sending, indeed, two companies to the assistance of

* It should be stated that the Officer Commanding the 1st Royal Dublin Fusiliers had every intention of resuming his proper direction as soon as he had dealt with the situation on his right. He left orders to that effect, when a wound compelled him to go to the rear. The Boers' fire attack on the right, however, proved more than a momentary demonstration, and indeed partook of the nature of a counter-attack, and only one and a half companies of the Dublin Fusiliers were able to rejoin the brigade before nightfall.

the 3rd mounted brigade,* whose movements must now be described.

The 3rd mounted brigade, and A. battery R.H.A., had from the first been engaged in sharp fighting amongst the broken ground radiating from Iketeni towards Alleman's Nek. The enemy here was numerous, not only on the front, where a staircase of four ridges led upwards to the main crest behind, but also on the right, where the high ground curled southwards, almost encircling Dundonald's flank in that direction. After shelling the heights south-east of the Nek, Dundonald pushed forward Thorneycroft's mounted infantry on the left, and on the right Gough's composite regiment, who were confronted directly by the four above-mentioned terraces. The Boers were upon them all, and Gough's progress was difficult and dangerous. Having by dint of heavy dismounted fire cleared the first two, Gough then found himself checked before the third ridge, upon the high peaks of which the enemy stood stubbornly; and it was not until A. battery concentrated the whole of its fire upon the position, that he was able to advance and occupy it. The Boers then retired to the fourth and final crest-line, some 1,500 yards back, and here, collecting in strength behind some hastily-constructed sangars, they once more brought to a halt the advance of Gough's regiment, which had now lost three officers and five men. Nor could a reinforcement of two companies Thorneycroft's mounted infantry with two Colt guns, and the rapid shelling of the R.H.A. battery, sufficiently diminish the volume of the hostile musketry to warrant Dundonald venturing upon a last assault. The enemy therefore lay confronting Dundonald to the end, and the success of the right appeared at first somewhat doubtful. But the Boers here were, in reality, as willing to flee as those in other parts of the field; only the fact that their line of retreat across the flats behind was at this time swept by the dropping shell-fire of the British long-range guns and the Howitzers, kept them so long on the crest. Their position was in any case untenable; the rest of the Nek was in British hands, and the only other line of retreat, the difficult

* Less the S. A. Light Horse, still doing duty as rearguard to the whole force.

THE CLEARING OF NORTHERN NATAL. 279

route to Laing's Nek by Iketeni Mountain, was now useless, since Laing's Nek itself must shortly be abandoned by their comrades. After nightfall, therefore, they drew off and left Sir R. Buller's troops in sole occupation of the last portal into the Transvaal.*

As for the 2nd brigade on the left of the road, the difficulties of its advance had practically ceased when the Dorset regiment had captured the conical hill and Nek from which the heaviest fire had come. At 3.30 p.m., moreover, the above-mentioned action of the 7th and 64th Field batteries, the Howitzers and the 12-prs., besides clearing a path for the attack of the Dorset, did much to quell the cross-fire beating upon the line of advance. The 2nd brigade then pushed out from the donga, and meeting with little further opposition, gained the heights north-west of Alleman's Nek by dusk, and bivouacked, as did the whole force, upon the positions it had won.

Whilst the troops, once more robbed of rest by bitter frost, passed the night upon the battlefield, the Boers on Laing's Nek, outflanked, and with their line of retreat nearer to their enemy than themselves, were evacuating their stronghold in such hot haste that by next morning not a gun nor a burgher remained in any part of the ground from Majuba to Pougwana. Sir F. Clery, after reconnoitring the Nek, sent forward first his mounted troops, and next the 4th brigade with artillery, and by 6 p.m. had quietly occupied the most colossal position in South Africa. Colonel Dartnell, pushing on with his scouts, then crossed the frontier, was in Volksrust the same evening, and was able to report that Natal was clear of the enemy who for ten months had made war in British territory. *Laing's Nek evacuated.*

At dawn on June 12th the force upon Alleman's Nek advanced once more, and pressed for the road and railway above Volksrust, hoping to strike at Botha's retreating columns. But though the latter were descried, and harmlessly shelled at ten thousand yards' range on the Zandspruit road, Botha had made good use of his time and escaped unscathed, veiled by a whole countryside of burning grass, leaving only a searchlight apparatus,

* For casualties, etc., see Appendix 2.

and miles of empty entrenchments, as trophies to the victors. Sir R. Buller then ordered his force into bivouac at Joubert's Farm, receiving next day (13th) the formal surrender of Volksrust. Thence he marched to Charlestown, which, unlike the Boer town, had been ruthlessly damaged, and established Headquarters upon Laing's Nek. There, at Charlestown, and at Volksrust, the whole army of Natal was concentrated during the day, and the various Headquarters connected by telegraph wire. The neighbourhood was ransacked for forage, meat, and transport; wagons, especially, being assiduously collected and repaired in the shops of the town. Some fighting occurred on the 14th upon the left rear, where two companies Thorneycroft's mounted infantry and a section Telegraph battalion R.E., which had gone back on the 13th to Gansvlei to pick up the telephone line used in the recent operations, were attacked in superior numbers by a roving band of Boers who had apparently issued from the Orange Free State. After standing at bay all day, the mounted infantry commander judged it best to save his force by a retirement, which he safely effected under cover of darkness by Botha's Pass.

June 13th, 1900. Sir R. Buller at Laing's Nek.

On the 15th, Lyttelton despatched the mounted infantry of his division, with six companies 1st King's Royal Rifles, and six companies 1st Liverpool regiment, under Major-General F. Howard, across the Buffalo river to receive the submission of Wakkerstroom. But so large a number of the enemy collected in front of this column, that Sir R. Buller, recalling Lyttelton to Coetzee's Drift, ordered Hildyard to undertake the same operation with a stronger force,* in co-operation with Lyttelton, whom he further reinforced† for the purpose. At the same time Talbot Coke, moving into Volksrust with the 10th brigade, occupied De Jagers Nek and Hout Nek with two battalions. Hildyard moved on the 16th, not by the direct Volksrust—Wakkerstroom road which traversed several dangerous defiles,

June 17th, 1900. Occupation of Wakkerstroom.

---

* Composition—3rd mounted brigade, 61st (Howitzer) battery, 12-pr. battery R.G.A., 13th and 69th batteries R.F.A., the 11th infantry brigade (Wynne).

† By the 53rd battery R.F.A., one Vickers-Maxim, six companies 1st Leicester regiment, six companies 2nd King's Royal Rifles.

but towards Zandspruit, whence he could descend upon Wakkerstroom by an easier route over De Jagers Nek from the northwest. On the morning of the 17th, he was before the town, Lyttelton, who had resumed his previous line of march from Coetzee's Drift, coming up a little later. The Landrost surrendered at once; many rifles were handed in, and the object of the expedition being accomplished, Lyttelton returned to Ingogo on the 18th, whilst Hildyard retraced his steps towards Zandspruit, which he reached on June 20th, having received 193 surrenders, and captured 197 rifles, 80,000 rounds of ammunition and large quantities of supplies.

Meanwhile Sir R. Buller, in compliance with urgent communications from Lord Roberts,* who was at Pretoria, had been strenuously preparing for an advance upon Standerton. To the occupation of this town, which lay over fifty miles north-west of Volksrust, the Field-Marshal attached the greatest importance. It was not only a large railway centre, containing much rolling stock and extensive repair shops, but it formed the nucleus of telegraphic and transport communication with the Orange Free State. Both President Steyn and General Christian De Wet were drawing their supplies therefrom, and using the wires as their only means of communication with the now peripatetic President Kruger and his Government. But whilst Sir R. Buller fully agreed that it was most desirable to seize Standerton, there were several considerations which rendered it impossible to start immediately. His army was in need of supplies, and the tunnel under Laing's Nek being destroyed, all transport across the steep Nek had to be hauled painfully by wagons with double spans, and often by man-handling, for the draught oxen were much weakened. The disturbed state of the Piet Retief and Wakkerstroom districts on the right flank, too, seemed a serious obstacle to an immediate advance; for to leave them behind unpacified would be to expose the communications to certain attack.† Both Gras Kop and the Belela's Berg

---

* Telegrams Nos. C. 2053, June 13th; C. 2108, June 15th; C. 2114, June 15th; C. 2119, June 16th; C. 2152, June 19th; C. 2167, June 20th.

† Telegram No. 0707, June 16th.

on this flank were occupied by the enemy, and Commandant C. Botha was reported to be concentrating a force at Vryheid for the express purpose of a raid upon the communications when the army had gone forward.* So unsettled, indeed, did the situation appear in these districts that Sir R. Buller doubted whether he ought not to constitute them his line of advance upon Standerton, instead of proceeding, as Lord Roberts desired, by the shortest route.† The eastward expeditions of Hildyard and Lyttelton were in any case essential. Only less troublesome was the left flank, which the attack on Thorneycroft's mounted infantry on June 14th, and the constant appearance of bands of the enemy, showed to be by no means safe. The enemy here had, in the Drakensberg, an undeniable covered way up to the Natal communications; and it seemed to Sir R. Buller unwise to leave this country behind him until the force under Lieut.-General Sir L. Rundle, who was then near Ficksburg, should have advanced sufficiently far northward to secure it.‡ Whilst recording these obstacles, however, Sir R. Buller made all possible haste to remove them. At 3 p.m. on the 18th, the first of thirty trains loaded with supplies came through the Laing's Nek tunnel; and next day Sir R. Buller, advancing his Headquarters from Laing's Nek to Volksrust, moved the IInd division§ under Sir F. Clery, up to Joubert's Farm about four miles north-west of Volksrust, on the first stage of the march to Standerton, Lyttelton's division being left in charge of the lines of communication from Laing's Nek to Newcastle. On the 20th Clery marched to Zandspruit, where in the evening he effected a junction with Hildyard's force‖ which had come in to the line over Graskop. At Zandspruit the army received a valuable

June 19th, 1900.
The advance on Standerton.

* Telegrams Nos. 282, June 18th; 283, June 19th.

† Telegram No. 282, June 18th.

‖ Telegrams Nos. 280, June 15th; 281, June 17th.

§ Composition—2nd and 4th brigades; three squadrons Bethune's M.I.; 7th, 63rd and 64th batteries R.F.A.; 86th (Howitzer) battery; two Vickers-Maxims; two 4.7-in., two 12-pr. guns and four 5-in. guns, all manned by R.G.A.

‖ Composition—3rd mounted brigade; two 4.7-in. and two 12-pr. guns (Naval); 61st (Howitzer) battery; 13th and 69th batteries R.F.A.; 11th infantry brigade (Wynne).

THE CLEARING OF NORTHERN NATAL. 283

reinforcement in Strathcona's Horse, a body of Canadian roughriders unsurpassed for daring and endurance in the field. Their arrival compensated for the departure of 800 Natal Volunteers, who had now, under the terms of their contract, to remain unwillingly, since there was yet work to be done, in their own Colony to which they had rendered such invaluable services.*

On the 21st Clery's and Hildyard's columns marching abreast, covered by the 3rd mounted brigade, reached Paarde Kop, Zandspruit being garrisoned by a detachment† from Brocklehurst's 2nd cavalry brigade from Charlestown. At Zandspruit, Hildyard himself, taking with him two 4.7-in. and two 12-pr. Naval guns, had left the force to go to Volksrust to command the Volksrust—Zandspruit section of the communications, his late command merging into that of Sir F. Clery.

Next day, Sir F. Clery, leaving a garrison at Paarde Kop, pushed on in two divisions, across twenty-two miles of rolling grass-lands to Kromdrai and Katbosch Spruit, Wynne following in rear with the 11th brigade and supply park, halted for the night at Platrand. Clery marched on June 23rd, covered as before by the 3rd mounted brigade, and these enterprising horsemen, dropping a link of two companies on the kopjes at Katbosch Spruit, rode thence straight on into Standerton, which was entered by Gough's mounted infantry and the Intelligence Staff at 2 p.m. without opposition. But for the complete demolition of the railway bridge spanning the Vaal river, the town, a collection of villas and shops disposed about a depression north of the Vaal, was undamaged, though the majority of the inhabitants had fled, and there were no supplies. The road bridge was intact; in the railway yards were 148 carriages and eighteen locomotives. Although the connecting-rods of the engines had been removed and buried by the railway employés, by the ingenuity of the Field Intelligence Department in discovering, and the labour of a hastily organised railway staff in refitting the parts, in a few days the engines were ready for work. Only

June 23rd, 1900.
Occupation of Standerton.

* Telegram No. 282, June 18th.

† Composition—18th Hussars; two 12-pr. guns (Naval); battery R.F.A.; section R.E.; 2nd Dorset regiment.

an immense pile of burnt sleepers marked the commencement of destruction which haste alone had evidently prevented being more thorough. Sir R. Buller entered Standerton on the morning of the 23rd, and on the 24th the whole force marched in, and was disposed in defensible positions about the crests of the basin, and upon the lofty Stander's Kop which commanded the country to the west.

Standerton thus secured, Sir R. Buller at once opened correspondence with Lord Roberts with reference to his next move, suggesting that, when he had filled Standerton with sufficient supplies to enable him to use it as a forward base, he should close the gap to Heidelberg (which he had just heard was about to be occupied by the troops of Lieut.-General Ian Hamilton),* and advance thence on Belfast to co-operate with the Field-Marshal's columns in their eastern operations along the Pretoria—Komati Poort line.† To this Lord Roberts consented‡ naming, however, Balmoral instead of Belfast as the point of coincidence on the eastern railway, and laying much stress on an early union with Heidelberg.§ On June 25th the line was re-opened for the carriage of supplies as far as the southern bank of the Vaal at Standerton. On the 27th Sir R. Buller received information of the occupation of Heidelberg by a detachment under Major-General Hart from Sir A. Hunter's division. Two days later he recalled an expedition which, commanded by Sir F. Clery, had started with the intention of reconnoitring Vrede, where the commandos of C. De Wet were reported to be concentrating;∥ on the 30th Sir F. Clery marched northwards with a column of all arms,¶ carrying eight

June 30th, 1900. Advance on Heidelberg.

---

* Telegram No. C. 2238, June 23rd.

† Telegram No. 287, June 23rd.

‡ Telegram No. C. 2267, June 24th.

§ Telegrams Nos. C. 2267, June 24th ; C. 2351A, June 28th ; C. 2394, June 30th ; C. 2453, July 2nd.

∥ Telegrams Nos. 289, June 27th ; 290, June 28th.

¶ Composition—Thorneycroft's M.I. ; Strathcona's Horse ; a squadron 13th Hussars ; A. battery R.H.A. ; 4th infantry brigade ; 63rd battery R.F.A. ; 86th (Howitzer) battery ; two 5-in. guns R.G.A.

THE CLEARING OF NORTHERN NATAL. 285

days' supplies, reaching Vlaklaagte in the evening. Some trifling skirmishing attended the next day's march to Val, and on July 2nd a strong body of the enemy was close in front of Greylingstad, where Sir F. Clery halted for the night. These merely remained in observance when on July 4th, Sir F. Clery, leaving a garrison with the 5-in. guns upon the commanding heights of Greylingstad, pushed on, and at 5 p.m. met Major-General Hart near the Zuikerbosch Spruit.* In this manner the two armies, which had started their respective campaigns from sea bases more than a thousand miles apart, joined hands after ten months of battles and marches, connecting, at this obscure spot, the last link of over 1,500 miles of railway, the larger portion of which had been wrested from the enemy, and much of it rebuilt. The work of the Natal army as a unit seemed now to be accomplished. One hand grasping that of Lord Roberts' invading forces, the other touching the sea five hundred miles away, it could stretch no farther, and at more than one point in the space between, its muscles appeared somewhat dangerously strained. As in the Orange Free State, the enemy, brushed from the line, lay in scattered bands on either side of it, watching for opportunities to sever the slender thread upon the integrity of which the masses of British troops in the van depended for their maintenance. There were at this time portions of commandos at Wakkerstroom, Amersfoort, Ermelo, Bethel, in the Verzamel Berg and at Vrede, at Blaauw Kopje on the Vaal, at Plat Kop on the Waterval, at Van Kolder's Kop, north-east of Greylingstad, and at many other places on either side of the line from Volksrust to Heidelberg. On July 6th Sir R. Buller, having consolidated as far as possible his lines of communication from end to end, took train to Pretoria to confer with Lord Roberts upon the subject of subsequent operations.

July 4th, 1900. Junction of the armies of Lord Roberts and Sir R. Buller.

* Sergeant A. H. L. Richardson, Lord Strathcona's corps, was awarded the Victoria Cross for an act of gallantry on July 5th during a skirmish at Wolve Spruit, near Standerton.

CHAPTER XI.

OPERATIONS IN THE ORANGE RIVER COLONY* (*continued*).

TOWARDS the end of June, 1900, when the columns which Lord Roberts had organised (see p. 135) were in motion in the east of the Orange River Colony, C. De Wet had under him some 8,500 men, with twenty or more guns. His principal lieutenants were Marthinus Prinsloo, J. H. Olivier, Fourie, Froneman, Haasbroek, Visser, De Villiers (of Harrismith), Paul De Villiers, Crowther, Roux and Piet De Wet.

Sir L. Rundle, based on Winburg, and on Basutoland through Ficksburg, held a line Winburg—Trommel—Ficksburg, with entrenched bodies (2nd Worcestershire regiment) at Ladybrand and Thabanchu. With the VIIIth division he occupied the following posts: Ficksburg, Willow Grange, Hammonia (17th brigade, Major-General Boyes), Klip Drift or Scheeper's Nek (1st Leinster regiment), Laager Spruit (Headquarters Colonial division), six miles south of Senekal, and Trommel, where he himself was. North of Sir L. Rundle was Clements, with Headquarters at Senekal, also based on Winburg; north-east of Clements, Paget was at and near Lindley; north again, MacDonald was at Heilbron; while Ian Hamilton had just arrived at Heidelberg (Transvaal). The northern and western columns were now to act against Bethlehem, which was still in the occupation of the enemy; and after its capture Clements was to operate against Harrismith.

June 27th, 1900.
Sir A. Hunter leaves Heidelberg.

On June 27th Sir A. Hunter, now in command of Ian Hamilton's force, after the latter's accident, marched south from

* See maps Nos. 38, 53 and 54, and Freehand sketches in the map case.

OPERATIONS IN THE ORANGE RIVER COLONY. 287

Heidelberg, crossed the Vaal at Villiersdorp, and at midday, July 1st, occupied Frankfort. Two days later he was joined by MacDonald, with the Heilbron column,* and on July 4th both forces moved towards Reitz in parallel columns, the western under Sir A. Hunter, the eastern under Bruce Hamilton. Early on July 7th Reitz was reached without fighting.

Clements and Paget, after clearing the country between Senekal and Lindley, joined hands on July 2nd, and, marching abreast six miles apart, advanced on Bethlehem. The enemy fell back in a south-easterly direction. On July 3rd, Paget's left front and flank were guarded by about 800 mounted men, under Colonel A. M. Brookfield, who was to make a wide sweeping movement and rejoin the main body that night near Bakenkop. Brookfield's artillery consisted of four guns of the 38th battery R.F.A., and two of the C.I.V. battery; his mounted troops were a detachment of Australians, chiefly men of the 4th contingent from South Australia, 14th battalion I.Y., one company I.Y. Scouts, and part of Prince Alfred's Volunteer Guard, a corps raised in Cape Colony. From the beginning of his march Brookfield was harassed by the enemy's sharpshooters. At about 10.30 a.m. his scouts discovered that the Boers were awaiting him with three guns on some ridges which crossed his path. Brookfield posted his own artillery on a long kopje running parallel to and about 4,000 yards' range from that held by the enemy. At the foot of the hill stretched a wide field of mealies, or Indian corn, which was carefully searched, and found to be unoccupied by the enemy. The guns above were then posted in sections, with an interval of 100 to 150 yards between each section, that of the C.I.V. on the left; but owing to the configuration of the ground, each pair was invisible to the others. The party of Imperial Yeomanry, escorting the 38th battery, at first lined the edge of the mealie field, a little to the right front of the guns; but as the engagement opened, Major H. E. Oldfield, who commanded the battery, ordered the escort to the right rear, as he considered the men to be too much exposed to the enemy's

July 3rd, 1900.
The affair at Bakenkop.

* Less 1st Argyll and Sutherland Highlanders, and two 4.7-in. Naval guns left to hold Heilbron.

shells. On reaching the ground allotted to him, the Yeomanry officer found that from it he could see neither the guns nor the enemy, and was therefore useless as an escort. More than once he reported this to Oldfield, but was ordered to remain where he was. The gap between the central and left sections of guns was filled by the Australians, and the outer flank of the guns of the C.I.V. was protected by a party of mounted men. The main body of the Imperial Yeomanry was kept in reserve, some distance back on the plain behind the hill crowned by the artillery; two miles still further back a strong party of the same corps held high ground to watch the rear.

Now for some hours proceeded an artillery duel, during which the enemy developed two more guns, one from his main position, the other from a knoll which partially enfiladed the right of Brookfield's line. But the shells which burst incessantly over the British kopje did little harm; and Oldfield, who was beginning to run short of ammunition, ordered his guns to cease fire, as he wished to reserve his strength to co-operate effectually with the main column, which he expected was soon to make itself felt on the left flank of the Boers. His men accordingly lay down about twenty yards from the guns, and only the C.I.V. detachment kept up a slow fire. The right and centre of the kopje thus appeared lifeless and deserted, and the Boers, believing that they had silenced one battery, determined to capture it. Whilst a swarm of marksmen demonstrated strongly against the side of the kopje where the C.I.V. guns were in action, about 100 stormers crawled unnoticed through the thick mealies below the hill, scaled the slope, and at 3.15 p.m. suddenly sent a heavy volley at very short range upon the right-hand section of guns, commanded by Lieut. W. G. Belcher. The gunners rushed to their posts, but could only fire a single round of case before the attackers were upon them. Belcher fell dead; all his men who were not killed or wounded were captured, and the two guns taken. At this moment, Oldfield, who had been to the left of the line of guns, hurried up towards Belcher's detachment; he, too, was struck down, mortally wounded. In the centre matters were equally grave. On the first alarm Captain

G. A. Fitzgerald, who was in charge of the second section of guns, sent for his limbers. One only managed to reach him; and largely owing to the exertions of a sergeant named Adams, a gun was rescued, and driven to assist the C.I.V. pieces. The second limber fared badly. The three drivers and all the horses of the team were killed or wounded, whilst attempting to restore order Fitzgerald was disabled, and thus a third gun passed into possession of the enemy. On the left the C.I.V. detachment, commanded by Major G. McMicking, was in great straits. The guns were run trail to trail, shelling the Boers advancing on the left, and in the direction from which Mauser fire appeared to be coming from the right. Not a single British rifleman was to be seen on the ridge. The escort on the left of the C.I.V. detachment had disappeared; of the Australians who had been distributed in three detachments, two parties, in obedience to an order received by their commanding officer, Major J. Rowell, were in full, though orderly, retreat. Over all the field there was uncertainty and confusion; and had the enemy followed up his successful surprise by a vigorous offensive, the whole of Brookfield's command might have been routed. But the burghers lost time in securing their prisoners, and it was well employed by Captain C. E. D. Budworth, R.A., attached to the C.I.V. artillery. Galloping to Rowell, who, with Captain A. E. M. Norton and B. troop of the South Australian Bushmen, still lay in rear of the ridge, he urged him to order an attempt to recapture the guns. Without hesitation Norton's men turned and charged uphill full in the face of a venomous fire. For a moment the Boers stood; then they broke and fled down the hill, followed by a hail of bullets from the Australians, who, greatly to their disappointment, were prudently forbidden to pursue them. It was noticed that many of the burghers wore helmets and military cloaks of British pattern, taken from prisoners who had been captured elsewhere; so that if their advance had been seen at all by any of Brookfield's column, they must have been mistaken for friends.

As soon as the Boers were off the ridge, their guns began to play heavily upon it. But the drivers of the battery, helped by two Yeomanry officers and some of their men, succeeded in dragging the derelict guns to the C.I.V. detachment, which, thus reinforced, finally drove off the party which was threatening the left of the position. One of the rescued guns was served throughout the remainder of the day by drivers from the C.I.V. detachment.

The casualties in the 38th battery were one officer killed and two wounded (one mortally); other ranks, one killed, six wounded and eight missing. As soon as order was restored the advance was resumed. The Boers fell back altogether, and Brookfield's detachment went on to rejoin the main body, as arranged, near Bakenkop. Paget's guns had for some time been heard on the right, and the complete withdrawal of the enemy from before Brookfield had been largely due to his operations.

Operations around Bethlehem. Paget had found the enemy in a strong position which barred his way between Bakenkop and Bronckhorstfontein. Attacking the former with the 1st Royal Munster Fusiliers, the 2nd King's Own Yorkshire Light Infantry, a squadron of the Middlesex Yeomanry, and two guns of the City Imperial Volunteers, Paget drove all before him back on Bethlehem, and bivouacked at Leeuwkop, where his outposts were continually disturbed by fire. Clements, co-operating on the south, had shelled the enemy's artillery positions all day, but had taken no further part in the engagement. Next morning, July 4th, Paget and Clements continued their movement. Paget sent out a reconnaissance to the north-east, to make certain that his left was clear, and then went on, over open country, to Blaauwkopje, fifteen miles north-west of Bethlehem. Clements bivouacked at Sterkfontein, after pushing the Boers from Bankfontein on to Kaffir Kopje, whence they covered the passage of their wagons over the Valsch with two guns. On July 5th, in accordance with instructions from the Commander-in-Chief, Clements sent the 2nd Bedfordshire regiment and the Malta M.I. back to garrison Lindley, and with the remainder of his force advanced to Bontjeskraal without opposition. Simultaneously, Paget reconnoitred the positions which the Boers were reported to be holding in front of Bethlehem, and following his mounted troops further to the south than he had intended, was forced to fight to extricate them, which caused a few casualties. He had thus crossed Clements' line of advance and coming up on the latter's right he bivouacked at Waterval. It was now found that the enemy, with his left strongly posted on Wolhuters Kop, was holding the hills to the south-west, west, and north-west of the town—on an arc the chord of which was the Reitz—Bethlehem—Fouriesburg road. At daybreak on the 6th, the British piquets were heavily shelled, and Paget, moving forward, took up a position north-west of the town. Soon afterwards Clements, the senior officer, sent a flag of truce into Bethlehem, with a message demanding surrender before 10 a.m. De Wet's refusal was received about noon, and at 12.30 p.m. operations were resumed. The mounted troops were pushed out widely right and left to turn the enemy's flanks; but so extended was the position, and consequently so great the distances to be traversed, that the infantry advance was much delayed. Paget moved to his right front, against Wolhuters Kop, while Clements directed his attack on Vogelsfontein, a kopje to his left front. The stubborn resistance of the Boers had not been overcome when night fell. Paget gained ground by an assault delivered by the 1st Royal Munster Fusiliers and the 2nd King's Own Yorkshire Light Infantry; but the mounted troops, owing to the difficult nature of the country and the obstacle presented by the Liebenbergs Vlei river, failed to turn the flanks. Neither could Clements' own force do more than hold the enemy on the left. The result of the day was a thorough reconnaissance of the enemy's position, which Clements hoped to seize on the next.

On the morning of the 7th, after a searching artillery preparation, in which the firing of the two 5-in. guns (6th company Eastern division R.G.A.) was most effective, a general assault was made on Wolhuters Kop and the ridge west of it. Clements launched the 1st Royal Irish regiment, supported by four companies of the 2nd Wiltshire and covered by a cross-fire of artillery, at the hostile centre, about half a mile north-west of Bethlehem. The resistance was slight, and at 8.45 a.m. the Royal Irish had carried the position, capturing a 15-pr., which proved

July 7th, 1900. The action at Wolhuters Kop.

to be the gun of the 77th battery lost at Stormberg.* Paget and Clements then advanced, and occupied Wolhuters Kop and Vogelsfontein, while two companies of the Royal Irish pushed on to the north-east crest of the former. The Boers were now seen to be in full retreat, and stragglers were shelled as they left Bethlehem. Early in the afternoon the troops entered the town, the capture of which had cost Clements and Paget 106 casualties.

The comparative ease with which De Wet had been driven from strong positions was to be explained by the fact that he was only fighting to delay the British advance until his main body should have secured its retreat to the mountains in the neighbourhood of Retief's Nek. On the previous day, the Boer leader had learned that Sir A. Hunter was moving on Bethlehem from the north, and was already approaching Reitz. Knowing that he was not strong enough to resist the triple combination being brought against him, De Wet at once decided to abandon Bethlehem, and to fall back on the mountain strongholds surrounding the Brandwater basin, whither the bulk of the forces of the Orange Free State had already retired.

On entering Reitz on the morning of July 7th, Sir A. Hunter ordered the 2nd cavalry brigade to Viljoenshoek, twenty miles to the south. From that place Broadwood was able to open heliographic communication with Clements, who informed him that he had just occupied Bethlehem. Two days later, Sir A. Hunter reached that town; on the 11th he received orders to assume command of the combined forces, that is, the VIIIth division and the columns of Paget and Clements, the last-named of which had marched on the 9th towards Senekal to refit. The troops now under Sir A. Hunter were as follows :—

VIIIth division and Colonial division (Lieut.-General Sir L. Rundle), disposed on a general front, Ficksburg—Biddulphs Berg.
  12th brigade (Major-General Clements), awaiting at Biddulphs Berg, near Senekal, the arrival of supplies from Winburg.

* See Volume I., page 301.

OPERATIONS IN THE ORANGE RIVER COLONY.

2nd cavalry brigade (Brig.-General Broadwood), at Bethlehem ; 800 men, six guns R.H.A., and one Vickers-Maxim.
2nd Mounted Infantry brigade (Brig.-General Ridley), at Bethlehem ; 1,400 men, six guns R.H.A.
Highland brigade (Major-General MacDonald), at Bethlehem ; three battalions.
20th brigade (Major-General Paget), at Bethlehem.
21st brigade (Major-General Bruce Hamilton), at Reitz, under orders to march on Bethlehem.
Two batteries R.F.A. and two 5-in. guns, also at Bethlehem.

The 3rd cavalry brigade (Brig.-General J. R. P. Gordon), which had accompanied Sir A. Hunter as far as Reitz, was on its way back to Heilbron, bound for Pretoria, in strength 800 sabres, six guns R.H.A., one Vickers-Maxim, and 375 mounted infantry.

The situation was now clear. The Boers, reported to be 6,000 to 8,000 strong with some 20 guns, had retired to the south of Bethlehem, and were holding entrenched positions of great natural strength in the recesses of the Brandwater basin. The tract in which they sought refuge lies on either side of the Brandwater river, which flows, from north to south, to join the Caledon river at a point some twenty miles above Ficksburg. On the south the Caledon river formed the boundary of the neutral state, Basutoland ; the three other sides are walled by a mountain range which rises in an almost continuous chain, though its sections were known by various names, such as the Witte Bergen on the west and the Roode Bergen opposite. These mountains are pierced only at a few points ; throughout their entire length there are but five passes or neks suitable for wheels, viz. : Commando Nek, Slabbert's Nek, Retief's Nek, Naauwpoort Nek, and the Golden Gate, the road over the last being so difficult that it was rarely used by wagons. Not all the enemy had as yet withdrawn behind these passes. On July 11th his dispositions were discovered to be as follows : At and north of Naauwpoort Nek was the Bethlehem commando, 600 men and eight guns, under Prinsloo ; Retief's and Slabbert's Neks were held in strength by C. De Wet, with about 4,000

The Brandwater Basin.

men and numerous guns, the main laager being at Kaffir Kop, six miles from Retief's Nek; Nelspoort was watched by piquets, and Commando Nek strongly guarded. On July 13th, a party of Royal Engineers, with an escort, engaged in repairing the Bethlehem—Senekal telegraph, had a brush with the enemy, suffering eight casualties.

<small>Sir A. Hunter's plan to enclose the Basin.</small>

Sir A. Hunter proposed to close in on the gathered Boers from the west and north simultaneously, moving on Nelspoort from the west, to block, and if possible force, Slabbert's Nek; to attack Retief's Nek, and close the pass of Naauwpoort. After clearing the passes, the target was to be the Brandwater basin and the bull's-eye Fouriesburg, which the Free Staters had now proclaimed the capital of the Orange Free State. Yet, until he should have obtained provisions for his troops, and ammunition for his guns, Sir A. Hunter did not feel justified in making a forward movement.

Sir L. Rundle, who had already been instructed by Lord Roberts to hold in strength the line Ficksburg—Hammonia—Biddulphs Berg, moved the Headquarters of the VIIIth division, the 16th brigade, and the Colonial division to Wit Kop, from which he drove the enemy's piquets. On July 12th and 13th, he reconnoitred towards Witnek, which was found to be strongly held, and established the Colonial division in a position within 2,000 yards of the Nek, whilst the Klip Drift Nek garrison was pushed in towards Rooikranz. Sir L. Rundle had been originally intended to operate against Slabbert's Nek; but, on the 14th, consequent on information received from Sir Godfrey Lagden, the British Resident in Basutoland, that the Boers were concentrating on Commando Nek with the intention of attacking Ficksburg and breaking out to the south-west, Sir L. Rundle was ordered to block the line from the Basuto border to Nelspoort. Sir L. Rundle, therefore, having received from Clements a reinforcement of 400 mounted men (Colonial division), moved his Headquarters, on July 15th, towards Rooikranz. He took with him three companies Imperial Yeomanry, two guns R.F.A., four companies 2nd Scots Guards, mounted infantry of the 2nd Manchester, 700 mounted men and six guns of the

OPERATIONS IN THE ORANGE RIVER COLONY.

Colonial division (Colonel E. H. Dalgety), as well as Driscoll's Scouts, 400 mounted men, Colonials and Imperial Yeomanry (Lieut.-Colonel H. M. Grenfell), and the 21st Bearer company. At Wit Kop, and opposite Witnek, he left Major-General B. B. D. Campbell, with two companies Imperial Yeomanry, four guns R.F.A., 2nd Grenadier Guards, four companies 2nd Scots Guards, 700 dismounted men of the Colonial division, and half the 21st Field hospital.

As the advance guard of this force approached Rooikranz, the enemy opened with musketry fire from the two hills at Bezuidenhouts Kraal, but were soon dislodged and driven back to Nelspoort, to the east of Rooikranz.* Rooikranz itself was found to be held in force, and Sir L. Rundle proceeded to shell the position from the west. Towards evening the enemy brought up considerable reinforcements from Nelspoort. On the same day, July 15th, the 2nd cavalry brigade (Broadwood) and the 20th infantry brigade (Paget) were sent out along the Senekal road, with the object of heading the enemy if he should attempt to break out in that direction, and pinning him to the ground until Sir A. Hunter could strike at his rear. On that very night the quarry most desired escaped the closing net.

General C. De Wet had for some time marked with foreboding the trend of the British operations. From the first he had opposed this retreat into mountains, which he knew would prove not a sanctuary but a trap. So strongly had he represented the dangers to his colleagues, that a plan for a universal break-out in three divisions was agreed to, and its details actually settled. De Wet's own party, escorting Steyn and the Government, was to be the first to depart; and on the night of the 15th he made his way with 2,600 men, four guns and 460 wagons over Slabbert's Nek, and struck for the north, fully expecting the rest to follow him on the next evening. It will be seen how, his strong grasp removed, the force which he quitted fell to pieces behind his back. Only one small band of Free Staters was to come after him over the passes; as for the rest, their leader saw them no more.

Escape of C. De Wet.

---
* Casualties in Sir L. Rundle's force, July 15th—Two killed, four wounded.

The flight of De Wet's commando was quickly discovered, though some time elapsed before it was known whose leadership had contrived the escape. Broadwood and Paget, with Ridley, were soon on his heels, and all through July 16th harassed his rear in the neighbourhood of Klipscheur and Bultfontein. But to pursue De Wet was not now the main issue; and Paget, desisting, left to Broadwood and Ridley an eventful chase of which the history must be deferred.

Whilst they began the hunt, Sir L. Rundle's mounted troops scouted south of Rooikranz, and a force under Lieut.-Colonel H. Martin from Klip Drift Nek advanced to about three miles west of the same place. Sir L. Rundle now realised that, before moving further southward, the Rooikranz position must be blocked. He therefore requested Sir A. Hunter to send a part of Clements' force to relieve Campbell from the duty of holding Haasbroek about Wit Kop—Witnek, and thus to prevent him from joining De Villiers at Rooikranz. This relief was carried out, two days later, by the arrival of Colonel G. W. Hacket Pain, in command of the 2nd Worcestershire and 2nd Wiltshire regiments and four guns; and on the 19th Campbell brought his troops down to Rooikranz North. At the same time, Sir L. Rundle's mounted troops began to close in towards the south of Rooikranz, plying the enemy with artillery and long-range rifle fire, and Grenfell's force was despatched to rejoin Clements, who was then about a mile to the west of the Zand river. Sir A. Hunter, also, had made a reconnaissance towards Retief's Nek and Slabbert's Nek, whilst Rimington's Guides had moved in the direction of Naauwpoort, meeting with small but constant opposition.

On July 20th, Bruce Hamilton was despatched, with the 1st Cameron Highlanders—the only battalion of his brigade with him at the moment—the 7th M.I., and the 82nd battery R.F.A., to occupy Spitz Kranz (Spitz Kop), about nine miles south-east of Bethlehem; this kopje was reported to overlook and command the approaches to Naauwpoort Nek, whilst possession of it was necessary to enable Bruce Hamilton to get into touch with the columns on his right. Some 400 Boers

OPERATIONS IN THE ORANGE RIVER COLONY.

were on it whom Bruce Hamilton engaged throughout the day. Progress was slow, but by nightfall the British had gained a position about a mile and a half from Spitz Kop, with the loss of two officers and seven men wounded. At 8 a.m. on the following day, the operations were resumed: with loss of three men killed and three officers and sixteen men wounded, Bruce Hamilton seized the kopje with the Cameron Highlanders, and held it, with a view to blocking Naauwpoort Nek.

Leaving Campbell's force opposite Rooikranz, Sir L. Rundle moved on the 20th to Hammonia, with the Headquarters of the VIIIth division. There he assembled three and a half companies Imperial Yeomanry, Driscoll's Scouts, thirty mounted Colonials, seven guns R.F.A., two guns Cape Mounted Rifles artillery, 2nd Scots Guards, and the 1st Leinster regiment.

The following is a summary of the dispositions on July 21st: *Dispositions on July 21st, 1900.*

Sir L. Rundle's Force.

Ficksburg and Willow Grange.—One and a half battalions of infantry, one company Imperial Yeomanry, four guns R.F.A., fifty Colonial division.

Hammonia.—One and a half battalions of infantry, one company Imperial Yeomanry, two guns R.F.A., 280 Colonial division.

Rooikranz.—One battalion of infantry, one company Imperial Yeomanry, four guns R.F.A., 100 Colonial division.

Rooikranz, north of Bezuidenhouts Kraal.—One battalion of infantry, two companies Imperial Yeomanry, four guns R.F.A., 700 dismounted Colonial division.

Biddulphs Berg.—Half a battalion, one gun, thirty Colonial division.

Senekal.—Half a battalion, one gun, seventy Colonial division.

Trommel.—Three companies of infantry, two guns.

Rietspruit (twenty miles west of Senekal).—Two companies of infantry, two guns.

Ladybrand.—Five companies of infantry, one and a half companies Imperial Yeomanry.

Thabanchu.—Three companies of infantry, one and a half companies Imperial Yeomanry.

Near Hammonia (Rundle's Movable column).—One battalion of infantry, three companies Imperial Yeomanry, ten guns, 700 Colonial division.

Major-General Clements' Force.

Wit Kop—Witnek.—Two battalions of infantry, four guns, about 100 mounted infantry.

Palmietfontein.—One battalion, one section Field guns, two 5-in. guns, 400 mounted infantry.

Major-General Paget's Force.

Bultfontein.—One and a half battalions of infantry, six guns, 250 mounted infantry.

Southern Corner Sebastopol.—One battalion, two guns, sixty mounted infantry.

Sir A. Hunter's Original Force.

Bethlehem.—Four battalions of infantry, twenty guns R.F.A., two 5-in. guns, 200 mounted infantry (Major-General MacDonald).

Half-way between Bethlehem and Naauwpoort.—One battalion of infantry, six guns R.F.A., one Vickers-Maxim, 550 mounted infantry (Major-General Bruce Hamilton).

Now that De Wet had escaped, the strength of the enemy holding the passes and inside the Brandwater basin was estimated at 5,500 fighting men, exclusive of the Harrismith and Vrede commandos, which were also said to have made their way out by Witzies Hoek and the Golden Gate. Sir A. Hunter now issued orders for closing in on the enemy, and arranged for a combined forward movement to be made on July 23rd. Sir L. Rundle was to bombard the position with every gun; Clements and Paget to concentrate for an assault on Slabbert's Nek, while Sir A. Hunter himself intended to attack Retief's Nek with MacDonald's Highland brigade, two 5-in. guns, the 5th battery R.F.A. and two sections 76th battery R.F.A., Lovat's Scouts, and Rimington's Guides, with the addition of Lieut.-Colonel B. D. A. Donne's force from Meyer's Kop (1st

OPERATIONS IN THE ORANGE RIVER COLONY.

Royal Sussex, and the 81st battery R.F.A.). To carry out these orders, Sir L. Rundle, on the 22nd, moved to Willow Grange, four miles north of Ficksburg, with the following troops: Three and a half companies Imperial Yeomanry, Driscoll's Scouts, four guns R.F.A., 2nd Scots Guards, 1st Leinster regiment and (detached from the garrison of Ficksburg) two companies 2nd Royal West Kent, two companies 1st South Staffordshire regiments and two guns R.F.A. He first pushed three companies South Staffordshire across the Willow Grange plateau, towards July's Kop, with skirmishing which cost him seven casualties. Sir A. Hunter, on the same day, marched from Bethlehem, and bivouacked for the night at Bishop's Farm, under Vaal Kranz, about eight miles north of Retief's Nek. This completed the preparations, and next morning fighting began all along the line.

On the south Boyes advanced from Ficksburg on Zoutkop; Sir L. Rundle from Willow Grange on July's Kop; Colonel T. R. Main, with part of the garrison of the town, from Hammonia on Abrikoo's Kop; Dalgety's Colonial division on Moolman's Hoek; and Campbell bombarded the enemy's position at Rooikranz. On the north Hacket Pain, at Wit Kop, pushed forward towards Witnek, and kept up a heavy fire on the Boers in that position; Clements, having marched from Besters Kop, at 10 a.m. joined hands with Paget, some two and a half miles north of Slabbert's Nek, and while their combined forces proceeded to attack that pass, Sir A. Hunter and MacDonald launched their assault on Retief's Nek, a few miles to the north-east.

As soon as they had effected a junction, which had been somewhat delayed by a stampede of the horses during a gale, Clements and Paget moved on towards Slabbert's Nek. Their mounted troops reconnoitred the Nek and watched the flanks; the artillery and infantry advanced to the foot-hills at the entrance to the pass. The Boers were found to be strongly entrenched on a ridge barring the Nek, and upon high hills which rose on either side of it; the ground, which sloped like a mansard roof from its summit, forbade a direct attack. The

July 23rd, 1900. Attack on Slabbert's Nek.

best approach seemed to be a spur which ran down from the enemy's left, and this Grenfell's mounted troops on Clements' right flank were ordered to capture. But the Boers, sweeping the spur from the caves and rocks which crowned it, checked the attack at the lower slopes, and Clements reinforced Grenfell with two companies 1st Royal Irish regiment, ordering him to hold on whilst he tried elsewhere. Still refusing his own left and feeling that of the enemy, he then threw two companies 2nd Wiltshire regiment against a second spur beyond Grenfell, that is still more to his right, and at the same time pushed forward the 1st Royal Munster Fusiliers, of Paget's force, near enough to hold the enemy in his central trenches. The Wiltshire, essaying to attack, were checked, as the mounted troops had been, when half-way up the spur, and darkness fell with success by no means assured. There had been forty-two casualties. But the work had been more effective than it appeared, especially that of the artillery, which, incessantly bombarding, had silenced the four guns brought against them, and severely shaken the enemy in his trenches. That night a patrol of Brabant's Horse, reconnoitring the western heights of the position, gained the summit unopposed. Seizing the point of vantage with a squadron of the same corps, at 4 o'clock next morning (24th), Clements sent four companies Royal Irish regiment and two companies Wiltshire regiment, under Lieut.-Col. H. W. N. Guinness, up by this side, and at 8 a.m. the highest peak was gained under cover of a cloud which fortunately lay upon the summit. There was a little firing; for the Boers, completely turned, beat a hasty retreat, whilst Guinness, swinging southward, cleared the crests below which Grenfell and the Wiltshire companies had been checked the night before. At 11 a.m. Clements ordered a general advance, and his force took possession of the evacuated positions without further losses.

July 23rd, 1900.
Attack on Retief's Nek

An arduous march throughout a night of rain, snow, and intense cold, had brought Sir A. Hunter's force within striking distance of Retief's Nek on the 23rd. That obstacle was even stronger than Slabbert's. Precipitous heights stood like gateposts of colossal proportions on either side of the entry. A third, of a conical shape, projected from the main ridge further away towards the British left front. This Sir A. Hunter perceived to be his only *point d'appui*, and at 9 a.m. he sent against it the 2nd Black Watch, whilst all his artillery thrashed the hostile ridges. The General then decided to await the arrival of the force from Meyer's Kop, whence Donne was bringing the 1st Royal Sussex regiment and the 81st battery R.F.A.; and a pause ensued. These troops came up about 1.30 p.m. and Sir A. Hunter developed his attack. Against the height to his right of the Nek went the Royal Sussex; against that on the left the 1st Highland Light Infantry. Both encountered strong opposition, which was only kept from being decisive by the powerful practice of the united artillery. The Royal Sussex, definitely checked, progressed not at all; the Highland Light Infantry fared better, clinging stubbornly to the base of their hill, though for a long time they could do no more. From the Black Watch came the action which loosened the enemy. Covered by the 5th battery R.F.A., that battalion had first gained a footing on the conical projection on the left, then pushed on to the main crest behind, thus coming up on the flank of the defence, which instantly began to crumble. Darkness enabled the Highland Light Infantry to win the height above them. At dawn on the 24th the 2nd Seaforth Highlanders, circling wide around the left, completed the turning movement by getting upon the crest beyond the Black Watch. By midday Retief's Nek had fallen, and the troops of Sir A. Hunter and MacDonald, amongst whom there had been eighty-six casualties, bivouacked in the Brandwater basin, near Retief's Nek Farm. The position at Witnek was also abandoned during this afternoon, and the Boers were reported to be retreating, from all directions, towards Fouriesburg.

The enemy was now hemmed in on three sides, and his sole chance of breaking out of the basin was in the direction of Harrismith, by way of Naauwpoort Nek, or the Golden Gate. To seal these exits at once was imperative, and Sir A. Hunter ordered MacDonald and Bruce Hamilton to hasten to bar them from outside.

July, 25th, 1900.
Occupation of Commando Nek.

On the morning of the 25th Sir L. Rundle occupied Commando Nek with his mounted troops, and then advanced through the Nek, to a farm three miles on the road to Fouriesburg, with four companies Imperial Yeomanry, Driscoll's Scouts, six guns R.F.A., 2nd Scots Guards and 1st Leinster regiment. At the same time the troops at Hammonia, Ficksburg and Rooikranz were ordered to close in on Fouriesburg.

Despatching MacDonald (Highland brigade, two 5-in. guns, Lovat's Scouts, and the 5th battery R.F.A.) to join Bruce Hamilton, and leaving Donne (six guns R.F.A., 1st Royal Sussex and 2nd Bedfordshire) to hold Slabbert's and Retief's Neks, Sir A. Hunter moved the remainder of the troops to Uithoek, nine miles in the direction of Fouriesburg, within three miles of which he pushed a mounted reconnaissance. That day MacDonald, marching by a bad cross-road towards Naauwpoort Nek, joined Bruce Hamilton, near midday, when the united forces moved on to Middelvlei and bivouacked.

July 26th, 1900.
Occupation of Fouriesburg.

At 5 a.m. on the 26th, Sir L. Rundle advanced to General's Nek, and sent Driscoll's Scouts on to Fouriesburg. Arriving there at 11.45 a.m. the Scouts found that the Boers had just evacuated the town, leaving behind 115 British prisoners of war. These told the Scouts that the burghers intended to return and take them away. As soon as this had been reported to Sir L. Rundle, he sent forward the remainder of his mounted troops, and followed with four companies Scots Guards, four companies Leinster regiment, and two guns R.F.A., who made a forced march of twenty-five miles during the day. Sir A. Hunter also entered Fouriesburg with his mounted troops in the afternoon, but finding it already in Sir L. Rundle's possession, returned to his camp, three miles north of the town. The enemy having retired to the east, Hacket Pain was now ordered to move from Witnek to Retief's Nek, to relieve Donne, who was instructed to proceed with his force and an additional 300 mounted men under Colonel C. R. Burn (6th battalion I.Y.), from Fouriesburg, to join the Highland brigade outside Naauwpoort Nek.

On July 27th, Sir A. Hunter's northern force marched into Fouriesburg; and, on the 28th, the pressure on the enemy was

OPERATIONS IN THE ORANGE RIVER COLONY.

kept up by Sir L. Rundle with two battalions, and by Clements and Paget, each with a battalion and a half. Clements, who commanded the advance guard, was soon engaged with the Boers, who fought a tenacious rearguard action all day in the vicinity of Slaap Kranz ridge. The action, which resembled that at Retief's Nek in its tactical features, was opened by a wing of the 2nd Wiltshire and the 1st Royal Irish regiment, who advanced against the heights flanking the precipitous Nek which they were unable to take before dark. At midnight the Scots Guards, who had seized a commanding knoll in front of the Boer left at dusk, went on and rushed the main position behind, finding it abandoned. The casualties during the day amounted to four men killed, three officers and twenty-seven men wounded.

<small>July 27th, 1900. Action at Slaap Kranz.</small>

In the meanwhile, the main body of the enemy was striving to make its escape from the Brandwater basin by Naauwpoort Nek and the Golden Gate. The former loophole had already been blocked from outside by MacDonald, who had established at H. Naude's Farm, facing it, the 2nd Seaforth Highlanders, two guns 82nd battery R.F.A., one 5-in. gun, 5th M.I., and Burma M.I. In effecting this MacDonald and Bruce Hamilton had met with considerable resistance on the 26th, to the north and north-east of the Nek; but they succeeded in driving the enemy out of the kopjes, and taking up a strong position, commanding the pass, at a distance of three and a half miles.

This now left open to the Boers only the Golden Gate, towards which, on July 27th, MacDonald and Bruce Hamilton marched with all speed, bivouacking at Darvel's Rust, ten miles from Naauwpoort Nek, that night. At 6 a.m. next day, leaving MacDonald's brigade at Darvel's Rust, Bruce Hamilton, with the 1st Cameron Highlanders, four guns 82nd battery R.F.A., one 5-in. gun, Lovat's Scouts, and the 7th M.I., drove the enemy from successive positions, and reached Stephanus Draai Nek at nightfall. Lovat's Scouts now returned to Darvel's Rust, where also Donne's troops from Slabbert's and Retief's Neks joined MacDonald, who immediately disposed them as follows: Four guns 76th battery R.F.A., Bedfordshire regiment, and

Burn's mounted troops (about 350) were despatched to H. Naude's Farm, to release the two guns 82nd battery R.F.A., 5th M.I., and Burma M.I., all of which, together with the Royal Sussex regiment, were sent on to join Bruce Hamilton.

On the 29th, that General, before he was aware that reinforcements were on the way, moved on with the small force at his disposal, viz.: 1st Cameron Highlanders, one 5-in. gun, four guns 82nd battery R.F.A. and the 7th M.I. The country was difficult, and the Boers opposed his advance; but at midday he was reinforced by the Royal Sussex, and gained a bivouac some six miles north of Solomon Raatze's Farm (Eerste Geluk).

July 29th, 1900. Occupation of Naauwpoort Nek. On the same day, MacDonald took his troops back to H. Naude's Farm, and thence reconnoitred Naauwpoort Nek, which he found deserted by the enemy. He consequently occupied the pass with a garrison of the Bedfordshire regiment, four guns 76th battery R.F.A., and Prince Alfred's Volunteer Guard, returning with the remainder of his troops to Darvel's Rust. At 5 p.m. he received a message from Sir A. Hunter telling him to suspend hostilities unless attacked, as General Prinsloo had surrendered unconditionally.

This event had thus come about: No sooner had C. De Wet disappeared from the Brandwater basin than the commandos which remained behind, dissatisfied with, or uncertain of his successor in command, thought it necessary to elect a fresh Commandant-General. Three candidates were present of equal rank, viz.: Prinsloo, P. H. Roux and Olivier. On July 27th the election took place, and caused immediate confusion; certain commandos nominated Prinsloo, others stood by Roux, who had been De Wet's own choice; but the chaos was increased by the fact that the votes of the more distant commandos had not been received at the time when Prinsloo, thinking himself elected, and abandoning hope at the same time, asked for an armistice. Even then the other commandants, although they had authorised Prinsloo to treat for peace, had forbidden him to agree to any terms until they had been submitted to them; and they had declared that they would not consider unconditional surrender. Whether he exceeded his authority or not,

OPERATIONS IN THE ORANGE RIVER COLONY. 305

whether, indeed, he were in truth Commandant-General or not, Prinsloo unreservedly capitulated, in the name of all the commandos present in his jurisdiction. He had, indeed, attempted negotiation. At 7.15 a.m. on the 29th, Sir A. Hunter received a request for a four days' armistice. This was refused, and the troops advanced beyond Slaap Kranz ridge. At 4.30 p.m. Sir A. Hunter received a second message, in which Prinsloo agreed to surrender next morning. At 9 a.m. on the 30th, Prinsloo and Crowther gave themselves up at Slaap Kranz, their example being shortly followed by the whole of the Ficksburg and Ladybrand commandos. Next day the Senekal and Winburg commandos laid down their arms, and a large number of Boers came in from outside the Golden Gate to Bruce Hamilton, who by that evening had gathered in 1,216 rifles, 671 horses and a 12-pr. gun. On the same day flags of truce had been sent to all the Boer leaders in the neighbourhood informing them of the capitulation. This news was received by, amongst others, Commandant Olivier, who was not within the basin, but outside the Golden Gate with 1,500 to 2,000 men and nine guns. Olivier would consent to do no more than halt, pending news from Prinsloo; getting none, he marched off, refusing to abide by a decision which he considered unjustifiable, and made by an officer whom he did not allow to have any authority over the army and himself. Roux, on the other hand, who was within the cordon, surrendered, though unwillingly; for he too disallowed the authority of Prinsloo. Nevertheless that leader, whether usurper or not, assuming command, like de Wimpffen at Sedan, only to be forced to surrender it immediately to his enemy, had sealed the general fate. *[July 30th, 1900. Capitulation of over 4,000 Boers.]*

The catastrophe took place near Slaap Kranz. The total number of prisoners taken (inclusive of those who surrendered to Bruce Hamilton) was 4,140, with three guns, two of which proved to be those captured from U. battery R.H.A. at Sannah's Post.* Over 4,000 horses and ponies, a large number of rifles, and upwards of a million rounds of ammunition, besides wagons and stock, also fell into Sir A. Hunter's hands. The majority

* See Volume II., Chapter XVII.

of the burghers appeared to greet with relief the turn of events; they were exhausted physically and morally, and Sir A. Hunter granted them certain concessions, such as permitting them to ride their horses, instead of walking, into captivity ; and, on reaching Winburg, the weakly amongst them and the old men and boys were to be allowed to proceed to their homes, in charge of such private wagons and draught oxen as the British Government did not wish to hire or purchase for its use. After giving in their arms, the surrendered burghers were conducted to Fouriesburg, marching in batches of 200, each party under escort of twenty Imperial Yeomanry from the VIIIth division. During the next few days the whole were conducted on, in two columns, by Paget and Bruce Hamilton, to Winburg, whence they were conveyed by rail to Cape Town.

CHAPTER XII.

OPERATIONS IN THE EASTERN TRANSVAAL.

JUNE 16TH TO AUGUST 21ST, 1900.*

THE exhaustion of men and animals and the wear and tear of material caused by the unbroken advance on Pretoria, forbade any immediate resumption of an active offensive after the battle of Diamond Hill. The sovereign need of the Army was to be remounted and refitted.

On June 16th Pretoria, with its garrison of the VIIth division (less the 15th brigade at Johannesburg), was covered upon its eastern side by the following troops :— Situation east of Pretoria.

XIth division (Pole-Carew) encamped some two miles east of the town;

1st M.I. brigade (Headquarters and 1st and 3rd corps) at Derde Poort;

Cavalry division (1st and 4th brigades) around Kameel Drift.

On June 19th Ian Hamilton's force,† destined for the Orange River Colony, marched from Pretoria towards Heidelberg. At Springs it was joined by the 81st battery R.F.A. and drafts of 500 mounted men, and after slight opposition reached Heidelberg

---

* See maps Nos. 38 and 48.

† 2nd cavalry brigade,   7th corps mounted infantry,
 3rd cavalry brigade,   72nd and 82nd batteries Royal Field
 2nd corps mounted infantry,   artillery,
 5th corps mounted infantry,   Two 5-in. guns,
 6th corps mounted infantry,   21st brigade.

on the 23rd. On the same day Sir A. Hunter, who was under orders from Lord Roberts " to be ready either to stretch a hand towards General Buller at Standerton, or to move upon the left flank of any enemy attacking Pretoria from the east," left Johannesburg, with Hart's troops,* and reached Heidelberg on the 25th. Meanwhile, around Pretoria the eastern outposts were being pushed further out. By the latter part of June, Pilcher,† detached by Hutton from Derde Poort, had reached Rietfontein. Thence he touched the garrison of Irene (19th brigade) with his right hand, and with his left Henry's patrols, which covered the front of the XIth division. The Guards' brigade now formed a cordon of outposts from Donkerhoek to Eerstefabrieken, with Headquarters at Donkerhoek; and Hutton, after accompanying a small column,‡§ detached on June 16th to open communication with Baden-Powell, had returned to his position at Derde Poort.|| At Eerstefabrieken were the Headquarters of the XIth division, the front of which was covered by the 18th brigade to about Edendale. French (1st and 4th cavalry brigades) was still at Kameel Drift. On the 27th the outpost line was strengthened by troops under Brigadier-General B. T. Mahon,¶ who arrived at Rietfontein (near Irene) from Johannesburg, and reinforced Pilcher.

* One company Imperial Yeomanry,   2nd Royal Dublin Fusiliers,
  28th battery Royal Field artillery,   Wing 2nd Somerset Light Infantry,
  G. section Vickers-Maxims,   Marshall's Horse.

† 400 mounted infantry,
  Four guns G. battery R.H.A.

‡ 300 of the 10th M. I., Canadian M.R., and New Zealand M.R.
  18th battery R.F.A. } from VIIth division.
  2nd Lincoln regiment

§ See page 234.

|| 1st corps M.I. (less 140 with Pilcher),
  C. section Vickers-Maxims,
  C. section galloping Maxims.

¶ Three squadrons I.L.H.,   1st Border regiment,
  M. battery R.H.A.,   1st Connaught Rangers.

OPERATIONS IN THE EASTERN TRANSVAAL. 309

The sole offensive act by either army in this area during the month of June was a feeble attack on the garrison* of Springs by some 300 Boers on June 28th.

To recapitulate the situation in South Africa at the beginning of July :—

Lord Methuen was about Lindley; Lieut.-General Sir L. Rundle's troops formed a chain of strongly entrenched posts, extending from Winburg to Ficksburg; Lieut.-General Sir A. Hunter, having succeeded to the command of Ian Hamilton's force, was in occupation of Frankfort. General Sir R. Buller was moving up the Natal railway, and had reached Standerton. In the Western Transvaal Baden-Powell, at Rustenburg, was engaged in pacifying that district. The Eastern Transvaal was the only area in which large hostile bodies were to be found; and, commanded by Louis Botha, they threatened danger.

Early in July Botha's forces, now reinforced by part of those commandos which Sir R. Buller had manœuvred out of Laing's Nek, showed signs of renewed activity. Lord Roberts determined to forestall them by moving his own troops eastward. On July 4th Major-General Hutton, with the 1st brigade of mounted infantry, strengthened by the 20th company Imperial Yeomanry, 66th battery R.F.A., two 5-in. guns, the 2nd Royal Fusiliers and 2nd Royal Irish Fusiliers, was despatched to Rietfontein to stiffen that flank; and, whilst covering the railway, to clear the country in the neighbourhood of Springs. On the same date Lieut.-Colonel Pilcher, having received from Hutton part of the Queensland M.I. and two Vickers-Maxims, was moved about three miles further to the east, to Zwavelpoort on the Tigerpoort—Witpoort ridge. On the morning of the 6th Hutton moved south-east to the neighbourhood of Bapsfontein. He had first sent on Mahon, with M. battery R.H.A., the Imperial Light Horse, 1st corps M.I. and C. section Vickers-Maxims, to seize the high ground above Bapsfontein and surprise a Boer

marginal note: Operations east of Pretoria.

---
* 8th mounted infantry (47),
Two guns 74th battery Royal Field artillery,
Royal Canadian regiment (370).

piquet which was usually stationed there. Mahon, after occupying the position, was himself attacked in the morning, but the effort was half-hearted, and on Hutton's arrival at 11 a.m. Mahon was despatched to aid Pilcher, who could be seen six miles to the north-west, engaged in clearing the Tigerpoort—Witpoort ridge. Next day Hutton decided to reconnoitre the district thoroughly. He instructed Mahon to push east with the mounted troops to the Bronkhorst Spruit, and thence to strike south to Witklip. Pilcher, from Tigerpoort, was to advance towards Witpoort; whilst the 8th corps M.I., two guns 74th battery R.F.A. and five companies of the Royal Canadian regiment were sent by Major-General Smith-Dorrien from Springs towards Witklip to screen Mahon's right flank. Hutton himself, with his infantry, moved three miles eastward in support. Shortly before noon scouts of the Imperial Light Horse, on the outer flank of Mahon's left flank-guard, came upon the enemy in force near Witklip, and being reinforced by a squadron joined in a brisk fight. The Boers worked in dangerously close under folds of the ground, and Mahon called the squadron back whilst he brought up his Horse artillery battery, proposing to check the advance with shrapnel. He also began a movement round the enemy's right flank with the rest of his troops. The Imperial Light Horse, which had lost several men in the skirmish, suffered further in obeying the order to retire, nineteen officers and men of the squadron being killed and wounded. The Boers, commanded by Commandant A. J. Dirksen, of Boksburg, then showed a strong front and unmasked three guns; and at 3 p.m. Mahon, receiving no support, began a general retirement towards Hutton's right, being later covered by a battalion of infantry and some guns sent forward for the purpose. Two hours before he had asked for reinforcements; but Hutton did not receive the request until Mahon was about to fall back, when he sent his Horse artillery battery to Mahon's assistance, considering that the hour was too late to bring up the infantry. Moreover, it was not Hutton's intention to commit himself to a general engagement so far to the south. Mahon, closely followed by the Boers, reached the previous night's bivouac with

July 7th, 1900. The affair at Witklip.

OPERATIONS IN THE EASTERN TRANSVAAL. 311

the total loss of two officers and six men killed and twenty-three men wounded.

Botha, who joined Dirksen after this engagement, now planned to harass the troops stationed around Pretoria. It had been reported to him that the capital was but lightly held, De Wet having drawn off so many troops upon himself. Ordering Commandant Grobelaar and General De la Rey to threaten the town from the north, and Lemmer to occupy the attention of Baden-Powell in the west, the Commandant-General reserved to himself the task of dealing with Hutton's advancing troops. Throughout July 8th and 9th Botha vainly attempted to force a passage through Hutton's lines, and skirmishing was general along the whole front. On the 9th the 1st Suffolk regiment was sent from Irene to Tigerpoort to support Pilcher, who on the previous evening had discovered an attempt by 400 Boers to pass between his outposts and those of the XIth division to the north. *[The Boers attempt to reach Pretoria.]*

Fresh disturbance in the Western Transvaal now called Smith-Dorrien from Irene to Krugersdorp on July 10th. Taking two battalions—the 1st Gordon Highlanders and 2nd Shropshire Light Infantry—Smith-Dorrien left on the line the 2nd Duke of Cornwall's Light Infantry, who came under Major-General Sir H. Chermside, the new commander of the communications from Kroonstad to Pretoria. The threatened neighbourhood of Springs was thus weakened by the withdrawal of troops. The expected arrival in Pretoria of a force from Senekal,* under Colonel T. E. Hickman,† enabled Lord Roberts to strengthen Hutton's right flank by despatching the 1st cavalry brigade, with Lieut.-General French, to the neighbourhood of Bapsfontein on the 9th. French joined Hutton near Rietvlei on the 10th and assumed command. At this moment Hutton's troops were disposed as follows :—Alderson was five miles south-west of Rietvlei, in touch with Springs on one side, and on the *[July 10th, 1900. French joins the forces east of Pretoria.]*

---
* See page 139.

† 1st, 2nd and 3rd regiments M.I.,
   Elswick battery,
   Section Vickers-Maxims.

other with Hutton's main body which held the lesser of two ridges running north-west towards Tigerpoort, the enemy being upon the greater; next, on the left, stood Mahon, who was in communication with Pilcher at Tigerpoort. Orders were now issued for an advance on the 11th, with the object of driving the Boers on the higher Tigerpoort—Witpoort ridge eastwards and southwards over the Bronkhorst Spruit. This move was fortunate, for Botha had appointed that very day for a general attack on the outposts around Pretoria. Thus the Boers' minor successes at Onderste Poort and Zilikat's Nek received no support from the Commandant-General, who, instead of attacking, found himself thrown on the defensive by French and Hutton. French menaced both flanks of the enemy on the Tigerpoort—Witpoort ridge with his mounted troops, and held the centre with a small force of infantry and heavy artillery. To the north Alderson, brought up from the other flank, circled with the 1st corps mounted infantry, 1st Canadian Mounted Rifles, New Zealand Mounted Rifles, 20th company I.Y. and G. battery R.H.A., together with Pilcher's mounted infantry (350 men and two Vickers-Maxims) and Henry's 4th corps mounted infantry with a battery R.F.A. sent by Lieut.-General Pole-Carew. All these threatened the Boers from the north, whilst Porter's 1st cavalry brigade manœuvred to turn their left flank. As soon as Alderson had made his attack felt the infantry were to advance, covered *He drives the enemy eastward,* by the guns, and seize the ridge about Witpoort. These tactics proved successful. By 12.30 p.m. the Boers were in retreat, and French was preparing to follow them up when he received a telegram from the Commander-in-Chief stating that " the enemy are pressing us all along the line of the Magaliesberg, and we require more troops in Pretoria;" requesting, further, that Mahon's and Pilcher's commands should return at once to the capital. This was complied with; and French occupied the ground he had gained with an infantry battalion and a battery. At 7.15 p.m. the news of the reverse at Zilikat's Nek* was sent by Lord Roberts to French, accompanied by the following

---

* See page 238.

OPERATIONS IN THE EASTERN TRANSVAAL.

instructions :—" Now that the enemy has been driven off by you from our right front, that might I think be safely held for the next few days by Porter's brigade, Hutton's mounted infantry, two 5-in. guns and the battalion now at Tigerpoort (1st Suffolk). If you concur in this order send in at once the four battalions of infantry* and two of the 5-in. guns and come in yourself to take command of the cavalry on the northern flank." To this French replied the same evening by urging the advisability of a vigorous offensive from the Tigerpoort—Witpoort position against Botha's line of communication at Balmoral, as he considered that the descents in the west were merely in the nature of raids. To Lord Roberts, however, the outbreak in that area appeared of a more serious character; and in consequence French, with three battalions of infantry (the fourth—the Royal Irish Fusiliers—was left with Hutton on French's recommendation) moved into Pretoria on July 12th. On the same day the 2nd Duke of Cornwall's Light Infantry was brought into Pretoria from Irene.

From July 12th to the 15th there was a pause which Lord Roberts used to secure his position. Two battalions of infantry, the 2nd Buffs and 1st Argyll and Sutherland Highlanders, and D. battery Royal Canadian artillery, were brought up by rail to Pretoria from Kelly-Kenny's command in the Orange River Colony. Such was the regularity and excellence of the railway service at this time that a single line, a scanty staff, and limited engine power were able to convey, in twelve hours, twenty loaded trains from the south to Pretoria through regions infested by the enemy. The Commander-in-Chief had provided against any repetition of such attacks as those of July 11th. But before he could be free to march on Balmoral it was necessary to clear the country north-east of Pretoria, where roved the commandos of Commandant Grobelaar. To this end a new column was formed and placed under Ian Hamilton, who now again took

* 2nd Royal Fusiliers,
1st Border regiment,
2nd Royal Irish Fusiliers,
1st Connaught Rangers.

the field. It consisted of an infantry brigade (Brigadier-General G. G. Cunningham) made up of the 1st King's Own Scottish Borderers, the 1st Border regiment, 2nd Royal Berkshire regiment and 1st Argyll and Sutherland Highlanders; Hickman's mounted infantry, D. battery Royal Canadian artillery, the Elswick battery, two 6-in. Howitzers, two 5-in. guns and two Vickers-Maxims. The rest of the infantry in and around Pretoria were redistributed. The 2nd Royal Fusiliers and 1st Connaught Rangers became corps troops under Colonel L. Brooke, and were attached to Mahon's force; the 2nd Norfolk regiment, 2nd Lincolnshire regiment, 2nd Duke of Cornwall's Light Infantry, and 2nd Hampshire regiment formed the garrison of Pretoria, under Lieut.-General C. Tucker.

The plans of the enemy to reach Pretoria. In the Boer camps Commandant-General Botha had been also re-arranging his forces preparatory to another attempt on Pretoria. On July 14th De la Rey's triumph at Zilikat's Nek was officially announced to the burghers, and Botha summoned a Krijgsraad at Balmoral to decide how best to draw the British off his colleague in the west. A renewal of the attack on Hutton at Rietvlei was agreed upon. Grobelaar's command to the north was broken up, some 800 men proceeding south-east to join Botha, the remainder, numbering 300, riding westwards as a reinforcement to De la Rey. Monday, July 16th, was fixed on for the assault. Commandants D. Erasmus and Grobelaar were to threaten the XIth division; General B. Viljoen and Commandant Dirksen to strike at Hutton. The Commandant-General himself would direct the whole attack from a high hill, a short distance in rear of his commandos, and in heliographic communication with all parts of his line. The movement was to be timed to coincide with a rising of all the burghers in Johannesburg, but, unknown to Botha, this plot had been discovered by the British officials on the 14th.

When French, with Pilcher's and Mahon's columns and three battalions of infantry, had moved into Pretoria on July 12th, Hutton had joined hands with the outposts of the XIth division northward by a series of posts stretching along the Tigerpoort—Witpoort ridge. Tigerpoort itself was occupied by the 1st

OPERATIONS IN THE EASTERN TRANSVAAL. 315

Suffolk regiment; at Witpoort were stationed three companies 2nd Royal Irish Fusiliers (180) under Major F. H. Munn, and some sixty New Zealand Mounted Rifles with two Vickers-Maxim guns. Southward, at Rietvlei, Hutton was encamped with his 1st mounted infantry brigade, four companies of the 2nd Royal Irish Fusiliers, G. battery R.H.A., the 66th battery R.F.A. and one 5-in. gun; his right flank, thrown slightly forward, was guarded by the 1st cavalry brigade, with T. battery R.H.A., two Vickers-Maxims, one 5-in. gun, and one company Royal Irish Fusiliers. The total strength of Hutton's command was now about 4,650 officers and men, eighteen Field guns, two 5-in. guns, three Vickers-Maxims and two machine guns. He took every precaution against surprise; his patrols and scouts were vigilant, and late on the evening of the 15th gave him information of increased activity in the Boer lines which led him to expect an attack. He consequently reinforced his outposts with 200 men of the 1st corps M.I. and two guns of G. battery R.H.A. This was a timely step. At 6.45 a.m. on the 16th the piquets at Rietvlei were hotly set upon; almost simultaneously Munn's detachment at Witpoort was heavily shelled. Hutton thereupon sent forward Lieut.-Colonel Alderson to take charge of the outposts about Rietvlei, keeping his own troops in hand until the direction of the Boers' real attack should be revealed.

<small>Hutton in command east of Pretoria.</small>

At 8 a.m. the enemy developed an encircling manœuvre against the 1st cavalry brigade (Lieut.-Colonel P. L. Clowes, 8th Hussars*) which formed Hutton's right flank. This was at first successful; the advanced posts were driven in and the right rear threatened; but at 1 p.m. this movement was completely checked, and Hutton sent all his available troops to reinforce Alderson, who had moved northward to assist Munn at Witpoort. Munn's party was posted on three hills, which faced roughly north-east and commanded the road through Witpoort Nek. Of the trio of kopjes, that in the centre was the lowest, and the western higher than the eastern. The troops

<small>July 16th, 1900. The enemy attacks Hutton.</small>

* Commanding in the absence of Colonel Porter, who had been temporarily disabled by an accident. On July 18th Brigadier-General Gordon from the 3rd brigade arrived and assumed command of the 1st cavalry brigade.

had been under shell fire for some two hours when heavy musketry was also directed against them. Munn, who had entrenched his men, manned the right-hand hill with two companies of the Irish Fusiliers with a Vickers-Maxim gun, the centre height with one company and another Vickers-Maxim, whilst a small party of the New Zealand Mounted Rifles was sent to the western kopje, the remainder of this corps being kept in reserve. The Boers, led by B. Viljoen, at first turned their attention chiefly to the eastern hill, and although suffering some losses from the fire of the 5-in. guns at Rietvlei, they succeeded in ensconcing themselves on dead ground within a few yards of the Irish Fusiliers. About 9 a.m. Boers could be seen advancing against the New Zealanders on the other flank, and Munn ordered the reserves of that corps to reinforce. At 11.30 a.m., however, a determined attack, supported by machine guns, fell upon the New Zealanders, and before they could be strengthened by a section of infantry which Munn had sent to their assistance, they were overpowered and driven off the hill, leaving nineteen wounded and unwounded men in the hands of the enemy. Munn's position was now critical; he himself could barely hold his own; should the Boers occupy this, the highest of the three hills, they would command and enfilade the whole of his line, not only with rifles but with the artillery and machine guns which they had pushed forward in this quarter. They were only kept from doing so by the well-directed shrapnel from G. battery R.H.A., which Alderson had brought from near Rietvlei when it was clear that the outposts there were in no danger.

The engagement at Witpoort.

The Boers having overwhelmed Munn's left, now lay so near to his line that they continually shouted to the troops to surrender, and only awaited the moment to rush in and complete their task. Both Munn's flanks were closely invested. A party whom he had sent at 12.30 to try and clear the face of the eastern hill had been unable to reach it. Alderson, who had assumed command in this part of the field, at once decided to renew the attempt with his fresh men, and sent some of the 1st Canadian Mounted Rifles, with Munn's section which had already failed, across the Nek, whilst the 2nd Canadian Mounted

Rifles, under Colonel T. D. B. Evans, were despatched from the reserve to strengthen the New Zealanders and re-occupy the lost ground upon the left. The counter-attack on the right, a throw as hazardous and vital to the issue as that of the Devonshire men at Wagon Hill, was executed with similar *élan*, and was immediately successful, though at the loss of both the officers of the 1st Canadians (Lieuts. H. L. Borden and J. F. Burch) who led it forward. Pressed hard on both flanks, the enemy wavered, and when at 2 p.m. Hutton arrived with all his available troops upon the scene of action, the scales fell against the Boers and they abandoned what had seemed a certain prey. By sundown the whole front was clear and Hutton re-occupied his original line of outposts. His losses during the day had been: Killed, two officers and five men; wounded, three officers and twenty-seven men; missing, two officers and twenty-two men, a total of sixty-one casualties. The following commandos took part in the engagement: On the right the Johannesburg and Germiston; in the centre the Krugersdorp and Johannesburg Police; on the left the Boksburg and Middelburg; in all about 2,000 men, with eight guns, four Vickers-Maxims and several machine guns, under Commandants Dirksen, Gravett, and Pienaar, the whole commanded by General B. Viljoen. The Boer casualties were nearly the same as those of their opponents. Whilst this attack on Hutton was in progress Botha kept the attention of Pole-Carew fixed on himself by skirmishing with the 18th brigade (Stephenson) at Edendale, and the Guards' brigade (I. Jones) at Donkerhoek. These demonstrations were answered by the fire of Pole-Carew's two 5-in. guns and two Naval 12-prs.

On the same day Ian Hamilton's column set out to clear the country north of Pretoria, moving along the Pietersburg railway, supported by Hickman's column. On arriving at Hamanskraal Hamilton was to strike south-east, and traversing the country between the Pienaars and Elands rivers, to cut the Delagoa Bay line at Bronkhorstspruit station. Mahon with 1,000 mounted infantry, M. battery R.H.A., two 4.7-in. guns, two Vickers-Maxims, and the 2nd Royal Fusiliers and 1st Connaught

July 16th, 1900. Ian Hamilton's flank movement begun.

Rangers, was stationed at Kameel Drift to keep the enemy from Hamilton's right flank when he should turn to the southeast, to assist him should he become seriously engaged, and finally to move eastward in line with him. The XIth division held its original outpost line about Eerstefabrieken, facing Botha's main body. On July 17th Lieut.-General French moved with the 4th cavalry brigade to join the 1st cavalry brigade near Rietvlei, that is, on the right of Hutton's line. French now resumed command of all the troops in that neighbourhood, and the whole front faced eastward, being thus composed :—

July 17th, 1900. French resumes command.

Disposition of the forces east of Pretoria.

On the extreme left, working in towards the railway at Bronkhorstspruit station, was Ian Hamilton, his right linked by Mahon's force to the left flank of Pole-Carew (XIth division) on the railway in the centre. Hutton's column joined Pole-Carew to French, who, with the 1st and 4th cavalry brigades, was thrown well forward on the right of all. The length of front covered by the combined forces, from Doornkraal on the left to near Rietvlei on the right, was at one period about thirty-five miles, but it contracted daily as the flanks converged upon the railway.

On July 18th Botha's laager was reported to be about five miles east of the Bronkhorst Spruit, and the same distance south of the railway. His force, composed chiefly of those commandos which had attacked Hutton on the 16th, was posted along the spruit itself, with parties to the front watching French and Hutton. North of the railway, facing the XIth division and Mahon's troops, were the commandos of T. Pretorius, Erasmus and Uys; but these were already showing signs of uneasiness as Ian Hamilton's column turned and bore down upon them. Botha's strength seemed to be about 5,000 men with eight Field, one 6-in. gun, and several Vickers-Maxims and machine guns. Lord Roberts had anticipated that by the 19th Ian Hamilton's force would have changed direction at Hamanskraal and made sufficient headway to the south-east to warrant the whole line being set in motion. Hamilton and Mahon were, however, delayed by difficult country, and the general advance was postponed. On the 21st Pole-Carew demonstrated to the south-east of the railway with Henry's M.I., his artillery and the Guards'

OPERATIONS IN THE EASTERN TRANSVAAL. 319

brigade ; but, finding the enemy holding a formidable position in the hills to his right front, and not feeling himself strong enough to surround them, he withdrew his force. On receipt of the information from this reconnaissance Lord Roberts telegraphed it to French at 6.15 p.m., and suggested that he should co-operate with Pole-Carew on the morrow. But French had his own road to fight for ; moreover, not anticipating an immediate advance, he had sent his wagons to refill at Springs, and they were not to return until next day. In any case Pole-Carew's front would be automatically cleared by the action of the widely-thrown flanks of the line. These views he telegraphed to the Commander-in-Chief, who agreed and deferred the general advance until the 23rd.

Meanwhile Ian Hamilton's column, accompanied by Hickman's force, had moved, according to the programme, as far north as Hamanskraal, thence east and south-east, *via* Walmansthal and Doornkraal to Rustfontein, north of Elands River station. There Mahon joined on the 22nd, and Hickman's force, which was urgently wanted in Pretoria, left on the same day with an empty convoy, leaving with Hamilton the Queensland Imperial Bushmen and the Elswick battery. During the preceding five days Hamilton had several skirmishes, but only five casualties, the enemy losing three prisoners and some wagons. Owing to the delaying of the general movement, Hamilton, at Doornkraal, was now somewhat too far in advance of the XIth division. On the 22nd Lord Roberts sent him instructions to march on Elands River station instead of Bronkhorstspruit station. When he received this order Hamilton was already at Rustfontein ; and, as he pointed out to the Commander-in-Chief, his position made it impossible for the enemy to remain in front of Pole-Carew's left.

Ian Hamilton continues his flank movement.

At 10.30 a.m. on the 22nd Lord Roberts again telegraphed to French, near Rietvlei, that the first object of the march on the morrow " must be to clear Pole-Carew's right, where the enemy are evidently in considerable strength. This we shall not be able to do without your direct assistance." At 2 p.m. French once more replied that before he could operate northward down the valley of the Bronkhorst Spruit, it would be necessary to dislodge the Boers in his own front, where they were holding strong positions in the hills between the Bronkhorst Spruit and Wilge river, due east of Rietvlei. He added that he had already issued orders for his brigades to march at 6 a.m. the next day with this end in view; he further suggested that if the XIth division were in reality blocked, it should await the result of his operations. If the enemy did not, as he expected, withdraw from Pole-Carew's right front, it would be an easy matter to turn northward, and in conjunction with Hamilton on the opposite flank, close upon the railway with a fair chance of enveloping those commandos which were obstructing Pole-Carew. Lord Roberts approved of French's plans, and directed Pole-Carew to push his left forward to Elands River station on the following morning, but to withhold his right until the effect of French's action should be apparent.

July 23rd, 1900. General advance eastward.

At 6 a.m. on July 23rd French advanced. The 1st cavalry brigade (Gordon) led, covering a front of eight miles, and moving in a south-easterly direction to turn the Boers' left flank. Gordon's orders were to secure the passage of the Wilge river at a drift named Dieplaagte (map No. 38). This he succeeded in doing, meeting with no opposition until he crossed the river, when Lieut. A. Ebsworth, 1st Australian Horse, was killed. The 4th cavalry brigade (Dickson), on Gordon's left rear, came under both rifle and shell fire during the day, but sustained no casualties. Hutton, who was in touch with Dickson on the left of the cavalry, was also opposed by both musketry and shell fire, but had no losses, and after a hard march of twenty-three miles, seized the drift over the Wilge river. The whole of French's force bivouacked on the line of the Wilge that night. During the day Pole-Carew pushed forward the 18th brigade (Stephenson) to Elands River station without opposition. Ian Hamilton's force remained halted at Rustfontein. Early in the morning Lord Roberts had telegraphed to French to "push round to the east and cut off the enemy, if possible." In reply French reported, at 10.20 a.m., that he was making good progress, and asked whether he was not to carry out the original scheme, namely, to cross the Oliphant river and break the railway east of Middelburg? At 2 p.m. the Commander-in-Chief telegraphed that so wide a movement was not desirable, and that the railway in the neighbourhood of Brugspruit station should be French's objective; adding, "As we have no other cavalry with the force, I do not like you being so far away." Upon receipt of these instructions French, on arrival at the bivouac, issued orders for the movements on the next day. Hutton was to march towards Balmoral; Dickson, moving wide on his right, to halt at a farm about six miles east of the Oliphant river; Gordon would seize and hold the drift on the river, about five miles north of its junction with the Steenbok Spruit, and about the same distance due east of Dickson's brigade.

During the night information was received that the Boers had evacuated Balmoral. Hutton's orders were therefore modified, and on the 24th he was directed to march to a point about ten miles south of the railway midway between Balmoral and Brugspruit stations. During this day's march several dead and wounded Boers, left behind from the fighting of the previous day, were found by the cavalry. About 1 p.m. the enemy made a determined stand, over a five mile front, west of the Oliphant river, covering the drift, and shelling the advancing force vigorously. Dickson was ordered to threaten him in front, Hutton endeavoured to turn his right, and Gordon made a détour to the east to envelop his left. The batteries advanced to 3,800 yards range, the dismounted cavalrymen pushing forward to within 1,000 yards of the position. It was nearly 5 p.m. before Gordon's turning movement developed sufficiently to compel the Boers to evacuate their position and retire, which they did to the north-east. French's force bivouacked on the position vacated by the enemy west of the Oliphant river. (Casualties, one officer and one man wounded). Ian Hamilton had marched from Rustfontein to Bronkhorstspruit station, where he met the XIth division, and also Lord Roberts, who arrived that evening.

July 24th, 1900. The Boers fall back eastward.

On the 25th Hamilton occupied Balmoral; Pole-Carew (XIth division) marched to Wilge River station; and French established himself on the line of the Oliphant river, about ten miles south-east of Groot Oliphants station, with Hutton in close support. About 4 p.m., from the high ground on the east bank of the river, the enemy could be seen hurriedly retreating in apparent disorder through Middelburg. The next day the cavalry and M.I. bivouacked just outside the town, which was occupied by French and Hutton, who drew a line of outposts along the Klein Oliphant river. On the night of the 25th a tempest raged over the area of operations, and the troops in their shelterless bivouacs suffered severely, one officer dying from exposure. The transport animals perished in hundreds; in many places whole spans of oxen and mules lay heaped together, killed by the severity of the weather.

<small>British advance continued to Middelburg.</small>

Lord Roberts now decided to break off his operations. The moment, indeed, was unfavourable for a prolonged campaign in the east. To fill Middelburg, his future base, with supplies, demanded a secure and uninterrupted line of communication. Many bridges and culverts had yet to be repaired or rebuilt between that town and the capital; and he could spare no troops for the proper guardianship of so great a length of unsafe railway. Finally, there was every hope that assistance would soon be available, both in troops and means of supply, from Sir R. Buller and the Natal line of railway. There was thus more to be gained than lost by a brief delay; on July 26th the Commander-in-Chief returned to Pretoria. To hold what he had won he prescribed the following dispositions: Pole-Carew's division (XIth) was distributed along the railway between Bronkhorstspruit and Groot Oliphants stations, with Headquarters at Brugspruit. French was left in command at Middelburg, with the 1st and 4th cavalry brigades, Hutton's mounted troops, two battalions of infantry and artillery. Ian Hamilton's column, including Mahon's force, was sent back to Pretoria, where it arrived on the 30th, having dropped on the way the Canadian battery, 2nd Royal Fusiliers and 1st Connaught Rangers, all under Colonel L. G. Brooke, at Pienaars Poort station. During the last few days of July and early August the cavalry and mounted infantry holding the front were busily employed sending out small columns and patrols from Middel-

<small>Lord Roberts suspends the eastward advance,</small>

burg to the north and east, and in entrenching the many advanced posts. The railway repairs were rapidly carried out, supplies pushed up, and every preparation made for a general advance at the earliest possible date. The strategical results of these almost bloodless operations were invaluable in effect. The main Boer army had been pushed back nearly eighty miles farther eastward from Pretoria. A large number of troops were thus liberated to deal with the altered situation to the west of the capital, where the enemy was much in need of a lesson.

By August 2nd the cavalry division, south of the railway, and Hutton's mounted troops, north of it, held a line of observation, roughly fifty miles long, from a point on the Oliphant river, about thirty miles north of Middelburg, across the railway at Wonderfontein, thence *viâ* Strathrae Farm to near Twyfelaar overlooking the Komati river, where Sir R. Buller's cavalry was expected to join hands at no distant date.* The line was connected with French's Headquarters, at Middelburg, by a system of telephones installed by the Royal Engineers, which proved invaluable for the quick transmission of orders and reports. Patrols, pushed out to the front and flanks, were constantly in touch with the enemy's scouts, and casualties in men and horses were of frequent occurrence in the skirmishes. On August 4th Pole-Carew moved the Headquarters of the XIth division to Middelburg; and on the 5th he and French disposed the troops and guns for the defence of the town. On the 8th French changed his Headquarters from Middelburg to a farm five miles south-east of Wonderfontein, close behind his outpost line, the right of which was held by Gordon's brigade. Some of the posts to the north of Middelburg, hitherto held by Hutton, were taken over by units of the XIth division; the mounted troops thus set at liberty were formed into a reserve mobile column at Pan, under Lieut.-Colonel Alderson. Between August 9th and 20th nothing of importance occurred. On the 21st Pole-Carew advanced along the railway from Middelburg to Wonderfontein and subsequently to Belfast, timing his movements with those of Sir R. and awaits junction with Sir R. Buller.

* See Chapter XVI.

Buller, who was now approaching the Delagoa Bay railway from the south. The junction of the army of Natal was to be the signal for the invasion of the last untraversed province of the Transvaal. Therein, it was hoped, Botha and his main body, beset by superior forces, and pent between walls of mountainous and fever-stricken districts, would make their final stand.

CHAPTER XIII.

OPERATIONS IN THE ORANGE RIVER COLONY (*continued*).

THE PURSUIT OF DE WET AND OLIVIER.*

BRILLIANT as had been the results of Sir A. Hunter's operations in the Brandwater basin, they were yet shorn of completeness by the escape of C. De Wet and Olivier. The chase of De Wet had already been begun. As for Olivier, the circumstances of his evasion in the face of the general capitulation appeared so questionable that it was thought for a moment that he might yet consent to be bound by his superior's formal act of surrender. This, however, was not the case. Olivier, like De Wet, struck for the open veld, and for the next few weeks the chief interest in the Orange River Colony centred on the pursuit of the two leaders.

It has been seen how Paget and Broadwood, when on the march from Senekal on July 16th, had been the first to discover and to interfere with the flight of De Wet, an occurrence which much disconcerted the fugitive, who had hoped to put many miles between himself and the fatal basin before his absence should be detected. Paget, who had other and more important duties, then left De Wet to Broadwood, who hurried after him with 700 sabres, 250 M.I. (Dawson) and Q. battery R.H.A. of his own brigade, with 700 M.I. under Ridley, and 200 mounted men with P. battery R.H.A. lent by Paget himself. On the 18th Broadwood was further strengthened by the 1st Derbyshire regiment and two guns R.F.A., the escort of a convoy which he met on the road. Two days earlier the 3rd Broadwood follows De Wet, July 17th, 1900.

* See maps Nos. 38, 53 and 54.

cavalry brigade (Little),* when on the march from Heilbron to Kroonstad, had been ordered to co-operate at once with Broadwood, and this corps came in touch with De Wet (but not with Broadwood) some ten miles north-west of Lindley on the 19th, fighting an action which cost the brigade under a score of casualties but De Wet considerably more, and much damaged his organisation. On the same day Broadwood also struck at the Boer rearguard, coming up with it at Palmietfontein, and losing twenty-one officers and men in a sharp and effective engagement. Thus made fully aware of the hue-and-cry, the Boer General determined to break across the railway at all costs, a task of no small difficulty, hampered as he was by the Government officials—a timorous band—by herds of cattle, and a train of 450 wagons, which no threats or exhortations could induce his burghers to reduce. Covered by the rearguard which Broadwood and Little had already encountered, on the night of July 21st he approached the line near Honing Spruit, where he not only succeeded in crossing, but actually captured a train guarded by 100 men and full of ammunition which steamed across his path at that moment. He then made for Vredefort. On that night Broadwood, who had lost touch somewhat as he hastened along the north bank of the Rhenoster, was at Vaalkrans, and next day at Roodewal, where he filled up with supplies, and got news of De Wet's movement on Vredefort. Thither he followed on the 23rd, getting so close to De Wet's rear on the next day that five of the Boer wagons fell into his hands. But pressing on through the town, Broadwood's leading troops ran against a strong position five miles beyond it, and had to fall back before a counter-attack which inflicted thirty-nine casualties.† In the afternoon Little with the 3rd cavalry brigade, who had marched by Roodewal Spruit, arrived and came under the orders of Broadwood, who even with this reinforcement saw that mounted

July 21st, 1900. De Wet crosses the railway,

and stands at bay at Vredefort.

---

* Colonel M. O. Little had succeeded Brig.-General Gordon in command of the brigade consisting of 9th, 16th and 17th Lancers (738 men), and R. battery R.H.A.

† For gallantry in carrying a wounded man into shelter during this engagement, Captain N. R. Howse, New South Wales Medical Staff Corps, was awarded the Victoria Cross.

troops alone could make little impression on an enemy standing at bay with determination and in such numbers. The opportunity of running down a quarry so swift and cool as De Wet had in reality passed; and Lord Roberts now prepared more elaborate measures. On July 27th the 2nd Northumberland Fusiliers were sent by Kelly-Kenny from Bloemfontein to join Broadwood. On the 30th Major-General A. Hart detrained at Kopjes station with the 2nd Royal Dublin Fusiliers, half the 2nd Somerset Light Infantry, the 71st company Imperial Yeomanry, 200 Marshall's Horse, the 28th battery R.F.A., and G. section Vickers-Maxims, all from Heidelberg. Hart, who became the senior officer present, marched at once to Kopje Alleen, twenty-five miles north of Kroonstad. His orders were to take command of the columns under Broadwood, Ridley and Little, in addition to his own; to endeavour to drive De Wet northwards, to prevent his moving eastwards, and to attack him if he took up a position. The Colonial division from Rundle's force was also ordered (July 27th) to Kroonstad to co-operate with a column under C. E. Knox, composed of the 1st Oxfordshire Light Infantry, 3rd Royal Scots, a battery R.F.A., two Vickers-Maxims, and 250 mounted men. Reaching Kroonstad by forced marches on August 3rd, the Colonial division was in position on the 6th. Broadwood himself was further reinforced by the Royal Canadian regiment from Springs, and thus, in addition to his mounted men, had now three battalions of infantry under his command. With this force he watched a line from Wilgebosch Drift, through Wonderheuvel and Leeuw Spruit to Vredefort. Hart was at Kopje Alleen; and C. E. Knox, on August 1st, marched north from Kroonstad towards him, driving off on the way a band whom De Wet had sent on to Rhenoster Kop, a strong height covered with bush, which, held with determination, would have proved an expensive capture. Knox was up in line with Hart on August 3rd. The night before he arrived, his recent opponents avenged their discomfiture at Rhenoster Kop by capturing a mail train near Holfontein, but were afterwards again put to flight by troops and an armoured train from Ventersburg Road.

Aug. 5th, 1900. Lord Kitchener assumes command of the pursuit.

On August 4th, Lord Kitchener left Pretoria to command the combined operations against De Wet. Reaching Wonderheuvel next day, he first despatched the Colonial division to watch Winkel's Drift and the other passages of the Rhenoster river. De Wet now seemed cut off from the Orange River Colony; his only way of escape was by crossing the Vaal into the Transvaal, an event only less desired by the British Commander-in-Chief than it was dreaded by himself, for his men had no mind to leave their country, and even his iron rule would have failed to prevent wholesale desertion. Lord Roberts, however, hoped to close even this loophole, and on August 5th ordered Lord Methuen to Scandinavia Drift, and Smith-Dorrien, in support, to Frederikstad, the former with the 5th and 10th battalions Imperial Yeomanry, 2nd Northampton regiment, a wing of the 1st Northumberland Fusiliers, four guns 4th battery R.F.A. and two Howitzers—the latter with his brigade, a battery and 250 mounted infantry. The narrative of subsequent events, involving a separate and elaborate scheme of operations, will be related in its proper place.* It is necessary now to return to Sir A. Hunter and his dealings with the other fugitive from the Brandwater basin, the Free State General Olivier.

Aug. 1st, 1900. MacDonald follows Olivier.

On August 1st Sir A. Hunter sent MacDonald after Olivier towards Harrismith. Taking with him 700 mounted men, two 5-in. guns, sixteen guns R.F.A. and four battalions of infantry, MacDonald moved on Harrismith, which he occupied on the 4th without opposition, the enemy having gone to the north. Next day, Colonel H. J. Blagrove, with a strong patrol of the 13th Hussars, rode into Harrismith from Besters in Natal, returning to Albertina when he found the town in British possession.

Distribution of the forces in the Orange River Colony.

When MacDonald commenced his march, Sir A. Hunter's force was disposed as follows:—

At Slaap Kranz: Divisional Headquarters; nine companies Imperial Yeomanry, escorting prisoners-of-war to Fouriesburg; Driscoll's Scouts; 16th infantry brigade (Campbell), consisting of the 2nd Grenadier Guards, 2nd Scots Guards, 1st Leinster

* See Chapter XIV.

OPERATIONS IN THE ORANGE RIVER COLONY. 329

regiment. The 2nd Royal West Kent regiment, and Royal West Kent M.I. were employed in guarding the camp of the prisoners of war.

At Fouriesburg (Boyes) : One section R.F.A. ; 1st South Staffordshire regiment ; 2nd Manchester regiment.

Also at Fouriesburg (Paget) : 1st Royal Munster Fusiliers, 2nd King's Own Yorkshire Light Infantry, 4th Scottish Rifles, 4th South Staffordshire regiment ; one section C.I.V. battery ; detachments of Imperial Yeomanry and Colonial mounted troops. (Queenstown Volunteers joined August 1st.)

At Klerksvlei Farm (Bruce Hamilton) : 1st Royal Sussex ; 1st Cameron Highlanders ; the 5th M.I. ; the Derbyshire M.I. and the C.I.V. M.I. ; four guns 76th battery R.F.A. ; one section No. 9 company R.E. (Half 2nd Bedfordshire regiment joined August 5th.)

At Slabbert's Nek (Clements) : 1st Royal Irish, 2nd Worcestershire and 2nd Wiltshire regiments ; 81st battery R.F.A. ; No. 5 company Eastern division R.G.A. (One squadron 2nd Brabant's Horse joined August 4th.)

At Commando Nek : Half company Gloucestershire Imperial Yeomanry ; one gun 2nd battery R.F.A. ; one company 2nd East Yorkshire regiment.

At Ficksburg : Half company Gloucestershire Imperial Yeomanry ; one gun 2nd battery R.F.A. ; three companies 1st Worcestershire regiment.

At Hammonia : Half company Wiltshire Imperial Yeomanry ; one gun 77th battery R.F.A. ; two companies 2nd East Yorkshire regiment.

At Senekal : Half company Wiltshire Imperial Yeomanry, one gun 2nd battery R.F.A. ; four companies 2nd East Yorkshire regiment.

At Ladybrand : Half company Wiltshire Imperial Yeomanry (furnishing a post at Leeuw River Mills) ; two companies 1st Worcestershire regiment.

At Thabanchu : Half company Wiltshire Imperial Yeomanry ; two companies 1st Worcestershire regiment.

At Israel's Poort : One company 1st Worcestershire regiment.

On August 3rd, Sir A. Hunter's original force was broken up and reorganised. Bruce Hamilton and Paget marched at once with the Boer prisoners of war to Winburg ; Clements proceeded to Kroonstad and the Transvaal ; and Sir L. Rundle received orders from the Commander-in-Chief to resume independent control of the VIIIth division, and to follow Olivier, who was now reported to have moved northwards through Vrede. Accordingly, Sir L. Rundle, leaving Colonel E. A. W. S. Grove in command of a column* with orders to follow the main body at the distance of a day's march, moved to Harrismith, where he established himself on August 6th. MacDonald's column was directed to rejoin Sir A. Hunter at Bethlehem, preparatory to moving on Kroonstad, *via* Lindley.

Aug. 10th, 1900. Sir A. Hunter joins in the pursuit.

On the 10th Sir A. Hunter left Bethlehem with a column consisting of the Highland brigade (MacDonald), half 2nd Bedfordshire regiment, Lovat's Scouts, 6th and 15th battalions Imperial Yeomanry, a detachment of mounted infantry, 5th, 8th and 82nd batteries R.F.A., and one 5-in. gun. On the 12th he arrived near Paardeplaats, about six miles from Lindley on the Kroonstad road, when instructions were received from the Commander-in-Chief to move either on Heilbron or on Reitz, in order to head Olivier, who was said to be moving through Frankfort on his way to join De Wet, who was then at Reitzburg. Sir A. Hunter decided that the best means of effecting this was to march on Heilbron. On the 13th he reached the Rhenoster river, and next day encountered a Boer force under Froneman. The enemy, about 1,800 men with six Field and two machine guns, was found to be holding a position on the right of, and parallel to,

Aug. 13th, 1900. Engagement with Olivier at Spitzkop.

the Lindley—Heilbron road, covering some five miles of front. His right rested on Spitzkop, a hill overlooking Reitfontein, his left near Witpoort (about twelve miles south of Heilbron). With Froneman was Olivier himself, besides Haasbroek, Visser, and Fourie, and all were bent on a desperate effort to join De Wet.

* One squadron Imperial Yeomanry, one company mounted infantry, two guns 79th battery Royal Field artillery, one section Royal Engineers, 2nd Royal West Kent regiment, two companies 1st South Staffordshire regiment, two companies 2nd Manchester regiment.

At 11.15 a.m. the Boers opened fire with their guns on the head of the column as it approached Witpoort. Sir A. Hunter at once attacked, having to execute an awkward change of his entire front to the right to do so. Holding the enemy in front with the 5-in. gun, the 5th battery R.F.A. and four companies Black Watch (subsequently reinforced by the Seaforth Highlanders), he despatched Lovat's Scouts, the 82nd battery R.F.A., and the Highland Light Infantry to turn the left. At 1.30 p.m. the Highland Light Infantry and Lovat's Scouts drove the Boer flank from its first position back to a second. Here the commandos stood more firmly, and Sir A. Hunter, planting his reserve (three companies Bedfordshire regiment) on the ground already won, sent the Highland Light Infantry along the ridges from right to left, towards Spitzkop, the key of the position. A heavy fire followed the battalion across the crests, but by 4.30 p.m. it was so near Spitzkop that the General ordered the Black Watch and Seaforth Highlanders, covered by the 5th battery R.F.A., to co-operate with a frontal attack. At dusk the enemy fell back, retiring in a south-easterly direction. In the engagement three men were killed, two officers and forty-three men wounded, mostly in the Highland Light Infantry, which bore the brunt of the fighting. Next day, August 15th, the force occupied Heilbron. *Olivier disappears.*

Turning now to the VIIIth division, Sir L. Rundle had at this time garrisons at Bethlehem (2nd East Yorkshire), Senekal, Hammonia, Ficksburg, Ladybrand and Thabanchu (1st Worcestershire, with Headquarters at Senekal); at Harrismith were posted the Headquarters and the bulk of the command, viz.:— nine and a half companies Imperial Yeomanry, Driscoll's Scouts, one section 2nd battery R.F.A., 77th and 79th batteries R.F.A., 2nd Grenadier Guards, 2nd Scots Guards, 1st Leinster, 2nd Royal West Kent, 2nd Manchester, and 1st South Stafford. On August 9th, railway communication between Harrismith and Ladysmith was re-established after being severed for ten months, and henceforward troops at Harrismith were based for supplies on Natal. On the same day Major-General Boyes marched north, along the Harrismith—Vrede road, with two companies Imperial *Other columns pursue Olivier.*

Yeomanry, four guns R.F.A., 1st South Staffordshire and 2nd Manchester regiments, a column organised for the pursuit of Olivier. On the 11th, information having been received that Olivier was to the north-east of Reitz, a second column (Colonel E. A. W. S. Grove, with two squadrons Imperial Yeomanry, one company M.I., four guns R.F.A., and 2nd Royal West Kent regiment) was ordered to move on Boyes' left—the latter changing his direction and marching upon Reitz. On the 13th Grove's order was cancelled. Detaching a part of his column to move to Bethlehem, he, with one squadron I.Y., one company M.I., two guns R.F.A. and his infantry battalion, left Harrismith to join Boyes. Next day Boyes, and two days later Grove, reached Reitz. But Olivier's force had already got away, and as described above, was on this very day fighting with Sir A. Hunter outside Heilbron.

As soon as Lord Roberts knew of these events, he ordered Boyes to proceed to Vrede, and to gain touch with Standerton as quickly as possible, and Sir L. Rundle to organise mobile columns, with a view to clearing the district of supplies, horses, stock and forage, and, above all, of rebels and oath-breakers. Two mobile columns were formed: the northern (Boyes, 17th brigade), based on Vrede, was to work towards Reitz, Frankfort, Standerton, and the Natal railway; the southern column (Campbell, 16th brigade), based on Harrismith, to operate to Fouriesburg, Bethlehem, Reitz, and eastward through Newmarket. These districts were carefully patrolled throughout the month of August, quantities of arms and ammunition being found and destroyed, and very little resistance met with. Many thousands of oxen, sheep and horses were captured, and about 1,000 Boers surrendered to Sir L. Rundle. By the end of August, that portion of the Orange River Colony lying eastward of the road Frankfort—Reitz—Bethlehem—Fouriesburg was clear of any organised fighting body of the enemy. Nor was any hostile force known to be south of the road from Bethlehem to Winburg.

Olivier's party, however, having moved rapidly south-west from Heilbron on August 14th, was below Kroonstad, its presence being accidentally discovered on the 19th in the following manner. For some weeks it had been known that a small independent party of Boers had established themselves sixteen miles to the north-east of Ventersburg, into which they rode two or three times a week, to the great annoyance of the inhabitants. In order to rid the neighbourhood of these raiders, Lieut.-Colonel W. H. Sitwell, on August 18th, was sent out with a mounted infantry company (five officers and sixty-five men), and Captain J. E. Pine-Coffin was ordered to Ventersburg with thirty-five Malta M.I. On the following day, Sitwell engaged the enemy some ten miles to the west of the town, but soon discovered that he had more to deal with than he could manage. His flanks were almost immediately turned, and it was with the greatest difficulty that he was able to extricate himself. Pursued for some miles by 400 Boers on fresh horses, the small British force was only saved by the self-sacrifice of a handful, who stubbornly held a cattle kraal on the line of retreat, and occupied the attention of the enemy whilst the rest made off. The defenders (five officers and nineteen men) held out for an hour and a half, when the kraal was rushed by overwhelming numbers, the British losing two men killed, two officers and four men wounded, and thirteen horses killed, the Boers, three men killed and fourteen wounded. Two days later two of the captured officers were released, and reported that at the Boer laager, about seven miles from the scene of action, there were 1,500 to 2,000 men, seven guns, and two machine guns, besides 200 wagons, and that Olivier, Fourie and Froneman were present. This information reached Kroonstad on the 21st, and Bruce Hamilton's column, which had arrived from Winburg the previous day, was despatched at once to Ventersburg Road.

On August 24th reports were received that Olivier, with 1,000 men and two guns, had suddenly appeared north of Winburg, and had surrounded a British force about nine miles from that town. This party, which consisted of 190 mounted men and thirty infantry, was under the command of Lieut.-Col. H. M. Ridley (16th battalion I.Y.), who had been sent out by Major-General R. E. Allen on reconnaissance towards Ventersburg.

Aug. 19th. Olivier's position discovered by accident.

Bruce Hamilton was immediately ordered to proceed to his aid with the 1st Cameron Highlanders, half the 1st Royal Sussex, 5th M.I., Brabant's Horse, and eight guns R.F.A., and succeeded in extricating him at 9 a.m. on the 26th. The relief came only just in time. For two days and three nights Ridley's men had withstood, almost without cover, shrapnel and common shell from three guns and the unceasing fire of a thousand rifles. Twice they had been summoned to surrender ; but surrounded though they were by vastly superior numbers they held out with determination, losing thirty-two officers and men before they were rescued and withdrawn to Winburg by Bruce Hamilton. Next day Olivier attacked the town from the north, north-east and north-west, but was repulsed on every side, losing twenty-five of his men by capture. Finally he himself with his three sons rode into a trap set by the Queenstown Volunteers, from which he emerged a prisoner of war.

Aug. 27th, 1900. Capture of Olivier.

CHAPTER XIV.

OPERATIONS IN THE WESTERN TRANSVAAL* (*continued*).

THE PURSUIT AND ESCAPE OF DE WET.

THE westward drift of hostile forces from Rustenburg, and the surrender of Klerksdorp, made Lord Roberts anxious for the safety of the small isolated posts on the route to Mafeking. A runner was sent to Lieut.-Colonel C. O. Hore at Elands River, directing him to call in the detachment of sixty men from Wonderfontein, and warning him to prepare for a siege. The garrisons of Lichtenburg and Zeerust were also ordered to Otto's Hoop. These changes, and the presence of a commando near Woodstock, half-way between Magato Nek and Elands River, increased the difficulty of supplying Baden-Powell's force; and the retention of Rustenburg had to be reconsidered. The evacuation of this stronghold of the old Boer spirit would mean a great revival of hope amongst the despondent enemy, and would probably lead to the re-establishment of a new seat of government in the heart of the Transvaal, with consequent persecution of all who had sided with the British. These views Baden-Powell insistently laid before Lord Roberts, pointing out that the holding of Rustenburg and Zeerust was necessary alike for moral effect, to give sanctuary to peacefully disposed Boers, and to provide bases of supply for mobile columns. *[margin: Proposed evacuation of Rustenburg.]*

In the eyes of the Commander-in-Chief the strategical gain of evacuation outweighed the political loss. He judged that the force at his disposal was best employed in guarding the railway, and in beating the enemy in the field. Despite the temporary

* See map No. 38.

loss of prestige involved in withdrawing from Rustenburg, he ordered Baden-Powell to evacuate it. Writing later to Baden-Powell, the Field-Marshal gave his reasons: " Had I not to send Ian Hamilton's force with supplies for you, I should have employed it with Broadwood's against De Wet [in the Orange River Colony], and should practically have been able to surround him. Moreover, I have not a single battalion to spare to garrison Rustenburg, nor can I undertake to supply it, as all troops are required for what, I venture to think, is more important duty."

Sir F. Carrington had reached Mafeking on July 26th, in advance of his troops. He there received orders to move on Rustenburg, and co-operate with Ian Hamilton. He was not ready to march till August 1st, on which date Ian Hamilton's movement from Pretoria on Rustenburg was to begin. The order for Hamilton ran : " You will occupy and hold Commando Nek, leaving there a suitable force as garrison to entrench themselves. . . . As soon as you are in touch with Baden-Powell, you should arrange to evacuate Rustenburg and Olifants Nek, withdrawing the battalion at Olifants Nek *viâ* Hekpoort and the south side of the Magaliesberg, if this can be conveniently arranged. . . . It is important that you should be back in Pretoria not later than the 9th or 10th of August." Sir F. Carrington was told that Baden-Powell had supplies up to August 10th, and must be relieved before that date.

Ian Hamilton's march along the Magaliesberg.

When it was decided to let Rustenburg go, Sir F. Carrington was directed not to go further east than Elands River. The garrison on the river was to be withdrawn when Rustenburg was given up. The concentration at Otto's Hoop of Colonel the Earl of Erroll's small force, which was now placed under Sir F. Carrington's orders, had been made in anticipation of the march to Elands River.

Ian Hamilton's force, numbering about 7,600 men, was made up of Brigadier-General B. T. Mahon's and Colonel T. E. Hickman's mounted forces, and Brigadier-General G. G. Cunningham's infantry brigade, with the 75th battery Royal Field artillery, the Elswick battery, and two companies of Garrison artillery. The infantry brigade, recently formed, consisted of

OPERATIONS IN THE WESTERN TRANSVAAL.

four strong battalions (1st King's Own Scottish Borderers, 1st Border regiment, 2nd Royal Berkshire regiment, and 1st Argyll and Sutherland Highlanders), with S. section of Vickers-Maxims. Mahon's force comprised M. battery Royal Horse artillery, the Imperial Light Horse, Lumsden's Horse, a battalion of Imperial Yeomanry, the 3rd corps of mounted infantry, the New Zealand Mounted Rifles, with detachments of Queenslanders, Bushmen and 18th Hussars, about 1,700 mounted men altogether. The mounted infantry, under command of Colonel T. E. Hickman, was composed of details from the 2nd brigade of mounted infantry, of released prisoners, and convalescents from all irregular horse in South Africa, formed into two complete regiments, under Major S. B. Von Donop, R.A. and Lieut.-Colonel A. N. Rochfort, R.A. The 3rd Queensland Imperial Bushmen and a Vickers-Maxim section were afterwards added to the force, which at the beginning of these operations numbered about 1,500 men.

Starting on August 1st, Hamilton's main body, with Hickman's force as advance guard, marched along the Rustenburg road, while Mahon's mounted troops moved in a parallel direction, north of the Magaliesberg. Desultory firing from the crest of the mountains did not delay the advance of the main column, but Mahon's march was somewhat obstructed. In order to keep touch with his northern force, Ian Hamilton considered it necessary to break through the mountains next day, and he selected Zilikat's Nek, the first gateway west of the neighbourhood of Pretoria. The pass was believed to be held by three or four hundred of the enemy, without guns, under Commandant Coetzee, who was acting under the orders of General De la Rey. The enemy's main body, about 1,500 strong with four guns, was reported near the Sterkstroom river, five-and-twenty miles distant.

Aug. 1st, 1900. Ian Hamilton starts.

The road across the Nek penetrates through walls of sheer cliffs which run east and west for many miles. The ground open to frontal attack was therefore limited, and a turning manœuvre difficult. Cunningham was ordered to force the pass with his brigade and a Field battery, whilst Hickman sent a small party of his mounted infantry to a point some three miles to the east, where it appeared possible for men to scale the cliffs and help the attack. The battery shelled the enemy from 3,000 yards to the south, assisted by the Elswick and 5-in. guns in rear, which fired at groups of men visible on the bluffs each side of the Nek.

Advancing with the 2nd Royal Berkshire on the right, under cover of a long shoulder, and the Argyll and Sutherland Highlanders working through thick bush on the left, the brigade made good progress till 9.15 a.m., when Hamilton, seeing that the heights must be crowned, kept Cunningham back till this had been done. At 10.30 a.m. fifty men sent eastward by Hickman had reached the summit of the range, and moved unopposed along the top towards the Nek. Half an hour later two companies of the Royal Berkshire managed to climb, under a heavy cross-fire, up the very steep cliffs on the east of the pass, Sergeant A. Gibbs, the first man up, being shot down as he reached the top.* The centre now resumed its advance, the defenders were forced backward, and a number of horses and wagons captured, the casualties being four men killed and two officers and thirty-five men wounded, nearly all belonging to the Royal Berkshire regiment. Meanwhile Mahon's troops on the north side of the pass had been delayed by a party of the enemy, and the orders heliographed from Hamilton not being received till 9.15 on the morning of the action, when the cavalry were still some six miles away, the Nek was carried before they arrived. Touch with Mahon's force was duly made. Leaving Hickman's troops, with the 1st King's Own Scottish Borderers and a section of the Elswick battery, to garrison Commando Nek, the column marched towards Rustenburg without sign of the enemy. At Kroondal, Baden-Powell's force came under Hamilton's orders. Before starting for Pretoria, Hamilton, on August 5th (4.15 p.m.), had telegraphed to Lord Roberts, forwarding Baden-Powell's proposal to retain Rusten-

---

* Private W. House, Royal Berkshire regiment, was awarded the Victoria Cross for gallantry in attempting to succour a wounded sergeant, and for his coolness in warning his comrades not to come to his assistance when he himself was severely wounded.

OPERATIONS IN THE WESTERN TRANSVAAL. 339

burg, which, Baden-Powell believed, could be held by a battalion, a squadron and four guns, even if Olifants Nek were abandoned. Lord Roberts the same day ordered the evacuation and the abandonment of Olifants Nek.

Orders for the evacuation of Olifant's Nek.

The troops holding Elands River, which had been originally a post on the line of communication between Mafeking and Rustenburg, were commanded by Lieut.-Colonel C. O. Hore, and consisted of 140 Australian Bushmen, 80 men of the Rhodesia regiment, and 80 Southern Rhodesia Volunteers, with a 2.5-in. Mountain gun and two machine guns. They had skilfully applied the lessons learned from adventurous life in the open to the trenches and shelters, and Hore's experience in the siege of Mafeking served him well. The camp was at Brakfontein, about half a mile east of the river, which here cuts the Zeerust road north and south; but as there are numbers of easy drifts above and below the road, the river, which was the only water supply, offered no efficient barrier against attack. The eastern end of the Schure Berg here merges into the northern slopes of the Zwart Ruggens, and the country, broken with scattered kopjes, made it difficult to hold the camp with a small force; but the garrison were confident of their ability to defend against all attack the accumulation of stores and wagons for which they were responsible.

Strong patrols of the enemy were seen on August 3rd, when Sir F. Carrington telegraphed that he hoped to reach Elands River in two days' time. After leaving Mafeking, he was joined by Lord Erroll's column at Otto's Hoop, but his whole force was still under 1,100 strong, viz.: Four squadrons of Paget's Horse, one squadron Kimberley Mounted Corps, five and a half squadrons New South Wales Imperial Bushmen, and sixty of Cameron's and the Imperial Yeomanry Scouts, with the 1st battery of Rhodesia Field Force 15-pr. guns, manned by New Zealanders, and four Vickers-Maxims. As it was proposed to get supplies at Elands River, this column took little of its own. On reaching Wonderfontein, on the Marico river, heavy firing was heard to the east, and a report came that Hore's camp was surrounded. Information was also received of a Boer commando approaching

Sir F. Carrington advances to relieve Elands River.

from the north. Colonel H. Paget was therefore left with 350 men, two guns, and a Vickers-Maxim, to guard the fifty ox-wagons that had been brought to remove Hore's supplies and ammunition. On August 5th the remainder of Sir F. Carrington's force was within eight miles of Brakfontein, and was further weakened by the Kimberley squadron and a Vickers-Maxim detached to protect the parked mule transport. Only 650 of all ranks with four guns and two Vickers-Maxims now remained with Sir F. Carrington, who, moving along the main road, located the enemy on some hills to his left front. The Boers before him were the Lichtenburg and Marico commandos under Lemmer, and exceeded Sir F. Carrington's force in strength. A rocky kopje right ahead was attacked and taken, but on surmounting it, the assaulting party was shelled by a gun concealed to their right. The ground intervening between these hills and the camp two or three miles away was flat and devoid of cover, and Sir F. Carrington saw that the Boers were on a wider front than he had supposed, and appeared to be working round both his flanks. An attempt was then made to continue the advance, until Sir F. Carrington came to the conclusion that to persist in face of the force opposed to him could only lead to disaster, when he gave the order to retire. A patrol of an officer and five men was sent to get through to Hore's camp. This and another patrol on the extreme right were promptly made prisoners. The only other casualties, in addition to these, were one officer and eight men slightly wounded, and two men severely wounded. On returning to Wonderfontein the same night Sir F. Carrington found that his expected supplies had not come in, and his force marched back to Zeerust next day with trifling loss by skirmishing fire from the hills.

Sir F. Carrington abandons the relief of Elands River.

Sir F. Carrington now considered that a concentration of his force at Mafeking was the only course open to him. The garrisons of Zeerust and Otto's Hoop were again withdrawn, and the enemy thereupon closed in on Mafeking. The post at Elands River was left to its fate. The echo of Sir F. Carrington's guns, faintly heard at Rustenburg, caused Baden-Powell to report that the relieving force had retired westwards, and that the

OPERATIONS IN THE WESTERN TRANSVAAL.

garrison had either been withdrawn or lost. Lord Roberts decided that Baden-Powell's force should accompany Ian Hamilton's column back to Pretoria. After dismantling the defensive works at Rustenburg and destroying about 400,000 rounds of Boer ammunition, Baden-Powell evacuated the town and joined Hamilton's force on August 7th ; on the previous night Colonel R. G. Kekewich's garrison had left Olifants Nek, and having demolished their defences, joined Hamilton. On the return march to Pretoria the column had reached Wolhuter's Kop and Bokfontein, near Commando Nek, when late on the night of the 8th, news came that a Boer force under Christian De Wet was moving northwards from the Vaal. There were no British troops to check De Wet between Commando Nek and Mafeking, save the beleaguered garrison at Elands River. The whole country was at the mercy of a bold leader. The opportunity for a junction of the enemy's forces from south and west had come, and with the time, the man. How De Wet had broken the toils surrounding him and emerged into the Western Transvaal must now be described.* His force was made up of the Bethlehem burghers under Commandant Michael Prinsloo; the Heilbron and Kroonstad men under Commandants L. Steenkamp and F. Van Aard ; the Boshof commando under Field Cornet C. C. Badenhorst, with a few Transvaalers from Potchefstroom, and a detachment of rebels from Griqualand. Mr. Steyn and the Government officials who entrusted themselves to the care of De Wet were guarded by a body of scouts under G. J. Scheepers, and a corps of highly-trained men recruited from many European nations, commanded by Captain Daniel Theron, to whose reconnaissance work De Wet himself more than once owed his escape from apparently hopeless situations. This party had, as related, broken through Slabbert's Nek on July 15th, and when the surrender of Prinsloo's force was complete, De Wet's column was the only considerable body of the enemy at large in the Orange River Colony. To destroy or disperse it, and to capture its famous leader, became, therefore, a matter of the first importance. It was at first believed that De Wet would

Aug. 7th, 1900. Evacuation of Rustenburg and Olifants Nek.

De Wet in the Western Transvaal.

* See also Chapters XI. and XIII.

try to join the remnant of the main Boer force about Middelburg in the Eastern Transvaal; but his information was accurate, and he knew that there was little hope of running the gauntlet between the British brigade at Heidelberg and Standerton, where Sir R. Buller had his Headquarters. Telegraphing to Sir R. Buller, Lord Roberts said : " De Wet with Steyn, instead of making for the eastern part of the Transvaal, is moving towards Potchefstroom. We have not too many troops in that direction, and I must remove Hart's force from Heidelberg." Accordingly when Lord Methuen's column, less the battalion left at Olifants Nek, reached Bank station on July 25th, there was more work before him than the punishment of train wreckers, for which he had come south.* He was directed to move on Potchefstroom at once, in order to deal with De Wet as soon as that leader should be forced to the north across the Vaal. The 1st division had arrived at Bank station short of supplies, and was obliged to wait there to obtain them. When on July 28th it moved on, the enemy, 600 strong, under General P. J. Liebenberg, vacating the ridges commanding the railway line, retired over the passes into the Gatsrand, a range of hills running parallel to and about 4,000 yards from the Bank—Frederikstad road. Constantly manœuvring them from their positions in the Gatsrand, Lord Methuen's column arrived with little loss at Potchefstroom on July 30th. Smith-Dorrien's force, consisting of one section of 20th battery R.F.A., one section of 37th (Howitzer) battery, a section 11th Field company R.E., the 2nd Shropshire Light Infantry, and the 1st Gordon Highlanders, remained at Bank station to escort a convoy, and await the arrival of the City of London Imperial Volunteers, who were relieving the Gordon Highlanders, now refitting in Krugersdorp. When reinforced, the brigade marched off, a train loaded with supplies following along the line in the wake of the column. While running down an incline, the engine was wrecked upon a broken rail, and the leading trucks were telescoped; of the company of Shropshire Light Infantry travelling as escort, fourteen men were killed and forty-five injured. On the following morning General

Sidenotes: Lord Methuen in pursuit of De Wet. Smith-Dorrien in pursuit of De Wet.

* See page 247.

OPERATIONS IN THE WESTERN TRANSVAAL. 343

Liebenberg demanded the surrender of Smith-Dorrien's force under threat of attack in half an hour. Before the Boer messenger who brought the demand had time to reach the General's tent, the enemy, some 500 strong with two guns, opened fire from the south-western end of the hills, under which the City Imperial Volunteers lay bivouacked, and shortly afterwards attacked the outposts. The latter were promptly reinforced, and the enemy, failing to gain any ground, retired towards Ventersdorp, after firing for an hour and a half.* Guns and Yeomanry were sent in pursuit, but on the approach of a body of mounted men from the south, who proved to be the escort of the wagons from Potchefstroom, they were recalled, and pursuit was taken over by the reinforcements, but too late to do much damage. In consequence of this attack, Smith-Dorrien, reinforced by 120 men of the 15th regiment Imperial Yeomanry and two guns, was ordered to remain at Frederikstad to keep open the line to Krugersdorp, and a regiment of Yeomanry, half a battalion, and two guns, were sent by Lord Methuen to Machavie to patrol the Klerksdorp railway, and to the junction of the Vaal and Mooi rivers. On August 3rd another patrol, while reconnoitring from Potchefstroom towards Venterskroon on the Vaal, on approaching Tygerfontein, was attacked by a detachment from Liebenberg's commando. The troops at Machavie were therefore recalled, and Lord Methuen prepared to move with all his strength from Potchefstroom to Roodekraal, to watch the Vaal drifts and confront De Wet as soon as he should cross. On August 4th Lord Kitchener went down to Rhenoster to take general charge of the operations against De Wet.† The situation in this area was then as follows :— *(Lord Kitchener assumes command of the pursuit of De Wet.)*

De Wet's commando, occupying the hills in the neighbourhood of Reitzburg, was hemmed in at Grooteiland and Parys. To the north-east was Brigadier-General Ridley's mounted infantry, consisting of Legge's, Dawson's and de Lisle's corps, together with Roberts' and Kitchener's Horse, and a contingent of Imperial Bushmen, about 900 men in all, with P. battery Royal Horse artillery. Thence the cordon was carried along

* Casualties—Two killed and seven wounded.   † See page 328.

Plans to surround De Wet.

the east and south by the 2nd and 3rd cavalry brigades, under Brigadier-General R. G. Broadwood and Colonel M. O. Little, and on their left by two mixed forces under Major-Generals A. FitzRoy Hart and C. E. Knox.* The line along the south bank was to be carried on westwards by the Colonial division, about 1,000 strong, commanded by Lieut.-Colonel Dalgety; but they did not arrive till August 6th. With Lord Methuen and Smith-Dorrien on the north bank, and these detachments closing in from the south and east, De Wet's escape seemed impossible. The cordon to the west of Reitzburg was not so tightly drawn, and Lord Methuen's column (5th and 10th regiments Imperial Yeomanry, half battalion 1st Northumberland Fusiliers, 2nd Northamptonshire regiment, two sections 4th battery Royal Field artillery and two Howitzers 37th battery R.F.A.) was ordered to Scandinavia Drift on the Vaal, fifteen miles west of Venterskroon. On arrival there on August 5th, information was received that De Wet was at Rhenosterpoort, and about to cross the river. Lord Methuen at once started back with his mounted troops and guns towards Venterskroon, instructing Major-General C. W. H. Douglas to follow with the infantry and baggage, after leaving two companies entrenched at Scandinavia Drift. Lord Methuen also ordered the Potchefstroom garrison, composed of four companies of the 2nd Royal Scots Fusiliers and 1st Royal Welsh Fusiliers, two guns of the 78th battery, and a squadron, to march to Roodekraal; two companies of the 1st Northumberland Fusiliers and two guns of the 20th battery R.F.A. took their place at Potchefstroom. Late that night orders were received from Lord Kitchener to send

---

* The 2nd cavalry brigade was made up of the Composite regiment of Household cavalry, 10th Hussars, 12th Lancers, and Q. battery R.H.A. The 3rd cavalry brigade included 9th, 16th, and 17th Lancers, and R. battery R.H.A. Hart's force comprised the 2nd Royal Dublin Fusiliers, half battalion 2nd Somerset Light Infantry, the 28th battery Royal Field artillery, G. section Vickers-Maxims, 200 Marshall's Horse, and the 71st company of Imperial Yeomanry. The 2nd battalion Northumberland Fusiliers, 2nd battalion Royal Canadian regiment, and two Naval 4.7-in. guns under Commander W. L. Grant, R.N., joined it before the chase after De Wet. Knox's force consisted of 1st Oxfordshire Light Infantry, 3rd Royal Scots, 250 mounted infantry from the Royal Irish Rifles and Malta contingent, the 17th battery R.F.A., and one Vickers-Maxim.

next day a detachment of three companies of infantry, two guns, and a squadron, under Lieut.-Colonel C. G. C. Money, to Winkel's Drift on the Rhenoster river,* about thirteen miles south-west of Reitzburg, for this portion of the enclosing line was weak until the Colonial division arrived.

De Wet, with his main body, crossed the river before day-break on August 6th, at Schoeman's Drift—the principal wagon ford from Potchefstroom to Reitzburg—leaving many of his men to pass later in the day. His force was then reorganised into two separate columns; he himself and Steyn went with one detachment along the Venterskroon road, and thence by the river bank to the bend of the stream towards Van Vuurens Drift south of Leeuwfontein; the other wing was sent to guard the left flank. Early on August 7th, Lord Methuen's guns turned the enemy's rearguard out of their first position on the hills south of Tygerfontein, whence they retired to another and stronger line of resistance. A heavy fire of Howitzers, guns, and Vickers-Maxims was opened on them, and after a short delay three companies of the 2nd Royal Scots Fusiliers and 1st Royal Welsh Fusiliers from Roodekraal and the dismounted Yeomanry were sent forward to clear the kopjes. The enemy held on with tenacity, but the heights were slowly won, and a brisk rifle fire hastened the Boer retirement. Their next position was upon the heights west of Venterskroon, and along a high ridge south-west of the village. Between this ridge and the river runs the road which De Wet had followed from Schoeman's Drift. Here the enemy held on stubbornly.† When the section of the 4th battery reached the crest of the hills, the huge convoy could be seen passing through the village, covered by a rearguard of about 1,000 men. At three o'clock, the hills in the neighbourhood of Venterskroon having been cleared, Lord Methuen's force returned to Tygerfontein, while the enemy encamped at Buffelshoek, near Van Vuurens Drift. The day illustrated the skill

margin note: Lord Methuen on the heels of De Wet.

* On map 38 the words "Kromellenboog Spruit" are wrongly printed along the lower waters of the Rhenoster river. Kromellenboog Spruit is the stream joining the Vaal south of Lindequee.

† British casualties—Two killed; six officers and nine men wounded.

of the Boers in rearguard fighting, as they manœuvred to cover the mass of wagons which De Wet had entreated them to leave in the Brandwater basin. The continual firing was heard by Lord Kitchener south of the river at Wonderheuvel, and he at once ordered Broadwood's cavalry brigade* to push on towards De Wet's Drift, four miles west of Schoeman's Drift, followed by Hart's brigade and Knox's force, while the Colonial division was sent across Scandinavia Drift to gain touch with the enemy. The 3rd cavalry brigade was also ordered to move north-west towards the Vaal, and Brigadier-General C. P. Ridley to send a patrol over the river at Parys.

Ridley's patrol reported that about 3,000 men and many wagons were moving out from Buffelshoek, and it was clear that De Wet was making for the north. To endeavour to intercept him, Ridley's mounted infantry at Parys, the nearest to the enemy, were ordered to move to Lindequee, whither Lord Kitchener himself was following with the 2nd and 3rd cavalry brigades; Hart's brigade was also sent to the same place. From Parys to Lindequee is seventeen miles by road over a bad drift, and the time required for Ridley's march was invaluable to De Wet. After the action on August 7th, Lord Methuen received the following telegram from Lord Roberts: "Kitchener is arranging to follow up the enemy as quickly as possible, and I trust you will be able to place your force in such a position as will prevent their moving on until Kitchener can overtake them. This is a matter of supreme importance. I understand you have got your supplies, and I feel sure you will do everything in your power to prevent the enemy escaping." A message was also sent to Lord Kitchener, urging him to cross the river and capture the convoy. Lord Roberts added: "If I hear that De Wet is able to give Methuen the slip, I will see if we cannot head him somewhere in the neighbourhood of Commando Nek or the Crocodile, where Ian Hamilton should be to-morrow." On August 8th, Lord Methuen's column remained in camp during the morning, orders being issued to march early in the

* A patrol of Broadwood's was attacked on this day. For gallantry on the occasion Sergeant T. Lawrence, 17th Lancers, was awarded the Victoria Cross.

afternoon towards Leeuwfontein, where De Wet was reported to have gone. False information, however, reached Lord Methuen that the Boer leader had re-crossed the Vaal at Venterskroon, and the order was countermanded. Lord Methuen decided to halt till he had definite knowledge of the enemy's movements; his horses were tired, and he wished to collect his detachments from Winkel's Drift and Scandinavia Drift. These arrived late that night, the former having marched twenty-one miles through heavy ground. Thus De Wet gained twenty-four hours' start at a time when minutes were of value. Patrols to Venterskroon and Parys proved that no re-crossing had taken place, and confirmed the report of De Wet's movement northwards. As Potchefstroom was not in the line of advance, its garrison was ordered to evacuate the town after dark on the 8th and march to Rietfontein, after destroying surplus ammunition and supplies.

Liebenberg's commando, reinforced by the Transvaalers from De Wet's force, entered the old Boer capital next day, once more hoisting the Vierkleur; on the 11th they marched again to join De Wet.

Meanwhile, after the rest at Tygerfontein, Lord Methuen's column marched early on the 9th, and on reaching Leeuwfontein, found that the tail of De Wet's convoy was inspanning three miles ahead. Yeomanry and guns at once galloped forward, but were soon checked by the Boer riflemen on the successive ridges, each of which was duly defended and timeously evacuated by the rearguard. At 4.30 p.m. further pursuit was abandoned, the enemy's main convoy being then about seven miles to the north-east, covered by a rearguard on a mass of kopjes on the right flank and a ridge in front. A few Boers were found dead, and the British losses were Lieut. A. M. Knowles and three men of the 3rd Imperial Yeomanry killed, and Lieut.-Colonel G. J. Younghusband and seven men wounded. Six wagons, two loaded with ammunition, were taken from the enemy, who also abandoned 350 cattle and 1,000 sheep. On the same day Lord Kitchener, with the 2nd and 3rd cavalry brigades and Ridley's force, arrived at Lindequee, with Hart's column four or five miles in rear at Kromellenboog Spruit. The mounted infantry and a Horse artillery battery at once crossed the river, and threw a few shells into the Boer rearguard. De Wet had intended to double back across the Vaal; but the presence of Lord Kitchener's column forced him to swerve to the west, and it was reported to the Commander-in-Chief that the enemy's main body was heading towards Bank station.

In that neighbourhood Liebenberg's commando, 600 strong, was marked near Cyferbult, north-west of Frederikstad. In view of the supposed trend of De Wet's flight, Smith-Dorrien's detachment was ordered on August 8th from Frederikstad to Welverdiend and Bank, between which stations, reinforced by the 2nd West Yorkshire regiment and a 6-in. gun mounted on a railway truck, sent from Krugersdorp, it was distributed; another party at Doornfontein watched the chief pass over the Gatsrand.

Aug. 8th, 1900. Ian Hamilton ordered to intercept De Wet.

Lord Roberts on this day sent the following telegram to Ian Hamilton at Bokfontein:

"Since you started from Rustenburg, De Wet and Steyn have crossed the Vaal, and are now moving in a north-easterly direction, making apparently for Commando Nek. You would be admirably placed at that Nek, if there were no other road through the Magaliesberg; but when they hear of your force being in their way they may, and probably will, go for Olifants Nek. Under these circumstances I think you must move towards Hekpoort. To-morrow you will probably not be able to get beyond Grootplaats or Scheerpoort. You must then try and find out which way the enemy are moving. They were attacked by Methuen yesterday morning near Venterskroon, and some of their wagons were reported by a patrol of Ridley's, which crossed the Vaal at Parys, to be moving yesterday in a north-easterly direction near Buffelshoek. Broadwood followed them across De Wet's Drift, and Kitchener, with Little, was to cross to-day at Lindequee. These troops will do all they can to get up with the enemy, but their movements are so rapid I fear they will not overtake them unless you can delay them. It is of the utmost importance that De Wet should

OPERATIONS IN THE WESTERN TRANSVAAL. 349

not be allowed to get north of the Magaliesberg, and this I hope you will be able to prevent. If he escapes you, he will assuredly join Botha, while if you can stop him the war will be practically over. . . . Supplies for three or four days will be sent to-morrow for your whole force. . . ."

On receipt of this, Hamilton moved his main body on the 9th through Commando Nek to Grootplaats, about five miles to the south-west, Mahon's brigade marching thither *via* Zilikat's Nek, which he found unoccupied by the enemy. Simultaneously, Baden-Powell's force took up a position at Rietfontein, thus covering the Neks from the south, and Hickman's mounted infantry were sent into Pretoria as escort to the refugees from Rustenburg.

Aug. 9th, 1900.
Ian Hamilton marches along the Magaliesberg.

At this moment reliable information of De Wet's movements was as rare as it was vital, and the situation not being clear, Lord Roberts telegraphed on the 9th to Hamilton not to leave Commando Nek that day. Should De Wet be moving north, news must soon be received as to where he would cross the Krugersdorp—Potchefstroom railway. For that eventuality Hamilton was well placed. If De Wet were bound east, he would be certain to cross the main line south of Johannesburg, in which case Hamilton's force would hurry in to Pretoria, whilst Paget's and Clements' brigades would be in readiness at the junction of the Natal and Transvaal railways, where they were being concentrated for the emergency. Everything promised well, and every contingency had apparently been provided for. De Wet was within the corral formed by the railways and the river, with British troops behind, in front, and along the railways on either flank.

On August 10th, Lord Methuen's column reached Enzelpoort at mid-day, without opposition. During the march it was learned that De Wet, who had laagered near Losberg for the night, had changed direction northwards, and was reported to be making for the Gatsrand by the Losberg—Wolvaardt route. By this time the Boers, trekking rapidly, were well ahead of their pursuers. After a short rest, Lord Methuen pushed on to

Lords Kitchener and Methuen in pursuit.

Taaibosch Spruit, whence the rear of the enemy's convoy could be discerned ascending the pass north of Buffelsdoorns, a rearguard covering the movement from a strong position to the south. The artillery shelled the ridge hard, but Douglas' infantry were too tired to carry out further operations that night, and an attack was ordered for the following morning.

Meanwhile, Lord Kitchener had brought his infantry, by a long and rapid march east of the Losberg, as far as Droogeheuvel, Broadwood, with the mounted troops, being sent to reconnoitre the passes of the Gatsrand towards Bank station.

The columns were now in want of supplies, Lord Methuen at Welverdiend, Lord Kitchener at Bank. The Colonial division, marching fast and light, had caught up Lord Methuen's column near Enzelpoort, and thence marched to Frederikstad.

The enemy dashed over the railway in two divisions on the night of August 10th between Frederikstad and Welverdiend, De Wet's immediate following blowing up the bridge north of the former place, while his wagons and the rearguard were thrown across three miles south-west of Welverdiend. A few scouts left behind to watch the Gatsrand were seen by Lord Methuen's mounted troops next morning at the Buffelsdoorns Pass; but it was soon evident that the enemy had vacated the position, and the division was ordered to march to Frederikstad. Learning that De Wet's force had moved westwards, Lord Kitchener changed the direction of his column to Welverdiend, where he arrived with Broadwood, Little and Ridley late on the 11th, and was met by Smith-Dorrien with the 19th brigade. De Wet was then supposed to be at Cyferbult, ten miles northwest of Frederikstad, and a combined attack by Lord Methuen from the west and by Lord Kitchener from the east of that place was suggested. It was now clear that Ian Hamilton's force, to be of service, must be posted west of Hekpoort as the enemy was moving away from the direction of Commando Nek; and Lord Methuen realised that, unless he continued the pursuit with mounted troops and mule transport, there was little chance of heading De Wet. Accordingly, leaving his infantry and heavy transport, he started at 3 a.m. on the 12th, with 600

Imperial Yeomanry, 600 men of the Colonial division with four 15-pr. guns, the 4th battery R.F.A. (four guns), one section of the 78th battery, a Howitzer section, and three Vickers-Maxims. The Yeomanry had but two and a half days' forage, and the Colonial division but one day's feed for the horses; yet a long march had to be faced. Major-General Douglas was to follow with the 9th infantry brigade as rapidly as possible after the Potchefstroom convoy should arrive, and the rest of the Colonial division were to await their remounts from Krugersdorp.

Crossing the Mooi River bridge, which had been repaired by the Royal Engineers during the night, the column at daybreak on August 12th was six miles south of Cyferbult, when the scouts reported that a large convoy had been seen trekking the previous evening a few miles north of that place. Pressing on, Lord Methuen's leading troops, the 5th and 10th I.Y., and the section of the 78th battery, overtook the Boers' rearguard early in the afternoon. The 5th I.Y. were at once sent off to the left front to head off the enemy's wagons, still four miles away, but were checked by gun and rifle fire. On the right, the 10th I.Y. and the two guns, working round the enemy's flank, captured without loss a gun with which De Wet was covering his retreat. The piece in question proved to be one which had been taken from the 77th battery R.F.A. at Stormberg. The speed of the flight had begun to tell on the Boers. Position after position was quickly seized. The road was littered with abandoned animals and supplies. Many of the enemy's mules dropped dead; it was observed that their oxen trotted as well as the mules and stood the strain better. Sixteen wagons, some full of ammunition, fell into Lord Methuen's hands; and sixty British prisoners, whom De Wet could no longer guard, were set free. Lord Methuen's advanced column had now marched thirty-two miles since early morning, and both horses and men were exhausted. A halt had to be called after dark; there was no water, and it was not till 11 p.m., when the transport arrived, that the troops had anything to eat. In rear, the 9th infantry brigade had left Frederikstad at noon, and Douglas stopped his force at Witpoortje, whence Broadwood's cavalry were seen some eight miles away toward the east. Coming up from Welverdiend as quickly as possible were Smith-Dorrien's infantry, followed by Hart's brigade.

Marching through the long winter night, De Wet, making for Rustenburg, crossed the southern slopes of the Witwatersrand, leaving Tafel Kop well to the left, and thereby achieved salvation. Every effort was made by Lord Methuen and by Lord Kitchener, who was now in personal command of Smith-Dorrien's, Broadwood's, Little's and Hart's columns, to force the pace. Both started at 3 a.m. next day, Broadwood's men moving without baggage of any kind. By noon, Methuen's advanced troops were at Rietfontein, south of Tafel Kop. There they discovered that De Wet had turned eastward and laagered at Vlakfontein, on the direct road to Olifants Nek. As it seemed likely that the enemy might turn off the main road when the scent became too hot, it had been arranged that only Douglas' troops and Smith-Dorrien's column should directly follow Lord Methuen towards Rietfontein, and that Lord Kitchener's forces should keep to the east of De Wet's track.

De Wet apparently surrounded.

Instead of this, all the columns, following the tracks left by the Boers, moved from Welverdiend by the same road. It was taken for granted that Olifants Nek was occupied. The Commander-in-Chief had telegraphed to Lord Kitchener, Smith-Dorrien and Broadwood, that Lieut.-General Ian Hamilton had been ordered to march down the Hekpoort valley in time to occupy the Nek on the morning of August 13th, whilst Baden-Powell blocked Commando Nek. There seemed no loophole of escape for De Wet, provided only he could be prevented from moving westward, or passing to the north of the Magaliesberg, through Magato Nek.

Thus every officer and man engaged in the chase felt sure that Olifants Nek would be closed against De Wet. The prospect of capturing the famous guerrilla filled all ranks with the keenest determination to spare no exertions. Privations, lack of rest, indifferent tracks over masses of bush-covered hills were unable to check the eager marching of the infantry ; the mounted troops scouted boldly through the blind and thicketed valleys

OPERATIONS IN THE WESTERN TRANSVAAL. 353

Every mile seemed to seal more certainly the fate of De Wet, who was dropping so many horses and oxen on the road that it was plain that his powers of flight were fast diminishing. The few prisoners who were taken told a tale of exhaustion and despair amongst the burghers, who saw no way of escape open. De Wet himself did not dare to hope that Olifants Nek would be unoccupied. After leaving Vlakfontein, he changed direction to the north-west, and darted towards the Selous river. The moment this move was discovered Lord Methuen was convinced that De Wet was making for the Magato Nek. But that, too, should be held by British troops, as it had been during the occupation of Rustenburg. To head the fugitives away from the west Lord Methuen sent off his mounted column, without baggage and with only half a day's rations, at 1 a.m. on August 14th. Marching by the light of the moon the column made a wide détour over the slopes of the eastern Zwart Ruggens range, getting well to the west of the enemy. At Selous Kraal, which was reached at 11 a.m., there appeared through the smoke of the veld fires a great cloud of dust raised by the enemy's convoy near Buffelshoek, four miles west of Olifants Nek.

De Wet, then, had turned from Magato Nek towards the east and Olifants, hastening, it was thought, to certain doom at the hands of Ian Hamilton and 8,000 men. But De Wet had not doubled blindly from the western pass. Hard pressed by Lord Methuen up to the Selous river, with his convoy at least in momentary peril, his scouts had suddenly reported that Olifants Nek was free of British troops. Hardly crediting the information, he threw off Lord Methuen's pursuit by a rapid swing southward under the mountains, and on the morning of August 14th his commandos and wagons streamed over the undefended Nek unhindered and unharmed. *De Wet turns towards Olifants Nek and escapes.*

The absence of Ian Hamilton was even more unaccountable to his own side than to the fugitive Boer. His orders had been clear, his information as full as the speed of the quarry allowed. On August 10th, Hamilton had been in camp at Groetplaats, forty-four miles from Olifants Nek, awaiting definite news of De Wet's movements, and receiving a convoy and remounts from

Ian Hamilton's absence. His orders.

Pretoria. At 9.45 a.m. on the 11th, the following telegram (sent at 7.45 a.m.) came from the Commander-in-Chief:—

" Our information points to De Wet crossing the Gatsrand and making for the railway between Frederikstad and Welverdiend station. It seems likely, therefore, that he will move northwards, towards Olifants Nek; anyhow, we require troops in that direction, and you should move to the westward at once towards Hekpoort. To-morrow you will probably be at Zeekoehoek, where the road from Krugersdorp passes through the Witwaters Berg. Barton will be instructed to send supplies to meet you at that point to-morrow afternoon or Monday morning. A cable cart will accompany them to enable you to communicate with us. The Hekpoort valley is full of supplies and you should help yourself freely from the well-stocked farms. Baden-Powell's force with the battalion that Methuen left at Olifants Nek should remain for the present at Commando Nek."

This was followed by another:—

" As soon as you reach Zeekoehoek, send on such force as you think sufficient to occupy Olifants Nek, with as many days' supplies as you can spare. You will then be available to move about with the remainder of your troops in any direction that may be required. It is important that we should prevent De Wet from moving north of the Magaliesberg, and if he can only be delayed anywhere for a couple of days Methuen and Kitchener should close in upon him."

General Ian Hamilton wired that he would do his best. On receipt of the first telegram at 9.45 a.m. on August 11th, the whole force started off at 11 o'clock, the 1st Border regiment, belonging to Cunningham's brigade, being left behind (as it was on duty on top of the hills), and Colonel R. G. Kekewich's battalion of the Loyal North Lancashire being taken in its place.

Yet a third message reached the General on the same date; this read:—

" Report just received that at 8.30 this morning De Wet

OPERATIONS IN THE WESTERN TRANSVAAL.

was trying to cross the railway line near Welverdiend station. Your force should just be in the right place to-morrow to head him should he go north and prevent him going north-east, or to follow him should he go west."

To Hamilton there seemed nothing in these communications implying urgency. If De Wet's passage of the Magaliesberg were imminent, by far the shortest route by which to block him was the Commando Nek—Rustenburg road, an interior line commanding the egress not only of Olifants but of Magato Nek; whereas Hamilton was moving by the circuitous track south of the range, which is here itself bowed southward. He replied to Headquarters:—

" If I have to go west, I propose not to lose time by occupying Olifants Nek, as my westward movement would cover that pass, which is sure to be held, and is now strongly fortified." Ian Hamilton's reply to his orders.

An hour after receipt of Lord Roberts' first message, Hamilton, leaving the 1st Border regiment on Commando Nek, marched to Bultfontein (thirteen miles), screened by Mahon's cavalry. Next day (12th), he moved on to Zeekoehoek (fourteen miles), which was reached at 1 p.m. Before he started on this second day's march a despatch rider from Commando Nek brought news (sent from Army Headquarters at 6.15 p.m. the night before), that: " De Wet is heading N.W. and is now being engaged by Smith-Dorrien at Welverdiend station." Hamilton was further informed that a convoy was about to leave Krugersdorp, and that he was to send mounted troops to meet it from Zeekoehoek along a road which, he learned from Barton, was strongly held by the enemy. Finally, intelligence was received at Zeekoehoek at 5 p.m. that De Wet was reported to have crossed the Mooi river, closely pursued by Lords Kitchener and Methuen.

The night of the 12th confronted Hamilton with a decision of more moment to the issue at stake than he appreciated. No more information was to be expected from Pretoria, the cable-cart wire to which had now been cut. From Zeekoehoek two roads run westerly; one, by Wagenpadspruit, leading directly on Ian Hamilton's alternatives, and decision.

Olifants Nek, twenty-six miles distant, over the foothills of the Magaliesberg; the other, by Hartebeestfontein and Vlakfontein, following the crest of the Witwatersrand. The former, from the nature of its course, was steep and difficult, and shut in by two ranges, gave no view on either side, whilst it was commanded from both; from the other road there was an unbroken outlook over the open veld towards Ventersdorp, and fair command over three routes converging from the south on Olifants Nek. Hamilton, as he had reported, was aware that the Nek was already in possession of the enemy, who, unknown alike to De Wet and Lord Methuen, his pursuer, had manned it directly the British garrison had been withdrawn from Rustenburg. Of their presence Hamilton had evidence more certain than reports; for the country between his camp and the Nek was full of skirmishers. He knew also that he must keep watch towards the south-east, whence his convoy was to come along an infested road, where, too, De Wet himself might elect to dash for Commando Nek or over the Johannesburg railway. Finally, he had already informed Headquarters that he did not propose to occupy Olifants Nek itself, hoping to block it automatically from a distance. These considerations caused him to adopt the southern of the two above-mentioned roads from Zeekoehoek; and his decision left Olifants Nek open long enough for De Wet's purpose, though it in no way affected Magato Nek, which had been the Boer leader's first objective. Even thus, Hamilton all but cut in upon the flank of the flying commandos. On August 13th his cavalry were sent forward, carrying three days' supplies, to endeavour to gain touch with De Wet. They moved so slowly that the infantry closed up on them before 8.30 a.m., when they were again pushed on. When they finally halted at Hartebeestfontein, De Wet, in the act of crossing the Witwatersrand and Hamilton's line of advance, was going into laager at Vlakfontein, eighteen miles from the cavalry bivouac. Many of his men had already passed over Olifants Nek; the rest followed next morning, and the chase was over.

CHAPTER XV.

OPERATIONS IN THE WESTERN TRANSVAAL (*continued*).*

AUGUST AND SEPTEMBER, 1900.

FATIGUE followed closely upon the disappointment of the troops at the escape of De Wet in the face of their utmost exertions. Energy and supplies were for the moment alike exhausted, and a pause in the chase was necessary to replenish them. The pursued were in similar case; and De Wet, whose salvation had lately depended on rapid motion, now saw that his command could only be saved from destruction by a halt.

Sending General Liebenberg with 500 men to block Magato Nek, and placing a rearguard at Olifants Nek, he crossed close to the pass with the main body, turned south-east, and laagered at the foot of the Magaliesberg, where pasture was good. Of the pursuing British forces Lord Methuen's mounted troops were at Doornlaagte on August 15th, Douglas being under orders to join him with the infantry the same evening; Lord Kitchener with the 2nd and 3rd cavalry brigades, Ridley's M.I., Colonial division and Smith-Dorrien's two battalions, was at Syferwater; Hart's brigade at Groenfontein, some five miles behind. Ian Hamilton's force had moved to Vlakfontein, nearly twenty miles from the pass with a bad road in front of him. At Commando Nek, Baden-Powell had 1,480 of all ranks, not including the infantry battalion holding the Nek. Close to Pretoria lay Hickman's force, with half of Paget's column at Horne's Nek, the other half near Onderstepoort. Lord Methuen was eager to pursue on August 16th; but Hamilton, still a day's march from the Nek, could not attack before the 17th. Thus De Wet's main force remained unmolested for three days, while

* See map No. 38.

Mr. Steyn, who had left him for Mr. Kruger's Headquarters, was given a long start. Meantime, on the 13th the troops were consoled by the surprising news that Hore's detachment on the Elands river was holding out, and its relief became at once as momentous as the pursuit of De Wet.

<small>The investment of Elands River.</small>

The garrison of Elands River—Imperial Bushmen from Australia and Tasmania, Volunteers from Rhodesia, and a few British South Africa Police—totalled 300 fighting men, with a Maxim and an old 7-pr. screw gun. Their camp was on a slight rise which commanded the only water supply—a creek half a mile away. This rise was in its turn overlooked by high hills to the north, east and south at an average range of 2,500 to 3,000 yards. Daily, since August 4th, the camp had been shelled by the enemy, who numbered about 500 men with four guns, three Vickers-Maxims and a machine gun. The first day's casualties among the defenders were six men killed and twenty-five wounded, with a loss in addition of 475 animals belonging to the convoy of eighty mule and ox wagons, for which it was impossible to provide shelter, as every hollow was searched by the enemy's fire. Next day the garrison learnt that Sir F. Carrington's attempt at relief had failed. A heavy bombardment followed, which killed and wounded twelve men and about fifty horses and mules during an hour before dark. The arrival of De la Rey with reinforcements brought the investing force to some 2,000 men and seven guns from the commandos of Fourie, D. Botha, Theunissen, De Beer, Lemmer and Steenkamp. Determined night attacks then began, with the object of cutting off the water supply of the garrison. These were repulsed by a party of Southern Rhodesia Volunteers, and a small detachment of Australian Bushmen, posted on kopjes near the creek, always with losses to the defence.

Judging that the garrison had been reduced in numbers and spirit by five days' bombardment, De la Rey, on August 9th, demanded a surrender, which was refused. The shelling was renewed, but with less vigour; and shortly afterwards a large portion of the investing force was withdrawn in order to occupy Rustenburg and Olifants Nek, the last a movement

OPERATIONS IN THE WESTERN TRANSVAAL.

of which the importance has been seen. By the evening of the 10th, the cordon was so far relaxed that a runner was able to get through on the 13th to Sir F. Carrington. Lord Roberts at once took steps to succour the post. Sir F. Carrington, whose force had been refitting at Mafeking, and had been increased by drafts from the north, was ordered to re-occupy Zeerust, and co-operate in the relief of Elands River. Lord Methuen's division, the nearest force, was also ordered to move thither with all speed. Lord Kitchener had, however, started before this order arrived. Taking with him the 2nd and 3rd cavalry brigades, Ridley's mounted infantry and Smith-Dorrien's battalions, he left at 2 a.m. on August 15th, and, after a rapid march of thirty-five miles, rode into Elands River camp early on the following morning, Broadwood's cavalry having reported by 4.30 p.m. on the 14th that the road was clear. Hart's force was to follow. Hore's casualties amounted to twelve killed and thirty-seven wounded, irrespective of natives; he also lost 1,329 animals.

Aug. 15th, 1900. Relief of Elands River.

Meanwhile Sir F. Carrington had reached Otto's Hoop on August 15th with 2,914 men.*

* 1st Brigade (Earl of Erroll).

Staff	13
Imperial Yeomanry Scouts	45
Paget's Horse	341
South Australian Bushmen	81
New South Wales Bushmen	140
Tasmanian Bushmen	105
Victorian Imperial Bushmen	88
Kimberley Mounted Corps	108
Bechuanaland Rifles	43
2nd Brigade (Colonel Grey).	
4th New Zealand regiment	423
5th New Zealand regiment	243
6th regiment New South Wales Imperial Bushmen	647
4th Bedfordshire regiment	267
Cameron's Scouts	25
Signallers	20
Artillery.	
1st battery Rhodesian Field Force Artillery	118
88th battery R.F.A.	105
Vickers-Maxim battery	64
Colt gun detachment	7
Four Maxims	31
	2,914

Next morning he found the enemy under Commandants Botha, Schwartz, and Snyman occupying a position above Lemmer's Farm near Buffelshoek. After a preliminary shelling and clearing of the flanks by Lord Erroll's brigade, the 4th New Zealand regiment attacked and carried two lines of kopjes in succession, losing one officer and two men killed, and three officers and nine men wounded. The enemy gave way when the attack was within fifty yards of them, leaving six dead on the ground. Next day the commandos were seen riding over the hills about twelve miles to the west. News of Hore's relief was received, and Sir F. Carrington was ordered to await Lord Methuen's arrival.

Aug. 16th, 1900. Lord Methuen resumes the pursuit of De Wet.

Whilst Lord Kitchener was engaged at Elands River, Lord Methuen, as the senior officer in the Magaliesberg, decided to continue the pursuit of De Wet. He arranged to move himself against Magato Nek on August 16th, and for Ian Hamilton to force Olifants Nek from Middelfontein early the following morning. Accordingly the advance guard of the colonial troops with the Ist division seized a commanding hill on the left of the mouth of Magato Nek, and the artillery coming into action, six guns on the left and the remainder in the centre, shelled the position. The Boers hurriedly abandoned it, and Lord Methuen's column, having lost one man killed and five wounded, crossed the Nek and encamped at Rietvlei.

It had been reported to Ian Hamilton that Olifants Nek was held by 4,000 to 5,000 men under the personal command of De Wet and De la Rey. He therefore prepared for a heavy engagement; but the Imperial Light Horse and supporting infantry soon found that they had only a weak rearguard before them. The pass was easily forced with only two casualties, two Krupp guns and three wagons being captured. Mahon's cavalry took up the pursuit, but the Boer rearguard, falling back towards Rustenburg, lured them off the real direction of the main body. The remainder of Hamilton's column halted at Waterkloof, four miles north of Olifants Nek, and followed the cavalry to Waterval on the Rustenburg road. De Wet's main body remained as before, resting south-east of the pass.

By this time Lord Methuen had received orders to proceed to Elands River, preparatory to clearing the country thence towards Mafeking. Lord Kitchener was directed to return to Pretoria by way of Rustenburg and Commando Nek, sending Ridley's mounted infantry to join Ian Hamilton's force. Hart's column, having reached Tweefontein in the Zwart Ruggens by strenuous marching, was to proceed to Krugersdorp, whither also the 2nd cavalry brigade was ordered to return, en route to Pretoria.

The fortunes of De Wet and the commandos which he had carried to the foot of the Magaliesberg must now be followed.

The Free State leader had now three objects in view. First, President Steyn was to be escorted to Machadodorp, President Kruger's Headquarters, to inspire with his unabated enthusiasm the councils of the leaders of the two Republics. De Wet himself, having no wish to be involved in the inhospitable country to the north, intended to break back with a small band to keep alight the fires of resistance in the Free State. Finally he must leave in the Transvaal a leaven of his own Free Staters so as to encourage the local burghers and show them that they were not deserted by their allies.

Movements of De Wet.

Finding that Ian Hamilton's force barred the Magaliesberg in the neighbourhood of Olifants Nek, he moved with his main body along the north-eastern arm of that range, striking the Rustenburg—Pretoria road, and arrived at Wolhuter's Kop on the evening of August 17th. Thence, in order to gain time and information, he sent a message to Commando Nek, stating that he had 2,000 men and eight guns, and demanding the surrender of the garrison. Baden-Powell, divining the ruse, caused a junior officer to reply that the message was not understood, and in the interval Hickman's mounted men were ordered by Lord Roberts to move to Zilikat's Nek. The summons to surrender was repeated on the following morning, signed as before by De Wet, who nevertheless had departed with his wagons and most of his men northwards during the night. When Hickman arrived near Zilikat's Nek, Baden-Powell with all his available mounted troops reconnoitred, and espied De

Wet's laager near Krokodil Drift, whence it moved to (the Hebron) Roodekopjes, twelve miles beyond the advanced scouts. The remainder of Paget's force had meanwhile arrived at Waterval; and Lord Roberts concurred in Baden-Powell's suggestion that Lieut.-Colonel C. Barter with the King's Own Yorkshire Light Infantry should relieve the mounted troops at Commando Nek, and that Baden-Powell and Hickman should join Paget at Waterval, and together endeavour to head De Wet, who was now reported to be moving in a north-easterly direction so as to join Botha by a long circuit. The combined force under Baden-Powell, numbering 800 mounted troops and a half battalion of the West Riding regiment, carried in ox-wagons, reached Onderste Poort on the 19th, and learnt that the Waterberg commando under Grobelaar was at Pyramids moving northwards, covering the march of the Free Staters. Ian Hamilton had previously been ordered to return to Pretoria; but on De Wet's appearance at Commando Nek, he was directed to push on his mounted troops with all speed, and delay the enemy at any cost until he himself could close up with the infantry. Mahon's brigade was on the Rustenburg road at Bokfontein, fourteen miles east of Sterkstroom, while Hamilton's main column was on the same road at Roodekopjes, three miles west of Sterkstroom. Hamilton started at 3.30 a.m. on August 19th, and by evening was at Kareepoort, where he found that the cavalry under Mahon had been engaged throughout the day. Marching in the early morning, they had found the enemy in position on the east side of the Crocodile river in such strength that no progress could be made. Colonel Pilcher had crossed the river with some of his mounted infantry to turn the flank, but after trifling loss was forced to fall back on Bokfontein for the night.

On the morning of the 19th, De Wet himself, in pursuance of his design to break back into the Free State, had left the laager on the Crocodile river. Commandant L. Steenkamp, who had been nominated Assistant Commander-in-Chief of the Free Staters, was to lead the main body and the convoy through the Bushveld. Steyn and the members of the Government, with a small escort, had left him on the 14th with intent to

OPERATIONS IN THE WESTERN TRANSVAAL.

cross the Pietersburg railway line and meet the Government of the Transvaal. This they succeeded in doing near Machadodorp.

The small band with De Wet, consisting of General Philip Botha and Commandant Michael Prinsloo, with 200 men, and Scheepers' corps of scouts, in all 246 mounted men, rode southwards from Krokodil Drift towards Wolhuter's Kop, the route lying between Hamilton's camp at Kareepoort (as yet reached only by an advanced detachment) and Mahon's camp at Bokfontein, six miles away, now only in charge of camp guards. When two miles from Wolhuter's Kop, another British force was reported on the Rustenburg road. This was Ridley's mounted infantry brigade, which had been sent on by Lord Kitchener. Another force under Major E. B. Urmston, consisting of a convoy for Hamilton, with an escort of the 1st Argyll and Sutherland Highlanders, two Elswick guns, and fifty M.I., which had just left Zilikat's Nek, was also discovered. De Wet's case was as critical as it had ever been. To retreat was impossible. His only hope was to cross the Magaliesberg at once, though all the passes were closed to him. Only a goat track led over the mountains, a path considered too steep even for cattle. But to the desperate band it was a road to safety; and, leading their horses, they began to clamber up the precipitous slopes. Once more fortune favoured men so deserving of it. A couloir, scarring the mountain side, hid them at first from sight. This failed half way up the ascent, and they became fully exposed to view; but then all eyes in the British camp were fixed on the skirmish in progress on the flats below, and none saw, nor might have trusted their eyes if they had, the exhausted men and horses scaling the heights. In this manner did De Wet snatch his men once more from the very jaws of destruction. *Aug. 19th, 1900. De Wet recrosses the Magaliesberg.*

Broadwood's cavalry, returning from Elands River to Krugersdorp, nearly came into contact with the party next day; but riding all night, De Wet led southward over the railway, ten miles north of Bank station, whence he passed unmolested to Van Vuurens Drift, and recrossed the Vaal. For a time he remained at Rhenoster Kop, making small excursions to Potchefstroom and elsewhere, before he re-opened active operations in his old haunts near Kroonstad.

Lord Roberts had fully expected that De Wet would try to double south again from the uncongenial Bushveld. He therefore ordered Hamilton to close Olifants Nek if there were but a chance of the Free State leader attempting it. The very smallness of De Wet's escort now stood him in good stead. Hamilton, having heard nothing of the movements of the party, reported that he felt sure that De Wet was east of the Crocodile river, making for Pienaar's River station. A rapid pursuit thither was therefore ordered. Hope still centred on a capture north of the Magaliesberg. "It was worth a supreme effort," wired the Commander-in-Chief on August 20th.

Steenkamp, left behind, proved himself a capable successor to his departed chief. Leaving a rearguard under Commandant Coetzee at Roodekopjes to cover his movements, he led his commando northwards. The previous march of Steyn and his escort towards the north-east helped to mislead the columns as to the position of the main Boer force, while the activity of Grobelaar's commando north of Pretoria added to the confusion; for each pursuing British commander believed that he had De Wet before him.

Ian Hamilton's main force was too far behind to support Mahon effectively on August 19th. Early on the 20th the cavalry again went to Roodekopjes, and there awaited the rest of the column. The Imperial Light Horse crossed the river eastwards and, supported by Lumsden's Horse, occupied the Roode and Zwart Kopjes, which were vacated by the Boer rearguard. Pilcher's mounted infantry pursued the enemy's convoy, now seen seven miles ahead, but the horses were too exhausted for success. The troops encamped near Krokodil Kraal, eight miles beyond the river; the infantry advancing next day to Nooitgedacht, twelve miles further, and the cavalry to Zoutpan. The Boers increased their lead considerably; at Zoutpan it was heard that a large commando had left there twenty-four hours before. On the 22nd the whole of Hamilton's column was at Zwartbooys Location. There Lord Roberts stopped it, for Paget and Baden-Powell were now at Pienaar's River station, and could deal with the fugitives.

A report that Grobelaar's commando had joined the Free Staters, raising the combined strength to 5,500 men and fifteen guns, and that these were only fifteen miles ahead, north of the Pienaar's river, caused Hamilton's return to Pretoria to be postponed. His march was continued as far as Rhenostervlei, on the Plat river; but even Mahon's cavalry at Cyferkuil picked up no trace of the enemy, who by this time was beyond Warmbad. A final effort to gain contact was made by sending two and a half battalions of infantry, the 75th battery Royal Field artillery, and a section of Elswick guns to Langkuil, in support of the cavalry brigade, whom Hamilton took as far as Warmbad. Although a few stragglers were taken, it was then seen that further pursuit was useless, and Hamilton's column was ordered to return. He reached Pretoria on August 28th, and was joined by Smith-Dorrien's brigade, come from Beestekraal, north-east of Rustenburg, by way of Hebron.

The Boers had not yet escaped from the meshes. In accordance with Baden-Powell's suggestion he himself and Hickman, with some 800 mounted men and a half battalion of the West Riding regiment in ox-wagons, marched from Commando Nek on August 19th to join Paget's force, and overtook it near Hamanskraal next morning. Paget's column by the evening of August 16th had been concentrated at Wonderboom Poort. His instructions were to be ready to intercept a movement due east, should the Free Staters escape Baden-Powell at Commando Nek. His force consisted of the following:— *(Operations by Paget and Baden-Powell north of Pretoria.)*

Mounted Troops (Colonel T. E. Hickman).
† 5th, 49th, 63rd and 66th companies Imperial Yeomanry.
Headquarters 4th battalion Imperial Yeomanry and one squadron of the Tasmanian contingent.

In addition to the above, detachments of the City Imperial Volunteers Mounted Infantry and Roberts' Horse had joined Hickman by August 17th; and the 2nd battalion Wiltshire regiment joined Paget on August 19th.

† The 5th company Imperial Yeomanry joined on August 18th.

Artillery (Colonel L. J. A. Chapman).
38th battery R.F.A. (four guns).
C.I.V. battery (four guns).
Two 5-in. guns.
Two Vickers-Maxims.

Engineers.—No. 3 Section 11th Field company.

Infantry (Lieut.-Colonel G. E. Lloyd).
1st battalion West Riding regiment.
Draft for 2nd battalion King's Own Yorkshire Light Infantry.
1st battalion Royal Munster Fusiliers.

On August 17th, leaving Hickman to hold Klein and Horne's Neks, Paget reconnoitred with the remainder of his force towards Doornpoort, where the 49th company and Headquarters 9th battalion Imperial Yeomanry and one squadron Tasmanians under Lieut.-Colonel H. R. L. Howard, Imperial Yeomanry, had a skirmish with a body of the enemy, 400 strong, who attempted to seize the low kopjes at Kameel Drift, north of the Derde Poort Nek. The Yeomanry, reaching the kopjes first, drove back the enemy with a loss of several men and horses. When on August 18th, after De Wet's summons, Hickman was sent to support Baden-Powell at Commando Nek, Paget moved the remainder of his command to Waterval and thence to Hamanskraal, in order to secure the railway line. On the morning of August 20th the rearguard of the party which he had driven from Kameel Drift Kopjes, and had been following since daybreak, tried to outflank the advanced troops, but were repulsed at noon by the 2nd Wiltshire and the 5th and 49th companies Imperial Yeomanry, who lost an officer and one man killed, and seven wounded. Baden-Powell and Hickman joined the column whilst fighting was still going on. Paget in the afternoon followed the enemy along the northern road east of the railway, leaving half a battalion of the West Riding regiment and two guns at Hamanskraal. Baden-Powell's force was on the right across the Pienaar's river. Two squadrons of the Rhodesia regiment which covered his advance came suddenly upon a party of 100 mounted Boers of the Waterberg commando, which had been detailed by Steenkamp to work round Paget's right flank. Both sides alike were completely sur-

OPERATIONS IN THE WESTERN TRANSVAAL.

prised. A fight ensued, in which the Rhodesia regiment lost one officer and four men killed, and two officers and six men wounded. Upon reinforcements with guns reaching the firing line, the enemy were driven off, losing nine killed and ten wounded. Paget's march was also impeded by fire from some high ground between the road and river, but the enemy was rapidly pushed aside by the 1st Royal Munster Fusiliers. Baden-Powell occupied Pienaar's River station on August 21st, followed by Paget next morning. Reinforced by Hickman's mounted troops and the 38th battery, he was sent forward to Warmbad to head Grobelaar's commando and the Free Staters, now reported to be trekking in combination along the Plat river. When approaching Cyferkuil, Baden-Powell learnt that the Boers had already passed through that place; and the march was diverted to the north-east of Warmbad, in order to cut off the enemy from the Buiskop Pass, or at least overtake his convoy while passing through the Nek. Pushing on across the Springbok Flats, a distance of twenty-two miles over a waterless desert, the force reached high ground some six miles from Warmbad, whence the Boers were descried hastening towards the Buiskop Pass, almost abreast of Plumer's Rhodesian brigade, which was leading the advance. Seeing that they were likely to be anticipated at the pass, part of the enemy's main body, with the convoy, swerved to the left, and went towards Roodepoort Pass to the north-west of Warmbad. Here they were followed and shelled as they entered the Nek. In the confusion thus caused, the wagons in rear moved off rapidly westward. It was now nightfall. Baden-Powell's men and horses were exhausted. The mouth of the pass was occupied in order to prevent any more wagons passing through in the darkness, and a camp formed near Warmbad village. Several Boer officers were captured, and during the night 141 British prisoners escaped and came into the camp. Next morning (August 23rd) both passes were found occupied by the enemy; but as the supplies carried on the saddles had run out, Baden-Powell before attacking waited for a convoy bringing four days' rations for Hickman's troops, which would enable his men to keep the field.

As the enemy was known to be weary and short of supplies, Lord Roberts urged Baden-Powell to press hard, believing that the entire Boer main body would break up, and the artillery and convoy fall into his hands. As Mahon's cavalry and Ian Hamilton's force were coming up behind, Baden-Powell again set off to turn the enemy by the north. The Boers, numbering 3,000 men with eight guns, had been broken up into three parts by the attack on the 22nd, the main body of the Free Staters being at Rietpoort, ten miles west of Nylstroom, while Grobelaar and the Transvaalers were near Achaaphoek to the north-east; the bulk of the transport had moved to the west. In Buiskop Pass a rearguard had been left, which it took the whole day to dislodge. As the pass was long and dangerous, Baden-Powell decided to withdraw at sunset, and during the night he marched round the hills, camping next day at Middelfontein, to the north of Nylstroom. On the morning of the 26th Nylstroom was occupied without opposition, although the Free Staters' rearguard was at Buffelspoort, six miles to the south of the village, and Grobelaar in a strong position six miles north of it. Baden-Powell's force was thus between two hostile bodies, and would have been in great danger from a more sophisticated foe. The Boers, however, were imposed upon by Baden-Powell's offer to negotiate; and Commandant Grobelaar, coming in to discuss the situation, showed no astonishment when he was gravely advised to surrender by a commander who was himself between two fires and without hope of support. Steenkamp and Grobelaar had now been driven so deep into the Bushveld that they could not interfere with Lord Roberts' advance against the main Boer army in the east. Baden-Powell was therefore recalled to Warmbad. When passing the Free State laager, on the way back to Warmbad, Baden-Powell addressed to Commandant-General De Wet a summons to surrender, with the object of discovering if he were really there.

As a result of these movements the Free Staters abandoned the idea of joining Botha, and concentrated their force some twenty-five miles north-west of Nylstroom, with a strong rearguard at Rietpoort. During these rapid manœuvres of the

OPERATIONS IN THE WESTERN TRANSVAAL.

mounted troops, Paget, having left a half battalion and two guns at Pienaar's River, and a small detachment to hold the water supply at Vaalboschbult, had reached Warmbad on August 24th. There he found Mahon's brigade starting to rejoin Hamilton's force. Reduced by so many detachments along the railway, Paget was weak, and the arrival of Baden-Powell's brigade at Warmbad on August 27th was welcome. The 2nd Wiltshire was sent to Hamanskraal and Waterval to relieve the 2nd battalion Worcester regiment which formed part of Major-General Clements' force; and Clements was ordered to concentrate on the last day of the month at Commando Nek. Paget's column remained at Warmbad for some days, and received on August 29th thirty-four released prisoners, whom Grobelaar found it fnconvenient to retain. On that date also, Baden-Powell, who had gone to Cape Town, prior to taking over the organisation of the police force for the new colonies, handed over his column to Brigadier-General Plumer, and Lieut.-Colonel A. J. Godley was placed in command of the Rhodesian brigade.

Whilst the pursuit of Steenkamp and Grobelaar was proceeding, operations had been carried out under Lord Methuen, with the object of restoring order throughout the district lying between Rustenburg and Mafeking. Lord Kitchener had been obliged to rely largely upon the supplies prepared for Lord Methuen's division to make his dash for Elands River. Forage and groceries were running very short in the Ist division. A convoy was awaiting them at Zeerust—sixty-five miles distant. Lord Methuen accordingly started for the west on August 17th. Elands River was reached next evening after a long march, and Colonel Little's brigade of cavalry, consisting of only 320 men of the 9th, 16th and 17th Lancers and R. battery R.H.A., there came under Lord Methuen's command. No forage being left, the force was dependent on what the country itself supplied. Zeerust was reached on the 22nd, and large stores found there. Lord Methuen had been sent into this district partly in order to disperse the Boers gathered in it between his force and that of Sir F. Carrington, and partly to carry out the wishes of the

Lord Methuen's operations in the Mafeking district.

Home Government that the latter General should, as soon as possible, return to Rhodesia.

Leaving Lord Erroll's brigade at Buffelshoek, both Lord Methuen and Sir F. Carrington now marched to Mafeking, which was reached with little opposition on August 28th. The local garrison, augmented by a battery from Buluwayo, had previously reconnoitred towards Lichtenburg, and found the enemy in that neighbourhood, and also to the north-east, in some strength. Thrice the troops had been attacked in camp, and on one of these occasions two officers and two men had been killed. On August 22nd, Lord Erroll had inflicted considerable loss on the enemy eight miles to the south-west of Otto's Hoop, at small cost to his own brigade, and Commandant Piet Liebenberg had been taken prisoner. Sir F. Carrington and his staff were now sent back to Salisbury; and Lord Erroll, who took over the command of the Rhodesian Field force, remained at the disposal of Lord Methuen, and was placed in charge of the district— Mafeking, Lichtenburg, Tafel Kop, Elands River, Zeerust.

Now that Lord Erroll's mounted troops were under Lord Methuen, the Commander-in-Chief recalled the 3rd (Colonel Little) cavalry brigade and the Colonial division (Colonel Dalgety) to Krugersdorp for Pretoria. Leaving Zeerust on August 25th these corps came into contact with some 200 to 300 of the enemy at Kalkfontein, about six miles distant on the Ventersdorp road. Little was wounded almost immediately, and the command devolved on Dalgety, who decided to remain there for the night. Advancing next morning, the same enemy was met in a position commanding the roads about four miles south of Jacobsdal, and the price of dislodging them was five casualties. The march was continued without incident till August 31st, when an engagement took place at Quaggafontein, south of Olifants Nek, with an advanced body thrown out by De la Rey, who had now re-occupied the Rustenburg district. With his main body posted upon the Magaliesberg, De la Rey was able to threaten the road to Krugersdorp; and whilst Dalgety was delayed by the detachment (some 450 men with two guns and a Vickers-Maxim), De la Rey himself arrived on

Aug. 31st, 1900. Affair at Quaggafontein.

OPERATIONS IN THE WESTERN TRANSVAAL.

the field with 600 more men and reinforcements of artillery. The position was such that guns could with difficulty be used against it, and an enveloping attack was attempted about 9 a.m. by the Kaffrarian Mounted Rifles and Border Horse, both belonging to the Colonial division, with a portion of the 9th Lancers in support. Three squadrons of the Kaffrarian Rifles were sent forward to within four hundred yards of the enemy, and maintained an exposed position till sunset, the 9th Lancers being unable to advance or retire from the fighting line all day. As the enemy's line was extended by his reinforcements, it became necessary to throw the reserves of the 16th and 17th Lancers into the fight, which continued till nightfall.

Dalgety's convoy had meanwhile been moved across the veld southwards from the road, which ran roughly parallel to the enemy's position, and at dark the force fell back and joined the convoy. The losses during this fight were eleven men killed, and six officers and twenty-six men wounded.

Next morning, the march for Krugersdorp was resumed, when General Lemmer, with about 200 men, attempted to bar the way about a mile east of Syferfontein. The intention of the Boer General was to obstruct the advance of the column until De la Rey, with 800 men and seven guns, could arrive from Quaggafontein and attack its rear. Lemmer's men were fortunately driven off with a loss to the British of three men killed and four wounded, and De la Rey finding that he was too late to attack Dalgety in rear, forbore any further attempt to harass the march of the cavalry, who arrived at Krugersdorp on September 2nd without further fighting.

Meanwhile Lord Kitchener, with Smith-Dorrien's brigade and Ridley's mounted infantry, had not reached Rustenburg till August 19th. On his way back to Pretoria he detached, on the 22nd, Smith-Dorrien's brigade from Wolhuter's Kop, sending it in a northerly direction to Beestekraal, so as to prevent the Free Staters doubling back across the Crocodile river, while he himself, with Ridley's mounted infantry, marched to Rietfontein next day. But though some days later the enemy appeared in strength at Quaggafontein from the Magaliesberg, the absence of any organised body in that neighbourhood at the time was certain, and Smith-Dorrien was recalled to Pretoria, his brigade being required for duty at Belfast.

To the south near Johannesburg, a small mixed column of 800 men with four guns, two Vickers-Maxims and three machine guns, under Lieut.-Colonel C. E. Bradley of the North Staffordshire regiment, encountered a party of 100 of the enemy near Modderfontein, on the Potchefstroom—Johannesburg road, on August 28th; on the 29th, taking advantage of a fog, Bradley surprised and engaged without much loss on either side a Boer force of from 200 to 300 men under Theron. The column returned to Johannesburg on the 30th.

On September 1st all the commandos of Transvaalers in the western district had been broken up, except that under De la Rey in the Lichtenburg district, while Steenkamp's Free Staters had been driven into the Bushveld beyond the zone of effective operations. Henceforward, the British columns in the west were mainly employed in clearing the country of marauding bands, supplies and stock. Paget was to clear the country westwards between the northern railway and the Crocodile river; Clements, operating from Commando Nek, was responsible for the district north and south of the Magaliesberg. To Methuen had already been assigned the whole of the west, from Zeerust in the north to Lichtenburg in the south; and his parties joined hands at Schweizer Reneke with those of Major-General H. H. Settle, who was based on Vryburg. A force under Major-General Hart, mainly composed of the 5th brigade, was to sweep the south-eastern district, which bordered the Potchefstroom—Klerksdorp railway.

Fighting north of Pretoria.

The northern force had several encounters. Plumer, with a small flying column, had been successfully engaged with the enemy on August 31st and September 1st and 2nd, to the east of the railway at Rooikop on the Elands river, capturing in the three days fifty-eight prisoners, sixty-one wagons, 2,100 cattle and a large quantity of ammunition and supplies. A squadron of Tasmanians from Paget's force at Warmbad, when searching ter cattle, rode into an ambush at Zwartkloof, and had to retire, with two officers and two men wounded and two others taken prisoners.* On September 3rd the enemy, having isolated Paget's camp by tearing up the railway seven miles south of Warmbad, attacked him from the east, opening with a 4.6-in. Howitzer at Buiskop Pass, followed by heavy rifle fire on the station buildings and camp. When their leader, Commandant Piet Coetzee, was killed, the Boers retired, not, however, before they had caused a loss to the garrison of one man killed and seven wounded, and had taken five prisoners. Upon reports being received, a few days later, of the approach of the enemy's patrols to Hebron, west of Waterval, Hickman's brigade of Imperial Yeomanry, with the C.I.V. battery, left for Pienaar's River station, where the remainder of Paget's force arrived on September 10th, Hickman's command proceeding to Waterval the same afternoon. The clearing work was to begin by marching towards Hebron. Paget moved his centre column, consisting of two guns 7th battery R.F.A., two 5-in. guns, eight companies 1st West Riding regiment, two companies 1st Royal Munster Fusiliers and a detachment R.E., to Zoutpan, by way of Stinkwater; Plumer, with his 700 mounted men, crossed the Aapies river to Makapan Stad, and Hickman co-operated from Waterval. All reached Hebron with little opposition. The fertile valley in which the town lay was devastated, and a herd of captured cattle sent into Pretoria. As the enemy was said to be retiring on Zoutpans Drift to join De la Rey in the west, Paget moved by night to Roodekopjes on the Crocodile river, where the force rested whilst the Engineers destroyed the irrigating channels and the river dam, and the animals devoured the growing crops of this well-cultivated district. Here Plumer and Hickman on either bank of the river burnt the farms and destroyed the crops of irreconcilables and oath-breakers.

Paget's column was now recalled eastwards, and arrived at Waterval on September 19th. A laager under Assistant-General Erasmus being reported east of the railway at Elim and Zuster-

* For gallantry on this occasion, Lieutenant G. G. E. Wylly and Private J. H. Bisdee, both of the Tasmanian Imperial Bushmen, were awarded the Victoria Cross.

hoek, an abortive attempt was made to surprise it. The expedition resolved itself into a stock raid, and, as such, was successful, for 3,250 cattle, 8,000 sheep, fifty horses, fifteen wagons and twenty-three prisoners were taken at the cost of one Bushman wounded. Paget had an interview with Erasmus, Commandant Dirksen and other Boer officers, and an armistice was agreed upon, during which Commandant Dirksen was permitted to proceed to interview Commandant-General Botha. The armistice was limited both in time and area, for on September 27th, two days later, Pienaar's River station was attacked by the enemy on three sides, and Paget immediately despatched Nicholson's brigade of Bushmen to Hamanskraal in support.

Sept. 27th, 1900. Attack on Pienaar's River.

The attacking force consisted of a detachment from the Waterberg commando, 600 strong, and the Pietersburg commando, under Commandant Beyers, numbering 400 men. Believing that Pienaar's River station was weakly held, only about 500 men of the two commandos were sent to attack the camp, which was occupied by a mixed force of 968 men of the Royal Munster Fusiliers, details of Bushmen and Rhodesia regiment, with two 15-pr. guns of the 7th battery R.F.A. and two 7-pr. M.L. guns belonging to the British South Africa Police, the whole under the command of Colonel L. J. A. Chapman, R.A. The post was well entrenched and the approaches mined. The Boers attempted their customary enveloping attack, opening fire from the north, south and east at the same time. A donga running about 200 yards north of the position afforded the enemy an avenue of approach. A number of men of the Waterberg commando creeping up it were routed by the explosion of a mine, and took no further part in the attack. The Pietersburg men, on the east and south, pushed their assault with boldness, capturing a sergeant and two men in an advanced trench, owing to the men in the next trench withholding their fire in the belief that the Boers were their own comrades. In some places the enemy came to within 200 yards of the defenders, but a short bombardment sent them off. The British casualties were one man killed and one wounded. Paget's column then went into

OPERATIONS IN THE WESTERN TRANSVAAL. 375

camp at Sybrand's Kraal, where it halted until the end of the month.

Further to the south, Major-General Hart commanded the Potchefstroom column, composed thus:—

Hart's operations in the Potchefstroom district.

Mounted Troops.

12th battalion Imperial Yeomanry, under Lieut.-Colonel R. H. F. W. Wilson.
Marshall's Horse.

Artillery.

One 4.7-in. Naval gun.
28th battery Royal Field artillery.
One Vickers-Maxim.

Infantry.

Half battalion 2nd Somersetshire Light Infantry.
2nd battalion South Wales Borderers.
2nd battalion Royal Dublin Fusiliers.

He left Krugersdorp on August 30th, moving in a south-easterly direction. On the following day, hearing that a detachment holding the Johannesburg Waterworks, ten miles south-west of the town, had been attacked, he made a diversion to his left with the mounted troops and battery, the rest continuing the march. A party of the enemy had been reconnoitring the Waterworks with a view to an attack later. They then retired to a high rocky ridge three or four miles away, obstructing the line of advance of Hart's mounted troops. Finding the ridge too strong for direct attack, Hart sent a detachment of the 2nd South Wales Borderers and two guns from the main column to the western end of the ridge, the infantry marching along the crest of the hills. Nine men of the Yeomanry were wounded in the first attempt to take the heights, and the Boers effected their escape without loss. Foraging along the route, Hart's column arrived at Leeuwpoort, south of Bank station, on September 4th, where the advanced patrols came in touch with a few of the enemy's riflemen, who fled when the guns opened fire; but a party of Marshall's Horse in the mounted screen, surprised by a heavy rifle fire at short range, were only extricated by the shrapnel of the Naval 4.7-in. gun with the main body (five casualties). Hart was now in the Gatsrand, a favourite haunt of the Boers, and one abounding in positions suitable for their tactics. He advanced westward from Leeuwpoort in three columns abreast, the main column following the valley, with detachments along the hills on each flank. Near the scene of the previous day's encounter the guns fired on a party of the enemy, killing four, of whom one was Commandant Daniel Theron, a well-known captain of scouts, the last exploit of whose career had been the wrecking of a train on the main line south of Johannesburg.

Continuing his march Hart, on arrival at Welverdiend, turned to the north-west across the Mooi river to deceive the local Boers as to his intended movements. On September 9th instructions were given for a surprise of Potchefstroom by night. The mounted troops, with four guns and a Vickers-Maxim and 150 men of the Royal Dublin Fusiliers, carried in wagons, arrived without mishap on the hills above Potchefstroom at 3.30 a.m., having made a détour round a bog near Frederikstad to avoid any likelihood of being discovered by a commando reported to be holding that place. The exits were occupied, and before dawn the troops had surrounded the town. As day broke some of the inhabitants ran the gauntlet of the piquets and escaped; others were killed or wounded, and seventy-eight were taken prisoners, but most of the fighting burghers of the district had been spirited away by De Wet a few days before.

On the night of September 12th, in the hope of surprising a party which was said to be moving south, Hart left a temporary garrison in Potchefstroom and withdrew from the town in two bodies—one commanded by himself moving north-west towards Ventersdorp; the other, under Lieut.-Colonel H. T. Hicks, northwards towards Frederikstad. The commando trekked rapidly through the night, and Hart's guns could merely reach the rearguard in the morning. On the 13th Frederikstad was gained, and on September 15th Hart evacuated Potchefstroom, bringing the prisoners and refugees into Frederikstad. These, with their household goods, made a large convoy, and to escort it Hart sent two squadrons, one battalion and two guns from Frederikstad.

Commandant Douthwaite, in the neighbourhood of the town, had received orders from General P. J. Liebenberg to attack this convoy, but the appearance of the Frederikstad troops was impressive, and Douthwaite respected them. He was, in consequence, relieved by Liebenberg of his office as Commandant.

Hart's column remained several days in Frederikstad, the stock-collecting parties having daily skirmishes. An advance was made on September 20th to Witpoortje and thence to Bulskop. At Eleazar a Boer laager was surprised; but after marching thirty-seven miles in twenty-five hours the mounted troops and artillery were too exhausted to pursue, and the enemy escaped, leaving several hundred cattle. Hart was now ordered to return to Krugersdorp, which he reached on September 30th, by way of Potchefstroom and Leeuwspruit, with little hindrance. Since leaving Krugersdorp the column had marched 310 miles.*

Meanwhile Major-General Barton's force at Krugersdorp had not been idle. Early in September the railway was cut eight miles east of Welverdiend, and a few days later another attempt was made to blow up the bridge near Bank. Punitive and stock-raiding expeditions were consequently sent out in various directions. On the night of September 16th the cairn of stones under the Paardekraal monument at Krugersdorp was removed by order of Lord Roberts; for the prolonged resistance of many simple Boers was fostered by the legend that the independence of the Transvaal would continue as long as the stones stood beneath the monument.

In the west, Lord Methuen's force had remained resting and re-fitting at Mafeking since August 28th. After the return of Sir F. Carrington to Rhodesia, a reorganisation of the whole command became necessary. A re-adjustment was made of Baden-Powell's and Lord Methuen's forces. The Loyal North Lancashire regiment rejoined by rail from Pretoria, and the detachment of Australian Bushmen at Mafeking proceeded to

---

* Casualties—Three killed, twenty-four wounded, three missing.

Pretoria to reinforce Baden-Powell. The reorganisation of Lord Methuen's troops, completed by September 7th, was:—

Reorganisation of the forces in the west.

No. 1 column, under Lord Methuen's direct command:—
    1st brigade Imperial Yeomanry.
    Mounted infantry of 1st Royal Munster Fusiliers.
    4th battery Royal Field artillery.
    Two guns 2nd battery Rhodesian Field Force.
    Two Vickers-Maxims.
    One section 11th Field company R.E.
    1st battalion Loyal North Lancashire regiment.
    Half 2nd battalion Northamptonshire regiment.

No. 2 column, under Major-General Douglas:—
    2nd brigade Rhodesian Field Force.
    Four guns 88th battery Royal Field artillery.
    Two guns 2nd battery Rhodesian Field Force.
    One section (Howitzers) 37th battery Royal Field artillery.
    Two Vickers-Maxims.
    One section 11th Field company R.E.
    1st battalion Northumberland Fusiliers.
    Half 2nd battalion Northamptonshire regiment.

No. 3 column, under Brigadier-General Lord Erroll:—
    Remainder of Sir F. Carrington's troops.

After providing a garrison of 400 mounted troops, 800 infantry and four Field guns for the local defence of Mafeking, the mobile columns started on September 8th, Lord Methuen towards Lichtenburg, Major-General Douglas to Otto's Hoop, where Lord Erroll's column had been encamped for some days. As a commando under Commandant Vermaas was reported to be at Molopo Oog, Lord Methuen changed his direction next day towards the north-east, ordering Douglas to move by the Lichtenburg road east of the enemy's laager, and Lord Erroll to conform, moving by Klipplaat. Douglas found the enemy occupying a ridge, near Molopo Oog, with detached parties holding some kopjes and bushes on both flanks. The position was at once attacked in front, and after a short engagement the Boers retired, those on the kopjes on the left of the position falling into the hands of Lord Erroll's force. The remainder retreated towards the south-east, only to be pursued by

Sept. 9th, 1900.
Affair at Molopo Oog.

the mounted troops of the other columns; during the day thirty-two prisoners, twenty-two wagons and 40,000 rounds of rifle ammunition were taken at a cost of four men wounded. Douglas then marched to Klipkuil, where there was a sharp engagement with a body of the enemy with one Vickers-Maxim, under Commandant Lemmer, who tried to seize the convoy.* Fighting was continued from 6 a.m. till noon, when the enemy, leaving six dead on the field, was driven eastwards.

Lord Methuen had meanwhile received orders from the Commander-in-Chief that the Ist division was to hasten to the relief of Schweizer Reneke, in co-operation with Major-General Settle. This township, the most considerable of the Bloemhof district, was reported to be surrounded by a body of the enemy 2,400 strong, with a large number of guns. Lord Erroll's command, therefore, remained for local defence at Otto's Hoop, while the other two columns marched southward with all speed.

* British casualties—One officer and six men wounded.

CHAPTER XVI.

THE ADVANCE TOWARDS KOMATI POORT.*

Effect on Natal of the successes in the Orange River Colony.

LIEUT.-GENERAL SIR A. HUNTER'S victory in the Brandwater basin had valuable effect in Natal and the Southern Transvaal. It removed in a moment the possibility of attack in force from the west which had kept Sir R. Buller's army chained fast to the railway from Heidelberg down to Ladysmith. True, De Wet, Olivier and other guerrillas were still at large; but, vagrant and weakened, they were unlikely seriously to raid Natal across the Drakensberg, an eventuality which had never been absent, and with reason, from Sir R. Buller's mind. None had known better than he how vulnerable still that many-gated colony was to incursions which would have undone in a few hours the heavy work of months. Nor had the enemy himself realised the weakness of the re-conquered fortress, to the very walls of which covered ways ran from all sides. Entry, subsistence, and escape were alike easy, and Boer forces, wandering in the Orange River Colony, or the Eastern Transvaal, in search of damage, might have stirred the whole theatre of war with the news of their passage of the Buffalo river or the Drakensberg.

Now, however, the west was safe; no large bodies of the enemy were to the east, and the strength of the garrisons and posts along the railway could be halved. Lord Roberts had long been waiting for the moment which would bring actual co-operation from Sir R. Buller's command. It is an example of how

* See maps Nos. 48, 49, 50.

THE ADVANCE TOWARDS KOMATI POORT. 381

war, even when successful, disappoints preconceived hopes and plans, that only now, after seven months, could the Commander-in-Chief call to his side a force which he had originally designed to be a member of his own army. On July 30th, Sir R. Buller received orders to prepare a division of infantry and a brigade of cavalry for a march to Middelburg. The route was to be by Amersfoort, Ermelo and Carolina; the last-named place, near which touch would be gained with French's cavalry, was to be reached if possible by August 15th.

<small>July 30th, 1900. Sir R. Buller ordered northward.</small>

Sir R. Buller immediately set about the concentration of the force from his widely scattered units. The task, with its manifold reliefs, entrainments, and marches of detachments was necessarily slow. Especially difficult was it to collect quickly transport sufficient to render self-supporting an army of 11,000 officers and men and over 3,000 horses, besides a large body of native drivers, etc., during a march of a hundred miles through country bare of supplies, remote from a railway, and occupied by the enemy. Sudden problems such as this—of frequent occurrence in South Africa—constitute the real difficulty of campaigning, yet are frequently disregarded as either of minor importance, when the tactical operations become of absorbing interest, or as matter of routine when they are uneventful. The orders received by Colonel G. Stanley, the Director of Transport, Natal army, were to provide carriage for fourteen days' rations, etc., as much as possible to be drawn by mules. By August 4th he had gathered together at Paarde Kop 451 mule-wagons and 304 ox-wagons, of which 240 constituted the supply park. Two days later the whole train, fully packed, moved to the place of assembly, Meerzicht, six miles north-east of Paarde Kop, where the fighting column had just completed its concentration.

The force selected by Sir R. Buller was composed as follows :—

2nd Cavalry brigade (Major-General J. F. Brocklehurst).
    5th Lancers.
    18th Hussars (3 squadrons).
    19th Hussars.

3rd Mounted brigade (Major-General the Earl of Dundonald).
  South African Light Horse.
  Strathcona's Horse.
  A. battery Royal Horse artillery.
  No. 2 Field troop Royal Engineers.

 IVTH DIVISION (Lieut.-General the Hon. N. G. Lyttelton).

7th brigade (Brigadier-General F. W. Kitchener).
  1st Devonshire regiment.
  1st Manchester regiment.
  2nd Gordon Highlanders.
  2nd Rifle Brigade.

8th brigade (Major-General F. Howard).
  1st Liverpool regiment.
  1st Leicester regiment.
  1st Royal Inniskilling Fusiliers.
  1st King's Royal Rifles.
  IVth division mounted infantry battalion.
  21st battery Royal Field artillery.
  42nd ,, ,, ,, ,,
  53rd ,, ,, ,, ,,
  23rd company Royal Engineers.
 61st (Howitzer) battery R.F.A.
  No. 16 company Southern division Royal Garrison artillery (two 5-in. guns).
  No. 10 Mountain battery Royal Garrison artillery (two 12-prs.).
  No. 10 company Western division Royal Garrison artillery (two 12-prs.).
  No. 6 company Western division Royal Garrison artillery (two 4.7-in. guns)
  Two Vickers-Maxim guns (one detached from the Vth division and one with the IVth division).

The withdrawal of these troops from the line had necessitated a redistribution of the guards and garrisons remaining behind, which were thus sub-divided :—

  1. Heidelberg—Kromdraai.—Lieutenant-General Sir C. F. Clery with IInd division, Thorneycroft's Mounted Infantry, Composite Mounted Infantry regiment, and three 4.7-in. guns, two 5-in. guns and two Naval 12-prs.

2. Platrand—Imbezane. — Lieutenant-General H. J. T. Hildyard with Vth division (less two battalions), 5th Dragoon Guards and Bethune's Mounted Infantry.

3. Newcastle—Ladysmith.—Major-General J. Wolfe Murray, commanding lines of communication, with 1st (Royal) Dragoons, one squadron Bethune's Mounted Infantry, one battalion detached from Vth division, and other details.

Whilst his column was in process of concentration, Sir R. Buller had taken the opportunity of despatching a force from Ladysmith* under Major-General C. M. H. Downing, to seize Van Reenen's Pass. The occupation of that long debatable gateway might have been effected earlier; but was now doubly necessary, because Sir L. Rundle was at this time on the opposite side of it on the march to Harrismith, and on arriving there was to depend upon the Natal railway for supplies. Downing, by a forced march, crossed the pass without fighting at 1 a.m. on August 5th; the repair of the railway which had been broken since October 12th, 1899, was put in hand; and Sir R. Buller, the western border of Natal thus further safeguarded, was able to leave it with an easier mind.

<small>Aug. 5th, 1900. Occupation of Van Reenen's Pass.</small>

At 8.30 a.m. on August 7th, Sir R. Buller's column left its bivouacs at Paarde Kop and Meerzicht, and pointed on Amersfoort. Hildyard had already (on July 30th) reconnoitred that place (seven casualties), finding the enemy entrenched west of it, and disposed to fight. Patrols from Paarde Kop on August 6th having confirmed the previous reconnaissance, Sir R. Buller parked the whole of his baggage, and advanced in battle formation, pivoting on Rooi Koppies and Strydkraal. A long running skirmish ensued. The Boers, some two thousand in number, with five guns, falling back slowly to the north of Amersfoort, kept at arm's length, though the 8th brigade pushed them

<small>Aug. 7th, 1900. Sir R. Buller marches northward.</small>

* Composition—Two squadrons of cavalry; 73rd battery R.F.A.; a section 4th Mountain battery; 90 men South Lancashire regiment; 480 men 1st Gloucester regiment.

hard, and Dundonald and Brocklehurst, on left and right respectively, felt at their flanks all day. At 5.15 p.m. the 1st King's Royal Rifles, on whom the brunt of the work had fallen, passed through Amersfoort, and seized the heights beyond. The Boers disappeared in the direction of Ermelo, and the column, whose casualties numbered nineteen wounded (two officers and seventeen men), of whom thirteen were of the King's Royal Rifles, bivouacked on both sides of the town. The discomforts of a bitterly cold night were increased by the absence of blankets, the baggage, which had only moved off at 1 p.m., failing to come in by nightfall. It did not arrive until midday on the 8th, and the troops, unable to proceed without it, enveloped, moreover, in a dense fog all the morning, remained motionless on that day. On the 9th the force, marching on two parallel roads, covered only eight miles, though unopposed by the enemy, and halted for the night on the farms, Klippaal Drift and Riet Spruit. Next day the Vaal river was reached and crossed at Beginderlyn, where an excellent stone bridge and a good drift were available. Sir R. Buller now discovered that the Boers, keeping out of reach, were marching parallel to his right. A cavalry skirmish with some four hundred of them took place near the bivouac ground on the right bank of the Vaal in the afternoon; otherwise the column was unmolested. On August 11th, the infantry and baggage again made but a short march of nine miles to Klipfontein, on the Ermelo road; but Lord Dundonald, preceding them with his brigade, occupied Ermelo at 3 p.m. and bivouacked on the south side of the town. Here he was joined next day (12th) by the rest of the force, to which upwards of a hundred burghers surrendered on its arrival. A fourteen-mile march on the 13th brought the column to the source of the Vaal river at Klipstapel, with no more opposition than an affair of patrols on the right, which cost the enemy four men and the South African Light Horse one man wounded. A sudden rupture of all telegraphic communication with the south proved that the Boers were active in rear of the expedition as well as in front of it. On the 14th the infantry reached Witbank and Kranspan,

Aug. 11th, 1900. Occupation of Ermelo.

THE ADVANCE TOWARDS KOMATI POORT.

and the cavalry Twyfelaar on the Vaalwater river, where, as arranged, they duly gained touch with French's outposts on Strathrae Farm. Carolina itself was entered by a squadron of Strathcona's Horse, who drove some fifty Boers from its precincts, and blew up a small magazine in the town. Next day, Sir R. Buller advanced his main body to Twyfelaar, losing two men by sniping fire at the bivouac, and there halted both to draw the supplies which awaited him at Wonderfontein, and to receive the instructions of the Field-Marshal as to his future co-operation with the forces on the Delagoa Bay railway. His northward march had been unexpectedly easy; and that from a cause which was the kernel of innumerable difficulties in many months of campaigning yet to come. True to the principles of guerrilla warfare, which the Boer leaders in the south had adopted earlier than their colleagues opposing Lord Roberts, the burghers of the districts traversed had made no pretence of opposition to a force so greatly superior to them in numbers, and so obviously bent on the very purpose which suited them best, an evacuation of their particular territories. Dogging the British column only to the confines of their own counties, each commando in turn had then fallen back, and was once more exactly where it had been when the column first set out—in troublesome, though harmless, proximity to the still adequately defended railway and frontiers of Natal.

Aug. 14th, 1900.
Junction with French.

Sir R. Buller was as fully aware of this avoidance of him as of the inadmissibility of preventing it. The bands left behind were not strong enough to do damage. He was marching under orders, and for a definite purpose. Had he, by turning aside to demolish his opponents, delayed his arrival at Twyfelaar, the cost of clearing the south-east of the Transvaal might have been the dislocation of far more important operations in course of preparation in the north-east. Of such a state of things as he and other Generals had left behind them, it may be hazarded that there is but one preventive and one cure; the preventive, an untiring pursuit of fugitives, and a ruthless harrying of farms, townships and all other sources of supply immediately after the battles which force guerrilla warfare

Disturbed state of the Eastern Transvaal.

on the beaten side; the remedy, the permanent occupation of each centre of unrest. How effective is the latter was shown at this very time by the surrendering on August 12th and following days of all but a fragment of the Standerton commando, whose capital and most of its hamlets were firmly in the hands of Sir F. Clery's troops. Rarely, however, in remote theatres of war is either method possible to the victor. As for instant pursuit, he is never less prepared for it than after a series of successes, when both his mobility and supply are at their lowest ebb; nor can troops be spared or risked for garrisons so long as hostile bodies, large enough to be respected as armies, still exist in the field. In short, that commander has a difficult problem who is forced to conduct regular and irregular operations at the same time. The necessity of doing so was at this moment taxing severely the resources of the Commander-in-Chief at Pretoria, whose columns, drawn largely from the only striking force at his disposal, were ranging over a vast area in chase of now this leader, now that, succouring beleaguered posts, or warding off attacks on the lines of communication; the main operations, those against Botha and his army, remaining meanwhile in suspension. Only the arrival of the troops from Natal enabled him to resume them.

On August 17th, Sir R. Buller despatched every available mule-wagon to Wonderfontein, where ten days' supplies had been collected for him by Lieut.-General French. Two days later the convoy returned, loaded with stores for five days, which, together with those already in hand, made up sufficient for eight days, all that could be carried by a transport already weakened by two hundred oxen during the northward march. From this time onward Sir R. Buller cast off the chain of direct supply which had connected him with Natal, and depended for subsistence upon the rail-head. The Director of Supplies in Natal, therefore, despatched all his trains to Pretoria, where Colonel E. W. D. Ward, ably presiding over the distribution, thus focussed in himself the products of two lines of railway, 1,800 miles in length. On the 18th, French, handing over Middelburg to Pole-Carew, advanced his Headquarters to Wonderfontein and resumed command of his cavalry division (1st and 4th brigades) which was linking Sir R. Buller's force to the railway through Strathrae and Witkloof. Hutton remained for the present on a semi-circular front, covering the northern side of Middelburg, where Pole-Carew was occupied in gathering up the XIth division, which had for some time past been strung out in small detachments along the line from Bronkhorstspruit eastwards. As some days were to elapse before it could be concentrated, Sir R. Buller, rather than remain idle, on August 21st advanced his force nine miles north-eastward to Van Wyk's Vlei, with the double object of gaining ground towards the enemy's left flank, and of covering the cavalry, whose outposts had already suffered losses from the constant skirmishing which occurred on the Belfast road. It was as yet too early to employ French actively on the outer flank. Not only was he required to preserve Sir R. Buller's connection with the railway, but it was desirable also to keep the cavalry division in the background, and to spare men and horses for a sudden entry into the heavy work which would fall to them in the general advance now in course of preparation. Sir R. Buller's own short march, which was much delayed by difficulties with the baggage at the drifts, was not without incident.

On the arrival of the leading troops at Van Wyk's Vlei, Dundonald's cavalry, who were covering the right flank, were pushed out towards the Komati river to occupy a ridge running parallel to the road by which the main body was advancing. Here they came in contact with a party of the enemy lurking in the Komati valley. These engaged them so seriously that first the 5th Lancers, the 18th Hussars and the 21st battery, and, later, four companies of the 2nd Gordon Highlanders and two of the 1st Leicester regiment had to be sent to their support. Aug. 21st and 22nd, 1900. Affairs at Van Wyk's Vlei.

The Boers, who held a strong position with three tiers of fire, resisted strongly. The battery, singled out by their marksmen, had difficulty in remaining in action, though the Gordon Highlanders, advancing to short range, maintained a hot musketry duel with the concealed riflemen. Heavy firing continued until

8 p.m., when the British detachments withdrew to bivouac with the loss of seven men killed, two officers and twenty-four men wounded, and three men missing.* A force,† despatched next day (August 22nd) under Major-General F. W. Kitchener, found this party of Boers still disposed to fight on the same ground. The country was extremely broken, and the enemy so scattered over the bouldered salients falling to the Komati river, and amongst the numerous kraals below them, that it was difficult to know where to strike. By a dexterous division of his forces, which he covered on the left flank with the 21st battery, and on the right with the Howitzers, Kitchener succeeded in manœuvring each band in succession from its hold, and by 2.30 p.m. was in possession of the field. He then returned to Van Wyk's Vlei with the small loss of two killed and five wounded. Sir R. Buller, confined by order to the Komati valley for the present, decided not to relax pressure on what was evidently the fringe of Botha's extreme left flank, and he arranged with French a further advance for next day, Pole-Carew having meanwhile kept in touch by moving on to Wonderfontein. On the morning of the 23rd, both Generals marched, French with his cavalry wide on the left between Sir R. Buller's column and the railway, both forces pointing on Geluk, which was reached about noon. A rocky ridge, running north and south, traversed the farm, so high that neither the nature of its summit nor its reverse slopes could be determined from below. As it commanded the proposed bivouac ground about the farmstead, it was necessary to occupy it, and the 8th brigade, the advance guard of the day, with Dundonald's cavalry on the right, moved upon it from the west. A few Boers visible on the crest-line made off at the approach of the troops; but the South African Light Horse, who were working through rough ground beneath the southern end of the ridge,

Aug. 23rd, 1900.
Action at Geluk.

---

* For gallantry on this day Sergeant H. Hampton and Corporal H. J. Knight, both of the Liverpool regiment, were awarded the Victoria Cross.

† Four squadrons South African Light Horse, 1st Devonshire and 1st Manchester regiments, 21st battery R.F.A., and two Howitzers 61st battery R.F.A.

THE ADVANCE TOWARDS KOMATI POORT.

came upon a party who fired hotly with rifles and three guns, killing an officer and wounding another officer and two men.

Two guns of the 21st battery, under Lieut. F. Rainsford-Hannay, were then pushed forward to assist, and were immediately severely handled, having a gunner killed and the officer and two others wounded. Rainsford-Hannay and his men stood firm, however, and though they could not by themselves silence the heavy bombardment directed on them, they kept on even terms until the arrival of the other four guns of the battery forced the enemy from the contest. With regard to the infantry, the vanguard, formed of the 1st (King's) Liverpool regiment, meanwhile climbed the western slopes unopposed. The battalion consisted of nine companies, of which, after sundry changes on the march, F., H., G. and A. companies (in this order from left to right) were in front line, the remainder, viz.: C., E., the Volunteer company, B. and D. companies in support. When near the crest, the last-named company was detached to the right to support the cavalry, from whose direction both gun and rifle fire sounded heavily. On arriving at the top the four leading companies of the Liverpool regiment found themselves on the lip of an extensive plateau, the summit of which sloped gently for about two miles back towards the Komati river to the east—a feature common in South Africa, of which Tabanyama, the Onderbrook Kopjes, and Diamond Hill may be recalled as instances. As in those cases, the Boers, ignoring the nearer crest, had ensconced themselves along the further, whence they opened with rifles and a Vickers-Maxim automatic gun on both right and left fronts of the leading companies of the Liverpool regiment. In response, the firing line spread outwards, F. company, which was to clear the way for a battery, inclining to the left, the remaining three to the right, a gap opening between. The battalion had received orders to take up a line of outposts on the first advantageous ground met with; and as the nearly flat table-land provided no field either of fire or view, the companies pushed on to seek a suitable spot. So doing, and descending the while, they approached the eastern crest, until a sharp discharge from the front forced them to halt and lie down. F. company, on the left, was still further separated by this time from the rest. Checked by shrapnel from behind, the Boer firing soon subsided; but the commander of F. company, having suffered losses, and becoming aware of his isolated situation, sent back to the main body for stretchers and reinforcements. C. and E. companies were promptly ordered to advance in that direction. But F. company was still out of touch with H. on its right, a wide interval intervening, so that C. and E. companies, seeing neither F. nor H. as they lay prone on the ground, instead of halting in line with them, pushed on through the gap and far beyond, until they were suddenly smitten by a withering volley from the Boer trenches only five hundred yards in front. Many fell at once; the remainder, though fully exposed at point-blank range, replied with vigour. Heavy and prolonged though the interchanges of fire now became, yet, owing to a roaring wind which swept the plateau, not a sound reached the supports in rear, who were long unaware of the predicament of their comrades. C. and E. companies unsheltered, outnumbered, and unassisted, fought resolutely. By 4 p.m. nearly the last cartridge had been expended; a private soldier, William Heaton* by name, then made his way back over the bare ground, safely reached the main body, and asked for reinforcements and ammunition. The former it was impossible to send; more troops would only have added uselessly to the losses already suffered; for the position of C. and E. companies, accidentally taken up, was of no value, and could not be retained. Nor were men who volunteered to carry forward ammunition able to reach the hard-pressed detachment, whose prospects looked dark indeed. Even artillery support was not to be had, for the guns had left the exposed surface of the broad plateau, which hid the enemy from view. As dusk began to fall, the Boers left their schanzes and advanced boldly. The fate of the two companies so far out in front seemed sealed, for to remain was to be surrounded, whilst many hundreds of yards of open was the only line of retreat. Retirement, however, was the sole chance, and the order was given.

* Awarded the Victoria Cross.

THE ADVANCE TOWARDS KOMATI POORT.

Whilst the officers and a handful of men remained, plying the last few rounds of ammunition, the remainder fell back with further losses. The Boers, in a last bid to secure them, came within forty yards of the covering party, only to be beaten back by their well-sustained shooting. Then about 5.30 p.m. the main body of the battalion was led forward to the rescue, and received in its midst the remnants of the two companies, who had lost in dead and wounded seventy-four officers and men. Casualties in other parts of the scattered field brought the losses for the day up to 105. At night French, who had been lightly engaged towards the north, threw out a line of outposts from Geluk nearly to Belfast.

It was now evident to Sir R. Buller that he was in close contact with the Boer left flank, and the incidents at Van Wyk's Vlei and Geluk, though unimportant in themselves, augured a keen fighting spirit amongst Botha's commandos. He could no longer operate single-handed; and, arranging with French to halt on the morrow, he informed Pole-Carew that his next advance must be made in conjunction with the XIth division. During the night the troops fortified the Geluk ridge, where cover was prepared for two 5-in., two 4.7-in., four 12-pr. guns, the 61st Howitzer and two Field batteries; and at dawn the outposts were strongly reinforced. These precautions proved necessary. Throughout the 24th the Boers kept up a constant fire, their strength being disclosed by the practice of six guns, including a 6-in. Creusot, which caused a dozen casualties in Sir R. Buller's force. French, who on the left flank reconnoitred in all directions, was also fired upon by heavy artillery. Still further north Pole-Carew's division as it approached Belfast from Wonderfontein came under a severe bombardment; in fact, the heights surrounding the township had to be taken from General B. Viljoen's men by manœuvres very like an attack in form. The enemy held a line from below Bergendal on the railway up to Elandsfontein towards the north, and both the 18th brigade in the centre and the Guards' brigade on the right were received by a line of artillery which clearly showed them to be close against a prepared position. Pole-Carew entrenched on the hills to the south and north-east of Belfast, the 4th mounted infantry on the Lydenburg road, the 18th brigade on a height called Monument Hill, outside Belfast, the Guards' brigade south of the station. During the day the XIth division had eighteen casualties.

<small>Aug. 25th, 1900. The Commander-in-Chief arrives at the front.</small>

At noon on August 25th, Field-Marshal Lord Roberts, who had left Pretoria the previous day, arrived at Belfast, where Sir R. Buller, French and Pole-Carew met him to receive his orders for the imminent action. The tactical problem, though resembling that of Diamond Hill, was even more difficult. Once more the enemy, barring the eastern road, lay astride of the railway, holding a front of twenty miles of heights which were apparently impervious to a frontal attack. As to the flanks, whilst the Boer right was lost in the intricate maze of the Lydenburg hills, the left was so encumbered with bogs and almost impassable spruits, that not only was it forbidden to French's cavalry, which had been designed to move in this direction, but Sir R. Buller declined to take even his infantry further towards the east, suggesting instead a northerly move on Waaikraal and Dalmanutha, where rested the Boer left. Assenting to this, Lord Roberts then decided to employ his cavalry on the opposite flank. French was, therefore, instructed to bring his division up to Belfast, whence, supported by the Guards' brigade, he would manœuvre north-eastward against the enemy's right, whilst Sir R. Buller struck at his left. The 18th brigade would meanwhile stand fast in its entrenchments in front of Belfast, both to hold the hostile centre and to await the arrival from Pretoria of troops to garrison Belfast on the departure of the Field force.

<small>His tactics.</small>

For these operations Lord Roberts had at his disposal some 18,700 officers and men, of whom about 4,800 were mounted, 82 guns of all calibres, and 25 machine guns.* Against him Botha could muster but 7,000 men, with 20 guns; but several of the latter were of heavy calibre, whilst as usual his mobility and the strength of his entrenched positions went far to make up

<small>The enemy.</small>

---

* Exclusive of troops still west of Belfast, and of Departmental Corps. For full state, see Appendix 2.

THE ADVANCE TOWARDS KOMATI POORT.

for disparity of numbers. Moreover, the spirit of the burghers was at this time higher than it had been at previous, and far less hopeless periods of the campaign. The dismissal of six incompetent Generals had increased the efficiency of their forces. Exaggerated accounts of successes elsewhere, the careful concealment or distortion of failures, fabricated reports of the terrible state of health of the British army, and reports not so false of the support of sympathisers in the British Parliament itself, stories of the desperate straits of Great Britain in China, where 350,000 Chinese troops, with nearly 500 guns, were said to be surrounding Pekin, of enthusiastic meetings in favour of the Boer Republics in Germany, America, France, and even in England, all this had re-grafted a measure of hope upon the credulous burgher's deep-seated patriotism and his natural tenacity.

Whilst the British Generals conferred at Belfast, their troops remained motionless throughout the 25th; Sir R. Buller's at Geluk, those of Pole-Carew to the east and south of Belfast. Both were, from dawn to dusk, under shell and rifle fire, which caused but few casualties owing to the cover thrown up during the previous night. Moreover, the enemy had by no means the better of the exchanges with the heavy guns of both divisions, one of the 6-in. Creusots near Bergendal being reduced to silence by a 5-in. shell from Pole-Carew's position.

At 5 a.m. on August 26th, the cavalry division left Geluk, and was in Belfast by 8 a.m., where the Commander-in-Chief gave French final instructions. The part assigned to the cavalry leader—the clearance of the enemy's right from the country north of Belfast and Machadodorp—was of importance; for unless it could be thoroughly carried out, the XIth division in the centre, its flank exposed, would be reduced to immobility. Ground less favourable to cavalry movements could not well be imagined. Precipitous hills bounded the view on every side, growing only more rugged in the direction of the intended advance. Such a terrain, but a few years earlier, might have kept mounted troops tied fast to the infantry; but French's men, inured to resigning and resuming almost hourly the *rôles* in turn of cavalry and mounted infantry, threaded their way

Aug. 26th, 1900. Operations of the cavalry on the left.

amongst strong positions with confidence. By noon the steep ridges east of the Steelpoort river were in their possession, the enemy, some four hundred in number, who opposed them with four pieces of artillery along the line of the Steelpoort, being gradually brushed away northward. At 2 p.m. French was able to send the assurance for which Pole-Carew was waiting—that his left flank was clear. Since dawn the Guards' brigade had been mustered on the left of the 18th brigade on Monument Hill, where also stood the 4th mounted infantry, the Naval 12-prs., the 5-in. guns, and the 85th battery R.F.A. The Guards had been relieved on the hills south of Belfast by two battalions brought up from Wonderfontein, the 84th battery and two 4.7-in. guns taking the place of the 85th battery, the Naval 12-prs. and the 5-in. guns. Half an hour after receipt of French's message the Guards' brigade and the 4th mounted infantry moved northward against the Boer flank, which seemed to rest about Swartkopjes on the Lydenburg road. This was in a measure a flank march across the face of the main hostile position to the east, and the right flank of the Guards was immediately assailed by shell and rifle fire which followed them all the way to Lakenvley, where a halt was called. The 18th brigade, extended from Monument Hill down to Belfast, also shared the bombardment, the casualties in both units throughout the day numbering thirty-five.

<small>Aug. 26th, 1900. The centre.</small>

<small>Aug. 26th, 1900. Sir R. Buller's operations on the right.</small>

Meanwhile Sir R. Buller, to the south, had been gradually fighting his way towards the railway. As previously mentioned, the direct line against the enemy's left was barred to him by the nature of the ground; and he had to march some distance northward before the necessary turn to the east could be made. Even this road was rendered so difficult by the bogs, that before moving off, Sir R. Buller, in order to lighten his train, despatched the whole of his supply park to Belfast, a service made possible by the presence of French's division on the same road on its way to that town. Sir R. Buller's force then pointed on Vogelstruispoort.* From the first he was harassed, not only on the right front, but in rear, where the baggage laboured amongst

* See map No. 49.

THE ADVANCE TOWARDS KOMATI POORT.

the marshy hollows. Besides the smaller pieces brought into action by the enemy, a 6-in. gun threw shrapnel over the troops at 8,700 yards, being so well concealed behind a low-lying kopje that the united efforts of the 5-in. and two 4.7-in. guns were unable to silence it. For the infantry the day's march was a long skirmish in widely-extended order. But the advance, though hampered throughout, was uninterrupted. The 1st Devonshire regiment, the leading battalion of the 7th brigade, long practised beyond the Indian frontier in this mode of warfare, worked by companies over a front of two miles and a half, and shouldered aside band after band of the enemy, many of which stood at close quarters. Echeloned on left and right respectively, the 1st Manchester regiment and the 2nd Gordon Highlanders kept the Boers from the flanks, whilst the Howitzers of the 61st battery and the 53rd battery R.F.A. continually found out the rapidly manœuvring commandos, their shooting being directed with wonderful accuracy by signal from the infantry. In rear, the 3rd mounted brigade and the 8th brigade fended off the attacks which came intermittently from the Komati valley, two of Howard's battalions also supporting the right of the Devonshire. In the evening the column, having turned eastward from Vogelstruispoort, bivouacked on Waaikraal, with the small loss, considering the incessant and often close contest, of forty-eight killed and wounded, bringing the total casualties of the entire forces to eighty-six.

With Sir R. Buller the day's fighting yielded results far more valuable than the few miles of progress made. It had enabled him to mark the key of the whole Boer position in front of Belfast, and not only to mark, but to arrive within striking distance of it from the most favourable point. On the north, now facing French and Pole-Carew, the enemy's entrenchments curved, as described, in a southerly direction from Swartkopjes down to the railway, forming a strong barrier against attack from the west. But the approach of Sir R. Buller from the south had long been known to the federal leaders. From the day of his departure from Paarde Kop the head of his column had pointed directly against the Boer left; and in

Sir R. Buller's deductions from the day's fighting.

order to face him, Botha had been compelled to throw that flank sharply backward, facing south, and south of the railway. The enemy's positions thus assumed here that weakest of all defensive forms, a salient angle; the apex of the salient, its most vulnerable point, was at Bergendal Farm, five miles to the west of Dalmanutha. A very brief scrutiny had disclosed its weakness to Sir R. Buller. Like all defences of that nature, its front was narrow; it could not be effectively supported by fire from either receding flank, or from the rear, since its projecting bulk hid much of the ground in front of it from artillery or riflemen posted behind. Most important of all, it was situated very near to the centre of the entire Boer line of battle, which its capture would break in two, exposing the line of retreat of both dismembered portions. Yet the actual ground was strong enough to defy assault to all but determined troops unafraid of close quarters. South of the railway, and parallel to it, ran a ridge, the lip of the high veld, and the watershed of the Crocodile and Komati rivers.* From its eastern end protruded a long, and from the western a short spur, both frontleted with parapets of boulder. That to the east fell southward by easy gradients, across which schanzes had been thrown up, facing nearly westward, by the burghers of Germiston, Bethel and Heidelberg. The western spur, some 1,500 yards distant from the other, and not well seen from it by reason of the formation of the ground and clumps of intervening trees, was of very different nature. At the summit of a smooth and gentle glacis, five hundred yards in length, arose suddenly a tumbled heap of boulders, of immense size and piled in fantastic shapes, a fortress as strongly built and as adroitly placed by Nature as ever by the most careful science of the military engineer. Three hundred yards to the east of it, and between it and the eastern spur, stood Bergendal Farm, backed by a coppice of fir trees, of which a few also dotted the slopes in front. Such was the joint in the harness of the Boer army, its topographical strength well calculated to disguise its tactical defects. Fully aware of both, General Botha had posted his best troops on and behind

The enemy's position at Bergendal.

* See map No. 50.

THE ADVANCE TOWARDS KOMATI POORT.

the kopje. The remnant of the Johannesburg Police remaining after many destructive engagements lined the rocks on the crest, one Vickers-Maxim gun in their midst, another on their left rear near the farm. They were commanded by Commandant Philip Oosthuizen, and still numbered amongst their officers that Lieutenant Pohlmann whose skill and courage had contributed so largely to the triumph at Nicholson's Nek nearly a year before. On a knoll in rear, separated from the Police by a depression, the Krugersdorp men, also famous in battle, were placed in support.

Before his troops had settled in their bivouacs after their day's hard work on the 26th, Sir R. Buller had informed Lord Roberts that he intended to assault Bergendal next day. A suitable base for the attack was already in the hands of his cavalry outposts, namely, a long ridge, henceforward known as Gun Ridge. This, at a distance of under four thousand yards faced nearly squarely the centre of the thrown back Boer flank, from which it was separated by a broad and marshy hollow. Though in itself only valuable as an artillery position, high ground, prolonging its northern end, led up to the level of the very plateau whereon stood Bergendal Farm and the fortified kopje. Thence the plateau undulated westward, running far from the zone of the Boer defences, beyond which its knolls and hollows offered a secure gathering ground for an assaulting force.

At dawn on August 27th, the 2nd cavalry brigade (Major-General J. F. Brocklehurst), together with the IVth divisional mounted infantry, A. battery R.H.A. and two Vickers-Maxims mustered behind the ridge (Gun Ridge) held by the mounted piquets. Their orders were to "cover the front of the advance, and at the same time to throw their left forward across the Belfast—Dalmanutha ridge, and obtain artillery positions whence they could shell from the north Bergendal and the northern slopes of the ridge, thus attacking in reverse any of the enemy who might attempt to reinforce Bergendal and the ridge behind it from the north," whilst the infantry attacked it from the south. All this Brocklehurst carried out with complete success, the

Aug. 27th, 1900. The battle of Bergendal.

nature of the ground in great measure concealing his movements. Gaining the rim of the heights west of Bergendal, he pushed his men out towards the railway in advance of the batteries, which first from one place and then from another opened fire on Bergendal. Meanwhile, covered by the 1st Manchester regiment, the whole of the rest of the artillery had deployed along Gun Ridge, being placed in the following order from right to left: The 42nd battery R.F.A., entrenched amongst the Manchester and Liverpool; two 4.7-in. guns; two 5-in. guns; two 12-prs.; 61st (Howitzer) battery; somewhat detached on the left, the 21st battery R.F.A.; and, still further to the north, the 53rd battery R.F.A. Behind the ridge the 7th brigade was kept concentrated in readiness to move. The 2nd Rifle Brigade was in the front line.*

Bravery of the defence. Now, about 11 a.m., swelled a bombardment such as had not been heard since the days of Vaal Krantz and Pieters Hill. Only some forty guns formed the broadside, but many were of heavy metal, and all were turned upon the rocky fort which held the Johannesburg Police, a target not to be missed, so plainly did it stand out upon the crest-line, nor to be struck without effect, so restricted the area within its walls. From Belfast a third 4.7-in. gun, placed by the Field-Marshal's order, threw shell into the back of the position. The Police were well covered; but the great boulders which shut them in, cracking under the blows of projectiles designed for the bursting of the armour of battleships, were as often a danger as a shield, and every splinter whirled like the fragment of an exploding shell. But the Police, firmer than their parapets, lay immovable. In three hours, during which the earth beneath them quaked, and the air above was full of flying rock and iron, none turned, though the hollow behind momentarily invited retreat. True, the way of escape was perilous enough; the hollow itself was so beaten by shrapnel that not a man of the supporting Krugersdorpers ventured to cross it to join his comrades on the powdering ridge. The Police therefore crouched alone, their handful dwindling rapidly. Their artillery gave them little

* See map No. 50.

THE ADVANCE TOWARDS KOMATI POORT. 399

help. Their own Vickers-Maxim was early overwhelmed by a deluge of shrapnel; the rest of the pieces, badly placed on the surrounding heights, had but to fire to be instantly crushed. Only a 6-in. Creusot, from the direction of Dalmanutha, and two smaller pieces east of Bergendal made spasmodic efforts to intervene.

The British gunners, masters of the situation, practised fatal experiments upon their helpless prey. When the Howitzers fired a salvo against the kopje, the gunners of the Field batteries, their pieces already loaded and trained, watched for the bursting of the six great shells amongst the rocks, and on the instant launched in their turn flights of shrapnel upon the identical spot, so that those of the enemy who were stirred by the first cataclysm, were beaten down by the second. If ever troops are to be moved or destroyed by artillery, the small band upon Bergendal might well have vanished. For three hours without respite they endured the storm, and then Sir R. Buller set his attack in motion. He had conceived a double and converging assault: by the Rifle Brigade, supported by the Devonshire from the west; by the Royal Inniskilling Fusiliers, supported by the Gordon Highlanders from the south, continuity of front being preserved by the advance of the two supporting corps in the gap between the inner flanks of their respective first line battalions. The Manchester regiment, replaced in the 7th brigade by the Royal Inniskilling Fusiliers, would remain with the guns on the right.

About 2.30 p.m., whilst the bombardment continued unabated, Lieut.-General the Hon. N. Lyttelton, who controlled the attack, ordered Major-General F. W. Kitchener to take his brigade to the front. To gain the flank of Bergendal, the path of the Rifle Brigade must needs follow approximately that already taken by the cavalry, their object, the western extension of the plateau, being the same. By this time Brocklehurst had established himself firmly on a rise of the plateau some 2,500 yards west of Bergendal Kopje, his artillery being now strengthened by the arrival of the 53rd battery from the left of the main line. Towards this point of vantage the Rifle Brigade, led by Lieut.- *The infantry advance.*

Col. C. T. E. Metcalfe, moved from behind the cover of Gun Ridge in the following formation—First line : two companies (E. and C.), each with half a company in front and half a company in support ; Second line : two companies (F. and G.) ; Third line : the remaining four companies (A., B., D. and H.), the men wherever possible preserving an interval of ten paces. Whilst they pursued their march towards the flank, the Royal Inniskilling Fusiliers (Lieut.-Col. R. L. Payne) moved up to the left of Gun Ridge, in readiness to develop their attack, the Gordon Highlanders closing up on their left rear, the Devonshire, still further to the left, keeping touch with the Rifle Brigade. Meanwhile, the target of all these movements, Bergendal Kopje, gave no more sign of life than a dropping rifle fire, and appeared to be smothered by bursting shell. The Vickers-Maxim at the farm fired an occasional string of missiles, chiefly against the left of Gun Ridge, where it did little or no damage. The Rifle Brigade pressed northward unhindered, and having arrived behind a knoll between Brocklehurst's position and Bergendal, swung eastward and were steadied for the assault. Hidden for the moment from the enemy, the battalion was now some 1,200 yards from the kopje, and facing that side of it which had been least affected by the artillery fire. The left extended near to the railway, so near that Metcalfe, thinking that he had gone too far in that direction, pushed another company (G.) up on the right of the two in the firing line, so as to broaden his front southward. Then the battalion breasted the knoll, crossed its top, and beginning to descend the eastern slope came into full view of Bergendal Kopje. The explosions of the British shells drowned the sound of the growing musketry which came from that battered heap of rock and began to take effect upon Metcalfe's ranks. The lines of the Rifle Brigade rolled on, and they had come within eight hundred yards of the kopje, when the Police, who were watching keenly through the interstices of their toppling ramparts, showed that some of them still lived by delivering a fierce volley. It was followed by a withering magazine fire, not only from the kopje itself, but from some schanzes which, thrown up in advance of the main Boer position north of the

THE ADVANCE TOWARDS KOMATI POORT.

line, took the battalion in flank. Halting his men for a few moments to reply, Metcalfe deflected to the left one company (A.) from his reserve to deal with the northerly trenches, and another (B.) to the right to gain touch with the line of advance of the Royal Inniskilling Fusiliers. With the Rifle Brigade had gone the machine gun of the Gordon Highlanders, in charge of Corporal W. Macdonald, who, utilising the pause, audaciously took his weapon into the foremost line, whence he poured bullets against the kopje. From Gun Ridge the artillery redoubled the avalanche descending upon the fort; yet the Mausers, once awakened, were not to be silenced, and the ranks of the Rifle Brigade were swept from end to end. Metcalfe then reinforced his first line, and gave the word to close.*

By this time the other wing of the attack was well on its way to the mark. The Royal Inniskilling Fusiliers had come under fire sooner than the Rifle Brigade. They advanced in échelon of half companies from the left, four companies in firing line, four in support, the men extended to eight paces interval. Immediately the head of their lines showed themselves over the western crest of Gun Ridge the Vickers-Maxim at Bergendal Farm assailed them with a stream of shells, which played upon them all the way down the slopes. Arrived at the foot of the ridge, which a marshy valley bounded, the Inniskillings were then wheeled half-left, and at a run made for a rocky spur which projected from the southern edge of the plateau, about eight hundred yards distant from Bergendal Kopje. The climb was steep and stony, and it was some forty minutes before the men, with many pauses to answer the fire which beat upon them, were disposed across the top for the final stage.

They were here in sight of the Rifle Brigade, at that moment lying down under a hot fusilade during the brief pause above described. The gap between the battalions was promptly filled by a company of the Devonshire, who were closely supporting the left attack. Then, whilst the artillery hurled a last annihilating downpour upon Bergendal, both regiments advanced

* For gallantry displayed in this attack, Private E. Durrant, 2nd Rifle Brigade, was awarded the Victoria Cross.

upon the scarcely visible kopje. The onset of the Rifle Brigade was swift and irresistible. Sweeping across the open glacis they dashed upon the rocks in the face of a roaring wind and of a still louder blast of bullets. Many were struck down, their Colonel amongst the foremost, three officers and eighty men falling around him upon the naked slope, whilst many who were wounded kept on, hoping to reach the enemy before they sank. Still the Police stood firm, crushed though they were up to the very last moment by the falling canisters of lyddite and the all-searching shrapnel. The final shell from Gun Ridge burst but ten yards in front of the leading infantry of the battalions of the attack. The burghers had lost fifty per cent. of their numbers; of the remnant many were too dazed to run when flight would have been but another service to their cause. But had the devoted band been a hundredfold stronger, they would have been unable to withstand the onslaught which converged upon their little fort. The Rifle Brigade were upon them on one flank, the Inniskilling Fusiliers, charging up in the nick of time, enclosed them on the other; and in another moment both battalions poured over them, obliterating them rather than forcing them to yield. Less than twenty men, of whom eight were wounded, were captured alive; about thirty made off, pursued by the shrapnel of Brocklehurst's and the 21st battery's gunners, who had long been watching for a break-away. The remainder lay amongst the rocks where they had fought; and of those who died, none was mourned more deeply than the brave young Lieutenant Pohlmann. The commander, Oosthuizen, who was wounded, stayed with his men to the last, and yielded up his arms only with his charge.

The assault.

No sooner had the victorious troops rushed through the works than they were re-formed for pursuit. Eastward swept the chase, the infantry across the top of the ridge, supported by the Horse and Field batteries which had galloped for the farm; the 2nd cavalry brigade over the slopes below. But the burghers were not to be caught by either horse or foot; and having cleared the plateau, the troops were stopped and withdrawn to bivouac at Bergendal Farm.

THE ADVANCE TOWARDS KOMATI POORT.

Thus was beaten in the Boer left flank, with a loss to the British of 120 officers and men killed and wounded.* The stroke, dealt so summarily at exactly the right spot, broke up immediately all the enemy's formations. Early in the day sinister rumours of the impending fate of the Police, flying along the federal positions, had stirred uneasily the wide line of battle. French, working eastward, met with little or no opposition, and was able to push forward up the Lydenburg road, which he held from Swartkopjes on the north down to Pole-Carew's left flank at Lakenvley. During the night the Boers abandoned their ruptured line, and fell back through Machadodorp to Helvetia. Here, where the mountains again stood across the path, they were encountered next day (August 28th) by Dundonald's cavalry brigade, which, in advance of Sir R. Buller's column, was pushing back the Boer rearguard. The enemy displayed many guns along a front formidable at any rate in topographical strength, and Sir R. Buller halted at Machadodorp to prepare another attack. French meanwhile closed in to Elandsfontein, where from a high hill he gained heliographic communication with Buller, whilst Pole-Carew supported the cavalry at Middlepunt. Neither General had to fight, the commandos being in full flight.

About noon on the 29th, Dundonald's and French's mounted troops arrived together in front of Helvetia, the infantry of Sir R. Buller's and Pole-Carew's columns uniting later at the same spot. This rapid convergence upon them of the entire British force struck awe into the fast demoralising commandos. There was a cry of "*de Engelse kom*" (the English are coming), and all gave way once more.† Those who still preserved a semblance of discipline were ordered to fall back upon the railway and defend it foot by foot; for Kruger, dragged eastward from station to station, was now nearing the end of his resources. In front of him pressed the British armies; behind him lay the Portuguese frontier; on either hand the precipitous

* For full casualties, see Appendix 2.

† General Ben Viljoen—"The Anglo-Boer War."

country offered no refuge to one of his advanced years. He stopped his train at Nelspruit, still exhorting his adherents, but preparing secretly for a flight which would carry him far beyond the reach of his pursuers. By evening on the 29th, French and Dundonald were close upon Waterval Boven, holding hills which commanded both that place and Waterval Onder. All the infantry bivouacked at Helvetia.

There were now good hopes of rescuing the prisoners of war who, since the Boer evacuation of Pretoria, had been interned at Nooitgedacht. Whilst on August 30th French and Pole-Carew occupied the hills above Waterval Onder, Sir R. Buller, leaving a fraction of his force at Helvetia, pushed across the precipitous country north of the line to a point whence he overlooked Nooitgedacht. The Boer Government, now in straits to guard itself rather than its captives, had already released the prisoners, who, numbering 9 officers and 1,697 men, made their way up the line into the camps at Waterval.

Aug. 30th, 1900. Release of British prisoners of war.

So ended what was virtually the last of the regular operations against the Boers. For from this point their army, breaking up into its constituent parts, scattered both north and south of the railway, some (reported as 2,000) towards Lydenburg, some (2,000) towards Barberton, and some (3,000) clinging to the line towards the frontier. Amongst the conflicting reports concerning the movements of the President and his *entourage*, one, that he intended to make a dash for Pilgrim's Rest, came too frequently to be ignored. Lord Roberts thus found it necessary to break up his own army, and to despatch it in separate columns in all these directions. He entrusted the movements northward on Lydenburg to Sir R. Buller; Lieut.-General Pole-Carew was to continue to operate along the railway; whilst Lieut.-General French, returning to Belfast, was to strike for Barberton, where, besides the fighting commandos, a number of Boers who had refused to fight on were reported to be incarcerated, awaiting release. By this time the army had been reinforced by the reappearance of Ian Hamilton's column, an addition more welcome because of its commander than its numerical strength; for Hamilton, one of whose brigades

(Cunningham's) was absent, brought with him less than three thousand men.*

On September 1st, Lord Roberts formally annexed the Transvaal to the British Crown by proclamation. This Mr. Kruger, from Nelspruit, lost no time in declaring "null and void," as the ex-President of the Orange Free State had done with regard to his own State from Reitz two months earlier.

<small>Sept. 1st, 1900. British annexation of the South African Republic.</small>

* See Appendix 2.

CHAPTER XVII.

THE ADVANCE TO KOMATI POORT.*

Sept. 1st, 1900.
Sir R. Buller marches on Lydenburg.

On September 1st, Sir R. Buller's troops set out in two columns along the Lydenburg road. Leaving a post (a squadron 19th Hussars, two guns 21st battery R.F.A., four companies 1st Royal Inniskilling Fusiliers) on the southern crest of the valley of the Crocodile river, an uneventful march brought the force to Badfontein, where an iron bridge spanned the stream. Sir R. Buller was now entering that wild region where the Drakensberg range, beginning, as it were, to disintegrate after its unbroken procession up from the Natal border, shattered the country in all directions with gorges and precipitous peaks. The road itself, crossing the spurs, rose and fell steeply. North of Badfontein it climbed high across a lofty shoulder which completely shut out all further view, whilst mountains flanking it on either side rendered it a defile as well as an obstacle. Advancing to prove this stronghold next day (September 2nd) the troops met with a severe reception. Three 6-in. guns, a 4.7-in. Howitzer, and many Field and automatic pieces opened from the elevated rim of the horse-shoe shaped position, firing with such unusual rapidity that it was evident that the road to Lydenburg was to be barred at all cost. To attack in front, and there was no other way, seemed to the General likely to be too expensive an operation to be undertaken by but five battalions and a half.

Is checked at Badfontein.

Without assistance, therefore, it appeared that the northward expedition must be brought to an early check; and Sir R. Buller, reporting to the Field-Marshal in the evening, suggested that an auxiliary column should be despatched from

* See map No. 49.

Belfast along the Dullstroom road. This route, which converged on that to Lydenburg, by a fortunate coincidence struck the hostile position just outside its western flank, turning it, therefore, at a point not too far for Sir R. Buller to co-operate by a frontal demonstration with a force advancing along it. On receipt of this information Lord Roberts immediately ordered Ian Hamilton to Sir R. Buller's assistance, holding also the 18th brigade in readiness at Helvetia to support him if necessary. Hamilton, marching on September 3rd, with Smith-Dorrien's brigade (1st Royal Scots, 1st Royal Irish, 1st Gordon Highlanders, the C.I.V. mounted infantry, two 5-in. guns and two Field batteries), halted at Zwartkopjes for the night. As he was without cavalry—his proper brigade (Mahon) not having joined before he set out—Sir R. Buller detached from his own force the 2nd cavalry brigade (Brocklehurst) with two guns R.H.A. to join Hamilton. By nightfall Brocklehurst had gained touch with Hamilton from Helvetia; and though still behind him at Zwartkopjes on the next night, sent on the 18th Hussars by a forced march in time to take part in his operations. Up to Dullstroom Hamilton met with continual opposition on the 4th; but he circumvented every effort of the Boer rearguard, and, passing through Dullstroom, camped on Palmietfontein, whence he was able to communicate with Sir R. Buller. On September 5th Ian Hamilton pushed on unopposed through a vast defile under the Steenkamps Berg to Wemarshoek, sending on half a battalion to seize the important gateway at Zwagershoek. He had thus not only placed himself almost in rear of the Boer position north of Badfontein, but was sure of access to Lydenburg itself, for the mouth of the valley approaching the town from the west was commanded from Zwagershoek. These movements had their inevitable effect on Badfontein. On the 5th the enemy drew off somewhat toward the east, covered by his heavy guns, which shelled Sir R. Buller's bivouacs, taking them in enfilade from the right at 10,000 yards range. During the morning the Boers fell to preparing a gun position in the same direction, but nearer by 3,500 yards, and Sir R. Buller despatched Major-General

Sept. 3rd, 1900. Ian Hamilton marches to co-operate.

Howard with three battalions and a battery to drive them off. Howard duly seized the hill, and though subjected to a hot musketry fire from a crest beyond, made good his hold. On the 6th the Boers fell back altogether, abandoning the powerful and carefully-prepared entrenchments near Badfontein to Sir R. Buller, who marched over them to Witklip. There Hamilton, whose rapid and well-directed dash had manœuvred Botha out of a tremendous fastness only comparable to Laing's Nek, joined Sir R. Buller with all his forces in the afternoon.

Sept. 6th, 1900. Occupation of Lydenburg. The 2nd cavalry brigade, riding on, entered Lydenburg, which was formally surrendered by the sheriff. The Boer force, which was commanded by Commandant-General Louis Botha in person, now broke up once more, part retreating northward to Pilgrim's Rest, part drawing back eastward only to Paardeplaats, where a great hill, an offshoot of the Mauchberg, hung over Lydenburg. To capture this position was absolutely necessary; for it guarded the Mauchberg Pass, which in its turn lay between Sir R. Buller and Spitz Kop, some thirty miles to the east. Now Spitz Kop, standing on the Nelspruit—Pilgrim's Rest road, was the key of the north at this moment, and had from the first been designed as the goal. Its occupation, by denying the road to the commandos on the railway, and perhaps to the President and his officials, would cut them off from breaking back into the open Transvaal, and imprison them in the inhospitable region into which they had been herded, just as French's march was penning them in on the south.

Sept. 8th, 1900 Action at Paardeplaats. On September 8th Sir R. Buller and Ian Hamilton delivered a combined attack on Paardeplaats. The place was immensely strong. Barring the Lydenburg—Spitz Kop road rose a steep semi-circular mountain, 1,800 feet high, whose horns, on each of which was emplaced a 6-in. gun, enveloped the track. Deep watercourses, with sides so sheer as to be almost impassable even by infantry, seamed the base of the hill.

Assigning the road as a line of demarcation between the two portions of his attack, Sir R. Buller sent Ian Hamilton against the Boer left, ordering Lyttelton to move against the right, the two commanders thus operating south and north of the road

THE ADVANCE TO KOMATI POORT. 409

respectively. To reach a point of extension it was necessary for Lyttelton's troops to march from their bivouacs on the southern side of Lydenburg out by the northern outskirts. So doing, they had to cross an open stretch, the range of which was known so accurately to the enemy's gunners that a series of 6-in. shells, launched from a distance of 11,000 yards, began to fall amongst the ranks as soon as they appeared upon the clearing. One of these, bursting over the Volunteer company of the Gordon Highlanders, laid low no less than 22 men, only one of whom was killed on the spot. Thus have modern weapons widened the zone of danger; and since death may be dealt by guns many hours' or, in certain circumstances, many days' march removed from their victims, a soldier is required to maintain his nerve through periods of strain many times longer than those which taxed the endurance of his ancestors. The outer flank of each attack was kept by cavalry, the 3rd mounted brigade (Dundonald) advancing on Lyttelton's left, the 2nd cavalry brigade (Brocklehurst) on the right of Ian Hamilton. The 5-in. guns fired from rising ground within the town of Lydenburg, the 12-prs. and Howitzers from near the road. The 7th brigade (F. W. Kitchener) led the left attack, the 1st Devonshire in first line; Hamilton on the right deployed two battalions of Smith-Dorrien's brigade in front, the Royal Irish and Royal Scots on left and right respectively, the combined fighting line covering some six miles from flank to flank. In this order the troops began a long and arduous climb up the mountain spurs. Once upon their steep sides there was little actual opposition. The enemy early withdrew his heavy guns; the Field and automatic pieces, which kept up the defence, did little damage from the very height of their stations. All day, from 9 a.m. to 5 p.m., the soldiers struggled up the precipitous gradients; yet in spite of the wide separation at starting, and the extreme difficulties of the ground, both wings of the attack converged upon the summit at precisely the same moment, and the Boers decamped. Their only line of retreat lay along an elevated razor-backed ridge, only a few yards wide, flanked on either side with precipices; and great

Moral effect of modern artillery.

would have been the execution done amongst them here had not a thick mist, dropping suddenly, shrouded the fugitives just as the troops rushed over the mountain top to cut them off.

The British losses in the affair were 31 killed and wounded, bringing the total casualties since the time of leaving the railway on September 1st to 44. This action, though it did not give Sir R. Buller the Mauchberg and the pass over it, had placed him so favourably for an attack thereon that he could safely attempt it alone. On September 9th, therefore, Ian Hamilton, whose presence was urgently required on the railway, quitted the force which he had so notably assisted, and marched southward with his own command to Klipspruit, on the way back to Machadodorp. Sir R. Buller, leaving Howard with the 1st Leicester, the 2nd Rifle Brigade, the 2nd cavalry brigade and four guns 42nd battery R.F.A. to garrison Lydenburg, then turned to reduce the Mauchberg. Reconnaissance disclosed the Boers to have taken up a position covering that mountain and the important gateway to the east which penetrated it. But the country itself was now the chief adversary of the troops. The road, a mere mountain track, indescribably steep and rough, would have completely baffled the guns and baggage of any army not inured to the utmost difficulties of campaigning. The Boers themselves were not now more skilled than the British troops in the management of wheeled transport, though the rapid retreat of the commandos with heavy artillery along this very route testified once more that they were past-masters. Between Sir R. Buller and the Mauchberg intervened a deep depression, and the troops had arrived at the crest of this before Botha's men showed their intention to stand in front of the Berg by sending a heavy fire of all arms across the hollow. They were smartly shelled by A. battery R.H.A.; the 1st King's Royal Rifles and the 2nd Gordon Highlanders, who were in front, poured a continuous musketry upon the further crest. After an hour of these interchanges, the two battalions, supported by the IVth divisional mounted infantry, descended to the attack, swept across the valley, and, breasting the opposite

Sept. 9th, 1900. Ian Hamilton returns to the railway.

THE ADVANCE TO KOMATI POORT.

slopes, carried the Mauchberg, with the loss of only some half dozen wounded. From the top the enemy's train was then descried far below, hurrying southward towards the Devil's Knuckles, and Dundonald immediately started in pursuit. But the nature of the country, more suited for mountain goats than for troop horses, kept the cavalry from closing on the Boer rear until late in the evening. By that time a rearguard too strong and too well posted to be dislodged covered the guns and wagons, and Dundonald, after engaging it closely until dark, withdrew into bivouac on the Mauchberg. Next day (September 10th), pursuers and pursued resumed the eastern movement. Daylight showed the Boer convoy to be still within range of the Mauchberg, whence the 5-in. guns threw shell along its path. In reply, one of the enemy's 6-in. pieces attempted to check pursuit by bombarding the track leading down the Mauchberg from a ridge 7,500 yards distant. The Gordon Highlanders, followed by the 53rd battery, Strathcona's Horse, and the 1st King's Royal Rifles descended without loss, then pressing on, made such speed towards the ridge that the enemy all but lost his cannon. Part of its equipment and ammunition were found abandoned, and when Strathcona's Horse reached the summit, the retreating gun itself was still so near that some of its escort fell to rifle fire. A second 6-in. gun from a position further eastward then opened to cover the withdrawal of the first; and once more a strong rearguard, aided by Field guns, kept the chase at arm's length. Derelict stores and wagons, strewing the way, showed how hard pressed was the enemy, of whom, thus hustled through a maze of precipices, it was more to be wondered that he saved anything than that he abandoned so much. For the Boers there was now but one possible success, to get clear; and this they finally effected, leaving Sir R. Buller to occupy Spitz Kop, his ultimate object, peacefully on September 11th. By so doing he brought to a successful conclusion an operation of enormous difficulty and the greatest tactical importance. Botha had been desirous at all costs to keep open the northern roads, even, as has been seen, leaving the main body to command in person the detachment

Sept. 9th, 1900. Sir R. Buller captures the Mauchberg.

Sept. 11th, 1900. Sir R. Buller occupies Spitz Kop.

detailed for the purpose. For wild as was the country, and rough the ways, by these routes alone was there any chance of breaking back when the oncoming forces of Lord Roberts should drive his commandos against the wall of the Portuguese frontier. Now, however, the key of those roads was in Sir R. Buller's hands, and though a long détour into the desolate and unhealthy hinterland might carry small bodies of men into freedom, neither artillery nor regular transport could follow.

French's operations against Barberton.During all this time French had been as much absorbed in his task southward of the line as Sir R. Buller to the north. His object, to enmesh the Boers about Barberton, could best be attained by first making Carolina from Machadodorp, and by skirting eastward along the road which ran thence parallel to the railway. At Carolina he would be joined by Mahon's brigade, which, hurrying up from the west, was at Middelburg on September 3rd. On that day French, who had busily circulated reports that he was about to make a dash on Standerton and Ermelo, despatched the 1st brigade in advance along the Machadodorp—Carolina road to Zevenfontein, where he himself joined it next day with the 4th brigade. The 1st brigade then moved on, and after a slight skirmish secured the bridge which spanned the Komati river. On the 5th the division, again only slightly opposed, crossed the Komati, and by evening was well on the way to Carolina, which was entered by a reconnoitring squadron.

Sept. 6th, 1900. French occupies Carolina.On the 6th French occupied the town, being duly joined there by Brigadier-General Mahon with the following troops: Imperial Light Horse, three companies New Zealand Mounted Rifles, Lumsden's Horse, the Queensland mounted infantry and Bushmen, the 3rd mounted infantry, the 1st Suffolk regiment and 2nd Shropshire Light Infantry, a 4.7-in. Naval gun, M. battery R.H.A., two guns 66th battery R.F.A., and two Vickers-Maxims.

At Carolina French remained until September 9th; for there was much to arrange. It may here be pointed out with what difficulties bristle those wide flanking movements which appear so easy, or even obvious, that they are apt to be hastily advocated by observers far from the scene. To supply a collected and stationary army is hard enough; its wants are so vast, its channels of communication commonly so restricted. But when that army spreads its wings for a flight, bringing broad tracts of country under their shadow, every difficulty increases tenfold; for the parts in most active motion, the extremities, require nourishment in ratio to their remoteness from the source of it, and every mile adds an anxiety to Headquarters. Nor is it only a question of supply, nor even of telegraphic or signal communication, though both are essential enough. The military requisite of actual tactical touch between the widely separated parts has usually to be fulfilled; otherwise each part, lost to the others, becomes a mere expedition, wasted if it be strong, or, if it be weak, in hourly danger. Problems of such a nature had many times presented themselves for solution to every considerable commander in South Africa. They had been met with such uniform success, despite the intensified difficulties imposed by the roadless, railless, and inhospitable theatre of war, that their extreme complexity had been known only to those who overcame them. Yet further such problems were the divergent marches of Sir R. Buller and French at this moment, the one burying himself in the mountainous wilds of the Mauchberg, the other in the torrid gorges of the Komati valley, marching more than sixty miles apart, and each drawing further away from the fountain of supply, which was already heavily drained by large bodies of troops upon the railway and all along that lengthy line of communication. Add to this the diagonal movements of supporting columns, of Ian Hamilton toward the north and of Mahon on the south, each requiring sustenance, communication, orders, and advices as to times and places of concentration; each liable to delay, to interference by the enemy, by the weather, by the nature of the country, and it will be seen what an infinity of calculation must precede and accompany all such enveloping manœuvres. As the best evidence of their difficulty, it may be adduced that war has more often seen them fail than succeed; as the best proof of the excellence of the conduct and economy of the British army at this period, let it be remembered that in South Africa they more often succeeded than failed.

The difficulty of flanking movements.

In order to preserve touch with French's column, Lord Roberts now ordered Hutton, whose command since the occupation of Belfast had been split up at various defensive posts on either side of the communications, to place himself between French and the railway, and to work eastward parallel with his line of march, *via* Rietvlei and Uitkomst, to Tafel Kop and Kaapsche Hoop, the latter being two lofty buttresses of the De Kaap goldfields, which dominated Barberton and the southern tracks, much as the Mauchberg and Spitz Kop commanded the northern. Hutton, who took with him Alderson's mounted infantry corps, with J. battery R.H.A., two 15-pr. and four Vickers-Maxim guns, in all some 1,600 men, started from Belfast on the 8th September, and reached Rietvlei, intending next day to pick up Henry and his mounted infantry, whose point of departure had been Waterval Onder. Hutton's task was by no means easy; information as to roads was of the vaguest description, and without roads the difficult country between him and Tafel Kop might well prove impassable. Moreover, his march was intended to serve another and more important purpose than that of merely linking with French. The time had now come for the centre to push on; and in front of Pole-Carew, at the head of the dangerous gorge in which flowed the Elands Spruit, the enemy was reported to have entrenched himself for a last stand at Godwaan Station. If Hutton could seize Tafel Kop and Kaapsche Hoop, he would completely turn this position, and Pole-Carew would be free to advance.

On the 9th September French struck eastward from Carolina. The question of his supply was still uncertain, for the Carolina—Belfast road was too unsafe for convoys, and no man knew what tracks, if any, he or Hutton might discover threading the maze between the railway and the Komati valley. At 10 a.m. the Boers were encountered, 600 in number, with three guns, on what proved to be the first of three prepared positions, each bestriding and flanking the road at the western and eastern mouths of the Roodehoogte defile. A long day's fighting ensued. The first position, attacked in front at close range by the guns of the 66th Field battery, and turned on the south by Gordon's brigade and four guns of the R.H.A., was won in two hours. The second, a much stronger line along the hills forming the walls of the pass, took longer. An attempt to turn the Boer right was foiled by the strength of their flanking parties; and after a bombardment of two hours French deployed his two battalions of infantry for an assault, whilst Gordon's brigade, which had remained on the south, felt at the enemy's left. Before the determined advance of the Suffolk regiment the opposition gradually crumbled, the Boers being heavily punished by shrapnel as they gave way in small bands. Their own artillery, however, shooting rapidly, from the third position, nearly 9,000 yards further eastward, forbade any close pursuit, and when evening fell they were still at Silver Kop, across the path to Barberton.

On the same evening Hutton, now joined by Henry, reached Welgeluk, some twenty miles to the north. Like French, he came upon the Boers—a commando of four hundred men with three guns under A. Viljoen—soon after setting out, and he too fought all day to push them back. This he did with great vigour, inflicting considerable loss on the enemy, and, except in horses, suffering none himself. By nightfall he was in possession of a strong tactical position, from Elandshoek to Welgeluk, commanding the valleys of both the Komati and Elands rivers.

On the morning of September 10th French, disposing his forces for the expected battle, found that his opponents of the previous day had vanished, and pursued his march uneventfully. Hutton, following the crest of a lofty plateau, and still driving A. Viljoen before him, reached his first point, Uitkomst, and thence made a fruitful reconnaissance of the line Kaapsche Hoop—Tafel Kop, which was his aim. He learned that henceforth he would find no practicable roads leading eastward. Moreover, Kaapsche Hoop and Tafel Kop were divided by country of such difficulty that, so far from being *en rapport*, they could only form separate tactical centres of influence. For this, however, both were valuable; Kaapsche Hoop safeguarding the right flank of troops upon the railway, by turning the whole of the Elandspruit defile; whilst from Tafel Kop communication could be maintained with French, in the Komati valley. On September 11th, Hutton reconnoitred in both directions. Alderson felt towards Godwaan, and Henry southward along the Glades river, where he gained touch with French who, again unopposed, had made the passage of the Komati river, and halted in the fork between the Komati and Glades rivers at Hlomohlom.

<small>Sept. 12th, 1900. French forces the Nelshoogte Pass.</small>

September 12th proved a difficult day for French's men. After crossing the Glades river, the road ran through a dangerous defile known as the Nelshoogte Pass; and this it was necessary to turn by tracks so precipitous that throughout the day the troopers went afoot, whilst many of the transport oxen perished as they strove to drag their heavy loads up the rough track. Fortunately the enemy resisted but feebly. By noon the guns, pulled by sixteen horses each up a gradient of 1 in $4\frac{1}{2}$, and the infantry, crowned the head of the pass. The 1st cavalry brigade, attempting to gain the same point, was baffled by the obstacles, and had to seek an easier approach. Meanwhile Hutton, persisting by day and night, in the face of great topographical difficulties, was getting a foothold upon the Kaapsche Hoop plateau from Godwaan down to Tafel Kop. The edge of it, towards Godwaan, was in Alderson's hands by noon, and the nek between Kaapsche Hoop and Tafel Kop was occupied before dark; but many hours of descending and climbing followed. Dawn of

<small>Sept. 13th. Hutton in possession of the Kaapsche Hoop plateau.</small>

September 13th had nearly broken before Hutton himself seized the lofty township of Kaapsche Hoop, which stood like a turret on the long roof overhanging the valleys of the Komati, Crocodile and Kaap rivers, forming the key of the railway from Godwaan to Kaapmuiden, and of the countryside from Alkmaar down to Barberton.

Meanwhile, the long motionless centre was once more set in motion; Pole-Carew, both his flanks now secure, advancing to Nooitgedacht on September 12th. Next day he moved on to Godwaan, followed to Waterval Onder by Ian Hamilton, now returned to the railway after his northern expedition with Sir R. Buller. The Boers at Godwaan, three thousand in number, under General B. Viljoen, abandoned their carefully-prepared trenches, which Hutton's presence almost on their rear had now made useless. They fell back with apprehension, scarcely knowing whither to go; for a report was rife that Buller, swooping down from Spitz Kop, was already in possession of the line at Nelspruit, thereby cutting them off. But Viljoen, pressing on to fight a way through, found only a crowd of disorderly looters in the station. Thence, through scenes of ever-increasing chaos and despair, he made his way along the line. On September 15th he rejoined, at Hector Spruit, Commandant-General Botha, whom he found sick in body, but with a heart as stout as ever, and still proclaiming himself hopeful amidst the wreck of all his hopes.

The enemy breaks up.

Even the Government, the necessity of protecting which had dictated all Botha's tactics since the fall of Pretoria, had now vanished. On September 11th President Kruger, granted "six months' furlough" by the Executive Raad, took train across the border, and sought refuge with the Portuguese Governor at Lourenço Marques. Thence, after more than a month of dubious existence, part prisoner, part guest, he sailed for Europe in a man-of-war provided by the Queen of Holland. On November 22nd he landed at Marseilles, and set out on that progress through Europe from which he and his countrymen hoped so much.

Botha had now the bitter task of breaking up his army and of ordering the well-worn guns to be thrown into the Hector Spruit. He well knew that such an act marked the end of the regular warfare of the Republics; but it was inevitable. His policy of uncompromising resistance remained unchanged; but it was not now a question of future policy but of immediate escape. Botha was hemmed in, and it is due to his military talent to repeat that such a blunder was not his own, but one forced upon him, as many such have been imposed upon generals in the field, by the demands of his political superiors. To protect Kruger and his *entourage* had been neither a military nor a political object of much importance. Such an aim was trivial in comparison with the guardianship of the roads and passes, the tactical avenues to the north and south, and the sallyports to freedom. Both Government and outlets were now lost; and escape was to be made, if at all, only by stealth and in small bands, as partisans rather than as soldiers, and over tracts denied to guns and transport, and even to men on foot. Of dismounted burghers Botha was now encumbered with many hundreds; and knowing full well that he would see them no more, he ordered them to retreat on Komati Poort, to enrol themselves as frontier guards under a certain General Coetzee. They set out, many in tears, and of them about eight hundred men were next heard of in the midst of the Portuguese, who disarmed them. With them, or into the British camps, or disappearing singly into the wilderness, went many who, though still horsed, had no stomach for further fighting for a cause which appeared irretrievably lost. The remainder of the Boer forces, men well mounted, well led, and of stout heart, made for the little-known tracks leading northward into Zoutpansberg and southward along the Swaziland border, trusting to avoid both Buller and French. In the first direction went Botha and B. Viljoen with 2,500 men; in the second Smuts, leading 1,800 with six guns. Meanwhile the British army, getting rumours how its adversaries were fading away before it, was rolling on to its goal. On September 13th French, leaving his baggage, followed a rough, little-used bridle path, and appeared before Barberton so suddenly that the defending commando only made off out of one end of the town as the troopers entered it at the other. Their transport was less fortunate; fifty wagons fell into the hands of French, whose booty besides included herds of sheep and of oxen, both food and draught, large quantities of supplies of all kinds except the much needed forage, forty-four locomotive engines and two complete trains, many rifles and much ammunition, and the sum of £10,000 in gold, captured in the cart of the Landrost as he attempted to escape. A hundred burghers were likewise taken prisoners; the same number of British captives, officers and men, released; whilst in the prison a number of burghers who had been incarcerated for abiding by their oath of allegiance to the British Crown were discovered and set free. On September 14th, Pole-Carew, leaving the railway where it curved northward, took

Sept. 13th, 1900. French occupies Barberton.

THE ADVANCE TO KOMATI POORT.

his division to Kaapsche Hoop, relieving Hutton, who marched to Godwaan to replenish. Ian Hamilton, in the wake of the XIth division, reached Nooitgedacht, advancing next day (September 15th) to Godwaan, as Pole-Carew pushed on to the North Kaap river. On the 16th and 17th Pole-Carew, moving still further eastward across the goldfields, detached the 18th brigade (Stephenson) and 84th battery R.F.A. to hold the railway at Alkmaar, Nelspruit and Poort City. Behind him, Ian Hamilton came up to Kaapsche Hoop and Joubertsdal, whilst French, reconnoitring east and south from Barberton on the 17th, captured fifty more engines beyond Avoca, and located part of Smuts' evading forces at Steynsdorp. On the 18th, Pole-Carew passed Avoca and halted on the Honeybird Creek, his scouts finding a weak Boer rearguard in front of Kaapmuiden. By this time reports of the President's flight, and of the break-up of Botha's forces had reached the Field-Marshal (then at Nelspruit), and he urged his commanders forward. Pole-Carew, pressing on in great heat and over execrable tracks, was in Kaapmuiden on the 19th, seizing there 19 locomotives and 114 trucks loaded with supplies. Here he halted on the 20th, to allow his straggling and sorely tried transport and rearguard to come up; Ian Hamilton meanwhile, now only one day's march behind, reaching Honeybird Creek on this day, and the railway south of Kaapmuiden on the 21st, when Pole-Carew halted three miles east of Malalsene. Next day Ian Hamilton entered Kaapmuiden and Pole-Carew Hector Spruit, where he inherited the legacy of dismantled and submerged cannon, fourteen in number, left by the defunct regular army of the South African Republic. On the 23rd Pole-Carew covered half the remaining distance to the frontier, and Ian Hamilton toiled after to Malalsene. Next day the Guards' brigade and Henry's mounted infantry (which had been attached to Pole-Carew) fell upon Komati Poort, surrounding there no enemy indeed, for all had long fled, but an immense and chaotic mass of stores and railway material. Nine miles length of rolling stock, including eighty engines, blocked the lines and sidings, some burnt, some loaded with stores, some derailed. On the

The final stage of the advance eastward.

Sept. 24th, 1900. Occupation of Komati Poort.

Lebombo hills, commanding the railway, a 6-in. gun lay blown up; the station itself had been destroyed by fire which still fed upon the piles of coal and other inflammables stacked in the yards. Everywhere was destruction and filth, and those who witnessed it might well imagine that in these heaps of abandoned wastage they saw an emblem of the débris of a cause. Ian Hamilton, at Hector Spruit on the 24th, came up to Komati Poort on the 25th. He and Pole-Carew now lost no time in preparing to entrain their commands for return to Pretoria. At Komati there was nothing to do. No enemy lined the frontier wall, at which the British forces, impelled so strongly against it, could only gaze somewhat blankly. By September 30th all of Pole-Carew's men were on their westward journey; Ian Hamilton, leaving Smith-Dorrien's brigade at the Poort, was recalled to the capital (whither the Field-Marshal had himself returned on the 21st) on the same date; whilst French, for whom a fresh task was waiting, left Barberton on October 3rd for Machadodorp, where he arrived on the 8th.

<small>Sept. 26th, 1900. Sir R. Buller marches against Pilgrim's Rest.</small>

Meanwhile, far removed from these scenes, Sir R. Buller had resumed activity in the mountain strongholds, which he had secured in August. In pursuance of a plan suggested by him, on September 26th he marched northward from Spitz Kop with the 1st Devonshire, 1st King's Royal Rifles, 2nd Gordon Highlanders, 3rd mounted brigade, two 5-in., two 12-prs., A. battery R.H.A., No. 10 Mountain battery, 61st Howitzer battery and other guns, his object being Pilgrim's Rest, where a commando under A. J. Gravett disquieted the otherwise pacific district. In traversing Burgers Pass, a defile connecting the valleys of the Sabi and Blyde rivers, Sir R. Buller encountered the enemy, who engaged him all day in that precipitous country. The pass was well carried by the 1st Devonshire, covered by the fire of all the artillery, and in the evening bivouac was made at Geelhoutboom with the loss of five men wounded. Next day, the infantry column and baggage, more harassed by the terrible gradients than by the enemy, halted by the Blyde river, four miles short of Pilgrim's Rest. That township was, however, entered amidst a dropping rifle fire, by Dundonald with the

THE ADVANCE TO KOMATI POORT.

3rd mounted brigade, and on the 28th by the main body, which passed by it, intending to occupy a mountain situated on its north-western outskirts. A track cut up by seven difficult drifts delayed the column; but the mounted troops, led by Colonel the Hon. J. Byng, after a four hours' scramble in the dark, surmounted the mountain just before daylight, surprising and inflicting casualties on a Boer piquet which was in the act of taking up position there for the day. The height was of importance in that it commanded the cross-track to the main road to Lydenburg, to reach which was Sir R. Buller's eventual object. To get the infantry and train up its almost vertical sides took the whole of the day and night of the 29th, and on the 30th Sir R. Buller rested his force on the summit. On October 1st Sir R. Buller pushed across to Krugerspost, meeting there a mounted force, which he had ordered out from Lydenburg. Toward the evening the Boers shelled the bivouacs from the west with two heavy guns, causing with their powerful shrapnel sixteen casualties—including two officers of the Devonshire—amongst the exposed troops. Thereupon Major D. Henderson (Argyll and Sutherland Highlanders), the D.A.A.G. for Intelligence, sallied out with a party to destroy them, an enterprise recalling that in which he had taken so successful a part during the siege of Ladysmith. The guns, however, more warily guarded than Henderson's victims of a year before, were withdrawn out of reach.

Oct. 1st, 1900. Sir R. Buller at Krugerspost.

On October 2nd, the force reached Lydenburg without incident, having suffered fifty-five casualties since its departure from Spitz Kop. At Lydenburg, Sir R. Buller received orders to hand over the command of the Lydenburg—Middelburg line, and to return to Natal preparatory to leaving for England. Thus for him, after a year of hard and unremitting labour, ended another campaign, during the varied fortunes of which he had retained, unvaried, the affection and confidence of his men. No General in South Africa had more often encountered the enemy, and under more difficult conditions of spirit, numbers and country; and few had exacted more respect from their opponents.

Oct. 2nd, 1900. Sir R. Buller re-enters Lydenburg, and terminates his service in South Africa.

CHAPTER XVIII.

OPERATIONS IN THE EASTERN TRANSVAAL.*

OCTOBER AND NOVEMBER, 1900.

AT the end of September, 1900, the Intelligence department at Headquarters estimated the Boer forces in the Eastern Transvaal to number about 6,300 men and sixteen guns. As the disintegration of the commandos increased it became, however, daily more difficult to form reliable estimates of their numbers and whereabouts.

To cope with the enemy's protean organisation and fighting strength Lord Roberts partially remodelled his army, dividing it into smaller columns, and giving to each the greatest possible mobility. On October 1st the Transvaal Government, under Acting-President Schalk Burger, together with Mr. M. T. Steyn and Commandant-General Louis Botha, were reported to be at Leydsdorp in the Zoutpansberg district (see general map of South Africa, Volume I.). Botha, who had been obliged on account of illness to hand over the command of the Boer forces to General B. Viljoen after the battle of Bergendal, now resumed control. At this juncture the scattered bands of burghers became more than usually active.

Brigadier-General J. C. Barker, commanding at Middelburg, had received warning that the enemy intended to break the railway, and capture a supply train near Dalmanutha; the line was also to be attacked near Wonderfontein and Pan, simultaneously from the north and south. The presence of a laager

* See maps Nos. 48 and 49.

twenty-four miles south of Pan was notified by telegraph on September 30th to all stations between Middelburg and Machadodorp. Another party of Boers, estimated at 200 men, was reported about eight miles south of Middelburg, at 8 p.m. on October 1st. Notwithstanding the enemy's proximity to the railway and his openly avowed threat of falling upon it, Barker did not think the situation demanded the suspension of the all-important traffic. He was aware that a general order existed that trains were not to run at night; but the transport of troops from Komati Poort to Pretoria was urgent and in full progress, and outweighed the risk of the continuance of the train service during the hours of darkness. The line was carefully watched at Pan and other points; after dusk a trolley patrolled the track east of Pan. The trains, however, were unfortunately not warned of impending danger. About 9.30 p.m. a train from the east was derailed near Pan. It contained sixty Boer prisoners for Pretoria, escorted by three companies 2nd Coldstream Guards, Major H. Shute in command. After being hurled off the line the men behaved with admirable steadiness, promptly manning the ditches on both sides of the railway. Some Boers had placed themselves astride of the line behind the train and brought an enfilade fire to bear upon it. The Guards, exposed and out-flanked though they were, met the attack with well-directed volleys, and after losing twenty-six officers and men killed and wounded, drove off the burghers. The completeness of the enemy's information was shown by the fact that although the engine was bespattered with bullets the three trucks next to it were untouched, for they contained the Boer prisoners.

Oct. 1st, 1900. Attack on a train.

Middelburg, from its position, was an important centre for the protection of the railway; and Lord Roberts saw the necessity of providing a movable column there, to be in readiness to march at short notice. For this purpose Barker was instructed to employ the 3rd mounted infantry. The precaution was timely. On the following day, Barker discovered that in addition to the hostile parties already notified, another laager of 200 to 300 Boers lay north-west of Pan. There were also commandos on the Moos river, and in the angle of the Wilge and

Oliphant rivers (map 48). These accumulating dangers brought Major-General A. H. Paget's force again into the field. During the first half of October he was engaged in clearing the country between the Middelburg and Pietersburg line of railways, taking, with little fighting, 150 prisoners, fifty wagons, and 12,000 sheep. The Boers then disappeared into the bushveld to the north-east, and Paget was sent westward across the Pietersburg line.

There was every prospect of difficulties in guarding the railway from Machadodorp east to Komati Poort and the road from Middelburg to Lydenburg. On October 3rd Lord Roberts telegraphed as follows to Sir R. Buller at Lydenburg and to Lord Kitchener at Komati Poort:—

"It is proposed, as a temporary arrangement, to distribute the troops east of Middelburg as follows:—

"On the line east of Machadodorp.—18th brigade, Headquarters; Royal Scots, Welsh regiment, Warwick regiment, Yorkshire regiment, 20th battery R.F.A., Steinacker's mounted infantry and a portion of Hutton's mounted infantry.

"On the line Lydenburg—Machadodorp—Belfast—Middelburg.—Lyttelton's division; Brocklehurst's brigade forming a movable column at Machadodorp, and another at Middelburg, as well as guarding the line.

"Please let me know how these troops can best be disposed so as to hold the places named and effectually protect the line of railway.

"The various posts off the line of railway to be provided with sixty days' supplies and the others with thirty days'."

Again on October 5th the Commander-in-Chief telegraphed to Sir R. Buller:—

"I would wish you to suggest the best distribution for Lyttelton's troops, which it is proposed to divide between Lydenburg, Machadodorp, Belfast and Middelburg. There are the following heavy guns which you can use: One 5-in. gun at Middelburg, one 4.7-in. gun at Dalmanutha, one 4.7-in. gun at Helvetia. It would be advisable to arrange the distribution so that there should be two small movable columns, one at Machadodorp, the other at Middelburg."

At this date Sir R. Buller was in the act of handing over his command to Lieut.-General the Hon. N. G. Lyttelton; and he left Lydenburg on the 6th. Lyttelton then distributed his command as follows: Major-General F. W. Kitchener (7th brigade), with Headquarters at Lydenburg, in command from Lydenburg to Schoeman's Kloof, about eight miles north of Helvetia (map 49). The 1st Manchester regiment guarded the road between these two places, with posts at Witklip, Badfontein, and Schoeman's Kloof, with two guns 21st battery, two guns 42nd battery R.F.A., and one 12-pr. R.G.A. The 1st Devonshire regiment and 2nd Rifle Brigade, with the 53rd battery R.F.A., and one 5-in. gun, and the supply column, were to garrison Lydenburg, whilst the 2nd cavalry brigade (Brocklehurst) left Lydenburg for duty at Machadodorp. Lyttelton, with the 18th Hussars, two companies mounted infantry, four guns 21st battery R.F.A., one 5-in. gun, manned by 16th company Western Division R.G.A., part of the 23rd company R.E., and the 8th brigade (128 officers; 4,119 men) marched on the 9th for Middelburg, where he established his Headquarters on the 16th. The column was opposed* all the way by small bodies of the enemy, who on the 12th brought a Vickers-Maxim gun into action. Large numbers of sheep, cattle and horses were collected, besides forage, etc.

About this time the 19th brigade (Smith-Dorrien) was being withdrawn from the unhealthy low veld; and the garrisons of the posts from Waterval Onder to Komati bridge, now held almost exclusively by units of the 18th brigade, were reduced to a minimum.

On October 10th, Major-General T. E. Stephenson went out from Alkmaar Station ten miles west of Nelspruit, with 100 mounted infantry, seven companies of the 1st Essex regiment, and four guns, to burn a farm called "In de Middel," about fourteen miles up the valley of the Crocodile river. The Boers held a

*Casualties—Killed, one man; wounded, six men; missing, one man.

strong position with unassailable flanks, and reserved their fire until the mounted infantry had come to close quarters. On the approach of the infantry they retired to a fresh position further north, but still covering the farm. Owing to the lateness of the hour and the reported advance of another force of the enemy to cut off his retreat, Stephenson at nightfall directed a retirement on Houtboschhoek, five miles north-west of Godwaan Station. He had lost two killed and four wounded.

<small>Commands on the railway.</small>
On the 16th Stephenson moved with the 18th brigade to Barberton and there established his Headquarters, with his troops holding the railway from Komati Poort to Waterval Onder; and Brigadier-General J. Reeves took over command of the line from Waterval Onder to Dalmanutha.

Meanwhile Major-General Smith-Dorrien (19th brigade), some of whose units had gone to Pretoria, had made Belfast his Headquarters. On October 25th he was given command, under Lyttelton, of the railway from Dalmanutha to Pan, whence Brigadier-General J. C. Barker was in charge to Bronkhorstspruit.

So early as September 27th the Commander-in-Chief had telegraphed to Lord Kitchener, who was superintending the withdrawal of the troops from Komati Poort, that he did not think it necessary to keep the cavalry division at Barberton.

<small>Orders for the cavalry division.</small>
Instead, French might leave his two battalions of infantry there, and with the rest of his force repair to Machadodorp, thence to make for Ermelo and Bethel, and clear those districts.

On September 29th French lost the services of the Imperial Light Horse, of Mahon's mounted brigade, who were ordered to Pretoria for disbandment under the scheme which was to release twenty per cent. of the Colonial division on October 10th.

During the last few days of September the cavalry reconnoitred to the south-west of Barberton as far as the Nelshoogte Pass, and found the country in that direction clear of the enemy.

On October 3rd French left Barberton with the 1st and 4th cavalry brigades, Mahon's brigade and three companies of the 1st Suffolk regiment, the other five companies of which had gone ahead two days earlier to improve the precipitous road up to

Kaapsche Hoop. Colonel J. Spens took over command of Barberton, which was garrisoned by 300 New Zealand Mounted Rifles, one section 66th battery Royal Field artillery and the 2nd battalion The King's Shropshire Light Infantry, besides 700 dismounted men left behind by French to be sent on by rail. No enemy was met on the way to Machadodorp, and except for an appalling thunderstorm which burst over the column on the first day, killing two men, two horses and six mules, French's force arrived on the 8th without incident. Whilst it halted until the 12th, refitting, obtaining remounts and resting the jaded transport animals, the Field Intelligence gave information of parties of Boers south of the railway at the following places: On the Dalmanutha—Carolina road, about midway between the two towns, 200 men; in Carolina, sixty men; near Lake Chrissie, under T. Smuts, 800 men; four guns and two Vickers-Maxims, with a laager about thirty miles due east of Carolina.

Oct. 8th, 1900. French at Machadodorp.

On October 10th the brigades of the cavalry division were reorganised as follows :—

> 1st brigade (Brigadier-General J. R. P. Gordon).
> 6th Dragoon Guards (Carabiniers).
> 2nd Dragoons (Royal Scots Greys).
> 6th (Inniskilling) Dragoons.
> T. battery Royal Horse artillery.
> C. and J. sections Vickers-Maxims.
> Field troop Royal Engineers.
> 13th company Army Service Corps.
> 9th Bearer company.
> 11th Field hospital.

> 4th brigade (Major-General J. B. B. Dickson).
> 7th Dragoon Guards.
> Lumsden's Horse.
> Imperial Guides (transferred from the Natal army).
> O. battery Royal Horse artillery.
> E. section Vickers-Maxims.
> Half battalion 1st Suffolk regiment.
> Ox transport, 150 wagons.

Mahon's brigade (Brigadier-General B. T. Mahon).
    8th Hussars.
    14th Hussars.
    M. battery Royal Horse artillery.
    F. section Vickers-Maxims.
    Detachment Royal Engineers.
    New South Wales hospital.
    Ammunition and supply columns.

The combined strength of the three brigades was :—183 officers, 3,169 men, with sixteen 12-prs., four Vickers-Maxims, and seven machine guns. To compensate for the greatly reduced strength of the regiments, due to insufficient remounts, Lumsden's Horse were added to French's command.

The cavalry division was now to begin the clearance first of the Ermelo and Bethel districts, subsequently the country down to Heidelberg, on the Natal railway. The division was to move slowly and to do its work thoroughly. As the troops would be out of touch with the railway during the operations, fourteen days' food and forage were to be carried, one day's supply on man and horse, two days' in regimental mule-wagons, three days' in brigade mule-wagons, and eight days' in the ox-wagons of the supply park.

French's orders for the march, which he issued on the evening of the 10th, provided for the advance on Ermelo,* *via* Twyfelaar and Carolina, in two columns with a reserve. Mahon's and Gordon's brigades, with brigade supply columns, would leave Machadodorp on the morning of October 12th and 13th respectively; the brigadiers were to dispose their men to cover a wide front, and to arrange to reach Ermelo on the 18th. Dickson would start on the second date, taking the ox supply column, and point on Carolina, arranging each day's march according to the country and the condition of the transport animals.

Mahon left Machadodorp at 7 a.m. on the 12th, *via* Dalmanutha for Geluk, where he arrived at 3 p.m. On approaching

* See map No. 49.

OPERATIONS IN THE EASTERN TRANSVAAL. 429

Geluk a small party of the enemy began to shoot from the ridge in front, but retired on two guns being brought into action. Their main body was seen to be holding a position in strength on the Vanwyksvlei ridge. At 4.30 next morning the brigade stood to arms. Fifteen minutes later the enemy threw shell into the camp from a hill south-west of Geluk, near the Vanwyksvlei ridge, and immediately afterwards opened a heavy musketry upon the front and left flank of the British camp. Mahon soon had his own guns in action and his outposts reinforced, disposing his force facing west on a high ridge on the left bank of the Geluk stream. The south end of this ridge was very broken, and covered with rocks, amongst which the burghers crept round to attack the right flank. About 5.45 a.m. the advanced parties of the 8th and 14th Hussars on the front and left were hard pressed, and finally driven in upon the trenches, a piquet of two officers and ten men of the 8th Hussars losing an officer and two men killed, and the same number wounded. The transport, which had been inspanned at the first shot, was now sent to the rear in the direction of Dalmanutha, escorted by a squadron. The firing increased in severity in front and on both flanks; by 6.15 a.m. it had become intense; but it was imperative that the position should be maintained to allow the transport to make good its retreat. Not until 7.30 a.m. were the wagons in safety, when Mahon decided upon a retirement. He could only communicate his predicament by the most circuitous means. There was no sun for the heliograph; an aide-de-camp had to be sent to Belfast, whence a message was despatched to French informing him of the situation. At 7.45 the guns were withdrawn to a position in rear, covered by the Field troop Royal Engineers. The cavalry were then ordered to evacuate the position; they fell back slowly, each regiment covering the other alternately. Manœuvring in this manner with great skill and steadiness they successfully performed the difficult feat of disengaging from a defensive action.

By 8.45 a.m. the transport had crossed the Waai Kraal Spruit on the Dalmanutha road, along which Major E. Rhodes, Royal Berkshire regiment, had sent from the garrison of Dalmanutha,

Oct. 12th, 1900. French marches southward.

Oct. 13th, 1900. Affair at Geluk.

which he commanded, one and a half companies of infantry to assist the retreating convoy ; and Mahon, relieved of all further anxiety about it, took up a new position on a ridge, south-west of Waai Kraal Farm, near a point where it was crossed by the road to Geluk. The 8th Hussars were on the right, the 14th Hussars on the left, the guns posted on each flank. The enemy's pressure now ceased. The Boers themselves had lost heavily ; Mahon's casualties—three officers and six men killed, four officers and twenty-five men wounded—were less than might have been expected in a force recoiling from the embrace of 1,100 horsemen, armed with four guns, and led by General T. Smuts.*

On receipt of Mahon's message, French directed Gordon, who had left Machadodorp that morning at 4.30 and was then nearing the Komati, to secure the passage over that river and to reconnoitre well to the west. Gordon ordered two squadrons of the 7th Dragoon Guards and the Vickers-Maxims, at Zevenfontein, to cross to the right bank of the Komati river and check any approach of the enemy from the direction of Geluk. French also sent Colonel D. Haig to find out Mahon's situation. At 11.15 a.m. this officer reported all quiet on Mahon's front, and later (12.45 p.m.) that the Boers were retiring on Vanwyksvlei, followed by a portion of Mahon's troops. Gordon then resumed his original line of march.

Mahon bivouacked near Welgevonden with his left thrown forward towards the Komati river. Gordon, who had crossed the river farther eastward, halted for the night at Bonnefoi.

At daybreak on October 14th Mahon sent out patrols of the 14th Hussars, one to the right rear of the camp and one to the front. The former was fired upon, but the enemy declined to meet a stronger force with guns sent against him. The patrol in front passed over the ground on which the fighting had taken place the day before, and at 9 a.m. reported all clear. About an hour afterwards the whole brigade moved forward, leaving the baggage in camp. But the Boers were too strong to be

* Major E. D. Brown, 14th Hussars, was awarded the Victoria Cross for three separate acts of gallantry performed during the engagement.

moved. Once more the advance guard found itself overmatched, and at 1.30 p.m. was driven back on the main body. Mahon, thinking he was blocked, withdrew his force, fell back upon his camp, and communicated with French. He was informed in reply that nothing more than a rearguard opposed him, and that a strong force from Carolina would be sent to Twyfelaar, where Mahon was to march at daylight on the morrow.

Gordon, who had established his outposts the night before near Everard, left that place at 3 a.m. on the 14th for Carolina, which he reached and found deserted early in the day. The enemy had retreated to the south and south-east. Gordon had earlier detached the Carabiniers, with a section of guns, to hold the right bank of the Komati river, to assist the passage of Mahon, who crossed next morning, and continued his march unmolested to Vaalbult, where he bivouacked. Dickson, following Gordon, arrived at Carolina at 9.30 p.m. on the 14th, with the ox transport, and with three wagons of ammunition, which had been sent from Machadodorp to replace that expended by Mahon on the 13th. The escort was fired on, and had two men wounded. <small>Oct. 14th, 1900. Carolina occupied.</small>

On October 16th the entire division moved out of Carolina, covering a front of fifteen miles, Mahon's brigade on the right, Gordon's on the left; Dickson's brigade, with the heavy transport, followed behind Mahon, with whom French had made his Headquarters. Mahon's march was unopposed throughout the day, and he halted for the night at Roodebloem. Dickson camped about three miles north of that place. Gordon, who followed the Lake Chrissie road, was ordered to halt about ten miles south-by-east of Carolina, which he did shortly after midday. About 2 p.m. the outpost line, which was held by the 6th (Inniskilling) Dragoons, was boldly attacked by Mahon's former adversary, General Smuts, with the Ermelo commando, some 700 strong, one gun and a Vickers-Maxim. The foremost dragoons were driven back as far as their supports with the loss of an officer and five men killed, three officers and seventeen men wounded. During the afternoon Gordon's <small>Oct. 16th, 1900. Boers attack the outposts.</small>

brigade was called in four miles westward, within nearer hail of the main body of the division.

On the 17th Mahon's brigade, covering Dickson's front, marched unopposed, and camped at a farm three miles to the south of Klipstapel. Dickson's brigade and the supply column advanced on Klipstapel, the right flank and rear being subjected to constant annoyance. Gordon, who had been lightly engaged with the enemy all day, bivouacked near the source of the Vaal about six miles east of Klipstapel. Towards evening when all was quiet, and the troops resting, about 300 Boers were observed collecting behind a ridge south-east of the bivouac. The warning, so rarely given, was accepted. The outpost line was at once strengthened by a regiment and a Vickers-Maxim. As the sun sank below the horizon the enemy suddenly charged the piquets. The troops were fully prepared and met the attack with a blast of fire which threw the Boers back, and laid low eight of their number. Three men of the Carabiniers were wounded.

Oct. 17th, 1900. Renewed attack on the outposts.

On the following day the whole force marched in the same order as before. The route of Mahon and Dickson lay *via* Kaffirspruit, five miles north-west of Ermelo. Mahon's column was fired at by individual burghers, but otherwise unhampered. Gordon's left and rear were harassed by about 300 of the enemy with a gun and a Vickers-Maxim; but they were kept off, one man of the Carabiniers being wounded.

Oct. 18th, 1900. Ermelo occupied.

About 3 p.m. forty of French's Scouts* entered Ermelo, and found that the burghers had quitted the town the day before. French received from Mr. A. B. Fisher, manager of the local branch of the Natal Bank, £550 in gold and £785 in notes on the National Bank of the South African Republic. A few supplies were found in the stores, but the town was almost bare of foodstuffs. French made Ermelo his Headquarters for the night, and Gordon occupied the slope north of the town, placing a line of outposts south and east.

---

* A body of 100 irregular troops, who performed the duties of divisional cavalry to Lieut.-General French.

OPERATIONS IN THE EASTERN TRANSVAAL. 433

Early on the 19th French marched on Bethel.* His movement, which hitherto had been in a southerly direction, now turned to due west. The order of march also was slightly altered, Dickson's brigade leading, followed by his own and the transport of the other two brigades, whilst Mahon covered the right (north) flank of the long convoy, and Gordon the left and rear. About 6 a.m. Dickson was opposed by a small commando occupying a strong position on a kopje commanding the road. Lumsden's Horse and O. battery Royal Horse artillery soon drove the enemy off, capturing two of their number. Later in the day Gordon called upon Dickson to disperse small parties threatening his right, and the 7th Dragoon Guards and O. battery successfully dealt with them, having only one man wounded. Gordon's troops, however, were at one period annoyed considerably by a Field and an automatic gun which shelled the left. Here, too, the enemy was eventually beaten off, but not before the Carabiniers had lost Second-Lieut. N. L. Calvert and one man killed, eleven men wounded and two missing. Mahon was unopposed during the day.

The next day (20th) Gordon's rearguard was fired on continually, the Boers coming so close that they captured a tonga ambulance with its medical officer and four stretcher bearers. The personnel was subsequently released; but the enemy kept the ambulance and horses. About 1 p.m. Gordon was sent forward, with his brigade and the mule transport, to occupy Bethel, which he did at 4 p.m., leaving Mahon's brigade to take over the duties of rearguard and to endure the incessant skirmishing in that quarter. The casualties in the division were one man killed and two wounded. French entered Bethel without opposition, and disposed his division as a cordon of outposts around the town. A telegram received from Lord Roberts congratulated him upon the good work done, and directed him to scatter the commandos which were threatening the railway from the east, between Heidelberg and Irene. The troops remained at Bethel on the 21st, their outposts under fire all day, and the Vickers-Maxim guns constantly engaged in keeping the

Oct. 20th, 1900. Bethel occupied.

* See map No. 48.

enemy's sharpshooters at arm's length. The only casualty was the loss of a sergeant of Carabiniers, whom two Boers, who rode close in to the line, dressed in khaki uniform, shot dead as they were hailed as comrades by the unfortunate non-commissioned officer.

On October 22nd the division marched at 4 a.m., having Heidelberg as its goal, Dickson's brigade as before screening the front, Gordon's covering the left and rear, and Mahon's the right (northern) flank. A commando of 300 Boers hung on the rearguard when it cleared Bethel. Hoping to give them a lesson the officer commanding the Carabiniers concealed his men behind a ridge and ordered them to reserve their fire until the enemy came within 400 yards. The burghers pushed on unsuspectingly; a smart fire at close range was poured into them in front, and an officer with a few men charged their flank. They broke and fled with much loss, and thereafter were more wary in pressing the rearguard. Another incident of the march was more questionable. French, who was anxious to alleviate the lot of his sick and wounded, sent an ox convoy of fourteen wagons, containing sixty-two officers and men, to Standerton under the Red Cross. When it was about ten miles out from Bethel it was stopped by the enemy, who doubtless suspected the General of trying to disembarrass himself of some of his troublesome transport. At any rate the Boers crowded the men into six wagons, and appropriated the remaining eight. On October 24th French was in heliographic communication with Greylingstad.

The remaining days' marches up to the arrival of the force at Heidelberg call for no special description; for beyond the incessant and dangerous sharpshooting nothing noteworthy occurred. Bands varying in numbers and boldness clung to the rear of the column all the way to Heidelberg; and though they displayed more caution than in the earlier portion of the march, their presence entailed such sleepless vigilance by day and night, that French's troops were practically on the defensive throughout.

At Heidelberg, on October 26th, ended one of the most

arduous, and in some respects the most expensive, operations of the campaign. The division had marched a distance of 220 miles, through drenching thunderstorms, over heavy roads and swollen spruits, with a long train and enfeebled oxen, and continually beset by a confident and aggressive enemy. In men the casualties had not been excessive, five officers and fourteen other ranks having been killed, seven officers and seventy-two other ranks wounded; and, though the Boers never ceased to watch for stragglers, only two men were missing. Against these losses were to be set nine Boer prisoners, forty-nine surrenders, and an unknown but not insignificant number slain or wounded in action.

Oct. 26th, 1900. French reaches Heidelberg.

But the severity of the strain upon the force was best to be gauged by the expenditure in animals. No less than 1,230 oxen, 128 mules, and 320 horses were lost outright, and of the rest 286 were unfit for further work. Fifty-five wagons had to be abandoned for want of draught. Nor did the moral effect of the operation add to the credit side of the British account. The results achieved fell far short of the wastage incurred. The enemy encountered on the road saw the force disappear into Heidelberg with feelings rather of exultation than of relief; for the veld behind it was strewn with its débris, and they plumed themselves that they had driven a whole division of cavalry to seek shelter under the guns of the railway guards.

At Heidelberg French received orders to leave his ox transport behind, and to march *via* Springs to Pretoria to refit. There, on November 12th, the cavalry division was finally broken up. French, whilst retaining command of all the cavalry in South Africa, was appointed to the Johannesburg district, and took with him thither the 1st (Gordon) cavalry brigade, the 2nd (Broadwood) being in the neighbourhood of Magato Nek. Of the remaining brigades of the original cavalry division, the 3rd was split up amongst the various columns now operating from Bloemfontein, and the 4th (Dickson) remained in Pretoria refitting

The cavalry division is broken up.

Returning now to the eastern railway; during October several small parties of the enemy attempted to destroy the line.

Fighting on the Delagoa line.

On the 5th a dynamite cartridge was exploded by a train between Brugspruit and Balmoral, fortunately with no other damage than the derailment of the engine. Brigadier-General J. C. Barker and his few troops were kept busily employed day and night endeavouring to frustrate these minor attacks. On the 7th he sent out from Middelburg the 3rd mounted infantry, accompanied by four guns of the Royal Horse artillery, to head off a detachment of the enemy approaching from the south. The Boers had obtained too great a start, and made good their retreat on Bethel, the troops exchanging a few shots with their rearguard. Again, on the 11th, another small column under Lieut.-Colonel T. D. B. Evans, Canadian Mounted Rifles, was sent north from Pan Station to disperse a band ten miles from the railway. The column encountered the party, shelled it heavily, causing several casualties, and pushed it back towards the bushveld. Evans then returned to Pan with the loss of two men wounded. On October 26th a mounted infantry patrol, from the IVth division, was ambushed near the railway about seven miles south-west of Middelburg, and had one man killed, six men wounded, and four captured.

On October 25th Major-General F. W. Kitchener, having received intelligence of a Boer laager, 400 strong, under Commandant Erasmus, near Krugerspost (map 49), marched from Lydenburg by night with a small column of all arms,* and at dawn occupied the valley. The enemy, who were holding a bridge across the Spekboom river, were driven back at daylight and the laager captured. Three shells from the 5-in. gun and Howitzers were then fired over the town of Krugerspost, and a flag of truce was sent in to demand the surrender of the commando. The town, however, was occupied by women and children only, the men having escaped to the hills; but the summons was delivered to Erasmus, who pleaded that in the cause of humanity the town might be spared. He added that, as he was only in temporary command, he had no authority to order a surrender. As nothing was to be gained by bombarding

---

* Four guns R.F.A., two Howitzers, two companies M.I., ten companies infantry, six machine guns.

Krugerspost the force returned to Lydenburg without loss or profit. The Boer casualties were a few killed, two prisoners and several wounded.

On the 30th Schoeman's laager had been located on the hills to the west of Lydenburg, and a "Long Tom" was also reported as in position there. Hoping to capture both gun and camp Kitchener assembled two small columns of all arms, one* to march from Lydenburg after 8.30 p.m., the other† from Witklip at 11 p.m. Soon after daylight on the 31st the two columns joined hands on the hills overlooking the enemy's camp, which was immediately abandoned, the "Long Tom" and another gun being removed. Kitchener pursued for a short distance, and shelled, at a range of 5,000 yards, Schalk Burger's camp, which had come into view. The force then retired (about 9 a.m.), the enemy attempting no pursuit, and firing only a few long-range shots, by which four men were wounded, one mortally. The captures consisted of the contents of the laager, large quantities of ammunition, telegraph and telephone instruments, and many tents. One prisoner only was taken.

Towards the end of October Mr. Steyn, having concluded his mission with the South African Republic Government, reached Nylstroom (map 48), on his way back from the east to the Orange River Colony, attended by Commandant-General L. Botha. There the officials were joined by General B. Viljoen, who had left Pietersburg‡ about October 27th. A large popular meeting was held; speeches were made by both Mr. Steyn and Botha exhorting the burghers "to do their duty towards their country and themselves, and to remain faithful to the cause, as the existence of the nation depended on it." Mr. Steyn immediately afterwards departed westward to join De la Rey. Later in the day a Council of War was held under the direction of the Commandant-General. Plans were discussed and arrangements

marginal note: The enemy's plans in the Eastern Transvaal.

* Four guns R.F.A., two Howitzers, one 5-in. gun, one company M.I., nine companies infantry, three machine guns.

† One gun R.F.A., one 12-pr. Q.F. gun R.G.A., one squadron 19th Hussars, one company M.I., two companies infantry, one Vickers-Maxim, one Colt gun.

‡ See general map of South Africa, Volume I.

made for the future. It was decided that Viljoen should march with his commando to Witnek, about nineteen miles north of Bronkhorstspruit, in the Pretoria district, as " the state of the commandos in those parts was reported to be very sad." These were the Boksburg and Pretoria commandos, which had lost heavily in prisoners of war and deserters. On October 31st the Intelligence Department had news of Viljoen thirty-seven miles north of Balmoral, with a force of 1,200 men, which included parts of Erasmus' and Dirksen's commandos.

The continued wet weather, which rendered the bushveld uninhabitable, had much to do with the increase of the hostile forces north of the Delagoa railway. On November 6th they began to show activity by pushing forward their patrols to within five miles of the line, between Bronkhorstspruit and Balmoral. Laagers were reported at Rhenoster Kop, eight miles due east of Rhenosterpoort, west of the Wilge river, and a commando under Spruyt was in the Steelpoort River valley. To the north-east of Pretoria Erasmus, Piet Uys, T. Pretorius and Dan Opperman, with about 400 men, were moving south from Zusterhoek, *viâ* Rhenosterpoort, in the hope of capturing a train to replenish the failing stores of food and clothing. Besides these there were numerous small bands roving both north and south of the railway. To Viljoen was entrusted the work of re-organising these widely scattered and incoherent bands.

Columns from the Delagoa railway.

On November 1st Lyttelton sent a small column* under Lieut.-Colonel R. L. Payne, 1st Royal Inniskilling Fusiliers, from Middelburg to find a party of Boers reported to be laagered about fourteen miles to the south-east of that place, and to drive in cattle and sheep. After two days of continuous rain and thick mist the column had to return without having effected its object. Payne's rearguard was attacked during the retirement, but the enemy was shaken off without difficulty, the column losing one man killed and one wounded.

At the same time, forty miles to the east, Major-General Smith-Dorrien (19th brigade) was engaged in protecting the railway,

* Three hundred 18th Hussars and M.I., four guns G. battery R.H.A., 500 1st Royal Inniskilling Fusiliers.

OPERATIONS IN THE EASTERN TRANSVAAL.

which was threatened between Belfast and Machadodorp. About the end of October a large Boer force was marked south of Vanwyksvlei, a place which had already been the fighting ground of Sir R. Buller, French and Mahon. On the evening of November 1st Smith-Dorrien sallied out of Belfast to attack this laager and another five miles further south on the Carolina road (map 49). The force was divided into two columns. Smith-Dorrien himself led the left, which consisted of:—

The 5th Lancers, Canadian Mounted Rifles, two guns 84th battery Royal Field artillery, one 5-in. gun Royal Garrison artillery, one section Royal Engineers, 1st battalion Gordon Highlanders.

The right column was commanded by Lieut.-Colonel J. Spens (The King's Shropshire Light Infantry), and consisted of:—

The Royal Canadian Dragoons, two guns 84th battery Royal Field artillery, two guns Royal Canadian artillery, one 5-in. gun Royal Garrison artillery, S. section of Vickers-Maxims, 2nd battalion The King's Shropshire Light Infantry.

The left column marched *via* Bergendal southward along the ridge to Frischgewaagd; the right was directed upon Vanwyksvlei, *via* Leeuwbank (map 49). The force started at 7.15 p.m. and marched through the night in a blizzard of mingled snow and rain, in which horses lay down and perished. Both columns reached Vanwyksvlei about 7 a.m. on the 2nd, the troops suffering greatly from exhaustion. In consequence of their condition, and the still tempestuous weather, Smith-Dorrien felt compelled to abandon the final part of his programme, the attack on the more distant and main laager at Witkloof. The enemy at Vanwyksvlei, unprepared for resistance, disappeared; only a party near Welgevonden hotly engaged the Canadian Mounted Rifles, who had become somewhat detached; but they too vanished on guns being sent to the left flank. As soon as the columns began their retirement, however, the Boers fell upon that of Smith-Dorrien, which was now on the right. They boldly pressed the rearguard, composed of one squadron 5th Lancers, two guns 84th battery and two companies Gordon Highlanders, who successfully repulsed them. Belfast was reached at 3 p.m.,

Smith-Dorrien's operations.

the infantry having covered twenty-eight miles in twenty hours in terrible weather. The casualties were one officer and one man killed; two officers and thirteen men wounded.

On November 6th Smith-Dorrien made a second attempt in the same direction. This time he took with him one squadron 5th Lancers, Royal Canadian Dragoons, Canadian Mounted Rifles (in all 250 mounted men), four guns 84th battery Royal Field artillery, two guns Royal Canadian artillery, two 5-in. guns Royal Garrison artillery, S. section Vickers-Maxims, one section Royal Engineers, and 900 infantry of the 1st battalion Suffolk regiment (four companies), and 2nd battalion The King's Shropshire Light Infantry.

<small>Nov. 6th, 1900. Fighting by Smith-Dorrien.</small>

The column left Belfast at 3.30 a.m. and marched on Witkloof and Leliefontein (map 49), where laagers were known to be. At 7.40 a.m. the Boers appeared at Eerstelingfontein (map 49) and hovered around the column, which bore them back across the Vanwyksvlei Spruit, until they turned at bay on an immensely strong position extending along the Komati river from Witkloof to Leliefontein. Smith-Dorrien at once opened fire with his guns, sending the Shropshire Light Infantry forward to hold the Boers in front. The ground was very open and the troops much exposed; but four companies fought their way up to within 500 yards of the Boer line, where they held on for over three hours under a heavy fire. Two guns of the 84th battery were also under a galling musketry at 1,400 yards range.

Smith-Dorrien had now great difficulty in discovering the enemy's flank; manœuvre as he would, everywhere riflemen appeared in front of the troops. At 2 p.m. he detached the Royal Canadian Dragoons, with two guns Royal Canadian artillery, supported by two Vickers-Maxims and two companies of the Suffolk regiment (Major W. R. De la p. Lloyd), to work round the Boers' left. At 4 p.m. the Suffolk companies, ably handled, obtained a lodgment on that flank, completely turning the enemy who were confronting the Shropshire Light Infantry. The result was instantaneous; the stronghold was hurriedly evacuated and all the commandos fled across the Komati river. The troops then took possession of the position, and advanced along

OPERATIONS IN THE EASTERN TRANSVAAL. 441

the high ground to Leliefontein where they bivouacked at sunset. Their casualties were six killed and twenty wounded, nearly all sustained by the Shropshire Light Infantry during their long blockade of the hostile front. Throughout the day the enemy's convoy had been seen to be crossing the Komati river, and the determined fighting of the burghers had been chiefly to secure its safe retreat. The wagons, collected behind a hill on the opposite side of the river, about 9,000 yards distant, were driven out and along the road to Carolina by the shells of the 5-in. guns.

At 7.30 the next morning, instead of crossing the Komati river and making the expected descent on Carolina, Smith-Dorrien misled the enemy by turning north-east along the left bank of the river. As soon as the Boers were assured of this several hundreds of them raced down to the river to re-occupy their position of the day before. In this they were frustrated by Lieut.-Colonel T. D. B. Evans with the Canadian Mounted Rifles and Major E. Guinness with two guns of the 84th battery, who formed for the day the mobile reserve which it was Smith-Dorrien's invariable habit to keep at his personal disposal for such emergencies. These galloped about two miles and seized the key of the position before the burghers, of whom they held some 300 fast in the river bed. At the same time the 5-in. guns came into action, and made destructive practice at the Boers, who were exposed in mass as they descended the open slopes from Carolina. Large numbers were visible, and it was evident that the commandos had been considerably reinforced, possibly beyond the powers of Smith-Dorrien's small force to cope with them. He at once sent three companies of the Shropshire Light Infantry to strengthen Evans and Guinness in their command of the river. The Boers quickly realised that nothing could be done against this strongly-posted force ; they began, instead, to work their way to the north-east down the right bank of the river. Smith-Dorrien perceived the threat to his flank and line of retreat, and ordered Spens and the advance guard to occupy the high ground at Vanwyksvlei with the 5th Lancers and a section of the 84th

Nov. 7th, 1900. Sharp affair on the Komati river.

battery, whilst the infantry, baggage and heavy guns withdrew, covered by Lieut.-Colonel F. L. Lessard and the Royal Canadian Dragoons with their Colt gun and two Canadian Field guns.

As soon as the transport began to file out of camp the Boers, scenting a retreat, openly crowded round the rearguard and fiercely assailed it. By 10.30 a.m. the convoy had withdrawn sufficiently for the rearguard to fall back. The Boers were upon it in a moment, some 200 of them charging up to within seventy yards, firing wildly from the saddle. The guns were only saved by the devotion of Lieut. H. Z. C. Cockburn and his troop of Royal Canadian Dragoons, of whom sixteen were captured, the rest killed or wounded. Foiled in this onslaught the Boers for the next two hours kept up a running fight. At 1.30 p.m. they again made a desperate effort to snatch the guns, galloping in as near as 200 yards. Once more disaster was averted by a fine stand by another party of Royal Canadian Dragoons under Lieut. R. E. W. Turner. At this crisis the Colt gun, in charge of Sergeant E. J. Holland, which was doing invaluable work covering the retreat of the Field guns, was almost surrounded; the horse was exhausted, so Holland coolly detached the carriage and rode off with the gun into safety.*

The enemy's bolt was now shot; and though they still followed the column, they kept fully 2,000 yards away and no more seriously menaced the troops. By 4 p.m. they had given up the pursuit, and the force encamped at Blyvooruilzicht (map 49), on the road to Belfast.

In spite of the close fighting the casualties during the day were small; for most of the Boer firing had been random shooting from horseback, intended more to intimidate than to do execution. The rearguard had only two killed and twelve wounded, all Canadians, including Lieuts. Cockburn, Turner and J. H. Elmsley. The men of the Royal Canadian Dragoons who had sacrificed themselves to allow the guns to escape, were well treated by the enemy, and released after a few hours. The Boer losses were heavier than those of their opponents, especially in officers.

* Lieuts. Cockburn and Turner and Sergeant Holland were awarded Victoria Crosses for gallantry on this occasion.

OPERATIONS IN THE EASTERN TRANSVAAL. 443

Amongst their killed were General Joachim Fourie, Commandant H. Prinsloo and Field-Cornet De Lange of Carolina; whilst Commandant J. Grobelaar was wounded. *Boer losses.*

The Commander-in-Chief congratulated Smith-Dorrien's troops upon their conduct on the 6th and 7th, expressing especial admiration of the rearguard action of Lieut.-Colonel Lessard and his men. Nevertheless, the operations had had an unexpected result; and Smith-Dorrien represented that to drive the strong and well-led Carolina and Ermelo commandos from this district, two columns were needed, each with at least 500 mounted men. Lord Roberts agreed, and telegraphed that arrangements would be made with Lyttelton for a corresponding increase of Smith-Dorrien's mounted force.

On November 13th Smith-Dorrien took another column of 1,200 horse and foot* from Belfast, this time to the north of the railway, his object being to co-operate with a similar force from Middelburg in driving back the Boers from the line between Belfast and Middelburg stations, and clearing that part of the Steelpoort River valley and adjacent country of cattle and sheep. The troops marched at 6 a.m. and about 7.30 collided with the Boer outposts, the mounted troops becoming engaged until 9 a.m. on the Langkloof heights, six miles north of Belfast. From this point the direction was changed to the north-west, into the valley of the Steelpoort river. In the afternoon a patrol on the left flank, engaged in driving cattle, was fired on by invisible sharpshooters, who were silenced by shell fire. The force bivouacked at Schoongezicht Farm (map 49). Up to this point no communication had been established with the column from Middelburg. *Nov. 13th, 1900. Smith-Dorrien raids north of the Delagoa railway.*

At 7 a.m. on the 14th Smith-Dorrien resumed his march, having been delayed for two hours in getting his transport across a difficult swamp. When about one and a half miles from camp

* 5th Lancers, eighty men and one Maxim; 3rd mounted infantry, eighty men; Royal Canadian Dragoons, eighty men and two Colt guns; Canadian Mounted Rifles, sixty men; total, 300 mounted men under Lieut.-Colonel A. C. King. Four guns 84th battery Royal Field artillery; two guns Royal Canadian artillery; S. section Vickers-Maxims; two 5-in. guns Royal Garrison artillery; one section Royal Engineers; 1st battalion Royal Irish regiment, 400 men; 1st battalion Gordon Highlanders, 500 men.

he found the enemy posted across his line of march. The mounted men soon drove them back, whereupon they took up another and much stronger line about five miles to the north, from which they repulsed the advanced troops with a well sustained fire. For an hour all the guns concentrated their fire upon the position; the mounted men were sent to turn the enemy's right flank, whilst four companies Royal Irish regiment and two companies Gordon Highlanders went forward to attack, and quickly cleared the road. Several farms in the neighbourhood used as depôts by the Boers were then burnt. During the morning the guns of the Middelburg column were heard. Later in the day communication by signal was opened between the columns, which were about seven miles apart. Whilst the main body of Smith-Dorrien's force encamped south of Witpoort, the mounted men went into the town and destroyed the mill and some houses. To deceive the enemy a report was circulated in Witpoort that the column would pass through that place on the morrow. The ruse was successful; for while the Boers assembled in the rough ground near the town, the column moved unopposed south-by-east to Witbooy and thence to Swartkopjes. Some difficult country was cleared, a large number of cattle driven in, and two prisoners taken without interference; but if the enemy had been deluded they were likewise left undamaged at Witpoort.

On the 16th, leaving the camp at Swartkopjes in charge of Colonel F. Macbean with four companies of infantry and two Field guns, Smith-Dorrien, with the remainder of the force, started at 4 a.m. for Dullstroom. He arrived with slight opposition, destroyed the mill, and returned to camp, having had one man killed. The column returned to Belfast on the 17th.

Smith-Dorrien returns to the line.

The force from Middelburg, commanded by Lieut.-Colonel G. D. Carleton, 1st Leicestershire regiment, left early on the morning of November 13th.* During the 13th the enemy hovered in front and on the flanks, especially the left; but a few rounds from the guns dispersed them. Towards the end of

---

* 18th Hussars, 200 men; 21st battery R.F.A.; one 5-in. gun R.G.A.; 1st Leicester regiment, 600 men; 1st King's Royal Rifles, 400 men.

OPERATIONS IN THE EASTERN TRANSVAAL.

the day's march a party of about 100 Boers closed upon the rearguard for about ten minutes as it entered the valley near Elandslaagte, ten miles due north of Pan Station (map 48). They were soon put to flight by the Vickers-Maxim gun, and the troops bivouacked in the village. At 4.30 a.m. on November 14th the force marched again, meeting with slight opposition from 150 Boers, who were driven off by gun fire. Later in the day, as the column left the main Witpoort road, a ridge was seen to be occupied by about 500 to 600 Boers, who greeted the advancing cavalry with musketry, but were easily dispersed by the artillery. The cavalry and 1st King's Royal Rifles then occupied the crest and opened fire on the Boers in the valley below. Carleton had no casualties. On the 15th and 16th all farms in the neighbourhood were visited and much corn and cattle collected. The column returned to Middelburg on the 17th without further incident. A third small column, under Lieut.-Colonel Payne, which had gone out from Middelburg on the 15th to block the roads leading south from the zones of Smith-Dorrien and Carleton, returned also on the 17th.

Beyond the movement of troops along the line as occasion required, the arrival of an armoured train at Belfast with two Naval 12-pr. guns, and the departure of the Canadian units for Pretoria, nothing of importance occurred during the next few days.

On November 19th two daring raids on the railway were carried out simultaneously at Balmoral and Wilge River stations by the commandos under General B. Viljoen. Viljoen fixed on a post on a kopje to the south-west of Balmoral, garrisoned by two officers and forty-nine men 2nd battalion of The Buffs. Believing that the entrenchments contained a gun which he would be able to use against the station and other posts, he led the attack here in person. The sides of the kopje were in places very steep; the summit was defended by stone breastworks, separated by intervals of 150 to 200 yards. About 3.30 a.m., just as the men were standing to arms, the enemy, about 300 strong, who had surrounded the hill under cover of darkness and mist, crept in between the sangars, poured volleys from all sides, and

Nov. 19th, 1900. Boers attack posts on the railway.

rushing in amongst the ranks overwhelmed them. Three men escaped, six were killed, thirteen wounded and the remainder were captured. The Boers then descended the northern slope towards the railway with the intention of destroying the line; but fell back on being confronted by another detachment of The Buffs. During their retirement they suffered several casualties under a severe cross-fire from a small piquet at an adjacent farm.

At the same time the hill immediately south of Balmoral was feebly attacked, and the girder bridge two miles east of Balmoral was also assailed; the enemy were in both cases beaten off by the half companies on guard.

During the night the Boers had placed a gun on a kopje 3,000 yards north of Balmoral, and a Vickers-Maxim on another hill 3,600 yards north-east. At dawn they bombarded the station, damaging the buildings and breaking the telegraph instrument. One of these guns soon burst; the other jammed, and the fire of the 6-in. Howitzer scattered the burghers, who about 10 a.m. made off for their old haunt on the Wilge river, about ten miles north of Balmoral. The British casualties were six men killed and thirteen wounded; one officer and twenty-four men were taken prisoners, but released the same day. Five unwounded and four wounded Boers were captured, one of whom reported their losses at sixty killed and wounded. Generals Lyttelton and Barker, after investigating the affair on the south-west kopje, exonerated the officers and men of The Buffs, more than a third of whom were shot down at once, the remainder being overcome by superior numbers. It was clear, nevertheless, that the post had been insufficiently fortified, and that the gaps between the sangars were too wide. It was not, indeed, yet fully understood how narrow must be the loophole, and how strong the wall, to keep out and check an enemy who was fast adding resolution to cunning as his fortunes grew more broken. The Boers had broken the railway and telegraph lines between Balmoral and Brugspruit; but these were quickly repaired. Reinforcements, summoned from Middelburg by signal, arrived during the afternoon.

The attack on the garrison at Wilge River station was carried out by Commandant Muller with about 300 men and two guns. At dawn a piquet was driven in from the ridge which commanded the line from north of the river. The entire crest was then occupied by the enemy, who opened fire with guns and rifles upon the station buildings and entrenchments; but, thanks to the excellence of their defences, the troops suffered only one casualty. About 150 burghers then approached within medium range of the station, but were met by a rifle and shell fire which they were unable to face; and after their own guns had injured the station buildings and telegraph wires they withdrew at 1 p.m. The railway was found to be damaged east and west of the Wilge river; but communication was speedily restored.

At 5 a.m. on the 20th Brigadier-General Barker with G. battery Royal Horse artillery left Middelburg to assist Balmoral. On arriving at 11 a.m. he took out the battery and thirty mounted infantry with three companies of the 1st battalion King's Royal Rifles, which had been sent from Middelburg in response to the signal the day before. With these he reconnoitred four miles south, shelling the Balmoral colliery, and seeing only a few Boer patrols. The same evening he went on to Wilge River station, and from thence to Bronkhorstspruit, where he stayed that night. On the 21st, having ascertained that the whole of the enemy had retired to the north-west, he returned to Middelburg. In consequence of the partial success of the attack on Balmoral, an order was issued on the 22nd that all outposts along the lines of communication were to construct "closed works."

The Intelligence Department had now received reliable information of various laagers assembled in the angle between the Wilge and Oliphant rivers, north of the Delagoa Bay railway. Viljoen had led back 800 men from the attack on Balmoral to Rhenoster Kop, eight miles east of Rhenosterpoort, and about twenty miles north of Balmoral station. Further to the north-west Erasmus was reported to be near Sybrand's Kraal. To deal with these Major-General Paget, who at this time was at Rietfontein, nine miles west of Pretoria, was ordered to Eerste- *Paget called eastward.*

fabrieken, on the eastern line, to "clear the country between the Pietersburg railway and the Wilge river."

On the 25th Paget had concentrated his troops and moved north-east to De Wagen Drift, five miles east of Elim (map 48). There he divided the force. The mounted troops formed one column under Brigadier-General Plumer, and consisted of two brigades under Colonel T. E. Hickman and Lieut.-Colonel M. Cradock, with the 1st, 2nd and 3rd regiments Australian Bushmen; New Zealand M.R.; Queensland Imperial Bushmen; Tasmanians; 5th, 49th and 66th companies I.Y., and Q. section Vickers-Maxims. The other column, under Paget's personal command, was composed of four guns 7th battery and four of the 38th battery Royal Field artillery; No. 6 company Eastern Division R.G.A., with two Naval 12-pr. guns; 1st West Riding regiment (seven companies), and 1st Royal Munster Fusiliers (four companies). Approximate strength, 2,500 officers and men, with ten guns and two Vickers-Maxims.

Paget decided to move in the first instance against Erasmus at Sybrand's Kraal, and to endeavour, by getting to the north of him, to compel him either to fight or to fall back on Viljoen at Rhenoster Kop, where the columns could deal with both. Erasmus chose the second alternative; and Paget, moving his infantry by the shorter route, *via* Sybrand's Kraal to Hartebeestefontein, about four miles north-west of Rhenosterpoort, and his mounted troops *via* Zusterhoek to Albert Silver Mine, placed himself well to the north-west of Viljoen. He was here in a position either to give battle or to force the enemy down towards the railway, or north-east along the Wilge River valley. On the 25th Lyttelton inquired of Paget by telegram what were his intended movements, suggesting co-operation. In reply Paget announced his intention of attacking the enemy at Rhenoster Kop on the 29th. Thereupon Lyttelton detailed two columns to co-operate from Middelburg, under Lieut.-Colonels R. L. Payne and G. D. Carleton. In the course of successful manœuvres on the 26th and 27th, Plumer twice drove the enemy in the direction of Rhenoster Kop. The Boers left eight men on the field and had several wounded; Plumer had no casualties.

OPERATIONS IN THE EASTERN TRANSVAAL.

On the 28th two guns which the enemy disclosed on a hill due north of the Kop were shelled heavily. Patrols reported the Boers in strength on an adjoining hill further to the north. The mounted troops forced the outlying parties of burghers back and held them to their main position. During the day several small bodies, about 400 in all, were seen to arrive from the north and south, and there were many indications as to where Viljoen intended to make his stand. The Boer General had full information of his adversary's numbers, and of the movements from Middelburg which began this day. His position was of great natural strength and of peculiar configuration. Facing north-west, and with its horns coming forward nearly 12,000 yards apart to the Bronkhorstspruit—Rhenoster Kop track, lay a semi-circular necklace of small and separate kopjes, each covered with bush and boulder, and divided from its neighbours by ground so broken as to afford safe communication between them all. About the centre of the arc, a rocky knoll projected like a salient towards the north-west, separated by the road from the main position behind, and from the British by open meadow land which stretched along the whole front of the position. Rhenoster Kop itself, the highest of the series by many hundreds of feet, lay somewhat detached on the Boer left (south-western) flank. Their right was guarded by deep and rocky ravines; the staircases to lofty and level grass land which stretched north-eastward. Across this plateau ran Viljoen's line of retreat, and his only one, for Paget barred his front; the ground below Rhenoster Kop on his left was impassable, and Carleton was coming up from the east, or right rear. When an attack seemed likely, Viljoen had taken the precaution to send his transport along the plateau road into the bushveld to the north-east, enjoining his men at all costs to keep this route open in case he and his commandos should have to follow. He then decided to accept battle, undoubtedly a bold resolution, for either victory or retreat would demand the most exact calculation of time and distance in order to deal with each opponent singly or to avoid being crushed between them both. Paget was already almost within striking distance; Carleton, he heard, was fast

The Boer position at Rhenoster Kop.

approaching. To ensure instant communication between his units, Viljoen established a close chain of heliographs, and himself took stand on the highest part of the right flank, whence he commanded the whole field, and was nearest to the line of retreat. He posted his men, who numbered about 1,200, with two guns, as follows :—On Rhenoster Kop, and the adjoining kopje on the left, the Johannesburgers, under his brother; in the centre, the Johannesburg Police, under Lieut. D. Smith; on the right, the Boksburgers, under Muller, some of the Pretoria commando, under D. Opperman, and Erasmus' force, which Paget had manœuvred back to him from Sybrand's Kraal. A party were also entrenched on the projecting kopje across the road. Carleton's line of advance, Viljoen's chief anxiety, was watched by a field-cornetcy.

On Paget's side there were difficulties which, had the Boer leader been aware of them, would have rendered him less sensitive about his right and line of retreat. A deep ravine skirted Paget's left flank, denying him all access to the Boer right wing, and limiting his tactics either to a frontal attack, or one on the strongly posted riflemen on Rhenoster Kop, the hostile left. Everywhere in front of the British troops spread hundreds of yards of bare grass land, which afforded a perfect field for the rifle fire of the defence, and a dangerous glacis to the attack. Viljoen's situation, then, was as tactically formidable as it was strategically risky, and none could foretell how the cards would fall.

Nov. 29th, 1900.
The action at Rhenoster Kop.

Early on November 29th Paget broke camp four miles northwest of Rhenosterpoort (map 48), where Plumer's mounted troops had joined the infantry the night before. The distance between the British and Boer camps was then about 7,000 yards. From the former the ground first sloped down to the Steelkraal Spruit, a feeder of the Moos river, and then gently upwards, ending in the irregular crest of a flat hill, on the farther edge of which was the enemy. The trend of these crests was generally parallel to those held by the Boers; their windings brought the respective positions now as far apart as 700 yards, now as near as 350 yards. In one place, namely, at a rocky salient previously mentioned, the hostile centre was actually wedged into the British line, which for some distance it raked in enfilade on both sides.

The advance began at 4 a.m., the infantry on the right, Plumer's two mounted brigades continuing the line to the left. Hickman's brigade led, followed by Cradock's Bushmen, until the Steelkraal Spruit had been crossed, soon after which Hickman changed direction to the east. The Field artillery came after, making use of the few positions obtainable to fire over the heads of the advancing lines. The hollow of the Steelkraal Spruit kept the advancing troops almost completely hidden from the enemy until the crest of the ridge was reached. In like manner the Boer position was entirely invisible to the attacking force. Colonel G. E. Lloyd, 1st West Riding regiment, who commanded the leading infantry, had at his disposal seven companies of his own battalion and four of the 1st Royal Munster Fusiliers (Major P. T. Chute), which he disposed in the following order: Two half companies in the first line extended to ten paces interval, their respective half companies 200 yards in rear extended to five paces. In the second line—three companies about 1,000 yards behind the first, and the remaining companies in reserve, with the exception of one guarding the transport. A squadron of the Imperial Yeomanry protected Paget's extreme right flank.

As the infantry ascended the incline towards the crest of the hill a small Boer piquet disappeared across the summit. The projecting height now on the right of the advance was disregarded, as it was thought to be unoccupied; but as the line drew near, musketry broke fiercely from its ridges. At 6 a.m. Lloyd diverted two half companies to attack it, and if possible turn the enemy's left; but these infantry were themselves outflanked, and about 7 a.m. had to be reinforced by another half company which prolonged the line to the right. But all here found it impossible to make headway against the overwhelming fire. Meanwhile the other leading companies had been absorbed, the whole line becoming deeply engaged. Lloyd himself moved towards the left, and led a company to the top of the ridge, the heavy rifle fire from which prevented further advance. About 9.15 a.m. he went forward alone to obtain a better view, and was immediately shot dead. The momentum of the infantry was now spent, and they were held to the crest, upon which beat a continuous rain of bullets. Ammunition and water were supplied to the men by comrades who crawled through the grass backwards and forwards all day for this purpose. Under these conditions they remained until 7 p.m.

Turning to the mounted brigades on the left—first a squadron of the Queensland Imperial Bushmen, in front of Hickman's brigade, galloped forward and seized a ridge on foot within 500 yards of the enemy. This party immediately came under hot fire, and were supported by the remainder of their regiment and by three squadrons of the 4th Imperial Bushmen contingent, under Lieut.-Colonel J. Rowell, who lined up on the left of the Queenslanders. In the meantime Cradock's brigade had circled round to the left of Hickman's, where the Bushmen soon drove off a commando about 100 strong. The New Zealanders, who were on the right of the brigade, were warmly received when they came to 1,200 yards range. Dismounting, they skirmished rapidly forward until within 400 yards of the enemy's position and in line with the left of Hickman, whose brigade thus became the centre of the firing line. It was about 5.30 a.m. when the whole force, horse and foot, thus found itself well committed to a frontal attack.

The 3rd regiment (West Australians and Victorians, under Major H. G. Vialls), on the extreme left, now pushed directly against two isolated kopjes which marked the enemy's right flank. A wider movement was rendered impracticable by the above-mentioned ravine intervening on that side. The 2nd regiment (Queensland mounted infantry, under Major W. H. Tunbridge) supported, and both were covered by a section of the 38th battery R.F.A. and a Vickers-Maxim. The advance was well led and resolutely carried out; but the kopjes were too strongly held to be taken by direct attack; and though the leading troops fought their way within 200 yards of the Mausers, they could advance no nearer. The two regiments established

OPERATIONS IN THE EASTERN TRANSVAAL.

themselves on a rocky ridge about 1,000 yards from the kopjes, and at least closed the north to the Boers. This was at 7.30 a.m., before it was known that the infantry had been checked on the right. The mounted troops were now occupying a front of about three and a half miles. Every man was in action, with the exception of 200 of the 1st Royal Munster Fusiliers, and 150 men of Hickman's brigade, fifty of whom were now sent as a reserve to Cradock's unsupported brigade. The soldiers on the extreme left had some slight cover, but there was none for those in the centre and right of the line; all were exposed to a heavy and incessant rifle fire, and all remained pinned to their positions till sunset. Thus for nearly twelve hours the attenuated line of infantry and dismounted troopers lay in the open under a vehement fire from invisible opponents, refusing to retire and unable to advance. Fortunate it was that Viljoen had either insufficient information or resolution to advance upon what was nothing more than an overmatched and unsupported firing line. The utmost efforts of the British artillery could little improve the situation. Throughout the day the artillery officers, try as they would, experienced the greatest difficulty in finding good positions for their guns. The 7th battery R.F.A. and one Vickers-Maxim advanced to a ridge only about 900 yards distant from the enemy's defences; but it was impossible to bring the guns into action on the crest, and the gunners could do no more than fire indirectly from behind it. A section commander with two guns of the 38th battery R.F.A., in searching for a favourable spot, found his detachment suddenly exposed to a fusilade at 700 yards range. But their quickness in replying with shrapnel saved the party; the burghers only fired one more volley before taking to flight, when the guns had time to draw back from such close contact. The two Naval 12-prs. R.G.A. (Major A. B. Shute) fired 200 rounds at 7,000 yards range from the bivouac of the previous night; but the Boer guns changed their position too frequently, and were too well protected by the rocks to be damaged.

Towards evening orders were issued for the men to entrench after dark, and for those in the firing line to be then as far as possible relieved by any who had been less severely engaged during the day. By some alteration of the order as it was passed from mouth to mouth down the line, the New Zealanders commenced to withdraw about 6 p.m., while it was still light. Instantly the watchful Boers seized the opportunity to launch a vigorous counter-attack, supporting it by a heavy fire from two guns and a Vickers-Maxim. The New Zealanders were soon informed of their mistake by Cradock, and turning, beat off the enemy. This was the last incident of the day. The British casualties numbered eighty-six: killed, one officer and fourteen men; wounded, ten officers and sixty-one men. The Boers lost twenty-four: two killed and twenty-two wounded.

Nov. 30th, 1900. The Boers evacuate Rhenoster Kop.

Paget had every intention of renewing the assault at dawn next day, but Viljoen declined a second bout. His ammunition was running short, his transport was getting out of touch far to the north on the Geluk road; the evident determination of Paget's troops had not been without its effect, and the troops from Middelburg might arrive at any moment. During the night he withdrew to the north-east along the Wilge river, slipping past Carleton's Middelburg column on his right, and by morning was out of reach of the British forces.

It is necessary now to turn to the forces from Middelburg, the movements of which had influenced the tactics of both sides at Rhenoster Kop, where the appearance of either column on the field might well have changed that drawn action into a victory for Paget. On November 28th, as recorded, Lyttelton sent two columns to co-operate with Paget—one under Lieut.-Colonel R. L. Payne, consisting of fifty men 18th Hussars, four guns G. battery R.H.A. and one 5-in. gun, four companies 1st Royal Inniskilling Fusiliers and two companies 1st King's Royal Rifles; the other, under Lieut.-Colonel G. D. Carleton, was composed of 240 men 18th Hussars, four guns 21st battery R.F.A., one 12-pr. Q.F. gun, one Vickers-Maxim, and six companies 1st Leicestershire regiment.

Movements of the co-operating columns.

Payne's column bivouacked the first night twelve miles north of Middelburg, watching the drift over the Klein Oliphant river. Small parties of Boers had been shelled and driven northwards

OPERATIONS IN THE EASTERN TRANSVAAL.

during the day. On the 29th a farm was raided; on the 30th the column marched north-east quite out of the sphere of Paget's operations and returned to Middelburg on December 1st. Payne had two men wounded. His absence, then, from Rhenoster Kop is easily to be explained.

Carleton had been directed by Lyttelton to place his column at the junction of the Wilge and Oliphant rivers on the 30th, so as to intercept any Boers who might escape from Paget towards the south. He marched on November the 28th to Groot Oliphants station on the railway, twelve miles west of Middelburg. On the 29th he proceeded in a north-westerly direction, capturing a small laager and driving before him T. Pretorius' commando towards the drift on the Wilge river. At 5.30 a.m. on the 30th he continued his advance to the Wilge, to a point due east of Rhenosterpoort, shelling on his way a few small parties of Boers, and here on a position commanding the drift over the Wilge, he established himself. Signalling communication was opened on this day with Paget's force to the north of Rhenoster Kop until the sun was hidden. Carleton did not wish to involve himself in the intricate country which lay before him, without definite news from Paget, and the failure of the sun brought him to a halt. About 5 p.m. a Kaffir brought intelligence that the Boers were holding a strong position at Rhenoster Kop, and that Carleton's co-operation was wanted. He thereupon prepared to advance. Later, however, on establishing lamp signal communication, it was ascertained that the enemy had evacuated his position the previous night. Thus it was that neither column from Middelburg was of any assistance to Paget, whose force encamped at Rhenoster Kop. The hill was then fortified and held in strength for some months as an outpost for the protection of the railway against raids in force from the north.

On November 28th, Middelburg having been denuded of troops by the absence of Carleton's and Payne's columns, a mobile column,* under Colonel F. Macbean, Gordon Highlanders, was detailed to proceed west from Belfast along the railway and to

---

* 5th Lancers, sixty men; four guns 84th battery R.F.A.; one 5-in. gun R.G.A.; 1st Royal Irish regiment, 350 men; 1st Gordon Highlanders, 500 men.

cover Middelburg from the south. Macbean marched to Wonderfontein, where he bivouacked. The next day he visited a farm about eight miles south of the line, and on the 30th returned to the railway at Pan station with one wounded man. On November 30th an escort of 132 men was sent from Belfast to Dalmanutha, to bring in ninety wagons and a number of oxen, which had formed part of the supply park of Sir R. Buller's army when it came up from Natal.

By the end of November fortified posts had been established the entire length of the eastern line of railway, with guards at every bridge and culvert from Pretoria to Komati Poort bridge. In addition, strong garrisons and mobile columns held and linked the towns of Belfast and Middelburg, whilst to the north Lydenburg, and to the south Barberton were held in force, each with a Major-General in command.* With the troops available protection could go no further; yet time was to show that it by no means went far enough.

* See Appendix 7.

CHAPTER XIX.

EVENTS ON JOHANNESBURG—DURBAN LINE.
JUNE TO NOVEMBER, 1900.*

BRIEF reference must here be made to events on the Natal—Johannesburg railway, which had now become an important line of communication and supply. Since June 25th Major-General A. FitzRoy Hart† had occupied Heidelberg. By the beginning of July his detachments held the railway from Zuikerbosch to Rietvlei, where they linked with the troops of the 19th brigade. From July 4th, when Hart's patrol joined hands with the advance guard of the Natal army, the railway from Elandsfontein to Ladysmith was held by a chain of entrenched posts, which week by week grew in number and in strength. Vlakfontein, Greylingstad, Waterval, Standerton and the intervening points were gradually garrisoned by the IInd division: Major-General A. S. Wynne's 11th brigade was responsible for the section Standerton—Paarde Kop; Lieut.-General H. J. T. Hildyard, with the 2nd cavalry brigade, and Major-General J. T. Coke's 10th brigade held Zandspruit and Volksrust: Lieut.-General the Hon. N. G. Lyttelton's section included Laing's Nek and Ingogo Heights, with detachments at Ingogo Station and Coetzee's Drift; Major-General J. Wolfe Murray was in general command of the line from Newcastle southward;

<small>Distribution of troops.</small>

---

* See maps Nos. 45, 46 and 48.

† 28th battery Royal Field artillery; G. section Vickers-Maxims; a wing of the 2nd Somerset Light Infantry; 2nd Royal Dublin Fusiliers; Marshall's Horse (14 officers, 288 other ranks); Manchester I.Y. (4 officers, 80 men). Total—65 officers, 1,835 other ranks.

Brigadier-General J. F. Burn-Murdoch, with the 1st cavalry brigade and detachments from the 7th infantry brigade, held Rooi Pont, six miles south of Newcastle, Ingagane and Dannhauser; Brigadier-General J. G. Dartnell, with the Natal Volunteer brigade, garrisoned Dundee, Glencoe and Waschbank, and Major-General C. M. H. Downing, from his Headquarters at Ladysmith, provided for the defence of the Drakensberg passes.

On June 28th Major-General J. T. Coke, with a column composed of two squadrons 19th Hussars, four 12-pr. guns (Naval), 69th battery R.F.A., one Vickers-Maxim, 2nd Middlesex regiment, and 1st Royal Dublin Fusiliers, moved from Volksrust with the object of clearing Gras Kop, and reconnoitring towards Amersfoort. Gras Kop was occupied without opposition on the evening of the same day. On the 29th the advance was resumed, now covered upon the left flank by the 18th Hussars and a Field battery, detached from the 2nd cavalry brigade at Zandspruit. Upon the high ground six miles to the south of Amersfoort a strong Boer force with several guns was encountered, and with this Coke soon became engaged. After driving the enemy from their ground at a cost of two killed and seven wounded, the column returned to Volksrust, which was reached on the 30th.

Throughout July the attitude of Sir R. Buller's force was purely defensive. The sole mobile body within the area was that of Sir F. Clery,* which, largely composed of infantry, and equipped with four heavy guns, had chiefly the passive duty of protecting the railway and reconstruction parties between Standerton and Heidelberg. Clinging to the line throughout the early portion of July, this ponderous column was constantly shadowed and stung by the active sharpshooters of the Heidelberg commando; and the section of the line which it patrolled could rarely be kept intact. On July 20th news was received of De Wet's escape from the Brandwater Basin, and with it an order from the Commander-in-Chief that Sir F. Clery should hold his

---

* 3rd mounted brigade (500); two and a half battalions 4th brigade; 63rd battery Royal Field artillery; two Howitzers 86th battery R.F.A.; two 5-in. guns R.G.A.

column in readiness at Greylingstad to prevent De Wet from breaking into the Transvaal between Standerton and Heidelberg. Sir F. Clery, who at the moment was moving upon Bethel, thereupon returned to Greylingstad.

Though minor affrays were numerous, the only sustained attack upon any post on the railway was made upon Zuikerbosch. The garrison under Major F. P. English, 2nd Royal Dublin Fusiliers, consisted of two companies of his own battalion, ten men Imperial Yeomanry, and 110 men Royal Engineers, the latter employed upon the broken bridge over the Zuikerbosch stream. At dawn on July 21st they were suddenly assailed by a strong commando with three guns and a Vickers-Maxim. The Boers, pushing in to close quarters, poured an exceedingly hot rifle and artillery fire on the defenders; but English signalled to Heidelberg, thirteen miles distant, that, although entirely surrounded, he was holding his own with confidence. Hart, with two Field guns, a Vickers-Maxim, 130 infantry, and 140 mounted men, hurried from Heidelberg to relieve the little post; but the attack was already repelled by the vigorous resistance of the garrison, and the approach of Hart only hastened the Boer retirement. July 21st, 1900. Boers attack Zuikerbosch.

On July 27th Hart, ordered by Lord Roberts to entrain his force for the Orange River Colony, withdrew to Klip River Station, being transferred southward on the 28th by train. On the same day Major-General C. D. Cooper, covered by Sir F. Clery's column, took over the posts evacuated by Hart, and moved into Heidelberg with one squadron Strathcona's Horse, two guns 63rd battery R.F.A., five companies 3rd King's Royal Rifles, and six companies 1st Rifle Brigade. July 27th, 1900. Hart leaves for the Orange River Colony.

Meanwhile the lower sections of the railway had been threatened by a force which had concentrated in the neighbourhood of Gras Kop and Rooi Koppies, and was not dislodged by a small column sent out from Platrand* under Lieut.-Colonel E. C. Bethune on July 12th. Hildyard then collected a strong force around Zandspruit and Volksrust, and by July

* Six guns, four companies mounted infantry and four companies 1st York and Lancaster regiment.

Hildyard collects troops for operations towards Amersfoort.

21st had three columns ready to move under Brocklehurst, Howard and Coke.*

Next day Gras Kop was occupied with slight opposition, and two 12-pr. guns were emplaced on its lofty summit. Using the mountain as his pivot, Hildyard, on July 24th, turned to Rooi Koppies, whither the local commandos had retired. Here he found himself before an entrenched position strongly held by several hundred Boers with two heavy guns and a Vickers-Maxim. After a preliminary bombardment by the 4.7-in. guns, the 12-prs., and the 13th and 69th batteries, Brocklehurst threatened the right of the position, and Howard's infantry deployed and advanced, the 2nd Gordon Highlanders in first line, the 1st King's Royal Rifles in support and two companies of the 1st Leicester in reserve—the whole covered by fire from their machine guns. The leading half battalion of the Gordon Highlanders rushed the main Boer position without a check, and Hildyard drove the enemy from their ground towards Amersfoort, with a loss to his own force of four men killed, one officer and twenty-one men wounded. The column bivouacked at Meerzicht; and the following days were spent in reconnoitring towards Amersfoort, and entrenching posts upon the neighbouring

---

* LEFT COLUMN.
(Major-General J. F. Brocklehurst.)

18th Hussars.
Two companies B.M.I.
Two companies 4th M.I.
Four guns 7th battery R.F.A.
Two 12-prs. (Naval).
Wing 2nd Lancashire Fusiliers.
Wing 1st Royal Dublin Fusiliers.

MAIN BODY.
(Major-General F. Howard.)

One squadron 19th Hussars.
13th battery R.F.A.
Two guns 69th battery R.F.A.
Two 4.7-in. guns (Naval).
Two Vickers-Maxims.
Wing 1st Leicester regiment.
1st King's Royal Rifles.
1st Manchester regiment.
2nd Gordon Highlanders.

RIGHT COLUMN.
(Major-General J. T. Coke.)

One squadron 19th Hussars.
Two 12-prs. (Naval).
Four guns 69th battery R.F.A.
2nd Dorsetshire regiment.
Wing 2nd Middlesex regiment.

heights for the protection of Paarde Kop and Zandspruit stations.

With the departure of General Sir R. Buller on August 7th, the redistribution* of the guards and garrisons of the Natal—Standerton line took effect. To recapitulate—Sir F. Clery, with the IInd division, was responsible for the section Heidelberg to Kromdrai; the Headquarters 4th brigade being at Heidelberg, that of the 2nd brigade at Standerton. Hildyard's troops joined hands with those of Sir F. Clery by Kromdrai, and held the line to Coetzee's Drift; the Headquarters 11th brigade being at Platrand, and that of the 10th at Ingogo. Sir F. Clery himself was in personal command of a column which early in August was composed of one squadron 13th Hussars, three companies Thorneycroft's mounted infantry, four guns 63rd battery Royal Field artillery, one 5-in. gun Royal Garrison artillery, 17th Field company Royal Engineers, 1st Durham Light Infantry, and a Naval detachment manning two 12-prs. *(Aug. 7th, 1900. Redistribution of troops.)*

The month of August passed in improving the defences of the posts along the line, in entrenching positions upon the hills to the north of Paarde Kop, Zandspruit and Volksrust, in accumulating reserves of supplies at the posts, and in repairing the frequently interrupted railway in order that the flow of stores to Pretoria along this, the shortest, the least exposed, and therefore the most reliable artery of supply for the army in the Transvaal, should not be checked.

As in July, Sir F. Clery's column, closely followed by Buys' Heidelberg commando, remained in the immediate neighbourhood of the railway, making a few reconnaissances and punitive raids on the farms of irreconcilables. The most noteworthy patrol during the month was that made by Lieut.-Colonel E. C. Bethune, who, with two companies Bethune's mounted infantry and four guns, left Platrand on the 24th. He reached Vrede next day, and after receiving 120 submissions, returned to Platrand on the 26th.

Towards the end of the month the enemy hovered in strong numbers within striking distance of the Volksrust—Newcastle

* See Appendix 8.

section of the line. On the 20th large parties were seen beyond the Buffalo, and two posts upon the eastern side of Newcastle were heavily attacked and forced to retire, until the Royal Dragoons arriving from Ingagane drove the Boers over the river. The outposts to the east of Newcastle, supported by the fire of the heavy guns, were unsuccessfully threatened again on the 21st and the 22nd, a post held by a squadron 13th Hussars reinforced by two companies 2nd Middlesex and four Field guns, being attacked with especial vehemence; and each day the railway was cut north of Dannhauser.

On August 22nd, General Sir R. Buller, in a telegram* sent from Van Wyk's Vlei, informed the Commander-in-Chief that "now that General Chris. Botha has broken back from Ermelo, there is a considerable force of the enemy threatening the line between Laing's Nek and Newcastle, which is much exposed." For the reasons given in Chapter XVI., he himself was unable to attend to them. In order to release some of Hildyard's troops for more active duties, Sir F. Clery's division had by the end of August taken over charge of the line as far as Zandspruit, where Wynne now assembled his 11th brigade.

Hildyard collects troops for operations towards Wakkerstroom, Utrecht and Vryheid.

In pursuance of instructions from Sir R. Buller to occupy Wakkerstroom, Utrecht and Vryheid, the 11th brigade, and other units detailed for the movement, had concentrated towards the end of August and the early days of September about Zandspruit and Volksrust. By September 4th there had assembled at Hout Nek, on the road to Wakkerstroom, the following troops, which were there re-organised in two columns, under Lieut.-General H. J. T. Hildyard's command :—

MAIN COLUMN.
(Major-General A. S. Wynne.)

Bethune's mounted infantry, five companies.
Vth division mounted infantry, two companies.
67th battery Royal Field artillery.
Two guns 86th (Howitzer) battery Royal Field artillery.
Two 4.7-in. guns 10th company Eastern division R.G.A.
Two 12-pr. guns (Naval).
11th infantry brigade (less one battalion).

* No. 341, August 22nd.

RIGHT FLANK COLUMN.
(Lieut.-Colonel C. J. Blomfield, Lancashire Fusiliers.)
Three companies composite mounted infantry.
69th battery Royal Field artillery.
2nd Lancashire Fusiliers.

At dawn on the 5th this force moved on Wakkerstroom, Blomfield's column crowning the eastern heights as right flank guard. From the hills some four miles to the south of Wakkerstroom parties of Boers were seen in the plain on which the town lies, and a train of wagons passing thence along the Piet Retief road. The mounted men of the main column pushed into the town and, after light skirmishing,* the hills north of Wakkerstroom were occupied. On the same day, in order to divert some of the enemy, Major-General J. T. Coke,† based on his own section of the line (Dannhauser—Newcastle), crossed Coetzee's Drift, and acting in co-operation with a force under Burn-Murdoch, took up a position on the high ground some five miles beyond the Buffalo river, losing two killed and three wounded.

_{Sept. 5th, 1900. Occupation of Wakkerstroom.}

On September 9th Hildyard marched for Utrecht, leaving the garrison of Wakkerstroom‡ with fourteen days' supplies entrenched upon the hill which commands the town from the south. Some ten miles were covered, with a loss to the mounted screen of two killed and three wounded, when information was received that General C. Botha lay across the road with a concentration of all the neighbouring commandos. Hildyard advanced at dawn on the 10th, expecting resistance at the passage of the Wonderhoogte defile, which covers Utrecht from the north. Bethune's mounted infantry on the right flank at once reported the high ground above the pass to be strongly held; and the head of the column was checked whilst the 67th, 69th and 86th (Howitzer)

---

* One man Bethune's mounted infantry killed; two men Bethune's mounted infantry wounded.

† 5th Dragoon Guards, 13th battery Royal Field artillery, six companies 2nd Dorsetshire regiment, two Naval 12-prs.

‡ Lieut.-Colonel W. J. Kirkpatrick, with half company mounted infantry, two 12-prs. (10th company Eastern division R.G.A.), six companies York and Lancaster regiment.

batteries and the 4.7-in. guns heavily bombarded the crest. The Boers soon retired, leaving a few dead ; the infantry advance was resumed, and the column bivouacked on the further side of the Pass, some eight miles from Utrecht.

Sept. 11th, 1900. Occupation of Utrecht.

By September 11th Coke and Burn-Murdoch had cleared the Belela's Berg, and the area within a radius of eighteen miles from Coetzee's Drift ; and when, marching through open country Hildyard reached Utrecht on that day, he found no Boers, but a detachment of Burn-Murdoch's cavalry already upon the high ground north of the town.

The force halted in Utrecht until the 17th, when, dropping an entrenched garrison* in and around the town, Hildyard made for Vryheid. Camp was reached that day midway to Vryheid with little opposition ; while Dartnell, moving from Dundee with the Natal Volunteer brigade, reached the Doorn Berg, whence he was in signalling communication with Hildyard. On the 18th the movement was resumed in combination, Dartnell having for his point of direction the southern slopes of the prominent Bemba's Kop, whilst Hildyard marched upon the landmark afforded by the northern brow of that mountain. In the evening Hildyard was on Scheeper's Nek, a height which from a distance of seven miles overlooks the town of Vryheid ; and Dartnell reached the bridge over the Blood river. Early on the 19th, Hildyard closed in on Vryheid ; and the Boers, who till then had clung to a position which covered the town itself, retired in haste towards the north. A garrison with supplies for one month was thus disposed at Vryheid :—

Sept. 19th, 1900. Occupation of Vryheid.

Lieut.-Colonel J. M. Gawne.	Forces	Location
	Five companies 2nd Royal Lancaster regiment / Two 12-prs. (Naval)	On a hill to north of the town.
	Two companies 1st South Lancashire regiment / One company mounted infantry	At Blood River Bridge.
	Two companies 2nd Lancashire Fusiliers / One company mounted infantry	At Scheeper's Nek.
	Two companies 2nd Royal Lancaster regiment	Holding the town itself.

---

* Major H. S. Scholes, York and Lancaster regiment, with half company mounted infantry, one 12-pr. gun, three companies 1st York and Lancaster regiment, two companies 2nd Royal Lancaster regiment.

Hildyard's division was now distributed as follows :—

With him at Vryheid, supplied from Dundee : Headquarters Vth division; Vth divisional mounted infantry, one company; Composite regiment mounted infantry, Headquarters and two companies ; Bethune's mounted infantry, Headquarters and four companies ; 67th battery Royal Field artillery, four guns ; 69th battery Royal Field artillery, four guns ; 86th (Howitzer) battery Royal Field artillery, two guns ; 10th company Eastern division, Royal Garrison artillery, two 4.7-in. guns ; two 12-prs. (Naval) ; Vth division ammunition column ; 2nd Royal Lancaster regiment, seven companies ; 2nd Lancashire Fusiliers, six companies ; 1st South Lancashire regiment, eight companies ; 11th brigade Field hospital ; 11th brigade Bearer company. *Distribution of Hildyard's troops.*

At Utrecht and Wakkerstroom, supplied from Wools Drift and Zandspruit : The garrison already stated.

At Volksrust : Vth divisional mounted infantry, Headquarters and two companies ; 2nd Lancashire Fusiliers, one company. At Laing's Nek : 5th Dragoon Guards, half a squadron ; one 12-pr. (Naval) ; 1st Royal Dublin Fusiliers. At Ingogo : Headquarters 10th brigade ; 5th Dragoon Guards, one and a half squadrons ; 13th battery Royal Field artillery ; 2nd Dorsetshire regiment. At Blood River—supplied from Dundee : Bethune's mounted infantry, one company ; 67th battery Royal Field artillery, two guns ; 1st South Lancashire regiment, one company. At Scheeper's Nek—supplied from Dundee : Composite regiment mounted infantry, one company ; 69th battery Royal Field artillery, two guns ; 2nd Lancashire Fusiliers, two companies. At Coetzee's Drift : 5th Dragoon Guards, one squadron.

By the end of September Hildyard's troops had received the following surrenders : At Wakkerstroom, 119 burghers ; at Utrecht, 186 burghers ; at Vryheid, 144 burghers.

Meanwhile Sir F. Clery's column moved throughout September between Standerton and Greylingstad; and except for losses in ambush incurred by two patrols, the first near Waterval bridge on the 6th,* the second near Heidelberg

---

* Killed, four men ; wounded, one officer and two men, Thorneycroft's mounted infantry.

on September 27th,* the month passed without noteworthy incident.

On September 23rd, in answer to a request forwarded through Sir R. Buller, Lord Roberts had authorised the disbandment on October 1st of the Natal Volunteers, with the exception of 300 (to be called the Natal Volunteer composite regiment) who had undertaken to serve till the end of the war. The Commander-in-Chief bade farewell with regret to troops who had served loyally, and with distinction, from the earliest and most critical period of the campaign.

<small>Oct. 1st, 1900. Loss of a convoy.</small>

At 5.30 a.m. on October 1st, a convoy of thirty-six wagons for the force at Vryheid left De Jager's Drift, escorted by sixty men of the newly-formed Volunteer composite regiment, with one 3-pr. Hotchkiss gun manned by a detachment of the 2nd Middlesex regiment. At 10 a.m., covered by outposts, the convoy was outspanned in a donga midway between De Jager's Drift and Blood River post. On receiving reports from natives that parties of Boers were in the neighbourhood, the officer in command despatched a patrol of twenty men to reconnoitre. Hardly had the patrol passed the outpost line when it rode into a commando of some 400 Boers, who drove it back upon the piquets, and pressing in on all sides in one converging movement, pushed the piquets, one and all, into the convoy. The Hotchkiss had fired one shot when the Boers from the high ground above the donga, bringing an intolerable point-blank rifle fire to bear upon the encircled escort and convoy, silenced the gun and soon forced the whole to surrender. On receipt of news of this, Hildyard at dawn on the 2nd despatched Lieut.-Colonel Bethune with five companies mounted infantry, 67th battery and one company infantry to strengthen Blood River post. There were further reports that the enemy was concentrating to attack Utrecht; and Hildyard himself, leaving at Vryheid its allotted garrison, followed Bethune with the rest of his force on the 6th. A standing camp was formed at Rooi Koppies, near Bemba's Kop and the junction of the Utrecht and Vryheid roads, a central

---

* One killed, four wounded; an officer and one man prisoners, Thorneycroft's mounted infantry.

position from which Hildyard could rapidly supply, communicate with and assist both Utrecht and Vryheid.

Meanwhile, in Sir F. Clery's section of the line, the British railway and the neighbouring Boer farms were being demolished by each side in turn, incidents too insignificant to need particular record—with one exception. On October 9th, the line having been broken between Zuikerbosch and Vlakfontein, Captain G. L. Paget, 1st Rifle Brigade, with Lieutenants J. W. S. Sewell and J. H. Stubbs, Royal Engineers, and sixteen men of the 1st Rifle Brigade from the garrison of Vlakfontein, sallied out in a short train to inspect the damage, and were promptly ambushed and cut up by a band of Boers concealed beneath a culvert.* Twenty-five men of the 1st Rifle Brigade under Captain A. D. Stewart, who endeavoured to extricate their comrades, were driven back upon their post at Vlakfontein, with the loss of their officer mortally wounded and a soldier. Sir F. Clery's column, which was at the time encamped some four miles to the south-east of Vlakfontein, marched by night to the spot, and at dawn on the 10th found a force of Boers of unknown strength upon the hills, which from the east command at close rifle range the railroad between Vlakfontein and the Zuikerbosch river. The position was lofty and extensive, and Sir F. Clery thought it prudent to halt until, in answer to his request, four companies 3rd King's Royal Rifles and four companies 1st Rifle Brigade joined him from Heidelberg on the 12th. Thus strengthened, he attacked the kopjes on the 13th. The Boers retired with slight opposition, and Sir F. Clery, after establishing a post of half a battalion 1st Rifle Brigade, one Vickers-Maxim and twenty-five men of Thorneycroft's mounted infantry under Lieut.-Colonel A. E. W. Colville on the position, marched into Greylingstad on October 25th.

Oct. 9th, 1900. Affair at Vlakfontein.

At the end of October General Sir R. Buller's order of October 19th, in which he relinquished command of the Natal army, and whereby that army, as such, ceased to exist, began to take

* Killed, one man ; wounded, Captain Paget (mortally), Lieut. Stubbs and five men and guard of train (the latter mortally); prisoners, Lieut. Sewell and ten men and engine driver.

effect. On the 27th Hildyard arrived at Newcastle to command all troops in Natal and in the Transvaal south of Zandspruit. On October 31st the IInd division, as a unit, also disappeared, and Wynne took over command of Sir F. Clery's section of the line.

A general redistribution of troops and commands therefore occurred, which took effect in November.* The troops of the Vth division, and of lines of communication, and their respective staffs, were amalgamated. General progress was made in the work of strengthening the posts along the line, and in throwing large reserves of supplies into Wakkerstroom, Utrecht and Vryheid. Sir F. Clery's mobile column, now under Lieut.-Colonel R. C. A. B. Bewicke-Copley, spent the early part of the month in intermittent skirmishing whilst clearing the country between Standerton and the Vaal (one killed, six wounded). On the 19th this column was in Standerton, whence it moved to the neighbourhood of Zuikerbosch in order to deal similarly with that area. Here on the 27th the infantry with the column were reduced, the 2nd Devonshire and the 3rd King's Royal Rifles being relieved by the 1st Rifle Brigade. Lieut.-Colonel A. E. W. Colville, as senior officer, then took command of the mobile column.†

* See Appendix 8.

† Thorneycroft's mounted infantry, 13 officers, 187 men, one machine gun; four guns 63rd battery Royal Field artillery; two Vickers-Maxims; detachment 17th company R.E.; 1st Rifle Brigade, 16 officers, 949 men, one machine gun.

CHAPTER XX.

OPERATIONS IN THE ORANGE RIVER COLONY* (*continued*).

SEPTEMBER TO DECEMBER, 1900.

At the end of August the movements of C. De Wet once more gave cause for uneasiness. It was known that on the 23rd he had recrossed the Vaal with 300 men, and had marched south, with the intention, so it was thought, of joining forces with Olivier, or at any rate of doing damage on his own account. The commandos were short of provisions and ammunition, and they were certain to attempt to replenish both by the capture of such places as they knew to be weakly garrisoned. Guerrillas are never more dangerous than when in straits. In order to lessen the number of small, isolated posts, the troops were withdrawn from Senekal and Hammonia, and sent to Ficksburg; while the garrison of Thabanchu was at first called in to the Waterworks (Sannah's Post), but a few days later was reinforced by two guns and two companies of infantry, and ordered to re-occupy the place.   *De Wet again in the Orange River Colony.*

Thwarted in the attempt to capture Winburg, the enemy separated into two parties, a small force proceeding in the direction of Senekal, while the majority, commanded by Fourie, advanced into the Koranna Berg, designing to attack Ladybrand and Thabanchu. But their ambition did not stop there; the full programme included the capture of Bloemfontein, and even, so it was said, the invasion of Cape Colony. To check them, Bruce Hamilton was ordered to go by rail from Winburg to Bloemfontein, where he arrived on the evening of August 31st. On the same date Sir A. Hunter's mounted troops

* See maps Nos. 38, 53 and 54.

(about 900, with one section R.H.A., one section R.F.A., and one section Vickers-Maxims), under the command of Lieut.-Colonel P. W. J. Le Gallais, started for Bloemfontein, where Sir A. Hunter himself proceeded, in order to confer with Kelly-Kenny on the general situation.

State of the Orange River Colony.

The surrender of Prinsloo had reduced the number of fighting Boers in the Orange River Colony by about one-half. Indeed, but for the freedom of the chief firebrands, De Wet and Olivier, armed resistance in this part of the theatre would probably have cooled early in August. But with them at large the hopes of the enemy were kept alive and his energy revived. The British force available for coping with their raiding bands was wholly insufficient, not only in numbers, but also in mobility. By strenuous efforts on the part of the mounted troops, invested garrisons might indeed be relieved, and the enemy possibly driven off; but effective pursuit of a swifter quarry was then never feasible. The situation in the south-east of the Orange River Colony, though at no time actually grave, was constantly troublesome. Troops, which could be ill spared, had to be sent south, if only for the purpose of reassuring the inhabitants, especially those of outlying places from which the garrisons had been withdrawn, such as Smithfield, Wepener and Rouxville.

During August the requirements of the Transvaal had drawn away from the Orange River Colony the Colonial division, Paget's force and Clements' force, so that Sir A. Hunter's command, by the end of the month, was reduced to the Highland brigade (MacDonald), Bruce Hamilton's column and Le Gallais' mounted troops. Of these, the Highland brigade was at Kroonstad (with a detachment at Heilbron), and Bruce Hamilton and Le Gallais had just reached Bloemfontein. Sir L. Rundle's two mobile columns were still engaged in clearing the country to the east; and C. E. Knox, based on Kroonstad, was manœuvring between that town and the Vaal with a force too weak in the mounted arm to be effective. The remainder of the troops in the Colony were employed either as small garrisons at important strategic points or pinned fast to the line of communication.

On September 1st Bruce Hamilton, with about 200 mounted

OPERATIONS IN THE ORANGE RIVER COLONY. 471

men, two guns 39th battery R.F.A., and the Cameron High- Sept. 1st—5th, landers, Royal Sussex and Bedfordshire regiments (1,750 men), Relief of started from Bloemfontein, to succour Ladybrand, which was Ladybrand. reported to be surrounded by a force under Fourie, Olivier's successor. The garrison consisted of a company of the 1st Worcestershire regiment and forty-three Imperial Yeomanry, and it was feared that without immediate aid surrender would be inevitable. A small column under Lieut.-Colonel W. L. White, R.F.A. (300 men of the 29th, 30th and 31st companies I.Y., two guns 39th battery R.F.A., two companies Royal Irish Rifles and sixty mounted infantry), had for some time been operating in the neighbourhood of Ventersburg, and had been directed by Kelly-Kenny to Thabanchu, where Bruce Hamilton arrived on September 2nd. Next morning White was ordered to move with all speed on Ladybrand, ahead of Bruce Hamilton, who, leaving a small garrison at Thabanchu, followed and closed up with White on September 4th some thirteen miles from Ladybrand. By that time White's advanced troops had already encountered the enemy at Leeuw River Mills, getting the better of a skirmish, which cost them three casualties, and the Boers about a dozen. Late on that night Le Gallais, who had reached Bloemfontein on September 1st, arrived from Thabanchu with 250 M.I. and two Vickers-Maxims, bringing Bruce Hamilton's numbers to 3,000 men, six guns R.F.A. and three Vickers-Maxims.

Like most of the towns in the Orange River Colony, Ladybrand lies in a hollow. It is completely commanded by the Platberg, a high hill roofed by an undulating plateau and having steep, and in some places precipitous sides. About thirty miles west of the town, the Thabanchu—Ladybrand road forks, the northern branch leading direct to Ladybrand, the southern passing through Leeuw River Mills, and thence (on its way to Jackman's Drift and Maseru) crossing the Wepener—Ladybrand —Ficksburg road a few miles south-west of Ladybrand. Each road runs practically parallel to opposite sides of the Platberg, and both are at many points within rifle range of the spurs and western crest of the hill. On the morning of September 5th, Bruce Hamilton sent Lieut.-Colonel E. G. T. Bainbridge, with ninety M.I. and one gun, along the northern road, to demonstrate in that direction, while Lieut.-Colonel White, with one gun and 280 mounted men, was instructed to take the southern road, and endeavour to gain the plateau of the Platberg. Le Gallais, with 250 mounted men and two Vickers-Maxims, supported White, who was soon under a brisk long-range fire from a spur which the enemy had occupied in considerable strength on his left flank. With the 5th M.I. Le Gallais attacked the spur and the valley west of it; but as soon as the Boers became aware of the superiority of the force opposed to them, they beat a hasty retreat, allowing Le Gallais' men to reach the plateau without further opposition, while White moved on to Ladybrand. The enemy then fell back northwards, covering the retirement with a strong rearguard, which, keeping off Bainbridge's M.I. about Modder Poort, eventually fell back on the main body.

Defence of Ladybrand.

The small garrison of Ladybrand, commanded with energy by Major F. White, R.M.L.I. (Commissioner of the District), had been posted in a strong and well-prepared position on the heights outside the town. For three days they had successfully withstood the attacks of about 3,000 Boers, who brought nine Field guns and two machine guns within effective range, whilst their riflemen shot continuously from the close cover of the walled gardens of the outskirts. So well had White sheltered his men that their casualties amounted to only seven wounded, though many horses, mules and oxen were destroyed by the enemy's shell fire, from which it was impossible to protect them on the exposed hillside.

Columns in the Doornberg.

Foiled at Ladybrand, the Boer commandos withdrew in the direction of Allandale, with the reported intention of falling back to the Koranna Berg and Doornberg. Sir A. Hunter decided to follow them up, and, if possible, surround them in the mountains. To effect this it was necessary that the VIIIth division should co-operate, and it was therefore placed at Sir A. Hunter's disposal. On September 6th he left Bloemfontein for Thabanchu, where he arrived next day with Rimington's Guides, 76th battery R.F.A., two guns 43rd (Howitzer) battery, four companies Royal Sussex and one company Highland Light

Infantry. Bruce Hamilton's column had now moved to Leeuw River Mills, and Le Gallais was camped some four miles to the west; a few days later, White's column (Welsh and Wilts I.Y., four Field guns, one Howitzer, and four companies Royal Irish Rifles) marched on Brandfort.

During the following week, September 8th to 15th, the various columns began to close in. MacDonald, who had been despatched on September 3rd from Kroonstad to Winburg, was ordered to search the Doornberg for a supply of ammunition said to have been secreted there, and to lay waste the district. Before this was carried out, however, information was received that a force, under Haasbroek, was in the neighbourhood of Brandfort, and MacDonald was sent in pursuit. Marching southward to Tafelkop on September 13th, he discovered the enemy's laager some eight miles west of that hill. The scouts which screened it were quickly driven in, and the commando broke away in confusion to the north-west, pursued by MacDonald to the north of the branch line from Smaldeel to Winburg, a number of wagons and oxen, and large quantities of supplies and ammunition, as well as a few prisoners, being captured. On the following day, MacDonald reached Kareefontein, midway between Smaldeel and Winburg, where he was reinforced by the Heilbron garrison. At the same time Sir L. Rundle's troops were moving westward. Boyes' column (with which was Sir L. Rundle himself) arrived at Bethlehem on September 11th, and, reconnoitring towards Lindley and Senekal, observed parties of the enemy hovering about the hills. Leaving Bethlehem on September 13th, the column occupied Senekal on the 15th, when it was immediately attacked by a commando of about 400 men with three guns under Hattingh of Vrede and De Villiers of Harrismith. The engagement was of short duration, and the enemy retired on being shelled in the direction of Lindley. Campbell's column left Ficksburg for Trommel on September 8th, but on the 12th was ordered to halt at Spitzkop, twelve miles west of Ficksburg and nine miles north-east of Clocolan. On the same date Sir A. Hunter set out for Allandale, being joined by Bruce Hamilton and Le Gallais next day.

Sept. 15th, 1900. Sir L. Rundle attacked at Senekal.

Various encounters.

On September 17th, Sir A. Hunter's force, except C. E. Knox, who was near Kroonstad, was disposed in the triangle between Ventersburg, Winburg, and Senekal. On that day Boyes' column, midway between Ventersburg and Senekal, engaged a party of about 800 Boers with two guns and two Vickers-Maxims under Van Tonder, and drove it towards the Doornberg. As the commando retired it found another British column advancing against its flank from the south. Van Tonder, caught unawares, thereupon changed his direction, and turning east up the Zand river, made off in disorder towards Senekal, being forced to abandon a gun, much ammunition and thirty wagons. Le Gallais also fell in with a Boer force, which trekked rapidly eastwards from the head of the Zand river towards Ficksburg. Finally Knox, on the march from Kroonstad towards Senekal, intercepted a band of 600 fugitives, and turned them with loss to himself of five killed and wounded.

The Doornberg laid waste.

On September 18th heliographic communication was established between the various columns; but it soon became evident that the Boers, in order to avoid being surrounded in the Doornberg hills, had broken up and dispersed. Sir A. Hunter knew that the main body had evacuated the hills; but uncertain as to the strength of the small parties remaining in the neighbourhood, he determined to lay waste the whole country and ruin the Doornberg as an asylum for wandering commandos. Sir L. Rundle, MacDonald and White were ordered to ravage the district in the following manner:—White and MacDonald were to join hands just outside the north-west corner of the range, and to march across the Doornberg hills towards Bruce Hamilton and Sir L. Rundle, who were holding the eastern side of the Doornberg. As soon as MacDonald approached Sir L. Rundle, Boyes was to be employed in destroying the country and in searching for arms. Le Gallais and Campbell were to move on Senekal. These movements were duly carried out. MacDonald marched south-east, burning such farms in the Doornberg district as were proved to have harboured the enemy; White, moving eastward, did the same. It was thought probable that the scattered commandos would now ride north, and

OPERATIONS IN THE ORANGE RIVER COLONY. 475

re-assemble in the Heilbron and Frankfort districts. To meet this contingency Hunter made a fresh disposition of his columns. His immediate intention was a combined " drive " northwards in the hope of pushing all independent parties of the enemy in front of him. The columns were soon set in motion ; on September 21st, Sir A. Hunter, Bruce Hamilton and Le Gallais were at Senekal ; MacDonald on the left at Veelgepraat (near Ventersburg) ; with Boyes and Campbell (22nd) on the right, at Bethlehem. Next day, a further forward movement was ordered : MacDonald to march to Kaalfontein bridge, on the Valsch river ; Bruce Hamilton and Boyes to converge on Lindley ; while Campbell was directed to proceed towards Reitz.

On the 23rd, Haasbroek, in command of the main Boer force retreating north, was at Blaauwkopje (twelve miles from Bethlehem), with his commando and five guns ; and C. De Wet was reported to be a few miles north of Kaalfontein bridge. Small parties of the enemy were visible on the flanks as Bruce Hamilton and Le Gallais advanced on Lindley. On September 25th, the several columns had reached the following places :— MacDonald, Kaalfontein bridge ; Le Gallais, Hopefield ; Sir A. Hunter, with Bruce Hamilton, near Klipfontein ; Sir L. Rundle and Boyes, Blaauwkopje ; Campbell, near Mosbank on the Liebenbergs Vlei river. Then, as the advance was resumed on the following day, Boyes, moving from Blaauwkopje northwards to the Lindley—Reitz road, in pursuit of the enemy's main force (estimated at 1,500, with two guns and a Vickers-Maxim), engaged the rearguard, which, after a display, fell back on the main body, which was now retreating in a north-westerly direction. On the 25th, Campbell had been successful in a skirmish in which he had but one casualty, and took from the enemy a mountain gun, which had last been in British hands in the disastrous affair at Nicholson's Nek, and a few wagons.*

On September 27th, Sir A. Hunter received a telegram from the Commander-in-Chief, ordering the adoption of a new scheme for the discomfiture of the enemy throughout the Orange River Colony. The general idea was similar to the plan formulated

* See Volume I., page 186.

Scheme for the pacification of the Orange River Colony. by Lord Roberts in his telegram of June 17th, viz. : To garrison certain centres, upon which mobile columns were to be based, and supplied as they roved about destroying all subsistence for the enemy. Sir A. Hunter was directed to exercise a general control over the forces in the north of the Orange River Colony, keeping Le Gallais' mounted troops with him, and moving wherever he could best supervise the operations. Sir L. Rundle, with Campbell's column, was ordered to proceed to Vrede; Boyes' column to Reitz and Frankfort; Bruce Hamilton to Lindley; and MacDonald to Kroonstad. Lord Roberts mentioned that on September 26th there had been a meeting of Boers at Heilbron, where De Wet had exhorted the burghers to continue fighting. About 1,000 Boers and two guns were at Heilbron; but on the approach of a British column, they had retired to the Klip river, in the direction of Frankfort. The Field-Marshal estimated the number of fighting burghers in the Orange River Colony to be now under 3,000.

At this time Sir L. Rundle reported that the Boers in his front had broken up into three parties, under Cornelius Olivier, Haasbroek and Michael Prinsloo. The first was being followed by Boyes' column; the second, engaged by Campbell on September 27th, was moving towards the Liebenbergs Vlei, west of Reitz; and the third was trekking west, towards Lindley. Thus at the end of the month, it seemed as though practically the whole of the Boer force in arms in the Orange River Colony was within the quadrilateral Heilbron—Frankfort—Reitz—Lindley, into which it had been steadily pushed not only by Sir A. Hunter's columns, but also by that of C. E. Knox, based on Kroonstad. Heilbron was now occupied by Knox; Reitz, by Boyes; Lindley, by Bruce Hamilton; while Sir L. Rundle, with the Headquarters of the VIIIth division and Campbell's column, established himself at Conveniente, on the Liebenbergs Vlei river, eighteen miles south of Frankfort; Sir A. Hunter with Le Gallais was near Roodepoort; MacDonald at Kaalfontein.

Colonel Grove was now detached with a column consisting of the 33rd (East Kent) company I.Y., two guns 2nd battery R.F.A., 2nd Royal West Kent regiment and its M.I. company to garrison Frankfort, with supply base at Heilbron. On October 1st Grove, on his way to Frankfort, arrived at Conveniente, where he joined Sir A. Hunter and Le Gallais. Two days later, Frankfort was occupied. Leaving Grove there with three companies Royal West Kent regiment and a gun in strong entrenchments, Sir A. Hunter proceeded to Heilbron with Le Gallais' mounted troops, to find the place already occupied by two battalions from C. E. Knox's column. In accordance with Lord Roberts' original instructions, MacDonald marched to Kroonstad on October 3rd, while Sir L. Rundle, with Campbell's column, moved on the 2nd to the Wilge river, laying waste the country and collecting supplies. He arrived at Vrede on the 5th. A commando of 400 Boers was met with near Tafel Kop (east of the Wilge), which dispersed in various directions on the approach of the column. With garrisons established at Harrismith, Vrede, Reitz, Lindley, Frankfort and Heilbron, from all of which mobile columns continuously patrolled the surrounding country, this portion of the Orange River Colony was so scoured that the bulk of the enemy soon turned their attention to less dangerous quarters. A few small bands remained, contenting themselves with firing on the British columns at long range, with insignificant results.

Meanwhile information had reached Headquarters on September 29th that some 200 Boers, under Fouché, had suddenly appeared in the south-east of the Orange River Colony, and had raided Wepener, robbing the bank, commandeering horses, clothing and supplies. As the town was without a garrison resistance had been out of the question, and the only British representatives (the District Commissioner and a few police) had been forced to take refuge in Basutoland. These Boers, with others, had come south after being driven out of the Koranna Berg and Doornberg, and had been joined by many who were living on their farms, in less danger from the British than from their own countrymen. Strong forces were also reported to be moving on Dewetsdorp, Zastron, Rouxville and Smithfield, none of which places were then garrisoned. Within the next few days, Dewetsdorp, Rouxville and Zastron were

Oct. 3rd—7th, 1900.
Occupation of Dewetsdorp, and other towns.

entered by parties of Boers, who looted what supplies they required. Kelly-Kenny had, however, already taken steps to send aid to the inhabitants of these towns. On October 3rd a column from Bloemfontein, consisting of three companies 2nd Gloucestershire regiment, four guns 68th battery R.F.A. and 150 M.I., occupied Dewetsdorp, from which the enemy had already withdrawn. On the same day, the Black Watch and the Highland L.I. were railed from Kroonstad to Bloemfontein, whence five companies Highland L.I. were despatched to Dewetsdorp, arriving there on October 7th. On the 4th Rouxville and Smithfield were both garrisoned, the former by police from Aliwal North, the latter by a detachment from Springfontein. On the 8th, three companies Highland Light Infantry, two guns 68th R.F.A., and 100 M.I. left Dewetsdorp for Wepener. Zastron alone remained practically in the hands of the enemy for many weeks; near it, on October 24th, a party of ten police from Rouxville captured by surprise a like number of Boers and 17 horses. Thus by the end of October most of the towns in the south-east of the Colony were guarded by British troops.

During this month the Boers showed signs of increased activity in the country to the west of the main railway line. Hitherto the small garrisons occupying the scattered towns and villages had been able to hold their own against such independent raiding parties as roved the districts, although it was sometimes necessary to send a relieving force from Bloemfontein or Brandfort in order to disperse unusually strong bodies. Early in October it became known that the Boers were collecting in the neighbourhood of Hoopstad and Bultfontein, which had been twice heavily attacked. On October 4th, Captain C. G. Henty, with fifty of the Volunteer company 2nd Royal Irish Rifles, and a few mounted men, moving out from Bultfontein with the object of dispersing a neighbouring force, was driven back by superior numbers with a loss of one officer killed, and one officer and six men wounded. Kelly-Kenny, hearing that MacDonald with the Highland brigade was on the way from Kroonstad to Bloemfontein, decided to utilise a portion of the brigade for the purpose of clearing the country and escorting a convoy to the garrisons of the two above-named towns. On arriving at Smaldeel on October 8th, MacDonald received instructions to form a small column for this purpose; and on the following day he himself, with a force consisting of 140 Lovat's Scouts, four guns 82nd battery R.F.A. and four companies Seaforth Highlanders, marched out of Smaldeel towards Bultfontein, with ten days' supplies, the remainder of the brigade proceeding direct to Bloemfontein under Lieut.-Colonel J. W. Hughes-Hallett. Bultfontein was reached on October 11th, and MacDonald was ordered to remain there until a month's supplies had been thrown both into that place and Hoopstad from Brandfort. This occupied a week, when, telegraphic communication being re-opened with Hoopstad and the enemy having disappeared, MacDonald was despatched to Bloemfontein, where he arrived on October 25th.

Before this, incidents had occurred which taught the Boers that the arts of secrecy and surprise were not theirs alone. On the night of the 10th Colonel E. A. W. S. Grove, the commandant at Frankfort, moved out and surrounded a Boer laager about seven miles south-east of the town, and opening fire at dawn forced a capitulation in a few moments. The Boers lost thirty-four men, with horses and rifles, Grove but one man wounded; and though he was pressed by another commando as he returned, he beat off the attack and gained camp with his booty. Again, Captain J. E. Pine-Coffin (Malta M.I.) twice fell upon Boer laagers near Ventersburg Road, namely, on October 8th and 14th, capturing on both occasions all their camp equipment, cattle and horses. From the second of these adventures he only extricated himself from the midst of greatly superior forces, which came to the rescue of their comrades, by doubling backwards and forwards between the converging commandos, finally escaping an apparently certain fate with seven casualties. *Minor British successes.*

In the meantime, the towns in the south-west had been repeatedly attacked by several commandos, which manœuvred independently. As early as October 4th, a Boer force was reported to be advancing on Koffyfontein; and on the 12th Commandant Visser summoned the garrison (fifty miners under *Boers attack the southern townships.*

Captain Robertson, Kimberley Light Horse) to surrender. Instead, Robertson's men took up a position, and throughout the month successfully resisted several attacks before being relieved on November 3rd. Not so fortunate or so alert were some other towns. Jacobsdal, by the treachery of some inhabitants, was entered by the Boers on October 25th, the garrison (Cape Town Highlanders) being surprised in its tents, into which the enemy fired, killing fourteen and wounding eleven. Relief, however, came at once from Modder River; the Boers were driven off, and the houses of the guilty townspeople were razed. In a similar manner the enemy gained admittance to Jagersfontein on the night of October 16th. On the following morning, aided by the inhabitants, they attacked the garrison, which consisted of a half company of the 2nd Seaforth Highlanders and the town guard under Major W. King Hall. These inflicted heavy losses upon a determined assault, and held out, suffering twenty-one casualties, until relieved by a force under Lieut.-Colonel J. W. Hughes-Hallett, consisting of forty mounted irregulars, two guns R.F.A. and a wing 2nd Seaforth Highlanders from Edenburg. On the 18th, 600 Boers got into Philippolis. Here there had been only eleven armed men of the police until Mr. H. Gostling, the Resident Magistrate, beat up a town guard of eighteen men, whom he entrenched near water. Relying on these he flatly refused Fouché's repeated summons to surrender. For six days this handful, who were very short of ammunition, defied every effort to reduce them, though half their number fell, and were finally relieved on the 24th by a party of Imperial Yeomanry. A few days earlier Fauresmith had maintained the flag against similar odds and with equal honour. Here was a company (117 men) of the 2nd Seaforth Highlanders, twenty Imperial Yeomanry and a town guard of seventeen men, under Captain A. B. A. Stewart, of the Seaforth. At 4.15 a.m. on October 19th, the Boers, who held commanding positions, attacked hotly, only to be driven away after four hours' fighting. There were eight casualties amongst the garrison. In all these affairs determination and gallantry were shown by members of the defence, which consideration of space alone causes to be

OPERATIONS IN THE ORANGE RIVER COLONY. 481

left undescribed. When such attacks are foiled, though every circumstance—numbers, position, mobility and surprise—is in their favour, it is with regret that the deeds of the individual soldiers, whose devotion contributed to success, must be passed over in silence.

While the Boers were thus overrunning the south-west of the colony, they were displaying no less activity in the north-west. Sir A. Hunter, at Kroonstad, learned that Bothaville was being used by the enemy as a base of operations for their attacks on the railway and telegraphs. The place had no British garrison, and the inhabitants, breaking the oath which it was almost impossible to keep, openly sided with the burghers. Sir A. Hunter, therefore, determined upon the only efficacious remedy, namely, to destroy the village, all but the churches and such buildings as were used as hospitals. With this intention, and having been informed that 1,600 Boers were moving on Bothaville from the south-east, he left Kroonstad on October 16th. He took with him Bruce Hamilton's column (four companies Cameron Highlanders, four companies Royal Sussex, half 39th battery R.F.A. and 70 mounted men), which, based on Lindley, had been laying waste the country between that town and Kroonstad, and had gone into Kroonstad for the purpose of escorting a convoy back to Lindley. The 3rd cavalry brigade coming from Kroonstad, as well as Rimington's mounted troops and those of Le Gallais, which now numbered over 1,000, with five guns, were ordered to co-operate. During the march only small parties of the enemy were encountered (five casualties), and Bothaville was occupied without resistance on the 20th. The 3rd cavalry brigade was then sent westward to Commando Drift, to reconnoitre and to get in touch with a column which, under Major-General H. H. Settle, had been ordered to join hands with Sir A. Hunter at Bothaville. Settle's force, consisting of 600 mounted men, ten guns and 1,350 infantry, had been operating for some time in the country east of the Modder River—Vryburg railway, and had worked its way to Christiana. Leaving that place on October 13th, Settle occupied Bloemhof on the 14th, and Hoopstad on the 17th. Marching thence towards Bothaville, he was briskly attacked at night for forty-five minutes at Elizabethsrust on the 19th, losing one officer and fifteen men wounded. On the 21st he met the 3rd cavalry brigade. It now seemed that the enemy had disappeared north of the Vaal, and none were reported to be in the neighbourhood. Consequently, on October 22nd, Settle marched back towards Hoopstad. On the way he was set upon by nearly 700 Boers, who appeared unexpectedly, and for two hours pressed hard upon the column. So closely did they beset the seventy-three wagons which formed the train, that the Cape Police, part of the escort, had to abandon two Maxim guns, owing to the destruction of the teams of horses, and at the close of the action Settle's losses were thirty-six killed, wounded and missing. A week later Settle reached Boshof, where he was at once called upon to provide for the relief of Koffyfontein.

<small>Oct. 22nd, 1900. Settle attacked.</small>

Sir A. Hunter, after destroying some fifty houses in Bothaville, left on October 23rd to return to Kroonstad, which he reached on the 26th. Here he learned that a party of the enemy with guns had taken up a position and was threatening the line to the east of the railway, between Ventersburg Road station and Ventersburg Town. Lord Roberts, being apprised of this, ordered Sir A. Hunter to clear the district forthwith, and on October 28th and 29th, the troops detailed for the operations left Kroonstad. On the 28th, the 3rd cavalry brigade and the mounted troops of Bruce Hamilton's column (viz.: Rimington's Guides, 120; Imperial Yeomanry, 70; mounted infantry, 70) marched *viâ* Geneva Siding from Ventersburg Road; and on the following day Sir A. Hunter and Bruce Hamilton (the latter's force augmented by two companies 3rd battalion Buffs, one company 4th Argyll and Sutherland and one 5-in. gun), reached Ventersburg Road by rail. Hearing that Ventersburg Town, as well as a farm north-west of it was still in the occupation of the enemy, Sir A. Hunter at 8 p.m. sent on the 3rd cavalry brigade, with orders to make a détour and get astride the Senekal road east of Ventersburg; while the remainder of the force moved at midnight direct on the town. Before it was reached a Boer outpost was discovered holding a nek some two miles

OPERATIONS IN THE ORANGE RIVER COLONY. 483

outside Ventersburg Town, and the burghers stoutly defended themselves until their flank was turned, when they rode off. No further resistance was offered ; but this incidental engagement had caused several casualties in Sir A. Hunter's force, the officer commanding the battery (Major J. Hanwell) being killed, and fourteen men wounded. Ventersburg Town was occupied by the 16th Lancers at 6 a.m. (October 30th), and Bruce Hamilton at once took in hand the removal of the male inhabitants, the destruction of the houses and farms of suspects, and the devastation of the surrounding country.

When Sir A. Hunter left Bothaville, Le Gallais' mounted force was ordered to proceed to Reitzburg, for the purpose of co-operating with C. E. Knox. That officer had been instructed by Lord Roberts to move at once from Vredefort Road into the Transvaal, taking with him de Lisle's M.I. (about 700 men, with three guns) and the Colonial division. The object of the movement was to assist Major-General G. Barton, who was practically invested at Frederikstad by a large force of the enemy under C. De Wet. Before Knox could join hands with him, Barton had been reinforced on October 25th by a battalion of infantry and 550 mounted men, and had scattered the Boers in all directions.* Knox reached Potchefstroom on the 26th, and then received information that De Wet was at Elandsfontein (near Lindequee), with the intention of recrossing the Vaal, and moving on Heilbron. At dawn next morning Knox, with the Colonial division, moved rapidly in the direction of Rensburg Drift. On the way he heard that De Wet, with 1,000 men and six guns, had the day before been pointing towards Schoeman's Drift, but had changed his direction towards Buffelshoek, on finding Le Gallais' force and some infantry waiting for him at Tygerfontein. At 5 p.m. on the 27th, Knox caught the enemy in the act of breaking laager at Rensburg Drift, midway between Venterskroon and Parys, and punished him severely. Not waiting to fight, the Boers broke and fled southwards ; but Le Gallais, who had previously been ordered to move on Vredefort *via* Venterskroon, succeeded in heading them off, and drove them

Le Gallais ordered to Reitzburg.

Oct. 27th, 1900. Knox gains touch with De Wet.

* See page 512.

up stream to Parys. The commando was completely disorganised; two guns and seven wagons were captured, and a shell, well placed by U. battery R.H.A., blew up an ammunition wagon; the mounted infantry lost but two men wounded. Darkness and a violent storm which raged throughout the night put an end to pursuit, and De Wet doubled and turned south-west, escaping in the direction of Bothaville. Next evening he laagered at Witkopjes, where he remained undiscovered for several days.

On October 28th, Barton reached Potchefstroom, and Le Gallais was despatched to near Parys, to endeavour to gain touch with the enemy; but he fell in with only a few. Knox, under the impression that De Wet was still moving up stream, intended to follow in the direction of Viljoen's Drift; but was forced to abandon the pursuit owing to the impassable state of the roads. Next day Knox returned to Vredefort Road, having disposed his force as follows: Le Gallais at Leeuw Spruit station; de Lisle at De Wet's farm, near Roodewal; the infantry at Rensburg Drift; and the Colonial division at Venterskroon, to be employed in clearing the hills and searching for buried ammunition. On the 30th the infantry were moved to Shepstone, the Colonial division to Geelbeksvlei, near Essenbosch, and Le Gallais further south along the line to Roodewal. On the 31st the movements were continued; for, although De Wet had not yet been located, information pointed to his being in the neighbourhood of Rhebokfontein. Le Gallais reached Honing Spruit, the infantry joined de Lisle near Roodewal, and Knox himself went by rail to Rhenoster. Minor incidents at this time were the capture of the mail for Pretoria, and the surprise and surrender of a post near Holfontein on the 28th.

Plans to enclose De Wet.

Once more a scheme was laid for closing in on De Wet. A section of Vickers-Maxim guns was sent to join the Colonial division to proceed with it to Witkopjes, and the infantry at Roodewal were strengthened by the Elswick battery. Le Gallais was instructed to clear away small parties of the enemy said to be on Rhenoster Kop, and then to continue his march to Tweekuil, in order to be on the west side of Rhebokfontein at

OPERATIONS IN THE ORANGE RIVER COLONY.

daylight on November 3rd. With Le Gallais on the west, and de Lisle's M.I. and the infantry blocking the passages of the Rhenoster river to the south and east, the Colonial division was to attack from the north. On the 2nd, however, it was discovered that De Wet had again disappeared, whether to the north or towards Bothaville could not be ascertained. It was, therefore, decided to block the drifts across the Vaal to the north and north-west, and on the 4th the infantry proceeded to Schoeman's Drift, the Colonial division to the vicinity of Scandinavia Drift, Le Gallais to Elandsvlei (north of Bothaville), and Knox, with de Lisle's M.I., reached Blesboklaagte. On the following day (November 5th), Knox, with de Lisle, marched on to Elandsvlei, meeting with some opposition on the way, and receiving conflicting reports about the enemy's movements. At first it was thought that the Boers were trending northward; but later a party of 200 were seen posting in the opposite direction, and Knox ordered the Colonial division to make for Kroonstad, the infantry to return to Rhenoster Camp, he himself intending to move on Bothaville next morning. Late that night he received a report from Le Gallais, whose force had spent the day in reconnoitring, that he had found the Boers holding the Bothaville Drift, had attacked and driven them off and secured the crossing, with the loss of five men wounded. Next morning Knox started for Bothaville.

Le Gallais, who had with him the 5th, 17th and 18th companies Imperial Yeomanry, the 5th, 7th and 8th battalions M.I. (about 1,050 men) and U. battery R.H.A., had moved rapidly on November 5th towards Bothaville, and by noon had reached a point about five miles to the west of the town. There it was intended to camp while a reconnaissance was pushed forward. In the afternoon, the 5th, supported by the 8th M.I. and two guns U. battery, drew towards the right bank of the Valsch river, which flows through Bothaville. A few Boers were seen on the distant skyline across the stream; but they made no reply to a shell which was fired at them, and the British advance guard carefully approached the houses dotted along the right bank. When the mounted screen reached a point within 1,000 yards'

Le Gallais in pursuit of De Wet.

range of the ridge beyond the river, a single shot was fired, and was immediately followed by a storm of shells and bullets. The advance guard, finding no cover at hand, hastily retired out of range, with only three casualties, and the guns shelled the Boer position until dark. When the moon rose, the 5th M.I. advanced on the town, and finding it unoccupied, pushed on (the 8th M.I. in support) across the river, which was in flood. The ridge, whence the Boers had opened fire, was soon reached and found untenanted. There the advanced troops spent the remaining hours of the night, while the main body of Le Gallais' force, with the baggage, moved up to Bothaville.

At 4 a.m. on November 6th, pursuit was resumed, following the tracks of the Boer guns, which were clearly marked in the wet ground. The 5th M.I. scouted rapidly ahead in the dark; the 8th M.I., Imperial Yeomanry and three guns of U. battery, followed in support; while the other troops, with one gun, held the drift and guarded the baggage at Bothaville.

<small>Nov. 6th, 1900. Le Gallais surprises De Wet.</small>

The first intimation that the enemy was near was the surprise within two miles of the river of a Boer piquet of five men, who were found asleep and captured before they could give the alarm. The mounted infantry went on. Suddenly, as day was breaking, the scouts, topping a low ridge, beheld a strange scene. Below them were grazing herds of oxen and horses, amongst which rode Boers engaged in collecting the beasts for the day's march. Within 300 yards of the British scouts lay De Wet's long-sought laager. The remainder of the advance guard was soon up, and lined the ridge. A heavy fire was then poured into the panic-stricken burghers, two guns of U. battery at the same time opening from a position slightly in rear.

The 5th M.I. (Major K. E. Lean) now became hotly engaged. They were disposed as follows: the Worcestershire company in the centre, the Royal Irish company holding a kraal on the left, and the Buffs company on the right and right front. After a few minutes a forward rush was made to rising ground a little in advance of the kraal held by the Royal Irish. This new position was actually on the edge of the Boer laager. In an enclosure barely twenty yards away crouched two Boer marks-

<small>The action near Bothaville.</small>

men, who, during the next five hours, remained undetected whilst they shot down any man of the 5th M.I. who showed himself on the ridge. Close by a desperate fight was in progress. The Boers at once realised their imminent peril. Those who could secure their horses made off with all speed, many bareback—De Wet and Steyn amongst them. There remained about 200 men, who, unable to find their mounts, took shelter in a square stone-walled kraal, behind two dams. A few State artillerymen brought three guns into action in the open, and bravely endeavoured to get the others away, and to inspan their Cape carts; but U. battery burst case and shrapnel over them at close range, effectually forbidding all movement, and driving every man to cover. Behind their stone shelters, the burghers then stood at bay, and fought with valour.

The 8th M.I. rapidly reinforced the 5th, coming up into a farmhouse and a kraal in échelon on the left. The farmhouse, being centrally situated, was unfortunately chosen by Le Gallais as his Headquarters, and no sooner did he enter it than it became a target for the enemy's rifles. Le Gallais and his staff officer, as well as Lieut.-Colonel W. C. Ross (8th M.I.) and some ten men, held the house; but the figures of the occupants, sharply relieved against a door open behind, were clearly visible through the windows, and bullets poured in. The house became a trap in which any movement brought instant death. Amongst the first Le Gallais fell mortally hurt about 6.30 a.m.; then Ross was dangerously wounded. The command devolved on Major P. B. Taylor, R.H.A. He soon observed that the Boers who had first escaped from the laager were now preparing counter-attacks against both flanks. The troops, in fact, were being fast thrown on the defensive; and, ordering up all available men from the rear, he despatched a call for help to Knox, at that time eight or ten miles away. At 8 a.m. 150 men of the 7th M.I. (Le Gallais' original force) came up on the flank, just in time to save the situation; and a Maxim, opening fire at 1,000 yards' range, held the Boers to their cover, and drove off others who were hovering about. The guns of U. battery, which were suffering severely in the open, continued in action; in one

Le Gallais killed.

instance a gun detachment was reduced to a single man, who served his gun alone, as a comrade had done under similar circumstances in front of Fort Wylie at Colenso (December 15th, 1899).

Now for two hours the situation on both sides remained unchanged. Taylor's men could do no more than pin the enemy to the ground, until help should arrive. The Boers still showed no sign of giving in, though their fire had been much subdued. At 10.15 a.m. the foremost of Knox's reinforcements began to appear. De Lisle's M.I. galloped on to the field, the Australians leading, and swept round to the Boers' left flank; while the Imperial Yeomanry closed around their right, thus hemming the laager in. Undaunted by the appearance of these fresh troops, the Boers continued to use their rifles with such effect that de Lisle, who had now assumed command, determined to put a summary end to the resistance, and ordered Taylor to go in with the bayonet. Forty men of the 5th M.I. were detailed; they were told to open magazine-fire for three minutes and then to storm. Their preliminary fusilade had not ceased before the white flag was hoisted over the laager. The Boers had done as much as they could, and enough for honour. The capture included one 12-pr. (from Q. battery R.H.A.), one 15-pr. (from 14th battery R.F.A.), four Krupp guns, one Vickers-Maxim, one machine gun, quantities of artillery and small-arm ammunition, a large number of horses, carts, saddles, spare arms, and one hundred unwounded and thirty wounded prisoners. The casualties on both sides had been heavy. Le Gallais' force lost three officers and ten men killed, and eight officers and twenty-five men wounded. Of the Boers, twenty-five were buried on the field. But well might Major-General Knox, in his report on the action, write that the success, however valuable, had been dearly bought with the blood of Le Gallais, than whom the British service had contained no officer more intrepid or more to be missed from a campaign which called forth his rare and peculiar military talents. Immediately after the surrender, Knox pushed on after De Wet and the Boers who had succeeded in breaking away early in the morning. After pursuing in a south-easterly direction for seven miles, Knox found that the enemy had broken up into small parties and had dispersed all over the district. He then returned to Kroonstad to refit.

The escape of De Wet boded trouble in the immediate future. It was not long before he had collected his scattered commandos. He then crossed the railway, and moved south-east, in the direction of the Koranna Berg. The centre of activity, therefore, once more shifted to the districts lying to the east and south-east of Bloemfontein, whither such British troops as were available were immediately despatched. Knox's force, which had returned to Kroonstad from Bothaville on November 8th, was sent on by rail to Bloemfontein. On the 22nd Knox, after conferring with the Commander-in-Chief at Johannesburg, arrived to superintend the operations of three columns commanded by Lieut.-Colonels T. D. Pilcher, J. S. S. Barker and E. B. Herbert. Lieut.-General Kelly-Kenny had now handed over his command at Bloemfontein to Sir A. Hunter.

At the end of October the situation in the Orange River Colony was as follows :—

The Boers were in occupation of Fouriesburg and Ficksburg, and small parties were scattered about the whole of the country situated to the east of the Bethlehem—Frankfort road, opposing the columns of the VIIIth division. On October 26th, Sir L. Rundle had met some hundreds of these six miles out of Bethlehem, and a brisk fight to clear them from his road to Harrismith had cost him seventeen casualties. Other parties were in the neighbourhood of Frankfort, Heilbron, Lindley and Senekal, and were raiding the districts further south, as far as the Orange river. De Wet, with a strong force, was moving on Dewetsdorp, on mischief bent.

All these hostile movements, independent and combined, had to be met by small mobile columns, assisted by the garrisons of the various towns. Harrismith, Vrede, Frankfort, Reitz and Bethlehem were garrisoned by the VIIIth division ; Heilbron was still held by the troops which C. E. Knox had thrown into it at the beginning of October ; Lindley had been evacuated, and the inhabitants removed, but was remanned in the middle of November by Bruce Hamilton, who detached a part of his force there, and with the remainder and the Colonial division operated towards Heilbron and Frankfort. Of the towns immediately south-east of Bloemfontein, Dewetsdorp was garrisoned by a mixed force, consisting of 2nd Gloucestershire regiment, six officers and 228 men; mounted infantry of the same regiment, twenty-three men; 1st Highland Light Infantry, three officers and 112 men; mounted infantry Royal Irish Rifles, one officer and thirty-five men; two guns 68th battery R.F.A., two officers and fifty-six men; and details three officers and eleven men, making a total of fifteen officers and 465 men.

<small>Nov. 14th, 1900.
De Wet approaches Dewetsdorp.</small>

On November 14th, Major W. G. Massy, R.F.A., Commandant of Dewetsdorp, received warning from the Intelligence Officer at Bloemfontein that De Wet and Haasbroek, with a force of 1,700 men and one or two guns, were moving south, and had reached a point some forty miles north of the Thabanchu—Ladybrand road. From Bloemfontein to Thabanchu and thence to Ladybrand a line of blockhouses had been established, with the object of checking a Boer movement to the south; but De Wet was not to be baulked, and approaching the line on the afternoon of the 16th, where there was a gap of 2,000 yards between two blockhouses, he decided to rush through. Accordingly, he opened fire with a Krupp gun on one of the blockhouses, near Thabanchu, and with his whole force successfully ran the gauntlet. Massy was duly informed of this, and further, that the Boers were apparently making for Daggafontein, in the direction of Dewetsdorp. Next day (November 17th), his mounted infantry observed a Boer laager near Grootfontein, having advanced scouts on Paul Schmidt's Berg, which overhangs the town on the east. On the 18th the enemy made a reconnaissance in force to within 4,000 yards of the town, retiring under fire from the guns of the garrison. The commandos did not go far, however; and on the following day they were discovered to be in laager four miles south of Damfontein.

<small>Investment of Dewetsdorp, Nov. 19th, 1900.</small>

Dewetsdorp is closely surrounded on three sides by steep hills, seamed with watercourses and strewn with boulders and rocks. The fourth side is flat and open, except for a deep nullah, or dry river-bed, which passes through the town. The garrison was disposed as follows:—One company Highland Light Infantry held a kopje to the south-east of and overlooking the town, with a small observation post on Lonely Kop, to the east; two Cossack posts were thrown out in a south-westerly direction, towards Reddersburg; the remainder of the troops were posted on the high ground to the north and west of the town. On November 19th Massy endeavoured to break the cordon which was enclosing him by sending out a force to shell the laager. The Boers replied by rushing two of the outlying posts the same night. They then practised the ruse of disappearing entirely from the neighbourhood, only to return on the night of the 20th, when they drove in two other small posts. At about 3.30 a.m. on the 21st the piquet on Lonely Kop was rushed, and the Boers, now in possession of high ground commanding the main camp of the garrison, poured in a vigorous fire. At 6 a.m. they brought a Krupp gun into action, but with little effect, as the guns of the 68th battery R.F.A. soon silenced it. Yet they continued to gain ground, driving the garrison of a fourth post back on the main camp. About midday, another strong commando was seen to be approaching, and Massy attempted to hold the eastern side of the town with his mounted infantry. This failed at once, the mounted infantry being forced back by a hot cross-fire from the nullahs running from the hills towards the town. Desultory firing went on all day; the trenches occupied by the Highland Light Infantry were attacked, the burghers establishing themselves in close proximity to them. By nightfall the enemy had gained possession of the heights to the west and north of the town.

Before daylight on the 22nd firing was resumed. As soon as the sun had risen Massy flashed a message to Bloemfontein, asking for assistance, and was answered that a column would start at once from Edenburg. At 8 a.m. the Boers drove in another post; and with their gun in action on Lonely Kop, in addition to the overwhelming rifle fire which they were now able to bring to bear, they soon raked the shelters occupied by the men of the Highland Light Infantry. These trenches were, however, held until dark, when the occupants were ordered to set fire to the stores at the south end of the town, and to fall back on the main position, which was done at 7 p.m. The night was spent in improving the defences of the main position, by strengthening the gun pits for the two Field guns, and by providing head cover and shelter from reverse fire.

At 2.30 a.m. on the 23rd, No. 1 outpost, composed of a detachment of the Gloucestershire regiment, and situated in an important position to the north of the town, was surprised by a party which crept stealthily up the side of the hill. A strenuous resistance was offered; but after losing half their numbers in killed and wounded, the men were forced to surrender, and the Boers gained yet another point of vantage. The capture of this post, coupled with the occupation of the ground evacuated on the previous evening by the Highland Light Infantry, enabled the enemy to pass through the town to the western edge of the plateau. From their new position the Boers now looked into nearly the whole of the defences at close rifle range. Moreover, by moving their gun on to the heights towards the Smithfield road, they commanded the ravine, wherein lay the water supply of the garrison; they had already shot down all the horses, which had been collected in another ravine.* With daylight came a tremendous cross-fire from every direction. The garrison, now crowded behind sangars and in trenches about the main camp, could do little; but the Field guns, one in a donga running down towards the town, the other near a trench occupied by some men of the Gloucestershire regiment, continued firing from their pits. At 2 p.m. Massy received a message that one of the guns had been put out of action, and most of the gun detachment wounded. At 4 p.m. a young officer, who with his men had all day been defending a trench near the other gun, was persuaded to send a message to the commandant asking permission to raise the white flag. Massy peremptorily refused; but his reply was not delivered, and at 4.45 p.m. he heard that the detachment had surrendered. Nevertheless, firing continued

* For two acts of gallantry, performed on November 22nd and 23rd, Private C. Kennedy, 2nd Highland Light Infantry, was awarded the Victoria Cross.

OPERATIONS IN THE ORANGE RIVER COLONY. 493

in other parts until 5.25 p.m. Then Massy was told that his wounded were being murdered. Giving credence to a statement neither well-founded nor likely to be, he ordered the white flag to be shown. Even had no such influence precipitated the surrender, it is doubtful if the garrison could have held out much longer. Three days of continuous and creditable fighting had exhausted the defence. On this final day the troops had been under fire for fifteen hours. The drinking water was in the hands of the enemy, and only at the point of the bayonet could a bottle have been filled. Of the garrison fourteen men were killed, four officers and seventy-one men wounded, and six men missing. The remainder were marched away along the Wepener road as prisoners of war.

<small>Nov. 23rd, 1900. Surrender of Dewetsdorp.</small>

That the promised succour from Edenburg did not reach the garrison was due to the facts that the relief column was late in starting and that its march was hampered by slow-moving ox transport. Leaving Edenburg on the 22nd, Barker, with 500 men of the 9th Lancers, Irish I.Y., 2nd Seaforth Highlanders and four guns, supported by Herbert, with 600 men of the 9th and 17th Lancers, 3rd Grenadier Guards, and four guns, reached Driekop, nine miles west of Dewetsdorp, on the morning of the 24th, and found himself confronted by an extensive and strongly-entrenched position, held by about 1,000 Boers, with two guns. Hearing no firing in the direction of Dewetsdorp, and obtaining no information about the garrison, Barker decided that he could not without reinforcements attack the Boers opposing him, and sent word to Edenburg to that effect. At 2.30 p.m. on the 25th, Pilcher's column (800 men, four guns R.H.A., two machine guns and a Vickers-Maxim), accompanied by Major-General C. E. Knox, left Edenburg for Dewetsdorp, and joined hands with Barker at a point some six miles west of Dewetsdorp, at 1.30 p.m. next day (26th). There Knox learnt that all had long been over at Dewetsdorp.

<small>Relief columns for Dewetsdorp.</small>

There had been no flaw in the plans of De Wet. Well aware that a column was marching to the relief of Dewetsdorp, he left a strong force to cover the march of himself and his prisoners towards Smithfield, and was well on his road before the pursuit

<small>De Wet escapes, and is pursued,</small>

commenced. A demonstration on November 28th against Boshof by another detachment served to draw some attention from his movements. On the 27th Knox and Pilcher caught up his rearguard nine miles south of Dewetsdorp in a position covering the laager of the main body, and after a protracted fight and capturing a few horses and wagons, drove it south and south-west. Helvetia, midway to Smithfield, was reached in the afternoon, when Barker and Herbert having joined from Dewetsdorp, the march was continued, on a wide front next day. From Smithfield on November 29th Knox moved to Carmel, fifteen miles along the Bethulie road, and Barker and Herbert to Waterval, four miles in rear of Knox; on the 30th, the former reached Slik Spruit, eight miles from Bethulie, and the two latter camped three miles behind. Every effort was now made to frustrate De Wet's evident design of invading Cape Colony.

and descends on Cape Colony. To that end he had gathered all available commandos on the banks of the Orange river, adding to his numbers by recruiting or impressing among the farmers of the district, who had either taken the oath of neutrality or were British subjects. On December 1st, the British troops at hand to head him back, exclusive of those employed in guarding the railway between the Orange river and Bloemfontein, were as follows:—

The Guards brigade (3rd Grenadier, 1st and 2nd Coldstream) held the bridges and drifts across the Orange river from Aliwal North to Orange River (Hopetown) bridge. The Guards had already received a hint of the plan of campaign from a three hours' tentative attack by De Wet's men on Zand Drift near Aliwal North (November 27th), four casualties resulting. C. E. Knox, with Pilcher's and Barker's columns, was at Bethulie; Herbert's column at Slik Spruit; Lieut.-Colonel W. H. Williams, with 300 of the 1st M.I., four guns, and three companies of the 1st Suffolk, was near Odendaal Stroom; other columns were on the way south from Bloemfontein. MacDonald, the Highland brigade having been broken up, had assumed command at Edenburg.

De Wet was at this time joined by Hertzog, and it was arranged that the latter should make an inroad into Cape Colony by crossing the river between Norval's Pont and Orange River bridge, while De Wet attempted to cross between Bethulie and Aliwal North. That they might have succeeded had the weather proved favourable is probable; but within a few days the climate changed the whole situation. Knox had moved his four columns (Pilcher's, Barker's, Herbert's and Williams') from place to place, in tune with the information which he received of De Wet's movements. On December 4th, Barker, Herbert and Williams were at Carmel, with Pilcher to the south on the Caledon. Then rain fell; the Orange river, which previously had been fordable almost anywhere, immediately rose to flood level, and became impassable except at the bridges and the best drifts. The Boers under De Wet now found themselves in an awkward predicament in the angle of the Orange and Caledon rivers, with one flooded river before them and another behind. Though he knew that the bridges were strongly held, De Wet yet hoped to find a drift unguarded, and made for Odendaal Stroom. He was too late; for Knox, guessing his intention, had placed Colonel C. J. Long in command of Herbert's and Pilcher's columns and the Suffolk regiment on December 5th, and ordered him to move at once from Karreepoort Drift, by Bethulie Bridge, to the south bank of the Orange river. At Bethulie next day Long met Lord Kitchener, who sent him with two days' supplies to bar the passage of the Orange with his mounted men at Odendaal Stroom, the Suffolk regiment being railed south to Knapdaar. Finding this his last hope gone, De Wet was forced to abandon the invasion of Cape Colony, and to devise instead means of escaping from the troops and floods which were in league to surround him. The Orange was a torrent; scouts whom he sent to examine the Caledon returned, pronouncing it impassable. The Boer leader began to despair of saving his commando.

De Wet in straits.

Knox, opening up heliographic communication with Long on December 7th, ordered him to march to Aliwal North, and sent the Suffolk regiment by rail to the same place. There Long, on the 8th, received instructions to leave Herbert at Aliwal North, and to proceed with Pilcher's column to Rouxville. Knox, with Barker and Williams, was then at Commissie Bridge, on the Caledon river, south of Smithfield, hoping to intercept the Boers' retreat. De Wet, searching the banks anxiously for a crossing, left everywhere a trail of dead horses behind him, and soon abandoned his Krupp gun and a wagon of ammunition. Finding the Commissie Bridge guarded, he moved rapidly northeast, discarding about 500 horses and many carts, as he made for a passage some miles upstream. Then fortune suddenly favoured the Boer leader; the rain abated; the Caledon fell as rapidly as it had risen; De Wet darted across the river and broke away in the direction of Dewetsdorp. On December 10th, Long had been ordered to clear the Zastron district and march on Wepener. On the 11th, hearing of De Wet's escape, he changed his direction to Smithfield, after which, in conjunction with Knox, he took part in the pursuit of De Wet towards the north. Thus signally failed the attempt to invade Cape Colony. But De Wet's abortive effort and apparently miraculous escape had rather increased than lessened his already high reputation. He was now the central figure of the campaign. Wherever he moved he attracted to himself large numbers of British troops, and kept under arms many a burgher whose courage for continued resistance was drawn from him alone. His influence extended to the most distant parts, for his deeds, losing nothing by report, resounded from end to end of the theatre of war.

De Wet again escapes.

Such, on December 11th, 1900, was the situation in the southeast of the Orange River Colony. In other parts no serious fighting had taken place since the beginning of November, though the main railway line had been wrecked at several points. The VIIIth division was still in the east of Orange River Colony, radiating continually mobile detachments, which collected masses of supplies and droves of cattle. Bruce Hamilton, with columns under Rimington and Maxwell, was clearing the country along the line of the Vaal between Parys and Viljoen's Drift. Finally Settle, who had been skirmishing and foraging for some time in the south-west of the Colony, had arrived at Edenburg, laden with booty of every description.

CHAPTER XXI.

OPERATIONS IN THE WESTERN TRANSVAAL * (continued).

SEPTEMBER TO NOVEMBER, 1900.

ON the day (September 12th) on which Lord Methuen marched from Otto's Hoop, Douglas, from Klipkuil, had a successful brush near Manana, in which, after a long chase, he captured sixteen prisoners, several wagons and a quantity of stock. Schweizer Reneke, elaborately fortified as it was, was found to be in no danger from a party of 400 men under T. De Beer, which had been little inclined to attack the formidable earthworks. The commando was easily dispersed, and from it Lord Methuen captured a Maxim and one of the guns lost nine months before at the battle of Colenso, as well as twenty-eight prisoners, twenty-six wagons, 800 cattle, 4,000 sheep, and 20,000 rounds of ammunition, while several Boers were killed during the pursuit.

After starting in an easterly direction towards a Boer laager at Korannafontein, Lord Methuen received orders to take his whole force to Rustenburg, as Mr. Steyn had left the Eastern Transvaal, and was on his way back to the Orange River Colony. Marching northwards on parallel roads both columns captured a few prisoners, and would have taken more had not parties of Boers avoided capture only by being disguised in British uniforms. On September 28th Douglas' column had a slight bout with the enemy. The rest of the march to the Magaliesberg, *viâ* Rietfontein (south of Tafel Kop), was without incident.

<small>Lord Methuen's movements.</small>

* See map No. 38.

Lord Roberts had now determined to deal more summarily with his opponents. He recognised that he had given too much credit to the honesty of those who yielded, too little, perhaps, to the undoubted difficulties of their position. Peace was remote indeed so long as his terms to the burghers led to no other result than this—that they abused the freedom gained by their oath of allegiance to assist, or actually reinforce, the commandos in the field. He resolved to employ columns to scour the country in all directions and to spare no farms which might contribute to the enemy's subsistence. Lord Methuen, though he had usually had to march too fast on special missions to have leisure for ravaging, had already begun the process, his wake showing bare amid the rich farm-lands between Lichtenburg and Olifants Nek.

Clements' movements.

Clements' column had at the same time been clearing the Rustenburg and Hekpoort districts and the country between Krugersdorp and Johannesburg. With Clements were a half squadron of the Protectorate regiment, the 8th battery Royal Field artillery (four guns), two 4.7-in. guns, manned by the 5th company Eastern division R.G.A., a section of the 38th Field company R.E., the 1st Border regiment and the 2nd King's Own Yorkshire Light Infantry. These concentrated at Commando Nek on August 31st, and were joined next day by the 2nd Northumberland Fusiliers, the 2nd Worcester regiment, 237 mounted infantry, and, a few days later, by Brigadier-General Ridley's brigade of mounted infantry (eighty-four officers, 1,139 other ranks, two Field guns and two Vickers-Maxims).

Leaving a garrison of the 2nd King's Own Yorkshire Light Infantry and half the 1st Border regiment, a 4.7-in. gun and two Field guns, to hold Commando and Zilikat's Neks, Clements moved westward on September 3rd. Marching along the Witwatersrand range he was opposed by only a few scouts, though General De la Rey lay near Boschfontein with some 1,200 men and five guns. De la Rey was short of ammunition, and after making a show of opposition on successive positions, he retired through Olifants Nek. Clements then moved southwards and returned to Hekpoort. A false rumour that President

Steyn had arrived at De la Rey's camp led to Ridley's brigade being sent to Zeekoehoek on September 18th. Next day the rest of Clements' troops followed as far as Thorndale, and Lord Roberts proposed to send Paget to Commando Nek to co-operate. Paget's column was at this time fully engaged with Erasmus' commando, and he represented that he could only spare one battalion and a few mounted men for the Magaliesberg. Moreover, there was danger lest the remnants of the Boer army, shattered in the Eastern Transvaal, might attempt to escape by crossing the Pietersburg line of railway. Paget's force, therefore, stood fast north-east of Pretoria watching the line; and on the 23rd Lord Roberts sent Broadwood's cavalry brigade and a column* under Lieut.-Colonel Bradley from Pretoria towards Rustenburg, to help Clements to break up De la Rey's detachment before it could be strengthened by the fragments of Botha's army. Cunningham's brigade was to garrison Rustenburg, and co-operate in the attempt to crush De la Rey and intercept Steyn. De la Rey's main force was now reported to be in laager near Olifants Nek, and plans were laid to surround it. Ridley's mounted infantry, with four days' rations, marched towards Quaggafontein, with orders to move to Elandsfontein on September 26th, to cut off the enemy's wagons. On the same day, eight miles east of Rustenburg, Broadwood's (the 2nd) cavalry brigade, accompanied by Bradley's column, drove Steenkamp with 500 burghers, a Vickers-Maxim and two Maxims, northwards. Clements, on arriving at Olifants Nek, found that De la Rey had left Steenkamp's commando to obstruct Broadwood, and had retired along the western slopes of the Magaliesberg beyond Magato Nek. Clements then marched to Doornlaagte, where he was joined by Ridley, whose force had been delayed by the opposition of 300 men and two guns, under Commandant Edwards. On September 30th the whole column crossed the mountains, Ridley's brigade by Magato Nek to

Plans to surround De la Rey.

---

* Composition—A composite infantry battalion (800), half 15th brigade Bearer company, half 15th brigade Field Hospital. Broadwood since August 28th had been at Pretoria.

Rustenburg, Clements' men through Olifants Nek, north of which they encamped.

On October 1st Cunningham's force (75th battery Royal Field artillery, one section of the Elswick battery, the 2nd West Yorkshire regiment and the 1st Argyll and Sutherland Highlanders), arrived at Rustenburg from Pretoria, whither it had been sent from the Delagoa Bay line. Cunningham now took over the Rustenburg defences from Bradley, who then returned to Pretoria. Meanwhile Clements, Ridley and Broadwood had been patrolling widely, capturing a few prisoners and wagons at various places.

On October 3rd Broadwood marched to Rustenburg with a convoy for Lord Methuen, who arrived this day at Olifants Nek with his two columns. Clements and Ridley then marched to Commando Nek, the communications of which with Pretoria, hitherto much infested by "snipers," had now to be cleared. With their usual response to any concentration of troops in a particular district the enemy had separated into three parties. De la Rey's commando, with five guns, was reported at Waterval, north-west of Magato Nek; Ricart, with 400 burghers, was at Kaffirskraal, north-east of Rustenburg, and Badenhorst, with 200, at Zoutpans Drift, on the Crocodile river. The small bands of marksmen which had habitually harassed the convoys between Pretoria and Commando Nek were dealt with early in October by Colonel A. N. Rochfort, R.A., who took with him a small party of the 2nd Royal Dublin Fusiliers, and captured all but one of the riflemen who haunted the precipitous kopjes and rocky dongas. The incident is typical of the difficulties of warfare throughout the whole mountain region. Insignificant parties, or even individuals, could hamper the movements of large bodies of troops by interfering with their means of supply, for it was impossible to be certain whether the sharp-shooting of a few outlaws might not be the precursor of more formidable attack by bands suddenly gathering from many quarters. In short, the risks attendant on campaigning beyond the Indian frontier were here repeated, and for convoys at least, intensified.

The Waterberg district and that area north of the Delagoa Bay line were full of roving partisans, against whom columns of infantry were of no avail. The ever present difficulty of forming mounted bodies to deal with them was now doubled by the withdrawal of the greater part of the first Colonial mounted contingents, whose year of service had expired. The mobility and efficiency of the army were seriously impaired till fresh horsemen could be improvised from the battalions of foot. To follow every wandering band of the enemy was impossible, but it was of the first importance to prevent Botha and Steyn from moving by the west of the Magaliesberg. To Major-General Paget this duty was assigned in the first instance, he being in the direct line between Krugerspost, the scene of the Transvaalers' last stand in the east, and the country north of Rustenburg, where De la Rey's men were in laager.

Moving from an entrenched camp at Sybrand's Kraal as centre, Paget and Plumer acted independently, clearing in the early weeks of October the country between the railway lines north and east of Pretoria. The local armistice which had been arranged to allow the Boer leaders to ascertain for themselves the true state of affairs ceased when Commandant Dirksen returned and surrendered after a fruitless attempt to reach Commandant-General Botha. Paget and Plumer captured 150 Boers and 12,000 sheep; and reaching Derdepoort on October 13th, Paget reported that the country south of a line from Pienaar's River bridge to the junction of the Wilge and Oliphant rivers (see map No. 48) was now clear. Botha was known to be at Warmbad, accompanied until the 19th by President Steyn, whose influence banished any thought of surrender. Steyn then went in a south-westerly direction with a small following. Sending Plumer with his own and Hickman's brigades, two 5-in. guns and three companies of infantry, to Pienaar's River station, Paget took the rest of his command, under Lieut.-Colonel G. E. Lloyd, to Waterval, whence he could co-operate in the combined movements.

Paget's and Plumer's movements.

Marching on Hebron, Lloyd's detachment, consisting of the Queensland Imperial Bushmen, two guns of the 38th battery

R.F.A. and two companies of the 1st West Riding regiment, surprised a party of Boers at Klipfontein, and afterwards returned to Waterval with eighteen prisoners, 1,550 cattle and many sheep. To strengthen Paget's hold on the Pietersburg line, the 1st battalion Scots Guards was added to his command at Pienaar's River.

A converging march on Jericho of three mounted columns from Pienaar's River, Hamanskraal and Waterval, was then made to clear up a district not previously visited. On the way Hickman's column, with the loss of one man, captured fifty-four prisoners, eighteen wagons and 3,500 cattle. Plumer, whose special duty it had been to discover Steyn, reconnoitred the Aapies river from Makapan Stad; but as both Steyn and Botha had passed westwards further to the north no certain information was gained. The mounted troops were joined at Jericho by the remainder of Paget's force on October 20th. A party of the enemy retired from Syn Kop. four and a half miles to the south-west of Jericho, to Beestekraal on the Crocodile river, after firing a few shells into Hickman's camp. They were followed up at once by Plumer's force. It was now ascertained that a large body, chiefly Free Staters, had crossed the Crocodile river near Ramakokskraal a few days earlier, and that there were two other large laagers at the junction of that river with the Aapies. Botha with 200 men was reported to be working along the Elands river, apparently intending to pass round the west of the Magaliesberg: the fact that De Wet had again crossed the Vaal and was trying to push northwards, pointed to an attempt at a union. The Commander-in-Chief, therefore, ordered Paget to Rustenburg, whither he marched with all his mounted forces, and on October 31st was joined by his infantry. Plumer was detached to watch Magato Nek.

Blockade of the Magaliesberg.

While Paget was thus engaged, Lord Methuen, moving from Rustenburg, was to drive De la Rey westwards, and to ravage the country towards Zeerust. The barrier of the Magaliesberg, all the passes of which were held by Clements' force, and the columns manœuvring north and south of the range, prevented any direct movement towards the Free State, so that the only route for the Boers was by the west of the mountains. Rustenburg having direct access to the west by Magato and Boschhoek Neks, became, therefore, a point of great importance.

On October 9th Lord Methuen endeavoured by moving over the Boschhoek Nek and sending Douglas through Magato Nek, to attack De la Rey from north and south. That leader, with 700 men and several guns, was reported to be holding a position from Tweerivier to Wysfontein, with his main laager at Bulhoek, about fifteen miles north-west of Magato Nek. Lord Methuen's column marched directly upon Bulhoek. *Lord Methuen pursues De la Rey.*

The country between the main roads is hilly, densely clothed with undergrowth, and broken by a succession of strong bushy kopjes. The enemy's laager could not be discovered, and the northern column, annoyed only by skirmishers, marched to Lindley's Poort. The southern column came upon a party of about 100 near the Selous river; these retired to the southwest. As the country favoured the enemy's tactics, both columns marched by the same road, and Douglas, crossing Magato Nek, turned northwards by Waterval, and joined Lord Methuen near Lindley's Poort with nine prisoners, twenty-three wagons, 1,080 cattle and 850 sheep. This concentration was effected in good time, for the enemy was so close at hand that an officer in the advance guard of the leading column was captured.

Reports were now received that De la Rey, with the commandos of Steenkamp, Van Tonder, Coster and Van Heerden, was moving on Roodewal, west of Lindley's Poort, where Generals Lemmer and Liebenberg had been ordered to join him. Finding that both columns were marching together the enemy dared not attack. When, however, Lord Methuen reached Nooitgedacht, on the Little Marico river, his camp was shelled by a Creusot gun, which killed four men and wounded six.

Zeerust was reached on October 18th with only two more casualties. A re-arrangement of the columns was again made— the 1st battalion Northumberland Fusiliers and half of the 1st battalion Loyal North Lancashire regiment joined Lord Methuen; the 2nd battalion Northamptonshire regiment and the other half of the Loyal North Lancashire, went to Major-General

Douglas. Douglas remained at Zeerust, Methuen moved towards Buffelshoek. The enemy then closed in on Zeerust, and, on October 20th, occupied some kopjes south-east of the town. After they had been shelled for some time, a reconnoitring party was sent out and the mounted men and guns of Lord Methuen's column, which was still near, attempted to work round the enemy's left flank to prevent his retiring.* The assailants proved to be only a small commando with one gun, and, on the approach of Methuen's mounted men, they rapidly retired to high ground near Quarriefontein, followed by the 3rd and 5th regiments of Imperial Yeomanry. While crossing cultivated ground some of the pursuers were checked in the standing crops by a hidden wire fence, and a heavy rifle fire was opened on them, an officer being killed and an officer and several men wounded. Whilst the wire was being cut the 3rd Yeomanry regiment worked further to the left, and advanced towards the Boers who were firing on the men checked beside the fence. Not until Lord Methuen reinforced the Yeomanry with a battalion of infantry and the guns did the enemy give ground. The losses during the day were one officer and one man killed, and an officer and eleven men wounded. Two companies and two guns being left to hold the position, Lord Methuen then moved to Buffelshoek. The two regiments of Imperial Yeomanry were sent to Otto's Hoop to relieve Lord Erroll's force, which now came under Lord Methuen's direct command, and was called the 1st mounted brigade.

Information having been received that a force under General Lemmer was in the neighbourhood, a combined movement of both columns took place on October 24th. The enemy numbered about 700, with one gun and a Vickers-Maxim, and included the commandos of Vermaas, D. Botha and Van Niekirk. To hold them in their position on the Kruis river, a demonstration was made by the garrison of Buffelshoek, and Lord Methuen proposed to force them back with Douglas' column from Zeerust,

* For gallantry in bringing out of action a private of the mounted infantry whose horse had bolted, Lieutenant A. C. Doxat, 3rd Imperial Yeomanry, was awarded the Victoria Cross.

OPERATIONS IN THE WESTERN TRANSVAAL. 505

while his own moved across the Boer line of retreat. To this end Lord Erroll's brigade made a wide turning movement northwards, while the rest of Lord Methuen's column moved towards Kaffirkraal.

Douglas found the enemy in position on a range of low hills beyond the Kruis river, with men on a kopje which stood in advance of their left. The Vickers-Maxims and Howitzers opened fire at a range of 3,400 yards against the centre of the Boer position, which was afterwards cleared by the infantry, while Lieut.-Colonel R. Grey's mounted brigade attacked the detached kopje on the Boer left. With the aid of the infantry and the guns, which had crossed the river, their right was also turned. Thus outflanked, the Boers at once retreated, their main body going in a south-easterly direction towards Kaffirkraal, vigorously pursued by Grey. Lord Methuen brought a battery into action some 3,000 yards south of Kaffirkraal, flanking the enemy's main line of retreat; his two squadrons of mounted troops then joined the 2nd Rhodesian brigade in the general pursuit, which resulted in the capture of twenty-one of Vermaas' wagons. A few of the advanced scouts of the turning column came into contact with the enemy from the south, but Lord Erroll's main body was unable to prevent the commandos making good their retreat eastward. The casualties were one man killed and eight wounded; the enemy left six dead and four wounded on the field. Twenty-five Boers were taken prisoners, and 242 cattle and 1,300 sheep were captured.

Instead of the circuit around the western end of the Magaliesberg, Botha had open to him a course which contained too much danger to be ignored, namely to continue his westward march into Bechuanaland, and thence harry Cape Colony. To provide against this, Lord Methuen was ordered to remain in the neighbourhood of Otto's Hoop, and fortify Zeerust, which was now to be permanently garrisoned. An attempt made shortly afterwards to surround a small party of the enemy at Waterkloof did not succeed, but in its flight northwards the commando left behind 950 head of cattle, 700 sheep and six wagons—one full of ammunition. Lord Methuen and Douglas then returned to Jacobsdal and Zeerust respectively, Douglas being ordered to move on Mabals Stad.

<small>Clearance of the Magaliesberg.</small>

During the month of October vigorous steps had been taken to clear the Magaliesberg. Cunningham's command remained in garrison at Rustenburg; Clements, working in co-operation with Broadwood, mainly concerned himself in clearing the mountains, in securing the passes, and in collecting stock in the valleys at the foot of the southern slopes, a task for which Barton was also ordered from Krugersdorp up the Hekpoort valley.

Clements, in co-operation with Barton, marched to Rhenosterspruit, sending Broadwood from Rustenburg to Wolhuter's Kop. Heavy firing was heard in the direction of Tweefontein on October 8th; but Barton was beyond the reach of Clements, who, nevertheless, sent patrols far and wide to prevent the enemy near him from reinforcing those with whom Barton was engaged. Clements, hearing on October 9th that Barton had been ordered south from the Hekpoort valley to keep De Wet, who had crossed the Vaal, from meeting Steyn, returned to Commando Nek on the 11th. He was there joined by Broadwood, who had made a wide sweep of three days' duration into the Bushveld, north of Rustenburg. The composite regiment of Household cavalry was now sent from Broadwood's brigade to Pretoria, for return to England; at the same time Brigadier-General Ridley, on appointment as head of the new police force in the Orange River Colony, handed over his command to Lieut.-Colonel N. Legge.

On October 13th, Clements began systematically to search the Magaliesberg, working westwards from Commando Nek. To the Northumberland Fusiliers fell the arduous task of following the crest of the mountains; the main force and Legge's brigade pursued the southern valley, and Broadwood's cavalry, strengthened by half the 2nd King's Own Yorkshire L.I., searched the country at the foot of the northern slopes. Cunningham assisted by sending a detachment eastwards to Waagfontein, and was also responsible for holding Olifants and Magato Neks.

The operation occupied six days, and resulted in thirty-eight prisoners being taken and a large amount of stock collected. The Boers, believing that no troops could march along the rugged hills, had long hidden themselves, their wagons and oxen in the sanctuaries, the remotest of which Clements now ruthlessly violated. In view of the possibility of Steyn attempting to cross the range, or of De Wet again making for the Magaliesberg, detachments were posted to block all the cattle paths, and Broadwood closed the Boschhoek Pass.

It was hoped to thus separate the Boers north of the range from their comrades to the south; but De Wet, as will presently be recorded, was soon to be driven back across the Vaal, while Steyn's movements remained inscrutable. Clements then withdrew his posts and moved westwards to Blaauwbank, where Legge's mounted infantry surprised a Boer laager by a night march, capturing five prisoners, 1,000 head of cattle and 600 sheep. At the end of the month Clements' brigade was at Syferfontein, eighteen miles south of Olifants Nek, awaiting communication with Douglas' column, which was expected at Mabals Stad.

De Wet had been so much pressed by the forces south of the Vaal that there was renewed danger of his breaking over the river and joining Botha and Steyn. Lord Roberts therefore placed Hart at Krugersdorp, sending Barton to clear the country north of that town. Barton took with him one 4.7-in. gun, the 78th battery R.F.A. (four guns), a section of the 28th battery R.F.A., a Vickers-Maxim, the 7th company R.E., the 12th battalion and the 19th company Imperial Yeomanry, 200 men of Marshall's Horse, detachments of Imperial Bushmen and mounted infantry, the 2nd Royal Scots Fusiliers, and the 1st Royal Welsh Fusiliers; with these he began to clear the country west of the Pretoria road. The column took seven prisoners and collected 300 cattle and 8,500 sheep with slight opposition, seven men being wounded. The local commandos then went into laager near Tweefontein, whence they were soon driven towards Dwarsvlei, losing more cattle. Reconnaissance showed that all the farmers in the neighbourhood had trekked west-

Barton's movements.

wards, and preparations were made to disperse them. All the mounted men, two guns and 300 infantry, under Major D. C. Carter, R.A., followed by the rest of the troops, marched before light on October 9th. A small party of Bushmen scouts became engaged in the early morning with a Boer outpost, and at once lost their leader. The alarm having been thus given, the enemy opened a heavy fire on Barton's troops advancing from the south-east. The commandos—those of Commandants Van Zyl, Van der Heuver and Piet De la Rey—were now marked in a strong position along a steep range of stony flat-topped hills, through which runs the road from Krugersdorp to Zeekoehoek. West of the road the range trends southerly, and then for several miles westerly, thus forbidding any attempt to turn the Boer right. As Barton wished to strike before the Boers could evacuate or strengthen their position and to drive them towards Clements, who was then in the Hekpoort valley, he decided to attack at once, although his troops were tired after a long march. To force the retreat in the required direction the hills west of the road were first secured, being stormed by the leading company of the 1st Royal Welsh Fusiliers. From the nature of the position the guns were able to fire to the last upon the eastern ridges, and so keep down the fire of the defenders there who were striving to cover the retreat of their comrades from the other height. After getting a footing on this kopje, which enfiladed the whole ridge, the Royal Welsh Fusiliers pushed on to attack the western end of the main position. When this had been carried the Fusiliers pressed along the top of the hills, while the Boers, with their wagons and cattle, disappeared into the deep gullies running down into the Hekpoort valley. The enemy had nowhere stood to close quarters; long-range fire caused all the casualties in Barton's force, viz.:—one officer and one man killed and three officers and twelve men wounded. Fourteen prisoners were taken during the three hours' engagement, together with 500 cattle, 5,000 sheep and a few wagons and horses.

Oct. 9th, 1900. Barton attacks.

Brigadier-General Ridley, then at Scheerpoort with his mounted infantry, was too far distant to co-operate with Barton

OPERATIONS IN THE WESTERN TRANSVAAL. 509

or intercept the fugitives. After driving the enemy north of the hills, Barton reached Dwarsvlei on the 9th; leaving his infantry there, he proposed to operate with his mounted men in conjunction with Clements in the Magaliesberg; but the situation was suddenly changed by news that De Wet, with 1,000 men and four guns, pressed from the south by the Colonial division and de Lisle's force, had crossed the Vaal at Schoeman's Drift and was at Venterskroon. Barton was ordered to move with all speed to the Gatsrand to turn him. As soon as the Dwarsvlei position was vacated the enemy re-occupied it, and the opportunity of placing them between two fires was lost. Barton marched to Welverdiend on October 13th, and had no sooner pitched his tents than the camp was shelled by two 9-pr. Creusot guns from a ridge 5,300 yards to the south. The two guns were quickly silenced and no damage was suffered; the hill whence they had fired was occupied as an advanced post. Clearing the Buffelsdoorn Pass, and leaving a strong detachment to hold it, Barton's main force drove before it the enemy's rearguard, and arrived at Frederikstad on October 17th, with a loss of two men killed and four wounded. *Barton moves to intercept De Wet.*

Oct. 17th, 1900. Barton at Frederikstad.

Two days later a large body of the enemy was seen approaching from the Gatsrand. General Liebenberg had been in the Gatsrand with a force of 700 men and four guns, and had reported Barton's arrival at Frederikstad to De Wet. Considering himself too weak to attack single-handed, he had suggested that De Wet should join him, and this had been arranged. Calling in his scattered commandos, Liebenberg attempted to isolate Barton from the north, but was unable to prevent him from receiving supplies by train from Welverdiend. The force now seen to be coming on were not Liebenberg's but De Wet's men, and included the burghers of the Heilbron commando and a part of the Vrede commando. It numbered from 900 to 1,000 men; but the large proportion of led horses gave it a far more formidable appearance.

Under the impression that De Wet was running from British troops on the other side of the Vaal, Barton took up an extended position about five miles long, covering the two bridges crossing the Mooi river, and the two passes over the Gatsrand. A mixed column, which had just arrived from Welverdiend, under Lieut.-Colonel Sir Robert Colleton, Royal Welsh Fusiliers, consisting of three companies of infantry, two guns, and 150 Imperial Light Horse, was sent out to reconnoitre, and saw nothing until it retired. It was then attacked, and lost one officer and two men killed and twelve wounded.

Meanwhile a general attack from the east and south by about 1,500 of the enemy with six guns and a Vickers-Maxim had developed, to be continued for seven hours, during which only two men were killed and nine wounded. Barton withdrew the detachment in the river valley to the higher ground east of the village. Early next morning some 300 Boers crossed the Mooi river and took up a position to the north-west. Rifle and gun fire was kept up on the garrison throughout that day and the next, causing a loss of one officer and one man killed and seven wounded. Barton's position was now virtually surrounded.

<small>Barton surrounded at Frederikstad</small>

Communication with Headquarters was still possible, for by an unusual oversight, the enemy had not cut the wire to Welverdiend. Lord Roberts immediately ordered Clements from Hekpoort, and Major-General C. Knox from Vredefort to Barton's assistance, arrangements which were modified when it was found that the Frederikstad force was able to hold its own. As there was no sign of any troops in pursuit of De Wet, Barton ordered his men to husband ammunition, for he could not tell how long he was to be shut up. The enemy closed in all round and attacked a strongly entrenched hill overlooking the railway station, held by a detachment of the Royal Scots Fusiliers. The attack was beaten off, with some loss among the defenders. As the Boers had tried during the day to cut off the water supply from the river, a company of the Royal Welsh Fusiliers seized a kopje on the further bank after dark, and before morning this was strongly fortified to protect the water piquet. The enemy, emboldened by the cautious expenditure of ammunition, made a fresh attack on the 24th. They appeared to have increased in strength, and a detach-

OPERATIONS IN THE WESTERN TRANSVAAL.

ment, consisting of two guns of the Elswick battery, the Essex regiment, a half battalion of the 2nd Royal Dublin Fusiliers, Strathcona's Horse and 150 men of the Colonial division, was pushed forward from Welverdiend, under Lieut.-Colonel H. T. Hicks, to relieve the pressure upon Frederikstad.

On the morning of October 25th the enemy opened a heavy fire on Barton's position from all sides. Impatient of the slow progress, De Wet had thrown more men across the river during the night to seize and entrench a position between the railway station and the river, while another party crept up under the railway embankment, close to the defenders. The advanced Boer position was comparatively open, and, once occupied, could not be abandoned by daylight without great risk. As the Boer piquets to the north had informed their General that no important British reinforcement need be feared from Welverdiend, De Wet detailed only eighty Free Staters and 120 Transvaalers to guard his rear. Neither order was fully obeyed. Liebenberg, instead of 120, sent only fifty-two of his men, and only sixty-eight Free Staters, under Field Cornets Cilliers and Wessels, went to take charge of this important post at the railway bridge. But these Boers held on against heavy shrapnel and Vickers-Maxim fire, which was employed against them. Barton then ordered Captain W. L. D. Baillie's company of the Royal Scots Fusiliers and a squadron of Imperial Light Horse to dislodge them. The attempt was unsuccessful, Baillie and four of his men being killed and several wounded. A stronger column of two companies Royal Scots Fusiliers and three companies Royal Welsh Fusiliers was next sent to make a frontal assault; a third company of the Royal Scots Fusiliers to assail the flank from a hill south of the station, and the Imperial Light Horse to cut off any who tried to escape between the river and the railway. The Boers, well concealed and entrenched, held their ground with great tenacity till midday, only giving way when the soldiers, with fixed bayonets, were within eighty yards of them. Up to this point the defenders, ably commanded by Sarel Cilliers, had been very little shaken by the fire of the attack. But their ammunition was running short when most needed; and

Oct. 25th, 1900. Barton defeats De Wet at Frederikstad.

another British force (Hicks') was seen coming from the direction of Welverdiend. To avoid capture, the defenders fell back on foot across the open ground. The river was a mile and a half away, and the bridge the only means of escape. But there was no pursuit, except by the shells of the 4.7-in. gun, the 78th battery and the Vickers-Maxims on the hills above the town which burst with great execution amongst the burghers as they ran over the open. Of the fifty-two Transvaalers only twenty-seven were able to rejoin their comrades across the river, and half of these were wounded.

The enemy left twenty-six dead on the ground, and thirty wounded and twenty-six unwounded prisoners were taken. The success was not gained cheaply by Barton's column. During the day one officer and twenty men were killed and four officers and fifty-one rank and file wounded. The reinforcements brought by Colonel Hicks with a convoy from Welverdiend arrived about noon on the 25th. As Frederikstad must be held, Barton did not feel justified in following up De Wet. In case some of the enemy might still be in the Gatsrand, he sent the Imperial Light Horse to occupy the Buffelsdoorn Pass. This rebuff at the hands of Barton put an end to De Wet's attempt to strike north. Much weakened he recrossed the Vaal near Wittekopfontein and there laagered. Knox's column followed him and shelled his laager from some kopjes north of the river with such effect that the burghers scattered hurriedly, abandoning two disabled guns and four wagons. Liebenberg withdrew west of the Mooi river into the Ventersdorp district.

Leaving a strong garrison at Frederikstad under Sir Robert Colleton, Barton next marched to Potchefstroom, which from this time to the end of the war was permanently occupied.

After the rough treatment he had received at Frederikstad, De Wet gave up all hopes of operating in strength north of the river. At a meeting which took place between him and Steyn at Ventersdorp on October 31st, it was settled that nothing remained but a descent into Cape Colony. To elaborate this scheme they again met at Bothaville, south of the Vaal, which

De Wet plans an invasion of Cape Colony.

OPERATIONS IN THE WESTERN TRANSVAAL 513

the Free Staters now crossed for the last time. General De la Rey, who had not been present at the conference, agreed to stay in the Transvaal to keep the British troops employed there.

Of De la Rey's commandos, De Beer's, near Schweizer Reneke, and those of Commandants Potgieter and De Villiers about Wolmaranstad were actively employed on both banks of the Vaal. Since the middle of October Major-General Settle, with a force of 600 mounted men, ten guns and 1,350 infantry, had been operating between Christiana and Bothaville.* Settle did not consider himself strong enough to act north of the Vaal. As no other force was available for the purpose the Wolmaranstad commando remained unmolested, and Settle went south towards Boshof. The main line of communication along the Central Transvaal railway was undisturbed during the month, though an attempt was made to injure it near Kaalfontein on October 20th.

During November stock-collecting marches were continued. The centre of interest at the beginning of the month was west of Rustenburg. Paget, leaving the 1st Scots Guards with Cunningham at that place, moved on November 1st to Tweerivier, in support of Plumer's force, which was there engaged. The enemy, 800 strong, were in position on some parallel ridges about two miles west of the Selous river. The stronghold was carried with small loss by the British South Africa Police, and a detachment of the Yorkshire and Warwickshire Yeomanry under Colonel H. R. L. Howard. When the second position was turned by the 3rd regiment Imperial Bushmen, under Major H. G. Vialls, and the 49th company I.Y., the Boers fled precipitately. A reconnaissance next day to Groenfontein discovered that Steyn had already gone south with a small escort. After getting into touch with Legge's mounted infantry covering Clements' advance, Paget returned towards Rustenburg. On the way a party of 300 Boers made a faint-hearted attack on the Bushmen acting as Plumer's rearguard, who, supported by Howard's Yeomanry and the Tasmanians of Hickman's force, drove off the enemy

Paget's movements.

* See page 481.

Lord Methuen's movements.

without difficulty, and took five prisoners. The return march to the Pietersburg line was accomplished without fighting.

In the west Lord Methuen remained for a week at Jacobsdal destroying all the crops; he then moved to Kaffirkraal to take the place of Douglas' column which was now at Mabals Stad. Information being received that Lemmer's commando was near Wonderfontein, south of Kaffirkraal, Lord Methuen, at 1 a.m. on November 9th, directed the Otto's Hoop garrison to demonstrate towards the enemy's laager, and Lord Erroll's brigade to make a wide out-flanking movement to the south-east. As soon as fire was opened by the main force the Boers fled, abandoning all their transport. Meanwhile the mounted brigade forced the Boers westwards towards the Otto's Hoop column. At a cost of two men wounded, seven of the enemy were killed and twenty-four prisoners taken. Marching towards Lichtenburg, destroying mills and crops, the column was received with artillery fire near Manana. The enemy did not remain to dispute the advance and in their rapid retreat they lost a Vickers-Maxim, retiring then to a farm eleven miles south-west of Lichtenburg. On November 14th an attempt was made to surround this party during the night, but the Boers had warning, and when Lord Methuen's guns opened fire on them at long range, they were already in full retreat.

Having scoured the Lichtenburg neighbourhood the column returned to Otto's Hoop. To keep open the road to Lichtenburg, the 5th battalion I.Y. and a section of the Rhodesian Field Force battery, under command of Lieut.-Colonel F. C. Meyrick, marched there on November 24th, and were checked by superior numbers with a gun, in a strong position a few miles north of the town. Hearing of this, Lord Methuen marched at once, covering the last forty-three miles in twenty-three hours. On arrival he found that the enemy had evacuated their position during the night, after keeping Meyrick's detachment from the town all day. They only retired when a convoy coming from Mafeking late in the afternoon had increased Meyrick's force by over 500 men and two guns. A garrison, made up of 100 men of the 10th I.Y., two guns, a company of the 1st Loyal North

Lancashire regiment and 350 men 2nd Northamptonshire regiment, was left at Lichtenburg, and the column returned to Jacobsdal.

Major-General Douglas' column* arrived on November 5th at Mabals Stad, and then turned northwards towards Brakfontein, to collect stock and to be in position to co-operate with the other columns from Rustenburg.

From various sources frequent reports were now received of an approaching attempt to invade Cape Colony, and that all the Boer forces north of the Vaal intended to assemble on the border near Warrenton, and thence join the Free Staters in the neighbourhood of De Aar. The combined levies were then to carry the fiery cross amongst the Cape Dutch and spur them to rebellion. Lord Roberts, therefore, ordered Douglas to hurry to Klerksdorp, which he reached on November 16th. On the way, after a march of twenty-seven miles across a waterless desert, a halt was made at Ventersdorp to reassure the inhabitants who bemoaned their isolated and helpless position. Reconnaissances found the enemy in the neighbourhood, in strength about 600 men, with one gun and a Vickers-Maxim. Their main laager, under General Liebenberg, was at Kaffirkraal, some twenty miles south-west of the village. The whole country teemed with supplies and stock, which were collected with little opposition.

Douglas' movements.

During the month Douglas' column captured twenty-nine prisoners, 4,700 cattle, 11,200 sheep, ninety horses and mules, 138 wagons and a large quantity of supplies. Klerksdorp was now to be permanently held, and Barton and Douglas marched in on the same day. Both columns then came under the orders of Lieut.-General French, who, on the break-up of the cavalry division, had been appointed on November 12th to command the

---

* Detail of Major-General Douglas' column : —
    Colonel R. Grey's mounted brigade (827 all ranks).
    Two sections 88th battery Royal Field artillery.
    Four Vickers-Maxims.
    Headquarters and two companies 1st battalion
        Loyal North Lancashire regiment } 750 all ranks.
    2nd battalion Northamptonshire regiment

Johannesburg district, which extended westwards as far as Klerksdorp, and included the valley of the Vaal.* French first proposed to clear the country to the south and south-west of Johannesburg. In pursuance of this plan, Douglas, after fortifying Klerksdorp and providing detachments to watch the adjacent drifts over the Vaal, took the rest of his column to Tygerfontein, a few miles north of Venterskroon. As the Losberg was supposed to be a Boer stronghold, an enveloping movement was made on December 4th in conjunction with the columns of Hart and Gordon, coming east and west. Nothing, however, was seen of the enemy in the southern section of the cordon, and Douglas proceeded to Potchefstroom with the captures made since leaving Klerksdorp, namely, eight prisoners, 5,700 cattle, 14,400 sheep, 240 wagons and carts, 350 horses, as well as 1,000 refugees.

After the successful engagement with De Wet in the Mooi River valley, Barton's force paused at Frederikstad, repairing the bridges and railway, and throwing up defences to cover the crossings and culverts. These posts absorbed a considerable number of men, so the 2nd Coldstream Guards from Pretoria were added to Barton's command, five companies being sent to Potchefstroom. Potchefstroom was then well provisioned, a police force organised, and the bank re-opened in this disaffected centre. The repairs of that section of the railway were then undertaken. When the train service was re-established, a further step towards settling the country was made by the occupation of Klerksdorp by Douglas. In clearing the neighbourhood, forty-two prisoners and 7,000 head of cattle and 5,000 sheep were taken. It was now intended to form smaller columns to cope with the attenuated and dispersed commandos, and there was no longer work for two general officers in this district. Hart was ordered to remain at Krugersdorp, and Barton to take over control of the lines of communication from Pretoria to Wolvehoek from Colonel J. M. Babington, who replaced him in command of the Potchefstroom column. A reconnaissance carried out by the new commander showed that the Tygerfontein position was clear

* See page 435.

OPERATIONS IN THE WESTERN TRANSVAAL.

of the enemy, and a convoy was sent to meet Douglas' column when it reached that place. Whilst Douglas took part in the combined movement on the Losberg, Babington's force relieved his detachments at the Vaal drifts. It was now possible to reduce the number of troops in the command; the Coldstream Guards were, therefore, sent to Bloemfontein, and Strathcona's Horse to Aliwal North to be ready for De Wet's descent on Cape Colony. Minor operations were also carried out by Hart in the Gatsrand during the month of November; but as these took place after his relief by Clements at Krugersdorp, the movements of the Magaliesberg force will first be considered.

While Cunningham's brigade, stationed at Rustenburg, made daily forays in the neighbourhood, Clements, clearing the country, circled round the western arm of the Magaliesberg, and arrived at Doornkom, in the Zwart Ruggens, on November 6th. At this date Paget was ten miles to the east at Groenfontein, and Douglas about the same distance to the southwest. There were thus ample troops in the district to prevent any general movement of Botha's commandos towards the south, of which, however, there was no sign. The few Boers seen retreated northwards, and were reported to have gone to the Pilandsberg. In that region they were harmless, so to meet the rumoured descent upon Cape Colony, Clements' force was ordered to march to Krugersdorp, to be ready to entrain in case of need. There it arrived on November 12th, and came under the orders of Lieut.-General French. During the march the column captured fifteen prisoners, 2,400 cattle and 3,600 sheep. After taking over the defences of Krugersdorp from Hart, Clements made the town his Headquarters until the end of the month, whilst Legge's mounted infantry were actively employed clearing the country west and north of Krugersdorp.

Clements' movements.

On November 23rd detachments of Kitchener's Horse and Roberts' Horse, supported by a company of the Northumberland Fusiliers, moved out against a small commando in the high ground at Zwart Kop in the upper reaches of the Crocodile river. Marching by night, the former surprised a party of seventy Boers, who fled, leaving three of their number behind.

Meanwhile, Lieut.-Colonel G. A. Cookson, with a small force, by a wide turning movement, seized the end of the Zwart Kop ridges. After a few rounds of shrapnel the enemy ran in confusion towards Hekpoort, losing considerably.

Broadwood's movements.

During this period Broadwood's column, strengthened by the 8th Hussars, cleared the rich country west of the Magaliesberg mountains and along their northern slopes. On the march to Kosterfontein, a party of 100 Boers were seen. They fled at once on being shelled, but returned next day to attack a squadron of the 12th Lancers, of whom, owing to a stampede amongst their horses, 6 men were taken prisoners and 2 wounded. The return march, *viâ* Olifants Nek, was opposed throughout by 300 Boers, who wounded an officer and three men of the 8th Hussars.

Hart's movements.

After French took over the command of the Johannesburg district, 200 mounted men were added to Hart's force at Krugersdorp. This was in anticipation of a combined movement of Hart's column and Gordon's 1st cavalry brigade to Klip River Station, where 300 Boers were reported to be threatening the railway. Being now relieved of responsibility for Krugersdorp by the arrival of Clements, Hart, with a force as under,* crossed the Roodepoort Pass of the Witwatersrand and arrived at Klip River Station on the 18th November. Gordon was already there with the Carabiniers, Scots Greys, Inniskilling Dragoons, T. battery Royal Horse artillery and a Vickers-Maxim. A tem-

---

* Detail of Major-General Hart's column :—

1st battalion Imperial Yeomanry
Detachment Imperial Yeomanry
Detachment Kitchener's Horse
Detachment Roberts' Horse
Detachment Imperial mounted infantry
Machine Gun section
} About 300 mounted troops, under Lieut.-Col. R. H. F. W. Wilson.

Four guns 28th battery R.F.A.
G. Section Vickers-Maxims
Detachment 6th coy. E.D.R.G.A. with 4.7-in. gun
} Major A. Stokes, R.F.A.

2nd Royal Dublin Fusiliers—Lieut.-Col. H. T. Hicks.
2nd South Wales Borderers—Lieut.-Col. the Hon. U. Roche.
No. 44 company A.S.C.—Major St. J. W. T. Parker.
No. 8 Bearer company—Major Townsend.
No. 15 Field hospital—Major Younge.

OPERATIONS IN THE WESTERN TRANSVAAL. 519

porary exchange of 300 men of the South Wales Borderers for two squadrons (160 sabres) of the Carabiniers having been made, the two columns moved through Allewyn's Poort. Slight resistance was encountered near Elandsfontein (two killed), and in the difficult ground about Orange Grove. Changing direction southward along the top of the Gatsrand, the rearguard was engaged in the Buffelsdoorn Pass, where an officer and two men were wounded. Hart's column then remained encamped on the north side of the pass till the end of the month, being there reinforced by 240 men of the Royal Scots Fusiliers and 1st Derbyshire regiment.

Gordon's cavalry brigade, which had started westwards with Hart's column, wheeled northwards, collecting stock, and returned to Varkensfontein by rail. Both columns took part in a fruitless effort to capture the Boers reported to be in the Losberg. Moving east and west they joined hands on December 4th with Douglas, who was advancing from the south, but the enemy had disappeared. Gordon then returned to Meyerton, collecting 1,200 head of cattle and 9,000 sheep on the way. Hart, leaving the 2nd South Wales Borderers and thirty Imperial Yeomanry to hold the Modderfontein Pass, returned to Krugersdorp, whence he guarded the railway to Welverdiend.

Other duties now called Field-Marshal Lord Roberts from the scene of his labours in South Africa. He had been appointed Commander-in-Chief at the War Office, and he could no longer delay his departure. On November 29th he handed over command of the forces in the field to General Lord Kitchener, and soon after sailed for England, honoured by the dignity of an Earldom. He left behind him a campaign of uncertain duration, but of certain issue. He well knew what trouble he bequeathed to his successor by his very success in grinding the federated Boer forces into desperate and scattered fragments; but he knew, also, that he left the cause in no danger. The reins which he had taken in hand at a time of grave peril to British ascendancy in South Africa he did not lay down until he had made all safe. The Republican Governments, which he had found triumphant, he had banished into hiding; their strong and elated armies

Nov. 29th, 1900. Field-Marshal Lord Roberts relinquishes command in South Africa.

he had broken to pieces. To the troops he bade farewell in the following terms :—

"SPECIAL ARMY ORDER.
"Army Headquarters,
"Johannesburg, 29th November, 1900.

<small>Lord Roberts' farewell to the Army.</small>

"Being about to give up the command of the Army in South Africa into the able hands of General Lord Kitchener of Khartoum, I feel that I cannot part with the comrades with whom I have been associated for nearly a year—often under very trying circumstances—without giving expression to my profound appreciation of the noble work they have performed for their Queen and Country, and for me personally, and to my pride in the results they have achieved by their pluck and endurance, their discipline, and devotion to duty.

"I greatly regret that the ties which have bound us together are so soon to be severed, for I should like to remain with the Army until it is completely broken up; but I have come to the conclusion that, as Lord Kitchener has consented to take over the command, my presence is no longer required in South Africa, and that my duty calls me in another direction. But I shall never forget the Officers and men of this force, be they Royal Navy, Colonials, Regulars, Militia, Yeomanry, or Volunteers; their interests will always be very dear to me, and I shall continue to work for the Army as long as I can work at all.

"The service which the South African Force has performed is, I venture to think, unique in the annals of war, inasmuch as it has been absolutely almost incessant for a whole year—in some cases more than a year. There has been no rest—no days off to recruit—no going into winter quarters, as in other campaigns which have extended over a long period. For months together, in fierce heat, in biting cold, and in pouring rain, you—my comrades—have marched and fought without a halt, and bivouacked without shelter from the elements; and you frequently have had to continue marching with your clothes in rags and your boots without soles—time being of such great consequence that it was impossible for you to remain long enough in any one place to refit.

"When not engaged in actual battle you have been continually shot at from behind kopjes by an invisible enemy, to whom every inch of the ground was familiar, and who, from the peculiar nature of the country, were able to inflict severe punishment while perfectly safe themselves.

"You have forced your way through dense jungles and over precipitous mountains, through and over which, with infinite manual labour, you have had to drag and haul guns and oxwagons. You have covered, with almost incredible speed, enormous distances, and that often on a very short supply of food; and you have endured the sufferings inevitable in war to sick and wounded men far from the base without a murmur —even with cheerfulness. You have, in fact, acted up to the highest standard of patriotism; and by your conspicuous kindness and humanity towards your enemies, and your forbearance and good behaviour in the towns we have occupied, you have caused the Army of Great Britain to be as highly respected as it must henceforth be greatly feared in South Africa.

"Is it any wonder that I am intensely proud of the Army I have commanded, or that I regard you—my gallant and devoted comrades—with affection as well as admiration, and that I feel deeply the parting from you? Many of you—Colonials as well as Britishers—I hope to meet again; but those I may never see more will live in my memory and be held in high regard to my life's end.

"I have learnt much during the war, and the experience I have gained will greatly help me in the work that lies before me, which is, I conceive, to make the Army of the United Kingdom as perfect as it is possible for an army to be. This I shall strive to do with all my might.

"And now farewell! May God bless every member of the South African Army; and that you may be all spared to return to your homes, and to find those dear to you well and happy, is the earnest hope of your Commander,

"ROBERTS, FIELD-MARSHAL."

END OF VOLUME III.

APPENDICES

APPENDIX I.

ARMY HEADQUARTERS STAFF, SOUTH AFRICAN FIELD FORCE.

April 29th, 1900.

Field-Marshal Comdg.-in-Chief	Field-Marshal the Right Honble. Lord Roberts, K.P., G.C.B., V.C., &c.
Military Secretary	Lieut.-Col. H. V. Cowan, R.A.
Asst. Military Secretaries	Capt. A. C. M. Waterfield, Indian Staff Corps. Capt. Duke of Marlborough, Imp. Yeo.
Aides-de-Camp	Capt. Lord Settrington, 3rd Royal Sussex regiment. Capt. Lord H. A. Montagu-Douglas-Scott, 3rd Royal Scots. Lieut. H. Wake, 3rd K. R. Rifle Corps.
Private Secretary	Col. N. F. FitzG. Chamberlain, Indian Staff Corps.
Asst. Private Secretary	Lord Elphinstone, S.H.
Naval Aide-de-Camp	Commander the Hon. S. J. Fortescue, R.N.
Extra Aides-de-Camp	Lieut. the Earl of Kerry, Irish Guards. Lieut.-Col. J. J. Byron, Roy. Australian Art. Major S. J. A. Denison, Royal Canadian rgt. Capt. J. H. H. Watermeyer, Cape Town Highlanders. Lieut. Duke of Westminster, Ches. Yeo.
Chief of Staff	Major-Gen. Lord Kitchener, G.C.B., K.C.M.G., Royal Engineers.
Aides-de-Camp	Bt.-Major J. K. Watson, D.S.O., K.R.R.C. Lieut. W. H. Cowan, D.S.O., R.N.
Dep.-Adjt.-Gen.	Major-Gen. W. F. Kelly, C.B.
Asst.-Adjt.-Gens.	*Col. I. J. C. Herbert, C.B., C.M.G. Col. B. Duff, C.I.E., Indian Staff Corps. Bt.-Col. J. M. Grierson, M.V.O., R.A. Bt.-Col. Sir H. S. Rawlinson, Bart. Coldstream Guards. Major (local Lieut.-Col.) R. B. Gaisford, R. Scots Fusiliers. Major (local Lieut.-Col.) J. Poett, Dorset regiment. Major (local Lieut.-Col.) H. I. W. Hamilton, D.S.O., R. W. Surrey regiment.
Dept.-Asst.-Adjt.-Gens.	Bt.-Lieut.-Col. G. F. Gorringe, D.S.O., R.E. *Bt.-Major F. Wintour, Royal West Kent regiment. Major R. C. B. Haking, Hampshire regt.
Director of Intelligence	†Lieut.-Col. G. F. R. Henderson, C.B. Bt.-Major C. J. Mackenzie, Seaforth Highlanders.

* At Cape Town. † Invalided.

526   THE WAR IN SOUTH AFRICA.

D.A.A.G. (Intell.)	Major F. J. Davies, Grenadier Guards. Major C. V. Hume, R.A. Major W. R. Robertson, D.S.O., 3rd D.G. Capt. G. F. Milne, R.A.
Cmdg. Art. (Maj.-Gen on Staff)	Col. (local Major-Gen.) G. H. Marshall.
Aide-de-Camp R.A.	Capt. A. D. Kirby, R.A.
A.A.G., R.A.	Major H. C. Sclater, R.A.
D.A.A.G., R.A.	Major J. Headlam, R.A.
Engineer-in-Chief	Col. (local Maj.-Gen.) E. Wood, C.B., R.E.
Aide-de-Camp R.E.	Bt.-Major R. S. Curtis, R.E.
Staff Officer R.E.	*Lieut.-Col. E. H. Bethell, R.E.
Staff Officer for Mil. Attachés	*Col. Visc. H. R. Downe, C.I.E.
Director of Telegraphs	Lieut.-Col. R. L. Hippisley, R.E.
Director of Transport	Col. (local Major-Gen.) Sir W. G. Nicholson, K.C.B.
A.A.G. Transport	Bt.-Col. H. N. Bunbury.
D.A.A.G. ,,	Capt. T. W. Furse, R.A.
Dir. of Supplies (Field Force)	Bt.-Col. E. W. D. Ward, C.B., A.S.C.
A.A.G. (Supplies)	Bt.-Col. F. F. Johnson, A.S.C.
Staff Lieutenants	Rdg.-Mr. and Hon. Lieut. W. Lyons, A.S.C. Qr.-Mr. and Hon. Lieut. A. G. Rose, A.S.C. Qr.-Mr. and Hon. Lieut. C. R. Law, A.S.C.
Director of Railways	†Bt.-Major (local Lieut.-Col.) E. P. C. Girouard, D.S.O., R.E.
Staff Officer	**Capt. (local Major) J. H. Twiss, R.E.
P.M.O. (Army)	Surg.-Gen. W. D. Wilson, M.B., R.A.M.C.
Medical Officer	Major W. G. A. Bedford, M.B., R.A.M.C.
Commandant Headquarters	**Capt. C. H. H. Gough, Indian Staff Corps.
S.O. to Commdt. Headquarters	***Capt. A. G. Maxwell, Indian Staff Corps.
P.M.O. (Field Force)	Col. W. B. Stevenson, M.B., R.A.M.C.
Medical Officer	Major G. H. Sylvester, R.A.M.C.
Medical Officers, Headquarters	Major W. R. Edwards, I.M.S. Kendal Franks, Esq., M.D., F.R.C.S.I.
Chaplain, Headquarters	Rev. H. T. Coney, M.A.
Staff Lieuts., Headquarters	Qr. Mr. and Hon. Lt. W. S. Cauvin, A.S.C. Qr.-Mr. and Hon. Lieut. J. Bowers, A.S.C.
Provost Marshal	*Bt.-Major R. M. Poore, 7th Hussars.
Press Censor	*Lieut. Lord E. G. V. Stanley, Reserve of Officers.
Principal Chaplain (Cape Town)	Rev. E. H. Goodwin, B.A., Chaplain to Forces (1st class).
Director of Signalling	**Bt.-Major T. E. O'Leary, R. Irish Fus.
Signalling Officers	***Capt. J. R. K. Birch, Cheshire regiment. ***Capt. J. Knowles, 15th Hussars.
Chief Ordnance Officer	Col. R. F. N. Clarke, Army Ordnance Dept.
Prin. Veterinary Officer	Vet.-Lieut.-Col. I. A. Mathews, V. Dept.
Dep. Judge Advocate-Gen. } Cape Dep. Judge Advocate } Town	Col. J. L. C. St. Clair. Lord B. Blackwood.
Body Guard	Major D. T. Laing.
Escort	Major W. M. Sherston, N. Somerset. Yeo.

* Graded as A.A.G. ** Graded as D.A.A.G.
† Graded as D.A.G. *** Graded as Staff Captain.

APPENDIX I.

SOUTH AFRICAN FIELD FORCE.
CORPS TROOPS (ORANGE FREE STATE).

Officer Commanding (Col. on Staff) — Davidson, Col. W. L., R.A.

Cavalry ....
- 26th, 28th and 48th companies Imperial Yeomanry.
- Headquarters and 1 company City Imperial Volunteers Mounted Infantry.

Royal Horse Artillery .... J. battery.

Royal Field Artillery ....
- Field Howitzer .. Brigade division ..
  - 43rd Field battery.
  - 65th ,, ,,
  - 87th ,, ,,
- C. I. V. battery 12½-pr. Q.F.

Heavy Artillery ....
- ½ No. 15 company S. div. R. Garr. Artllry.
- No. 36 ,, ,, ,, ,,
- Naval brigade.... Four 4.7-in. Q.F. / Four 12-pr. Q.F.

Royal Engineers ....
- 1st Field Park.
- 9th Field company (Headquarters and two sections).
- "C." Pontoon troop.
- 1st Balloon section.
- 1st Telegraph division.
- 6th, 8th, 10th, 20th, 30th, 42nd Railway companies. Railway Pioneer regiment.

Signallers .... 1st Mounted company.
Army Service Corps .... Supply Park.

CAVALRY DIVISION (ORANGE FREE STATE).

Lieut.-Gen. .... French, Maj.-Gen.(local Lieut.-Gen.) J. D. P.
Divisional troops .... Field Troop R.E.

1st Brigade.
Brig.-Gen. ...... Porter, Col. T. C., 6th Dragoon Guards.
6th Dragoon Guards.
2nd Dragoons.
6th Dragoons.
Australian Horse.
New South Wales Lancers.
T. battery R.H.A.
D. section 1-pr. Vickers-Maxims.
No. 13 company A.S.C.
½ No. 12 Bearer company.
½ No. 11 Field hospital.

2nd Brigade.
Brig.-Gen. ..... Broadwood, Bt.-Col. (local Brig.-Gen.) R. G., 12th Lancers.
Household Cav. (Composite regt.).
10th Hussars.
12th Lancers.
Q. battery R.H.A.
E. section 1-pr. Vickers-Maxims.
No. 19 R. Transport company.
½ No. 9 Bearer company.
No. 6 Field hospital.

3rd Brigade.
Brig.-Gen. ...... Gordon, Lieut.-Col. (local Brig.-Gen.) J. R. P., 15th Hussars.
9th Lancers.
16th Lancers.
17th Lancers.
R. battery R.H.A.
I. section 1-pr. Vickers-Maxims.
No. 20 R. Transport company.
½ No. 9 Bearer company.
½ No. 11 Field hospital.

4th Brigade.
Brig.-Gen. ...... Dickson, Col. (local Maj.-Gen.) J. B. B., C.B.
7th Dragoon Guards.
8th Hussars.
14th Hussars.
O. battery R.H.A.
J. section 1-pr. Vickers-Maxims.
No. 20 Bearer company.
No. 20 Field hospital.

MOUNTED INFANTRY DIVISION (ORANGE FREE STATE).

Major-General .... Hamilton, Col. (local Maj.-Gen.) I.S.M., C.B., D.S.O.
DIVISIONAL TROOPS .... Rimington's Guides.

1st Brigade.

Major-General.................. Hutton, Col. (local Maj.-Gen.) E. T. H., C.B., A.D.C.

Brigade Troops.

G. battery Royal Horse Artillery.
C. and K. Sections 1-pr. Vickers-Maxims.
C. and D. Sections Galloping Maxims.
Australian Pioneers.
1 Section New South Wales Ambulance (Bearer company and Field hospital).
Nos. 7 R. and 7 L. Transport companies.

1st Corps Mounted Infantry.
Commanding:
Alderson, Bt.-Lieut.-Col. E. A. H., Royal West Kent regiment.
South Eastern company ⎫
Cork　　　　　　　　,,　⎪　1st
Aldershot　　　　　　,,　⎬　Battn.
Southern　　　　　　,,　⎭　Mtd. Inf.
1st Canadian Mounted Rifles
2nd　　　　　,,　　　,,　　,,

3rd Corps Mounted Infantry.
Commanding:
Pilcher, Bt.-Lieut.-Col. T. D., Bedfordshire regiment.
North'd Fus. company ⎫
L. N. Lancs.　　　　,,　⎪　3rd
Northern　　　　　　,,　⎬　Battn.
K. O. Yorks. L. I.　,,　⎭　Mtd. Inf.
Munster Fus.　　　,,
Queensland Mounted Infantry.
New Zealand Mounted Rifles.

2nd Corps Mounted Infantry.
Commanding:
De Lisle, Capt. (local Lieut.-Col.) H. de B., D.S.O., Durham Light Infantry.
Wilts. company ⎫
Gordon　　,,　⎪　6th
Bedford.　,,　⎬　Battn.
Essex　　,,　⎪　Mtd. Inf.
Welsh　　,,　⎭
New South Wales Mounted Rifles.
West Australian Mounted Infantry.

4th Corps Mounted Infantry.
Commanding:
Henry, Bt.-Col. St. G. C., Northumberland Fusiliers.
D. of Corn. L. I. company ⎫
Shrops. L. I.　　　,,　⎪　4th
Yorks.　　　　　　,,　⎬　Battn.
Warwick.　　　　　,,　⎭　Mtd. Inf.
Victorian Mounted Rifles.
South Australian Mounted Infantry.
Tasmanian Mounted Infantry.

2nd Brigade.

Major-General.................. Ridley, Bt.-Col. (local Br.-Gen.) C. P.

Brigade Troops.

P. battery Royal Horse Artillery.
A. and B. Sections 1-pr. Vickers-Maxims.
B. Section Galloping Maxims.
Mounted Detachment Royal Engineers.
Nos. 36 R. and 36 L. Transport companies.
1 Section New South Wales Ambulance (Bearer company and Field hospital).

APPENDIX I.

5TH CORPS MOUNTED INFANTRY.
Commanding:
Dawson, Lieut.-Col. H. L., Indian Staff Corps.

Worcester company ⎫
Royal Irish   ,, ⎪ 5th
East Kent   ,, ⎬ Battn.
Gloucester   ,, ⎪ Mtd.
East Yorks.   ,, ⎭ Inf.
Roberts' Horse.
Marshall's Horse.
Ceylon Mounted Infantry.

6TH CORPS MOUNTED INFANTRY.
Commanding:
Legge, Maj. (local Lieut.-Col.) N., D.S.O., 20th Hussars.

Eastern company ⎫ 2nd
Western   ,,   ⎬ Battn.
Northern   ,,   ⎪ Mtd.
Dublin   ,,   ⎭ Inf.
Kitchener's Horse.
A. Section Galloping Maxims.

7TH CORPS MOUNTED INFANTRY.
Commanding:
Bainbridge, Bt.-Maj. (local Lieut.-Col.) E. G. T., East Kent regiment.

Norfolk company   ⎫ 7th
Lincoln   ,,   ⎪ Battn.
Scottish Bordrs. company ⎬ Mtd.
Hampshire   ,,   ⎪ Inf.
Durham L. I.   ,,   ⎪ Burma
Essex   ,,   ⎬ Mtd.
2nd West Riding ,,   ⎭ Inf.
Nesbitt's Horse.

8TH CORPS MOUNTED INFANTRY.
Commanding:
Ross, Maj. (local Lieut.-Col.) W. C., Durham L. I.

Cheshire company ⎫
E. Lancs.   ,, ⎪ 8th
S. Wales Bordrs. ,, ⎬ Battn.
N. Staffd.   ,, ⎪ Mtd.
1st W. Riding ,, ⎪ Inf.
Oxfordshire L. I. ⎭
Lumsden's Horse.
Loch's Horse.

1st DIVISION (KIMBERLEY).

Lieut.-General .... Methuen, Lieut.-Gen. P. S., Lord, K.C.V.O. C.B., C.M.G.

DIVISIONAL TROOPS.

Cavalry attached to Division ...... { 3rd, 5th and 10th Battns. Imp. Yeo. (comprising Nos. 9, 10, 11, 12, 13, 14, 15, 16, 37, 38, 39, 40 companies). Kimberley Mounted Corps.

Royal Field Artillery .... { 4th Field battery. 20th   ,,   ,, 38th   ,,   ,, 37th   ,,   ,, (Howitzer). Diamond Fields artillery.

Royal Garrison artillery............ No. 23 company W. Division.
Royal Engineers .... 11th Field company.

9TH BRIGADE.
Maj.-Gen....Douglas, Col. (local Maj.-Gen.) C. W. H., A.D.C.
1st Northumberland Fusiliers.
1st L. N. Lancashire regiment.
3rd S. Wales Borderers.
4th Scottish Rifles.
Det. Army Service Corps.
No. 1 Bearer company.
No. 19 Field hospital.

20TH BRIGADE.
Maj.-Gen.......Paget, Col. (local Maj.-Gen.) A. H., Scots Guards.
2nd Northamptonshire regiment.
2nd K. O. Yorkshire L. I.
1st R. Munster Fus.
4th S. Staffordshire regiment.
Det. Army Service Corps.
Bearer coy. (locally constituted).
No. 8 Field hospital.

OTHER TROOPS ON THE LINE AT, AND NORTH OF, MODDER RIVER.
Kimberley regiment.
5th Bn. R. Dublin Fusiliers.
3rd Bn. K. O. Scottish Borderers.

IIIRD DIVISION (ORANGE FREE STATE).

Lieut.-General .... Chermside, Lieut.-Gen. Sir H. C., G.C.M.G. C.B., R.E.

DIVISIONAL TROOPS.

Divisional Cavalry .... De Montmorency's Scouts.
Royal Field Artillery .... 5th Field battery.
9th ,,   ,,
17th ,,   ,,
Royal Engineers .... 47th Field company.
Mounted Infantry .... 1st company Royal Scots.
2nd   ,,   ,,   ,,
Northumberland Fusilier company.
1st company Derby.
2nd   ,,   ,,
1st   ,,   Berks.
2nd   ,,   ,,
Royal Irish Rifles company.

22ND BRIGADE.	23RD BRIGADE.
Maj.-Gen. ...... Allen, Col. (local Maj.-Gen.), R.E.	Maj.-Gen. ..... Knox, Col. (local Maj.-Gen.) W. G., C.B.
2nd Northumberland Fusiliers.	1st Royal Scots.
2nd Royal Berkshire regiment.	1st Suffolk regiment.
3rd East Kent regiment.	3rd Royal Scots.
4th Argyll and Sutherland Highlrs.	9th King's Royal Rifle Corps.

VITH DIVISION (BLOEMFONTEIN GARRISON).

Lieut. Gen. .... Kelly-Kenny, Maj.-Gen. (local Lieut.-Gen.) T., C.B.

DIVISIONAL TROOPS.

Divisional Cavalry .... Detachment Prince Alfred's Vol. Guard.
Royal Field Artillery .... 76th Field battery.
81st ,,   ,,
82nd ,,   ,,
Royal Engineers .... 38th Field company.

12TH BRIGADE.	13TH BRIGADE.
Maj.-Gen. ...... Clements, Col. (local Maj.-Gen.) R. A. P., D.S.O., A.D.C.	Maj.-Gen. ...... Knox, Col. (local Maj.-Gen.) C. E.
2nd Bedford regiment.	2nd East Kent regiment.
1st Royal Irish regiment.	2nd Gloucestershire regiment.
2nd Worcester regiment.	1st West Riding regiment.
2nd Wiltshire regiment.	1st Oxfordshire Light Infantry.
7 R. Transport company.	7 L. Transport company.
8th Bearer company.	7th Bearer company.
3rd section Cape Field hospital.	13th Field hospital.

APPENDIX I.

VIIth DIVISION (ORANGE FREE STATE).

Lieut.-Gen. .... Tucker, Maj.-Gen. (local Lieut.-Gen.) C., C.B.

DIVISIONAL TROOPS.

Divisional Cavalry .... { 1st company City of London Imperial Volunteers Mounted Infantry.

Royal Field Artillery .... { 18th Field battery.
62nd ,, ,,
75th ,, ,,

Royal Engineers .... 26th Field company.

14TH BRIGADE.	15TH BRIGADE.
Maj.-Gen.......Maxwell, Col. (local Maj.-Gen.) J. G., D.S.O.	Maj.-Gen.......Wavell, Col. (local Maj.-Gen.) A. G.
2nd Norfolk regiment.	2nd Cheshire regiment.
2nd Lincoln regiment.	2nd South Wales Borderers.
1st K. O. Scottish Borderers.	1st East Lancashire regiment.
2nd Hampshire regiment.	2nd North Staffordshire regiment.
26 R. Transport company A.S.C.	26 L. Transport company A.S.C.
14th Brigade Bearer company.	15th Brigade Bearer company.
14th Brigade Field hospital.	15th Brigade Field hospital.

VIIIth DIVISION (ORANGE FREE STATE.)

Lieut.-Gen. .... Rundle, Maj.-Gen. (local Lieut. Gen.) Sir H. M. L., K.C.B., C.M.G., D.S.O.

DIVISIONAL TROOPS.

Divisional Cavalry .... Unallotted.

Royal Field Artillery .... { 74th Field battery.
77th ,, ,,
79th ,, ,,

Royal Engineers .... 5th Field company.

R. A. Med. Corps............ 23rd Field hospital.

16TH BRIGADE.	17TH BRIGADE.
Maj.-Gen.......Campbell, Maj.-Gen. B. B. D., M.V.O.	Maj.-Gen.......Boyes, Maj.-Gen. J. E.
2nd Grenadier Guards.	1st Worcester regiment.
2nd Scots Guards.	1st South Staffordshire regiment.
2nd East Yorkshire regiment.	2nd Royal West Kent regiment.
1st Leinster regiment.	2nd Manchester regiment.
21st Bearer company.	22nd Bearer company.
21st Field hospital.	22nd Field hospital.

IXth DIVISION (ORANGE FREE STATE).

Lieut.-Gen..................... Colvile, Maj.-Gen. (local Lieut.-Gen.) Sir H. E., K.C.M.G., C.B.

DIVISIONAL TROOPS.

Divisional Cavalry .... Eastern Province Horse.

Royal Field Artillery .... { 83rd Field battery.
84th ,, ,,
85th ,, ,,

Royal Engineers .... 7th Field company.

IXTH DIVISION (ORANGE FREE STATE)—continued.

3RD BRIGADE.
Maj.-Gen.......MacDonald, Col. (local Maj.-Gen.) H. A., C.B., D.S.O., A.D.C.
2nd Royal Highlanders.
1st Highland Light Infantry.
2nd Seaforth Highlanders.
1st Argyll and Sutherland Highrs.
No. 21 R. Transport company.
Cape Med. Staff Corps Bearer company.
No. 3 Field hospital.

19TH BRIGADE.
Maj.-Gen.......Smith-Dorrien, Col. (local Maj.-Gen.) H. L., D.S.O.
2nd Duke of Cornwall's L.I.
2nd Shropshire Light Infantry.
1st Gordon Highlanders.
Royal Canadian regiment.
No. 42 R. Transport company.
No. 19 Bearer company (Cape Vols).
No. 19 Field hospital.

XTH DIVISION (KIMBERLEY).

Lieut.-Gen. .... Hunter, Maj.-Gen. (local Lieut.-Gen.) Sir A., K.C.B., D.S.O.

DIVISIONAL TROOPS.
Divisional Cavalry......... Imperial Light Horse.
Royal Field Artillery ...... { 28th Field battery. 66th ,, ,, 78th ,, ,,
Royal Engineers .... 9th Field company (1 section).

5TH BRIGADE.
Major.-Gen....Hart, Maj.-Gen. A. FitzR., C.B.
2nd Somersetshire Light Infantry.
1st Border regiment.
1st Connaught Rangers.
2nd Royal Dublin Fusiliers.

6TH BRIGADE.
Maj.-Gen....Barton, Maj.-Gen. G., C.B.
2nd Royal Fusiliers.
2nd Royal Scots Fusiliers.
1st Royal Welsh Fusiliers.
2nd Royal Irish Fusiliers.

XITH DIVISION (ORANGE FREE STATE).

Lieut.-Gen.................... Pole-Carew, Maj.-Gen. (local Lieut.-Gen.) R., C.B.

DIVISIONAL TROOPS.
Divisional Cavalry........ Detachment Prince Alfred's Vol. Guard.
Royal Field Artillery ...... { 2nd Field battery. 39th ,, ,, 68th ,, ,,
Royal Engineers .... 12th Field company.

1ST BRIGADE.
Maj.-Gen....Jones, Col. (local Maj.-Gen.) I. R., Scots Gds.
3rd Grenadier Guards.
1st Coldstream Guards.
2nd Coldstream Guards.
1st Scots Guards.
11 R. Transport company.
Guards' Brigade Bearer company.
Guards' Brigade Field hospital.

18TH BRIGADE.
Maj.-Gen....Stephenson, Col. (local Brig.-Gen.) T. E., Essex regiment.
2nd Royal Warwickshire regiment.
1st Yorkshire regiment.
1st Welsh regiment.
1st Essex regiment.
11 L. Transport company.
18th Bearer company.
18th Field hospital.

APPENDIX I.

21ST BRIGADE (ORANGE FREE STATE).
(Unattached.)

Maj.-Gen.	Hamilton, Bt.-Col. (local Maj.-Gen.) B. M., East Yorkshire regiment, p.s.c.
	1st Battn. Royal Sussex regiment.
	1st Battn. Derbyshire regiment.
	1st Battn. Cameron Highlanders.
	City Imperial Volunteers.
Mounted Troops (attached).......	One company mounted inf. Cameron Hghrs.
Royal Engineers	9th Field company (1 section).

COLONIAL DIVISION (ORANGE FREE STATE).

Brigadier-General......................................	E. Y. Brabant, C.M.G.
	1st Brabant's Horse.
	2nd Brabant's Horse.
	Border Horse.
	Cape Mounted Rifles (Detachment).
	Frontier Mounted Rifles.
	Kaffrarian Rifles,
	Komgha Mounted Rifles.
	Queenstown Volunteers.
	Warren's Horse.
	Cape Artillery—two 15-pr. and two 7-pr, guns.

HEADQUARTERS STAFF.—NATAL ARMY.

General Commanding	Gen. the Rt. Hon. Sir R. H. Buller, G.C.B., K.C.M.G., V.C.
Military Secretary	Col. the Hon. F. W. Stopford, C.B.
Aides-de-Camp	Capt. H. N. Schofield, Royal Artillery.
	Capt. C. J. Sackville-West, K.R.R.C.
	Lieut. A. R. Trotter, 2nd Life Guards.
Naval Aide-de-Camp	Lieut. E. Lees, R.N.
Extra Aide-de-Camp	Col. Lord Gerard, W. C. Lancs. Hussars.
Chief Staff Officer (D.A.G.)	Col. H. S. G. Miles, M.V.O.
Assistant-Adjutant-General	Bt.-Lieut.-Col. H. M. Lawson, R.E.
	Lieut.-Col. C. à Court.
Dep.-Assist.-Adjt.-Gens...........	Major L. E. R. Kiggel, Warwick. regiment.
	Major P. J. T. Lewis, A.S.C.
	Major Hon. F. Gordon, Gordon Highlanders.
Provost Marshal	Major A. G. Chichester, Royal Irish regt.
Assist.-Adjt.-Gen. (Intell.)	Bt.-Lieut.-Col. A. E. Sandbach, R.E.
Dept.-Assist.-Adjt.-Gen. (Intell.) ..	Bt.-Major D. Henderson, Argyll and Sutherland Highlanders.
Officer Commanding Royal Artillery	Col. C. M. H. Downing, Royal Artillery.
Aide-de-Camp (Royal Artillery)....	Capt. R. A. Bright, Royal Artillery
Staff Officer (Royal Artillery)......	Capt. E. S. E. W. Russell, Royal Artillery.
Chief Engineer	Lieut.-Col. (local Col.) C. K. Wood, R.E.
Staff Officer (Royal Engineers)	Capt. C. M. Hutton, Royal Engineers.
Director of Army Telegraphs	Major W. F. Hawkins, Royal Engineers.
Principal Chaplain	Rev. A. A. L. Gedge, M.A.
Director of Signalling	Capt. J. S. Cayzer, 7th Dragoon Guards.
Press Censor ....,,..	Major W. D. Jones, Wiltshire regiment,

CORPS TROOPS.

Royal Artillery
- 4th Mountain battery.
- 10th ,, ,, (detachment).
- 16th company Southern divn. Royal Garrison Artillery.
- 10th ,, Eastern ,, ,, ,, ,,
- 2nd ,, Western ,, ,, ,, ,,
- 6th ,, ,, ,, ,, ,, ,,

Royal Engineers
- 2nd Balloon section.
- Headquarters and 4 sections Telegraph Battn.
- "A" Pontoon Troop.

CAVALRY.

1st Brigade.
Maj.-Gen....Burn-Murdoch, Lt.-Col. (local Brig.-Gen.) J. F., 1st Royal Dragoons
5th Dragoon Guards.
1st Royal Dragoons.
13th Hussars.
A. battery R.H.A.
No. 6 company A.S.C. (part of).
No. 11 Field hospital.

2nd Brigade.
Maj.-Gen....Brocklehurst, Col. (local Maj.-Gen.) J. F., M.V.O. Eq.
5th Lancers.
18th Hussars.
19th Hussars.
No. 31 company A.S.C.
No. 18 Field hospital.

3rd Mounted Brigade.
Maj.-Gen...................... Dundonald, Col. (local Maj.-Gen.), D. M. B. H., Earl of, C.B., M.V.O.
Thorneycroft's Mounted Infantry.
South African Light Horse.
Bethune's Mounted Infantry.
Composite Regiment Mounted Infantry with Natal Vols.
No. 6 company Army Service Corps (part of).
No. 24 Field hospital.

IIND DIVISION.

Lieut.-Gen. .... Clery, Maj.-Gen. (local Lt.-Gen.) Sir C. F., K.C.B.

Divisional Troops.
Divisional Cavalry .... 1 Troop 13th Hussars.
Royal Field Artillery ....
- 7th Field battery.
- 63rd ,, ,,
- 64th ,, ,,

Royal Engineers .... 17th Field company.
Supply Column .... No. 1 Auxiliary Co. Army Service Corps.
Field Hospital .... No. 5 Field hospital.

2nd Brigade.
Maj.-Gen....Hamilton, Lt.-Col. E. O. F., R. W. Surrey regt.
2nd Royal West Surrey regiment.
2nd Devonshire regiment.
2nd West Yorkshire regiment.
2nd East Surrey regiment.
No. 16 company A.S.C.
No. 2 Bearer company.
Field hospital (Depôt company).

4th Brigade.
Maj.-Gen....Cooper, Col. C.D., Royal Dublin Fus.
2nd Scottish Rifles.
3rd King's Royal Rifle Corps.
1st Durham Light Infantry.
1st Rifle brigade.
No. 14 company A.S.C.
No. 14 Bearer company.
No. 14 Field hospital.

APPENDIX I.

IVth DIVISION.

Lieut.-Gen. .... Lyttelton, Maj.-Gen. (local Lt.-Gen.) the Hon. N. G., C.B.

Divisional Troops.

Divisional Cavalry .... Unallotted.
Royal Field Artillery .... { 21st Field battery.
42nd ,, ,,
53rd ,, ,,
Royal Engineers .... 23rd Field company.
Supply Column .... Auxiliary company A.S.C.
Field Hospital .... ½ No. 26 Field hospital.

7th Brigade.	8th Brigade.
Maj.-Gen....Kitchener, Col. (local Brig.-Gen.) F. W.	Maj.-Gen.....Howard, Col.(local Maj.-Gen.) F., C.B., C.M.G., A.D.C.
1st Devonshire regiment.	1st Liverpool regiment.
1st Manchester regiment.	1st Leicester regiment.
2nd Gordon Highlanders.	1st King's Royal Rifle Corps.
2nd Rifle brigade.	2nd King's Royal Rifle Corps.
No. 22 company A.S.C.	Auxiliary company A.S.C.
No. 17 Bearer company.	No. 16 Bearer company.
No. 11 Field hospital.	No. 24 Field hospital.

Vth DIVISION.

Lieut.-Gen. .... Hildyard, Maj.-Gen. (local Lieut.-Gen.) H. J. T., C.B.

Divisional Troops.

Divisional Cavalry .... 1 Troop 13th Hussars.
Royal Field Artillery .... { 13th Field battery.
67th ,, ,,
69th ,, ,,
Royal Engineers .... 37th Field company.
Supply Column .... { Locally organised from Army Service Corps details.
Field Hospital .... No. 16 Field hospital.

10th Brigade.	11th Brigade.
Maj.-Gen....Coke, Col. (local Maj.-Gen.) J. T.	Maj.-Gen.....Wynne, Col. (local Maj.-Gen.) A. S., C.B.
2nd Dorsetshire regiment.	2nd (King's Own)Royal Lancaster regt.
2nd Middlesex regiment.	2nd Lancashire Fusiliers.
No. 32 company A.S.C.	1st South Lancashire regiment.
No. 15 Bearer company.	1st York & Lancaster regiment.
No. 11 Field hospital.	No. 25 company A.S.C.
	No. 6 Bearer company.
	Depôt company Field hospital.

APPENDIX 2.

APPROXIMATE STRENGTHS AND CASUALTIES.

THE ADVANCE FROM BLOEMFONTEIN TO PRETORIA.

APPROXIMATE STRENGTH OF THE MAIN COLUMN UNDER FIELD-MARSHAL LORD ROBERTS, MAY 3RD, 1900.

Arms.	Officers.	Men.	Horses.	Guns.						
				5-in.	4.7-in. Naval.	12-pr. Naval.	15-pr. Field.	12-pr. Field.	1-pr. Q.F.	Machine.
CAVALRY DIVISION—LIEUT.-GENERAL FRENCH. (Joined May 8th, 1900.)										
Divisional & Brigade Staffs	24	84	125	—	—	—	—	—	—	—
Cavalry (3 brigades)	198	3,319	2,862	—	—	—	—	—	—	9
Royal Horse Artillery, Vickers-Maxims & Ammunition column	17	518	558	—	—	—	—	18	6	—
Royal Engineers	4	105	120	—	—	—	—	—	—	—
Army Service Corps	3	120	60	—	—	—	—	—	—	—
Royal Army Medical Corps	9	102	24	—	—	—	—	—	—	—
Total Cavalry Division	255	4,248	3,749	—	—	—	—	18	6	9
1ST MOUNTED INFANTRY BRIGADE—MAJOR-GENERAL HUTTON.										
Brigade Staff	10	25	45	—	—	—	—	—	—	—
Mounted Infantry (1st, 2nd (a) & 3rd Corps)	114	1,896	2,050	—	—	—	—	—	—	9
R.H.A. and Corps Troops	19	482	476	—	—	—	—	6	2	4
Total 1st Mounted Infantry Brigade	143	2,403	2,571	—	—	—	—	6	2	13

(a) Part of the 2nd Corps detached, not included.

APPENDIX 2.

VIIth Infantry Division—Lieut.-General Tucker.

VIIth Infantry Division Staff	12	67	51	—	—	—	—	—	—
Mounted Troops (City Imperial Volunteers)	5	140	95	—	—	—	—	—	2
R.F.A. and Ammunition column	20	482	342	—	18	—	—	—	—
Royal Engineers	7	112	17	—	—	—	—	—	—
Infantry (2 brigades)	172	5,931	60	—	—	—	—	—	9
Army Service Corps	8	74	52	—	—	—	—	—	—
Royal Army Medical Corps	10	127	18	—	—	—	—	—	—
Total VIIth Division	**234**	**6,933**	**635**	—	**18**	—	—	—	**11**

XIth Infantry Division—Lieut.-General Pole-Carew.

XIth Infantry Division Staff	12	55	46	—	—	—	—	—	—
The Naval Brigade	8	82	10	—	—	2	—	—	—
R.F.A. and Ammunition column	20	482	342	—	18	2	—	—	—
Royal Garrison Artillery	3	73	4	2	—	—	—	—	—
Royal Engineers	4	143	40	—	—	—	—	—	—
Infantry (2 brigades)	176	6,588	156	—	—	—	—	—	8
Army Service Corps	8	74	52	—	—	—	—	—	—
Royal Army Medical Corps	10	127	18	—	—	—	—	—	—
Total XIth Division	**241**	**7,624**	**668**	**2**	**18**	**2**	—	—	**8**

Mounted Infantry attached to the XIth Division—Lieut.-Colonel Henry.

Mounted Infantry Staff	3	6	10	—	—	—	—	—	—
Mounted Infantry (4th and 8th Corps)	58	1,548	1,731	—	—	—	—	—	6
Royal Horse Artillery	5	132	179	—	6	—	6	—	—
Det. Maxims	1	16	17	—	—	—	—	—	2
Total Henry's M.I.	**67**	**1,702**	**1,937**	—	**6**	—	**6**	—	**8**

Corps Troops—Unattached.

Mounted Signallers	1	25	26	—	—	—	—	—	—
Royal Engineers	15	541	446	—	—	—	—	—	—
Army Service Corps	4	100	20	—	—	—	—	—	—
Army Headquarters Staff and Escort	62	156	200	—	—	—	—	—	—
Total unattached	**82**	**822**	**692**	—	—	—	—	—	—
Grand Total Main Column	**1,022**	**23,732**	**10,252**	**2**	**36**	**2**	**30**	**8**	**49**

Note.—In addition to the above guns, a detachment of Royal Garrison Artillery with two 9.45-in. and four 6-in. Howitzers joined the main army at Johannesburg on June 2nd.

APPROXIMATE STRENGTH OF THE FORCE UNDER LIEUT.-GENERAL IAN HAMILTON, MAY 1ST, 1900.

Arms.	Officers.	Men.	Horses.	Guns. 5-in.	Guns. 15-pr.	Guns. 12-pr.	Guns. 1-pr. Q.F.	Guns. Machine.
Divisional Staff	11	25	20	—	—	—	—	—
2nd Cav. Bde. { Brigade Staff	3	7	16	—	—	—	—	—
Cavalry (3 regiments)	66	1,320	1,440	—	—	—	—	3
R.H.A. and Maxims	6	148	187	—	—	6	2	—
2nd M.I. Bde. { Brigade Staff	3	10	16	—	—	—	—	—
Mounted Infantry	182	4,100	4,305	—	—	—	—	8
R.H.A. and Maxims	8	180	226	—	—	6	4	2
19th Bde. { Brigade Staff	3	11	6	—	6	—	—	—
Royal Field Artillery	5	162	120	—	—	—	—	—
Infantry (4 battalions)	104	3,300	24	—	—	—	—	4
21st Bde. { Brigade Staff	3	11	6	—	6	—	—	—
Royal Field Artillery	5	162	120	—	—	—	—	—
Infantry (4 battalions)	103	3,650	24	—	—	—	—	3
Corps and Bde. Troops. { Royal Field Artillery	10	330	240	—	12	—	—	—
Royal Garrison Artillery	3	74	4	2	—	—	—	—
Ammunition Columns	6	212	159	—	—	—	—	—
Royal Engineers	2	45	4	—	—	—	—	—
Army Service Corps	11	131	81	—	—	—	—	—
Royal Army Medical Corps	16	202	34	—	—	—	—	—
Total	550	14,080	7,032	2	24	12	6	20

APPENDIX 2.

Approximate Strength of Lieut.-General Colvile's Column in support of Hamilton's Force, May 1st, 1900.

Arms.	Officers.	Men.	Horses.	Guns. 4.7-in.	Guns. 15-pr.	Guns. Machine.
Divisional Staff	12	55	46	—	—	—
The Naval Brigade	6	50	7	2	—	—
Eastern Province Horse	3	80	85	—	—	—
Royal Field Artillery and Ammunition Column	12	286	250	—	12	—
Infantry (4 battalions)	104	3,265	114	—	—	4
Royal Engineers, Army Service Corps, and Royal Army Medical Corps	9	115	61	—	—	—
Total	146	3,851	563	2	12	4

Field State of the Natal Army on June 1st, 1900.

Units.	Officers.	Other ranks.	Horses.	Guns. Naval.	Guns. Field.	Guns. Vickers-Maxims.	Guns. Machine.
Headquarter Staff & Attached	32	238	336	—	—	—	—
1st Cavalry Brigade	62	1,422	498	—	—	—	3
3rd Mounted Brigade	150	2,709	2,674	—	8	—	11
2nd Infantry Division	249	9,863	856	—	18	—	10
4th Infantry Division (General Lyttelton's Force)	260	10,498	2,295	—	26	1	9
Colonel Bethune's Force	26	495	567	—	2	—	1
5th Infantry Division	207	8,197	717	—	18	—	7
Corps Artillery	24	654	312	—	18	2	—
Ammunition Park	2	31	4	—	—	—	—
Naval Brigade	11	89	14	6	—	—	—
Royal Engineers	6	229	44	—	—	—	—
Army Service Corps	3	24	14	—	—	—	—
Drakensberg Defences	93	4,565	1,156	—	19	—	5
Line of Communication Troops	254	5,322	2,166	—	4	—	2
Totals	1,379	44,336	11,653	6	113	3	48

N.B.—The above figures are exclusive of sick, wounded, missing, &c.

APPROXIMATE STRENGTH OF LORD ROBERTS' AVAILABLE FORCE,
AUGUST 26TH, 1900.

Officers.	Lieut-General French.		Guns of all Calibres (exclusive of Maxims).
	Men.	Horses.	
163	2,545	2,441	14
	General Sir R. Buller.		
251	7,800	1,800	42
	Lieut-General Pole-Carew.		
261	7,756	1,174	26
675	18,101	5,415	82

APPROXIMATE STRENGTH OF IAN HAMILTON'S COLUMN (N.C.O.'S AND MEN ONLY), AUGUST 31ST, 1900.

Mounted Troops.	Infantry.	Guns.
80	2,300	14

ADVANCE ON KROONSTAD.
SUMMARY OF BRITISH CASUALTIES. MAY 1ST TO 13TH, 1900.

Ranks.	Killed.	Wounded.	Missing.	Total.
Officers	3	13	5	21
Other Ranks	29	149	43	221
Total	32	162	48	242

APPENDIX 2.

DOORN.KOP (near Johannesburg).
SUMMARY OF BRITISH CASUALTIES. MAY 29TH, 1900.

Ranks.	Killed.	Wounded.	Missing.	Total.
Officers	2	11	—	13
Other Ranks	26	123	—	149
Total	28	134	—	162

BIDDULPHS BERG.
SUMMARY OF BRITISH CASUALTIES. MAY 29TH, 1900.

Corps.	Killed and died of wounds.		Wounded.		Missing.		Total.
	Officers.	Other ranks.	Officers.	Other ranks.	Officers.	Other ranks.	
2nd Grenadier Guards	1	39	4	87	—	8	139
2nd Scots Guards	—	5	1	18	—	—	24
Other units	—	2	1	19	—	—	22
Total	1	46	6	124	—	8	185

SIX MILE SPRUIT (near Pretoria).
SUMMARY OF BRITISH CASUALTIES. JUNE 4TH, 1900.

Ranks.	Killed.	Wounded.	Missing.	Total.	Remarks.
Officers	—	2*	—	2	*1 died of wounds.
Other Ranks	1	24	—	25	
Total	1	26	—	27	

Diamond Hill.

Summary of British Casualties. June 11th to 12th, 1900.

Ranks.	Killed and died of wounds.	Wounded.	Missing.	Total.
Officers	9	14	—	23
Other Ranks	19	131	3	153
Total	28	145	3	176

Alleman's Nek.

Summary of British Casualties. June 11th, 1900.

Ranks.	Killed.	Wounded.	Missing.	Total.	
Officers	2	6*	—	8	*1 Officer & 3 men died of wounds.
Other Ranks	17	117*	—	134	
Total	19	123	—	142	

Bergendal.

Summary of British Casualties. August 27th, 1900.

Ranks.	Killed.	Wounded.	Missing.	Total.
Officers	1	7*	—	8
Other Ranks	12	96	4	112
Total	13	103	4	120

* Two died of wounds.

APPENDIX 3.

RAILWAY WORK, MAY AND JUNE, 1900.

THE chief difficulties before the railway staff consisted in *repairing* the vast damage done to bridges, buildings, permanent way and water stations; in the *paucity of rolling stock;* and in the necessity of providing an entirely *new personnel.*

A.—RECONSTRUCTION AND REPAIR.

As the enemy retired northwards they " completely disabled the line behind them in an unprecedented manner. Practically every bridge and culvert was destroyed, including the very large bridges at Vet Zand, Vaalsch, Rhenoster and Vaal rivers, consisting of several spans of 100 feet over deep ravines, while spans of from 7 feet to 75 feet were numerous. At most places the water supply had been destroyed, and in many the permanent way itself had been blown up for miles."*

Hasty temporary repairs were executed after the army left Kroonstad, both by an officer of the Works Department who accompanied the army as it advanced, and, wherever possible, made arrangements for work to be begun ahead of the " construction train," and also by Lieutenant H. A. Micklem, D.S.O., R.E., in charge of the construction train, who with a detachment of 150 Royal Engineers pushed forward the railhead hour by hour. The work of this detachment was supplemented by that of infantry, of working parties of civil gangers and of natives, varying in number from 300 to 1,500 men. Although the advance of the army was rapid, railway communication with Johannesburg was in this way opened in 11 days, and with Pretoria in 16 days, after the arrival of the Commander-in-Chief in those places.

In the case of the Zand, Vet, Vaalsch river bridges (each of which consisted of five spans of 100 feet), most of the original concrete piers of the low-level bridges previously used by the Cape Government Railways were standing, and the missing piers were in these as in

* History of Railways in South Africa, by Lieutenant-Colonel Sir E. P. C. Girouard, K.C.M.G., D.S.O., R.E.

almost every other case, replaced by crib piers of sleepers, the spans being crossed by timber baulks.

In the case of the Vaal bridge at Vereeniging the original cuttings had become silted up by floods, and heavy excavation was required. As before, a low-level bridge (all material for which had to be found in the neighbourhood and brought to the site by wagon) was constructed to take the place of the demolished high-level girder bridge. This occupied all available parties of Royal Engineers, infantry, and natives from the neighbouring colliery from May 27th till June 9th, when Lieutenant Micklem's party on the construction train brought railhead up to the Vaal and helped to finish this work on June 10th. On the evening of the eleventh day after its occupation the first through train reached Johannesburg from Bloemfontein.

In addition to some 16 spans of 100 feet, several of from 50 feet to 75 feet were erected, and the reconstruction of spans of lengths varying from 7 feet to 30 feet was common. Work on the Vet river bridge occupied from May 7th to 13th; that on the Doorn river bridge (one span of 100 feet and one of 20 feet) from May 14th to 17th; on the Zand bridge from May 17th to 23rd; on the Vaalsch bridge from May 13th to 23rd; on the Rhenoster bridge (six spans of 19 feet each) from May 25th to 30th; on the Taaibosch bridge (eight spans varying from 20 feet to 14 feet) from June 6th to 9th; on the Vaal bridge (17 spans of various lengths) occupied 14 days. In the case of each of the above bridges deviations of lengths, varying from half a mile to two miles, were entailed, the total deviations amounting to several miles. The reconstruction of culverts and permanent way, the repair of points, telegraph stations and water tanks, were too numerous to describe in detail.

B.—ROLLING STOCK.

The total amount of rolling stock on the line south of Bloemfontein was:—

Engines.	Coaches.	Trucks.
423	565	7,041

If this was inadequate at the outbreak of the war, it became daily more insufficient as the length of the railway line, handed over to the railway staff, extended. The enemy consistently withdrew, whenever possible, the bulk of their own rolling stock, or damaged whatever they were unable to withdraw.

APPENDIX 3.

The bulk of the locomotives, coaches and trucks on the enemy's side was not recovered till a later period,* and none of the new stock ordered to replace it could be brought into traffic until July, 1900.

Yet if the quantity was inadequate, the quality of the rolling stock was eminently suitable for military purposes. The long bogie trucks were invaluable for guns and wagons, and the ordinary trucks were well adapted for other freight.

C.—PERSONNEL.

" On arrival at Bloemfontein a new problem in railway organization was presented. Hitherto we had been working on a railway system the staff of which were loyal . . . . but now we had entered the enemy's country, captured 149 miles of railway from them, and would shortly be possessed of several hundred miles more. The railway officials were, some of them, loyal, and others either openly or, what was worse, secretly disloyal to us; and it was known that when we should arrive in the Transvaal we should find none of the railway employés friendly to us. Consequently, the Director of Railways decided on taking over complete charge of the railways and on working them under the Imperial Military Railways with the aid of a staff of employés, civil and military, appointed by himself."†

The military controlling staff continued as heretofore to act as intermediaries between the army and the technical working staff; but the latter had now to be treated by the Director of Railways, and the want of a larger reserve of trained railway men registered in Great Britain for war purposes was at once felt. The numbers normally required by the traffic and locomotive departments of the Transvaal and Free State railways in peace consisted of over 3,000 white men; and it was a heavy task suddenly to improvise so large a staff during actual war. The Chief Traffic Managers of the Cape Government and of the Natal Government railways handed over to the Director all officials that could possibly be spared, and all British employés who had left the Free State were, as far as possible, reinstated in their former positions. There were available, also, the officers and men

* Although 16 engines and 400 trucks were recovered at Pretoria, the station books disclosed the fact that in the preceding 48 hours 70 trains, many of which were drawn by two engines, had been sent east.

† History of Railways in South Africa, by Lt.-Col. Sir E P. C. Girouard, K.C.M.G., D.S.O., R.E.

of the 8th, 10th, 31st and 42nd Railway companies of Royal Engineers, strengthened by the special railway reserve men from home. These, however, were altogether insufficient, and other sources had to be sought. Only by depleting regular regiments—colonial, militia, yeomanry or volunteer corps—of such reservists as had previously been in railway employment in civil life might the deficiency be made good. The step was an unavoidable experiment, for the qualifications and the numbers of these men were entirely unknown. Nevertheless, induced by the offer of working-pay at Royal Engineer rates, some 800 to 1,000 offered themselves, and proved of great service.

Number of men provided by R. E. Railway Companies	79
,, ,, taken from the army	279
Found in the Free State and re-appointed	154
British refugees re-instated in Free State	303
,, ,, ,, Transvaal	54
Transferred from C. G. Railways	136
,, ,, Natal Government	57
Obtained elsewhere	965
Found in Transvaal and re-appointed	13
Received direct from England	12
	2,052

The Director thus succeeded in keeping the entire management of the railway system in his own hands. The works, locomotive and stores departments were controlled by Royal Engineer officers; the traffic and accounts departments by civilian officials with experience of the South African system.

APPENDIX 4.

THE DEFENCES OF PRETORIA.

THE capital of the Transvaal lies in a flat basin some 4,000 yards square. The plain, intersected by the dongas of the Aapies river, is enclosed on the north by two parallel ridges of the Magaliesberg Hills, on the south by two similar ridges trending east and west, and on its eastern and western sides by rough isolated hills.

Guarding the pass through which the Johannesburg railway enters the basin of Pretoria, lay Forts Schanzkop and Klapperkop. On the north stood the fort of Zandfontein barring the defile of Daspoort, and commanding the Rustenburg road. Further to the north, Wonderboom Fort closed the main avenue through the Magaliesberg range, by which the Aapies river finds its outlet to the north, and two smaller redoubts on the plain itself covered the artillery camp from surprise from the west.

The first three of these four forts were upstanding works built without attempt at concealment. Large lunettes formed traverses at the angles, with cover for a gun detachment. There was a brick defensible "gorge," and in the centre of each face with high parapet mounting, a gun was designed to be placed, so as to fire "en barbette." Each fort was purposed to be in telephonic and heliographic communication with the rest, to be provided with searchlights, to have its own water supply, and to be provisioned for three months.

FORT SCHANZKOP, on the ridge of hills to the south of the town, and upon the western side of the Poort, through which the Johannesburg rail and highway run, faced south and commanded both the line and the road. It was a three-gun redoubt without flank defences. The parapet (without ditch) was some 120 yards in length and some 12 feet thick, and it was designed solely for long-range artillery, for the slopes immediately to the south were dead to view and fire.

FORT KLAPPERKOP, a six-gun redoubt, resembled Fort Schanzkop in type. It stood some 2,000 yards to the east of the latter, and was separated from it by the valley along which the Johannesburg rail and road, and the Standerton highway, ran.

FORT WONDERBOOM, the first of the forts to be built, was of similar construction to the rest, but different from them in that it was excavated by blasting and digging. A cavity was thus formed of some 200 feet in length, 80 feet in width and 15 feet in depth. It was casemented into quarters and magazines with stone, brick, cement and concrete. ·This fort stood four miles from the town upon the northernmost of the two Magaliesberg ridges, and upon the eastern wall of the Poort itself, thus overlooking the Pietersburg road and railway.

The fort faced north, in which direction it held a good command over the valley before it for some four miles.

FORT ZANDFONTEIN (or Daspoort), of a type similar to Wonderboom, lay some two miles to the north-west of the town. It stood upon the northern slope of the ridge of hills to the west of the Daspoort, thus overlooking the avenues of approach from Rustenburg as well as from Pietersburg.

Of these forts, Schanzkop and Klapperkop might have supported each other, but Fort Wonderboom was isolated and could have been disregarded by an attack from the south.

Moreover, the eastern side of Pretoria was unprotected by works, although improvised defences might have been suitably constructed on an isolated ridge which flanked the Delagoa Bay railway at a distance of some 4,000 yards to the east of the town.

APPENDIX 5.

CASUALTIES IN ATTACK ON GAME TREE FORT, DEC. 26TH, 1899.

	Killed and died of wounds.	Wounded.	Missing.
Officers	3	1	—
Men	21	22	3
	24	23	3

Total 50

DETAIL OF CASUALTIES IN MAFEKING UP TO END OF MARCH, 1900.

COMBATANTS.

	Whites. Officers.	Whites. Men.	Natives.
Killed or died of wounds	6	53	13
Wounded	11	97	49
Missing	1	26	—
	18	176	62

Whites killed, wounded and missing ... 194

Total combined losses... 256

NON-COMBATANTS.

	Whites.	Natives.
Killed	4	32
Wounded	5	92
	9	124

133

Total whites ... 203 ⎫ 389 by shell or bullet, exclusive of
Total natives ... 18 ⎭ accident or disease.

RETURN OF SICK AND CASUALTIES IN MAFEKING UP TO END OF APRIL, 1900.

	Distribution.	Admissions.	Discharges.	Deaths.
October	Sick	49	19	—
	Casualties	34	4	4
November	Sick	50	51	1
	Casualties	28	22	6
December	Sick	73	72	1
	Casualties	57	23	14
January	Sick	43	38	3
	Casualties	25	33	15
February	Sick	52	35	9
	Casualties	24	14	9
March	Sick	82	61	9
	Casualties	41	34	8
April	Sick	103	68	20
	Casualties	24	22	7

TOTAL CASUALTIES DURING THE SIEGE OF MAFEKING.

	Killed and died of wounds.	Wounded.	Missing.	Died.	Accident.	Total.
I.—COMBATANTS.						
Whites:—						
Officers	6	15	1	—	—	22
N.C.O.'s & men	61	103	26	16	5	211
Total Whites	67	118	27	16	5	233
Coloured	25	68	—	—	—	93
Total Combatants.						326
II.—NON COMBATANTS.						
Whites	4	5	—	32	—	41
Natives	65	117	—	—	—	182
Barolongs	264	—	—	—	—	264
Total Non-combatants						487

Total all Casualties during siege, 813.

Out of 44 officers, 22 were killed, wounded, or missing = 50 per cent.
Out of 975 men, 190 were killed, wounded, or missing = 19.48 per cent.

APPENDIX 5.

Composition and Approximate Strength of Brigadier-General Mahon's Flying Column for the Relief of Mafeking, May 4th—17th, 1900.

	Officers.	Men.	Horses.	Guns. 12·pr.	Guns. Machine.
Staff	2	4	8	—	—
Imperial Light Horse					
Kimberley Mounted Corps (5 officers, 117 men)	36	900 ⎫	1,200		
Royal Horse Artillery	4	100 ⎭		4	2
Infantry (from the 6th Fusilier brigade)	3	100	—	—	—
Total	45	1,104	1,208	4	2

NOTE.—In addition 52 mule wagons (10 mules each) with supplies accompanied the column.

APPENDIX 6.

"TO ACT STRICTLY ON THE DEFENSIVE."

THAT some difference of signification was assigned to this expression by sender and recipient respectively will be gathered from the following quotation from (*a*) Sir R. Buller's Despatch of May 24th, 1900, and (*b*) Lord Roberts' covering letter to same.

(*a*) (Sir R. Buller's Despatch) " I have the honour to report that having on the 3rd March received orders from Field-Marshal Lord Roberts to act strictly on the defensive, the force under my command took up positions, etc."

(*b*) (Lord Roberts' covering letter) " As it might be inferred from the first paragraph of the despatch that the force in Natal could have taken a more active part in the campaign during the period extending from 3rd March to 2nd May, had I not ordered it to act strictly on the defensive, I would invite your Lordship's attention to the telegraphic correspondence between Sir Redvers Buller and myself, quoted in the appendix to the present letter. From this correspondence it will, I think, be clear that the inaction referred to in the despatch was not due to my order of the 3rd March, but should be ascribed to the conception formed by Sir Redvers Buller of the strength and distribution of the enemy, and to other difficulties, including the unfitness of the Ladysmith garrison to take the field for some time after its relief, which prevented him from attempting either of the schemes of offensive action which he proposed on the 5th March and the 24th March, and to both of which I assented."

APPENDIX 7.

DELAGOA BAY RAILWAY, EASTERN TRANSVAAL.

LINES OF COMMUNICATION EAST OF PRETORIA.
NOVEMBER 30TH, 1900.

IVTH DIVISION, LIEUT. GENERAL THE HON. N. G. LYTTELTON.

HEADQUARTERS AT MIDDELBURG.

Silverton.	{ 18th battery Royal Field artillery. { Volunteer company 1st West Riding regiment.	
Eerstefabrieken.	1st King's Own Scottish Borderers.	
Pienaar's Poort.	{ 2nd Duke of Cornwall's Light Infantry. { 1st Connaught Rangers.	Brigadier General J. C. Barker.
Bronkhorst-spruit.	{ 81st battery Royal Field artillery. { 2nd Royal Fusiliers.	
Balmoral.	2nd The Buffs, East Kent regiment.	
Oliphant River.	83rd battery Royal Field artillery.	

Middelburg.	18th Hussars. G. battery Royal Horse artillery. 21st battery Royal Field artillery. No. 3 section Vickers-Maxims. IVth division Ammunition column. 23rd company Royal Engineers. 8th Infantry brigade (Major-General F. Howard). 1st Leicestershire regiment. 1st Royal Inniskilling Fusiliers. 1st King's Royal Rifles. Supply column. 11th and 31st companies Army Service Corps. Bearer company. Field Hospital.

Pan. Wonderfontein. Belfast.	66th battery Royal Field artillery. 2nd Royal Berkshire regiment. 19th infantry brigade and corps troops (Major-General H. L. Smith-Dorrien).	Major-General Smith-Dorrien.
Corps troops.	{ 5th Lancers. { 84th battery Royal Field artillery. { 14th company S. D. Royal Garrison artillery. { S. section Vickers-Maxims. { Xth division Ammunition column. 1st Royal Irish regiment. 2nd Shropshire Light Infantry. 1st Gordon Highlanders. 43rd company Army Service Corps. 19th brigade Field Hospital. ,, ,, Bearer company.	

Machadodorp.	19th Hussars. 42nd battery Royal Field artillery. 61st ,, ,, ,, ,, Detachment 20th company W. D. Royal Garrison artillery. 2nd Royal Irish Fusiliers. 23rd company Army Service Corps.	Brigadier-General J. Reeves.
Dalmanutha.	Detachment 19th Hussars. ,, 6th company W. D. Royal Garrison artillery. Detachment 1st Royal Berkshire regiment.	
Waterval Boven.	{ ,, 1st Liverpool regiment. { ,, 4th Duke of Cornwall's M.I.	
Waterval Onder.	} ,, 19th Hussars. { 1st Liverpool regiment.	
Nooitgedacht.	Detachment 2nd Royal Warwickshire regiment.	
Godwaan.	2nd Royal Warwickshire regiment.	
Elandshoek.	Detachment 2nd Royal Warwickshire regiment.	
Alkmaar.	Detachment 1st Welsh regiment.	
Nelspruit.	1st Welsh regiment. Detachment Army Service Corps.	
Krokodil Poort.	,, 1st Welsh regiment.	
Kaapmuiden. Hector Spruit. Malalsene.	} Detachments 1st Yorkshire regiment.	
Komati Poort.	Steinacker's Horse. Detachment 4th M.I. One section 20th battery Royal Field artillery. 36th company Royal Garrison artillery. 12th company Royal Engineers. 1st Yorkshire regiment.	Major-General T. E. Stephenson.
Barberton.	18th infantry brigade (Major-General T. E. Stephenson). 3rd mounted infantry. 20th battery Royal Field artillery. 1st Royal Scots. Army Service Corps. Royal Army Medical Corps.	
Kaapschehoop mountain (7 miles south-east of Godwaan).	} 4th mounted infantry. { L. section Vickers-Maxims. { Detachment 1st Royal Scots. ,, Army Service Corps.	
Avoca (on the Barberton line).	} ,, 1st Royal Scots.	

APPENDIX 7.

Lydenburg.	7th infantry brigade (Major-General W. F. Kitchener). Mounted infantry of the IVth division. 1st Devonshire regiment. 1st Manchester regiment. 2nd Rifle Brigade. 22nd company Army Service Corps. Bearer company and Field Hospital.	
Witklip (on Lydenburg road).	One squadron cavalry. Two 15-pr. guns Royal Field artillery. One 12-pr. Q.F. gun. One Colt gun. Two companies infantry.	Major-General W. F. Kitchener.
Badfontein (on Lydenburg road).	Detachment Cape Garrison artillery. No. 4 section Vickers-Maxims.	
Helvetia (on Lydenburg road).	Detachment 1st Liverpool regiment. „ 6th company W. D. Royal Garrison artillery.	

Approximate total strength—24,586 men and 110 guns.

APPENDIX 8.

Mobile Column.

Lieut.-Colonel R. C. A. B. Bewicke-Copley, King's Royal Rifle Corps.
>Three companies Thorneycroft's mounted infantry (214).
>Four guns 63rd battery Royal Field artillery.
>One 5-in. gun Royal Garrison artillery.
>Two Vickers-Maxims.
>One Colt gun.
>Half 17th Field company Royal Engineers.
>2nd Devonshire regiment (640).
>3rd King's Royal Rifles (492).

(1.)

Natal District (Lieut.-General H. J. T. Hildyard).
(Delimited into three sub-districts.)

(a) *Volksrust Sub-district* (Major-General J. T. Coke).
>Zandspruit to Coetzee's Drift, including Wakkerstroom, Botha's Pass and Alleman's Nek.
>>Troops :—Two squadrons 5th Dragoon Guards.
>>One and a half companies mounted infantry.
>>13th battery Royal Field artillery.
>>Four Naval 12-prs. manned by Royal Garrison artillery.
>>One 4·7-in. gun, manned by Royal Garrison artillery.
>>2nd Dorset regiment.
>>1st York and Lancaster regiment (less one company).
>>1st Royal Dublin Fusiliers.

(b) *Newcastle Sub-district* (Brigadier-General J. F. Burn-Murdoch).
>Imbezane inclusive to Hatting Spruit exclusive, and on the east the drifts over the Buffalo river, within the latitudes of the above-named places; also Utrecht.
>On the west the Drakensberg Passes, from Botha's Pass exclusive to Normandien inclusive (near Sunday's River Pass).
>>Troops :—One squadron 5th Dragoon Guards.
>>Two squadrons 1st (Royal) Dragoons.
>>Half company mounted infantry.
>>19th battery Royal Field artillery.
>>Three Naval 12-prs. manned by Royal Garrison artillery.
>>One company Scottish Rifles.
>>One company 1st York and Lancaster regiment.
>>2nd Middlesex regiment.
>>Imperial Light Infantry.

(c) *Dundee Sub-district* (Lieut.-Colonel C. J. Blomfield, Lancashire Fusiliers).
>From Hatting Spruit to Sunday's river inclusive, and Vryheid, the drifts of the Buffalo, up to points parallel with Hatting Spruit and Sunday's river and the Passes of the Drakensberg from Normandien to Cundycleugh.
>>Troops :—Two and a half squadrons Natal Volunteers and Police.
>>Five squadrons Bethune's mounted infantry.
>>Three companies Composite regiment mounted infantry.
>>Two companies mounted infantry.
>>67th battery Royal Field artillery.

APPENDIX 8.

    69th battery Royal Field artillery.
    Two guns 73rd battery Royal Field artillery.
    Two guns 86th (Howitzer) battery Royal Field artillery.
    Two 4.7-in. guns, manned by Royal Garrison artillery.
    Three Naval 12-prs.
    37th company Royal Engineers.
    2nd Royal Lancaster regiment.
    2nd Lancashire Fusiliers.
    1st South Lancashire regiment.

(d) *Ladysmith Sub-district* (Lieut.-Colonel F. R. S. Carleton, Royal Irish Fusiliers).
    Sunday's river to Colenso inclusive. On the west the passes of the Drakensberg south of Cundycleugh.
    Troops :—One squadron 1st (Royal) Dragoons.
        One squadron 5th Lancers.
        Four guns 73rd battery Royal Field artillery.
        Four guns No. 4 Mountain battery Royal Garrison artillery.
        Seven companies infantry.

(e) Officers commanding Howick, Pietermaritzburg, Eshowe and Durban were to report direct to D.A.G. Natal District.

(2.)

Zandspruit—Heidelberg (Major-General A. S. Wynne).

General Wynne divided his command into two sections, under Brigadier-General E. O. F. Hamilton (Zandspruit to Waterval exclusive) and Major-General C. D. Cooper (Waterval to Heidelberg), who in turn sub-divided their sections into three sub-sections. The mobile column appertaining to this command was reorganised, the proportion of infantry composing it and the number of heavy guns with which it was hampered being reduced.

Sub-section A.

Zandspruit to Paarde Kop.

1. Zandspruit.—One troop Bethune's mounted infantry.
    Two companies 2nd Royal West Surrey regiment.
2. Gras Kop.—Half troop Bethune's mounted infantry.
    Two companies 2nd Royal West Surrey regiment.
    One Naval 12-pr. manned by Royal Garrison artillery.
3. Dublin Hill.—Half troop Bethune's mounted infantry.
    One company 2nd Royal West Surrey regiment.
    One Naval 12-pr. gun.
4. Paarde Kop.—One company 2nd Royal West Surrey regiment.
    One Naval 12-pr. gun.
5. Kopje Alleen and Paarde Kop Station.
    One troop Bethune's mounted infantry.
    Two companies 2nd Royal West Surrey regiment.
    One 4.7-in. gun.

Sub-section B.

Zandfontein to Katbosch.

6. Zandfontein.—One company 2nd East Surrey regiment.
7. Platrand.—One troop Bethune's mounted infantry.
    Two guns 64th battery Royal Field artillery.
    Four companies 2nd East Surrey regiment.

558 THE WAR IN SOUTH AFRICA.

   8. Leeuw Spruit.—One company 2nd East Surrey regiment.
   9. Kromdrai.—One company 2nd East Surrey regiment.
10. Katbosch.—One company 2nd East Surrey regiment.

Sub-section C.
Standerton to Vlaklaagte.

11. Standerton.—One squadron 13th Hussars.
               Thorneycroft's mounted infantry (re-organising).
               Two Howitzers 86th battery Royal Field artillery.
               One Naval 12-pr.
               Two 4.7-in. guns.
               Two guns 64th battery Royal Field artillery.
               Seven companies 1st Durham Light Infantry.

12 & 13. Kaffir Spruit and Vlaklaagte.—One company 1st Durham Light Infantry.

Sub-section D.
Waterval to Greylingstad.

14. Waterval.—Two troops 13th Hussars.
              Two guns 64th battery Royal Field artillery.
              Two companies 2nd Scottish Rifles.
15. Val.—One company 2nd Scottish Rifles.
16, 17, 18 and 19.—Groot Spruit—Doornhoek—Greylingstad.
              Two troops 13th Hussars.
              One 5-in. gun Royal Garrison artillery.
              Five companies 2nd Scottish Rifles.

Sub-section E.
Vlakfontein to Zuikerbosch.

20 and 21. Vlakfontein.—One company 1st Rifle Brigade.
22. Edens Kop.—Four companies 1st Rifle Brigade.
23. Zuikerbosch.—Two companies 1st Rifle Brigade.
              One Vickers-Maxim gun.

Sub-section F.
Botha's Kraal to Elandsfontein (exclusive).

24. Botha's Kraal.—One company 3rd King's Royal Rifles.
25. Heidelberg.—One squadron 13th Hussars.
              Two guns 63rd battery Royal Field artillery.
              One Naval 12-pr. manned by Royal Garrison artillery.
              1st Essex regiment (who relieved 1st Coldstream Guards on November 1st).
              Half company 3rd King's Royal Rifles.
26, 27, 28, 29 and 30.—Blesbok Spruit, Nigel Mine, Rietvlei, Rietspruit, Roodekop
              Three and a half companies 3rd King's Royal Rifles.

APPENDIX 9.

PROCLAMATIONS.

(a) ANNEXATION OF THE ORANGE FREE STATE.

WHEREAS certain territories in South Africa, heretofore known as the Orange Free State, have been conquered by Her Majesty's Forces, and it has seemed expedient to Her Majesty that the said territories should be annexed to, and should henceforth form part of Her Majesty's dominions, and that I should provisionally, and until Her Majesty's pleasure is more fully known, be appointed Administrator of the said territories with power to take all such measures and to make and enforce such laws as I may deem necessary for the peace, order and good government of the said territories.

Now, therefore, I, Frederick Sleigh, Baron Roberts of Kandahar, K.P., G.C.B., G.C.S.I., G.C.I.E., V.C., Field-Marshal and Commanding in-Chief the British Forces in South Africa, by Her Majesty's command, and in virtue of the power and authority conferred upon me in that behalf by Her Majesty's Royal Commission, dated the twenty-first day of May, Nineteen Hundred, and in accordance with Her Majesty's instructions thereby and otherwise signified to me, do proclaim and make known that, from and after the publication hereof, the territories known as the Orange Free State are annexed to and form part of Her Majesty's dominions, and that, provisionally, and until Her Majesty's pleasure is fully declared, the said territories will be administered by me with such powers as aforesaid. Her Majesty is pleased to direct that the new territories shall henceforth be known as the Orange River Colony.

God Save the Queen.

Given under my hand and seal at the Headquarters of the Army in South Africa, Camp south of the Vaal River, in the said territories, this twenty-fourth day of May, in the year of our Lord Nineteen Hundred.

ROBERTS, Field-Marshal,
Commanding-in-Chief Her Majesty's Forces in South Africa.

(b) ANNEXATION OF SOUTH AFRICAN REPUBLIC.

Whereas certain territories in South Africa, hitherto known as the South African Republic, have been conquered by Her Majesty's Forces, and it has seemed expedient to Her Majesty that the said territories should be annexed to, and should henceforth form part of Her Majesty's dominions, and that I should provisionally, and until Her Majesty's pleasure is more fully known, be appointed Administrator of the said territories, with power to take all such measures, and to make and enforce such laws as I may deem necessary for the peace, order, and the good government of the said territories.

Now, therefore, I, Frederick Sleigh, Baron Roberts of Kandahar and Waterford, K.P., G.C.B., G.C.S.I., G.C.I.E., V.C., Field-Marshal, Commanding-in-Chief of Her Majesty's Forces in South Africa, by Her Majesty's command, and in virtue of the power and authority conferred on me in that behalf by Her Majesty's Royal Commission, dated the fourth day of July, Nineteen Hundred, in accordance with Her Majesty's instructions thereby and otherwise signified to me, from and after the publication hereof, do proclaim that the territories known as the South African Republic are annexed to and form part of Her Majesty's dominions, and that provisionally, and until Her Majesty's pleasure is fully declared, the said territories will be administered by me with such powers as aforesaid. Her Majesty is pleased to direct that the new territories shall henceforth be known as the Transvaal.

God Save the Queen.

Given under my hand and seal, at Headquarters of the Army in South Africa, in the said territories, this first day of September, in the year of Our Lord Nineteen Hundred.

ROBERTS, Field-Marshal,
Commanding-in-Chief, Her Majesty's Forces in South Africa.

INDEX

INDEX TO VOLUME III.

AAPIES RIVER, 373, 502.
Abattis, 145.
Aberdeen, 187.
Abrikoo's Kop, 299.
Achaaphoek, 368.
Adams, Sergeant A., 289.
Administration, in the Orange Free State, 32, 65 ; of Bloemfontein, 32 ; of Johannesburg, 92.
Advance, The : from Kroonstad to Pretoria, 65–103 ; reasons for pressing, 66 ; to Kroonstad, 38, 40–64 ; towards Komati Poort, 380–405 ; to Komati Poort, 406–421.
Adye, Colonel J., 9–13, 15–17, 22–5.
Airey, Colonel H. P., 236, 246.
Airlie, Lieut.-Colonel D. S. W., Earl of, 45, 214.
Albert Silver Mine, 448.
Albertina, 328.
Alderson, Lieut.-Colonel E. A. H., 3, 6, 33, 47–8, 56, 75–6, 78, 90, 96–7, 209, 211, 312–13, 315–16, 323, 414, 416.
Alderson's Mounted Infantry. See INFANTRY, MOUNTED.
Alexander, Lieut.-Colonel the Hon. W. P., 238, 240.
Aliwal North, 478, 494–5, 517.
Alkmaar, and station, 416, 419, 425.
Allan, Captain P. S., 241.
Allandale, 472–3.
Alleman's Nek, action at, 273–9.
Allen, Major-General R. E., 134, 334.
Allewyn's Poort, 519.
Ambulances, 37 ; capture of, by Boers, 433.

America (U. S.), 393.
America Siding and Station, 60, 132.
Amersfoort, 285, 381, 383–4, 458–60.
Ammunition : Boers short of, 454, 469, 498 ; destruction of, 205, 332, 341, 347 ; expended, 97, 453 ; for Boers, 126 ; for British, 31, 37 ; for rebels, 2, 6 ; in Mafeking, 158, 163–4, 168 ; supply of, under fire, 452.
Ammunition columns. See REGULAR UNITS.
Annexation of : districts of Cape Colony, 2, 6–9 ; Orange Free State, 126 ; South African Republic, 405. See also APPENDIX 9.
Appendices, 525–60.
Appointments, 17, 36, 519 ; of Military Governors, 32, 92.
Arcadia (near Johannesburg), 70.
Arcadia (in Natal), 250.
Argentine horses, 214.
Argyll and Sutherland Highlanders. See MILITIA and REGULAR UNITS.
Armaments, Boer, 73, 89, 92 ; in Mafeking, 146, 163–4, 168–9.
Armistices, 95, 101, 227, 269, 374.
Armoured trains, 145, 147, 149, 153, 160–2, 195, 197, 327, 445.
Arms, collection of, 16, 50, 124, 229, 332 ; in Mafeking, 141.
Army. See BRITISH.
Army Order, Special, 520–1.
Army Medical Corps, Royal. See REGULAR UNITS.
Army Service Corps. See REGULAR UNITS.
Artillery, Royal. See REGULAR UNITS.

Artillery: in Great Britain, 34; in Mafeking, 163-4, 168-9; in South Africa, 34-5; modern, moral effect of, 409; positions for, difficulty in finding, 453.
Arundel, 9, 29-30.
Ashby, Private E. P., 24.
Ashby, General Turner, 141.
Avoca, 419.
Australian contingents: New South Wales, Queensland, South Australia, Victoria, West Australia. *See* COLONIAL UNITS.

BABINGTON, COLONEL J. M., 516-17.
Badenhorst, Commandant C. C., 341, 500.
Baden-Powell, Colonel R. S. S., 186-7, 198, 200, 202, 228, 230-1, 233-8, 240, 244-7, 308-9, 311, 335-6, 338-41, 349, 354, 357, 361-2, 365-9, 377-8; defends Mafeking, 140-85.
Badfontein, 406-8, 425.
Baillie, Captain W. L. D., 511.
Bainbridge, Lieut.-Colonel E. G. T., 471-2.
Bainbridge's Mounted Infantry. *See* INFANTRY, MOUNTED.
Baine's Drift, 189, 193, 232.
Bakenkop, the affair at, 287-90.
Balmoral, 284, 313-14, 321, 436, 438, 445-7.
Bangwaketse tribe, 199.
Bank, and Station, 75, 232, 247, 342, 348, 350, 363, 375, 377.
Bankfontein, 290.
Banks: of Africa, 28; of Natal, 432; National, The, 32, 432.
Baobab tree, 188.
Bapsfontein, 309-11.
Barberton, 404, 412, 414-16, 418-20, 426-7, 456.
Barker, Brig.-General J. C., 422-3, 426, 436, 446-7.
Barker, Lieut.-Colonel J. S. S., 489, 493-4.
Barkly West, 4, 19, 107, 109, 182.

Barolong tribe, 144, 151, 167, 180, 202, 231.
Barter, Lieut.-Colonel C. St. L., 362.
Barton, Major-General G., C.B., 35, 108-9, 111-12, 231-3, 242, 244, 354-5, 377, 483-4, 506-12, 515-16.
Bastard tribe, 8.
Bases for supplies, 30.
Basutoland, 286, 293-4, 477.
Bates Major A., 3-4.
Bathoen (native chief), 199.
Battles of, Diamond Hill, 204-25; Bergendal, 397-402.
Bavians Berg, 44-6.
Baxter, Corporal A., 24.
Bazaine, Marshal, 184.
Bearcroft, Captain J. E., R.N., 98, 217.
Bechuanaland, 17, 189, 505; defence of frontier of, 140.
Bechuanaland Rifles. *See* COLONIAL UNITS.
Bedfordshire regiment. *See* MILITIA *and* REGULAR UNITS.
Beestekraal, 365, 371, 502.
Beet, Corporal H. (awarded the Victoria Cross), 113.
Beira, 34, 188, 229, 231.
Beith, 252, 259-60, 263-4.
Beginderlyn, 384.
Belcher, Lieut. W. G., 288.
Belela's Berg, 281, 464.
Belfast, 284, 323, 372, 387, 391-5, 397-8, 407, 414, 424, 426, 429, 439-40, 442-5, 456.
Belmont, 17-18.
Bemba's Kop, 464, 466.
Bentinck, Captain Lord C., 147, 180-1.
Bergendal Farm, Ridge and Kopje, 391-393, 396, 422, 439; the battle of, 397-402.
Bergvlei, 92.
Berkshire regiment, Royal. *See* REGULAR UNITS.
Besters (Natal), 328.
Besters Kop, 299.

INDEX. 565

Bethanie, 230.
Bethel, 285, 426–7, 433–4, 436, 459.
Bethel commando. *See* COMMANDOS.
Bethlehem, and road, 93, 118, 122–3, 136, 138, 286–7, 290–4, 296, 298–9, 330–2, 473, 475, 489.
Bethlehem commando. *See* COMMANDOS.
Bethulie, and bridge, 29–30, 105, 112, 494–5.
Bethune, Lieut.-Colonel E. C., 252, 259–61, 266, 459, 461, 466.
Bethune's Mounted Infantry. *See* INFANTRY, MOUNTED.
Bewicke-Copley, Lieut.-Colonel R. C. A. B., 468.
Beyers, Commandant, 374.
Bezuidenhout Pass, 255.
Bezuidenhouts Kraal, 295, 297.
Biddulphs Berg, 93, 133–4, 292, 294, 297; action at, 122–4.
Biggarsberg mountains, 42, 65, 251–4, 257–65, 268.
Bird, Major W. D., 184, 190, 192, 197–8, 201.
Bisdee, Private J. H. (awarded the Victoria Cross), 373.
Bishop's Farm, 299.
Blaauwbank (Natal), 252.
Blaauwbank (north-west of Krugersdorp), 507.
Blaauwberg, 188.
Blaauw Kopje, 285.
Blaauwkopje (O. F. S.), 290, 475.
Blackburn, Captain L. D., 190.
Black Watch, The. *See* REGULAR UNITS.
Blagrove, Colonel H. J., 328.
Blake, Colonel J. F., 42.
Blesboklaagte (Natal), 263.
Blesboklaagte (O. F. S.), 485.
Blizzard, 439.
Blockhouse line, 490.
Bloemfontein, 5, 14, 76, 102, 104–7, 113, 115, 126, 128, 131–2, 134, 227, 229, 258, 327, 435, 469–72, 478–9, 489–91, 494, 517; the reorganisation at, 27–39; to Kroonstad, 40–64.
Bloemhof, 108, 379, 481.
Bloemhof commando. *See* COMMANDOS.
Bloemplaats, 52, 54.
Blomfield, Lieut.-Colonel C. J., 463.
Blood River, 266–7, 464–6.
Blyde River, 420.
Blyvooruilzicht, 442.
Bodle, Colonel W., 199–200.
Boekenhoutskloof Ridge, 207–8, 210–11.
Boers: abandon Kroonstad, 61; abandon the line of the Vaal, 71; activity of, 422–3; after the fall of Pretoria, 204–5; agents of the, 2; antipathy of, to serving out of their own districts, 226; breaking up of commandos of, 417, 419; British uniforms worn by the, 289, 434; commandeering by the, 2–6, 8–9, 14; demoralisation of the, 61, 71, 94, 268, 403; dispositions of the, 285, 422, 438, 447; dispositions of the, after Mafeking, 230, 450; dispositions of the, on the Northern frontier, 193; "Dopper," the, 233; movements of the, 2–7, 60, 69, 126, 128, 133–4, 136–7, 146, 157, 193, 230, 255, 326, 349, 361, 490–6; outworks, unwillingness of the, to occupy, 260; positions of the, 40, 68–9, 98, 108–11, 122, 272–3, 391–2, 396, 449; separation of the forces of the, 226; States of, 1; supplies for the, shortness of, 469; sympathisers with the, 393; unpreparedness of the, 42; works of the, around Mafeking, 156.
Bokfontein, 234, 341, 348, 362–3.
Boksburg, 86, 88, 310.
Boksburg commando. *See* COMMANDOS.
Bombardment: at Bergendal, 398–9; of Mafeking, 149, 156, 164–5, 167–8, 173–4.

Bombproofs, 145, 155, 165, 197.
Bonnefoi, 430.
Bontjeskraal, 290.
Boots, 31.
Borden, Lieut. H. L., 48, 317.
Border Horse. *See* COLONIAL UNITS.
Border regiment. *See* REGULAR UNITS.
Border Siding, 112.
Borderers, King's Own Scottish. *See* REGULAR UNITS.
Borderers, South Wales. *See* REGULAR UNITS.
Boschbank, 69, 71.
Boschbank Nek and Pass, 503, 507.
Bosch Kop, 54, 59, 61.
Bosch Kop (east of Pretoria), 215-18.
Bosch Kopje, 67.
Boschfontein, 498.
Boschrand, 60-2.
Boshof, 66, 104, 107-9, 112, 134, 482, 494, 513.
Boshof commando. *See* COMMANDOS.
Botha, Assistant-General C., 72, 227, 260, 268-9, 279, 282, 462-3.
Botha, Commandant D., 358, 360, 504.
Botha, Commandant-General L., 40, 68, 71-5, 87-9, 91, 93-5, 128, 204-7, 228-9, 235, 242, 254, 269, 309, 311-14, 317-18, 324, 349, 362, 368, 374, 386, 391-2, 396, 408-11, 417, 422, 437, 501-2, 505, 507, 517.
Botha, General P., 44, 50, 93, 128, 163.
Botha's Pass, 269-73, 280.
Bothaville, 66, 70, 104, 108, 124, 481-3, 485, 512-13; action at, 486-9.
Bothaville Drift, 485.
Boyes, Major-General J. E., 122, 286, 299, 329, 332, 473-6.
Braamfontein, 92.
Brabant, Brig.-General E. Y., C.M.G., 106, 122-3, 138-9, 229.
Brabant's Horse. *See* COLONIAL UNITS.
Brabazon, Major-General J. P., C.B., 34.

Brack river, 190-1, 193.
Bradley, Lieut.-Colonel C. E., 372, 499-500.
Brakfontein (Eland's river), 339-40, 515.
Brandfort, 40, 42-6, 61, 69, 105, 128, 473, 478-9.
Brandfort commando. *See* COMMANDOS.
Brand's Drift (Vet river), 106.
Brandwater Basin, 292-306, 325, 328, 346, 380, 458.
Brandwater river, 293.
Brawn, making of, in Mafeking, 174.
Brester's Flats, 107.
Brickfields, Mafeking, British attack on, 169-72.
Bridges, Lieut. H., 162.
Bridges: railway, 30, 61-2, 65-6, 72, 95, 112, 128, 131, 197, 205, 232, 251, 322, 350, 459; road, 30, 251, 283, 384, 494.
Brigades. *See* CAVALRY, INFANTRY and INFANTRY, MOUNTED.
British: administration in Cape Colony, 1; administration in Orange Free State, 32, 65; administration of Bloemfontein, 32; administration of Johannesburg, 92; rule, in South Africa, 187; soldier, traits of, 146; South African dominions, 1; subjects, 9.
British army, 226; casualties in— *see* CASUALTIES, *also* APPENDIX 2; composition of, May 3rd, 1900, 38; *see also* APPENDIX 1; dispositions of, July 21st, 1900, 297-8; dispositions of, east of Pretoria, 318; distribution of, in the Orange River Colony, 134-6; distribution of, in June, 1900, 228-33, 286, 292-3, 328-9; distribution of, on the Natal Railway, 382-3; distribution of, east of Pretoria, 424-5; *see also* APPENDIX 7; distribution of, on the railway, Johannesburg to Durban, 457-68; *see also* APPENDIX 8;

INDEX. 567

exhausted state of, 307, 357, 439; in Natal, 65; movements of, 3, 5–6, 11–17, 69, 106–13, 124, 131, 133–6, 139, 206, 230–1, 235, 258–85, 307–9, 313–14, 317, 326–8, 330, 342–3, 348, 420, 423, 498; wastage in, 207.
British Government, 186, 228, 306, 370.
British South African Police. *See* COLONIAL UNITS.
Britstown, 9, 11–13, 16.
Broadwood, Brigadier-General R. G., 6–7, 33, 45, 51, 59, 63–4, 78, 97, 135, 212–15, 222–4, 292–6, 325–7, 344, 346, 348, 350–2, 359, 435, 499–500, 506–7, 518.
Brocklehurst, Major-General J. F., M.V.O., 254, 274, 283, 381, 384, 397, 399, 402, 407, 409, 424–5, 460.
Bronckhorstfontein, 290.
Bronkhorst Spruit, 310, 312, 318, 320.
Bronkhorstspruit Station, 95, 223, 317, 319, 321–2, 387, 426, 436, 447, 449.
Brooke, Colonel L. G., 314, 322.
Brookfield, Colonel A. M., M.P., 137–8, 287–90.
Brown, Major A. D. (awarded the Victoria Cross), 430.
Browne, Inspector J. W., 145, 171.
Brugspruit Station, 321–2, 436, 446.
Bryce's Stores, 191–3.
Buchan, Mrs., 179.
Budworth, Captain C. E. D., 289.
Buffalo drifts, 266–7.
Buffalo river, 252, 268, 271, 280, 380, 462–3.
Buffelsdoorn and Pass, 230, 350, 509, 512, 519.
Buffelshoek, 345–6, 348, 353, 360, 370, 504.
Buffelshoek (north of Parys), 483.
Buffelspoort, 368.
Buffs, The (East Kent regiment). *See* MILITIA AND REGULAR UNITS.
Buiskop Pass, 367–8, 373.

Bulhoek, 503.
Buller, General The Right Hon. Sir R. H., G.C.B., K.C.M.G., V.C., 65, 136, 138, 227–9, 243, 308–9, 322–4, 342, 380–8, 391–7, 399, 403–4, 413, 417–18, 420, 424–5, 439, 456, 458, 461–2, 467; clears Northern Natal, 249–85; correspondence between, and Lord Roberts, 29, 255–8, 268; occupies Lydenburg and Spitz Kop, 406–12; returns to England, 421.
Bullock, Colonel G. M., 137.
Bulskop, 377.
Bultfontein (O. F. S.), 296, 298, 478–9.
Bultfontein (Western Transvaal), 355.
Buluwayo, 186, 189, 229, 231, 235, 370.
Burch, Lieut. J. F., 317.
Burger, Acting-President Schalk, 422, 437.
Burgers Pass, 420.
Burma Mounted Infantry. *See* INFANTRY, MOUNTED.
Burn, Colonel C. R., 302, 304.
Burnham, Mr. F. R., 60, 95.
Burn-Murdoch, Brigadier-General J. F., 253, 458, 463–4.
Bushmen, Imperial. *See* COLONIAL UNITS.
Bushveld, 362, 364, 368, 372, 424, 438, 506.
Buys, Commandant, 461.
Byng, Colonel the Hon. J. H. G., 421.

CALEDON RIVER, 41, 293, 495–6.
Calvert, Second Lieut. N. L., 433.
Calvinia, 8, 12.
Cameron Highlanders. *See* REGULAR UNITS.
Cameron's Scouts. *See* COLONIAL UNITS.
Cameronians (Scottish Rifles). *See* MILITIA *and* REGULAR UNITS.
Campbell, Major-General B. B. D., M.V.O., 295–7, 299, 328, 332, 473–7.

Campbell (town), 5, 17-20, 22, 25, 229.
Canadian regiment, The Royal. *See* COLONIAL UNITS.
Canadians, Royal (Leinster regiment). *See* REGULAR UNITS.
Cannon Kopje, 144, 149-50, 153, 159, 168, 178; Boer attack on, 154-5.
Cape artillery. *See* COLONIAL UNITS.
Cape Boy (coloured) contingent. *See* COLONIAL UNITS.
Cape Colony, 105, 108, 143, 193, 251, 255, 287, 505; annexation of districts in, by Boers, 2, 6-9; danger of rebellion in, 5; government of, 1; Imperial Yeomanry in, 34; invasion of, 469, 494-6, 512, 515, 517; lines of communication in, 6; militia to hold, 106; rebellion in the north-west of, 1-26; recruiting in, 141.
Cape Dutch, 515.
Cape horses, 21.
Cape Mounted Rifles. *See* COLONIAL UNITS.
Cape Police. *See* COLONIAL UNITS.
Cape Town, 6, 9-10, 12, 26, 30-1 33, 35, 94, 140, 157, 169, 306, 369.
Cape Town Highlanders. *See* COLONIAL UNITS.
Capitulation of General Prinsloo, 305.
Capper, Lieut.-Colonel J. E., 134.
Captures: by Boers, 120, 124, 127-8, 130-1, 133, 147, 192, 240, 246, 326-7, 433, 466, 493; by British, 18, 24, 59, 87, 91-2, 101, 108, 111, 124, 181, 184, 234, 283, 291, 305, 326, 332, 338, 347, 351, 372, 374, 379, 418-19, 424-5, 437, 473-5, 479, 488, 497, 501-3, 505, 507-8, 515-18.
Carabiniers. *See* REGULAR UNITS.
Carew, Colonel G. A. L., 232.
Carleton, Lieut.-Colonel G. D., 444-5, 448-50, 454-5.
Carmel, 494-5.
Carnarvon, 9-10, 12, 14-15.
Carolina, 381, 385, 412, 414, 427-8, 431, 439, 441.
Carolina commando. *See* COMMANDOS.
Carr, Captain C. C., 184.
Carrington, Lieut.-General Sir F., K.C.B., K.C.M.G., 229, 231-2, 235-6, 247, 336, 339-40, 358-60, 369-70, 377.
Carter, Major D. C., 508.
Casualties: Boer, 21-2, 25, 44, 49, 56, 59, 71, 111, 123-4, 148, 155, 181, 192, 245, 317, 333, 347, 360, 376, 430, 432, 435, 437, 443, 446, 448, 454, 471, 488, 505, 512, 514; British, 51, 59, 62, 134, 333, 446, 463, 465, 467, 471, 480; at Dewetsdorp, 493; Diamond Hill, 224; Onrust, 241-2; Selous River, 246; Zilikat's Nek, 240; in Adye's force, 11, 17, 24-5; in Baden-Powell's, 148, 154, 157, 161, 165, 173, 181, 367; in Barton's, 508, 510, 512; in Bethune's, 267; in Brabant's, 123-4; in Broadwood's, 326; in Brookfield's, 138, 288, 290; in Buller's, 254, 264, 270, 272, 384, 391, 403, 409-10, 421; in Carrington's, 340, 360; in Chapman's, 374; in Clements', 139, 292; in Colvile's, 114; in Dalgety's, 371; in Derbyshire regiment (4th), 131; in French's force, 91, 95, 97, 320-1, 431, 433, 435; in Hamilton's (Bruce), 297; in Hamilton's (Ian), 44, 64, 86, 319, 338; in Hart's, 375, 377; in Hildyard's, 460; in Hore's, 358-9; in Hunter's, 111, 331, 483; in Hutton's, 316-17; in Knox's (C. E.), 474; in Le Gallais', 488; in Little's, 370; in Lyttelton's, 425; in Mahon's, 311, 430; in Methuen's, 125, 245, 345, 347, 503-5; in Paget's, 137, 292, 373, 454; in Plumer's, 184, 192, 198-201; in Pole-Carew's, 220, 394, 423; in Rundle's, 121, 123-4, 295, 299, 301, 303, 489; in Settle's, 482; in the Shropshire

INDEX.

Light Infantry (train wrecked), 342; in Smith-Dorrien's force, 343, 440-2; in Spragge's, 120; in Warren's, 21.
Cattle, disease among, 1-2.
Cavalry Brigades :—
  1st (Porter, later Gordon), 33, 51-6, 59-60, 67, 70, 73, 75-6, 96-7, 101-2, 206-12, 307-8, 311-13, 315-24, 387, 391-418, 426-35, 516, 518-19.
  2nd (Broadwood), 33, 44-6, 51, 59, 64, 78, 97, 100-1, 135, 206, 212-17, 222-4, 292-3, 295, 307, 325-7, 344-54, 357, 359, 361, 435, 499-500, 506, 518.
  3rd (Gordon, later Little), 33, 51-6, 59, 61-2, 67-8, 70, 72, 74, 87, 91-2, 97, 135, 206, 212-17, 293, 307, 315, 325-7, 344-54, 357, 359, 369-71, 435, 481-3.
  4th (Dickson), 33, 51-6, 59, 67, 70, 73, 75-7, 96-7, 206-12, 237-9, 307-8, 318-24, 387, 391-418, 426-35.
  1st (Natal) (Burn-Murdoch), 249, 252-3, 265, 267, 458, 464.
  2nd (Natal) (Brocklehurst), 254-6, 265-6, 271-2, 274, 283, 381-421, 424-5, 457-8, 460-4.
  3rd Mounted (Natal) (Lord Dundonald), 249, 252-65, 271-2, 274, 277-8, 280, 282-3, 381-421, 458.
Cavalry division, 33, 51-64, 67-103, 206, 209-12, 224, 307-8, 311-24, 387, 391-418, 426-35; charge of, at Diamond Hill, 214; condition of, 222; congratulated on good work, 433; enters Transvaal, 69; mobility of, disappeared, 205; reorganisation of, 33, 37, 427-8; work of, 393-4.
Chapman, Colonel L. J. A., 366, 374.
Charleston, 72, 273, 280.
Chermside, Lieut.-General Sir H. C., G.C.M.G., C.B., 39, 105-6, 113, 134, 139, 311.
Chesham, Brigadier-General C. C. W., Lord, 34.
Cheshire regiment. *See* REGULAR UNITS.
Chief of the Staff. *See* KITCHENER, LORD.
Chief Staff Officer, Lines of Communication, 22.
China, 393.
Christiana, 107-9, 112, 481, 512.
Church, Captain B. E., 237-8.
Church of England Convents, Sisters of, 28.
Chute, Major P. T., 451.
Cilliers, Field-Cornet S., 511.
City of London Imperial Volunteers. *See* VOLUNTEERS.
Clearing columns, formation of, 332.
Clearing of Northern Natal, 249-85.
Clements, Major-General R. A. P., D.S.O., 9, 29, 113, 123, 134-6, 138-9, 286-7, 290-2, 294, 296, 298-300, 303, 329-30, 349, 369, 372, 470, 498-500, 502, 506-10, 513, 517-18.
Clery, Lieut.-General Sir C. F., K.C.B., 259, 265, 279, 282-4, 382, 386, 458, 461-2, 465, 467-8.
Clocolan, 107, 473.
"Closed works," 447.
Clothing, 31, 251; capture of, by De Wet, 131, 205.
Clowes, Lieut.-Colonel P. L., 315.
Cockburn, Lieut. H. Z. C. (awarded the Victoria Cross), 442.
Coetzee, Commandant P., 337, 364, 373.
Coetzee, General, 418.
Coetzee's Drift (Buffalo river), 280-1, 457, 461, 463-5.
Coetzee's Drift (O. F. S.), 47-8.
Coke, Major-General J. T., 269-70, 277, 280, 457-60, 463-4.
Coldstream Guards. *See* REGULAR UNITS.
Colenso, 250-1, 488, 497.
Colesberg, 209.

Collieries, The (Natal), 255.
Colleton, Lieut.-Colonel Sir R., Bart., 510, 512.
Colley, Major-General Sir G. P., K.C.B., 265.
Collins, Mr. J. A., 32.
Colonial Division. *See* COLONIAL UNITS.
Colonial Office, 140.
Colonial troops, expiration of service of, 501.
Colonial Units :—
  Australian Bushmen, 231, 358-9, 377, 448.
  Australian Horse, 33, 55, 320.
  Bechuanaland Rifles, 145, 160-2, 164, 169-72, 178-81, 359.
  Bethune's Mounted Infantry, 252, 260, 282, 383, 460-3, 465-6.
  Border Horse, 371.
  Brabant's Horse (1st and 2nd), 300, 329, 333.
  British South African Police, 145, 147, 158, 160-2, 171, 176, 178-81, 183, 187, 189, 198, 203, 230, 246, 358, 374, 513.
  Bushmen Brigade, 231-2, 245, 374.
  Cameron's Scouts, 339, 359.
  Canadian Artillery, 12, 14, 17-18, 203, 228, 230, 236, 245, 313-14, 322, 439-43, 445.
  Canadian Dragoons, Royal, 439-43, 445.
  Canadian Infantry regiment, The Royal, 80-6, 309-10, 327, 344, 445.
  Canadian Mounted Infantry, 12, 14, 43.
  Canadian Mounted Rifles (1st), 48, 78, 234, 308, 312, 316-17.
  Canadian Mounted Rifles (2nd), 47, 78, 137, 211, 308, 316-17, 436, 439-41, 443, 445.
  Cape Artillery, 18-19.
  Cape Boy (coloured) contingent, 145, 170-2.
  Cape Mounted Rifles, 297.
  Cape Police, 3, 32, 145, 149, 152-4, 170-2, 178-81, 482.
  Cape Town Highlanders, 18, 480.
  Colonial Division, 106-7, 121-4, 134-5, 138, 292-306, 327, 344-54, 357, 370-1, 426, 470, 483-8, 509, 511.
  Composite regiment of Mounted Infantry, 382, 463, 465.
  De Montmorency's Scouts, 224.
  Driscoll's Scouts, 122, 295, 297, 299, 302, 328, 331.
  Duke of Edinburgh's Own Volunteer Rifles, 17-18, 20-22.
  Eastern Province Horse, 113-14, 135.
  French's Scouts, 72, 432.
  Imperial Bushmen, 231, 235-7, 246-7, 337, 339, 343, 358-9, 374, 452, 507-8, 513.
  Imperial Guides, 427.
  Imperial Light Horse, 182-4, 230, 232, 308-10, 337, 360, 364, 412, 426, 510-12.
  Imperial Light Infantry, 252, 258.
  Kaffrarian Mounted Rifles, 371.
  Kimberley Light Horse, 480.
  Kimberley Mounted Corps, 232, 247, 339-40, 359.
  Kitchener's Horse, 13, 16, 45, 58, 343, 517-18.
  Lumsden's Horse, 89, 337, 364, 412, 427-8, 433.
  Mafeking Corps (railway and other employés), 145, 178-81.
  Mafeking Town Guard, 145, 178-81.
  Manitoba Dragoons, 234.
  Marshall's Horse, 84, 308, 327, 344, 375, 457, 507.
  Natal Carbineers, 260, 264.
  Natal Naval Volunteers, 251.
  Natal Volunteer Composite regiment, 466.
  Natal Volunteer Brigade, 458, 464.
  Natal Volunteers, 283, 466.
  Nesbitt's Horse, 13, 22.

INDEX. 571

New South Wales Artillery, 11, 16.
New South Wales Imperial Bushmen, 339, 359; 6th regiment, 359.
New South Wales Lancers, 33.
New South Wales Medical Staff Corps, 326, 428.
New South Wales Mounted Rifles, 3, 46, 48.
New Zealand Bushmen, 231, 339.
New Zealand Hotchkiss battery, 35.
New Zealand Mounted Rifles, 12, 14–15, 43–4, 48, 70, 90, 97, 234, 308, 312, 315–17, 337, 412, 427, 448, 452, 454; 4th regiment, 359–60; 5th regiment, 359.
Orpen's Light Horse, 11–12, 16, 17.
Prince Alfred's Volunteer Guard Mounted Infantry, 131, 287–90, 304.
Protectorate regiment, 143, 145, 147, 152–3, 160–3, 170, 178–81, 231, 245–6, 498.
Queensland Imperial Bushmen, 319, 337, 412, 448, 452, 501.
Queensland Mounted Infantry, 47–8, 203, 309, 337, 412, 452.
Queenstown Rifle Volunteers, 329, 333.
Railway Pioneer regiment, 30, 62, 130, 134.
Rhodesia regiment, 143, 186–7, 189–92, 196–203, 230–1, 245–6, 339, 366–7, 374.
Rhodesian Field Force (1st and 2nd brigades), 34, 231–2, 339–40, 359, 370, 378, 514.
Rhodesian Field Force Artillery (1st and 2nd batteries), 359, 378.
Rimington's Guides, 3, 43, 296, 298, 472, 482.
Roberts' Light Horse, 63, 343, 365, 517–18.
South African Light Horse, 263, 267, 269, 271–2, 274, 278, 382, 384, 388.
South Australian Bushmen, 359.
South Australian Mounted Infantry, 10, 13, 287–90.
Southern Rhodesia Volunteers, 196–8, 234, 339, 358.
Strathcona's Horse, 283–5, 382, 384, 411, 459, 511, 517.
Tasmanian Bushmen, 231, 358–9, 365, 372–3, 448, 513.
Tasmanian Mounted Infantry, 217.
Thorneycroft's Mounted Infantry, 261, 264, 278, 280, 282, 284–5, 382, 461, 465–8.
Steinacker's Mounted Infantry, 424.
Umvoti Mounted Rifles, 252.
Victorian Imperial Bushmen, 359, 452.
Victorian Mounted Rifles, 217, 245.
Warren's Scouts, 18–19.
Warwick's Scouts, 243.
West Australian Mounted Infantry, 12, 49, 217, 223, 452.
Colt guns, 120, 217, 241, 278, 359, 437, 442–3.
Columns, various. *See* FORCE.
Colvile, Lieut.-General Sir H. E., K.C.M.G., C.B., 41, 46, 50, 93, 106–7, 113–21, 124, 126–7, 132, 134–6, 205, 229.
Colville, Lieut.-Colonel A. E. W., 467–8.
Command in South Africa, Lord Kitchener to, 519.
Commandeering by Boers, 2–6, 8–9.
Commander-in-Chief. *See* ROBERTS, LORD.
Commando Drift, 481.
Commando Nek (O. F. S.), 293–4, 302, 329.
Commando Nek (Transvaal), 234–40, 248, 336, 338, 348–50, 352, 354–7, 361–2, 365–6, 369, 372, 498–500, 506.
Commandos:—
  Barkly West rebels, 4.
  Bethel, 88, 396.
  Bethlehem, 115, 118, 293, 341.
  Bloemhof, 4, 74, 108, 147.

Commandos—*continued.*
  Boksburg, 260, 317, 438, 450.
  Boshof, 108, 341.
  Carolina, 275, 443.
  De Beer's, T., 230, 358, 497.
  De la Rey's, 89, 247, 358, 503, 513.
  Douthwaite's, 247.
  Du Toit's, 88–9, 96.
  Edwards', 499.
  Erasmus', 438, 450.
  Ermelo, 43, 88, 431, 443.
  Ficksburg, 305.
  French Corps, 177.
  German Corps, 177.
  Germiston, 260, 317, 396.
  Griqualand West rebels, 2–5, 19–25, 108, 341.
  Grobelaar's, 50, 235, 313, 367–8.
  Harrismith, 298, 473.
  Heidelberg, 42, 86, 88, 396, 458, 461.
  Heilbron, 115, 341, 509.
  Hekpoort, 235.
  Irish Corps, 42, 260, 263.
  Johannesburg, 75, 275, 317, 450.
  Johannesburg Police (Zarps), 317, 397–8, 400, 402–3, 450.
  Kenhart rebels, 14.
  Klerksdorp, 108, 230.
  Kolbe's, 4.
  Kroonstad, 341.
  Krugersdorp, 74, 108, 317, 397–8.
  Ladybrand, 305.
  Lemmer's, 236, 240, 244–5, 358, 371, 514.
  Lichtenburg, 108, 146, 230, 340.
  Liebenberg's, 14, 108–9, 247, 347–8, 509, 515.
  Losberg, 247.
  Lotter's, 4–5.
  Lydenburg, 275.
  Marico, 74, 146, 177, 230, 340.
  Middelburg, 317.
  Orange Free Staters, 61, 68, 93, 104, 117–19, 122, 126, 128, 226, 228, 293–306, 361–3, 365–8, 371–2, 502, 511, 513, 515.
  Pietersburg, 374.
  Piet Retief, 260–1.
  Potchefstroom, 74, 146, 149–50, 341.
  Pretoria, 275, 438, 450.
  Pretorius', T., 438, 455.
  Prieska rebels, 14.
  Rustenburg, 74, 146, 177, 197.
  Scheepers' Scouts, 363.
  Senekal, 305.
  Smithfield, 115, 118.
  Spruyt's, 438.
  Standerton, 386.
  Steenkamp's, 499, 503.
  Swaziland Police, 260, 275.
  Transvaalers, 2, 6–7, 14, 61, 68, 107, 126, 226–8, 347, 368, 372, 438, 511–12.
  Theron's, 372.
  Utrecht, 465.
  Van Tonder's, 503.
  Vrede, 115, 298, 509.
  Vryburg rebels, 4.
  Vryheid, 465.
  Wakkerstroom, 43, 465.
  Waterberg, 195, 197, 362, 366, 374.
  Winburg, 305.
  Wolmaranstad, 4, 74, 108, 146.
  Zoutpansberg, 191–2, 260, 275.
Commissie Bridge, 495–6.
Commissioner, Resident, of Bechuanaland. See GOOLD-ADAMS.
Commissions, 36.
Composite regiment of Mounted Infantry. See COLONIAL UNITS.
Composition of the Forces in South Africa. See APPENDIX I.
Connaught Rangers, The. See REGULAR UNITS.
Connolly, Major, W. H., 220.
Conolly, Mr., 169.
Constantia, 44.
Conveniente, 476–7.
Convoy for Heilbron, loss of, 126–8, 205 ; for De Jager's Drift, loss of, 466.
Cooke, Sergeant L., 162.
Cookson, Lieut.-Colonel G. A., 518.

INDEX. 573

Cooper, Major-General C. D., 459.
Cornwall's, Duke of, Light Infantry. *See* REGULAR UNITS.
Correspondence between Lord Roberts and Sir R. Buller, 65, 255-8, 268-9, 281-4.
Coster, Commandant, 503.
Coughlan, Mr., 169.
Council of War, 437.
Courtesy of Germans on the border of Cape Colony, 9.
Cowan, Captain B. W., 145, 160.
Cradock, Major M., 14-15, 448, 451-4.
Craufurd, Miss, 179.
Creusot guns. *See* GUNS, BOER.
Crocodile Pools, 197-8, 200.
Crocodile river, 96, 100, 233, 238, 240, 248, 346, 362, 364, 371-3, 396, 406, 416, 425, 500, 502, 517.
Cronje, General A. P. J., 108-9.
Cronje, General P., 4, 6, 9, 13, 29, 49, 146, 149-50, 155, 157, 185.
Crowther, Commandant J., 122, 286, 305.
Cundycleugh Pass, 252.
Cunningham, Colonel G. G., 213, 215, 314, 336-8, 354, 405, 499-500, 506, 513, 517.
Currie, Sergeant, 170.
Cyclists, 16.
Cyferbult, 348, 350-1.
Cyferkuil, 365, 367.

DAGGAFONTEIN, 490.
Dalbiac, Major H. S., 121.
Dalgety, Colonel E. H., 295, 299, 344, 370-1.
Dalmanutha, 392, 396-9, 422, 424, 426-9, 456.
Damfontein, 490.
Dankbaarfontein, 50-1.
Dannhauser, 264, 266-7, 458, 462-3.
Dartnell, Colonel J. G., C.M.G., 279, 458, 464.
Darvel's Rust, 303-4.
Daspoort, 96.
Davis, Major Karri, 183.

Dawson, Colonel H. L., 325, 343.
Dawson's Mounted Infantry. *See* INFANTRY, MOUNTED.
De Aar, 6, 9-10, 12-13, 15-16, 515.
De Beer, Commandant T., 4, 230-1, 358, 497, 513.
De Beer's commando. *See* COMMANDOS.
Deelfontein Noord, 59.
Defence and Relief of Mafeking, 140-85.
Defence of Roodewal, 129.
Defences of Pretoria, 98-101. *See also* APPENDIX 4.
Defensive, Sir R. Buller to act on, 256. *See also* APPENDIX 6.
De Horsey, Commander S. V. Y., R.N., 98.
De Jager's Drift, 267 ; loss of convoy at, 466.
De Jager's Nek, 280-1.
De Kaap Goldfields, 414.
De Klerks Kraal Drift (Zand river), 52-3.
Delagoa Bay Railway, 95, 101, 207, 228, 317, 324, 385, 436, 438, 443, 447, 499, 501.
De Lange, Commandant, 448.
De la Rey, General H. J., 2, 42-3, 46, 50, 72, 74-5, 88-9, 183, 208-10, 218, 229-30, 235, 243, 247, 311, 314, 337, 358, 360, 370-3, 437, 498-503, 513.
De la Rey, Commandant P., 508.
De la Rey's commando. *See* COMMANDOS.
De Lisle, Lieut.-Colonel H. de B., 59, 78, 101, 219, 221-4, 343, 483-5, 488, 509.
De Lisle's Mounted Infantry. *See* INFANTRY, MOUNTED.
De Montmorency's Scouts. *See* COLONIAL UNITS.
De Naauwte, 14-15.
Derbyshire regiment. *See* MILITIA *and* REGULAR UNITS.

Derdepoort, and Nek, 222 224, 235, 238, 307-8, 366 501.
Destruction of stores, etc., 420.
Devil's Knuckles, 411.
De Villiers, General A. J., 122-3, 126, 133, 286.
De Villiers, Commandant (Griquatown), 20, 25.
De Villiers, Commandant P. H., 122-3, 286, 296, 473, 513.
Devonshire regiment. See REGULAR UNITS.
De Wagen Drift, 448.
De Wet, Hoofd Commandant C. R., 35, 40, 74, 93, 117, 126, 128, 130-3, 136-9, 205, 207, 227, 229, 281, 284, 286, 291-3, 295-6, 298, 304, 325-8, 330-1, 368, 376, 380, 458-9, 469-70, 475-6, 483-90, 493-6, 502, 506-12, 516-17; escapes through Olifants Nek, 353; pursuit of, in Western Transvaal, 335-64.
De Wet, General P., 64, 93, 118-19, 126, 227, 286.
De Wet's Drift, 346, 348.
De Wet's Farm, 271, 484.
Dewetsdorp, 105-7, 113, 134, 477-8, 489-94, 496.
De Wimpffen, General, 305.
Diamond Hill, 307, 389; the battle of, 204-25.
Dickson, Major-General J. B. B., C.B., 33, 51-2, 55-6, 209-10, 237-8, 320-1, 427-8, 431-5.
Dieplaagte Drift, 320.
Diepsloot, 96-7, 100.
Director of Railways. See GIROUARD.
Director of Supplies. See RICHARDSON *and* WARD.
Director of Transport. See NICHOLSON *and* STANLEY.
Dirks Berg Diamond Mine, 54-5.
Dirksen, Commandant A. J., 310-11, 314, 317, 374, 438, 501.
Disaffection of the Cape Dutch, 1.
Disbandment of Natal Volunteers, 466.

Distribution of troops. See BRITISH ARMY.
Doctors, 31.
Donker Poort, 208, 215, 219-22.
Donkerhoek, 208, 215-16, 220-3, 308.
Donne, Lieut.-Colonel B. D. A., 298, 301-3.
Doorn Berg, 267, 464.
Doornberg, The (O. F. S.), 472-4, 477.
Doornbergfontein, 13-16.
Doornfontein (east of Pretoria), 211; (Gatsrand), 348.
Doornkloof, 63.
Doornkom, 517.
Doornkop (O. F. S.), 58.
Doorn Kop, 54, 75-6, 87, 89, 91, 215; the battle of, 78-86.
Doornkraal, 318-19.
Doornkuil, 73-4.
Doornlaagte, 357, 499.
Doorn Poort, 206, 366.
Dorsetshire regiment. See REGULAR UNITS.
Douglas, Major-General C. W. H., 124-5, 132, 244, 344, 350-2, 357, 378-9, 497, 503-7, 514-17, 519.
Douglas (town), 4-6, 17-19, 22.
Douthwaite, Commandant, 247, 377.
Douthwaite's commando. See COMMANDOS.
Downing, Colonel C. M. H., 266, 383, 458.
Doxat, Lieut A. C. (awarded the Victoria Cross), 504.
Drachoender, 16, 22-3.
Drafts of troops, 31, 34-5, 251.
Dragoon Guards. See REGULAR UNITS.
Dragoons. See REGULAR UNITS.
Drakensberg Mountain and Passes, 65, 250, 252-7, 267-9, 273-5, 282, 380, 406; the defence of, 458.
Driefontein, 68, 76, 91.
Driekop, 493.
Driscoll's Scouts. See COLONIAL UNITS.

INDEX.

Dronfield, 3, 108, 112.
Droogeheuvel, 350.
Drury, Lieut.-Colonel C. W., 14–15.
Dublin Fusiliers, The Royal. *See* REGULAR UNITS.
Duke of Edinburgh's Own Volunteer Rifles. *See* COLONIAL UNITS.
Dullstroom, and road, 407, 444.
Dun, Civil Surgeon, 24.
Dundee, 250, 253, 257, 263–7, 458, 464–5.
Dundonald, Major-General D. M. B. H., The Earl of, C.B., M.V.O., 254, 259–65, 271, 277–8, 382, 384, 387–8, 403–4, 409, 411, 420.
Dunlop-Smith, Veterinary-Lieut., 179.
Du Preez, General, 108–9.
Du Preez Laager Drift, 52–4.
Durban, 138, 188, 253.
Durban—Johannesburg line, events on, June to November, 1900, 457–68.
Durham Light Infantry. *See* REGULAR UNITS.
Durrant, Private E. (awarded the Victoria Cross), 401.
Du Toit, General S. P., 41, 74, 88–9, 96, 107–9, 231.
Du Toit's commando. *See* COMMANDOS.
Dwarsvlei, 507, 509.
Dyer, Captain J. E. F., 237–8.
Dynamite, explosions of, Mafeking, 150, 155.

EAST LANCASHIRE REGIMENT. *See* MILITIA *and* REGULAR UNITS.
East London, 30, 35, 250, 253, 256, 258.
East Surrey regiment. *See* REGULAR UNITS.
East Yorkshire regiment. *See* REGULAR UNITS.
Eastern Province Horse. *See* COLONIAL UNITS.
Eastern Transvaal, 380; operations in, June 16th to August 21st, 1900, 307–24; October and November, 1900, 422–56.
Ebsworth, Lieut. A., 320.
Edenburg, 134, 480, 491, 493–4, 496.
Edendale, 210, 212, 308.
Edwards, Lieut.-Colonel A. H. M., 182–3, 230.
Edwards, Captain L., 239.
Edwards, Commandant, 499.
Edwards' commando. *See* COMMANDOS.
Eerstefabrieken, 308, 318, 447.
Eerstegeluk, 70.
Eerstelingfontein, 440.
Elandsfontein (near Johannesburg) 76, 86–9, 91, 457, 519.
Elandsfontein (Eastern Transvaal), 391, 403.
Elandsfontein (near Lindequee), 483.
Elandsfontein (Western Transvaal), 499.
Elandshoek, 415.
Elandslaagte, and Collieries (Natal), 249, 252–5, 259, 265.
Elandslaagte (Eastern Transvaal), 445.
Elands river (east of Belfast), 415.
Elands river (north-east of Pretoria), 209, 224, 317, 372.
Elands river (Western Transvaal), 230, 234, 245–6, 335–6, 339–41, 358–61, 363, 369–70, 502.
Elands River Station, 209, 223, 319–20.
Elandspruit, and defile, 414–15.
Elandspruit (O. F. S.), 63.
Elandsvlei, 485.
Eleazer, 377.
Elim, 373, 448.
Elizabethsrust, 482.
Elmsley, Lieut. J. H., 442.
Eloff, Field-Cornet S., 175–81.
Elsburg, 86.
Elswick battery, Royal Field artillery, 311, 314, 319, 336, 338, 363, 365, 484, 500, 510.
Engelbrecht, Commandant, 260.

Engelbrecht's Drift, 69, 72, 74.
Engineers, Royal. *See* REGULAR UNITS.
England, 393, 519.
English, Major F. P., 459.
English, horses, 21; inhabitants to German territory, 9.
Enzelpoort, 349–50.
Erasmus, Assistant-General, 373–4, 499.
Erasmus, Commandant D., 314, 318, 436, 438, 447–8.
Erasmus' commando. *See* COMMANDOS.
Ermelo, 285, 381, 384, 412, 426, 428, 432, 462.
Ermelo commando. *See* COMMANDOS.
Erroll, Brigadier-General C. G., the Earl of, 34, 236, 247, 336, 339, 359–60, 370, 378–9, 504–5, 514.
Escape of De Wet (Olifants Nek), 353.
Escort for Heilbron convoy, 126–7.
Essenbosch, 68–9, 484.
Essex regiment. *See* REGULAR UNITS.
Europe, 417.
Evans, Colonel T. D. B., 317, 436, 441..
Events on Johannesburg—Durban line, June to November, 1900, 457–68.
Everard, 431.
Executive Raad, 417.
Exhaustion of men and animals, 307, 357, 439.

FABER'S PUT, action at, 19–22.
Farms, burning of, 373, 444, 466, 474.
Fauresmith, 104, 480.
Feltham, Lieut. J. A. P., 170–1, 179.
Ficksburg, 121, 123, 131, 134, 136, 282, 286, 292–4, 297, 299, 302, 309, 329, 331, 469, 473–4, 489.
Ficksburg commando. *See* COMMANDOS.
Field Artillery, Royal. *See* REGULAR UNITS.

Field Intelligence Department. *See* INTELLIGENCE.
Fisher, Mr. A. B., 432.
FitzClarence, Captain C., 147–8, 152–3, 160–2, 170–2, 178; (awarded the Victoria Cross), 147.
Fitzgerald, Captain G. A., 289.
Flanking movements, difficulty of, 413.
Florida, 75–6, 78, 89–91, 96, 98.
Food. *See* SUPPLIES.
Forage, shortness of, 29, 37, 369.
Forbes, Lieut. J. S., 24.
Forbes, Mr., 179.
Force :—
  Babington's, 516–17.
  Baden-Powell's, 231, 240, 244–7, 349, 357, 361–9, 377.
  Barker's, 489, 493–5.
  Bethune's, 259–61, 266–7.
  Bradley's, 372, 499–500.
  Brookfield's, 287.
  Carleton's, 444–5, 448, 454–5.
  Carrington's, 339–40.
  Colleton's, 510.
  Colville's, 468.
  Cookson's, 518.
  Cradock's, 448–54.
  Cunningham's, 336, 499, 506.
  Downing's, 383.
  Erroll's, 247, 336, 359, 378–9, 504, 514.
  Grenfell's, 296.
  Grey's, 359, 505, 515.
  Godley's, 369.
  Grove's, 330.
  Hamilton's (Ian), 138, 286, 307, 317–22, 336–54, 357, 360–9, 404, 407–10. *See also* INFANTRY, MOUNTED.
  Herbert's, 489, 493–5.
  Hickman's, 317–19, 336, 349, 357, 361–9, 373, 448–54, 501–2, 513.
  Hicks', 376, 511.
  Hore's, 339, 358–9.
  Hunter's, 138, 286, 326–34, 469–89.
  Kekewich's, 246.

INDEX. 577

Le Gallais', 470, 472-7, 481, 483-8. *See also* INFANTRY, MOUNTED.
Lloyd's, 501-2.
Long's, 495.
Macbean's, 455-6.
Mahon's, 238, 307-22, 336-54, 360-9, 412, 426-35.
Maxwell's, 496.
Meyrick's, 514.
Nicholson's, 374.
Payne's, 438, 445, 448, 454-5.
Pilcher's, 489, 493-5. *See also* INFANTRY, MOUNTED.
Plumer's, 244-7, 367, 369, 372, 448-54, 501-2, 513.
Rhodesian Field, 159, 231. *See also* COLONIAL UNITS.
Rimington's, 481, 496.
Rochfort's, 500.
Settle's, 372, 379, 481-2, 496, 513.
White's, 472, 474.
Williams', 494-5.
See also BRIGADES *and* DIVISIONS OF CAVALRY, INFANTRY *and* INFANTRY, MOUNTED.
Forestier-Walker, Lieut.-General Sir F. W. E. F., K.C.B., C.M.G., 26, 31, 33, 106.
Forster, Commandant, 19.
Fort Wylie, 488.
Forte, H.M.S., 259.
Forts : in Mafeking, 159, 172-3 ; Johannesburg and Pretoria, 73, 94, 98-101. *See also* APPENDIX 4.
Fouché, Field-Cornet, 3, 477, 480.
Fourie, General, 72, 86, 88, 286, 331, 333, 443, 469, 471.
Fouriesburg, and road, 291, 294, 301-2, 306, 328-9, 332, 489.
Fourteen Streams, 4, 13-14, 51, 66, 89, 107-12.
Fowle, Major J., 132.
France, 393.
Frankfort, 74, 118, 126, 133, 136, 287, 309, 330, 332, 475-7, 479, 489-90.

Frans Poort, 218.
Fraser, Mr. J. G., 32.
Frederikstad, and road, 74, 88, 96, 232, 247, 328, 342-3, 348, 350-1, 354, 376-7, 483, 509-12, 516.
French, Lieut.-General J. D. P., C.B., 29, 51, 53-6, 59-62, 67-79, 81, 84-5, 87-92, 96-7, 206-7, 209-12, 217-18, 222, 224, 243, 308, 311-14, 318-23, 381, 385-8, 391-5, 403-4, 408, 419-20, 439, 515-18 ; marches, from Carolina to Barberton, 412-18 ; from Barberton to Heidelberg, 426-35.
French, Captain S. G., 198.
French Corps. *See* COMMANDOS.
French's Scouts. *See* COLONIAL UNITS.
Friend, The (newspaper), 32.
Frischgewaagd, 439.
Froneman, General C. C., 93, 128, 130, 286, 330, 333.
Frontiers, defence of, 140.
Furlough, grant of, to President Kruger, 417.
Fusilier regiments. *See* REGULAR UNITS.

GABERONES, 165, 197.
Game Tree Hill, and fort, 156 ; action at, 159-63.
Gansvlei Spruit, 272-4, 280.
Garrison Artillery, Royal. *See* REGULAR UNITS.
Garrisons : in Orange River Colony, 134-6, 139, 331, 477 ; of Mafeking, 145 ; of Heilbron, 247 : on lines of communication, 128, 134, 139.
Garsfontein, 206, 209.
Gatacre, Lieut.-General Sir W. F., K.C.B., D.S.O., 29, 250.
Gatsrand, The, 72-5, 342, 348-50, 354, 375, 509-10, 512, 517, 519.
Gawne, Lieut.-Colonel J. M., 464.
Geelbeksvlei, 484.
Geelhoutboom, 420.

VOL. III. 37

Geluk, 393, 428; action at, 388-91; affair at, 429-30.
Geluk road (north-east of Rhenosterpoort), 454.
General Officer Commanding Lines of Communication. *See* FORESTIER-WALKER, SIR F. W. E. F.
General's Nek, 302.
Geneva flag, 151.
Geneva Siding, 61, 482.
Genoa, 184.
German Corps. *See* COMMANDOS.
German frontier, 17.
German Government, South-West Africa, 9.
German territory, asylum in, for British subjects, 9.
Germany, 393.
Germiston, and road, 76, 87-91, 98-9, 233.
Germiston commando. *See* COMMANDOS.
Gibbs, Sergeant A., 338.
Girouard, Lieut.-Colonel E. P. C., D.S.O., 29, 62.
Glades river, 416.
Glen Siding, 128.
Glencoe, and Pass, 252, 264-5, 458.
Gloucestershire regiment. *See* REGULAR UNITS.
Godfray, Colonel J. W., 240.
Godley, Major A. J., 150, 155-6, 159-61, 176, 178-81, 369.
Godwaan Station, 414, 416, 419, 426.
Gold, capture of, 418, 432.
Golden Gate, 293, 298, 301, 303-5.
Goold-Adams, Major H. J., 166.
Gopani, 201.
Gordon, Brigadier-General J. R. P., 33, 51-2, 56, 135, 212-13, 215, 293, 315, 320-1, 323, 326, 415, 427-8, 430-5, 516, 518-19.
Gordon, Captain W. E., 241; (awarded the Victoria Cross), 242.
Gordon Highlanders. *See* REGULAR UNITS.
Gordonia, district of, 8-9.
Gostling, Mr. H., 480.
Gough, Captain A. P. G., 235.
Gough, Major H. de la P., 263, 278.
Governments: British, 186, 228, 306, 370; Orange Free State, 60-1, 63, 94, 226-7, 295, 341, 362; South African Republic, 94-5, 204-5, 226-7, 363, 404-5, 417, 422, 437.
Governor of Lourenço Marques, 417.
Granary of the Orange Free State, 105.
Grant, Commander W. L., R.N., 344.
Gras Kop, 281-2, 458-60.
Gravett, Commandant A. J., 317, 420.
Great Britain, 393.
Grenadier Guards. *See* REGULAR UNITS.
Grenfell, Lieut.-Colonel H. M., 138, 295-6, 300.
Grey, Colonel R., 232, 359, 505, 515.
Greyling, Commandant, 43.
Greylingstad, 74, 93, 126, 285, 434, 457, 459, 465, 467.
Greytown, 253.
Griqualand West, 2, 6, 17-18, 22, 34.
Griqualand rebel commando. *See* COMMANDOS.
Griquatown, 3, 6, 14, 17-18, 20, 22, 25.
Grobelaar, Commandant, 235, 238, 247, 311, 313-14, 362, 364-9, 443.
Grobelaar, General, 43, 50, 73, 75, 88, 189-93, 205.
Grobelaar, General (Vryheid), 267.
Grobelaar's commando. *See* COMMANDOS.
Groenfontein, 357, 513, 517.
Groetplaats, 353.
Groot Drink Drift, 16, 22.
Groot Oliphants Station, 322, 455.
Groot Varsh Kuil Drift, 13.
Grooteiland, 343.
Grootfontein, 490.
Grootplaats, 348-9.
Grootvlei, 68, 70.
Grove, Colonel E. A. W. S., 330, 332, 476-7, 479.

INDEX.

Guards' Brigade. *See* INFANTRY BRIGADES.
Guerrilla warfare, 93, 206, 223, 385, 469.
Guinness, Major E., 441.
Guinness, Lieut.-Colonel H. W. N., 300.
Gun Ridge (Bergendal), 397-8, 400-2.
Guns: Boer, 11, 40, 44, 46, 49-51, 57-8, 67, 73, 79, 81, 86-7, 90-4, 97-8, 109, 119, 122-3, 128, 130, 134, 138, 146, 149-50, 159, 162-85, 191, 197, 206, 212, 217, 223, 247-8, 252, 260, 268, 270, 286-8, 293, 295, 305, 310, 317-18, 330-1, 333, 337, 358, 368, 371, 373, 383, 391-2, 395, 399, 406, 408, 411, 414-15, 417-18, 420, 422, 427, 430, 433, 437, 449, 474, 483, 490, 498, 503-4, 507, 709; thrown into Hector Spruit, 419; British—35, 38, 41-2, 149, 187, 196-7, 234, 243, 392, 428; **Naval 12-prs.,** 99, 219-20, 249, 252, 259, 262, 265, 267, 270-1, 276, 279-80, 282-3, 317, 382, 391, 394, 398, 409, 420, 425, 445, 448, 453-4, 458, 460-5; **Naval 4.7-in.,** 46, 58, 87, 98-9, 261, 265, 267, 270-1, 282-3, 287, 317, 344, 375, 382, 391, 394-5, 398, 412, 424, 460, 462, 464-5, 498, 512, 518; **5-in.,** 57-8, 80-6, 99, 206, 212, 216, 218-19, 222-3, 243, 270-1, 284, 291, 293, 298, 302-4, 307-9, 313-17, 328, 330-1, 338, 366, 373, 382, 391, 394-5, 398, 407, 409, 411, 420, 424-5, 436-7, 439-41, 443-4, 454-5, 458, 461, 482, 501; **6-in.,** 109, 112, 132, 348; **Howitzers, 5-in.,** 135, 169, 243, 282; **6-in.,** 94, 314, 446; **9.45-in.,** 94. *See also* COLT, HOTCHKISS, KRUPP, NORDENFELT *and* VICKERS-MAXIM.
Guthrie-Smith, Major H., 221.
Gwynne, Mr. H. A., 32.

HAASBROEK, GENERAL, 286, 296, 330, 473, 475-6, 490.
Haig, Major A. E., 127, 129.
Haig, Colonel D., 430.
Haking, Major R. C. D., 126-7.
Halt, the, at Johannesburg, 92-6; Kroonstad, 62-4.
Hamanskraal, 317-19, 365-6, 369, 374, 502.
Hamilton, Major-General B. M., 57-8, 80-1, 83-4, 135, 212, 215-21, 287, 293, 296-8, 301-6, 329-30, 333-4, 469-71, 473-6, 481-3, 490, 496.
Hamilton, Lieut.-Colonel E. O. F., 255, 261, 270.
Hamilton, Lieut.-General I. S. M., C.B., D.S.O., 33, 38, 41, 44-6, 50-63, 66-81, 84-5, 88-92, 96-7, 100-1, 106, 114, 126, 135-6, 138, 206-7, 209, 212, 215-19, 222-4, 233, 243, 248, 251, 258, 284, 286, 307, 309, 313, 317-22, 336-8, 341, 350, 352-3, 357, 360-5, 368-9, 404, 407-10, 413, 416, 419-20; correspondence with Lord Roberts about De Wet, 348-9, 354-5; reasons for not holding Olifants Nek, 355-6.
Hammonia, 121, 123, 131, 134, 229, 286, 294, 297-9, 302, 329, 331, 469.
Hampshire regiment. *See* REGULAR UNITS.
Hampton, Sergeant H. (awarded the Victoria Cross), 388.
Hanbury-Tracy, Major the Hon. A. H. C., 236.
Hanwell, Major J., 483.
Harness, 38.
Harrismith, 257, 286, 301, 328, 320-2, 383, 473, 477, 489.
Harrismith commando. *See* COMMANDOS.
Hart, Major-General A. FitzR., C.B., 35, 111-12, 136, 243, 284, 308, 327, 344, 346-7, 352, 357, 359, 361, 372, 375-7, 457, 459, 516-19.
Hart river, 271.

Hartebeeste river, 15.
Hartebeestefontein, 448.
Hartebeestfontein, 356.
Hartebeestpoort, 233.
Harts river, 182.
Hatting Spruit, 265.
Hattingh, Commandant, 473.
Hay division, Griqualand West, 2, 19.
Heaton, Private W. (awarded the Victoria Cross), 390.
Headquarters Staff, 36, 124.
Hebron, 362, 365, 373, 501.
Hector Spruit, 417, 419–20.
Heidelberg, 69, 86, 93, 126, 135–6, 138, 232–3, 243, 284–7, 307–8, 327, 342, 380, 382, 428, 433–5, 457–61, 465, 467.
Heidelberg commando. See COMMANDOS.
Heilbron, and road, 63, 66–8, 93, 113–15, 119–21, 124, 126–9, 132, 134–8, 229, 247, 286–7, 293, 326, 330–3, 470, 473, 475–7, 483, 489–90.
Heilbron commando. See COMMANDOS.
Hekpoort, district and valley, 236, 241–3, 336, 348, 350, 352, 354, 498, 506–8, 510, 518.
Hekpoort commando. See COMMANDOS.
Helpmakaar, and Nek, 252–3, 259–63, 266.
Helvetia (Eastern Transvaal), 403–4, 407, 424–5.
Helvetia (O. F. S.), 494.
Henderson, Major D., 421.
Henry, Colonel St. G. C., 43, 54, 56, 59, 61–2, 67, 70, 86–7, 91–2, 98–100, 217–18, 224, 308, 312, 318, 414–16, 419.
Henry's Mounted Infantry. See INFANTRY, MOUNTED.
Henty, Captain C. G., 478.
Herbert, Lieut.-Colonel E. B., 489, 493–5.
Herbert district, Griqualand West, 5, 17.
Her Majesty, Queen Victoria, 173.
Hermann, Field-Cornet, 24.

Hertzog, Judge, 494.
Hickman, Lieut.-Colonel T. E., D.S.O., 139, 243, 247, 314, 317, 319, 336–8, 349, 357, 361–2, 365–7, 373, 448, 451–3, 501–2, 513.
Hicks, Lieut.-Colonel H. T., 376, 511–12, 518.
Hidden Hollow, 176.
Higginson, Captain C. P., 83.
High Commissioner of South Africa. See MILNER, SIR A.
Highland Brigade. See INFANTRY BRIGADES.
Highland Light Infantry. See REGULAR UNITS.
Hildyard, Lieut.-General H. J. T., C.B., 255, 259–60, 265, 267, 269–70, 276–7, 280–3, 383, 457, 459–68.
Hlomohlom, 416.
Holdsworth, Colonel G. L., 159, 195–6, 200, 234.
Holland, Her Majesty the Queen of, 417.
Holland, Sergeant E. J. (awarded the Victoria Cross), 338.
Holfontein, 327, 484.
Home Government. See BRITISH GOVERNMENT.
Honde river, 220, 223.
Honeybird Creek, 419.
Honing Spruit and Station, 67, 133, 137, 326, 484.
Hoopstad, 66, 104, 107–8, 479, 481–2.
Hopefield, 475.
Hopetown, and bridge, 5, 11, 13, 17, 494.
Hore, Lieut.-Colonel C. O., 143, 145, 147, 160–1, 176–7, 179–80, 236, 335, 339–40, 360; besieged at Elands river, 358–9.
Horne's Nek, 233, 357, 366.
Horse artillery, Royal. See REGULAR UNITS.
Horses, 21, 29, 31, 33, 62–3, 141, 214, 231, 246, 251, 332, 381, 387, 415, 427, 435, 439.

INDEX. 581

Hospitals, 28, 133, 151, 179; shelling of, 165; train wrecked by Boers, 246-7. *See also* ROYAL ARMY MEDICAL CORPS (REGULAR UNITS).
Hotchkiss guns, 146-7, 266, 466.
House, Private W. (awarded the Victoria Cross), 338.
Household Cavalry. *See* REGULAR UNITS.
Hout Kop, 71, 73.
Hout Nek, 258, 280, 462.
Houtboschhoek, 426.
Houwater, 10-13, 15.
Howard, Major-General F., C.B., C.M.G., 280, 382, 395, 408, 410, 460.
Howard, Lieut.-Colonel H. R. L., 366, 513.
Howitzers. *See* GUNS.
Howse, Captain N. R. (awarded the Victoria Cross), 326.
Hughes, Lieut.-Colonel S., 21.
Hughes-Hallett, Lieut.-Colonel J. W., 479-80.
Hungarian horses, 21.
Hunter, Lieut.-General Sir A., K.C.B., D.S.O., 35, 37-8, 51, 65-6, 107-12, 135, 138, 182, 228, 231-4, 250, 284, 286-7, 298-302, 305-6, 308-9, 325, 328, 330-2, 380, 469-70, 472-7, 481-3; Prinsloo surrenders to, 304.
Hunter-Weston, Major A. G., 60-1, 68, 95.
Huntingdon, Lieut. A. W., 21.
Hussars. *See* REGULAR UNITS.
Hutton, Major-General E. T. H., C.B., 33, 42-4, 46-9, 51, 53, 56, 59, 61, 63, 67-8, 70-1, 73, 76-8, 90-2, 96-7, 206, 209, 211, 224, 234, 308-15, 317-18, 320-3, 387, 414-16, 419.
Hutton's Mounted Infantry. *See* INFANTRY, MOUNTED.

IKETENI Mountains, 273, 275, 278-9.
Imbezane, 383.
Impati, 253.

Imperial Bushmen. *See* COLONIAL UNITS.
Imperial Guides. *See* COLONIAL UNITS.
Imperial Light Horse. *See* COLONIAL UNITS.
Imperial Light Infantry. *See* COLONIAL UNITS.
Imperial Yeomanry, 131, 133-7, 233, 235, 294-5, 297-9, 302, 306, 308, 328-32, 345, 351, 451, 471, 480, 482, 518-19; organisation of, 34.
1st brigade, 378.
Battalions :—
　1st, 34, 518.
　2nd, 16.
　3rd, 34, 124-5, 347, 503.
　4th, 15, 34, 122, 365.
　5th, 34, 109-12, 124-5, 243-4, 328, 344, 351, 503, 514.
　6th, 34, 302, 330-1.
　7th, 34, 67, 217.
　8th, 17-22, 34.
　9th, 34, 366.
　10th, 34, 124-5, 243-4, 328, 344, 351, 514.
　11th, 34, 122.
　12th, 34, 375, 507.
　13th, 34, 93, 113-25, 136, 205.
　14th, 34, 137-8, 289-90.
　15th, 34, 243-4, 330-1, 343.
　16th, 34, 333.
　17th, 34, 231.
　18th, 34, 231.
　19th, 17-22, 34.
　20th, 34.
Companies :—
　5th, 365-6, 448, 485-8.
　17th, 485-8.
　18th, 485-8.
　19th, 241, 507.
　20th, 309, 312.
　29th, 471.
　30th, 471.
　31st, 471.
　34th, 121.
　49th, 365-6, 448, 513.

Imperial Yeomanry—Companies—*con.*
  63rd, 365.
  66th, 365, 448.
  71st, 327, 344.
  Cheshire, 13,
  Derbyshire, 12.
  Devonshire, North, 217.
  East Kent, 476.
  Gloucestershire, 329.
  Hampshire, 15.
  Irish, 493.
  Lancashire, 23-4.
  Manchester, 457, 459.
  Middlesex, 290.
  Staffordshire, 15.
  Suffolk, 13, 15.
  Warwickshire, 23-4, 513.
  Welsh, 473.
  Wiltshire, 329, 473.
  Yorkshire Dragoons, 110-11, 513.
  Other Units :—
    Lord Lovat's Scouts, 114, 126, 132, 298, 302-3, 330-1, 479.
    Paget's Horse, 22, 247, 339, 359.
    Scouts, The I. Y., 129, 287-90, 359.
Inchanga Drift, 267.
" In de Middel " Farm, 425.
Indian, corn, 287 ; ponies, 31.
Indoda Mountain, 260, 265.
Indumeni, 253.
Infantry Brigades :—
  1st or Guards' (Jones), 49, 98, 217-23, 308, 317-24, 391-420.
  2nd (E. Hamilton), 249, 254-5, 261-5, 270-2, 274-80, 282, 460.
  3rd or Highland (MacDonald), 45-6, 50, 106-7, 113-21, 124, 134-5, 138, 293-306, 328-34, 470, 473-7, 494.
  4th (Cooper), 249, 263-5, 270, 279-80, 282, 284, 458, 460.
  5th (Hart), 111-12, 136, 231-3, 243, 250, 252, 327, 344-54, 357, 359, 372, 375-6, 457, 517-19.
  6th (Barton), 108-12, 231-3, 250, 252, 506-12, 515.
  7th (F. W. Kitchener), 249-50, 382-421, 425, 458.
  8th (Howard), 249-50, 267, 382-421, 425, 460-4.
  9th (Douglas), 124-5, 132, 134, 244-7, 350-4, 357, 378-9, 497-500, 503-7, 515, 519.
  10th (Coke), 254-5, 265, 269, 270-2, 274-80, 457, 460-1, 465.
  11th (Wynne), 255, 265, 267, 270-80, 282-3, 457, 461-2, 465.
  12th (Clements), 113, 123, 131, 134-5, 138-9, 286, 290-306, 349, 369, 470, 498-500, 502, 506-9, 517-18.
  13th (C. E. Knox), 132, 135, 139, 327, 344-6, 470, 474-7, 483-9, 493-6, 510.
  14th (Maxwell), 42-3, 47, 58, 99-101, 206.
  15th (Wavell), 42-3, 52, 58, 92, 99, 307.
  16th (Campbell), 122-3, 286-306, 328-34, 473-7.
  17th (Boyes), 122-3, 286-306, 328-34, 474-7.
  18th (Stephenson), 43, 50, 98, 217-24, 308, 317-24, 391-420, 424-6.
  19th (Smith-Dorrien), 45-6, 57-9, 63-4, 70, 80-6, 100-1, 131, 206, 231, 236, 241-4, 247, 342, 350-2, 357, 359, 365, 371-2, 407-20, 425-6, 438-44.
  20th (Paget), 109, 112, 132, 134-7, 286, 290-306, 349, 357, 362-9, 372-4, 424, 448-54, 470, 501-2, 513.
  21st (B. M. Hamilton), 45-6, 57-9, 63-4, 70, 80-6, 100-1, 135, 206, 212-17, 223, 293-307, 328-34, 470, 473-7, 481-3, 496.
  22nd (Allen), 134, 139.
  23rd (W. G. Knox), 134, 139.
Infantry Divisions :—
  1st (Methuen), 107-9, 112, 124-5, 131-3, 136-8, 243-7, 342-54, 357, 360, 369-72, 377-8, 497-500, 502-6, 514.

INDEX. 583

IInd (Clery), 249-52, 254-65, 279-85, 382, 457, 460, 462-8.
IIIrd (Chermside), 39, 105-6, 113, 139.
IVth (Lyttelton), 250-9, 265-85, 382-421, 424-6, 436.
Vth (Hildyard), 250-6, 259-85, 382-3, 460-8, 516.
VIth (Kelly-Kenny), 38-9, 106, 139.
VIIth (Tucker), 42-3, 49-64, 67-103, 231, 307-8.
VIIIth (Rundle), 34-5, 41-2, 105-7, 121-4, 134-8, 286-306, 328-34, 470, 472-7, 489, 496.
IXth (Colvile), 41, 46, 50, 106-7, 113-21, 126, 135-6, 377-8.
Xth (Hunter), 35, 65-6, 107-12, 136, 228, 231-3, 250, 252-3, 258.
XIth (Pole-Carew), 42-4, 47, 49-64, 67-103, 206, 217-24, 307-8, 311-12, 314, 317-24, 386, 391-420.
Infantry, Mounted :—
Infantry, Mounted, reorganisation of, 33-4.
Division (Hamilton, Ian), 33, 44-64, 67-103.
1st brigade (Hutton), 33, 47, 67-103, 206-25, 307-24, 387, 414-19.
  1st Corps (Alderson), 3, 6, 33, 42-3, 47-8, 56, 59, 74-6, 78, 96-7, 209-11, 307-17, 414, 424, 494.
  2nd Corps (De Lisle), 45, 78, 101, 219, 221-4, 307, 343, 483-5, 488, 509.
  3rd Corps (Pilcher), 42-4, 47-8, 59, 75-8, 90, 209-11, 307, 312, 314, 362, 364, 412, 423, 436, 443.
  4th Corps (Henry), 43, 54, 56, 59, 61-2, 67, 70, 74, 86-7, 91-2, 98-100, 217-24, 312, 318-24, 392, 394, 415-16, 419.

2nd brigade (Ridley, later N. Legge), 33, 67-103, 135, 206-25, 293-306, 325-7, 337, 343, 346-54, 357, 358, 363, 371, 498-500, 506, 508, 513, 517.
5th Corps (Dawson, later Lean), 52, 63, 303-4, 307, 325, 329, 333, 343, 473, 485-8.
6th Corps (Legge), 45, 217, 223, 307, 343.
7th Corps (including Burma) (Bainbridge), 33, 296, 303-4, 307, 471-2, 485-8.
8th Corps (Ross), 43, 59, 74, 86-7, 98-100, 206, 309-10, 485-8.
IVth division, battalion of, 382, 397, 410, 425, 436, 460.
Vth division, battalion of, 462.
Unattached units, etc. :—
  10th battalion, 308.
  1st regiment, 311.
  2nd regiment, 311.
  3rd regiment, 311.
  Derbyshire, 329.
  East Kent (The Buffs), 486.
  Gloucestershire, 11, 16, 22.
  Gough's, 263, 278, 283.
  Hickman's, 139, 243, 247.
  Le Gallais', 33.
  Malta, 290, 333, 344, 479.
  Manchester, 294.
  Martyr's, 33.
  Munster Fusiliers, The Royal, 18, 378.
  Royal Irish, 486.
  Royal Irish Rifles, 133, 344, 490-3.
  Royal Scots, 135.
  Royal West Kent, 329, 476.
  Sitwell's, 333.
  Suffolk, 16.
  Warwickshire, 10-11.
  Worcestershire, 486.
Ingagane, 266, 458, 462.
Ingogo heights, river and station, 229, 265, 268-9, 281, 457, 461, 465.
Inkwelo Mountain, 270-1.

Inkweloane Range, 269-72.
Inniskilling Dragoons. *See* REGULAR UNITS.
Inniskilling Fusiliers, The Royal. *See* REGULAR UNITS.
Intelligence: Boer—42, 132-3, 423; British—40, 53, 93-4, 283, 422, 427, 438, 447, 490.
Intintanyoni, 252.
Intombi hospital, 250-1.
Irene, 206, 308, 311, 313, 433.
Irish brigade (Boer), *see* COMMANDOS; (British), *see* INFANTRY, 5th brigade.
Irish Fusiliers, The Royal. *See* REGULAR UNITS.
Irish regiment, The Royal. *See* REGULAR UNITS.
Irish Rifles, The Royal. *See* REGULAR UNITS.
Isabellafontein, 41, 44.
Israels Farm, 184.
Israel's Poort, 329.

JACKAL TREE, 150, 154-5, 168.
Jackman's Drift, 471.
Jackson, General Stonewall, 205.
Jacobsdal (Western Transvaal), 370, 506, 514.
Jacobsdal (O. F. S.), 36, 104, 480.
Jacobsrust, 41.
Jagersfontein, 480.
Jameson, Doctor L. S., 234.
Jan Massibi's, 200-03.
Jellalabad, 146.
Jericho, 502.
Jervis-White-Jervis, Major Sir J. H., Bart., 210, 238.
Job's Kop, 252.
Johannesburg, 27, 40, 71, 73-6, 87-92, 96, 98-9, 101, 138, 143, 226, 231, 247, 307-8, 314, 349, 372, 375-6, 435, 489, 498, 516, 518, 520.
Johannesburg commando. *See* COMMANDOS.
Johannesburg Police. *See* COMMANDOS.
Johannesburg—Durban Line, events on, June to November, 1900, 457-68.
Jokeskei river, 90, 96. *See also* LITTLE JOKESKEI.
Jones, Captain E. P., R.N., 259.
Jones, Major-General I. R., 219-21, 223, 317.
Jones, Captain L. H., 23-4.
Jonono's Kop, 254-5, 265.
Jooste, Commandant, 9, 14.
Jordaan Siding, 62, 67.
Joubert, Commandant-General P., 32, 252.
Joubert's Farm, 280, 282.
Joubertsdal, 419.
Junction Drift (Zand river), 52, 54-5, 57-8.
July's Kop, 299.

KAALFONTEIN, 513.
Kaalfontein, and bridge (Valsch river), 475-6.
Kaap Range, 17.
Kaap river, 416.
Kaapmuiden, 416, 419.
Kaapsche Hoop, 414-16, 419, 427.
Kaffir Kopje, 290, 294.
Kaffirkraal (E. of Otto's Hoop), 505, 514-15.
Kaffirskraal, 500.
Kaffirspruit, 432.
Kaffrarian Mounted Rifles. *See* COLONIAL UNITS.
Kalkfontein, 370.
Kalkheuvel, 96-7.
Kalkoenkrans, 53.
Kameel Drift, 206, 209, 224, 237-8, 307-8, 318, 366.
Kameel Drift Kopjes, 366.
Kameelfontein Ridge, Valley, etc., 207-10.
Kameelzyn Kraal, 208.
Kanya, and road, 144, 169, 199-201.
Karee Boosch Poort, 10-11.
Karee Kloof or Plaats, 12-13.
Karee Siding, 40-1.

INDEX.

Kareefontein, 473.
Kareepoort, 362-3.
Kareepoort Drift (by Bethulie Bridge), 495.
Katbosch (O. F. S.), 137.
Katbosch Spruit, 283.
Kekewich, Colonel R. G., 246, 341, 354.
Kelly, Major-General W. F., C.B., 28, 39.
Kelly-Kenny, Lieut.-General T., C.B., 38-9, 106, 131, 134, 139, 313, 327, 470-1, 478, 489.
Kenhart, 5, 8, 12, 13-16, 23.
Kenhart rebels. *See* COMMANDOS.
Kennedy, Private C. (awarded the Victoria Cross), 492.
Khama (native chief), 191, 196.
Kheis, 16, 22-4.
Kimberley, 2, 4, 5, 29, 32, 34, 35, 37, 41, 51, 107-8, 112, 143, 147, 157, 185, 231.
Kimberley Light Horse. *See* COLONIAL UNITS.
Kimberley Mounted Corps. *See* COLONIAL UNITS.
King, Lieut.-Colonel A. C., 443.
King-Hall, Major W., 480.
King's Royal Rifle Corps. *See* MILITIA *and* REGULAR UNITS.
Kipling, Mr. R., 32.
Kirkpatrick, Lieut.-Colonel W. J., 463.
Kitchener, Major-General F. W., 382, 388, 399, 409, 425, 436.
Kitchener, Major-General H. H., Lord, G.C.B., K.C.M.G., 10, 13-16, 33, 53, 67, 71, 113, 115, 121, 123-4, 126-7, 131-2, 135, 206, 328, 343-4, 347-8, 350, 352, 354-5, 357, 359, 361, 369, 371, 424, 426, 495, 519-20; Lord Roberts urges, to pursue De Wet, 346; sent to North-west Cape Colony, 12.
Kitchener's Horse. *See* COLONIAL UNITS.
Klein Nek, 366.

Klein Oliphant river, 322, 454.
Kleinfontein, and Ridge, 208, 215-18, 220.
Klerksdorp, 66, 69, 72, 89, 228, 230, 232, 236, 247, 335, 343, 372, 515-16.
Klerksdorp commando. *See* COMMANDOS.
Klerksvlei Farm, 329.
Klip Drift, 286.
Klip Drift Nek, 294, 296.
Klip Dam, 4.
Klipfontein (O. F. S.), 475.
Klipfontein (north-west of Johannesburg), 90-1.
Klipfontein (Ermelo road), 384.
Klipfontein (north-west of Pretoria), 502.
Klipkuil, 379, 497.
Klippaal Drift, 384.
Klipplaat, 378.
Klip river (Drakensberg), 272.
Klip River, and Station, 73, 75-80, 83, 86-7, 459, 476, 518.
Kliprivers Berg, 71, 74-9, 88.
Klipriver's Oog, 75-7.
Klipscheur, 296.
Klipspruit (Eastern Transvaal), 410.
Klipspruit (near Johannesburg), 77-9.
Klipstapel, 384, 432.
Knapdaar, 495.
Knight, Corporal H. J. (awarded the Victoria Cross), 388.
Knight, Captain W., 129-30.
Knoffelfontein, 25.
Knowles, Lieut. A. M., 347.
Knox, Major-General C. E., 131-2, 134-5, 327, 344, 346, 470, 474, 476-7, 483-5, 487-9, 493-6, 510, 512.
Knox, Major-General W. G., C.B., 134.
Koedoes Poort, 206.
Koegas Pont, 16-17, 22.
Koffyfontein, 479, 482.
Kolbe, Commandant J., 4.
Kolbe's commando. *See* COMMANDOS.
Komati Poort, and Bridge, 95, 284, 323, 423-6, 456.

Komati Poort, the advance towards, 380-405 ; the advance to, 406-21.
Komati river, and valley, 387-9, 395-6, 412-16, 430-1, 440-1.
Koning, 25.
Koodoesberg, 4.
Kopje Alleen, 54-5, 327.
Kopje's Station, 68, 133-4, 327.
Koranna Berg, 469, 472, 477, 489.
Korannafontein, 497.
Korwe, 201.
Kosi Bay, 95.
Kosterfontein, 518.
Kraaipan, 147.
Kranspan, 384.
Kranzspruit, 63.
Krause, Doctor, 89-90, 92.
Krijgsraad, 108, 314.
Krokodil, Drift, Hill, and Spruit, 207-11.
Krokodil Drift (west of Pretoria), 362-3.
Krokodil Kraal (west of Pretoria), 364.
Kromdrai, 283, 382, 461.
Kromellenboog Spruit, 127, 345, 348.
Kroonbloem, 67.
Kroondal, 338.
Kroonspruit, 62.
Kroonstad, 38, 93, 113, 115-21, 124, 126, 128-9, 131-4, 137-9, 205, 243, 311, 326-7, 330, 333, 364, 470, 473-4, 476-8, 481-2, 485, 489; the advance to, 40-64 ; the advance from, 65-103 ; surrender of, 62.
Kroonstad commando. *See* COMMANDOS.
Kruger, H. E. President S. P. J., 68, 72, 88, 94-5, 175, 205, 227, 233, 281, 358, 403-5, 417, 419 ; leaves South Africa, 417.
Kruger, Mrs., 95.
Krugersdorp, 75, 81, 90, 139, 232-6, 240-4, 246-7, 311, 342-3, 348-9, 351, 354-5, 361, 363, 370-1, 375, 377, 498, 506-8, 516-19.
Krugersdorp commando. *See* COMMANDOS.
Krugerspost, 421, 436-7, 501.

Kruis river, 504-5.
Krupp guns, 11, 130, 146-7, 183, 246, 360, 488, 490-1, 496.
Kuki Hills, 18.
Kuruman, 2-4, 17, 23, 25, 236.

LAAGER SPRUIT, 286.
Ladybrand, 40, 106, 257, 286, 297, 329, 331, 469-72, 490.
Ladybrand commando. *See* COMMANDOS.
Ladysmith, 5, 36, 175, 183-4, 186, 249-56, 259, 263, 265-6, 331, 380, 383, 421, 457-8.
Lagden, Sir G. Y., K.C.M.G., 294.
Laing's Nek, 65, 72, 227, 264-5, 267, 270-1, 273, 279-82, 309, 457, 462, 465.
Lake Chrissie, 427, 431.
Lakenvley, 394, 403.
Lancashire Fusiliers. *See* REGULAR UNITS.
Lancaster regiment, The King's Own Royal. *See* MILITIA *and* REGULAR UNITS.
Lancers. *See* REGULAR UNITS.
Landon, Mr. P., 32.
Landrosts, 32, 112 ; of Barberton, 418 ; Kroonstad, 62 ; Wakkerstroom, 281.
Lane, Private W. F., 24.
Langeberg district, 23.
Langkloof Heights, 443.
Langkuil, 365.
Lansdowne, The Most Hon. H. C. K., Marquis of, K.G., G.C.S.I., etc., 31, 33-4.
Law, Martial. *See* MARTIAL LAW.
Lawrence, Sergeant T. (awarded the Victoria Cross), 346.
Lean, Major K. E., 486.
Lean's Mounted Infantry. *See* INFANTRY, MOUNTED.
Leary, Rev. J. W., 192.
Lebombo Hills, 420.
Leeuwbank, 439.
Leeuwfontein, 345, 347.
Leeuwkop (O. F. S.), 290.

Leeuwkop (Transvaal), 96-7.
Leeuwpoort, 375-6.
Leeuw River Mills, 329, 471, 473.
Leeuwspruit, 377.
Leeuw Spruit, and Station, 68, 133, 136, 327, 484.
Le Gallais, Lieut.-Colonel P. W. J., 33, 470-7, 481, 483-8.
Le Gallais' Mounted Infantry. *See* INFANTRY, MOUNTED.
Legge, Lieut.-Colonel N., D.S.O., 45, 216-18, 343, 506-7, 513, 517.
Legge's Mounted Infantry. *See* INFANTRY, MOUNTED.
Leicestershire regiment. *See* REGULAR UNITS.
Leliefontein (Eastern Transvaal), 440-1.
Leliefontein (O. F. S.), 138.
Lemmer, General, 73, 235-7, 240, 244, 340, 358, 371, 379, 503-4, 514.
Lemmer's commando. *See* COMMANDOS.
Lemmer's Farm, 360.
Lessard, Lieut.-Colonel F. L., 442-3.
Leydsdorp, 422.
Lichtenburg, 228, 231-2, 247, 335, 370, 372, 378, 498, 514-15.
Lichtenburg commando. *See* COMMANDOS.
Liebenberg, Commandant P., 370.
Liebenberg, General P. J., 6-10, 13-14, 108-9, 247, 342-3, 347-8, 357, 377, 503, 509, 511-12, 515.
Liebenberg's commando. *See* COMMANDOS.
Liebenbergs Vlei river, 291, 475-6.
Limpopo river, 142, 159, 182, 188-92, 194, 196, 231-2.
Linchwe (native chief), 163, 191, 195-7.
Lincolnshire regiment. *See* REGULAR UNITS.
Lindequee Drift (Vaal river), 70-2, 127, 345-8, 483.
Lindley, 61, 63-4, 93, 113-14, 121-6, 132, 134, 136-9, 227, 243, 286-7, 290, 309, 326, 330, 473, 475-7,

481, 489; garrison of, 135; Spragge's Yeomanry captured near, 115-20.
Lindley commando. *See* COMMANDOS.
Lindley's Poort, 503.
Lines of Communications: in Cape Colony, 6; "closed works" on, 447; in Eastern Transvaal, 322, 426; Johannesburg to Durban, events on, June to November, 1900, 457-68; in Natal, 257, 282, 285; Orange Free State, 70, 92, 104-6, 126, 128, 131, 134, 139, 205, 229; Pretoria to Wolvehoek, 516; Heidelberg — Ladysmith railway, 382-3.
Little, Colonel M. O., 326-7, 348, 350, 352, 369-70.
Little Jokeskei river, 90.
Little Marico river, 503.
Liverpool regiment, The King's. *See* REGULAR UNITS.
Lloyd, Lieut.-Colonel G. E., 366, 451, 501.
Lloyd, Major W. R. de la P., 440.
Lobatsi, 199-200, 231.
Local forces, South Africa. *See* COLONIAL UNITS.
Locomotives, 283, 418-19.
Lombard, Commandant, 195.
Lombard's Kop, 209.
London, 187.
Lonely Kop (Dewetsdorp), 491.
Long, Colonel C. J., 132, 495-6.
Longford, Captain the Earl of, 119.
"Long Tom," 437.
Losberg, 349-50, 516-17, 519.
Losberg commando. *See* COMMANDOS.
Lothian regiment, The Royal Scots. *See* MILITIA *and* REGULAR UNITS.
Lotter, Field-Cornet, 4-5.
Lotter's commando. *See* COMMANDOS.
Lourenço Marques, 417.
Louwbaken, 207, 209-11.
Lowe, Lieut.-Colonel W. H. M., 237-8.
Loyal North Lancashire regiment. *See* REGULAR UNITS.

Lucknow, 146.
Lumsden's Horse. *See* COLONIAL UNITS.
Lyddite, 49, 218.
Lydenburg, Hills and Road, 392, 394, 403-4, 406-10, 421, 424-5, 436-7, 456.
Lydenburg commando. *See* COMMANDOS.
Lynch, Colonel, 260, 263.
Lyttelton, Lieut.-General the Hon. N. G., C.B., 250, 267, 269, 271, 280-2, 382, 399, 408-9, 424-6, 438, 443, 446, 454-5.

MABALS STAD, 506-7, 514-15.
Macbean, Colonel F., 444, 455-6.
McDilling, native constable, 8.
MacDonald, Major-General H. A., C.B., D.S.O., 45, 113, 136, 138, 286-7, 293, 298-9, 301-4, 328, 330, 470, 473-9, 494.
Macdonald, Corporal W., 401.
Machadodorp, 361, 363, 393, 403, 410, 412, 420, 423-8, 430-1, 439; South African Government at, 95.
Machavie, 343.
Machine guns. *See* VICKERS-MAXIMS, etc.
Mackenzie, Lieut.-Colonel G. F. C., 13.
Mackinnon, Colonel W. H., 81.
MacLaren, Captain K., 190, 196.
McMicking, Major G., 289.
Mafeking, 37-8, 51, 66, 107, 110, 186, 188, 193, 196-203, 228, 230-1, 235-6, 247, 335-6, 339-41, 359, 361, 369-70, 377-8, 514; actions at, 147, 159-62, 169-72; ammunition in, 158, 164, 168; armaments in, 146, 163-4, 168-9; casualties, *see* CASUALTIES *and also* APPENDICES; communication with, 157; considerations of the siege of, 184-5; defence and relief of, 140-85; Eloff's attack on, 176-81; garrison and condition of, 145, 175; junction of Mahon and Plumer outside of, 182; municipal authorities, help of, 145; native village in, set on fire, 172; operations outside of, 183-4; organisation of forces in, 140-6; rations in, daily scale of, 174; relief column for, 181-4; rifles in use in, 145-6; signals used in, 152-3; sorties from, 152-3, 170-2; spies in, 166; trenches in, flooding of, 158-73.
Mafeking Corps (Railway and other employés). *See* COLONIAL UNITS.
Mafeking Town Guard. *See* COLONIAL UNITS.
Magaliesberg Range, 230-1, 233-40, 243, 247, 312, 336-57, 360-4, 370-2, 497, 499, 501-2, 505-9, 517-18.
Magalipsi, 194-6.
Magato Nek, 230, 234, 237, 245, 335, 352-3, 355-7, 360, 435, 499-500, 502-3, 506.
Magersfontein, 6.
Mahon, Colonel B. T., D.S.O., 13, 38, 107, 109-10, 181-4, 202-3, 231-3, 238, 308-10, 312, 317-19, 322, 336-8, 349, 355, 360, 362-5, 368-9, 407, 412-13, 426, 428-34, 439.
Main, Colonel T. R., 299.
Maitland Camp, 34.
Majuba, 264, 273, 279.
Makapan Stad, 373, 502.
Maklutsi river, 189-90, 192-3; village, 190, 196.
Malalsene, 419.
Malan, Commandant, 72.
Malmani road, 150, 172.
Malta Mounted Infantry. *See* INFANTRY, MOUNTED.
Manana, 497, 514.
Manassas, 205.
Manchester regiment. *See* REGULAR UNITS.
Mangani Spruit, 46.
Manitoba Dragoons. *See* COLONIAL UNITS.
Marandellas, 188.

INDEX. 589

March from Bloemfontein to Pretoria, considerations on, and conditions of, etc., 102–3.
Marico town, and district, 201, 228.
Marico commando. *See* COMMANDOS.
Marico river, 191, 195, 197, 339.
Marks' Farm, 217, 219, 224.
Marseilles, 417.
Marsh, Inspector C. S., 145, 170.
Marsh, Captain F. C., 180.
Marshall's Horse. *See* COLONIAL UNITS.
Marsham, Captain the Hon. D., 153–4.
Martial law: proclaimed by Boers, 7; by British, 25.
Martin, Lieut.-Colonel H., 296.
Martineau, Sergeant H. R. (awarded the Victoria Cross), 163.
Martini-Henry rifles, 146.
Martyr, Lieut.-Colonel C. G., D.S.O., 33.
Martyr's Mounted Infantry. *See* INFANTRY, MOUNTED.
Maseru, 471.
Masibi Drift, 189–93.
Masséna, Marshal, 184.
Massibi road, 150, 182.
Massy, Major W. G., 490–3.
Matlabas river, 193.
Mauchberg Mountain, and Pass, 408, 410–11, 413–14.
Mauser rifles, 263, 401, 452.
Maxwell, Lieut.-Colonel C., 496.
Maxwell, Major-General J. G., D.S.O., 42–3, 47, 99, 206.
Meerzicht, 381, 383.
Meran, 265.
Metcalfe, Lieut.-Colonel C. T. E., 400–1.
Methuen, Lieut.-General P. S., Lord, K.C.V.O., C.B., C.M.G., 35, 37, 66, 70, 93, 107–9, 112, 124–6, 131–6, 138–9, 227, 229, 243–7, 309, 328, 342–8, 350–61, 369–70, 372, 377–9, 497–8, 500, 502–6, 514.
Metz, 184.
Meyer, General L., 46, 260, 267.

Meyer's Kop, 298, 301.
Meyerton, 69, 72–3, 519.
Meyrick, Colonel F. C., 109–11, 514.
Middelburg, 94, 321–4, 342, 381, 386–7, 412, 421–5, 436, 438, 443–9, 454–6.
Middelburg commando. *See* COMMANDOS.
Middelfontein, 360, 368.
Middelvlei, 302.
Middle Drift, 189, 193.
Middlepunt, 403.
Middlesex regiment. *See* REGULAR UNITS.
Military districts, Western Transvaal, 228.
Military Governors, Bloemfontein, *see* PRETYMAN; Johannesburg, 92.
Military police, 32.
Militia Units :—
  Militia Units, 6, 35, 106.
  The Royal Scots (Lothian) (3rd), 327, 344.
  The Buffs (East Kent) (3rd), 482.
  The King's Own (Royal Lancaster) (3rd), 128–9, 133.
  The Bedfordshire (4th), 359.
  The Cameronians (Scottish Rifles) (4th), 135, 329.
  The East Lancashire (3rd), 128.
  The South Staffordshire (4th), 329.
  The Sherwood Foresters (Derbyshire) (4th), 128–31, 133, 136.
  The King's Royal Rifle Corps (9th), 128.
  Princess Louise's (Argyll and Sutherland Highlanders) (4th), 128, 131, 482.
Miller, Captain Sir J., Bart., 241.
Milner, The Right Hon. Sir A., K.C.M.G. (High Commissioner), 5, 9, 32.
Mina, General, 93.
Mines, explosive, 145, 172–3; at Johannesburg, 89, 92.
Misgund, 75–6, 78.
Mochudi, 194–6.

Modderfontein (O. F. S.), 43.
Modderfontein (Transvaal), 372.
Modderfontein Pass, 519.
Modder Poort, 472.
Modder river, 37, 49, 143, 480.
Modder Spruit and Siding, 249, 252, 255, 259.
Molloy, Sergeant, 161.
Molopo Oog, affair at, 378–9.
Molopo river, 144, 148–9, 152, 154–5, 163, 167, 177, 183, 200–1, 203.
Money, Lieut.-Colonel C. G. C., 345.
Montgomery, Lieut. H. F., 119.
Monument Hill (Belfast), 392, 394.
Monument, The, at Paardekraal, removal of, 377.
Mooi river (Natal), 251.
Mooi river, bridge and valley (Western Transvaal), 247, 343, 351, 355, 376, 510, 512, 516.
Mooiplaats (O. F. S.), 61.
Mooiplaats (east of Pretoria), 208, 217, 219–20, 223.
Mooiplaats Drift, 100.
Moolman's Hoek, 299.
Moos river, 423, 450.
Mors Kop, 208.
Mosbank, 475.
Mosilikatze's Nek. See ZILIKAT'S NEK.
Moshwane, 200.
Motsitlani, 182.
Mount Pougwana. See POUGWANA.
Mount Prospect, 265.
Mountain battery. See REGULAR UNITS.
Mounted Infantry. See INFANTRY, MOUNTED.
Mules, 31, 36–8, 141, 322, 381, 427, 435.
Muller, Commandant, 447, 450.
Municipal authorities, Mafeking, help of, 145.
Munn, Major F. H., 315–16.
Murray, Major-General J. Wolfe, 383, 457.
Murray, Lieut., 152.
Myer's Farm, 264.

NAAUWPOORT JUNCTION, 29.
Naauwpoort Nek (O. F. S.), 293–4, 296–8, 301–4.
Napoleon Bonaparte, Emperor, 154.
Natal, 35, 37–8, 69, 72, 75, 86, 108, 136, 182, 184, 193, 328, 349, 380, 383, 385–6, 406, 421, 428, 456; Bank of, 432; clearing of Northern, 249–85; disbandment of Volunteers of, 466; Johannesburg railway, events on, June to November, 1900, 457–68; local forces of, see COLONIAL UNITS; rebels, 266; situation in, 65.
Natal Spruit, 86, 88.
National Anthem, British, 92.
National Bank, 32, 432.
Natives, in Mafeking, 142–3, 166–7, 173, 181, 199; question of, in the West, 194–7; in Rhodesia, 232.
Naude's, H., Farm, 303–4.
Naval Brigade, The Royal, 98–9, 251, 254, 259, 461; guns of, see GUNS.
Nel, Commandant, 137.
Nelshoogte Pass, 416, 426.
Nelspoort, 294–5.
Nelspruit, 404–5, 408, 417, 419, 425.
Nesbit, Captain R. C., V.C., 147.
Nesbitt's Horse. See COLONIAL UNITS.
Newcastle, and road, 250, 252, 257, 264–6, 269, 282, 383, 457–8, 461–3, 468.
Newmarket (O. F. S.), 332.
Newspaper, *The Friend*, 32.
New South Wales, corps from. See COLONIAL UNITS.
New Zealand, contingents from. See COLONIAL UNITS.
Nichols, Farrier-Corporal, 179.
Nicholson, Colonel J. S., 157, 189, 194, 197, 374.
Nicholson, Major-General Sir W. G., K.C.B., 36.
Nicholson's Nek, 397.
Nickerson, Lieut. W. H. S. (awarded the Victoria Cross), 113.

Nooitgedacht (Delagoa Bay line), 101, 136, 404, 416, 419.
Nooitgedacht (O. F. S.), 70.
Nooitgedacht (north-east of Zeerust), 503.
Nooitgedacht (north-west of Pretoria), 364.
Nordenfeldt gun, 146, 159, 163-4, 167, 187.
Norfolk, H., Duke of, K.G., 86.
Norfolk regiment. *See* REGULAR UNITS.
North Kaap river, 419.
North Staffordshire regiment. *See* REGULAR UNITS.
Northern Natal, the clearing of, 249-85.
Northumberland Fusiliers. *See* REGULAR UNITS.
Norton, Captain A. E. M., 289.
Norval's Pont, 30, 105-6, 494.
Nqutu, 266.
Nuns (in Mafeking), 163.
Nurses, 31.
Nylstroom, 195, 368, 437.

OCCUPATION OF: Johannesburg, 91; Kroonstad, 62; Pretoria, 101-2.
Odendaal Stroom, 494-5.
Officers, paucity of, 35-6.
Oldfield, Major H. E., 287-8.
Old Viljoen's Drift, 70-2.
Olifants Nek, 234-7, 246-7, 336, 339, 341-2, 348, 352-8, 360-1, 364, 370, 498-500, 506-7, 518; attack on, by Lord Methuen, 244-5.
Olifantsvlei, 77.
Oliphant, Private, 170.
Oliphant river, 321, 323, 424, 447, 455, 501.
Olive river, 4.
Olivier, Commandant C., 476.
Olivier, General J. H., 6, 286, 304-5, 380, 469-71; pursuit and capture of, 325-34.
Omdraai Vlei, 8, 10, 13.
Onderbrook Kopjes, 389.

Onderste Poort, 237-8, 242, 312, 357, 362.
Onrust, affair at, 241-2.
Oosthuizen, Commandant P., 397, 402.
Oosthuizen, Field-Cornet S., 235.
Oosthuizen, General, 74, 108-9.
Operations: in the Eastern Transvaal, June 16th to August 21st, 1900, 307-24; October and November, 1900, 422-56; Orange River Colony, 104-39, 286-306, 325-34, 469-96; Rhodesia (Plumer's), 186-203; Western Transvaal, June and July, 1900, 226-48; pursuit and escape of De Wet, 335-56; August and September, 1900, 357-79; September to November, 1900, 497-520.
Opperman, Commandant D., 438, 450.
Orange Free State, 2, 7, 27, 32, 34-5, 37-8, 59, 93, 111, 131, 133, 205, 227-9, 250, 253, 255, 258, 268, 272, 274, 280-1, 285, 294, 307, 336, 361-2, 380, 405; annexation of, 126; description of, 104-5; government of, 60-1, 63, 94; pacification of, 112.
Orange Free State commandos. *See* COMMANDOS.
Orange Grove, 92, 519.
Orange river, 1-3, 5, 7, 9-10, 14, 16-17, 22-3, 25, 30, 41, 134, 139, 186, 209, 229, 489, 494-5.
Orange River Colony, 313, 341, 437, 459, 497, 506; distribution of troops in, 134-6; operations in, *see* OPERATIONS.
Order, valedictory, by Lord Roberts, 520-1.
Orders, 38-9, 42, 96, 135-6; issued by: Baden-Powell, 245; Sir R. Buller, 467; Sir F. Clery, 259; French, 53, 321, 428; issued to: Baden-Powell, 140; Sir R. Buller, 257; Sir F. Carrington, 232, 336; Clements, 510; Sir H. Colvile, 113; French, 312-13, 319, 426, 433; Hamilton

Orders—*continued.*
(Ian), 336, 348, 354-5; Sir A. Hunter, 308; Knox (C. E.), 510; Lord Methuen, 107-8, 124, 131-2, 328, 346; Paget, 448; Plumer, 187; Sir L. Rundle, 105-6, 123; Spragge, 115; for suppression of the rebellion in Cape Colony, 9.

Ordnance Corps, Army. *See* REGULAR UNITS.

Organisation, of artillery, 34-5; cavalry, 33; Imperial Yeomanry, 34; Mafeking and Rhodesian forces, 140-6, 230-2; mounted infantry, 33-4.

Orpen's Light Horse. *See* COLONIAL UNITS.

Orr-Ewing, Major J. A., 24.

Osfontein, 256.

Otto's Hoop, 231, 237, 247, 335-6, 339-40, 359, 370, 378-9, 497, 501-5, 514.

Oversea Colonials. *See* COLONIAL UNITS.

Oxen, 36-8, 141, 196, 322, 381, 416, 427, 435, 456.

Oxfordshire Light Infantry. *See* REGULAR UNITS.

PAARDEBERG, 9, 28, 31, 33.

Paarde Kop, 283, 381, 383, 395, 457, 461.

Paardekraal monument, removal of, 377.

Paardeplaats (Eastern Transvaal), 408.

Paardeplaats (O. F. S.), 330.

Pacification of the Orange River Colony, 112; scheme for, 476.

Paget, Major-General A. H., 109, 112, 132-8, 286-7, 290-300, 303, 306, 325, 329-30, 349, 362, 366-7, 369, 372-4, 424, 447-51, 454-5, 470, 499, 501-2, 513, 517.

Paget, Captain G. L., 467.

Paget, Colonel H., 340.

Pain, Colonel G. W. H., 296, 299, 302.

Palala river, 191, 193.

Palapye, 159, 190, 194, 196.

Palla, 193.

Palmietfontein (O. F. S.), 298, 326.

Palmietfontein (Eastern Transvaal), 407.

Pan Station, 323, 422-3, 426, 436, 445, 456.

Panzera, Major F. W., 158, 160-2, 168-70, 178.

Parliament, British, 393.

Parker, Major St. J. W. T., 518.

Parsons, Colonel Sir C. S. B., K.C.M.G., 10, 12-16.

Parys, 69-70, 108, 124, 343, 346-8, 483-4, 496.

Passage of Rhenoster river, 68; Vaal river, 69-73, 107; Vet river, 50; Zand river, 59.

Paton, Lieut. H. P., 161.

Paulet, Lieut. C. S., 24.

Paul Schmidt's Berg, 490.

Payne, Lieut.-Colonel R. L., 400, 438, 445, 448, 454-5.

Peace, negotiations for, 207, 227, 268-9; remoteness of, 498.

Pechell, Captain C. A. K., 153-4.

Pekin, 393.

Philippolis, 104, 480.

Philippolis commando. *See* COMMANDOS.

Philomel, H.M.S., 259.

Phokwani Siding, 112.

Pienaar, Commandant, 317.

Pienaar's Poort, 207-8, 218, 222-4.

Pienaar's Poort Station, 312, 317.

Pienaar's river, 208, 212-13, 215-16, 219, 365-6, 369, 374, 502.

Pienaar's River Bridge, 501.

Pienaar's River Station, 365, 367, 374, 501.

Piet Retief commando. *See* COMMANDOS.

Piet Retief district, and road, 281, 463.

Pietersburg railway, and road, 96, 189-90, 193-4, 196, 317, 363, 424, 437, 448, 499, 502, 514.

Pietersburg commando. *See* COMMANDOS.

INDEX. 593

Pieters Farm, 259.
Pieters Hill, 398.
Pilandsberg, 517.
Pilcher, Colonel T. D., 5, 47-8, 75-8, 90, 209, 211, 308-12, 314, 362-5, 489, 493-5.
Pilcher's Mounted Infantry. *See* INFANTRY, MOUNTED.
Pilgrim's Rest, 404, 408, 420.
Pine-Coffin, Captain J. E., 333, 479.
Pitsani Bakluku (Pothlugo), 199-200.
Plans of Boers, 128, 176, 193, 311, 314, 437-8, 469, 493-4, 512 ; British, 128, 135, 138, 186, 255, 257-8, 266, 268, 294, 392, 475-6, 484.
Platberg, 471.
Platrand, 283, 383, 459, 461.
Plat Kop, 285.
Plat river, 365, 367.
Plot at Johannesburg, 314.
Plumer, Lieut.-Colonel H. C. O., 144, 157, 159, 165, 169, 172-4, 182-4, 230, 234-5, 367, 369, 372-3, 448, 450-1, 501-2, 513 ; operations of, in Rhodesia, 186-203.
Pohlmann, Lieut., 397, 402.
Pole-Carew, Lieut.-General R., C.B., 206, 217-18, 222-3, 307, 312, 317-23, 386-8, 391-5, 403-4, 414, 416, 418 ; occupies Komati Poort, 419-20.
Pomeroy, 252-3, 260-1.
Ponies, 31.
Ponts, 16-17, 189-90, 193-4.
Poort City, 419.
Port Elizabeth, 30, 35.
Porter, Colonel T. C., 33, 51-2, 55, 209-11, 312-13, 315.
Portuguese, 418.
Portuguese frontier, 188, 243, 403, 412.
Portuguese Governor, Lourenço Marques, 417.
Posen Hill, 54, 56.
Postal services, 32.
Postmasburg, 20.
Potchefstroom, 66, 71-2, 74-6, 228, 232-3, 235, 246-7, 342-5, 347, 349, 351, 364-72, 375-7, 483-4, 512, 516.

Potchefstroom commando. *See* COMMANDOS.
Potchefstroom road, 76-9.
Potgieter, Commandant (Smithfield), 118, 513.
Pougwana, 264, 267, 270, 273, 279.
Pound Plateau, 254.
Powerful, H.M.S., 259.
Presidents of the Boer Republics. *See* KRUGER *and* STEYN.
Pretoria, 4-5, 27, 38, 40-1, 107, 126, 128, 135, 139, 143, 150, 173, 189, 192-3, 204, 206-8, 222, 224, 226-40, 242-3, 246-8, 252, 284-5, 293, 307-9, 311-15, 317-23, 328, 336-8, 341, 349, 354-5, 357, 361-2, 364-5, 370-3, 377-8, 386, 392, 404, 417, 420, 423, 426, 435, 438, 445, 447, 456, 461, 484, 499-501, 506-7, 516 ; the advance to, 65-103.
Pretoria commando. *See* COMMANDOS.
Pretorius, Commandant T., 318, 438, 455.
Pretorius' commando. *See* COMMANDOS.
Pretorius Drift, 47.
Pretyman, Major-General G. T., C.B., 32.
Prieska, 3, 5-10, 12-17, 22.
Prieska rebels. *See* COMMANDOS.
Prince Alfred's Volunteer Guard. *See* COLONIAL UNITS.
Principal Medical Officer (Natal), 250.
Prinsloo, Commandant H., 443.
Prinsloo, Commandant M., 118, 341, 363, 476.
Prinsloo, General M., 117-19, 126, 286, 293, 305, 470 ; surrenders, 304.
Prisoners of war: Boer—3, 22, 25, 49, 56, 58-9, 63, 71, 87, 91, 111, 124, 134, 179, 181, 305, 319, 333, 372, 374, 376, 379, 418, 423-4, 473, 488, 497, 502-3, 505, 507-8, 514-18 ; British—4, 8, 11, 64, 94, 120-1, 124, 131, 133, 147, 192, 240, 340, 351, 367, 446, 467, 493 ; exchange of, 64 ; release of, 101-2, 302, 404, 418 ; by Boers, 136, 442.

VOL. III. 38

Proclamations, 7–9, 16. See also APPENDIX 9.
Protectorate regiment. See COLONIAL UNITS.
Pursuit of De Wet and Olivier, 325–34; and escape of De Wet, 335–56.
Pyramids, 362.

QUAGGAFONTEIN, affair at, 370–1, 499.
Quaggas Nek, 271.
Quarriefontein, 503.
Queen of Holland, Her Majesty the, 417.
Queen Victoria, Her Majesty, messages from, 173.
Queensland, Corps from. See COLONIAL UNITS.
Queenstown Rifle Volunteers. See COLONIAL UNITS.

RAATZE'S, SOLOMON, FARM (Eerste Geluk), 304.
Railways, 29–31, 41, 104, 107, 138–9, 142, 207, 228, 231, 250, 257–8, 285, 313, 331, 349, 372, 383, 385, 424, 428, 513; cutting of, by French, north of Kroonstad, 60; east of Pretoria, 95; damage to and repair of, 62, 112, 128, 131, 205, 232, 247, 259, 265–7, 322–3, 373, 436, 446–7, 461, 467, 516; gauges of, 188; rolling stock, capture of, 87, 283, 418–20; safety of, arrangements for, 128, 135, 256.
Railway Pioneer regiment. See COLONIAL UNITS.
Rainsford-Hannay, Lieut. F., 389.
Ralph, Mr. J., 32.
Ramakokskraal, 502.
Ramathlabama, 147, 173, 182, 200–2.
Ramsden, Trooper H. E. (awarded the Victoria Cross), 163.
Ramutsa, 197, 199–200.
Rand, The, 73–4.
Rawlinson, Colonel Sir H. S., Bart., 251.

Rebellion in the north-west of Cape Colony, 1–26; recrudescence of, 515.
Rebels, 2–25, 108.
Reconnaissances, 46, 50–1, 61, 63, 75, 88, 109, 115, 130, 132, 173, 180, 190, 196, 201, 206, 268, 284, 290–1, 296, 302, 319, 410, 415, 426, 461, 485, 507, 513, 515–16.
Recruiting in Cape Colony, 141.
Red Cross flag, 434; fired on by Boers, 246.
Reddersburg, 30, 491.
Reeves, Brigadier-General J., 426.

REGULAR UNITS.

Cavalry :—
Household Cavalry, 33, 45, 214, 344, 506.
5th (Princess Charlotte of Wales's) Dragoon Guards, 140, 265, 267, 383, 463, 465.
6th Dragoon Guards (Carabiniers), 33, 55, 67, 427, 431–4, 518–19.
7th (Princess Royal's) Dragoon Guards, 13, 15, 33, 77, 209, 237–8, 427, 430, 433.
1st (Royal) Dragoons, 265–7, 383, 462.
2nd Dragoons (Royal Scots Greys), 33, 53, 55, 235, 237–42, 427, 518.
5th (Royal Irish) Lancers, 266, 381, 387, 439–41, 443, 455.
6th (Inniskilling) Dragoons, 33, 55, 73, 427, 431, 518.
8th (King's Royal Irish) Hussars, 33, 315, 428–31, 518.
9th (Queen's Royal) Lancers, 33, 56, 91, 180, 326, 344, 369–71, 493.
10th (Prince of Wales's Own Royal) Hussars, 33, 45, 58, 64, 213–14, 344.
12th (Prince of Wales's Royal) Lancers, 33, 45–6, 214, 344, 518.
13th Hussars, 259, 265–6, 284, 328, 461–2.
14th (King's) Hussars, 14, 77, 235, 237–8, 249–50, 428–31.

INDEX.

16th (The Queen's) Lancers, 33, 56, 91, 252, 326, 344, 369-71, 483.
17th (Duke of Cambridge's Own) Lancers, 33, 56, 91, 326, 344, 346, 369-71, 493.
18th Hussars, 267, 272, 283, 337, 381, 387, 407, 425, 438, 444, 454, 458, 460.
19th (Princess of Wales's Own) Hussars, 259, 381, 406, 437, 458, 460.

Artillery :—
Royal Horse :
A. battery, 262-3, 271-2, 274, 278, 284, 382, 410, 420.
G. battery, 43, 47-8, 90, 97, 211, 308, 312, 315-17, 438, 447, 454.
J. battery, 35, 56, 67, 86-7, 98, 217, 224, 414.
M. battery, 35, 109-11, 183-4, 308-10, 317, 337, 412, 427.
O. battery, 33, 90, 210-12, 237-8, 427, 433.
P. battery, 325, 343.
Q. battery, 33, 35, 212-13, 325, 344, 488.
R. battery, 33, 56, 91, 212, 326, 344, 369.
T. battery, 33, 315-17, 427, 519.
U. battery, 305, 484-7.
Royal Field, 6, 109, 132, 135-7, 267, 294-5, 297, 302, 328-9, 332-3, 391, 407, 436-7, 493.
2nd battery, 122, 329, 331, 476.
4th battery, 124-5, 243-4, 328, 344-5, 351, 378.
5th battery, 113-14, 132, 298, 301-2, 330-1.
7th battery, 249, 270, 276, 279, 282, 373-4, 448, 453, 460.
8th battery, 135, 330, 498.
13th battery, 269-71, 280, 282, 460, 463, 465.
14th battery, 488.
17th battery, 131, 134, 344.
18th battery, 57-8, 99, 234, 247, 308.

19th battery, 266.
20th battery, 124-5, 243, 342, 344, 424.
21st battery, 382, 387-9, 398, 402, 406, 425, 444, 454.
28th battery, 109-10, 231, 308, 327, 344, 375, 457, 507, 518.
37th (Howitzer) battery, 124-5, 342, 344, 378.
38th battery, 243-4, 287-90, 366-7, 448, 452-3, 501.
39th battery, 471, 481.
42nd battery, 382, 398, 410, 425.
43rd (Howitzer) battery, 35, 472.
44th battery, 10-11, 13, 22, 24-5.
53rd battery, 280, 382, 395, 398-9, 411, 425.
61st battery, 259, 270, 274, 280, 282, 382, 388, 391, 395, 398, 420.
62nd battery, 58, 99.
63rd battery, 282, 284, 458-9, 461, 468.
64th battery, 270, 276, 279, 282.
65th (Howitzer) battery, 35.
66th battery, 112, 231, 309, 315-17, 412, 414, 427.
67th battery, 462-3, 465-6.
68th battery, 13, 132, 478, 490-3.
69th battery, 270-1, 280, 282, 458, 460, 463, 465.
72nd battery, 307.
73rd battery, 266, 383.
74th battery, 57, 80-6, 100, 206, 309-10.
75th battery, 58, 99, 336, 365, 500.
76th battery, 57, 80-6, 206, 212-17, 219, 298, 303-4, 329, 472.
77th battery, 292, 329, 331, 351.
78th battery, 109-10, 231, 233, 241, 344, 351, 507, 512.
79th battery, 122, 330-1.
81st battery, 80-6, 206, 299, 301, 307, 329.
82nd battery, 57, 63, 80-6, 206, 212-17, 219-21, 296, 303-4, 307, 330-1, 479.

VOL. III.

Regular Units (Artillery)—*continued.*
  83rd battery, 99, 219–21.
  84th battery, 99, 394, 419, 439–43, 455.
  85th battery, 99, 394.
  86th battery, 283–4, 378, 458, 462–3, 465.
  87th battery, 35.
  88th battery, 359, 515.
  Vickers-Maxims :
  C. section, 308, 427.
  D. section, 33.
  E. section, 33, 427.
  F. section, 428.
  G. section, 308, 327, 344, 457, 518.
  I. section, 33.
  J. section, 33, 427.
  Q. section, 448.
  S. section, 337, 439–41, 443.
  Ammunition columns, 428, 465.
  Royal Garrison, 112, 259, 271, 280, 282, 284, 437, 440–1, 443.
  2nd company W. D., 262.
  5th company E. D., 329, 498.
  6th company E. D., 291, 448, 518.
  6th company W. D., 382.
  10th company E. D., 463, 465.
  10th company W. D., 382.
  16th company W. D., 270, 425.
  16th company S. D., 270, 382.
  36th company S. D., 99.
  4th Mountain battery, 259, 383.
  10th Mountain battery, 382, 420.

Engineers :—
  Royal Engineers, 30, 55, 60, 62, 86, 95, 113–14, 206, 243–4, 280, 283, 294, 323, 329–30, 342, 351, 366, 373, 378, 382, 425, 427–9, 439–41, 443, 459, 461, 467–8, 498, 507.

Foot Guards :—
  Grenadier Guards (2nd), 122–3, 295, 328, 331.
  Grenadier Guards (3rd), 49, 219, 493–4.
  Coldstream Guards (1st), 219–21, 494.
  Coldstream Guards (2nd), 219–21, 423, 494, 516–17.
  Scots Guards (1st), 219–20, 502, 513.
  Scots Guards (2nd), 122–3, 294–5, 297, 299, 302–3, 328, 331.

Infantry :—
  The Royal Scots (Lothian) (1st) [formerly 1st Foot), 407, 409, 424.
  The Queen's (Royal West Surrey) (2nd) [formerly 2nd Foot], 255, 261–2.
  The Buffs (East Kent) (2nd) [formerly 3rd Foot], 131, 313, 445–6.
  The King's Own (Royal Lancaster) (2nd) [formerly 4th Foot], 270, 464–5.
  The Northumberland Fusiliers (1st) [formerly 5th Foot], 135, 243–4, 328, 344, 378, 503.
  The Northumberland Fusiliers (2nd) [formerly 5th Foot], 327, 344, 498, 506, 517.
  The Royal Warwickshire (2nd) [formerly 6th Foot], 424.
  The Royal Fusiliers (City of London) (2nd) [formerly 7th Foot], 110–11, 184, 309, 313–14, 317, 322.
  The King's (Liverpool) (1st) [formerly 8th Foot], 280, 382, 388–91, 398.
  The Norfolk (2nd) [formerly 9th Foot], 314.
  The Lincolnshire (2nd) [formerly 10th Foot], 234, 239–40, 308, 314.
  The Devonshire (1st) [formerly 11th Foot], 137, 382, 388, 395, 399–402, 409, 420–1, 425.
  The Devonshire (2nd) [formerly 11th Foot], 262, 275, 468.
  The Suffolk (1st) [formerly 12th Foot], 13, 128, 206, 311–15, 412, 415, 426–7, 440–2, 494–5.

INDEX.

The Prince Albert's (Somersetshire Light Infantry) (2nd) [formerly 13th Foot], 112, 308, 327, 344, 375, 457.

The Prince of Wales's Own (West Yorkshire) (2nd) [formerly 14th Foot], 275, 500.

The East Yorkshire (2nd) [formerly 15th Foot], 122, 329, 331, 348.

The Bedfordshire (2nd) [formerly 16th Foot], 113, 135, 290, 302-4, 329-31, 471.

The Leicestershire (1st) [formerly 17th Foot], 280, 382, 387, 410, 444, 454, 460.

The Royal Irish (1st) [formerly 18th Foot], 291-2, 300, 303, 329, 407, 409, 443-4, 455.

The Princess of Wales's Own (Yorkshire) (1st) [formerly 19th Foot], 217, 424.

The Lancashire Fusiliers (2nd) [formerly 20th Foot], 460, 463-5.

The **Royal Scots Fusiliers (2nd)**, [formerly 21st Foot], 110-11, 232, 235, 344-5, 507, 510-11, 519.

The Cheshire (2nd) [formerly 22nd Foot], 52, 55, 57.

The Royal Welsh Fusiliers (1st) [formerly 23rd Foot], 110-11, 232, 235, 344-5, 507-8, 510-11.

The South Wales Borderers (2nd) [formerly 24th Foot], 375, 518-19.

The King's Own Scottish Borderers (1st) [formerly 25th Foot], 58, 314, 337-8.

The Cameronians (Scottish Rifles) (2nd) [formerly 90th Foot], 254.

The Royal Inniskilling Fusiliers (1st) [formerly 27th Foot], 266, 382, 399-402, 406, 454.

The Gloucestershire (1st) [formerly 28th Foot], 266, 383.

The Gloucestershire (2nd) [formerly 61st Foot], 132, 478, 490-3.

The Worcestershire (1st) [formerly 29th Foot], 329, 471.

The Worcestershire (2nd) [formerly 36th Foot], 135, 286, 296, 329, 331, 369, 498.

The East Lancashire (1st) [formerly 30th Foot], 55, 58.

The East Surrey (2nd) [formerly 70th Foot], 275.

The Duke of Cornwall's Light Infantry (2nd) [formerly 46th Foot], 80-6, 247, 311, 313-14.

The Duke of Wellington's (West Riding) (1st) [formerly 33rd Foot], 362, 365-6, 373, 448, 451-2.

The Border (1st) [formerly 34th Foot], 112, 233, 308, 313-14, 337, 354-5, 498.

The Royal Sussex (1st) [formerly 35th Foot], 57, 80-6, 215-16, 218-21, 299, 301-2, 304, 329, 333, 471-2, 481.

The Hampshire (2nd) [formerly 67th Foot], 58, 314.

The South Staffordshire (1st) [formerly 38th Foot], 299, 329-32.

The Dorsetshire (2nd) [formerly 54th Foot], 260, 265, 269, 275-9, 283, 460, 463, 465.

The Prince of Wales's Volunteers (South Lancashire) (1st) [formerly 40th Foot], 383, 464-5.

The Welsh (1st) [formerly 41st Foot], 98, 424.

The Black Watch (Royal Highlanders) (2nd) [formerly 73rd Foot], 46, 113, 132, 301, 331, 478.

The Oxfordshire Light Infantry (1st) [formerly 43rd Foot], 131, 134, 327, 344.

The Essex (1st) [formerly 44th Foot], 98-9, 511.

The Sherwood Foresters (Derbyshire) (1st) [formerly 45th Foot], 52, 57, 63, 80-6, 113, 213, 215, 217-18, 220, 325, 519.

The Loyal North Lancashire (1st) [formerly 47th Foot], 135, 243-4, 246, 354, 377-8, 503, 514-15.

Regular Units (Infantry)—*continued.*

The Northamptonshire (2nd) [formerly 58th Foot], 135, 243-4, 328, 344, 378, 503, 515.

Princess Charlotte of Wales's (Royal Berkshire) (2nd) [formerly 66th Foot], 314, 337-8, 429.

The Queen's Own (Royal West Kent) (2nd) [formerly 97th Foot], 122-3, 299, 329-32, 476-7.

The King's Own (Yorkshire Light Infantry) (2nd) [formerly 105th Foot], 137, 290-1, 329, 362, 366, 498, 506.

The King's (Shropshire Light Infantry) (2nd)[formerly 85th Foot], 80-6, 137, 236, 240-2, 244, 311, 342, 412, 427, 439-42.

The Duke of Cambridge's Own (Middlesex) (2nd) [formerly 77th Foot], 259, 265, 269, 275-7, 458, 460, 462, 466.

The King's Royal Rifle Corps (1st) [formerly 60th Foot], 280, 382, 384, 410-11, 420, 444-5, 447, 454, 460.

The King's Royal Rifle Corps (2nd) [formerly 60th Foot], 280.

The King's Royal Rifle Corps (3rd) [formerly 60th Foot], 459, 467-8.

The Duke of Edinburgh's (Wiltshire) (2nd) [formerly 99th Foot], 135, 291, 296, 300, 303, 329, 365-6, 369.

The Manchester (1st) [formerly 63rd Foot], 256, 382, 388, 395, 398-9, 425, 460.

The Manchester (2nd) [formerly 96th Foot], 329-32.

The Prince of Wales's (North Staffordshire) (2nd) [formerly 98th Foot], 372.

The York and Lancaster (1st) [formerly 65th Foot], 459, 463-4.

The Durham Light Infantry (1st) [formerly 68th Foot], 461.

The Highland Light Infantry (1st) [formerly 71st Foot], 301, 331, 472-3, 478, 490-3.

Seaforth Highlanders (Ross-shire Buffs, The Duke of Albany's) (2nd) [formerly 78th Foot], 301, 303, 331, 479-80, 493.

The Gordon Highlanders (1st) [formerly 75th Foot], 57, 80-6, 236, 241-2, 311, 342, 407, 439, 443-4, 455.

The Gordon Highlanders (2nd) [formerly 92nd Foot], 382, 387, 395, 399-402, 409-11, 420, 460.

The Queen's Own Cameron Highlanders (1st) [formerly 79th Foot], 57, 80-6, 215, 219, 296-7, 304, 329, 333, 471, 481.

The Royal Irish Rifles (2nd) [formerly 86th Foot], 471, 473, 478.

Princess Victoria's (Royal Irish Fusiliers) (2nd) [formerly 89th Foot], 110-11, 309, 313, 315-17.

The Connaught Rangers (1st) [formerly 88th Foot], 112, 233, 308, 313-14, 317-22.

Princess Louise's (Argyll and Sutherland Highlanders) (1st) [formerly 91st Foot], 113, 287, 313-14, 337-8, 363, 500.

The Prince of Wales's Leinster regiment (Royal Canadians) (1st) [formerly 100th Foot], 286, 297, 299, 302, 328-9.

The Royal Munster Fusiliers (1st) [formerly 101st Foot], 18, 290-1, 300, 329, 366-7, 373-4, 448, 451, 453.

The Royal Dublin Fusiliers (1st) [formerly 102nd Foot], 269, 275-7, 458, 460, 465.

The Royal Dublin Fusiliers (2nd) [formerly 103rd Foot], 112, 308, 327, 344, 375-6, 457, 459, 500, 511, 518.

The Rifle Brigade (The Prince Consort's Own) (1st), 254, 270, 459, 467-8.

INDEX. 599

The Rifle Brigade (The Prince Consort's Own) (2nd), 382, 398-402, 410, 425.
Provisional battalion, 247.

Army Service Corps, 26, 37, 129, 427, 518.
Royal Army Medical Corps (including Bearer companies, Field hospitals, etc.), 36, 113, 295, 427-8, 465, 499, 518.
Army Ordnance Corps, 129.

Reinforcements: Boer—51, 72, 108, 198, 371; British—31, 203, 246, 251, 446, 488.
Reitfontein (O. F. S.), 330.
Reitz, 136, 287, 291-3, 330, 332, 405, 475-7, 489.
Reitzburg, 66, 68, 104, 108, 124, 330, 343-5, 483.
Relief of Mafeking. See MAFEKING.
Remounts, 29-39, 67, 250, 427-8.
Rensburg Drift, 483-4.
Republican flag, 92.
Republican Government, 92, 422, 519.
Republics, Boer, 7, 226-7, 361, 393, 417, 432.
Reorganisation, the, at Bloemfontein, 27-39; of cavalry division, 427-8; of the forces in the west, 378; of the army into mobile columns, 422.
Retief's Nek, and Farm, 292-4, 296, 298, 303.
Rhebokfontein, 484.
Rhenoster Kop (O. F. S.), 67-8, 327, 364, 484.
Rhenoster Kop (Eastern Transvaal), 438, 447; battle of, 448-55.
Rhenoster river, 64, 66-9, 114-15, 127-31, 135, 326, 328, 330, 343, 345, 485.
Rhenoster Camp and Station, 484-5.
Rhenosterfontein, 219, 221, 223.
Rhenosterpoort (O. F. S.), 344.
Rhenosterpoort (Eastern Transvaal), 438, 448, 450, 455.
Rhenosterspruit, 506.

Rhenostervlei (Plat river), 365.
Rhodes, The Right Hon. C. J., 29.
Rhodes, Major E., D.S.O., 429.
Rhodes Drift, 189-91, 193, 196, 232.
Rhodesia, 143, 232, 358, 370, 377; frontier, defence of, 140; operations in, 186-203.
Rhodesian Field Force, regiment, Volunteers, etc. See COLONIAL UNITS.
Ricart, Commandant, 500.
Richardson, Sergeant A. H. L. (awarded the Victoria Cross), 285.
Richardson, Colonel W. D., C.B., 36.
Ridley, Colonel C. P., 33, 135, 212-13, 293, 296, 325, 327, 346-7, 350, 357, 359, 361, 371, 498-500, 506, 508.
Ridley, Lieut.-Colonel H. M., 333-4.
Ridley's Mounted Infantry. See INFANTRY, MOUNTED.
Rietfontein (north-east of Potchefstroom), 347.
Rietfontein (south-east of Pretoria), 308-9.
Rietfontein (Western Transvaal, south of Tafel Kop), 352, 497.
Rietfontein (west of Pretoria), 236, 349, 371, 447.
Rietfontein (Klip river), 73, 75-8.
Rietfontein Farm (O. F. S.), 126, 128.
Rietkuil, 71.
Rietpoort, 368.
Rietspruit (near Senekal), 71-2, 297.
Riet Spruit (near Ermelo), 384.
Riet Spruit (Zand river), 54-5, 134.
Riet Spruit Siding, 55, 59.
Rietvlei (east of Belfast), 414.
Rietvlei (south-east of Pretoria), 311, 314-20, 457.
Rietvlei (Western Transvaal), 360.
Rifle Brigade, The. See REGULAR UNITS.
Rifle practice, by rebels, 2.
Rifles, in Mafeking, 145-6; for rebels, 2, 6.

Rimington, Lieut.-Colonel M. F., 481, 496.
Rimington's Guides. *See* COLONIAL UNITS.
Rinderpest, 2.
Roberts, Field-Marshal, The Right Hon. F. S., Lord, K.P., G.C.B., V.C., etc. etc., 5, 6, 9, 12–13, 104, 107, 121, 124, 128, 134, 165, 174, 201–2, 226–9, 234–8, 243–4, 248–51, 253–6, 267–8, 281–6, 290, 294, 308, 312–13, 318–21, 327–30, 332, 335–9, 341–2, 346, 352, 359, 361–5, 368, 370, 377, 379–81, 385–6, 392–3, 397–8, 404–7, 412, 414, 419–26, 433, 443, 458–9, 462, 466, 475–6, 482, 489, 498–9, 502, 507, 510, 515; annexes Orange Free State, 126; Transvaal, 405; at Diamond Hill, 204–25; breaks off eastern march, 322; correspondence with Buller, 255–8; with I. Hamilton, 348–9, 354–5; enters Johannesburg, 92; Pretoria, 101; farewell order of, 520–1; instructions by, to Rundle, 105–6; moves from Bloemfontein to Pretoria, 40–103; plans of, to subjugate Orange River Colony, 135; precautions for guarding lines of communication, 131; reorganises at Bloemfontein, 27–39; returns to England, 519; strength of force of, on leaving Bloemfontein, 41.
Roberts, Colonel H. R., 239–40.
Roberts' Horse. *See* COLONIAL UNITS.
Robertson, Captain, 480.
Roche, Lieut.-Colonel the Hon. U., 518.
Rochfort, Lieut.-Colonel A. N., 337, 500.
Rolling stock. *See* RAILWAYS.
Roman Catholic Convents, sisters of, 28.
Roode Bergen, 293.
Roodebloem, 431.
Roodehoogte defile, 414.

Roode Kop Station, 86.
Roodekopjes (Hebron), 262, 364, 373.
Roodekraal, 343–5.
Roodeplaats, 210.
Roodepoort (Cape Colony), 12–13.
Roodepoort (south of Heilbron), 93, 114, 476.
Roodepoort, and Station (west of Johannesburg), 85, 90.
Roodepoort Pass (north of Pretoria), 367.
Roodepoort Pass (Witwatersrand), 518.
Roodewal (O. F. S.), 68, 126–7, 129–30, 132–3, 326, 484.
Roodewal (Transvaal), 96.
Roodewal (west of Lindley's Poort), 503.
Roodewal Spruit (O. F. S.), 326.
Rooi Koppies, 383, 459–60, 466.
Rooi Pont, 458.
Rooidam, 4, 109, 182; action at, 110–12.
Rooigrond, 154.
Rooikop (Elands river), 372.
Rooikrans, 96.
Rooikranz, 294–9, 302.
Rooipan, 18.
Rosmead, 30.
Ross, Lieut. C., 43, 67–8.
Ross, Lieut.-Colonel W. C., 487.
Ross' Mounted Infantry. *See* INFANTRY, MOUNTED.
Roux, General P. H., 93, 133–4, 286, 304–5.
Rouxville, 41, 470, 477–8, 495.
Rowell, Major J., 289, 452.
Royal Army Medical Corps. *See* REGULAR UNITS.
Royal Artillery. *See* REGULAR UNITS.
Royal Canadian regiment. *See* COLONIAL UNITS.
Royal Cavalry regiments. *See* REGULAR UNITS.
Royal Commission, on care and treatment of sick, 28, 31; on the war in South Africa, 38.

INDEX. 601

Royal Engineers. *See* REGULAR UNITS.
Royal Infantry battalions. *See* REGULAR UNITS.
Royal Navy. *See* NAVAL BRIGADE.
Rundle, Lieut.-General Sir H. M. L., K.C.B., C.M.G., D.S.O., 35, 41-2, 93, 105-7, 113, 116-18, 121-3, 131, 134-8, 229, 282, 286, 292, 294-9, 302-3, 327, 330-2, 383, 470, 473-7, 489.
Rustenburg, 228, 230, 233-8, 243-7, 309, 335-41, 348-9, 352-6, 358, 360-3, 365, 369-71, 497-503, 513-17.
Rustenburg commando. *See* COMMANDOS.
Rustfontein, 319-21.
Ryan, Captain C. M., 157.

SABI river, 420.
Sabi River railway, 188.
Sandford, Captain H. C., 161.
Saltpan, 193.
Sangars, 239.
Sanie, 182-3.
Sannah's Post, 30, 34-5, 37, 305.
Scandinavia Drift, 328, 344, 346-7, 485.
Schanz Kop fort, Pretoria, 98-9.
Scheeper's Nek, 286, 464-5.
Scheepers, G. J., 128, 341, 363.
Scheepers' commando. *See* COMMANDOS.
Scheerpoort, 348, 508.
Scheme for the pacification of the Orange River Colony, 476.
Schiffer's Pan, 12.
Schmidt Drift, 22.
Schoeman, General, 6, 437.
Schoeman's Drift (Vaal river), 70, 345-6, 483, 485, 509.
Schoeman's Kloof, 425.
Scholes, Major H. S., 464.
Schools, 32.
Schoongezicht Farm, 443.
Schuins Hoogte ridge, 265, 271.

Schure Berg, 339.
Schurveberg, 96, 100.
Schwartz, Commandant, 199-200, 360.
Schweizer Reneke, 2, 372, 379, 497, 513.
Scobell, Major H. J., 238-9.
Scots Fusiliers, The Royal. *See* REGULAR UNITS.
Scots Greys, Royal. *See* REGULAR UNITS.
Scots Guards. *See* REGULAR UNITS.
Sebastopol, 298.
Secretary of State for War, 31, 34.
Sedan, 305.
Sefetili, 200-3.
Segali (native chief), 195.
Sekwani, 191, 193-7.
Selika, 190-4.
Selous Kraal, 353.
Selous river, 246, 353, 503, 513.
Senekal, 41, 93, 107, 121-3, 131, 133-6, 138-9, 286-7, 292, 294-5, 297, 311, 325, 329, 331, 469, 473-5, 482, 489.
Senekal commando. *See* COMMANDOS.
Serfontein, 67.
Service of Colonial troops, expiration of, 501.
Settle, Brigadier-General H. H., C.B., D.S.O., 9-16, 228, 372, 379, 481-2, 496, 513.
Sewell, Lieut. J. W. S., 467.
Shashi river, 189, 193.
Shelters, for women and children, 149.
Shepstone, 484.
Shropshire Light Infantry. *See* REGULAR UNITS.
Shute, Major A. B., 453.
Shute, Major H. G. D., 423.
Sick, at Bloemfontein, 28, 31; Ladysmith, 250-1; treatment of, 28; by Boers, 434.
Silver Kop, 415.
Silverton, 206.
Simkins, Captain W. V., 21.
Sisters of Convents, care of sick, 28.
Sitwell, Lieut.-Colonel W. H., 333.

Sitwell's Mounted Infantry. *See* IN-
FANTRY, MOUNTED.
Situation, at Diamond Hill, 212, 214, 222; east of Pretoria, 307, 385; in Natal, 65; in Rhodesia, 197; in South Africa, 309; in the Western Transvaal, 65, 248; in the Orange River Colony, 470; on the Vaal river, 343-4.
Six Mile Spruit, 89, 95-6, 248; action at, 98-101.
Slaap Kranz, and ridge, 303-5, 328.
Slabbert's Nek, 293-6, 298-300, 302-3, 329, 341.
Slik Spruit, 494.
Smaldeel, 46, 49-50, 52, 473, 479.
Smith, Lieut. D., 450.
Smith's Crossing, 252.
Smith-Dorrien, Major-General H. L., D.S.O., 57, 80-2, 131, 134, 206, 231, 236, 239-40, 242-4, 247, 310-11, 328, 342-4, 348, 350, 352, 355, 357, 359, 365, 371-2, 407, 409, 420, 425-6, 438-45.
Smitheman, Lieut. F., 173, 202.
Smithfield, 105-6, 112, 134, 470, 477-8, 492-4, 496.
Smithfield commando. *See* COM-
MANDOS.
Smuts, General T., 418-19, 427, 430-1.
Snider rifles, 151.
Snyman, Commandant, 360.
Snyman, General, 75, 157-8, 165-6, 168, 177, 185, 200-2, 208, 210, 230.
Soldier, British, traits of, etc., 146.
Somersetshire Light Infantry. *See* REGULAR UNITS.
Sorties, 152-3, 170-2.
Soudanese, 145.
South Africa, command of troops in, taken over by Lord Kitchener, 519.
South African Colonial troops. *See* COLONIAL UNITS.
South African Light Horse. *See* COLONIAL UNITS.
South African Republic, 419, 432, 437; annexation of, 405.

South Australian corps. *See* COLO-
NIAL UNITS.
South Lancashire regiment. *See* REGULAR UNITS.
South Staffordshire regiment. *See* MILITIA *and* REGULAR UNITS.
Southern Rhodesia Volunteers. *See* COLONIAL UNITS.
Southern Transvaal, 380.
Spain, 146.
Special Army Order, 520-21.
Specie, at Bloemfontein, 28; capture of, 418, 432.
Spekboom river, 436.
Spence, Colonel W. A., 21.
Spens, Lieut.-Colonel J., 80-3, 132-3, 242, 439, 441.
Spies in Mafeking, 166.
Spion Kop, 263.
Spitz Kop (Eastern Transvaal), 408, 411, 414, 417, 420-1.
Spitz Kop (Northern Natal), 269-71.
Spitz Kop (O. F. S.), 330-1, 473.
Spitz Kranz (Spitz Kop), 296-7.
Spragge, Colonel B. E., 115-25, 205.
Spreckley, Lieut.-Colonel J. A., 190-2.
Springbok Flats, 367.
Springfontein, and junction, 30, 36, 478.
Springs, 86, 232, 307, 309-11, 319, 327, 435.
Spruyt, Commandant, 438.
Spruyt's commando. *See* COM-
MANDOS.
Staff, Army Headquarters, 36, 124. *See also* APPENDIX I.
Stander's Kop, 284.
Standerton, 93, 136, 138, 268, 281-5, 308-9, 332, 342, 412, 434, 457-61, 465, 468.
Standerton commando. *See* COM-
MANDOS.
Stanley, Colonel G., 381.
Starkey, Major L. E., 110.
State Secretary, Pretoria, 193.
Steelkraal Spruit, 450-1.

INDEX. 603

Steelpoort river, and valley, 394, 438, 443.
Steenbok Spruit, 321.
Steenkamp, Commandant L., 6-9, 128, 130, 341, 358, 366, 368, 372, 499; appointed Assistant Commander-in-Chief, 362.
Steenkamps Berg, 407.
Steenkamp's commando. *See* COMMANDOS.
Steenkamp's Pan, 67.
Steinacker's Mounted Infantry. *See* INFANTRY, MOUNTED.
Stephanus Draai Nek, 303.
Stephenson, Major-General T. E., 98, 317, 320, 419, 425-6.
Sterkfontein, 290.
Sterkstroom, 362.
Sterkstroom river, 337.
Stewart, Captain A. B. A., 480.
Stewart, Captain A. D., 467.
Steyn, H. E. President M. T., 6, 32, 61, 63, 95, 126, 128, 227, 229, 281, 295, 341-2, 345, 348, 358, 362, 364, 405, 422, 437, 487, 497, 499, 501-2, 506-7, 512-13.
Steynsdorp, 419.
Stinkwater, 373.
Stof Kraal, 23.
Stokes, Major A., 518.
Stores, 30, 35, 141, 411, 420, 461.
Stormberg, 29-30, 250, 292, 351.
Strategy, 268.
Strathcona's Horse. *See* COLONIAL UNITS.
Strathrae Farm, 323, 385, 387.
Strengths of: Boer forces—51-2, 66, 93, 96, 108-9, 138, 230, 247-8, 252, 267, 272, 293, 298, 333, 360, 368, 383, 414-15, 422, 476, 504; L. Botha's, 40, 318, 392, 418; P. Botha's, 44, 50; P. Cronje's, 146; De la Rey's, 46, 50, 235, 247, 337, 358, 371, 498, 503; De Villiers', 122; C. De Wet's, 40, 126, 128, 286, 295, 363, 483, 490; P. De Wet's, 118; Froneman's, 330;
Grobelaar's, 50, 235, 267, 365; Joubert's, 32; Liebenberg's, 247, 342-3, 509; Meyer's, 46, 260; Olivier's, 305; Roux's, 134; T. Smuts', 418, 427, 430; Van Rensburg's, 191; Van Tonder's, 474; B. Viljoen's, 317, 418, 438, 450; Visser's, 2; British forces—Alderson's, 3, 6; army at Bloemfontein, 27, 35, 38; Baden-Powell's, 228, 357; Barker's, 493; Bethune's, 266; Bradley's, 372; Broadwood's, 6, 293; Brookfield's, 287; Buller's, 256, 381; Carrington's, 231-2, 359; Colvile's, 41; Colville's, 468; Erroll's, 339; French's, 51, 67, 428; Gordon's, 293; B. Hamilton's, 471; Ian Hamilton's, 41, 214, 336; Hart's, 457; Herbert's, 493; Hickman's, 337; Hore's, 339; Hunter's, 292-3; Hutton's, 67, 209, 234, 315, 414; Imperial Yeomanry, 34; Le Gallais', 470, 485; Little's, 326, 369; Lyttelton's, 425; MacDonald's, 293; Mahon's, 181, 317, 337; main army, 41; Massy's, 490; Methuen's, 243; Militia, 35; Paget's, 448; Pilcher's, 493; Plumer's, 196-7, 200, 203, 230; Ridley's, 293, 498; Roberts' (Lord), 41, 392; Rundle's, 41; Settle's, 15, 481, 513; Smith-Dorrien's, 241, 443; Volunteers, 35; Williams', 494. *See also* APPENDIX 2.
Strydkraal, 383.
Stuart, General J. E. B., 141.
Stubbs, Lieut. J. H., 467.
Sunday's river, and bridge, 253-4, 259.
Sunnyside, 5-6.
Supplies, 93, 114-17, 124, 126, 132, 251, 259, 265, 269, 284, 322-3, 331-2, 336, 342, 349, 369, 383, 432, 463, 468, 473, 479; accumulation of, 30, 36-7, 131; at Tuli, 188; captured at, Barberton, 418; Komati Poort, 419; Roodewal,

Supplies—*continued*.
130-1; Waterval Drift, 28; collection of, 50, 107, 231, 372; destruction of, 347; difficulties of, in Rhodesia, 188-9; for, Cavalry division, 428; posts on Eastern railway, 424; the Natal Army, 281-2, 381, 385-6; in 141, 157, 164, 166, 169, 174, 202; Rustenburg, 246, 335; transit of, *viâ* Natal, 257-8, 461.
Surprise Hill, 252, 254, 259.
Surrender, discussion of terms of, 101.
Surrenders of: Boers, 25, 87, 107, 281, 305, 332, 461, 465; British, 120, 128, 130-1, 466, 493.
Swartkopjes, 394-5, 403.
Swaziland, 418.
Swaziland Police. *See* COMMANDOS.
Swinburne, Lieut. H., 162.
Sybrand's Kraal, 375, 447-8, 450, 501.
Syferfontein (north-west of Krugersdorp), 371, 507.
Syferfontein (Vaal river), 73, 75, 78.
Syferwater, 357.
Sympathisers with the Boers, 393.
Syn Kop, 502.

TAAIBOSCH SPRUIT (Vaal river), 71, 128.
Taaibosch Spruit (Vet river), 49-50.
Taaibosch Spruit (Western Transvaal), 350.
Tabanyama, 252, 389.
Tactics of: Boers, 256, 417; British, 41, 68, 392, 450.
Tafel Berg, 122.
Tafel Kop (Eastern Transvaal), 414-16.
Tafel Kop (Western Transvaal), 352, 370, 497.
Tafelkop (O. F. S.), 473.
Tafel Kop (O. F. S., Wilge river), 477.
Tartar, H.M.S., 259.
Tasmanian Corps. *See* COLONIAL UNITS.
Taungs, 182.
Taylor, Major P. B., 487-8.

Taylor, Sergeant-Major, 170-1.
Telegraphs, cutting of, 60, 95, 247, 446-7.
Telephones, 145, 178, 180-1, 323.
Terrible, H.M.S., 251, 259.
Tesebe Drift, 23.
Thabanchu, 40-2, 105-6, 138, 258, 286, 297, 329, 331, 469, 471-2, 490.
Tigerpoort, and ridge, 309-14.
Tintwa Pass, 255.
The advance from Kroonstad to Bloemfontein, 40-64; from Kroonstad to Pretoria, 65-103; towards Komati Poort, 380-405; to Komati Poort, 406-21.
The pursuit of De Wet and Olivier, 325-34.
The pursuit and escape of De Wet, 335-56.
The reorganisation at Bloemfontein, 27-39.
Theron, Captain Daniel, 72, 341, 372, 376.
Theron's commando. *See* COMMANDOS.
Theunissen, Commandant, 358.
Thorndale, 499.
Thorneycroft, Lieut.-Colonel A., 261, 264, 278, 280, 282.
Thorneycroft's Mounted Infantry. *See* INFANTRY, MOUNTED.
Tonga ambulance, capture of, by Boers, 433.
Town Commandant, Mafeking, duties of, 149.
Town Guards. *See* COLONIAL UNITS.
Townsend, Major S., 518.
Trains, armoured, 145, 147, 149, 153, 160-2, 195, 197, 327; capture of, by Boers, 130-1, 247, 326-7, 342; capture of, by British, 418; wrecking of, 423, 436.
Transport, 231, 381, 412, 416, 418; difficulties of, 61, 281, 386, 410; in Mafeking, 143; Methuen's, 107; in Natal, 251; reorganisation of, 36-8.

INDEX.

Transvaal, 7, 40, 69, 71, 143, 186-8, 228, 256, 258, 267-8, 273, 279, 286, 324, 328, 330, 405, 408, 459, 468, 470, 483, 513; Government of, 94, 101, 126, 226; Eastern, operations in, June 16th to August 21st, 1900, 307-24; October and November, 1900, 422-56; Western, operations in, June and July, 1900, 226-48, 335-56; August and September, 1900, 357-79; situation in, 65, 108-12.
Transvaalers. *See* COMMANDOS.
Trebu, 62.
Trommel, 107, 121, 286, 297, 473.
Troops, arrival of, at Cape Town, 6; distribution of, in Orange River Colony, 134-6; in June, 1900, 228-9; east of Pretoria, 424-5, *see also* APPENDIX 7; on Natal railway, 382-3; on the Johannesburg—Durban line, 457-68, *see also* APPENDIX 8.
Tucker, Lieut.-General C., C.B., 42-3, 52, 54-8, 99-100, 231, 314.
Tugela Ferry, 260.
Tuli, 144, 186-94, 196-7.
Tunbridge, Major W. H., 452.
Turner, Lieut. A. J., 241.
Turner, Lieut. R. E. W. (awarded the Victoria Cross), 442.
Tweedracht, 208, 213.
Tweefontein (Griqualand West) 19, 25.
Tweefontein (east of Pretoria), 224.
Tweefontein (Zwart Ruggens), 361.
Tweefontein (north of Krugersdorp), 506-7.
Tweekuil, 484.
Tweepoort, 63.
Tweerivier, 503, 513.
Twistniet, 61.
Twycross, Captain G., 20.
Twyfelaar, 323, 385, 428, 431.
Tygerfontein, 343, 345, 347, 483, 516.
Tyger Poort, 208, 212-15, 217.
Tyler, Lieut. A. J., 200.

Uitenhage (O. F. S.), 67.
Uithoek (O. F. S.), 302.
Uithoek Hill, 260-2.
Uitkomst, 414-15.
Umtali, 229.
Umvoti district, 252.
Umvoti Mounted Rifles. *See* COLONIAL UNITS.
Uniforms, British, worn by Boers, 289, 434.
Union Jack, 92, 232.
Upington, 8-9, 14-17.
Urmston, Major E. B., 363.
Utrecht, 267, 462-8.
Utrecht commando. *See* COMMANDOS.
Uys, Commandant P., 318, 438.

Vaalboschbult, 369.
Vaalbult, 431.
Vaalkrans, 326.
Vaal Krantz (Natal), 398.
Vaal Kranz (O. F. S.), 299.
Vaal river, 17, 19, 38, 40, 66, 68-74, 104, 107-10, 112, 127, 131, 138, 202, 209, 226, 235, 268, 283-5, 287, 328, 342-8, 363, 384, 432, 468-70, 482-5, 496, 502, 506-7, 509, 512-13, 515-17.
Vaalwater river, 385.
Val, 285.
Valedictory order by Lord Roberts, 520-1.
Valsch River bridge, 65, 475.
Valsch river and Drifts, 60, 116-17, 290, 485.
Van Aard, Commandant F., 341.
Van Aswegen, Commandant, 4, 108.
Van der Heuver, Commandant, 508.
Van Heerden, Commandant, 503.
Van Kolder's Kop, 285.
Van Niekirk, Commandant, 504.
Van Reenen's Pass, 249, 253-7, 383.
Van Rensburg, Commandant, 191.
Van Tonder, Commandant, 474, 503.
Van Tonder's commando. *See* COMMANDOS.
Van Tonder's Pass, 252, 260, 263.

Van Vuurens Drift, 345, 363.
Van Wyk's Hill, 269-71.
Van Wyk's Vlei, or Vanwyksvlei ridge (Eastern Transvaal), 387-8, 391, 429-30, 439-41, 462.
Van Wyk's Vlei (Griqualand West), 12, 14-15.
Van Zyl, Commandant, 508.
Vant's Drift, 266.
Vanwyksrust, 75, 77.
Varkensfontein, 519.
Vaughan, Sergeant, 234.
Veelgepraat, 475.
Veld fires, 123.
Venter, Commandant, 20-1.
Venter's Vallei, 29.
Ventersburg, 59, 113-15, 333-4, 471, 474-5, 482-3.
Ventersburg Road Station, 59, 134, 139, 327, 333, 479, 482.
Ventersdorp, and road, 228, 232, 343, 356, 370, 376, 512, 515.
Venterskroon, 235, 343-5, 347-8, 483-4, 509, 516.
Vereeniging, 69, 71, 74, 126, 131, 231.
Vermaaks Kraal, 260-1.
Vermaas, Commandant, 378, 504-5.
Vernon, Captain R. J., 160-2.
Verzamel Berg, 273, 285.
Vet river, 44, 128; action at, 46-50.
Vialls, Major H. G., 452, 513.
Vickers-Maxim guns, 11, 34, 41-3, 51, 57-8, 73, 75-6, 86, 90-1, 97, 100, 123-5, 128, 132, 134-5, 147, 163-4, 183-4, 197, 209-10, 212, 220-1, 230-1, 239, 243-4, 247, 259-60, 262, 267, 269, 271, 274-6, 280, 282, 293, 298, 308-9, 311-12, 314-18, 327, 337, 339-40, 344-5, 351, 358-9, 366, 370, 372, 375-9, 382, 389, 397, 399-401, 412, 414, 425, 427-8, 430-3, 437, 439-40, 445-6, 452-4, 458-60, 467-8, 470-2, 474-5, 484, 488, 493, 498-9, 504-7, 510-12, 514-15, 519.
Victoria, corps from. *See* COLONIAL UNITS.

Victoria Crosses, 113, 137, 147, 163, 242, 285, 326, 338, 346, 373, 388, 390, 401, 430, 442, 492, 504.
Victoria Road, 15.
Victoria West, 9-10, 12.
Vierkleur, 347.
Viljoen, Commandant A., 415, 450.
Viljoen, Commandant B., 73, 75, 260, 263, 314, 316-17, 391, 416-18, 422, 437-8, 445, 447-50, 453.
Viljoen's Drift (Vaal river), 72, 74, 484, 496.
Viljoenshoek, 292.
Villiersdorp, 287.
Virginia Siding, 54-6, 133-4.
Visser, Field-Cornet, 2-3, 109, 286, 330, 479.
Vlaakplaats, 96.
Vlakfontein (Heidelberg Line), 457; affair at, 467.
Vlakfontein (O. F. S.), 73, 85.
Vlakfontein (Western Transvaal), 352-3, 356-7.
Vlaklaagte, 285.
Vogelsfontein, 291-2.
Vogelstruisfontein, 79, 81, 85.
Vogelstruispoort, 394-5.
Volksraads, convening of, 72.
Volksrust, and road, 273-5, 279-83, 285, 457-9, 461-2, 465.
Volunteers: City Imperial, battery of, 35, 132, 287-90, 366, 373; infantry of, 10-13, 16, 57, 80-6, 215-16, 218-20, 247, 342-3; mounted infantry of, 206, 329, 365, 407; Colonial, 32, 458; British, companies of, 389, 409, 478; arrival of, 251'; disbandment of the Natal, 466; Post Office, corps of, 129; Southern Rhodesia, *see* COLONIAL UNITS; strength of, 35.
Von Donop, Major S. B., 337.
Vosburg, 12.
Vrede, 268, 284-5, 330, 332, 461, 473, 476-7, 489.
Vrede commando. *See* COMMANDOS.
Vredefort, 326-7, 483, 510.

INDEX.

Vredefort Road, and Station, 68, 70, 127–33, 483–4.
Vredes Verdrag, 54–6.
Vryburg, 2–3, 66, 112, 147, 173, 181–2, 201–2, 228, 231, 372, 481.
Vryburg rebels. *See* COMMANDOS.
Vryheid, 256, 282, 462, 464–8; affair at, 266–7.
Vryheid commando. *See* COMMANDOS.
Vyvyan, Lieut.-Colonel C. B., 149.

WAAGFONTEIN, 506.
Waaikraal (or Waai Kraal) Farm and Spruit, 392, 395, 429–30.
Wagenpadspruit, 244, 355.
Wagon Hill, 317.
Wagons, 36–8, 295, 346, 381, 411, 427, 435, 441, 466, 473.
Wakkerstroom, 256, 280–1, 462–3, 465, 468.
Wakkerstroom commando. *See* COMMANDOS.
Walford, Lieut.-Colonel, 145, 153–4.
Walmansthal, 319.
War, efforts to avert, 2; end of, discussed, 228.
War Office, 519.
Ward, Private C. (awarded the Victoria Cross), 137.
Ward, Colonel E. W. D., C.B., 36, 114, 386.
Warmbad, 235–6, 238, 365, 367–9, 372–3, 501.
Warren, Lieut.-General Sir C., G.C.M.G., K.C.B., 18–22, 25–6, 34, 153, 229, 236, 250, 254–5; attacked at Faber's Put, 19; to command in Griqualand West, 17.
Warren's Scouts. *See* COLONIAL UNITS.
Warrenton, 41, 107, 109, 112, 231, 515.
Warwick's Scouts. *See* COLONIAL UNITS.
Warwickshire regiment, The Royal. *See* REGULAR UNITS.

Waschbank river, 253, 259–60, 265, 458.
Water, supply of, under fire, 452.
Waterberg district, 501.
Waterberg commando. *See* COMMANDOS.
Waterkloof, 360, 505.
Waterval Boven, 404.
Waterval Drift (O. F. S.), capture of convoy at, 28.
Waterval (near Pretoria), 101–2, 235, 237–8, 247, 360, 362, 366, 369, 373, 501–2.
Waterval Onder, 404, 414, 416, 425–6.
Waterval (O. F. S.), 68, 291.
Waterval (south-east O. F. S.), 494.
Waterval (north-west of Magato Nek), 500, 503.
Waterval (Plat Kop), 285, 457, 465.
Waterworks, Bloemfontein, 106 Johannesburg, 375.
Weather, severity of, 322.
Weenen, 253.
Weil, Mr. Julius, 144, 166.
Welgegund, 96–7.
Welgelegen Siding, 51, 61.
Welgeluk, 415.
Welgevonden, 430, 439.
Welkom Drift, 46.
Welsh regiment. *See* REGULAR UNITS.
Welverdiend Station, 348, 350, 352, 354–5, 376–7, 509–12, 519.
Wemarshoek, 407.
Wepener, 35, 41, 105–6, 134, 470–1, 477–8, 496.
Wessels, Commandant C. J., 93.
Wessels, Field-Cornet, 3–4, 511.
Wessels (headman of Barolongs), 144.
Wessels Nek, 259, 265.
West Australia, corps from. *See* COLONIAL UNITS.
West Kent regiment. *See* REGULAR UNITS.
West Riding regiment. *See* REGULAR UNITS.
West Surrey regiment. *See* REGULAR UNITS.

West Yorkshire regiment. *See* REGULAR UNITS.
Western Transvaal, operations in, June and July, 1900, 226-48 ; pursuit and escape of De Wet, 335-56 ; August and September, 1900, 357-79 ; September to November, 1900, 497-521.
White, Major F., 472.
White, General Sir G. S., G.C.B., G.C.S.I., G.C.I.E., V.C., etc., 86, 251.
White, Lieut.-Colonel W. L., 471-4.
White flag, raising of, 120, 180, 492-3.
Wildebeestfontein, 74.
Wilgebosch Drift, 327.
Wilge river (O. F. S.), 477.
Wilge river (Transvaal), 320, 423, 438, 447-8, 455, 501.
Wilge River Station, 321, 445-7.
Wilkinson, Major G. E., 129-30.
Williams, Captain A., 147, 160, 171.
Williams, Lieut.-Colonel W. H., 494-5.
Willow Grange (O. F. S.), 286, 297, 299.
Wilson, Lieut.-Colonel R. H. F. W., 375, 518.
Wiltshire regiment. *See* REGULAR UNITS.
Winburg, 38, 43, 46, 107, 113-14, 121, 131, 134, 136, 138, 258, 286, 292, 306, 309, 330, 332-4, 469, 473-4 ; garrison of, 50.
Winburg commando. *See* COMMANDOS.
Windsorton Drift, Road, and Station, 4, 108-10, 112.
Winkel's Drift, 328, 345-7.
Wire entanglements, 239 ; fences, 503.
Witbank, 384.
Witbooy, 444.
Witklip (Lydenburg road), 408, 425, 437.
Witklip (south of Tyger Poort), the affair at, 310-11.
Witkloof, 387, 439-40.
Wit Kop, 294-6, 298-9.
Witkopjes, 484.
Witnek (Eastern Transvaal), 438.
Witnek (O. F. S.), 294-6, 298-9, 301-2.
Witpoort Nek, and ridge (east of Pretoria), 309-17.
Witpoort (north of Belfast), 444-5.
Witpoort (O. F. S.), 67, 330-1.
Witpoortje, 351, 377.
Witte Bergen, 293.
Wittekopfontein, 512.
Wittepoort (O. F. S.), 70.
Witwaters Berg, 96, 241, 354.
Witwatersrand range, 90, 143, 352, 356, 498, 518.
Witzies Hoek, 298.
Wolhuters Kop (O. F. S.), 291-2.
Wolhuter's Kop (Transvaal), 247, 341, 361, 363, 371, 506.
Wolmarans, Major, 94.
Wolmaranstad, 513.
Wolmaranstad commando. *See* COMMANDOS.
Wolvaardt, 349.
Wolvehoek, 70, 516.
Wolve Spruit, 285.
Wonderboom Fort (Pretoria), 101, 237.
Wonderboom Poort, 233, 365.
Wonderfontein (Eastern Transvaal), 323, 385-6, 388, 391, 394, 422.
Wonderfontein (Western Transvaal), 335, 339-40, 456, 514.
Wonderheuvel, 71, 327-8, 346.
Wonderhoogte defile, 463.
Wonderwater Drift (Vaal river), 71.
Work done on railways, 62. *See also* APPENDIX 3.
Works, defensive, Mafeking, 144-5, 148-9.
Woodcote Farm, 255.
Woodstock, 335.
Wools Drift, 267, 465.
Worcestershire regiment. *See* REGULAR UNITS.
Wounded. *See* CASUALTIES and APPENDIX 2.
Wylly, Lieut. G. G. E. (awarded the Victoria Cross), 373.

Wynne, Major-General A. S., C.B., 267, 270, 280, 282-3, 457, 462, 468.
Wysfontein, 503.
YELLOWBOOM FARM, 271.
Yeomanry. *See* IMPERIAL YEOMANRY.
York and Lancaster regiment. *See* REGULAR UNITS.
Yorkshire regiment. *See* REGULAR UNITS.
Young, Lieut. F. V., 234.
Younge, Major G. H., 518.
Younger, Captain D. R., 241; (awarded the Victoria Cross), 242.
Younghusband, Lieut.-Colonel G. J., 125.
Yule, Colonel J. H., 263.

ZAND DRIFT (Aliwal North), 494.
Zand river (O. F. S.), 32, 40, 50-55, 61, 128-9, 133-4, 296, 474; action at the, 54-9.
Zandspruit, and road, 279, 281-3, 457-62, 465, 468.
Zastron, 477-8, 496.
Zeekoefontein, 71.
Zeekoehoek, and Pass, 241-2, 244, 354-6, 499, 508.
Zeerust, 201, 228, 230, 234-6, 246, 335, 339-40, 359, 369-70, 372, 502-6.
Zevenfontein, 412, 430.
Zilikat's Nek, 233-42, 248, 312, 314, 337-8, 349, 361, 363, 498.
Zonderhout Farm, 59.
Zoutkop, 299.
Zoutpan (north-west of Pretoria), 364, 373.
Zoutpan (Griqualand West), 12-13.
Zoutpans Drift, 234, 373, 500.
Zoutpansberg, 188, 193, 418, 422.
Zoutpansberg commando. *See* COMMANDOS.
Zuikerbosch Rand, 88, 457.
Zuikerbosch river, and Spruit, 285, 467.
Zululand, 266.
Zusterhoek, 373-4, 438, 448.
Zuurbekom, 77-8, 85.
Zuurbult, 78, 85.
Zuurfontein, 43.
Zwagershoek, 407.
Zwartbooys Location, 365.
Zwartkloof, 372.
Zwart Kop (Crocodile river), 517-18.
Zwart Kop (near Pretoria), 98-100.
Zwartkopjes, 407, 444.
Zwartkoppies, 217, 219.
Zwart Koppies, 364.
Zwart Ruggens, 339, 353, 517.
Zwavelpoort, 206, 208-9, 212-13, 215-16, 219, 309.
Zween Kuil, 7.

www.ingramcontent.com/pod-product-compliance
Lightning Source LLC
Chambersburg PA
CBHW052008290426
44112CB00014B/2163